W9-AOS-406

FRANCE

FODOR'S TRAVEL PUBLICATIONS

are compiled, researched, and edited by an international team of travel writers, field correspondents, and editors. The series, which now almost covers the globe, was founded by Eugene Fodor in 1936.

OFFICES
New York & London

Fodor's France:

Area Editor: Dominique Sicot
Editorial Contributors: John Ardagh, Robert Brown, John P. Harris, Andrew Heritage, Mark Lewes, Ira Mayer, Vivienne Menkes, Susan Pritchard, Barry Tasner, Pamela Vandyke Price, Anne Willan
Executive Editor: Richard Moore
Deputy Editor: Thomas Cussans
Maps and Plans: Swanston Graphics
Drawings: Graham Byfield

FODOR'S

FRANCE
1988

FODOR'S TRAVEL PUBLICATIONS, INC.
New York and London

MANUFACTURED IN THE UNITED STATES OF AMERICA
10 9 8 7 6 5 4 3

CONTENTS

CONTENTS

CONTENTS

FOREWORD

France, often regarded as the world's most civilized nation—not least by the French—has for centuries exerted a powerful attraction for travelers. Today, as ever, it is a rewarding and delightful country to visit, and can provide a fascinating experience, whether for a full-scale vacation or for a briefer tour. For many Americans and Britons, France is the natural first choice on the Continent, as Europe used to be called.

In the last couple of decades the old France so beloved of the between-the-wars emigrés, the France of peasant farms and sleepy market towns, of the Paris enshrined in the stories of Scott Fitzgerald and Hemingway has changed almost out of recognition. A brisk, modern society has replaced the old order. In Paris, roaring highways sweep down beside the Seine, where once lovers wandered, but the towering modern blocks that disfigure so many cities have largely been banished to the outskirts. In the countryside smart new factories dot a landscape still haunted by lovely old châteaux or terraced with vines; along country lanes you can see smartly dressed girls, accompanying their black-shrouded grandmothers, grandmothers who may do their shopping in a nearby *supermarché*.

For the tourist this dichotomy presents a challenge. You can now get around the country, or parts of it at any rate, in the fast new T.G.V. trains, or meander gently along in quiet local buses; you can stay in excellent modern hotels, brash in their crispness, or in hidden country inns, where pet cats doze in overgrown gardens. You can join the incredible crowds along the Riviera, struggling for space on crowded beaches and food in close-packed restaurants; or you can drift through idyllic green waterways, sleepy in a silent skiff, with not a living creature in sight except the munching cows glimpsed through bordering trees. More than ever before France can offer all the best that life can afford—gourmet meals, delicious wines, an elegant, sophisticated way of life, art and history by the mile—and at prices that will not break the bank. Paris can be expensive, of course, if you let it, as can other chic destinations but, for the most part, France does not live up to its reputation as a costly destination. And, what is more important, you will be getting value, service and satisfaction for your money.

*

We would like to thank all those who have helped us in the task of updating this edition: the many helpful people in French Tourist Offices, both regional and national—especially in Paris and London, where we once again gratefully acknowledge the assistance of Mrs Pauline Hallam.

Our task of creating this new edition has been greatly lightened by the help of many who have put their expertise at our disposal. We are grateful for the discernment of Anne Willan, the distinguished teacher and writer on French cuisine, and for the continuing help of John P. Harris, whose amusing and sympathetic observation of the French way of life enlivens many breakfast tables. We would also like to extend our particular thanks to our Area Editor, Dominique Sicot.

*

All prices quoted in this Guide are based on those available to us at time of writing, mid-1987. Given the volatility of European costs and rates of exchange, it is inevitable that changes will have taken place by the time this book becomes available. We trust, therefore, that you will take prices quoted as indicators only, and that you will double-check so as to be sure of the latest figures.

Errors are bound to creep into any Guide. Hotels and restaurants can suffer instant decline in the quality of their service, acts of governments or God can change the travel picture overnight, and in many smaller ways we can find that items we have given as gospel appear to be untrue. For these reasons we greatly appreciate letters from our readers, telling us of their travel experiences or chastising us for apparent—or actual—errors. Not only do such letters help to keep us on the straight and narrow path, but they also give us a traveler's eye view that might have escaped our professional revisors.

Our addresses are—

in the U.S.: Fodor's Travel Publications, 201 East 50th Street, New York, NY 10022;

in the U.K.: Fodor's Travel Guides, 9-10 Market Place, London W1N 7AG.

MAP OF FRANCE

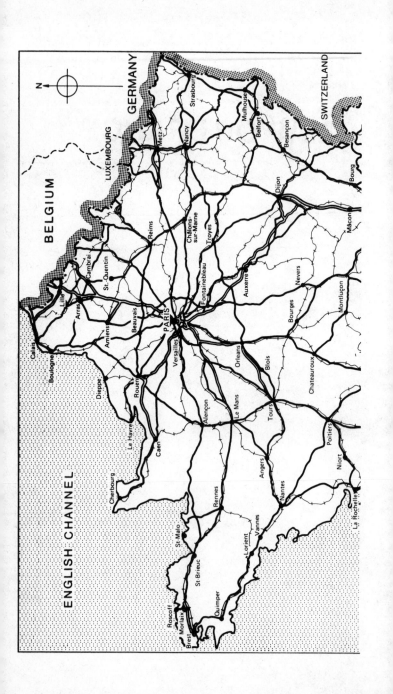

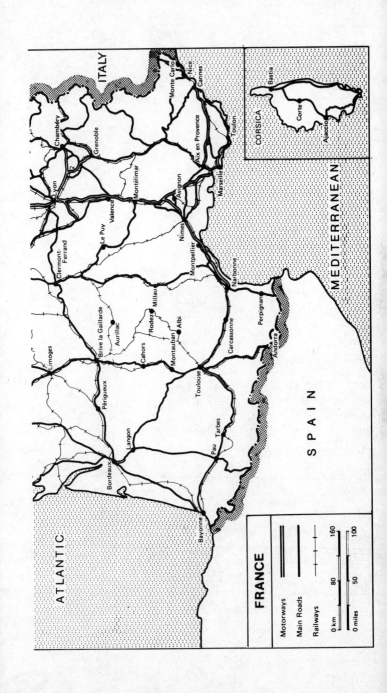

FACTS AT YOUR FINGERTIPS

FACTS AT YOUR FINGERTIPS

Planning Your Trip

NATIONAL TOURIST OFFICE. The major source of information for anyone planning a vacation in France is the French Government Tourist Office. They produce copious amounts of information, much of it free and all of it useful.

Their addresses are:

In the U.S.: 610 Fifth Ave., New York, N.Y. 10020 (212–757–1125); 645 North Michigan Ave., Chicago, IL 60611 (312–337–6301); 1 Hallidie, Suite 250, San Francisco, CA 94102; 9401 Wilshire Blvd., Suite 314, Beverly Hills, CA 90212 (213–272–2661).

In Canada: 1981 Ave. McGill College, Suite 490, Montreal, Quebec H3A 2W9 (514–288–4264); 1 Dundas St. West, Suite 2405, P.O. Box 8, Toronto, Ontario M5G 1Z3 (416–593–4717).

In the U.K.: 178 Piccadilly, London W.1 (01–491 7622).

TOURS. The range and variety of tours to France, whether fully-escorted or largely independent, is immense, and growing all the time. We can do no more than suggest a very few of the more characteristic here, but for comprehensive lists of tour operators contact either the French National Tourist Office or your travel agent. We give a representative list of American and British tour operators below. (All details and prices quoted here are for mid-'87; be sure to check for the latest information).

From the U.S.: For a basic, first-time budget overview of the whole of France, Globus Gateway offer a reasonable 15-day tour called, simply, "La France": hectic but comprehensive. The cost is around $900–$1,000 per person, excluding airfare to Paris. If you're not so keen on this type of whistle-stop broadside, there are plenty of good-value tours that take in only one or two areas of the country, though the sightseeing isn't necessarily any more in-depth. American Express has six tours, ranging in price from $350 to $1,300; several include side trips to Belgium and Luxembourg. Esplanade Tours' evocatively-titled "Medieval Southern France: Land of Troubadors, Crusades and Cave Artists" does much the same for southwestern France, though for a good bit more money: around $2,200, excluding airfare, per person.

A slightly more specialized, though not much less all-encompassing, tour is Maupintour's "Art of Paris and Southern France," just one of many art-oriented tours. This covers Paris, Versailles, Giverny, Fontainebleau and Barbizon in northern France and Provence in the south, plus a stop-over in Burgundy for wine tasting. 16 days, nine of them in Paris, works out at around $3,600 per person, excluding airfare.

1

A large number of self-drive vacations are available for those who are after greater independence. Auto-Venture, for example, offer five self-drive tours of various regions of France for around $600 per person for seven days. They also offer more expensively priced chauffeur-driven tours. A wide range of fly-drive vacations are also on offer from many tour operators.

For those after something distinctly different, a number of intriguing, and costly, vacations are available. Hemphill-Harris offers helicopter tours—yes, helicopter tours—featuring châteaux visits, among other delights. One day costs $750, 10 days cost $15,000, and there are several itineraries at prices in between. Buddy Bombard's "Great Balloon Adventures" offer a similar combination of graceful living, haute cuisine and adventure. Tours are based in either the Loire or Burgundy and include at least one balloon flight daily (weather permitting). Prices begin at around $2,000 per person for a half week.

From the U.K.: The range of tours from the U.K. is if anything even more immense. Art, history, ballooning, every species of sailing, self-catering, music, cookery, pilgrimages, walking, photography, even naturism, and much more beside, are all more than amply catered for. We strongly recommend you contact either the French National Tourist Office, whose *Guide for the Traveler in France* provides full lists of all tour operators and details of their vacations, or your travel agent.

U.S. Tour Operators

Abercrombie and Kent International Inc., 1420 Kensington Rd., Oak Brook, IL 60521 (312–954–2944).

Air France, 666 Fifth Ave., New York, N.Y. 10103 (212–247–0100).

American Express, 822 Lexington Ave., New York, N.Y. 10021 (800–241–1700); 12 Richmond St. East, Toronto, Ontario M5C 1M5 (416–868–1044).

Auto Venture, Division of Travplan Corp, 920 Logan Building, Seattle, WA 98101 (800–426–7502).

Bennett Tours, Inc., 270 Madison Ave., New York, N.Y. 10016 (212–532–5060).

Bombard Society, 6727 Curran St., McLean, VA 22101 (800–862–8537).

Caravan Tours, 401 N. Michigan Ave., Chicago, IL 60611 (312–321–9800).

Cartan Travel Bureau, 12755 Highway 55, Minneapolis, MN 55441 (800–422–7826).

Cortell Group, 770 Lexington Ave., New York, N.Y. 10021 (212–751–4200).

Cosmos/Globus Gateway, 95–25 Queens Blvd., Rego Park, N.Y. 11374 (718–268–1700).

Esplanade Tours, 581 Boylston, Boston, MA 02116 (617–266–7465).

Extra-Value Travel, 437 Madison Ave., New York, N.Y. 10022 (212–750–8800).

Floating Through Europe, 271 Madison Ave., New York, N.Y. 10016 (212–685–5600).

Four Winds Travel, 175 Fifth Ave., New York, N.Y. 10010 (212–777–0260).

Hemphill-Harris, 16000 Ventura Blvd., Suite 200, Encino, CA 91436 (818–906–8086).

Maupintour, 1515 St. Andrews Dr., Lawrence, KS 66044 (800–255–4266).

Pan Am Holidays, Pan Am Bldg., New York, N.Y. 10017 (212–687–2600).

Salt and Pepper Tours, 7 W. 36th St., Suite 1500, New York, N.Y. 10018

T.W.A. Getaway Vacations, 28 South 6th St., Philadelphia, PA 19106 (215–925–7885).

U.K. Tour Operators

Air France Holidays, 69 Boston Manor Rd., Brentford, Middx. TW8 9JQ (01-568 6981).

Allez France, 27 West St., Storrington, Pulborough, West Sussex RH20 4DZ (09066-5033).

American Express, American Express Europe Ltd., 6 Haymarket, London SW1Y 4BS (01-930 4411).

Brittany Ferries, The Brittany Center, Wharf Rd., Portsmouth, Hants. (0705-827701), and Millbay Docks, Plymouth, Devon (tel. 0752-221321).

British Airways Tours Operations, 101–102 Cheapside, London EC2V 6DT (01-726 8153).

Club Mediterranée, 106-108 Brompton Rd., London SW3 1JJ (01-581 1161).

Cosmos Coach Tours, Cosmos House, 1 Bromley Common, Bromley, Kent BR2 9LX (01-464 3400).

Eurogolf, 41 Watford Way, Hendon, London N.W.4 (01-202 0191).

French Travel Service, Francis House, Francis St., London SW1 1DE (01-828 8131).

Heritage Travel, 21 Dorset Sq., London NW1 5PG (01-730 9841).

Paris Travel Service, Bridge House, Ware, Herts. (0920-3922).

P.G.L. Adventure Holidays, 104 Station St., Ross-on-Wye, Herefordshire HR9 7AH (0989-65556).

Swan Hellenic Art Treasures Tours, 77 New Oxford St., London WC1A 1PP (01-831 1616).

Thomson Holidays, Greater London House, Hampstead Rd., London NW1 7SD (01-387 9321).

 WHEN TO GO. The main tourist season in France is June through September, but Easter is a favorite for many foreign visitors, especially those to Paris and Provence. Most of France is on vacation in July and August, when prices in holiday resorts soar, campsites and self-catering accommodations are jampacked, and travel is frequently unpleasant, with roads dangerously busy, and trains and buses uncomfortably crowded. On top of all that, many restaurants in Paris and other cities close for at least a month during this two-month peak period, as do theaters and shops. The plus points are good weather—July is generally the hottest month, with August more likely to be stormy—and less crowded city-center streets, and a wealth of events designed for summer tourists. Even Paris, once dead as a dodo in July and August, now organizes a number of jollities, such as firework displays and street festivals.

All the same, we advise you to pick June or September if you can: the weather is usually pleasanter for sightseeing (though June can be wet) and you won't have to stand in line to visit the country's wonderful historic buildings. October, too, is a good time to visit France, as you get a combination of the new season's exhibits, theater and opera, and more often than not golden days that show France's gloriously varied scenery at its best.

As for the fashionable resorts on the southeastern coast, the fabled Riviera, they're a long way from paradise in the height of summer, with beaches sardine-crowded, tent cities mushrooming along highways and all the sun-seeking world and his wife turning what was once a millionaires' playground into something more like Coney Island or Blackpool! The winter season, once ultra-chic, doesn't really exist now, though Nice is very lively at Carnival time in February or March. But once again, May, June and September or October are good bets.

Don't on any account travel on 1, 13/14 or 31 July, or 1, 14/15 or 31 August, or even the nearest weekends to these dates, unless you absolutely have to. The French are conformist about their holidays and everyone seems to be traveling at these peak periods, with two major national holidays (July 14 and August 15) only making matters worse.

The winter sports season in France (including Corsica) starts in late-November and continues until Easter, the busiest times being over Christmas and during the mid-semester vacations in February. A few high-altitude resorts in the Alps offer year-round skiing.

Climate. Average afternoon temperatures in degrees Fahrenheit and Centigrade:

	Jan.	Feb.	Mar.	Apr.	May	June	July	Aug.	Sept.	Oct.	Nov.	Dec.
Paris												
F°	42	45	52	60	67	73	76	75	69	59	49	43
C°	6	7	11	16	19	23	24	24	21	15	9	6

Nice

F°	56	56	59	64	69	76	81	81	77	70	62	58
C°	13	13	15	18	21	24	27	27	25	21	17	14

SEASONAL EVENTS. The visitor to France is never short of special events and festivals to entertain him or her. The list below covers only the principal annual events and celebrations. The French National Tourist Office as well as regional and local tourist offices within France can supply full details of events, from the national to the local village fête.

January. Monte Carlo Motor Rally.

February. Lemon Festival at Menton. Famous carnival at Nice (may run into Mar.). Mid-Lent carnivals (*Mardi-Gras*) in southwest and northeast.

April. Penitential processions in Corsica and in the southwest on Good Friday. *Prix du Président de la République,* internationally known horserace at Paris's Longchamp racecourse, at Easter. *Printemps de Bourges,* a major music festival.

May. Cannes Film Festival. Joan of Arc celebrations at Orléans, May 7–8. Monaco Grand Prix. International Tennis Championships at Roland-Garros stadium in Paris. "Musical May," concerts, dance and drama, at Bordeaux. *Festival de l'Ile de France* begins (continues to mid-July). Gipsy pilgrimage to Les Stes.-Maries-de-la-Mer, May 24–25. Pilgrimage and Blessing of the Sea at Honfleur, Whitsun. *Féria de la Pentecôte,* Nîmes, Whitsun.

June. *Festival du Marais,* Paris, with concerts in churches and courtyards of restored mansions (continues into July). *Tour de France,* the world's best-known cycle race, starts. *Fête de la Musique:* concerts and improvised street performances all over France. *Fêtes de la St.-Jean* (Feast of John the Baptist), celebrations all over the country, especially in places with names beginning with "St.-Jean," culminating in *Feux de la St.-Jean,* firework displays, on June 24. *Prix de Diane,* major horse race, at Chantilly. *Grand Fénétra,* fair at Toulouse. *Fêtes Musicales* (concerts), Tours. Gascony Festival at Auch. *Les 24 Heures du Mans,* motor-racing Grand Prix at Le Mans.

July. *Fête Nationale:* Bastille Day celebrations all over the country, with military parade in Paris, fireworks, dancing in the streets, July 14. *Festival Estival,* Summer Festival of concerts in Paris. *Festival de Cornouaille,* France's major folklore event, at Quimper. World-famous drama, dance and music festival at Avignon. *Festival des Nuits de Bourgogne,* Burgundy (may continue into Aug.). Final stage of the *Tour de France* cycle race, Champs-Elysées in Paris.

August. *Heures Musicales:* concerts in abbey at Mont St.-Michel. Feast of the Assumption pilgrimages, Lourdes and Le Puy, Aug. 15. Napoleon's birthday celebrations, Corsica, Aug. 15. *Les Grandes Heures de Cluny,* concerts in monastery at Cluny. Casals Festival at Prades.

September. *F.I.A.C. (Foire Internationale de l'Art Contemporain),* major contemporary art show, Paris. Wine festivals in Beaune and Dijon, Burgundy. *Musique en Côte Basque,* with concerts in centers such as Bayonne and Biarritz on the Basque coast. Commemoration of the martyrdom of the Huguenots, when Protestants from all over Europe assemble at the Musée du Désert at the Mas Soubeyran, Mialet, first Sun. in Sept.

October. Grape-picking fairs and festivals in the wine-producing regions. International Dance Festival, Paris (continues into Nov.). *Prix de l'Arc de Triomphe,* major horse race at Longchamp racecourse, Paris (first Sun. in Oct.). *Frairie des Petits Ventres:* traditional street festival, Limoges.

November. *Les Trois Glorieuses:* famous series of wine events in Beaune, Meursault and Nuits-St.-Georges, culminating in a wine auction at the Hospice de Beaune, Burgundy.

December. *Fête de la Lumière:* traditional ceremonies during which candles are lit in windows in honor of the Virgin Mary, in Lyon, Dec. 8. Midnight masses on Christmas Eve all over France, including Gregorian plainchant in some abbeys, most picturesque "living cribs" in Provence and the eastern Pyrenees, and famous celebrations with a medieval theme in Châteauneuf-en-Auxois and Pérouges.

National Holidays 1988. January 1; April 4 (Easter Monday); May 1 (Labor Day); May 8 (V.E. Day); May 23 (Whit Monday); July 14 (Bastille Day); August 15 (Assumption Day); November 1 (All Saints'); November 11 (Armistice Day); December 25.

 WHAT TO PACK. The golden rule is travel light. Baggage trolleys are in theory available at airports and rail stations, but in practice you may well have difficulty finding one, especially during peak holiday periods. Motorists should bear in mind that it is most unwise to leave baggage visible when you make daytime stops, so don't take more than will fit into your trunk. And unless you hit on one of the very rare hotels that has a garage watched over by a night attendant, you'll need to be able to carry it all to your room overnight. Remember too that you may well come back with more than you started with, as you find yourself buying gifts and souvenirs, perhaps even some new clothes in fashion-conscious France.

Your wardrobe will depend in part on where you'll be staying, in part on what you'll be doing. Weather in Paris and most of northern France is very variable, so be prepared for all eventualities, with a raincoat and umbrella at all times of year. Northeastern France can get very hot in summer but also very cold in winter. The south is naturally warmer than the north at all times of year, though you should always have a warm jacket in case the icy mistral wind is blowing. Parts of central France, especially the Loire Châteaux area, tend to get very steamy in July, so pack suitable clothes for sightseeing comfortably.

Despite having led the way in popularizing nude sunbathing (or perhaps because of it), the French are fairly formal socially. We advise you not to pack the jazzier and more casual items in your wardrobe if you're going to be visiting French families, eating in expensive restaurants, going to the theater and opera or the classier stores. A jeans-and-sneakers outfit will cause raised eyebrows in such establishments, as will wildly patterned shirts worn over shorts. Both men and women wearing shorts will probably be refused admission to churches and cathedrals, whether or not they are attending a service or mass, but there is no need to cover head and arms (though beach-style décolletés are frowned on).

Similarly, if you're invited to a dinner party in a private home, the golden rule is dress up rather than down. Frenchwomen take a great deal of trouble with their appearance and tend to dress up for entertaining, except in very young or bohemian circles, and you will feel awkward if you're in casual clothes when no one else is. On the other hand long skirts and dresses are rarely worn in France, so best pack a cocktail dress or a silk or chiffon blouse or shirt to go with a dressy skirt.

Practical, low-heeled shoes are better suited to sightseeing, wet weather and cobbled streets than daintier high-heeled styles. And avoid suede, which may well be ruined by the sandy sidewalks in Paris and the gravel walks and courtyards generally found outside châteaux and other historic buildings. Evening shoes won't be necessary for most visitors, but you'll be pleased to be able to exchange your daytime strollers for something more elegant for the evenings.

Handbags need careful thought. You'll need something big enough to hold passport (it is illegal not to have identification on you in France), travelers checks, tickets, glasses and maybe sunglasses, cosmetics and so on for all-day sightseeing. But if it's too big it will start feeling like a millstone after a while. We recommend that you choose a style that you can sling across your body, bandolier-style, as most Frenchwomen do, rather than carrying it on your shoulder, where it's an easy prey to bag-snatchers. A model with enough interior pockets (at least one with a zipper closing for your money) to keep things in some kind of order, and to keep passport and travelers' checks separated, makes life easier. Something with a positive fastening is protection against pickpockets. Take along a smaller bag for short excursions and for evenings; an evening bag will be needed only if you're going to dressy functions. Men used to carrying a shoulder bag should bear in mind our advice about bag-snatchers too. Either sling it across you, or go instead for the small type with a long handle you loop over your wrist.

COSTS IN FRANCE. France is basically a fairly expensive country, though regional differences are marked. The good news is that inflation in 1987 is at last under control: the 2.3% rate was the best since 1972. With a fluctuating dollar and a rather strong pound, it is difficult to say what the traveler will encounter. We must stress that it is essential to check the latest position when you're planning your trip, and to keep an eagle eye on exchange rates during your visit.

Paris can be expensive, but then again it has such a wide choice of sleeping and eating places that you can find both hotels and restaurants at reasonable prices in most districts. The same applies to the Riviera: in small side-streets away from the seafront in Cannes or Nice you'll find modest hotels and popular eating spots that certainly won't break the bank. And France has such a wide range of regions that you can pick and choose depending on your budget. Strasbourg, for instance, is a more expensive city, and the whole of Alsace is affected by this, except for very rural areas. The wine areas—especially Burgundy and the Bordeaux region—tend to be expensive too. But whole tracts of central France offer food and accommodations at unbeatable prices: the Auvergne and the Cévennes for instance. You'll find budget seaside resorts in Britanny, but also along the Languedoc and Roussillon coast. And in country districts everywhere you'll often be amazed at the value you'll get for your francs.

France has now become very conscious that its own citizens are curtailing their vacation spending in line with their diminishing budgets. Consequently a number of schemes have been put into operation to persuade the French that vacations needn't be too expensive. Everybody benefits. Good reductions are available on trains and planes for foreigners as well as French people, on top of which there is still the old-established *France-Vacances* rail pass for those non-resident in France. For details see "Getting around France." A number of resorts offer better deals in June and September than in high summer and an interesting new development is the launching of "Leisure Passports" giving you good reductions for sightseeing and many other leisure activities (see the "Loire Valley" chapter for details of the most important scheme).

Students and those under 26 do well in France, with reductions for most things except hotels and restaurants and the new Youth Pass, which even includes some fast-food restaurants.

Sample Costs. Cinema 30.35 frs.; theater 60 frs. upwards; opera 150 frs. upwards; museum entrance fee 15–25 frs.; bus journey in provincial city around 5 frs.; bus/metro journey in Paris around 4 frs.; glass of wine in café 5–10 frs., in wine bar around 10 frs.; draught beer in café around 8 frs., bottled beer around 10 frs.; soft drink in café around 10 frs.; taxi around 30 frs. for a 10-minute ride; cigarettes 5–10 frs. for pack of 20; newspaper around 4.50–5 frs. for French, 8 frs. upwards for foreign. For hotel and restaurant costs see "Staying in France."

French Currency. The basic unit of currency in France is the French franc (abbreviated as fr. or frs.), which is divided into 100 centimes. Coins in circulation are 5, 10 and 20 centimes (all copper-colored), 50 centimes, 1 fr., 2 frs., and 5 frs. (silver-colored) and 10 frs. (dark copper color). Notes or bills in circulation are 10 frs. (rapidly being superseded by the coins), 20 frs., 50 frs., 100 frs., 200 frs. and 500 frs.

At the time of writing (mid-'87) there were 6.00 frs. to the U.S. dollar and 10 frs. to the pound sterling. However, with exchange rates so unpredictable it is essential that you check the rate before you leave home, when you arrive and throughout your trip.

TAKING MONEY ABROAD. Traveler's checks are still the standard, and best, way to safeguard your travel funds; and you still usually get a better exchange rate in France for traveler's checks than for cash. In the U.S., many of the larger banks issue their own traveler's checks—just about as universally recognized as those of American Express, Cook and Barclays—as well as those of one or more of the firms mentioned above. In most instances there is a one percent charge for the checks; there is no fee for Barclays checks. Some banks also issue them free if you are a regular customer. The best-known British checks are Cook's and those of Barclays, Lloyds, Midland and National Westminster banks. It is also always a good idea to have some local currency upon arrival. Some banks will provide this service; alternately, contact *Deak-Pererra*, 630 Fifth Ave., New York, N.Y. 10111 (212–757–0100).

Britons holding a Uniform Eurocheque card and cheque book—apply for them at your bank—can cash checks for up to £100 a day at banks in France participating in the scheme and write checks for goods and services—in shops, hotels, restaurants, etc.—again up to £100 a time. Similarly, holders of Visa cards can withdraw money at over 750 post offices throughout France: look for the CB/VISA sticker in the window. You will also be able to change money at these same post offices: look for the CHANGE sticker posted on a window or wall.

Credit Cards. The conservative French have not taken easily to plastic money. As a result many shops, restaurants and hotels will not take some, or all, of the major cards and you should make sure you have cash or traveler's checks available at all times. As a general rule, establishments catering to foreign tourists are more enlightened on this matter, whereas those whose clientele is mainly French are less likely to accept your proffered card. This means that the price status of an establishment is no guide to its willingness or otherwise to take credit cards: a tiny bistrot near a famous château or in the middle of a tourist-frequented town may take the whole range of cards (and even foreign currency), whereas a deluxe restaurant mainly patronized by French businessmen may refuse the lot.

In our hotel and restaurant lists we indicate which, if any, cards are accepted. But bear in mind that in unpredictable France such details can and do change without warning. The abbreviations used are AE (for American Express), DC (for Diners Club), MC (for MasterCard, incorporating Access and Eurocard) and V (for Visa).

As a rule of thumb, Visa is the most likely to be accepted, with American Express and Diners Club about equal in the popularity stakes and MasterCard currently the poor relation.

If the worst happens and you lose your card or have it stolen, these are the numbers to ring in France (all are Paris numbers): American Express 47–08–31–21; Diners Club 47–23–78–05; MasterCard 43–23–42–49 on weekdays or 43–23–46–46 on weekends; Visa 42–77–11–90.

CHANGING MONEY. As with most countries, the best place to change money in France is at a bank. However, there are several official exchange offices in Paris and in some other major centers, and at most airports and some rail stations, where you can be sure of getting the official exchange rate. For convenience, or in emergencies, you may want to change money outside banking hours at tourist offices, hotels, some travel agents or privately run exchange offices, but you should be aware that they will give you a figure well below the official rate.

Banks are open Mon. to Fri. inclusive in Paris and some major cities; Tues. to Sat. in many provincial cities, towns, and villages; market-day only in rural centers. Opening times are by no means standardized, but run roughly from 9 to 4.30 or 5, with a lunchtime closure of at least an hour (frequently up to two hours) for the majority of banks in the provinces. In July and Aug., with many staff on vacation, a number of banks that stay open all day close their exchange counter at lunchtime.

PASSPORTS. Americans. Apply in person at U.S. Passport Agency Offices, local county courthouses or selected Post Offices. If you have a passport not more than eight years old you may apply by mail; otherwise you will need:

—proof of citizenship, such as a birth certificate.

—two identical photographs, either black and white or color, two inches square, on non-glossy paper and taken within the past six months.

—$35 for the passport itself plus a $7 processing fee if you are applying in person (no processing fee when applying by mail) for those 18 years and older, or, if you are under 18, $20 for the passport plus a $7 processing fee if you are applying in person (again, no extra fee when applying by mail).

—proof of identity such as a driver's license, previous passport, any governmental ID card that includes a photo and signature.

Adult passports are valid for ten years, others for five years; they are not renewable. Allow four to six weeks for your application to be processed, but in an emergency, Passport Agency offices can have a passport readied within 24–48 hours, and even the postal authorities can indicate "Rush" when necessary.

If you expect to travel extensively, request a 48- or 96-page passport rather than the usual 24-page one. There is no extra charge. When you receive your passport, write down its number, date and place of issue separately; if it is later lost or stolen, notify either the nearest American Consul or the Passport Office, Department of State, 1425 K St. NW, Washington, DC 20524, as well as the local police.

Canadians. Canadian citizens apply in person to regional passport offices, post offices or by mail to Bureau of Passports, Complexe Guy Favreau, 200 Dorchester West, Montreal, P.Q. H2Z 1X4. A $21 fee, two photographs and evidence of citizenship are required. Canadian passports are valid for five years and are non-renewable.

Britons. British subjects should apply for passports on special forms obtainable from main post offices or a travel agent. The application should be sent or taken to the Passport Office according to residential area (as indicated on the guidance form) or lodged with them through a travel agent. It is best to apply for the passport four to five weeks before it is required, although in some cases it will be issued sooner. The regional Passport Offices are located in London, Liverpool, Peterborough, Glasgow and Newport. The application must be countersigned by your bank manager or by a solicitor, barrister, doctor, clergyman or justice of the peace who knows you personally. You will need two full-face photos. The fee is £15; passport valid for ten years.

VISAS. A visa is required for nationals of all countries except members of the European Economic Community. Contact French consulates or tourist offices for details.

 HEALTH AND INSURANCE. The different varieties of travel insurance cover everything from health and accident costs, to lost baggage and trip cancellation. Sometimes they can all be obtained with one blanket policy; other times they overlap with existing coverage you might have for health and/or home; still other times it is best to buy policies that are tailored to very specific needs. Insurance is available from many sources, however, and many travelers unwittingly end up with redundant coverage. Before purchasing separate travel insurance of any kind, be sure to check your regular policies carefully.

Generally, it is best to take care of your insurance needs before embarking on your trip. You'll pay more for less coverage—and have less chance to read the fine print—if you wait until the last minute and make your purchases from, say, an airport vending machine or insurance company counter. If you have a regular insurance agent, he or she is the person to consult first.

Flight insurance, which is often included in the price of the ticket when the fare is paid via American Express, Visa or certain other major credit cards, is also often included in package policies providing accident coverage as well. These policies are available from most tour operators and insurance companies. While it is a good idea to have health and accident insurance when traveling, be careful not to spend money to duplicate coverage you may already have . . . or to neglect some eventuality which could end up costing a small fortune.

For example, basic Blue Cross-Blue Shield policies do cover health costs incurred while traveling. They will not, however, cover the cost of emergency transportation, which can often add up to several thousand dollars. Emergency transportation is covered, in part at least, by many major medical policies such as those underwritten by Prudential, Metropolitan and New York Life. Again, we can't urge you too strongly that in order to be sure you are getting the coverage you need, check any policy carefully before buying. Another important example: Most insurance issued specifically for travel does not cover pre-existing conditions, such as a heart condition.

Several organizations offer coverage designed to supplement existing health insurance and to help defray costs not covered by many standard policies, such as emergency transportation. Some of the more prominent are:

Travel Assistance International, the American arm of Europ Assistance, offers a comprehensive program providing medical and personal emergency services and offering immediate, on-the-spot medical, personal and financial help. Trip protection ranges from $35 for an individual for up to eight days to $220 for an entire family for a year. Full details from travel agents or insurance brokers, or from *Europ Assistance Worldwide Services, Inc.,* 1333 F St., N.W., Washington, D.C. 20004 (800–821–2828). In the U.K., contact Europ Assistance Ltd., 252 High St., Croydon, Surrey (01-680 1234).

Carefree Travel Insurance, c/o ARM Coverage Inc., 120 Mineola Blvd., Box 310, Mineola, N.Y. 11510 (516–294–0220), offers medical evacuation and other services arranged through Inter.Claim. Carefree coverage is available from many travel agents.

International SOS Assistance Inc., Box 11568, Philadelphia, PA 19116 (800–523–8930) has fees from $15 a person for seven days, to $195 for a year.

IAMAT (International Association for Medical Assistance to Travelers), 417 Center St., Lewiston, N.Y. 14092 (716–754–4883); 188 Nicklin Road, Guelph, Ontario, N1H 7L5 (519–836–0102).

The British Insurance Association, Aldermary House, Queen St., London E.C.4 (01-248 4477) will give comprehensive advice on all aspects of vacation travel insurance in the U.K.

Another frequent inconvenience to travelers is the loss of baggage. It is possible, though often complicated, to insure your luggage against loss through theft or negligence. Insurance companies are reluctant to sell such coverage alone, however, since it is often a losing proposition for them. Instead, it is most usually included as part of a package also covering accidents or health. Remuneration is normally determined by weight, regardless of the value of the specific contents of the luggage. Should you lose your luggage or some other personal possession, be sure to report it to the local police immediately. Without documentation of such a report, your insurance company might be very stingy. Also, before buying baggage insurance, check your homeowners policy. Some such policies offer "off-premises theft" coverage, including loss of luggage while traveling.

The last major area of traveler's insurance is trip cancellation coverage. This is especially important to travelers on APEX or charter flights. Should you get sick abroad, or for some other reason be unable to continue your trip, you may be stuck having to buy a new one-way fare home, plus paying for space on the charter you're not using. You can guard against this with trip cancellation insurance, usually available from travel agents. Most of these policies will also cover last minute cancellations.

STUDENT AND YOUTH TRAVEL. All student travelers should obtain an International Student Identity Card, essential for getting student discounts, youth bus passes, etc. It is available for $10 from the *Council On International Educational Exchange* (see below for addresses). Canadian students should apply to the *Association of Student Councils,* 187 College St., Toronto, Ont. M5T 1P7. The Canadian card is $10. The following organizations can also be helpful in finding student flights, educational opportunities and other information. Most deal with international student travel generally, but materials for those listed cover Israel.

American Youth Hostels, Box 37613, Washington DC 20013 (202–783–6161). Members are eligible for entree to the worldwide network of youth hostels. The organization publishes an extensive directory to same.

Council on International Educational Exchange (CIEE), 205 East 42 St., New York, N.Y. 10017 (212–661–1414); 312 Sutter St., San Francisco, CA 94108 (415–421–3473) provides information on summer study, work/travel programs and travel services for college and high school students and a free *Charter Flights Guide* booklet. Their *Whole World Handbook* ($7.95 plus $1 postage) is the best listing of both work and study possibilities.

Institute of International Education, 809 United Nations Plaza, New York, N.Y. 10017 (212–883–8200) is primarily concerned with study opportunities and administers scholarships and fellowships for international study and training. The New York office has a visitor's information center; satellite offices are located in Chicago, Denver, Houston, San Francisco and Washington.

HINTS FOR HANDICAPPED TRAVELERS. Facilities for the handicapped in France are generally good, or better than average at least. The French government is commendably aware of the difficulties facing disabled visitors and is doing much to ensure that public facilities make at least a minimum of provision for them. They have produced an excellent booklet— *Touristes quand même*—with an English glossary and easily understood symbols. This details facilities available to the disabled on transportation systems, and in public buildings—museums, historic buildings, etc.—on a region by region basis. It is available from the French National Tourist Office, the Paris tourist office or from the *Comité National Français de Liaison pour la Readaption des Handicapés,* 38 blvd. Raspail, 75007 Paris.

Regional hotel lists include a symbol to indicate which hotels have rooms accessible to the disabled. Similarly, the S.N.C.F., French railways, have special carriages on some trains reserved exclusively for the handicapped. They can also arrange to escort wheelchair-bound passengers on and off trains and help them catch connecting trains, but this later service must be requested some days in advance.

Otherwise, the principal sources of information are *Access to the World: A Travel Guide for the Handicapped,* by Louise Weiss, is an outstanding book covering all aspects of travel for anyone with health or medical problems. It features extensive listings and suggestions on everything from availability of special diets to wheelchair accessibility. Order from *Facts On File,* 460 Park Ave. South, New York, N.Y. 10016 ($14.95).

Tours specially designed for the handicapped generally parallel those of the non-handicapped traveler, but at a more leisurely pace. For a complete list of tour operators who arrange such travel write to the *Society for the Advancement of Travel for the Handicapped,* 26 Court St., Brooklyn, N.Y. 11242. *Moss Rehabilitation Hospital,* 12th St. and Tabor Rd., Philadelphia, PA 19141, answers inquiries regarding specific cities and countries as well as providing toll-free telephone numbers for airlines with special lines for the hearing impaired and, again, listings of selected tour operators.

Also very helpful is the *Information Center for Individuals with Disabilities,* 20 Park Plaza, Room 330, Boston, MA 02116.

In the U.K., contact *Mobility International,* 43 Dorset St., London W.1; the *National Society for Mentally Handicapped Children,* 117 Golden Lane, London E.C.1; the *Across Trust,* Crown House, Morden, Surrey (they have an amazing series of "Jumbulances," huge articulated ambulances, staffed by volunteer doctors and nurses, that can whisk even the most seriously handicapped across Europe in comfort and safety). But the main source in Britain for all advice on handicapped travel is the *Royal Association for Disability and Rehabilitation* (RADAR), 25 Mortimer St., London W.1.

Threshold Travel, Wrendal House, 2 Whotworth St. West, Manchester (061-236 9763) specialize in package tours for the disabled to France, principally to Nice.

 FRENCH TIME. France is six hours ahead of Eastern Standard Time and one hour ahead of Greenwich Mean Time. The French put their clocks forward an hour in the spring and back an hour in the fall at more or less the same time as both the U.S. and Britain, meaning that this six and one hour difference respectively remains the same.

Getting to France

From North America

 BY AIR. Flights from major departure points in the U.S. and Canada to France are frequent and generally easy to arrange. And, given the perpetual battle for business among the major airlines flying the Atlantic, fares are generally inexpensive. We give details of sample fares to Paris below.

However, be warned that though fares may be low and flights numerous, long-distance flying today is no bed of roses. Lines and delays at ever-more-crowded airports, perfunctory in-flight service and shrinking leg-room on board a giant jet with some 400 other people, followed by interminable waits for your luggage when you arrive, are the clearest possible signals that the glamor of air travel—if it ever existed—is very much a thing of the past.

Unfortunately, these problems are compounded when flying to Europe by the fact that most flights from the States are scheduled to arrive first thing in the morning. Not only are you in for a night's discomfort on the plane, but you arrive at the start of a new day to be greeted by the confusion (some would say chaos) of a modern airport. To make life even more difficult for the weary traveler, many hotels will not allow you to check in before noon or even 1 P.M. giving you as much as six hours with nothing to do and nowhere to go.

There are a number of steps you can take, however, in order to lessen the traumas of long-distance flying. The first and possibly the most important of all is to harbor no illusions about the supposed luxury. If you approach your flight knowing that you are going to be cooped up for a long time and will have to face delays and discomforts of all kinds, the odds are that you will get through it without doing terrible things to your blood pressure or being disillusioned—but there's no point expecting comfort, good service and efficiency because you won't get them.

The right attitude is half the battle, but there are a number of other practical points to follow. Wear comfortable, loose-fitting clothes and take off your shoes. Try to sleep as much as possible, especially on the night flights; this can very often mean not watching the movie (they are invariably dull anyway) as it will probably be shown during the only period when meals are not being served and you can sleep. If you have difficulty sleeping, or think you might, take along a light sedative and try to get a window seat in order to avoid being woken up to let the person next to you get to the toilet or being bashed by people walking down the aisle. Above all, avoid alcohol, or at least drink only a little. The dry air of a pressurized airplane causes rapid dehydration, exaggerating the effects of drink and jet lag. Similarly, drink as much water as possible. Finally, once you arrive, try to take things easily for a day or so. In the excitement of being in a new place, especially for the first time, you can very often not realize how tired you are and optimistically set out sightseeing, only to come down to earth with a bump. Whatever you do, don't have any business meetings for at least 24 hours after arriving.

Fares. With airfares in a constant state of flux, the best advice for anyone planning to fly to France independently (rather than as part of a package, in which case your flight will have been arranged for you) is to check with your travel agent, get him or her to explain the complex ins-and-outs of the fares available and then get them to make the reservations for you. Nonetheless, there are a number of points to bear in mind.

The best bet is to buy either an Apex or Super-Apex ticket. First Class, Business (or Club) and even the misleadingly-named Economy, though giving maximum flexibility on flying dates and cancellations, as well as permitting stop overs, are extremely expensive. Apex and Super-Apex by contrast are reasonably priced and offer the all-important security of fixed return dates (all Apex tickets are round trip). In addition, you get exactly the same service on board the airplane as flying Economy.

However, there are a number of restrictions; you must book, and pay for, your ticket 21 days or more in advance; you can stay in France no less than and no longer than a stated period (usually six days and six months); if you miss your flight, you forfeit the fare. But from the point of view of price and convenience, these tickets certainly represent the best value for money.

If your plans are sufficiently flexible and tighter budgeting is important, you can sometimes benefit from the last-minute bargains offered by tour operators otherwise unable to fill their plane or quota of seats. A number of brokers specializing in these discount sales have sprung up who can book seats of this type. All charge an annual membership fee, usually around $35–45.

Among them are: *Stand-Buys Ltd.,* 311 West Superior St., Suite 414, Chicago, IL 60610 (312–943–5737). *Moments Notice,* 40 East 49th St., New York, N.Y. 10017 (212–486–0503). *Discount Travel Intl.,* 114 Forest Ave., Narberth, PA 19072 (215–668–2182). *Worldwide Discount Travel Club,* 1674 Meridian Ave., Miami Beach, FL 33139 (305–534–2082).

Charter flights are also available to France, though their number has decreased in recent years. Again, a travel agent will be able to recommend the most reliable. You might also consider, though this too should be done via a travel agent, buying a package tour to France, but using only the plane ticket. As packages are able to get substantial discounts on fares through block booking seats, the price of the total package can sometimes be less than an ordinary air fare alone.

Typical fares as of mid-1987 for New York to Paris were: $1,781 one way First Class year-round; $972 one way Business Class year round; $1,450 round trip Economy Class; $700–$760 roundtrip APEX depending on season (can be even less pricey). Charter fares are about the same as, or slightly lower than, APEX.

 BY SEA. Cunard's *QE2* is the only luxury liner that makes transatlantic crossings on a regular schedule— four roundtrips annually that stop at Le Havre. Rates vary by season, but "intermediate" season (July) fares range from around $1,500 to $7,000, as of mid-1987, per person, double occupancy, each way. Contact *Cunard Lines, Inc.,* 555 Fifth Ave., New York, N.Y. 10017 (tel. 800–522–5262 or –7530).

Throughout the summer Polish Ocean Lines operate a passenger service between Montreal and London and Rotterdam, both of which have good transport connections with French cities. There are also several shipping lines which offer berths on their modern container ships which ply between North American ports and Europe. A round trip costs around $2,600. It is essential to book well in advance as the number of berths per ship is limited to twelve. Details from *Gdynia American Shipping Lines,* 238 City Rd., London EC1V 2Q1 (tel. 01–251 –3389).

For details on the possibility of freighter travel to or from France, consult *Air Marine Travel Service,* 501 Madison Ave., New York, N.Y. 10022 (tel. 212–371–1300) publisher of the *Trip Log Quick Reference Freighter Guide.*

From the U.K.

BY AIR. As you would expect, Paris has an excellent service from both London airports, Heathrow and Gatwick. British Airways and Air France operate some 12 flights daily from London (Heathrow) to Paris (Charles-de-Gaulle/Roissy) airport. The flying time is one hour. British Caledonian fly from London (Gatwick) to Paris (Charles-de-Gaulle/Roissy) and they offer six flights daily with departures approximately every two hours. The flying time from Gatwick is slightly shorter, at around 55 minutes. This, coupled with the efficiency of the Gatwick Airport Express service operated by British Rail from London (Victoria) to the in-terminal station at Gatwick and the swift Roissy Rail Service (Line B) from Charles-de-Gaulle/Roissy airport to the center of Paris (both journeys taking around half an hour) makes Gatwick–Paris the quickest and easiest route. The new London City Airport in London's Docklands will be in full operation in 1988, with up to four flights daily to Paris. Fares will be at Club Class levels.

Services from elsewhere in the U.K. to Paris are also good. Airports with direct flights to Paris include: Birmingham (British Airways), East Midlands (British Midland), Manchester (British Airways/Air France), Stansted and Southampton (Air U.K.).

There are also good direct air lines from London to French provincial centers. Flying out of London Heathrow, British Airways/Air France operate flights to Bordeaux, Lyon, Marseille, Mulhouse and Nice. On all these routes there is at least one flight a day, though Nice in high summer has at least three flights daily. Air France exclusively serve Lille, Strasbourg and Toulouse with at least one flight daily on week days. Air France also operate a number of seasonal services, normally on a couple of days per week in summer to Biarritz, Montpellier and Nantes. From London Gatwick there are direct flights by smaller airlines to a wide range of destinations. Dan Air fly to Toulouse throughout the year and during the summer to Lourdes/Tarbes, Montpellier, and Perpignan; Brit Air fly to Brittany, serving Caen, Le Havre, Morlaix, Quimper and Rennes. Finally there are direct charter flights from Gatwick to Calvi on Corsica by operators such as Planefair.

Fares. Fares from London to Paris are high, but less so than they have been. Expect to pay around £65 for an off peak round trip using scheduled services from London; for Club Class around £180 round trip. There are now "scheduled charter" flights which are available to all. One of the major French travel firms has broken into the market, offering return flights to Paris Orly from London Gatwick for as little as £55 return. Details from *Nouvelles Frontières,* 1–2 Hanover St., London W1R 9WB (tel. 01–629–7772). Their charters also serve other destinations including Strasbourg, Nice, Toulouse and Nantes. Air France have countered this threat by greatly increasing the numbers of flights from regional airports including Birmingham, Manchester and Southampton. The fares to Paris from the regions are better value for money: as a guide expect to pay around £100 round trip from Manchester.

BY TRAIN. France has never been so easily accessible by train from London. Thanks to the combination of the fast Hoverspeed City-Link service and the superb *Train à Grand Vitesse* (T.G.V.) and other French high speed trains (Corail 200) on several lines there are very few major cities which cannot be reached in a longish day from London. With a start from London around 10 A.M., and traveling via Paris, Lyon, Dijon and Grenoble can all be reached before 9 P.M.; Nantes, Bordeaux, Avignon and Strasbourg before 10 and even Marseille a little after 10.30 P.M.

Paris can be reached in under five and a half hours using the City-Link rail-hovercraft-rail service run by Hoverspeed. There are up to four through services from London (Victoria) on week days, and five at weekends during the summer. The interchanges between the different modes of transport are easy and there is no need to tote baggage for long distances. On the French side a special Turbotrain runs from the hoverport (Boulogne Aeroglisseurs) via Lille to Paris (Gare du Nord). Fares are good value for money. An ordinary Second Class round trip to Paris works out at around £75. In summer it is essential to book in advance. Full details from any British Rail Travel Center, or direct from *Hoverspeed,* Maybrook House, Queens Gardens, Dover, Kent (tel. 0304–216205).

It is also possible to travel to Paris using one of the conventional ferry services, though this extends the journey time to around seven hours via the Dover–Calais and Folkestone–Boulogne crossings, and ten hours via the Newhaven–Dieppe route. The boat trains for Dover, Folkestone and Newhaven all depart from London's Victoria Station. On all these routes the interchange between rail and ship is easy, but be prepared for lines in high season. All these crossings are only suitable for daytime travel.

The best way to get to Paris overnight is to use the Parisienne service run by British Rail and Townsend Thoresen. This service leaves from London (Waterloo) to Portsmouth in mid-evening, to connect with the overnight sailing to Le Havre, where the ferry docks at 7 A.M. local time. From Le Havre, a Corail express train whisks you to Paris, arriving in the Gare St. Lazare just after 10. A choice of cabin/couchette accommodations are available. Transfers between station and port are provided.

If bound for Normandy and Brittany there is a wide range of routes and operators to choose from. From Portsmouth there are direct sailings to Caen, Cherbourg and St.-Malo, but these are not through rail services so be prepared to make your own way from station to ship, and vice versa. Alternatively, travel from London (Waterloo) to Weymouth and then by ferry to Cherbourg, from where there are connecting trains to Bayeux, Caen, Lisieux, and Rennes. On this route bus connections are provided.

There are also special through trains from Calais and Boulogne to a wide range of French resorts —(destinations vary according to the season). In summer there is the Flandres–Riviera train. This has an early-afternoon connection from London (Victoria), and runs overnight from Calais (Maritime) to Marseille, St.-Raphael, Cannes, Juan les Pins, Antibes and Nice. First and Second class sleeping cars and couchettes are available. On three nights a week there is a through train to the resorts of Languedoc-Roussillon (Montpellier, Sète, Béziers and Perpignan). Sleepers and couchettes available. Pre-booked travelers can also use some of the French Travel Service (F.T.S.) weekly holiday trains: the "Brittany Express" (Calais–Nantes), the "Pyrenees Express" to Toulouse, and the "Aquitaine Express" to Bordeaux, Biarritz and St.-Jean de Luz. In winter there are through trains to the ski resorts, including Bourg-St.-Maurice, and St.-Gervais-le-Fayet for Chamonix.

Fares. Visitors from the U.S. and other non-European countries should investigate the Eurail pass. Though not valid for the U.K. portion of the journey, this is an excellent deal. The pass gives unlimited First Class rail travel in 16 European countries, including France, at a cost of $280, $350, $440, $620 and $760 for 15 days, 21 days, one month, two months and three months respectively. Details from *French National Railroads,* 610 Fifth Ave., New York, N.Y. 10020.

A wide range of through fares is available from the U.K. For short breaks the European Saver fares, valid for five days, are excellent value. 1987 prices were: Paris £50 round trip, Lyon £82, Avignon £96 and Cannes £115. All use the Hoverspeed Citylink service. For longer stays the full round trip fares, using the ordinary ferry service, are £72, £118, £138 and £165 respectively. By traveling off peak in France and staying away for at least six days you can save money on longer trips. Ask for details of the *Séjour* fares: Lyon £106 round trip, Avignon £121, Cannes £141.

Young people resident in the U.K. (for at least six months) should evaluate the Inter Rail card at around £140 for one month's unlimited rail travel in some 21 European countries, plus travel at half price on British Rail plus up to 50% discount on Sealink British Ferries, Hoverspeed and Townsend Thoresen ferries to and from France. The discount varies according to route. Details from any

FERRY SERVICES FOR TRAVEL TO FRANCE FROM BRITAIN

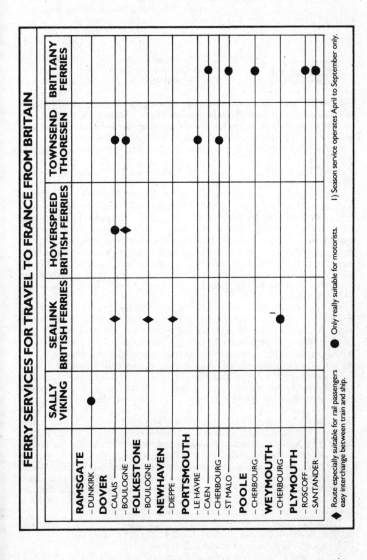

	SALLY VIKING	SEALINK BRITISH FERRIES	HOVERSPEED BRITISH FERRIES	TOWNSEND THORESEN	BRITTANY FERRIES
RAMSGATE					
– DUNKIRK	●				
DOVER					
– CALAIS		◆	●	●	
– BOULOGNE			◆	●	
FOLKESTONE					
– BOULOGNE		◆			
NEWHAVEN					
– DIEPPE		◆			
PORTSMOUTH					
– LE HAVRE				●	●
– CAEN					●
– CHERBOURG				●	●
– ST MALO					●
POOLE					
– CHERBOURG					●
WEYMOUTH					
– CHERBOURG		● 1)			
PLYMOUTH					
– ROSCOFF					●●
– SANTANDER					●●

◆ Route especially suitable for rail passengers: easy interchange between train and ship.

● Only really suitable for motorists.

1) Season service operates April to September only.

British Rail station. Also on offer, but only worth buying if you don't intend traveling around once you get there, are the discount youth tickets from *Eurotrain,* 52 Grosvenor Gardens, London S.W.1 (tel. 01–730 3402), or *Transalpino,* 71–75 Buckingham Palace Rd., London S.W.1 (tel. 01–834 9656). Paris £42, Lyon £81, Avignon £96, Cannes £116—from London, round trip.

 BY BUS. International Express, operating out of London's Victoria Coach Station, serve some 40 main centers in France, with the emphasis on the southern resorts.

Paris, for example, can be reached by using the Hoverspeed City-Sprint services, promoted under the International Express banner. These City-Sprint services are the fastest, taking full advantage of the 40-minute hovercraft Channel crossing. There are up to four departures daily in the summer, and the morning bus arrives in Paris by tea time. The actual traveling time is a little over eight hours. The fare is around £40 round trip, with slight reductions for students. For details contact *Hoverspeed,* Maybrook House, Queens Gardens, Dover, Kent (tel. 0304–216205).

International Express also run several services to Paris which make use of conventional ferry services across the Channel—with a commensurate increase in journey time. These International Express lines are operated by Eurolines. First, an overnight bus which leaves London (Victoria Coach Station) in mid-evening and reaches Paris (Port de la Villette) early the following morning; not the most restful of journeys as the ferry transfers are made in the middle of the night. Secondly, there is a daily daytime service during the summer. This leaves London in the morning and reaches Paris around 7 P.M. Thirdly, there is now a mid-day departure as well. Fares on these slower services work out at around £40 round trip.

Heading South? Then International Express' "Riviera Express"—run in conjunction with French Leave holidays—will take you in comfort to the resorts of the Riviera: St.-Maxime, Cannes and Nice. This runs twice a week from London (Victoria Coach Station), leaving in the morning. The Channel crossing is made in the afternoon and an overnight stop in a hotel at Auxerre. This makes the journey much more relaxed than the tiring overnight drives on many routes. Fares are also good value for money: around £140 round trip, excluding evening meal. Eurolines operate an express service which runs overnight to Grenoble. From here, there are connecting services to Nice and Marseilles. Using this route you leave London (Victoria Coach Station) in mid-afternoon and reach Grenoble the next morning. The connecting services leave around lunch time. The round trip fare to Nice is around £125. Eurolines also run a fast bus to Lyon four days a week in summer. This leaves London in mid-evening and reaches Lyon the following afternoon: around £75 round trip.

The beautiful Atlantic coast is also served by International Express. During the peak summer season there is at least one bus a day to Bordeaux. These buses continue on to Biarritz (the Queen of Beaches, the Beach of Kings), around £92 round trip. The journey takes up to 24 hours. Twice a week the service to Bordeaux is extended to Lourdes via Tarbes.

The Savoy Alps, Annemasse (for Geneva and Evian-les-Bains), and Chamonix have an almost daily service from London. The run to Chamonix takes some 21 hours: to Chamonix £82 round trip.

For details, contact *International Express,* The Coach Travel Center, 13 Regent St., London SW1Y 4LR (tel. 01–439 9368), or any National Express coach station or appointed travel agent. *Eurolines,* 52 Grosvenor Gardens, London S.W.1 (tel. 01-730 3433). For details of Europabus services contact *S.C.E.T.A.,* Europabus, Service Routier Voyageurs, 9 rue Pablo Neruda, 92532 Levalois Perret Cedex, France.

BY CAR. Traveling to and throughout France by car is easy, with a wide range of Channel crossings to choose from. The French autoroute network is like an octopus centered on Paris, its tentacles reaching out into the different corners of the country. Thus for many of the regions it is quickest to go via the French capital.

The shortest sea crossing is from Dover to Calais. Dover has good access from London via the M2/A2, the road going right to the entrance of the Eastern Docks. The Channel can be crossed by Hovercraft in 35 minutes or conventional ferry in around 75 minutes. Both Calais and Boulogne are served by Hoverspeed hovercraft and by the fast ferries of Townsend Thoresen and Sealink British Ferries. Departures are frequent, especially during the summer, so that it is only really necessary to book well in advance if a specific sailing is required at a peak weekend. Sealink also operate a frequent service from nearby Folkestone to Boulogne, and Sally Viking Line operate from Ramsgate to Dunkerque.

Getting to Paris from the French Channel ports is equally easy, with disembarkation and customs checks usually quick and efficient. Calais and Boulogne are served by the A26 motorway which now commences at Nordausque, only a few miles from the coast, and continues all the way to Paris. The roads leading to the motorway are as follows: from Calais take the N43; from Boulogne the N42; and from Dunkerque follow the signs for the A25 which runs to Lille and then the A1, which connects with the A26 near Arras. Don't forget that tolls are charged on the French motorways, so be sure to have some small denomination notes and change ready for toll booths, though credit cards (Visa, mostly) are more and more accepted.

Portsmouth, with its excellent motorway access from London and the Midlands, is now one of the major ferry ports, with services to Le Havre, Caen, Cherbourg and St.-Malo, though sailings are not as frequent as from Dover and Folkestone. The daytime sailings to the first three destinations take around five hours, and nine hours to St.-Malo (See Ferry Chart for operators). However, one of the most useful features of this route is that the overnight sailings to Le Havre, usually timed to leave late evening, berth in the French port at around 7 A.M. local time. This means that by booking a cabin or couchette it is possible to get a good night's sleep and an early start the next morning.

Other crossings worth considering are the Truckline (Brittany Ferries) service from Poole to Cherbourg (summer only), the British Ferries service (summer only: may not run in 1988—check for latest details) from Weymouth to Cherbourg, and, in the southwest, the Brittany ferries sailing from Plymouth to Roscoff.

Fares. These vary widely according to both the time of year and the convenience of the timing. Away from the peak weekends in high summer the ferry companies offer a wide range of special deals for motorists, with or without accommodations in France. Even in high summer it is possible to save substantially by traveling mid-week. To give an idea of costs, for two adults and a medium sized car the crossing from Dover to Calais works out at around £90 peak one way, falling to around £85 using an early-morning, mid-week sailing in summer. On the longer Portsmouth routes, budget around £95 using a daytime service and £120 going overnight with a cabin for two.

FRENCH CUSTOMS. There are two levels of duty-free allowance for travelers entering France: one, for those coming from an E.E.C. country; two, for those coming from any other country.

In the first category you may import duty free: 300 cigarettes or 150 cigarillos or 75 cigars or 400 gr. of tobacco; plus, five liters of wine or one and a half liters of alcohol over 22° proof or three liters of alcohol less than 22° proof; plus, 75 gr. of perfume and three-eighths of a liter of toilet water; plus, for those over 15, other goods to the value of 2,000 frs. (400 frs. for those under 15).

In the second category you may import duty free: 200 cigarettes or 100 cigarillos or 50 cigars or 250 gr. of tobacco (these allowances are doubled if you live outside Europe); plus, two liters of wine or one liter of alcohol more than

22° proof or two liters of alcohol less than 22° proof; plus, 50 gr. of perfume and a quarter of a liter of toilet water; plus, for those over 15, other goods to the value of 300 frs. (150 frs. for those under 15).

Any amount of French or foreign currency may be imported into France. Foreign currencies converted into francs may be reconverted into foreign currency only up to the equivalent of 5,000 frs. Similarly, no more than 5,000 frs. may be exported. No more than the equivalent of 2,000 frs. in foreign currency may be exported.

Staying in France

 HOTELS. Most areas in France offer a good range of hotels to suit all tastes and pocketbooks, though prices vary considerably from one area to another. The country's luxury hotels are found in Paris and in the chic resorts along the Mediterranean coast or the winter sports resorts in the Alps. Most cities have one or two top-class hotels plus many more in the moderate and inexpensive brackets. Country districts offer many peaceful inns, ranging from very comfortable places with pools and lovely grounds to modest little spots, often with excellent restaurants.

The official French system grades hotels into 4-star deluxe, 4-star, 3-star, 2-star and 1-star. But the grading depends as much on amenities (T.V., direct dialing and the like) as on price, which may vary substantially within one star grading. Accordingly, we have graded all the hotels in our listings by price alone, dividing them into three basic groups: Expensive, or (E), Moderate, or (M), and Inexpensive, or (I). In Paris we also suggest some Superdeluxe, or (S), and Luxury, or (L) hotels (see Paris chapter for details and prices).

Prices. In the rest of the country, as a rule of thumb, you should expect to pay 120–270 fr. for a double room without breakfast in an Inexpensive hotel; 270–450 in a Moderate hotel; and 450–850 in an Expensive hotel.

But it must be emphasized that prices vary enormously within each category and, confusingly, within each hotel. One establishment may well have a couple of special rooms costing considerably more than the majority of rooms, and/or some that have fewer facilities than other rooms and are priced at a lower rate. We have therefore based our grading on the *average* price of a room. You must check very carefully the cost of the room you are being offered when you make reservations.

To make matters worse, prices change frequently, with some hotels suddenly deciding to upgrade their rooms by adding bathrooms or other facilities in order to escape from government controls on lower-priced hotels. And the government itself has complicated the issue by deciding to de-control hotel room prices more or less overnight, making it even more difficult to predict how any one establishment will have reacted by the time you read this.

We recommend that you check the price posted up in your room and make sure that it is the same as the price you agreed when reserving. A small number of tourist resorts offering exceptional facilities, or with major historical monuments to maintain, are allowed to instruct hotels to charge a *taxe de séjour* (resort tax) to all visitors. The price of this tax is around 1–5 fr. per person per day, with half-price for children between 10 and 4 and exemption for children under 4; it must be clearly stated in each room, at the entrance to the hotel and at the local town hall.

The good news is that in France you mostly pay for the room, not on a per-person basis. This is tough on people traveling alone, especially as single rooms are becoming less common (and are often poky and run-down), but it does mean that couples or other visitors sharing a room can do a great deal better than in many other countries in Europe. Many hotels will now agree to three people sharing a double room with a double and single bed for only a small extra charge (around 30–40 fr. extra), a bargain for a couple traveling with a child. In the newer hotels most rooms, as elsewhere in the West, are twin-bedded. In older hotels they're more likely to have a double bed. Rooms with a private bathroom are now the norm, even in some (I) places, as new hotels are built and older ones renovated. But you should be aware that as more space is given over to bathrooms so the bedrooms seem to shrink: even in (E) hotels you may find double rooms uncomfortably cramped, with little space for baggage or nowhere to write letters and postcards. Television sets are found in most (E) hotel rooms, many (M) rooms and in city-center (I) hotels mostly used by businessmen and commercial travelers. In country districts you're less likely to find them.

General Points. One or two tips to help you sleep easy in your bed in France's hotels. First, bear in mind that *salle de bain* (bathroom) does not necessarily mean the room contains a bathtub; it may just have a shower. If you've a fondness for soaking in plenty of hot water specify that you want a *baignoire* (bathtub) not just a *douche* (shower). Secondly, plumbing may leave a lot to be desired in the less expensive hotels, in spite of genuine efforts in recent years to modernize and renovate. Noise can be a problem in city-center hotels too. Air-conditioning is rare, even in (E) hotels, and though doubleglazing is becoming more common, this doesn't help in summer temperatures when you'll need some air at night. We advise you to specify that you want a quiet room *(une chambre tranquille)*. The same applies to country hotels: even the most delightful place may be near a busy road, or even a motorway.

Another cause of insomnia can be lack of a pillow! The French favor a long bolster called a *traversin,* hard and lumpy to those not brought up on one. There may be pillows too, either on the bed or in the wardrobe or cupboard, but check this out as soon as you get to your room and ask for them immediately (the term is *oreiller*) if your search proves unsuccessful. Don't wait till bedtime when the linen closet will be locked up and the night porter or receptionist won't have the key.

In most hotels geared to receiving foreign tourists you'll find someone at reception who speaks at least a little English, but don't expect chambermaids and other staff to, except in the top-notch places.

Hotel Restaurants. Few hotels now include breakfast in the room price. Check the price posted up in the room by law to see if it specifies an extra charge for breakfast. In small, family-type hotels and many city-center hotels in all price ranges you can have breakfast in your room for no extra charge—indeed such hotels may well not have a breakfast room. This is a pleasant French habit we advise you to make the most of, but remember that you will be getting a "Continental breakfast" of tea, coffee or chocolate accompanied by rolls or croissants, plus butter and jam or honey—all in small quantities. If you want extras, such as eggs or fruit juices, you'll need to patronize an (E) hotel, and be prepared to pay heavily for the privilege; much better take full-scale breakfasts in a local café. The newer (I) and (M) hotels encourage guests to come down to a breakfast room, though it may still be possible to have breakfast in your room. (E) hotels with a full room service will almost certainly charge you extra for bringing breakfast to your room, *and* expect you to tip the waiter (see *Tipping*).

Most city-center hotels in the (I) and (M) price range do not have restaurants, though (E) hotels may well have one. In country districts and by the sea most do have a restaurant, at all price ranges. Indeed many are better-known for their restaurants, and the rooms may well be more modest (and considerably less expensive) than the quality of the meal might lead you to expect. An interesting recent development, however, is for the country's top-flight restaurants to provide a few luxurious rooms for their patrons to enjoy a day or two in their often beautiful surroundings. They are often reserved months ahead by French gourmets, but it's certainly worth trying.

Some hotels in all price categories offer special rates for those staying 5 days or longer, but this rarely applies to hotels without restaurants. Special weekend rates and off-season discounts may also be available. New regulations prevent hoteliers from refusing requests for rooms from patrons who do not wish to dine there, but in practice it is difficult to enforce this ruling, and anyway we recommend that you dine at least for the first night in family-type hotels—their restaurants are generally excellent, incidentally. In high season (roughly mid-June to mid-September) many hotels offer only halfboard terms. Bear in mind that French people prefer their main meal in the middle of the day, so you'll get more for your money if you have lunch rather than dinner when you're half-boarding. Full-board terms are generally marvelous value, but may be too constricting if you plan to do a lot of touring and sightseeing: you'll have to be in your hotel at around 12.30 for lunch and 7.30 to 8 for dinner.

Reservations. *Accueils de France* (Welcome Information Offices) in major centers can make reservations for you, but generally only for the same day or 2 or 3 days ahead. You'll pay a small fee, but all or some of it will be deducted when you present your voucher to the hotel reception for your bill to be prepared. A useful service called SOS Hôtels France offers a central reservation service covering the whole country; main office is in Paris (51 rue Notre-Dame de Lorette, 9e, tel. 45-26-08-07) with additional offices at rail stations in Avignon, Montpellier, Strasbourg, Toulouse and Tours, and on the following motorways: A4 (Reims), A6 (Nemours) and A7 (Mornas and Sorgues). If you pay for the first night when you reserve, you'll be sure of finding a bed even if you reach your destination late at night.

Hotel Chains. France's major chains are Frantel (the best and most expensive, generally in city centers, with good restaurants); Sofitel (modern and well-run, mostly expensive); Mapotel (affiliated to Best Western International); Holiday Inn (only a few of these in France so far); Novotel (widespread, modern, comfortable, usually on outskirts, and with light meals only); Mercure (similar to Novotel); and the small but growing chains of Arcade, Campanile, Climat de France and Ibis, catering mostly to families. All these are modern and efficiently run, but, except for the Frantel hotels, are generally somewhat impersonal, and have far less atmosphere than older hotels.

Hotel Associations. France-Acceuil hotels are a friendly 1– and 2–star chain covering the whole country and providing a useful inter-member reservation service; free handbook from *France-Acceuil,* 85 rue Dessous-des-Berges, 75013 Paris. The well-known Logis de France, with over 3,000 members, are small and medium-sized, family-run hotels with 1– or 2–stars and mostly in small towns and the countryside. Their "Quality Charter" puts the accent on comfortable bedrooms, well-prepared family-style cooking using local ingredients (only a few, town-center, hotels have no restaurant) and all-inclusive room rates (no extra charges or taxes). Auberges de France are members of the same association but are more modest, being generally small and in rural districts; but they too must comply with minimum standards of friendliness, comfort and regional cuisine. *The Official Guide to the Country Hotels and Inns of France* is published in the U.S. by Faber and Faber for $10.95. Regional lists with distinctive yellow covers are available from tourist offices; for a full list apply to the *Fédération Nationale des Logis et Auberges de France,* 23 rue Jean-Mermoz, 75008 Paris. *Relais du Silence* are particularly peaceful hotels, mostly in the country; for booklet write *Hôtel des Oiseaux,* 38640 Claix.

Relais et Châteaux are around 150 very pleasant, generally expensive converted châteaux, inns and manor-houses all over the country, each with its own distinctive atmosphere. The accent is on relaxation in peaceful surroundings, with elegant decor and fine cuisine, but the range is wide, from the deluxe Ritz in Paris or the fabulous Baumanière in Provence to more modest establishments. Many are accessible only by car and some are hard to find—ask for clear instructions. A booklet listing them all is obtainable from *Relais et Châteaux,* Hôtel Crillon, 75008 Paris, and some may be reserved as part of a package from Britain (run by Brittany Ferries for instance).

Residence Hotels. These are a cross between hotels and furnished apartments or villas. Known as *hôtel-résidence de tourisme* or *résidence hôtelière,* each offers rooms, or pairs of rooms, with kitchenettes, though self-service restaurants are also available; minimum stay is normally one week. So far they are mostly found in seaside resorts or ski centers.

STAYING IN A CHÂTEAU. An exciting new trend enables visitors to France to stay in genuine private châteaux, be greeted by the owners and made to feel more like true guests than paying customers. Accommodations vary and can be very pleasant, sometimes including dinner with the aristocratic hosts; advice will be given on excursions, sports opportunities and so on. Some châteaux offer suites or a whole wing, as well as individual rooms. We include some of these delightful places in our regional hotel lists, but you should also know about an association called Château Acceuil, whose members offer just such accommodations in their private châteaux, plus friendly hospitality and an introduction to local architecture, culture and gastronomy: brochure and information from Madame la Vicomtesse de Bonneval, Château de Thaumiers, Thaumiers, 18210 Charenton-du-Cher.

BED AND BREAKFAST. Known as *Chambres d'Hôte*, this service is gradually becoming more common (look for green and yellow signboards), with accommodations ranging from the very basic upwards, prices varying accordingly. Many tourist offices in rural districts or tourist centers keep card indexes of local families willing to take in guests on a b & b basis, and Accueil à la Ferme is a nationwide scheme for rooms in farmhouses or outbuildings, sometimes with meals.

SELF-CATERING. The best-known scheme here is called Gîtes Ruraux: furnished apartments or houses in rural districts that can be rented for a week, a fortnight or a month. Gîtes range from very modest farm cottages to quite luxurious accommodations. Prices rise in July and August, for which you must reserve well ahead of time. The *Fédération Nationale des Gîtes Ruraux de France,* 34 rue Godot-de-Mauroy, 75009 Paris will supply regional brochures, as will many tourist offices. A Gîtes de France booking service is available from the French National Tourist Office in London in return for a small membership fee, which entitles you to receive a fat brochure listing well over 1,000 gîtes set aside for British holidaymakers in particularly popular areas. Packages with reduced ferry rates are offered. *Vacances Franco-Britanniques,* 15 Rodney Rd., Cheltenham also specializes in gîte-type rentals.

FARM HOLIDAYS. These are run by local Chambers of Agriculture. Various formulas are available, including farm camping holidays and farm holidays for children. Write for details of local offices and organizers to *Agriculture et Tourisme,* 9 av. George-V, 75008 Paris.

VILLA RENTAL. The French Government Tourist Offices in London and New York publish extensive lists of agencies specializing in villa rental. Or write to *Rent-A-Villa Ltd.,* 3 W. 51st St., New York, N.Y. 10019. In France, *Interhome,* 88 blvd. Latour-Maubourg, 75007 Paris has a choice of weekly rentals, and local tourist offices may be able to supply lists of real estate agents specializing in short-stay rentals. Short-stay accommodations in Paris are like gold dust (see Paris chapter).

YOUTH HOSTELS. France has several hundred *auberges de jeunesse* or youth hostels where hikers or cyclists (no motorists!) may spend the night and eat inexpensive meals. A brochure giving details of number of rooms, access and facilities offered may be obtained from the *Fédération Unie des Auberges de Jeunesse,* 6 rue Mesnil, 75016 Paris.

For details of membership of the Youth Hostels Association see "Student and Youth Travel."

CAMPING. French campsites and caravan or trailer sites have a high reputation: most are large, well-run and offer a wide range of amenities. But they are jampacked in July and August and few will take advance reservations. In recent years unauthorized tent cities have been mushrooming in the summer along the Mediterranean, reducing once-famous stretches of coast to a nightmare of crawling traffic and unsanitary conditions. As the police and tourist authorities move campers on, so the problem spreads to previously unspoilt inland areas. The Atlantic Coast is becoming almost as crowded as the Mediterranean. We cannot, therefore, urge you strongly enough to avoid the high-summer season if you want to be near the coast.

In inland rural areas you stand a better chance of finding space on a campsite, or you may be able to pitch your tent on a farm. Some tourist offices issue *Camping à la Ferme* brochures listing farmers willing to rent out a corner of a meadow to campers, and maybe provide a farm breakfast. You can even take a trailer to winter sports resorts: national tourist offices abroad will supply details of *caravaneige* sites operating in winter conditions.

Camping is particularly popular in Corsica, but also very strictly controlled. No camping is allowed along the seashore and inland you must either keep trying till you find a space in one of the island's 100-odd campsites (lists supplied by regional tourist office) or obtain permission both from the local town hall and from the owner of the land you camp on.

The *Fédération Française de Camping at de Caravaning,* 78 rue de Rivoli, 75004 Paris, publishes a guide to the country's camp and trailer sites, *Le Guide Officiel Camping Caravaning;* also obtainable from national tourist offices abroad. Regional and departmental tourist offices issue local lists.

RESTAURANTS. French cuisine is generally considered the best and most varied in Europe, if not in the world. Indeed standards are so high that the choice of restaurants offering meals ranging from good to truly outstanding is quite astonishing, even in small towns or rural districts. Prices, too, are often reasonable, with many places offering value for money that no other country can beat. But to get good value you must follow the eating habits of the French, whose exacting standards are the spur to many a restaurateur.

The first tip is to choose places frequented by the French—that way you'll avoid the tourist traps. And best follow the French in setting more store by the food than by the décor: beware of elaborate menus and décor, except at the very top end of the price scale. You should also bear in mind that for most French people lunch is the main meal of the day, with the evening meal a light supper. This is especially true outside Paris. In country districts you may find it quite difficult to find a good restaurant for the evenings, particularly on Sunday, when most will have served a long-drawn-out lunch. And family-type hotels invariably offer the most elaborate meal in the middle of the day.

Another important tip is—read the menu! Apart from the very top spots, restaurants are compelled by law to post the menu outside, so that you can consult it *before* you go in. Look first to see whether there is only a *carte* (table d'hôte) or a series of fixed-price meals. The latter, known in French simply as *menus,* are always better value than eating *à la carte,* but watch for the sneaky way some restaurants add supplements to many dishes on their *menus.* The lowest-price meal will often be called a *menu touristique* and may well include some local specialties. The *menu gastronomique* will naturally be at the other end of the price scale, generally with some dishes invented or perfected by the chef.

French meals are structured into three, four or five courses: invariably a starter or *hors d'oeuvre;* sometimes an *entrée* (often fish); then the main dish, followed by cheese and/or dessert. A dressed green salad may appear between the main dish and the cheese board. These fixed-price *menus* vary considerably in price, but many include service (look for the words *prix nets* or *service compris*) and the lower-priced ones may include a quarter-liter carafe of wine (not of course the finest vintage). Check the menu carefully to see what is included.

If you want only one dish, much better go to a café, or perhaps one of the pizza houses, pancake places or snackbars that are now found everywhere. Skipping the starter or the dessert seems barbaric to the food-loving French and you will court the waiter's and the manager's disapproval by doing so in a proper restaurant. Even in the *brasseries,* where quick service and less elaborate dishes are the norm, it is standard practice to have at least two courses.

As for styles of cooking, classical *haute cuisine* is still very much alive and well, with its rich sauces and traditional accompaniments, in spite of the inroads made by *nouvelle cuisine,* the often-misunderstood "new" cooking that can arouse passionate admiration or violent irritation. "New" cuisine relies less on rich sauces to add taste and variety than on the natural flavor of fresh ingredients and unusual combinations to awaken jaded palates. Portions are frequently small but great attention is given to presentation, with many dishes (traditionally served directly on to your plate) extremely pretty to look at. Lightly cooked meat and fish are characteristic of the new cuisine (fish and shellfish may be almost raw), so be prepared for this, as well as for the sometimes bizzare combinations of ingredients. There has been something of a backlash against *nouvelle cuisine* in recent years, the main criticisms being small portions, high prices (inevitable when so many fresh ingredients are used) and a slavish devotion to fashion. But many American and British visitors are enthusiastic about the new note of lightness and freshness that has influenced classical cuisine as well as the newer variety.

Complementing these two main styles is regional cuisine. In our restaurant lists we have picked out many places where you can sample regional recipes and specialties. Our lists do not claim to be exhaustive: we have selected places we think you'll enjoy, covering a broad price range, but you'll certainly make many discoveries of your own once you've got your eye in.

Prices. As with hotels, we have graded the restaurants in our listings by price alone, dividing them into three basic categories: Expensive, or (E), Moderate, or (M), and Inexpensive, or (I).

As a rule of thumb, you should expect to pay 300 fr. upwards per person, without wine but including service, in an Expensive (E) restaurant; in the top spots a meal will cost 550–650 fr. In a Moderate (M) restaurant the price range is around 200–250; in an Inexpensive (I) restaurant, 80–200. Your choice of wine will govern your final bill: carafes of house wine start at around 15 fr., bottles at around 35 fr. for a local wine, 60 fr. for something a bit more special, and up to 150 fr. or even more. If you have a coffee at the end of your meal it will cost you 8–10 fr. in an (I) restaurant but may be considerably more in the other categories. A *digestif* (brandy or liqueur) will add another 30 fr. upwards.

Closing Times. These can be a problem, not least because they vary with alarming frequency. Most restaurants close for at least one day a week, and often for several weeks a year too. Many family-run restaurants close at mid-semester vacation time in February and November, and may also close in the summer if they cater mostly to French customers. Our lists tell you when we expect restaurants to shut, but as the position may have changed since our presstime, we advise you to double-check locally. Many tourist offices will supply restaurant lists with up-to-date opening times, or you might try telephoning. However, many restaurants are reluctant to take telephone reservations—either because they are too small or too busy to cope, or because they are afraid of being overrun by foreign tourists and scaring away the regular French customers on whom they rely for their year-round income. Credit cards are another problem: our lists tell you which cards the restaurant was willing to accept at our presstime, but again the position may have changed since then.

Budget Eating and Drinking Tips. The existence of so many restaurants offering fixed-price meals is in itself a boon to the budget traveler and the number one rule is: never choose from the *carte* in preference to a *menu,* as it will invariably work out more expensive. Snacks are expensive in France, since local eating habits ensure that restaurants can make out by offering 3– or 4–course meals at low prices. In particular soft drinks work out very costly, especially when imported. If you're traveling with children who need to be filled up with liquid at frequent intervals, do as the French do and order a *limonade* (sweetened fizzy mineral water) or a *sirop* (brightly colored fruit-flavored syrups topped up with still or fizzy water) rather than individual bottled drinks. And adults should go for the local tipple: a glass of wine in a café in a wine-growing area may well cost less than a coffee!

You can save money by eating or drinking in a café standing up at the bar counter, rather than sitting at a table, where the waiter service will be more expensive. But don't pay for your drink or sandwich and then sit at a table, as you would in an English pub. French beer is considerably less expensive than imported beer—you'll be brought the imported kind if you don't specify that you want *une bière française.* And draught beer is less expensive than bottled (ask for *un demi pression* for roughly half a pint of draught).

Relais Routiers (French for truckdrivers' pull-ins) are a well-known way of finding budget meals, but have become so popular, particularly with British visitors, that prices have risen. Places bearing the blue and red logo are still worth stopping for, or you might buy the annual *Guide des Relais Routiers* (English edition available) and pick out one that suits your needs. Don't expect *haute cuisine* or fancy décor—meals are family-type, structured into three or four courses, and the décor is plain and workmanlike.

In towns and cities, always keep an eye open for modest spots patronized by the locals rather than by tourists. There are far too many such places for us to be able to include more than a handful in our lists, but you'll need them on the days when you're not aiming for a gastronomic experience, merely a pleasant meal.

The tourist authorities have calculated that France now has over 7,000 fast-food outfits, newly christened *B.G.V.* or *bouffe grande vitesse,* meaning high-speed nosh and modeled, of course, on the famous *T.G.V.* or highspeed train! You'll find familiar names such as McDonalds, Free Time, Quick and the like in every provincial high street, but connoisseurs say standards are below those of North America and you'd probably do better to stick to "formula meals" for value, not to mention genuine French ambience.

 TIPPING. Tipping is a common custom in France, as in most of Europe, and many people providing you with service will expect a tip. However, a service charge is automatically added to your bill in hotels, restaurants and cafés and there is no need to leave anything on top of that unless you wish to demonstrate that you have been particularly pleased with the service offered. In practice many people leave a small amount in the saucer with the bill in restaurants and cafés—often merely some of the small change returned to them—and if you stay more than two or three days in a hotel it is customary to leave something for the chambermaid (say a round figure approximating to 5 frs. per day). Incidentally, you can check whether or not the service charge is included in prices posted in hotel rooms or on menus by looking for the words *prix nets* or *service compris.* If they're not there, bear in mind that the bill you receive will have 12 or 15 percent added.

In expensive hotels you'll probably use the services of a baggage porter (bell boy) and the hotel porter or *concierge,* and possibly the telephonist. All of them will expect a tip. Reckon on around 5 frs. per item of baggage for the baggage porter, but the other tips will depend on how much you've used their services—instinct must be your guide here. In moderate and inexpensive hotels you'll be lucky to find anyone to carry your baggage and the only person you'll come across regularly is the receptionist, who need not be tipped unless you ask for a special service.

In hotels providing room service, give 2–5 frs. to the waiter, but this does not apply to breakfast served in your room. If the chambermaid does some pressing or laundering for you, give her 2–5 frs. on top of the charge made.

In restaurant and nightclub cloakrooms with an attendant give 2–5 frs., but there is no need to proffer anything if the waiter merely helps you in to your coat. Give washroom attendants 2 frs. Washrooms at rail stations normally have a fixed charge (around 2 frs.), which you'll see posted up. The same applies to theater cloakrooms.

Anyone showing you to your seat, in theaters, opera houses or movies, and at sports events such as tennis tournaments, should be given a tip of not less than 2 frs.

If you're lucky enough to find a rail porter (they're a dying breed in France) you'll notice a metal tag pinned to his overalls stating the fixed charge per item of baggage, which will range from 5–9 frs. depending on the station. If he's been particularly helpful, add a franc or so extra.

Give around 15 per cent to taxi drivers and to hairdressers (though the service charge is included in many salons now—if in doubt, ask). Museum guides should be given 5–10 frs. if you've taken a full guided tour; it is also standard practice to tip couriers if you've taken an excursion, and the driver too if he's been helpful—the amount will depend on the length of your tour, the number of people you're traveling with and so on.

MAIL. Stamps can be bought either at post offices or at the cigarette counter in any café displaying the red TABAC sign outside. Paris post offices are open 8 A.M.–7 P.M. Mon. to Fri., 8–12 Sat.; on Sun., the main post office in each *arrondissement* is open 8–12. Paris has one post office that is open round the clock, at 52 rue du Louvre, 1er–be prepared to stand in line for some time in the tourist season. The post office at 71 av. des Champs-Elysées, 8e is open longer hours than usual: 8A.M.–10 P.M. Mon. to Sat., 2–8 P.M. Sun. Telegrams and cables can be sent by telephone at any time of the day or night; call 42-33-21-11 for telegrams sent in English. They can also be sent at night from the rue du Louvre post office or the telegram office at 8 pl. de la Bourse, 2e.

At our presstime the following postal rates were operating, but we advise you to check locally, as rises occur frequently: Letters weighing up to 20g. (¾ oz) cost 2 frs. within France and to all E.E.C. countries except Britain, Ireland and Denmark, for which the rate is 2.50 frs., and 3.20 frs. to all other countries by surface mail. Postcards cost 1.90 frs. to France, all E.E.C. countries, Canada (surface mail) and Switzerland, no matter how much you write. Airmail to the U.S. is 4.05 for 5g., plus 65 centimes per 5g. extra. Aerograms to all destinations cost 3.85. Airmail paper is a good investment, as postage mounts up quickly, but note that mail to the U.K. goes airmail anyway.

TELEPHONES. The French telephone service is efficient, and street pay stations common even in country districts. The whole network is automatic and linked to the international dialing system. You can make calls from street kiosks (including some at bus stops in towns and cities), post offices, and cafés in Paris and some other large towns.

For local calls from cafés in Paris you may need a slug or token (*jeton*) which is bought from the tobacconist's counter in *café-tabacs*. The cost varies, from 1 fr. upwards. Put in the slug or token, await the dialing tone, dial the number and when you hear your party answer, push the button on the front of the phone. However, for most phones, and for all street pay stations, coins are used, the minimum charge being 1 fr. Other coins taken are 50 centimes and 5 fr. Note that in Paris more and more street kiosks accept only *télécartes* (see *Reduced Rates,* below).

You can make international calls from most coin-operated pay stations, but check this on the instructions (in English too) inside the kiosk. To get on to the international network, dial 19, wait for a second tone, then dial the country code (1 for the U.S. and Canada, 44 for the United Kingdom, 353 for the Republic of Ireland, followed by the city or area code and the subscriber's number.

For calls within France, all numbers have eight digits. The system has conveniently been rationalized so that instead of a whole series of area codes, used only if you're dialing from a different area, the country has been divided into just two zones: Paris and the inner suburbs; and the rest of France. Thus, dialing from outside Paris merely dial the eight-digit number, even if you're dialing within the same area, for anywhere *except* Paris and the inner-suburb *départements* known as Hauts-de-Seine, Seine Saint-Denis and Val-de-Marne; for Paris and these *départements* only, dial 16, wait for a second tone, then dial 1 followed by the eight-digit number. If you're dialing from Paris or the inner suburbs, to make a call within the same area, merely dial the eight-digit number; to dial anywhere else in France, dial 16, wait for a second tone, then dial the eight-digit number.

Note, however, that this eight-digit system was introduced in October 1985 and that you're still likely to come across lists and leaflets with the old numbers through 1987. If so, this is what to do. For Paris and inner-suburb numbers, add a 4 at the beginning (thus 275-23-45 becomes 42-75-23-45); seven-digit Paris outer-suburb numbers, add the single-digit area code (3 or 6 in brackets) to the number (thus (3) 951-95-26 becomes 39-51-95-36 and (6) 063-39-72 becomes 60-63-39-72). For six- or seven-digit numbers outside *the Paris area*, add the bracketed one-digit or two-digit area code to the number to make a total of eight digits.

Telephone numbers in France are always spoken in pairs, not in single digits. Thus 34-56-78-99 is referred to as *trente-quatre, cinquante-six, soixante-dix-huit, quatre-vingt-dix-neuf*, and not *trois-quatre-cing-six*, etc.

Reduced Rates. to the U.S. and Canada between 10 P.M. and 10 A.M., French time, and all day Sun. and French public hols.; to Britain and other E.E.C. countries, between 9.30 P.M. and 8 A.M. weekdays and from 2 P.M. Sat. through to 8 A.M. Mon., as well as all day on French public hols.; to Israel between 8 P.M. and 8 A.M. and all day Sun. and French public hols.

You can now buy a handy *télécarte* from post offices, rail stations and various other places (particularly café-tobacconists) sporting the *télécarte* sign. It comes in two versions, entitling you to either 40 or 120 charge units, and can be used in any kiosk equipped with a card-operated payphone.

CLOSING TIMES. Shop hours vary considerably and may well be different from what you are used to. Most stores and services in the provinces have a lunchbreak of at least two hours, usually 12–2. (For Paris trading patterns see our Paris chapter.) Small and medium-sized non-food shops are generally open 9–12 and 2–7, while food stores are more likely to open earlier, around 7.30 or 8, and close later, around 7 or 7.30, but to shut between 12.30 and 3.30 or 4. In many small towns and villages and a fair number of large towns too, Mon. is closing day for most stores and services (including banks), though they remain open to around 7 on Sat.

Banks are a law unto themselves. Typical hours outside Paris are 9–12.15 and 2–4.45 or 5, Tues. to Fri., with earlier closing at around 4 on Sat. Banks open Mon. will shut. Sat. In some small market towns or villages the bank may be open only on market days.

Most shops and businesses (but not banks) close for at least four weeks a year. The annual closure comes in July or Aug. for those in areas catering little to tourists; closure in Feb. or Nov. is more likely in tourist centers. Public holidays bring confusion, with many food shops open in the morning (as on Sun.), and most other shops closed, except at the height of the tourist season. If a public holiday falls on a Tues. or Fri. many shops will take a long weekend break (i.e. Sat. to Wed. or Thurs. to Mon. or Tues.).

ELECTRICITY. Paris has officially finished the change-over to 220 volts (50 cycle), though if you're staying in a private home make sure that your hosts aren't still on 110 volts. Apparatus marked 220/240 volts will operate without problems in Paris, but not as efficiently as back home. A series of adapters to fit the wide range of lamp sockets and wall sockets in France will prove a godsend. Hotels with modern bathrooms will have special sockets for razors only, as will overnight trains. Best have an ordinary razor to hand in case of emergencies, though.

CONVENIENT CONVENIENCES. Visitors to France will soon discover that plumbing is not the nation's strong point. Even private homes seem to be remarkably short of toilets and many cafés and some restaurants (including some fashionable and expensive ones) still have toilets of the hole-in-the-ground variety. Sad to say, really clean and properly ventilated toilets are the exception rather than the rule and those in museums, métro stations and underground garages are best avoided. Those in rail stations generally have an attendant (and a fixed fee, around 2 frs) and are slightly better, and those at gas stations on motorways are usually reasonably clean. It is normal practice to have at least a coffee or a drink before using the toilet in cafés. The good news is that a self-cleaning coin-operated public lavatory called a *Sanisette* (now copied in London, incidentally) has blossomed in the streets of Paris and other big cities. Distinctly more hygienic than most alternatives, but make sure not to let children use them alone, as there have been some nasty accidents.

SIGHTSEEING. Museums. Museum opening times in France are frankly a nightmare. Except in a few enlightened towns and cities where the mayor or tourist office has persuaded all museums and other monuments to agree on identical opening hours, you will find that they vary enormously, causing visitors considerable frustration and frequently making it impossible to visit all a city's sights in a single day. Quite apart from the lack of standardization, times change from month to month and season to season. What's more, they are often changed arbitrarily, so that although our checklists were accurate when we went to press, the times may have changed out of all recognition by the time you read this. We advise you to double-check with local tourist offices whenever possible, especially if you intend to make a special journey to a single museum or château.

Many sights are closed for at least one day a week (though they may be open daily in July and Aug.). State-owned museums close on Tues., City of Paris museums on Mon. Private or city-owned museums may close at any time, with a slight preference for Tues. or Fri.

A large number of sights, even in big cities, are closed for at least two hours at lunchtime. Visiting hours are also generally shorter than in many other countries, so reckon on a early start if you want to fit in several places in a single day. The good news is that it is gradually becoming more common for the lunchtime closure not to be observed in July and Aug. Another point to bear in mind is that last visits are frequently *at least* half an hour before the official closing time. And we're sorry to say that some attendants at state-owned sites (this applies much less to privately-owned ones) have a nasty habit of closing considerably earlier than the stated time, so be prepared for disappointments.

Admission charges are again very varied, though it is safe to say that in the very great majority of cases there is at least a nominal charge for most visitors (some sights allow children under 12 in free). Reduced charges are frequently available for those over 65 (occasionally 60 or 62), for those under 18 and for students. Take your passport or student card along. Teachers and journalists may also be offered reductions.

Many state-owned museums and monuments and some private ones allow visitors in free or for half-price on Sun. and/or public holidays. But public holidays are a problem. Some museums stay open, others shut. Again, the decision whether to shut or not seems to vary at frequent intervals, depending on staff availability, the weather and what have you. The most frequently observed closures are Jan. 1, May 1, Nov. 1 and Christmas Day. On Easter Mon., Ascension Day, Whit Mon., July 14 and Aug. 15 you stand a better chance of getting in.

An increasing number of towns and cities are introducing all-in-one tickets (generally known as *billets globaux*) that are both convenient and good-value, as they enable you to visit all the sights for a fee well below the combined rates for single tickets. In some cases you can spread your visits over several days—or even weeks if you'll be passing back that way later.

Another recent tendency is to raise admission charges when a special exhibit is being staged—and that happens a great deal in the summer.

Art Galleries. Art galleries in Paris and other cities are a law unto themselves, but generally open the same times as shops, except that they may well not start in the morning till 10. Many are closed on Mon. They do not normally charge for admission, as they are, of course, hoping to sell what is on display.

Churches. Many of France's historic churches, cathedrals and basilicas are full of beautiful paintings and other objects that you'll want to admire, in addition to being beautiful in themselves. Alas, in these days of widespread thefts from churches all over Europe they are no longer open all the time. Most open quite early in the morning, around 7 A.M., when early masses are held. They may well close between around 12.30 and 3, then reopen until around 7 P.M. You should naturally maintain a respectful attitude when masses or services are in progress and it would be more than ill-mannered to wander around sightseeing at such times. Indeed, some churches state that no visits may be made during masses. If there is no such sign posted up, no one will object if you stay quietly at the back admiring the architecture. Although dress rules are not as rigidly enforced as in some countries, we recommend that you avoid shorts and skimpy beach-style wear, as you may be refused admission if your dress is deemed unsuitable. However, you do not need to ensure that your head and arms are covered.

Some churches have treasuries, cloisters or towers that can be visited for a small fee. In some outlying country districts churches are kept locked except during masses. Often, however, the key can be obtained from a sacristan, tourist office or even the nearest café.

Getting Around France

BY AIR. The principal internal airline in France is the state-owned Air-Inter. It works closely with Air France, in many cases offering flights that connect with international arrivals. The airline covers over 40 major business and vacation centers, with frequent daily flights.

France's major airports are the two Paris airports—Orly and Roissy/Charles de Gaulle, both of which are used by Air Inter—Bordeaux, Lyon, Marseille, Montpellier, Mulhouse/Basel, Nantes, Nice, Strasbourg and Toulouse. In addition, there are a host of minor airports, though flights to them are generally most frequent outside the peak vacation months as they are mainly used by businessmen.

In addition to Air Inter, there are also a good many smaller airlines serving both minor and major airports in France.

There are a number of reductions available at certain times of year or day on most French domestic airlines. These include: 25 per cent for young people between 12 and 22; 50 per cent for children between two and 12; free for children under two; ten per cent for groups of ten or more; 20 per cent for groups of 20 or more. Discounts of up to 60 per cent may be obtained on certain flights by families or couples flying together, students or senior citizens.

Full details are available from travel agents, including information on special fly-drive rates and combined international and domestic tickets.

BY TRAIN. France's rail service, operated by the *Société National des Chemins-de-fer Français,* or S.N.C.F., is excellent, among the best in the world. Trains are fast and comfortable, timekeeping exemplary, and fares reasonable, with good reductions available.

Pride of place goes to the famous T.G.V., or *Train à Grande Vitesse,* the swiftest train in Europe and now servicing a growing area of the country. By mid-'87, the service ran from Paris (Gare de Lyon) to Lyon, Valence, Montélimar, Avignon, Marseille, and Toulon, while other trains branch off at Avignon for Nîmes and Montpellier; to Grenoble or St.-Etienne; to Mâcon, Bourg-en-Bresse, Bellegarde and Geneva while another route goes to Chambéry and Annecy; to Dijon, Beaune, Chalon-sur-Saône, Dôle, Besançon and on to Lausanne. There is also a direct Lille–Lyon run, a great boon to travelers from Britain. By the end of the '80s the service will have been extended to the Atlantic coast, from Paris, and Brittany, stopping at Tours and Le Mans. There are also plans for it to run to Nice on the Mediterranean.

The T.G.V. is very stable and smooth, despite the high speeds, the only drawback being that the seats are slightly cramped and the ceilings a little low, and, surprisingly, the food rarely more than adequate, though efforts are being made to improve it. (There are no restaurant cars, all meals being served at your seat). All services are daytime only.

The next-best thing to the T.G.V. is the *Train Corail,* not as fast but with more leg and head room and airconditioning throughout. The Corails have "Grill Express" self-service meal cars at most times of day, where the food is not at all bad and the choice of dishes impressive. Outside mealtimes "Bars Corail" serve sandwiches and snacks as well as drinks. Trolley service is available on many trains, offering cold and hot drinks, sandwiches and confectionery. Most of the network is now served by these Corail trains, but on branch or country lines, and at peak times on main lines, you will find rather older rolling stock or the old-fashioned *Autorails,* noisier, slower and not airconditioned, but still adequate. These trains rarely offer any form of food or drink service, however.

Tickets and Fares. Seats may be reserved on virtually all trains (with the exception of a few country lines) up to the day before departure; the service is computerized and efficient. Reservations are compulsory for the T.G.V. service but may be made, subject to availability, up to five minutes before departure. Cost is around 12 frs. in second class.

Supplementary payments are required for the T.G.V. at certain peak times (particularly on the Paris–Lyon run) and on some other particularly fast main-line services. Buy your *supplément* in advance, as it will be more expensive on the train; booklets *(carnets)* of 15 *suppléments* may be bought and are handy if you're going to do a lot of traveling on fast trains; the inspector will take one or more coupons depending on the distance and the class in which you travel.

Virtually all trains have both first- and second-class compartments, though a few branch or country lines have only second-class seats. However, first-class only mainline trains have now been phased out and even the T.E.E. service has some second-class compartments.

Note, however, that your ticket will not be inspected as you enter or leave the platform. Instead you *must* insert it into one of the orange machines at the entrance to platforms or inside the station building, to have it date-stamped. Put the ticket in and move it to the left until you hear a click. This also applies to supplement vouchers, but *not* to international tickets. If you break your journey on the same day you don't need to have your ticket stamped again. But if you make an overnight stop it will have to be restamped. The French term for this is *composter,* a word with which you will become rapidly familiar if you do not follow this procedure and are automatically fined by the inspector who comes through the train.

All regular tickets are valid for two months from the date of issue and may be used at any time during those two months providing they have been date-stamped on the day of travel. If you unexpectedly cannot travel your money will be refunded automatically within the validity period and over the next three months (minus a small administrative charge); after that period you will need to make a special application for a refund.

Discount Fares. The key to the S.N.C.F.'s reductions system is the "red-white-and-blue calendar." Ask for a *calendrier voyageurs* and study it carefully. The basic schedule is that *blue* periods (when all the reductions we mention apply) run from Mon. noon to 3 P.M. Fri. and Sat. noon to 3 P.M. Sun., and the rest of the time is *white* (when no reductions apply); *red* periods correspond to certain peak holiday departure and return journeys (some journeys, mainly with cars, are more expensive than normal at such times).

Providing you start both outward and return journeys in a blue period, you are entitled to the following reductions:—Round-trip tickets *(billets séjour)* for trips of more than 1,000 km. (620 miles) and *either* lasting a minimum of five days *or* including part of a Sun. cost 25 per cent less than twice the one-way fare.

—Family tickets entitle all but one of the family to a 50 per cent reduction, providing two or more persons of the same family travel together.

—Couples traveling together can get a 50 per cent reduction on one of their tickets.

—Senior citizens get a 50 per cent reduction even if traveling alone.

To benefit from the "Family" or "Couple" fares you must first acquire a *carte famille* or *carte couple:* available free of charge from rail stations or S.N.C.F. tourist offices, but you must take along your passport and two passport-sized photos per person included; validity is five years. The senior citizens pass is called a *carte vermeil* and is available to men aged 62 and over and women 60 and over; it costs around 70 frs. and is valid for a year; again you must take along your passport and a photo. Holders of a British Rail Senior Citizens Rail Card can buy an additional "Europ-Senior" pass that gives half-price rail travel in France during the blue periods; this is more advantageous than buying a separate *carte vermeil.*

Youth Fares. The Youth Pass *(carte jeune)* is valid June through Sept. only. It entitles anyone between 12 and 26 to 50 per cent reductions on all journeys started in blue periods, and to various reductions on S.N.C.F. services, including one free couchette. The Youth Square *(carré jeune)* is again available to those between 12 and 26 but is valid for a year; it entitles you to a 50 per cent reduction on any four journeys during the year, providing they start in a blue period; if they start in a white period you can still get a 20 per cent reduction. Both these cost around 150 frs., and the *carte jeune* can be bought as often as you need one—no annual restrictions.

Rail Rover Passes. The *France-Vacances* Rail pass is now available for nine or 16 days unlimited travel in any month. You just fill in the dates on which you want to travel as you go along. The great thing is that you don't feel that you have to be on the move all the time. The first class ticket costs £137 for nine days, and £175 for 16; the second class ticket £94, and £120. Card holders do not pay the supplements charged on T.E.E. trains, and some T.G.V.'s—but seats must be reserved in the normal way. The card also gives you other goodies such as discounts on car hire, and up to 30% discount at some Frantel/PLM hotels.

The Eurail Pass and Eurail Youth Pass are both valid in France. For details, see "Getting to France—By Train."

 BY BUS. There are few long-distance bus services in France, mainly because the rail network covers the country so comprehensively. There are some regular buses linking towns within the same region, some of the time operated by the S.N.C.F. and connecting with trains. But for the most part buses only operate where there is no, or only an infrequent, rail service.

Bus tours are another matter, and there are plenty of opportunities here. The S.N.C.F.'s excursions service offers well over a thousand bus tours starting out from all over the country; details from tourist offices and rail stations. Cityrama has a 12-day "Magnificent France" tour leaving Paris just four times a year and taking in a very full program of sights and scenery all over the country. Paris Vision's "Tour de France" also lasts 12 days and is very slightly more frequent.

Both offer full-board terms but Paris Vision's tour may also be taken on half-board. All rooms have bath or shower; singles cost extra. Exhausting but rewarding! Both these operators also have a number of short tours. Cityrama has half- and whole-day tours in the Paris area and a number of Paris tours by day or by night. Whole-day tours also go to Reims (including champagne-tasting), Normandy and the Loire châteaux; two-day tours to the Loire Châteaux alone or the châteaux combined with Mont-St.-Michel; also three- and four-day tours combining the Loire Valley, Normandy and Brittany in various ways. Paris Vision's program is similar, but also offers a whole-day Burgundy tour using bus combined with the high-speed train (T.G.V.)

 BY CAR. You may use your home driver's license in France for up to one year, but must have—and be able to show proof of—third–party insurance (the "green card"). The *Automobile Club d'Ile-de-France,* 8 pl. Concorde, 75008 Paris (tel. 42-66-43-00) will deal with all inquiries about road travel in France. They have a 24-hour telephone, but their office is open weekdays only. They can offer help to foreign motorists in trouble, but have a charge for this.

In general, French roads are well maintained, with a full network of expressways *(autoroutes)* and a growing number of ringroads *(boulevards périphériques),* the latter enabling you to avoid many town centers. However, these ringroads get very crowded, especially those around Paris and Lyon, during rush hours, so time your trip to avoid these periods if at all possible.

You would also be well advised to avoid driving at certain peak times in the summer when the traffic, especially that leaving Paris, can be truly horrendous. The first and last weekends in July and August are the worst, while Easter and Whitsun can be nightmarish. One statistic emphasizes the problem: over the six days at the end of July and the beginning of August around six million French people set off on holiday and another four million come home—and around 4,000 of them are killed trying to do so.

Rules of the Road. The speed limit on French expressways—remember they are toll roads: have some 50 centime and 1 fr. coins, or even your credit card (Visa is the most widely accepted one), ready for the automatic machines used in some regions—is 130 k.p.h. (81 m.p.h.), though a good many French drivers take not the slightest notice of it. There is also a minimum limit of 80 k.p.h. (50 m.p.h.) in the fast lane. If it is raining the limit is automatically reduced to 110 k.p.h. (68 m.p.h.).

Other major roads are designated *routes nationales,* or "N" roads, this letter appearing in the road number. On these the speed limit is 110 k.p.h. (68 m.p.h.) where they are two lane and 90 k.p.h. (56 m.p.h.) where they are one lane. In built-up areas the limit is 60 k.p.h. (37 m.p.h.). These same limits apply to the smaller *routes départementales* ("D" roads) and on the much narrower side roads, known variously as "C" roads, meaning *communale,* or "V" roads, meaning *vicinale.* Confusingly, roads are renumbered frequently, with "N" roads becoming "D" roads and vice versa. So make sure you've got up-to-date maps. Tourist offices, garages and car-hire firms will normally supply them free.

The key road regulation to remember is that *traffic coming from the right has priority* (except on traffic circles), unless there is an international STOP sign. Many French drivers take this as a license to shoot out after scarcely a glance to see what's coming, so beware! In towns with many roads at right angles traffic can be slowed considerably by this tradition.

Seat belts must be worn at all times by front-seat passengers. Children under 12 may not sit in front seats. A red warning triangle is a compulsory piece of equipment and the car must also be fitted with flashing warning lights. There are severe penalties for failure to obey these regulations, and for drink-and-driving offences, for which on-the-spot fines are common—you can be sent to prison for a first offense in extreme cases. Another unexpected source of fines is the regulation that makes it illegal to lend your car to any French person, or any foreigner who has lived in France for more than six months.

Parking. Many towns now have parking meters, with charges ranging upwards from 1 fr. for 30 minutes. Meters do not usually need to be fed on Sun., on Sat. in business districts, and between 12 and 2 in many provincial towns and Paris suburbs. Check carefully, as times vary widely. In some places, such as outside rail stations, there is often a 15-minute limit. Best check out parking restrictions carefully if you're not using a meter, as Denver boots and tow-aways are becoming common. Underground garages are found in some large cities; prices vary widely but are generally high for short periods. Don't leave anything visible in your car if you're parking it in one of these garages—thefts are common.

Gasoline. At our presstime (mid-'87) gasoline cost around 5 frs. a liter for the top grade (called *super*) and around 4.50 frs. a liter for the regular *(essence)*. However, there is a price war in progress, with many super- and hypermarkets defying the government by selling at lower prices than regular service stations, and variations between regions, and between urban and rural districts, are marked; so it's worth shopping around.

Motorail. You can save many hours of tiring driving by taking advantage of the S.N.C.F.'s car-carrier services. Generally the car travels in a special section of the train you travel in yourself, but it may travel separately the previous day if you prefer. Best bet is to travel overnight, in a couchette or sleeper. Prices are reasonable if you stick to the blue periods (see "BY TRAIN" above) but early reservation is advised; the fifth journey, incidentally, comes free.

Most useful for drivers from Britain are Boulogne to Avignon, Biarritz, Bordeaux, Brive, Fréjus, Narbonne; Calais to Narbonne or Nice; Dieppe to Avignon or Marseille; and Amiens to Avignon, Biarritz, Fréjus, Narbonne and St.-Gervais may also be worth considering. There are over 20 destinations from Paris and all sorts of combinations may help you combine visits to different parts of France: Dijon to Nice, for instance, or Orléans to Toulouse. However, many services run summer only.

Car Hire. Renting a car is fairly expensive in France, not least because this service attracts the "luxury" rate of value-added tax at 33.3 per cent. If cost is important to you, bear in mind that automatic gears and airconditioning are uncommon in France and will add very considerably to the price. The main worldwide rental agencies naturally operate in France, but there are also many local agencies, details of which you can get from local tourist offices.

Special weekly rates and weekend rates may be available, with either unlimited mileage or a fixed figure after which you pay extra (typically 500 km. or around 310 miles for a weekend). Make sure that this is clearly stated on the documents when you take the car: otherwise you may find yourself paying a lot more than you were expecting.

For central reservations for major car-hire companies call the following numbers (English-speakers available):

Avis (1) 46-09-92-12; Citer (1) 43-41-45-45; Europcar 30-43-82-82; Hertz (1) 47-88-51-51; Inter-Rent (1) 42-85-32-03; Mattei (1) 43-46-11-50.

Citer has a special arrangement with Air Inter giving you all-inclusive set rates per day for car hire in conjunction with domestic air travel. Call (1) 43-41-45-45 and ask for *Passeport des Privilèges*. Similarly, SCETA is a service that offers car hire in conjunction with the S.N.C.F., with pick-up at any one of the 200 rail stations. For reservations, call 05-05-05-11 (toll free).

Conversion Charts. One of the most confusing experiences for many motorists is their first encounter with the metric system. The following quick conversion tables may help to speed you on your way.

Motor Fuel. An Imperial gallon is approximately 4½ liters; a US gallon about 3¾ liters.

Liters	Imp. gals.	US gals.
1	0.22	0.26
5	1.10	1.32

Liters	Imp. gals.	US gals.
10	2.20	2.64
20	4.40	5.28
40	8.80	10.56
100	22.01	26.42

Tire Pressure measured in kilograms per square centimeter instead of pounds per square inch; the ratio is approximately 14.2 pounds to 1 kilogram.

Lb per sq. in.	Kg per sq. cm.	Lb per sq. in.	Kg per sq. cm.
20	1.406	26	1.828
22	1.547	28	1.969
24	1.687	30	2.109

Kilometers into miles. This simple chart will help you to convert to both miles and kilometers. If you want to convert from miles into kilometers read from the center column to the right, if from kilometers into miles, from the center column to the left. Example: 5 miles = 8.046 kilometers, 5 kilometers = 3.106 miles.

Miles		Kilometers	Miles		Kilometers
0.621	1	1.609	37.282	60	96.560
1.242	2	3.218	43.496	70	112.265
1.864	3	4.828	49.710	80	128.747
2.485	4	6.347	55.924	90	144.840
3.106	5	8.046	62.138	100	160.934
3.728	6	9.656	124.276	200	321.868
4.349	7	11.265	186.414	300	482.803
4.971	8	12.874	248.552	400	643.737
5.592	9	14.484	310.690	500	804.672
6.213	10	16.093	372.828	600	965.606
12.427	20	32.186	434.967	700	1,126.540
18.641	30	48.280	497.106	800	1,287.475
24.855	40	64.373	559.243	900	1,448.409
31.069	50	80.467	621.381	1,000	1,609.344

BY BIKE. The S.N.C.F. rents bikes at around 20 fr. for half a day, 28 fr. a day, from close on 200 rail stations. You'll have to show your passport and leave a deposit of about 175 fr. (holders of Mastercard and Visa credit cards or *France Vacances* or *Carte Vermeil* passes need not pay the deposit). You generally have to return the bike to the same station. Bikes may, incidentally, be sent as accompanied baggage from any station in France, and some local trains in rural areas suitable for biking carry your bike free at certain times of the week—details appear in timetables. Tourist offices in towns and resorts will supply details of local shops which rent out bikes.

BY BOAT. Cabin cruiser and barge holidays on France's sizeable inland waterways network are a popular way of seeing the country. An increasing variety of packages includes almost anything from gourmet cuisine to ballooning. Tourist authorities issue *Tourisme Fluvial* brochures detailing what's on offer in their regions, covering both cruises with captain and cook and do-it-yourself holidays. The most popular regions are Burgundy (especially for wine-tasting) and the Canal du Midi in the southwest, but Champagne and Brittany also have many opportunities.

So many French companies offer boat excursions and holidays that we are unable to list them here (though we do give some advice in our regional chapters). But we should mention the long-established *Locaboat Plaisance,* Port-au-Bois, 89300 Joigny (tel. 86-62-06-14), which offers barge holidays from Easter through October on the Midi and Burgundy canals, and in Anjou, Brittany, Charente, Ile de France and Lorraine. The bus tour companies are getting in on the act too, with Cityrama now offering a luxury barge cruise in Burgundy along 100 miles of the Yonne river.

Many hotel barges can be reserved through U.S. and U.K. travel agents. For instance, the well-organized "Barge About France" with its large fleet of privately owned barges is represented by Salt and Pepper Tours in New York (212–736–8226). Possibilities include visits to châteaux and vineyards, wine-and-cheese-lover tours, golf cruises and gourmet touring, with hot-air ballooning an optional extra. Six-night cruises start at around $1400. The experienced Continental Waterways (tel. 800–227–1281) in Boston offers trips in many regions and now has three-day cruises for around $700. The large-scale operator Floating Through Europe (tel. 800–221–3140) now offers Alsace and Lorraine cruises as well as its old-established program. Esplanade Tours (617–266–7465) sails on the Canal du Midi and the Rhône Canal and also in Champagne, while Horizon (tel. 800–421–0454) has a popular six-day Loire cruise, and various ballooning offers.

Leaving France

V.A.T. REFUNDS. Visitors to France (i.e. normally resident outside the country) may be given the opportunity to save money by being exonerated from part of the value-added tax (*T.V.A.* in French) on certain goods. Discounts obtained in this way range from 13 to 23 per cent (on "luxury" goods such as jewelry or perfumes). You should be aware that offering this discount is not a legal obligation on shopkeepers, so you may not insist on it. You'll find that the easiest places to benefit from the system are the department stores, which have special staff dealing with it, and shops with a large foreign clientele. Small boutiques are emphatically not equipped to deal efficiently with the complicated paperwork involved, and the system is liable to break down.

This is how it works. For a start, the total value of your purchases in a single store must be at least 1,200 frs. if you live outside the E.E.C.; if you live in an E.E.C. member state (which of course includes Britain and Ireland), discounts are obtainable only on *single items* costing at least 2,000 frs. Some stores will simply state a price after deduction of the discount. But they'll be taking a risk, because if you don't do your bit by handing on the documentation to the customs, they'll be out of pocket. The great majority will ask you to pay the full amount and the discount will be sent to you in due course. The store will fill out a form in quadruplicate, giving you three copies and keeping one. Make sure that if you live outside the E.E.C. they haven't filled in an E.E.C. form by mistake and vice versa. You must give details of your bank account, or that of friends in France—reimbursements cannot be made to private addresses. If you live outside the E.E.C. you present two of the forms to the customs official on leaving the country—he will probably ask to see the goods in question to make sure that you haven't just been doing a favor to a French friend! Make sure to leave plenty of time for this operation. If you live in an E.E.C. country, the papers are dealt with by the customs official when you reach your own country.

Frankly, you may well think it's not worth the time and trouble, unless you're making really big purchases. And E.E.C. residents in particular should bear in mind that the customs official you present your forms to back home may decide to charge you customs duty on the goods—which will easily cancel out the V.A.T. refund!

CUSTOMS ON RETURNING HOME. U.S. Residents. You may bring in $400 worth of foreign merchandise as gifts or for personal use without having to pay duty, provided they have been out of the country more than 48 hours and provided they have not claimed a similar exemption within the previous 30 days. Every member of a family is entitled to the same exemption, regardless of age, and the exemptions can be pooled. For the next $1,000 worth of goods a flat 10 per cent rate is assessed.

Included in the $400 allowance for travelers over the age of 21 are one liter of alcohol, 100 non-Cuban cigars and 200 cigarettes. Only one bottle of perfume trademarked in the U.S. may be brought in. However, there is no duty on antiques or art over 100 years old. You may not bring home meats, fruits, plants, soil or other agricultural products.

Gifts valued at under $50 may be mailed to friends or relatives at home, but not more than one per day of receipt to any one addressee. These gifts must not include perfumes costing more than $5, tobacco or liquor.

If you are traveling with such foreign-made articles as cameras, watches or binoculars that were purchased at home or on a previous trip, either carry the receipt or register them with U.S. Customs prior to departure.

Canadian Residents. In addition to personal effects, and over and above the regular exemption of $300 per year, the following may be brought into Canada duty-free: a maximum of 50 cigars, 200 cigarettes, two pounds of tobacco and 40 ounces of liquor, provided these are declared in writing to customs on arrival. Canadian Customs regulations are strictly enforced; you are recommended to check what your allowances are and to make sure you have kept receipts for whatever you may have bought abroad. Small gifts can be mailed and should be marked "Unsolicited gift, (nature of gift), value under $40 in Canadian funds." For other details, ask for the Canada Customs brochure, *I Declare.*

British Residents. There are two levels of duty-free allowance for people entering the U.K.: one, for goods bought outside the E.E.C. or for goods bought in a duty free shop within the E.E.C.; two, for goods bought in an E.E.C. country but not in a duty-free shop.

In the first category you may import duty free: 200 cigarettes or 100 cigarillos or 50 cigars or 250 grams of tobacco (*Note:* if you live outside Europe, these allowances are doubled); plus one liter of alcoholic drinks over 22% vol. (38.8% proof) or two liters of alcoholic drinks not over 22% vol. or fortified or sparkling or still table wine; plus two liters of still table wine; plus 50 grams of perfume; plus nine fluid ounces of toilet water; plus other goods to the value of £32.

In the second category you may import duty free: 300 cigarettes or 150 cigarillos or 75 cigars or 400 grams of tobacco; plus 1½ liters of alcoholic drinks over 22% vol. (38.8% proof) or three liters of alcoholic drinks not over 22% vol. or fortified or sparkling or still table wine; plus four liters of still table wine; plus 75 grams of perfume; plus 13 fluid ounces of toilet water; plus other goods to the value of £250. (*Note:* though it is not classified as an alcoholic drink by E.E.C. countries for Customs' purposes and is thus considered part of the "other goods" allowance, you may not import more than 50 liters of beer.)

In addition, *no animals or pets of any kind* may be brought into the U.K. The penalties for doing so are severe and are strictly enforced; there are *no* exceptions.

 DUTY FREE. Duty free is not what it once was. You may not be paying tax on your bottle of whiskey or perfume, but you are certainly contributing to somebody's profits. Duty free shops are big business these days and mark ups are often around 100 to 200 per cent. So don't be seduced by the idea that because it's duty free it's a bargain. Very often prices are not much different from your local discount store and in the case of perfume or jewelry they can be even higher.

As a general rule of thumb, duty free stores on the ground offer better value than buying in the air. Also, if you buy duty free goods on a plane, remember that the range is likely to be limited and that if you are paying in a different currency to that of the airline, their rate of exchange often bears only a passing resemblance to the official one.

THE FRENCH WAY OF LIFE

La Douceur de Vivre

by
JOHN P. HARRIS

Born in England, John Harris has lived in a small village in the south of France since 1975. He has written numerous articles for both French and British newspapers and magazines, including the London Times, *and is the author of* France—a Guide for the Independent Traveler *(Macmillan, London 1986).*

France is neither too hot nor too cold; neither too wet nor too dry; neither too flat nor too crammed with inconvenient mountains. At any rate, that is what the French say. They think that countries should be hexagonal in shape, and about 600 miles across. Spain is too square; Norway is frayed at the edges; l'Angleterre (which is what they usually call Great Britain) awkwardly surrounded by cold water; Switzerland landlocked and too small; the U.S.A. too large (you cross three time zones and then get the same depressing dinner). After God created France He belatedly realized that He had gone too far: it was too near perfection. "How can I restore the balance?" He asked Himself. Then He saw what to do—He created the French. That is a French story. They enjoy grumbling about themselves, or rather about other French people, but in the same breath they admit that there is only one civilized

36

way for people to live, and that is the French way, *la civilisation française*.

On the other hand, the French, and every writer about them including myself, can be relied upon to talk of a nation of individualists; and indeed, at each corner of *l'hexagone* there are people speaking strange languages—Basque, Breton, Flemish, Alsatian, Provençal and Catalan —many of whom (especially Bretons) get rather prickly if you call them French. And yet almost all of them feel that non-hexagonal ways of life are deviations from the civilized norm: barbarous, if not verging on the extra-terrestrial.

Going Native

My wife and I have been living in France for more than ten years, and we have come to the conclusion that there is something to be said for this view. Our fellow-villagers are kind, patient and friendly, behaving with natural dignity and good manners, like most of the other French people we meet (except Parisians in the rush hour). If we were to try to live in outlandish ways, doing the wrong things at the wrong times, we might meet with greater tolerance than in some other countries, but our life would be less easy and pleasant. Visitors to France, whether they stay a week or a year, will have a better time if they "go native" as far as they find it practicable—and when and where they don't, they should be philosophically aware of the drawbacks of trying to behave as in dear old Birmingham (AL or U.K.). This chapter is about the French way of life as it impinges on the visitor, particularly the Anglo-Saxon visitor. (I am using the word "Anglo-Saxon" as the French use it: to them, Louis Armstrong, Robert Burns, James Joyce and Frank Sinatra are representative Anglo-Saxons; Beowulf and King Alfred have nothing to do with it.)

The Daily Round

Let us look at their time-table. They get up between 6 and 7. A recent survey in the Paris region shows that 49% of them have bread, butter and jam for breakfast, with *café au lait* (the only time of day when milk goes into coffee; *café* means black coffee in small doses). 21.5% have something more substantial, while 27% have nothing but *café au lait*. (Children might have cocoa instead, with a few of them getting those new-fangled cornflakes.) Standing up in the kitchen is how 32.6% of Parisians have this frugal meal, while 22.5% get it at a café on the way to work. A lucky 5.5% have it in bed, and a luckier 1% lying in the bath-tub.

By 8 France is at work. Many small shops have opened earlier (especially food shops, and bakeries in particular—breakfast bread and croissants should be warm and fresh). By 10, Parisian executives are fuming because their London contacts haven't yet answered the phone (it's only 9 in England).

There is no coffee break.

Out to Lunch

At 12 they are hungry. Work stops for two hours or longer. Shops, except hypermarkets and suchlike, close. *Le déjeuner* (called *le dîner* in the country) is a sacred rite. A few young or eccentric people in big towns might have a sandwich or a hamburger, but the ideal is a proper meal, taking an hour and a half; a surprising number, even of those who work in central Paris, manage to get home for it. However, the increasing number of women at work means that six lunches out of ten are eaten at restaurants or canteens; substantial freshly-cooked affairs, eaten with serious critical attention. The French grew rich in the '60s: back in 1920 they each ate nearly three pounds of bread a day—now it is just under a pound, with a corresponding increase in the consumption of meat, fish and cheese. Less wine is drunk, but more of it is of higher quality. Quality is important. Just watch the housewife at market. Bocuse, alleged to be France's top restaurateur (he has turned into a T.V. star and Foodie ambassador, spending as much time abroad as in his kitchen) insists that the excellence of his restaurant is due to the care he and his deputies take in selecting, not once a week but every day, the best raw materials at the big markets in Lyon; and growing some of them himself. Bread, butter (margarine is for Americans and such), eggs, chickens, cheese—basic things like these can be had in perfection in France if one takes time and trouble and pays the price. Even water. The French hold the world's record for the consumption of good water. Why drink the safe but chlorinated stuff from the tap when a franc or two will buy a liter from a good spring? I am not saying that the poor drink only Vichy or Badoit. Rather, that rich and poor alike pay as much attention to bread and butter and eggs and the contents of the water-jug as rich Anglo-Saxons might pay to the choice of fillet steak and claret.

There is a typical restaurant in our nearest market town (pop. 6,000). There is only one menu, costing 60 frs. in 1985, say $6.50, unlimited decent wine, service and tax included. Copious *hors d'oeuvre,* a fish dish or a light meat dish, a more serious meat dish, vegetables in season, a session with a good cheese board (half a dozen kinds, cut and come again) fruit or ice cream . . . It is always full by 12.30. A couple from San Francisco who stayed in a rented cottage in our village were hardly ever able to use it. They used to get up at 9 and have an Anglo-Saxon sort of breakfast, and so they were hopelessly out of phase with the commercial travelers (up at 6) who form the restaurant's main clientele. You can't start your lunch there at 1.30 or 2, and there are no doggy bags in France. We are in the Midi, where an early start and a siesta are convenient (many of the shops don't reopen until 3.30). However, the couple happily developed the picnic habit: France is God's own country for buying a picnic in, if only you get to the *charcuterie* and the *boulangerie* and the *pâtisserie* well before they close at 12. After that the roads are empty while the French take in half the day's calories.

Work and Play

Back to work for another four-hour stretch. No tea-break. Are the French mighty toilers? Yes and no. I have conducted oral language examinations in France and in England. The French expect me to keep on examining non-stop from 8 to 12.30, and again from 2 to 6.30. The merciful (lazy?) English think that six hours of attentive interviewing per day, with breaks mid-morning and mid-afternoon, is all the human mind can stand. French schoolchildren have a much longer day than Anglo-Saxon ones, and have more to learn (enormously more than

American ones, who seem to the French to leave serious learning until university, if then; though U.S. post-graduate degrees are respected).

On the other hand, wage-earners and schoolchildren have many leisure days. In the early '80s, the average industrial worker put in 1,872 hours of work in the U.S.A., 1,750 in the U.K., but only 1,650 in France. Five weeks' paid vacation is the official minimum, and there is a large number of public holidays. If a public holiday falls on a Tuesday, Monday may be taken off too, especially in banks (this is called making a bridge, *un pont*). The children have Europe's longest school day, but they also have the longest vacations. The French have become addicts of leisure in the last two decades. They are the world's champions in ownership of *résidences secondaires:* one family in ten has a second house in the country, where they go at weekends and in holidays, causing astounding traffic jams as they flee the cities.

But many French people want to be their own bosses. The price of independence is hard work. A motorized grocer comes to our village on Tuesdays and Saturdays. He and his wife seem happy on a 70-hour week (and in the evenings he rehearses with the brass band when he isn't training the junior rugby football team). He takes one week's vacation a year. To him, company men seem feather-bedded: 50% of all who work have secure tenure of their jobs; 37% get automatic salary increases in line with inflation; 27% buy their enterprise's products at reduced rates (electricity workers are given current almost free, for example); 24% get automatic promotion by seniority; 24% get six weeks' paid vacation or more, and there are all kinds of fringe benefits (free or subsidized housing, transport and so forth). But our grocer, and the butchers and bakers and others who open their shops on Sunday mornings, cling to their independence.

Café Society?

If he finishes his day's work at 6 or 6.30, will our average Frenchman call in at his favorite café for a chat and an aperitif on his way home? Probably not, nowadays. In the past, the café was used as a sort of extra living-room for meeting friends or professional contacts, or even for writing novels if you were Jean-Paul Sartre or Simone de Beauvoir. But today an average of two hours and 50 minutes is spent watching T.V. at home, reducing the time available for social life.

This is sad. The number of cafés has diminished. Fortunately there are still a lot left, and how convenient they are for the visitor! Anglo-Saxon bars and pubs may be seen by the French as sombre haunts where customers take refuge from the wife and kids while getting fuddled as rapidly as possible. On the terrace of a French café one can bask in the sun or enjoy the shade of a multi-colored parasol, sipping a cool lager and keeping an eye on life's passing show, while one's near and dear toy with icecreams or write letters . . . A small black coffee entitles one to spend an hour or two; no hurry. But in our market town the cafés do good business only in the summer, when the tables come out under the plane trees in the avenue, and then half the customers are "foreigners"—Parisians, Britons, the Dutch . . .

While we are on the subject: It seems odd to the Anglo-Saxon that in France beer is generally considered a non-alcoholic drink. When one tells the French that some people at home succeed in getting nastily drunk on it, they say "But they must drink several glasses!" Indeed. A

Frenchman will spend half an hour sipping a quarter of a liter. One sees few drunks in France, except in the north.

Nonetheless, alcoholism exists. The cause, usually, is excessive regular consumption of wine: the average is 73 liters a year, but it is those who drink substantially more than a liter a day who pay the price: they don't get rowdy, they succumb at last to cirrhosis of the liver. Let us not be gloomy. The French live fractionally longer than Americans or Britons, and a moderate amount of daily wine is thought to be good for the health.

La Politesse

I mentioned the aperitif hour to talk not only about cafés but also about friendliness. Some people—notably Americans—complain that the French are inhospitable and stand-offish. The fact is that they are great respecters of privacy. If the Englishman's home is his castle, the Frenchman's apartment or house is his lair. People simply do not pop into one another's lairs, drinking casual cups of coffee and borrowing half-a-pound of sugar. They need a neutral place in which to socialize. Britons (more or less, depending on whether they live in the north or the south) come somewhere between typical French people and the American middle class. According to Paul Fussell (*Caste Marks*, 1983): "Among the [American] middles there's a convention that erecting a fence or even a tall hedge is an affront." And he quotes William H. Whyte, Jr., who was told: "The street behind us is nowhere near as friendly. They knock on doors over there."

It is quite different in France. People in the country are more open and friendly than people in Paris (crowded capital cities are pretty bad for the character; Parisians are in a hurry, and are more likely to make casual acquaintanceship at the weekend, in their country cottage or camp-site). People in the Midi, where we live, just love to talk, and even to listen. But our village neighbors are timid about entering our house. If they want to ask us something they will wait until we meet, or stay on the doorstep, or phone (from 50 yards away). They penetrate our house, and we penetrate theirs, when specifically invited: for aperitifs, or dinner, and the occasion is rather formal. No pot-luck meals on the spur of the moment. That is how they behave among themselves, too. It's not because we are foreigners.

So when do we talk? If there were a café in our village, that would be the place, but the village is too small. Fortunately there are only a few days in the year when openair life is impossible, and there are benches everywhere, in the sun and in the shade. The villagers—and we—sit there for hours, chatting. Are you staying in a small country hotel, or renting a vacation place? The locals really are interested in you, your habits and tastes, the number and ages of your children, your work, where you come from, and so forth, and are longing to impart a discreet selection of their own personal details. Of course you *may* be invited home. There are no rules about this sort of thing. And if there were, the French would take pleasure in breaking them.

When talking with the French, there are conventions that should be observed if one does not want to be thought a barbarian by people who are unaware of Anglo-Saxon attitudes. One simply must say *Bonjour*, followed by *Monsieur, Madame, Mademoiselle, Messieurs, Mesdames* or *Messieurs-dames,* much more often than would be thought necessary (on entering a small shop, for instance); and *Au revoir Monsieur* (etc). Hands are shaken frequently (by colleagues at work, morning and evening, and by the most casual acquaintances). *Bon appétit* can replace *Au revoir* shortly before mealtimes. On going through a door a certain amount of *après-vous*-ing is normal, with *Pardon* if one goes through first, turning one's back. Getting on first-name terms is a sign of much greater intimacy than in England or America. Rush-hour Parisian life is more brutal, of course, and as elsewhere in the world the driving seat of a car exerts a malign influence. In England a headlight flash sometimes means "After you"; in France it means either "After me" or "I am a criminal and I expect you are too, so watch it, chum, the cops are round the corner."

The Political Spectrum

Café conversation will often turn to politics—a fascinating subject in France. The visitor who speaks French should exercise extreme caution and be prepared for surprises. The deep background is more complex than in Britain or America. The French have more often been placed in extreme situations, where radical choices have had to be made. Anglo-Saxon myths, traditions and experience are simple in comparison.

The revolution of 1789 still reverberates. So does the Dreyfus case, which took place at the end of the last century. One cannot understand France without knowing something about them. Dreyfus was innocent, but Church and State needed him guilty. They were defeated, but they got their revenge in 1940, when Pétain and the collaborators substituted *Travail, Famille, Patrie* (Work, Family, Our Country) in place of *Liberté, Egalité, Fraternité,* the revolutionary slogan. To them (one can hardly call them "the right," since de Gaulle was far from being a left-winger) the fall of France was a deserved punishment for wicked atheistical notions like education free from religious influence, and for the Popular Front government of 1936 which introduced shocking things like paid vacations (two weeks) under cosmopolitan intellectuals like Léon Blum. The Communist Party (except for dissidents) truckled to the occupying Germans until Hitler attacked Russia in 1941. Then they joined the resistance whole-heartedly, and at the liberation they were able, with some accuracy, to call themselves *le parti des fusillés,* the party of those who were shot. Rough justice at the liberation, with much paying off of old scores—war wounds still hurt. That extraordinary genius de Gaulle was able to prevent a communist take-over, and then to de-colonize Algeria in the teeth of the extreme right.

So there are: ex-Resistance heroes; ex-collaborators; Gaullists; anti-Gaullists of right and left; different kinds of Catholic influence (some Catholics were collaborators, including many of the higher clergy, though many of the lower ones resisted); communists who look back with nostalgia to the days of Stalin; communist dissidents who have left the party or been expelled for free-thinking; ex-colonists (*pieds noirs*) still seething with resentment; various tiny extreme groups; left-overs from 1968 (when there were student upheavals and the hippies arrived); anti-semites; xenophobes; a highly educated intelligensia; and a large number of people who just want to be left alone to get on with their job or have a good time, of whom a proportion regularly fall for some orator who says "down with politicians" and then proposes crudely simple political solutions. I am not saying that all the French are profound students of history; these issues and events are part of the mythic background, like Nelson's blind eye or the Boston Tea Party.

Americans, by the way, will be astonished to hear President Reagan described as a *libéral*. *Un libéral* means someone who believes in *laissez-faire* economics, even the law of the jungle—quite different from a British centrist or an American left-winger. In 1984 a Gallup poll, published by the weekly *L'Express*, suggested that *le libéralisme* was coming into favour: in ten years' time 67% hoped to live in "a society encouraging effort, risk-taking and individual enterprise, with the State playing the discreetest possible role." Those who looked forward to "a greater role for the State, with redistribution of incomes" numbered 19%, with 14% "don't knows" or "won't says." But nowadays *L'Express* is rather a right-wing paper . . .

The End of the Day

It has taken us a long time to get our average Frenchperson past that café. Back home, there is of course the television, about which the French have mixed feelings. At one and the same time they envy the number of channels available to American viewers (but cable T.V. is starting) and feel superior about the low intellectual quality of American television, as reported by French sources. The same sources suggest that British television is better than French, and everybody wonders why. Old movies are the favorites. Lengthy and serious discussion programmes have a wide audience, and so does *Apostrophes,* a literary programme devoted to new middlebrow and highbrow books (it has a remarkable influence on book sales).

Le dîner (called *le souper* in the country) is at around 8, for rich and poor. It's a lighter meal than at mid-day, with soup replacing *hors d'oeuvre.* The school-children will have finished their homework by then. Bed follows not long after. But the movies after a sharp fall as television established itself in every home, have resisted well. The number of attendances at theaters, music-halls and the like has considerably increased since the early '70s. Movies and theaters start at 9 or later; going out in the evening implies a short night's sleep. Except in Paris, films are dubbed into French, a practice deplored by intellectuals. (Visitors to Paris who want to see a movie in the language it was made in should look for the abbreviation *v.o.,* meaning *version originale;* otherwise they will experience such shocks as seeing the space-traveler in *"2001, A Space Odyssey"* pressing the button marked "English" at the satellite de-briefing computer, only to receive the question *"Quelle est votre nationalité?"* to which the able astronaut replies, without blinking an eyelid, *"Américaine."*) Record entries are scored by the most popular French films; American movies come next.

Le Weekend

Almost all employed people now have a two-day weekend, usually Saturday and Sunday, but Sunday and Monday for many shop workers. Schoolchildren have Wednesdays free. In recent years the French have revolutionised their leisure habits: jogging, swimming, soccer, gymnastics, tennis and vigorous bicycle-riding (for fun, not transport) are practised, mainly at the weekend, by large numbers of all social classes. 52% of men and 40% of women practise some form of sport, two-thirds of them regularly. (The figures for 1973 were 41% and 28% respectively.)

Sunday is a day for enjoying oneself. Movies, soccer matches, restaurants . . . the "continental Sunday," the British used to call it, though "godless" was a misnomer—the Roman Catholic church requires attendance at Sunday mass (which nowadays can take place on Saturday evening instead) but never wished to impose gloom and closed doors for the rest of the day. 85% of the population declare themselves Catholics, but only 15% of those go church every week. There is a fairly strong anti-church sentiment among many, even among those who say they are Catholics (but the traditional warfare between priest and primary schoolteacher, the one reactionary and the other attached to Republican ideals, is a thing of the past). Divorce, the pill and safe legal abortion are widely accepted, even by practising Catholics, who politely conceal their smiles when celibate ecclesiastics denounce such facilities. (The last female abortionist to be condemned to the guillotine was executed under the collaborationist Vichy government.)

The great Sunday ritual takes place at 12 or soon after. Four out of ten will visit friends or relations. This is the big day for restaurants: a special menu, with somewhat higher prices. 60% of families do more cooking on Sundays than on other days. Half the French end their Sunday lunch with a fresh fruit tart or some sort of *gâteau,* which is why the pastrycooks are open in the morning and why you see Frenchmen carefully carrying flat cardboard boxes. Then a quarter of the population takes a little siesta.

Vacation Variations

The yearly cycle is determined not only by climate but also by vacation patterns. The French may work long and hard on the days when they work, but they are also the world's champion vacation-takers (when they are not self-employed or farmers). According to the most recent statistics, 26% of them took a winter vacation of 14 days' average length. Rather more than half of these went skiing. There is a sharp division here between Parisians and country-dwellers: 47% of the first took a winter vacation, but only 14% of the latter. Schoolchildren have a week or two in February, and schools organize "snow classes" for pupils who cannot otherwise be taken to the ski-slopes.

The same figures show that 54% of the population took a summer vacation away from home (85% of the executives and members of the professions; 52% of the bosses; 51% of the blue-collar workers). The average length was 27 days. The majority—80%—went in July and August. Big factories close down completely. But only 5% went to hotels. 26% stayed with relations or friends (in the country, mainly); Parisians remember their provincial origins. 22% spent their summer holiday in tents or caravans; 17% rented holiday accommodations (this is well organized in France: visitors find that the lists of officially inspected rent-approved accommodations supplied by the *Gîtes de France* offices are remarkably useful if they want to cater for themselves in the "real" France). 14% went to their *résidence secondaire;* and 9% borrowed someone else's.

It follows that if the visitor wants to explore provincial France in a leisurely fashion, there is much to be said for May, June and September; October can be wonderful in the south. In July and especially August, Paris is relatively empty, and the visitor may or may not consider that to be a good thing. (One can actually have fun driving around Paris in one's own car if one starts at dawn on a Sunday in August.)

The Seven-Year Itch

There is also a seven-year cycle: presidential elections, under the present constitution (but French constitutions do get changed). The next one is due in 1988, when François Mitterrand's term of office ends. Presidential elections do not coincide with parliamentary ones; at the time of writing there is the uneasy cohabitation of a socialist president and a center-right government that came into power in 1986. Many people think that seven years is too long, and that a second term, making 14 years of the same president, *much* too long. It can be held that Giscard d'Estaing's defeat in 1981 was caused partly by profound boredom with Giscard d'Estaing: sleep descended like a conditioned reflex whenever he appeared on the television screen, and by 1985 François Mitterrand in his turn was producing a certain amount of *ennui* among the less politically motivated, coupled with disillusion among those who had thought that the human condition would be changed when the left came to power. Alas! one could still get only a pint out of a pint pot. France proved to be not immune to what was happening in the rest of the world, and in the '80s governments everywhere have been finding that they can make fewer changes than they thought.

Tastes and Aspirations

An essay such as this has to contain rash generalizations, unless it is to be five times the length, hedging every statement with ifs, buts and exceptions. Is there an average French person? Obviously not. There are the rich and the poor, for example. Hemingway, or was it Scott Fitzgerald?, said "The rich are different from us—they have more money." But in the Anglo-Saxon world there seem to be more class differences, apart from money, than in France. The Anglo-Saxon blue-collar worker—to speak only of food, an important enough subject—chooses different meals from the élite and eats them at different times. Not so in France where, however, income differences can be greater. The poor, in France, like champagne, oysters and *foie gras,* but they get them less often than the rich. The British picture, with one class settling down to sausage, chips and tea at 6; or having menu A at the Chinese restaurant, with another class dining, and probably wining, at 8, is not found in France.

The same is true of other aspects of life. The gulf between one class and another is not one of tastes and aspirations; rich and poor are in broad agreement on what constitutes a pleasant life. The poor are simply farther away from it than the rich.

Compared with the real poor in the Third World, the French poor are rich. They see the doctor when they need to, without financial worry; they have enough to eat; their children wear shoes; and have an excellent educational system at their disposal. But they still have a bad time compared with the rich. The statistics of life expectancy are revealing. At the age of 35 a university teacher can look forward to 43.2 more years of life, and an executive, lawyer or doctor 42 more years; but an unskilled labourer only 34 more years. Noise, dirt, accidents and constraints such as shift work cost him nine years of life.

Many of the unskilled section, and of the unemployed, are of North African origin, a reminder of France's colonial past. Frictions develop in run-down areas that have turned into ghettos. Extreme right-wing groups, notably the *Front National* under Le Pen, have picked up racist votes, capitalizing on the fear of insecurity. Theft and violent robbery have increased, but not as much as awareness of them. French enthusiasts for bringing back the death penalty are incredulous when told that the number of murders in France today is no greater than in 1825, when the population was half its present size. One is in no more danger of being murdered in France than in Britain, and in nine times less danger than in the U.S.A.

Plus ça Change . . .

Changing France . . . I was there in 1947, and I said to myself: "How wonderful! But it cannot last." On the whole it has. The surge of prosperity in the '60s brought improvements to French life, with some drawbacks (traffic in Paris, for example) but basic traditions die hard. The young ape foreign fashions, with a fast-food/motor-bike/hash/mid-Atlantic pop noise/comic-strip culture, but they grow out of it. Official morality has changed. Contraception used to be forbidden (condoms were allowed, on the grounds that they prevent infection—a macho notion), Paris was famed for its elegant brothels but women had to go to London for diaphragms and to Switzerland for abortions. All that has gone. *Le topless* is seen on most beaches, and total nakedness on some. But the family remains a powerful cohesive unit, *jeunes filles* are very often *sérieuses* (an important word: "responsible" rather than "gloomy") and foreign tourists looking for an easy lay can do better elsewhere.

What do they think of us? Corresponding to the Anglo-Saxon stereotype that depicts all Frenchmen wearing berets and pointed beards, waving their arms wildly and being saucy with the girls, there is a French picture of the Americans as rich, generous, and over-weight, and liable in world politics or personal relationships to behave like a well-meaning bull in a china shop; and of the English as either tall, silent, inhibited, masochistic and scrupulously honest, or as drunken, sadistic, soccer-watching vandals. Of course nobody really believes any of this, but if one is going to attach a national label to oneself one might as well be aware of the cliche lurking at the back of the mind.

"Happy as God in France" say the Germans, exaggerating a bit. Anglo-Saxons come in two sorts: those who love France and those who don't. It's a matter of taste and character. The former find it easy to slip into the French way of life for a week or a month or permanently. The latter are better off in Paris or the Riviera. There, at a price, arrangements can be made to suit inflexible millionaires from Texas or the Middle East; one might even be able to get a classic dish served with milky breakfast coffee at three in the afternoon, shielded from the shudders of the natives. But really, the French are canny operators when it comes to enjoying *la douceur de vivre,* the sweetness of life. If one follows their example while in France one will not go far wrong. (One way of going wrong might be to quote almost any paragraph from this chapter to them; at any rate it will start a vigorously French argument.)

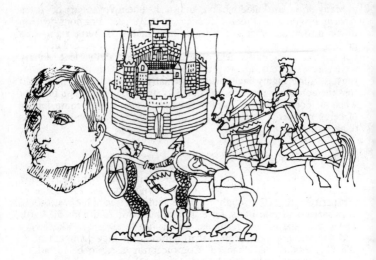

FRANCE—HISTORY AND CULTURE

Nexus of Europe

by
ANDREW HERITAGE AND MARK LEWES

France has traditionally benefited from its geographical location at the heart of Western Europe. Having coasts on the Atlantic and the Mediterranean, access to the North Sea, the Alpine passes, and exclusive control of the passes of the Pyrenees, France has always played a key role in European trade, travel and politics, as well as intellectual and artistic development. Within its present boundaries France encompasses Latin, Germanic, Celtic and Flemish racial types. These factors have combined to determine the nature of French culture—an interaction of ideas and influences from all over Europe, and, in the days of Empire, the world.

In this chapter we have counterpoised tables of significant events in France with brief descriptions of the cultural developments which accompanied them.

Romans and Franks

B.C.	
c.600	Marseille founded by the Greeks
390	The Gauls sack Rome
58–51	Caesar conquers Gaul; writes up the war in *De Bello Gallico*
A.D.	
1st cent.	Lutetia, later to become Paris, built by the Gallo-Romans
405–75	Barbarian tribes struggle for Gaul; 451 Attila invades but is defeated at Châlons
481	Clovis the Great becomes king; 486 he defeats Syriagus, the last Roman governor of Gaul, signalling the end of Roman influence; 500 Clovis is converted to Christianity; 507 he conquers the Visigothic realm of Toulouse; 508 makes Paris his capital; 511 on his death the kingdom is divided between his four sons
567	After more divisions following royal deaths, and subsequent reunions, the Frankish kingdom is divided into three parts— the eastern countries (Austrasia), later to become Belgium and Germany; the western countries (Neustria), later to become France; and Burgundy
771	Charlemagne (742–814) becomes king; 768 he is crowned Holy Roman Emperor and makes Aix-la-Chapelle his capital; 778 is defeated by the Moors at Roncesvalles in Spain, after which he consolidates the Pyrenees border; 782 Alcuin (735–804) leaves York to become Charlemagne's educational advisor; 813 Council of Tours indicates the growing strength of the French language
814	The Carolingian line continues until 987 through a dozen or so monarchs, with a batch called Charles (the Bald, the Fat, the Simple) and a sprinkling of Louis

Early traces of French culture include the cave paintings of wild beasts and hunters at Lascaux, in the Dordogne (c. 1500 B.C.), and the slightly earlier fertility figures found in neighboring regions, such as the *Venus of Lespugue*. France even boasts its own Stonehenge, in the megalithic stone complexes at Carnac in Brittany (c. 3500 B.C.).

The first known racial group to occupy France were the Celts, who inhabited most of northwest Europe during the last millennium B.C. Regarded as barbarians by the Romans, they were nonetheless skilled in metalwork and carving and produced beautiful artefacts and ornaments. Soon, however, these peoples were to be subjugated by the classical civilizations of the Mediterranean.

Traces of Greek trading colonies from the 5th century B.C. have been found at Marseille and Perpignan; however, it was not until the Roman Empire spread suddenly and rapidly north of the Alps, occupying southern France by 120 B.C. and penetrating the northern forests by 49 B.C., that the first unified culture was established, albeit by invaders.

Many examples of Roman architecture are found in the south of France, from the well-preserved amphitheaters at Arles and Nîmes, to the monumental arch at St.-Rémy and the functional beauty of the Pont du Gard at Nîmes. France, more than any other country north of the Alps, inherited a substantial foundation of classical Roman civilization, and although much was destroyed in the Dark Ages, enough remained to dominate the development of early Christian art and architecture. The cathedral baptisteries at Aix and Marseille owe much to this inheritance. It is no accident that the most famous modern example of a Roman triumphal arch—the Arc de Triomphe—should have been built in Paris.

By the 7th century A.D., Christianity was well established throughout France. Its interaction with an inherited classical tradition produced the first great indigenous French culture, the Frankish or Merovingian. The Franks, originally a group of Germanic tribes, established a huge empire over Western Europe, finally expelling the Romans from French soil.

Although most of the architecture of this period has been lost, Frankish sophistication is reflected in the ornate damascene silver and bronze work found in the many warrior cemeteries of northern France. France was soon to become part of the central core of Catholicism, and would remain so until the French Revolution. Many of the great monastic centers—Tours, Limoges, Auxerre, Reims, Chartres and Corbie—were established at this time and rapidly became cultural powerhouses.

Under Charlemagne not only did the Frankish Empire expand into Northern Italy, but the axis of European power shifted north of the Alps, to the newly constituted Holy Roman Empire, centered around Charlemagne's huge palace at Aix-la-Chapelle, regarded by contemporaries as a "second Rome." His chapel at Aix, now part of Aachen cathedral, was modeled on San Vitale in Ravenna. Little of the complex now remains, but Charlemagne, supported by his friend and teacher Alcuin, also promoted a renaissance of classical learning and creativity. He imported bronzes from Italy and numerous small votive pieces from Asia Minor as models for Frankish craftsmen working in gold, ivory, bronze and cloisonné. His interest in the written word led to the production of illuminated manuscripts in nearly all major monastic centers, especially at Reims and Tours. The *Ebbo Gospels* and the *Utrecht Psalter* (both at Reims) display a vivacity and technique not usually associated with early Medieval art. Following the achievements at Aachen, Carolingian architecture flowered, with its distinctive slender piers, round-headed arches and groin vaults; the oratory of Germigny des Prés (c. 820, restored) is a fine example of the period. In tandem with the rise of manuscript illumination and architecture was the development of fresco painting, based on the rather heavy style of Byzantine mosaics, such as those at St.-Germain in Auxerre.

Romanesque and Gothic

987	Hugh Capet (941–96) becomes king, the first to achieve the principle of hereditary kingship by having his son Robert crowned as co-ruler and his successor, thus ending the elective system; 996 Hugh dies of small pox after a short but influential reign, having begun the unification of France
1066	William, Duke of Normandy, invades England; crowned king of England at Christmas in Westminster Abbey; 1067 work begins on the Bayeax Tapestry
1095	Pope Urban II promulgates the Crusades at Clermont Ferrand; Philip I (1053–1108) excommunicated for adultery, thus excluding him from the Crusades and allowing him to consolidate royal power in the nobles' absence
1099	Jerusalem captured by the crusaders
1100	Bourges joined to France
1108	Louis VI, the Fat (1081–1137) ascends throne; he further strengthens the royal power, ably assisted by Abbot Suger

(1081–1151), one of France's greatest statesmen

1100s	Struggle between the Anglo-Norman kings and the French for territory; after switching husbands (from Louis VII of France to Henry II of England) Eleanor of Aquitaine's great possessions changed allegiance, too; 1199 Richard Coeur de Lion (1157–99) killed while beseiging Châlons
1225	England acquires Gascony
1229	Treaty of Meaux—region between rivers Rhône and Narbonne becomes French
1257	Sorbonne founded
1258	Treaty of Corbeil fixes the Pyrenees frontier
1270	Louis IX (1215–70). St. Louis, dies in Tunis on the 7th and last Crusade
1307	Philip IV (1268–1314), the Fair, disbands the Knights Templars to gain their wealth
1309–78	Breakaway popes resident in Avignon
1337–1453	*The Hundred Years War,* episodic fighting between France and England for control of large areas of territory; 1348 Black Death, plague rages in France for two years; 1349 The Dauphiné purchased, the title "Dauphin" becomes that of the king's male heir; 1350 France buys Montpellier from Aragon; 1356 the English advance; Jean II (1319–64) the Good, defeated at Poitiers by the Black Prince; 1360 two major lulls in the Hundred Years War were 1360–69 and 1396–1416, the latter a two-year truce; 1431 Jeanne d'Arc burned at the stake in Rouen; from the lowest point, French fortunes and morale revive; 1453 the War ends with the English totally defeated and confined to their last toehold on the Continent, Calais
1438	Pragmatic Sanction of Bourges, French Church gains some independence from Rome and the state treasury some relief from papal payments
1461	Louis XI (1423–83) crowned; nicknamed the "Spider" he was a cynically brilliant statesman; 1469 printing press first established; France acquired—1473 Cerdagne and Roussillon; 1477 Artois, Picardy and Burgundy; 1481 Maine, Anjou and Provence
1483–1515	Attempts of territorial expansion into Italy by Charles VIII (1470–98) and Louis XII (1462–1515); 1494 and 1501 the French armies twice reached as far south as Naples; by 1514 after a series of battles and treaties, France had lost all the land it had gained, but close contact with Italy gave impetus to the Renaissance in France

The more settled conditions in Europe during and after the 10th century saw the increasing prosperity of the church and the flowering of Romanesque, a style that developed under the protective wing of reformist monastic orders such as the Benedictines at Cluny in Burgundy. The rapid expansion of such orders, strategically placed on pilgrim routes, led to a profusion of building, painting and sculpture. Languedoc, Burgundy and the Loire valley have the best examples— the first fully-vaulted European church can be found at Saint-Benoît-sur-Loire (1083).

Romanesque architecture was an almost exclusively ecclesiastical style, characterized by immensely solid buildings, whose rounded arches are set on powerful columns with ornate floral capitals. Each region had its own variations, that of the south being quite different from that of Normandy, for example. During the 12th century a greater range of materials and techniques were developed; smoothly finished stone and ornate reliefs appear and the individual artist, as opposed to the mere anonymous artisan, became important—Giselbertus, who worked at

Autun Cathedral, was one such. The wonderfully sculpted relief of Christ in Majesty over the main Autun doorway is combined with a wealth of spontaneous detail. A similar vitality also marks the few remaining examples of Romanesque painting, in which detailed narrative was developed; although the best example of this story-telling power remains the famous tapestry at Bayeux (c. 1070).

The desire to span greater areas with stone and to admit more light to the building was to lead to the development of the pointed arch and the rib vault. The essentially skeletal structure that resulted could then contain large areas of glass. This style, the Gothic, first appeared at Saint-Denis (1140), today on the outskirts of Paris, but was soon to gain currency throughout Europe. It subsequently dominated ecclesiastical architecture from Portugal to Poland for the next 400 years. First fully developed at Notre Dame, Paris (from 1163), Chartres (from 1200), Reims (from 1211) and Amiens (from 1220), these cathedrals all contain distinctive Gothic forms; delicate filigree-like rose windows, tall lancet windows—both usually of richly-stained glass—and elaborately carved doorways and facades.

The Gothic style was long-lived and went through distinct evolutions. Conceived as organic wholes, the cathedrals took many years to build, and consequently reflect changes both in architecture and society as a whole. Often a single building demonstrates the progression from the purity of early Gothic line and form to the intricate tracery of the Flamboyant style (developed after about 1375), and so on to the highly complex and possibly febrile over-decoration of Late Gothic, from the 15th century. The best examples of the late style are in Normandy.

In secular buildings, ecclesiastical Gothic forms were combined with the more popular elements of wooden gable and round-spired turret, as in the Palace of Justice at Rouen (1499). Like its ecclesiastical counterpart, this style spread throughout France in the wake of the monarchy's gradual unification of the country, supplanting the many regional styles, especially in the south—a mirror both of the imposition of a central power and a slow progress towards national identity.

The Renaissance

1515	Accession of François I (1494–1547); 1519 the Habsburg Charles I of Spain elected Holy Roman Emperor as Charles V, the beginning of 450 years of Franco-German rivalry; 1521–44 a series of wars, treaties and alliances (François married Charles' sister in 1530) ended with the Peace of Crespy; France enters the High Renaissance under François and, simultaneously, religious divisions widen (Luther had published his Wittenberg protest in 1517)
1547	Accession of Henri II (1519–59); marries Catherine de Medicis who rules as regent after his death
1547	Mary, Queen of Scots (1542–87) brought to France as a dynastic pawn; marries the Dauphin, François, in 1558; 1559 he becomes king but lives for only a year; she returns childless to Scotland on his death
1558	France captures Calais, England's last territory on French soil
1572	August 24, St. Bartholomew Massacre in Paris; Protestants—celebrating the marriage of Henri de Navarre to Margaret, daughter of Catherine de Medicis—were slaughtered by the Catholics led by the Guise family; Admiral de Coligny, the Protestant leader, was among those who died; the killing spreads to other parts of the country with thousands dead

1547   Henri de Navarre (1553–1610) becomes king as Henri IV, first of
            the Bourbon line, turning Catholic to do so; his reign re-estab-
            lished peace and prosperity in France; 1598 Edict of Nantes
            grants Protestants (Huguenots) toleration; aided by his Su-
            perintendant of Finances, the Duc de Sully (1560–1641), Henri
            creates luxury industries, roads and canals, putting France
            back on her economic feet; 1608 Champlain founds Quebec;
            1610 Henri assassinated in Paris
1610   Louis XIII (1601–43); supported by the deviously brilliant Cardi-
            nal Richelieu (1585–1642), Louis begins the destruction of the
            Huguenot cause; 1618–48 The Thirty Years War, joined by
            France in 1635 when the Habsburg threat became too serious
            for further diplomatic shuffling; 1627 Siege of La Rochelle ends
            by the Huguenots losing nearly all privileges; 1635 Académie
            Français founded

From the late 15th century into the 16th, the golden light of the
Italian Renaissance slowly dawned over France. In its wake there came
a significant increase in secular artistic activity. The Renaissance in
France received its greatest impetus under François I, who imported
many Italian artists and craftsmen—among them Leonardo da Vinci,
who lived at Cloux from 1507. The climax of this process was the
building, under the supervision of the Venetian Serlio, of the Palace of
Fontainebleau (from 1528). For the decoration of the Palace a work-
shop was developed, whose members included such Italian painters and
sculptors as Cellini, Primaticcio and Rosso, as well as jewelers and
tapestry weavers. The school developed a distinct late Renaissance (or
Mannerist) style in obvious competition to its Italian contemporaries,
characterized by a use of rich colors, flowing, elongated forms and a
concentration upon allegory and eroticism. An earnest desire to rival
and outdo Italy in cultural pursuits was to dominate French culture for
the next 200 years.

Massive building programs were started, although constantly dis-
rupted by the religious wars of the 16th century they saw a rigorous
rejection of Gothic and vernacular forms in favor of classical models.
The first great examples of this development were the châteaux around
Paris and in the Loire valley. They were hybrid creations, combining
daring interpretations of Italian forms with more traditional spired
skylines. Fine examples are those at Blois (from 1498) and Chambord
(from 1519). The rebuilding of the Louvre, begun in 1546, marked the
final assimilation of Italian classical architecture into France.

This was also the age of the rise of the French court, and with it came
the appearance of the independent, free-thinking courtier, whose cultural antecedents can be found in the works of the sceptical essayist
Montaigne (1533–92), the political theorist Jean Bodin (1530–96) and
the poet courtier Pierre de Ronsard (1524–85). Ronsard in particular
was to contribute much to the reformation and modernization of the
French language by reference to and borrowings from the classics. The
establishment of humanist learning is probably best illustrated by the
philosophical works of René Descartes (1596–1650) and Blaise Pascal
(1623–62). The clarity, reason and severity of the Cartesian school
marked the ascendancy of France in the academic world.

By the beginning of the 17th century the strongly Italianate flavor
of the 16th had been replaced by something more distinctly French,
although the urge to better their southern neighbors was still pronounced. The formal and dramatic lessons of Roman Baroque architecture, for example, were fully absorbed by Salomon de Brosse in his

facade for St.-Gervais, and were to be developed in Bruant and Mansart's church of Les Invalides (1679). Similarly, in the reign of Henri IV, much emphasis was placed on one of the most characteristic of Baroque architectural concerns, the development of large scale town planning. Under Henri IV the Place des Vosges was built in Paris, the first of a number of *places* (squares) forming focal points within a city. The *place* continued as a central ideal in Parisian town planning until the 19th century.

From Sun King to Deluge

1643	Accession of Louis XIV (1638–1715), the Sun King; 1648–52 the Fronde insurrection leads to Louis' decision to rule absolutely from a safe powerbase outside Paris; he chooses Versailles and creates an environment which totally domesticates the nobility; war rages from 1661 to 1714 with the Dutch, English, etc.; 1683 at his wife's death Louis secretly marries Madame de Maintenon; 1685 Revocation of the Edict of Nantes forces mass emigration of Huguenots; from 1701–14 war crystallizes into the War of the Spanish Succession; 1715 at his death—aged 76 and after 72 years on the throne—he leaves behind a handful of great monuments, an insatiable national taste for glory and a ruined country ("After me comes the deluge")
1715	Louis XV (1710–74), great-grandson of Louis XIV; wars include Polish Succession (1733–35) and Austrian Succession (1740–48) which ended in the Treaty of Aix-la-Chapelle; 1756–63 Seven Years War loses France most of her overseas possessions and sees England becoming a world power; 1768 France buys Corsica where Napoleon was born in 1769
1774	Louis XVI (1754–92); married to Marie Antoinette, a frivolous and unpopular Austrian princess; 1776 the French assist in the American War of Independence, ideals of liberty cross the Atlantic with the returning troops to reinforce new social concepts; early 1780s government near to bankruptcy; 1785 Affair of the Diamond Necklace increases the monarchy's unpopularity; 1788 bad harvest further affects national economy; 1789 the Estates General called but breaks up in chaos, the Third Estate (the "Commons") split away and form a National Assembly (July 9)

It was under Louis XIV that the most grandiose schemes of post-Renaissance France were to be realized. In considering these massive works one should remember that France had, by the 17th century, regained its former position as the preponderant power of Europe—fully unified, heavily armed and defended, and administered by a carefully-ordered aristocratic bureaucracy which radiated from the absolutist court of the Sun King at Versailles. This was the golden age, in which patronage of the arts enjoyed almost equal expenditure to that lavished on Louis's continual wars. The palaces of the Louvre (1546–1878) and Versailles (1661–1756) bear witness to this in sheer scale, if nothing else. They were built as demonstrations of France's power and, more specifically, that of Louis. In their profusion of painted and sculpted decoration were performed the intellectually exquisite plays of Corneille (1606–84), and were hung the opulent portraits of their creators by painters such as Philippe de Champaigne (1602–74). Indeed, under Louis's patronage and the auspicious eye of his treasurer Colbert, the Académie des Beaux-Arts was established, by which the state could control the nature and quality of the Arts, often as a propaganda machine. It held sway as sole arbiter of taste until the famous Salon des Refusés in 1863.

It was perhaps unfortunate that the two greatest French painters of the age spent most of their working lives in Rome—Nicolas Poussin (1594–1665) reflects Corneille's admiration for classical order and Stoicism in his severe figure compositions and landscapes, whereas Claude Lorraine (1600–82) surveys a lost world of classical idyll in his pictorial imagination.

However, this was also the age of the Counter-Reformation, and of the persecution of the Huguenots—not all was lofty and grand. The devotional paintings of Georges de la Tour (1593–1652) and the genre pieces of the Le Nain brothers display a concern for the spiritual existence of the common man which seems far removed from the glories of Versailles. The fables of La Fontaine (1621–95) and the fairy tales of Perrault (1635–88) have retained their popular appeal, as have many of the products of the popular theater which flourished in the 17th century, none more so than the satirical comedies of Molière (1622–73). Less universally enduring, but as popular at the time were the tragic master-pieces of Racine (1639–99).

The beginning of the 18th century found France on the verge of bankruptcy; the court withdrew from the splendors of Versailles, and their cultural life reflected a taste for domesticity, albeit tempered by a pronounced taste for fantasy. It was in their elegant Parisian boudoirs and reception rooms that the French Rococo style of decoration and ornamentation developed—the grand gesture on a small scale. The theatrical fantasies and *fêtes champêtres* of the painters Watteau (1684–1721) and Fragonard (1732–1806), the intimate eroticism of Boucher (1703–70), and the dreams realized in stone by Clodion (1738–1814), provided civilized diversions for an aristocracy now withdrawn from the stage of power politics. A more social diversion which was to have lasting appeal was the development of the comic opera, a misnomer for the most popular and accessible art form of the century.

However, the age also produced artists given less to providing diversions for a pampered and frivolous aristocracy. The paintings of Chardin (1699–1779) display a placid stillness comparable with the solidity of Poussin. Houdon's sculpture, at its best, combines a profound classicism with a remarkable veracity, as his portrait of Voltaire (1778) shows. The development of the novel from its early picaresque form can be seen in the work of Abbé Prévost (1697–1763) whose *Manon Lescaut* looks forward to the sophisticated form of Laclos's *Les Liaisons Dangereuses,* probably the finest mirror of French aristocratic dalliance.

It was in the realm of literature that a new force was first apparent. The beady eye of Voltaire (1694–1778) surveyed contemporary society and declared, in novels such as *Candide* (1759), that maybe this wasn't the best of all possible worlds. Similar seeds of doubt were voiced by other writer/philosophers. The 18th century had seen the rise—not only in France—of a wealthy entrepreneurial middle class whose values were based in the main upon logic and empirical reason, whether in commerce, the arts or in science. The spokesmen were Voltaire, Diderot (1713–84), who recorded the state of human achievement in his *Encyclopaedia* (published from 1751) and J.-J. Rousseau (1712–78), who more than anyone defined the paradox at the heart of mid-18th-century France. In *La Nouvelle Héloïse* (1760 and *Confessions* (c.1770) he used a careful examination of the individual's faults and needs as a natural being as a basis for arguing for social and political reform—the need for Revolution.

Revolutionaries and Romantics

1792–1804	First Republic: 1792–95 The Convention: Robespierre, Danton, Marat etc., in control; 1793–94 The Terror: a bloodbath during which the King, Queen and hundreds of others were guillotined; reaction sets in and the instigators of the Terror were themselves executed; 1795–99 The Directory: with Napoleon Bonaparte as its champion; 1799–1804 The Consulate: with Napoleon as First Consul
1804–14	First Empire: Napoleon I; the rule of war; 1805–12 Napoleon conquers most of Europe; 1805 Trafalgar, British victory leading to her subsequent command of the seas; 1805 Austerlitz, French victory leading to land superiority; 1807 Code Napoleon promulgated, legal system still in use in many countries; 1812 winter and Russian determination defeats Napoleon outside Moscow; France exhausted by long conflict; 1814 the Emperor abdicates and is exiled to Elba
1814–48	Restoration of the Bourbons: Louis XVIII, brother of the executed Louis XVI (whose son probably died in prison—novels notwithstanding) regains throne; 1814–15 Congress of Vienna to settle peace terms; 1815 The Hundred Days—Napoleon returns from Elba, raises an army but lacks national support; is defeated at Waterloo (June 18) and exiled to St. Helena in the south Atlantic; dies there 1821
	The crown is now passed around the Bourbon family; 1824 Charles X, locked into a pre-revolutionary state of mind, abdicated 1830; a brief upheaval (Three Glorious Days) brought Louis Philippe, the Citizen King, to the throne; 1840 Napoleon's remains brought back to Paris; 1846–47 severe industrial and farming depression; 1848 Louis Philippe abdicates
1848–52	Second Republic: Louis Napoleon, nephew and step-grandson of Napoleon I, an ambitious adventurer, is elected President; decides to try for supreme power and stages a successful takeover bid (Dec. 2, 1851)

As often happens, art was one step ahead of history. Notions of political identity for the common man had made the plays of Beaumarchais (1732–99), including the *Marriage of Figaro* and the *Barber of Seville,* popular works. The design for the Panthéon by Soufflot (1757–90), Gabriel's refined Petit Trianon at Versailles (1762), and the paintings of Greuze (1725–1805) and David (1748–1825) display a concern for moral order in great contrast to the flippancies of Fragonard. The clear, apparently simple, frieze-like structure of David's *Oath of the Horatii* (1784), the first masterpiece of neo-Classicism, touched an artistic nerve which was to explode in the French Revolution five years later.

Many of the ideals of the French Revolution proved impracticable and short-lived, but the renewed taste for classicism remained a touchstone for the Establishment until the late 19th century—a tradition, best exemplified in the work of Ingres (1780–1867), which was to degenerate in a matter of 50 years into a voyeuristic justification for painting nudes.

With the rise to power of Napoleon from the ashes of the Revolutionary Directoire, a new intellectual force and esthetic mode came to the fore—Romanticism. While respecting many of the genuine tenets of the classical world, its adherents rejected the slavish emulation of them. The subject matter of Romanticism was the modern world, seen in all its heroism, adventure and horror, or more precisely the artist's means of expressing his reaction to it. Never strictly formulated—the very idea was against the Romantic grain—its dye spread to all the arts, demanding an immediacy of technique, emotionalism and the ability to convey the doubts and uncertainties of the human condition. It found its most successful outlet in literature, in the morbid speculations of Chateaubriand (1768–1848), the amoral and intensely psychological novels of Stendhal (1783–1842), and the all-encompassing fiction and dramatic works of Victor Hugo (1802–1885), Dumas (1802–70) and Balzac (1799–1850). In painting, its early master was Géricault (1791–1824), whose powerfully Romantic *Raft of the Medusa* (1819), at once hopeful and despairing, inspired Delacroix (1798–1863), the master of the expressive brush-stroke whose emotive use of color epitomized Romantic aspirations. In music, it found expansive expression in the works of Berlioz (1803–69). His *Symphonie Fantastique* is perhaps the most widespread and accessible of all Romantic works. On a smaller scale, but with no less intensity, the music of the expatriate Pole, Chopin (1810–49), crystalized the movement's lucid introspection.

The nebulous nature of Romanticism, which made it so adaptable to various art forms, reflected both the political turmoil of France in the 19th century, and the withdrawal of the artist from politics, growing industrialization and urbanization into a more subjective world. It also led to a rapid fragmentation of Romanticism into many different movements. Adherents of "Art for Art's Sake," for example, promoted extreme estheticism and intuitive psychological investigation; its major literary exponents were the poets Baudelaire (1821–67) and Théophile Gautier (1811–72), who combined a taste for the exotic with a concern for the extreme refinement of their art. This approach was to develop through the 19th century into the Symbolist movement, in which the wilder shores of art were explored by the poets Mallarmé (1842–98), and Verlaine (1844–96), and by painters such as Moreau (1826–98) and Redon (1840–1916).

Realism Rules

1852–70	Second Empire: Napoleon III, "the Empire means peace"; colonial expansion into Indochina, Syria and Mexico; 1852–70 Baron Haussman recreates the center of Paris; 1870–71 Franco-Prussian War; Napoleon III takes refuge in England; Paris besieged by the Prussians; France defeated; 1872 Napoleon dies in Chislehurst, England
1870	Third Republic established, lasts until 1940 and sees 14 presidents
1871	Paris commune abolished amid scenes of carnage and destruction; peace with Germany signed
1875	New constitution sets up bi-camaral government, with main power vested in a cabinet and a president who is elected for a seven-year term
1889	Paris World Exhibition, building of Eiffel Tower
1894–1906	Dreyfuss Affair, spy trial and its anti-semitic backlash shocks France
1904	Entente Cordiale signed between France and Britain
1907	Triple Entente (France/Britain/Russia) faces Triple Alliance (Germany/Austria/Hungary) foreshadowing World War I

Another development from Romanticism was Realism, often carrying strong social overtones. The close observation of life in a supposedly non-stylized fashion was taken up by Flaubert (1821–80)—probably the finest French writer of the century—and in a more sensational fashion by Zola (1840–1903), whose Rougon-Macquart series (inspired by Balzac's *Comédie Humaine*) set out to examine the consciousness of modern man in all its manifestations. The conclusions were inevitably depressing. Pictorially, however, the results were quite different. The Barbizon School of landscape painters—Millet (1814–75), Théodore Rousseau (1812–67) and Diaz (1807–76)—approached their subjects with a fresh eye, using clear, bright colors to produce paintings in which atmospheric effects and naturalistic observation replaced the idealized classicism prevalent in previous centuries.

It was primarily from the work of these painters that the Impressionist movement evolved. Taking modern life as their subject matter, Monet (1840–1926), Renoir (1841–1919) and Pissarro (1831–1903) proceeded to break down their visual perceptions in terms of light and color, an interpretation of "realism" which was to have lasting effect, culminating in Monet's late series of *Waterlily* paintings (from 1916).

The breaking down of established cultural barriers in favor of a new perception was not solely the province of the Impressionists, indeed they played only a small part in the process. The political commitment apparent in the work of Courbet (1819–77) looked forward to the republican ideals of the 1870s, and Manet's (1832–83) rejection of pictorial tradition in both subject matter and treatment caused great scandal in 1863 when, due to the number of works rejected at the annual Salon of the Academy, an alternative, the Salon des Refusés, was held. It was this period of disruption, in both politics and the arts, which gave rise to the popular myth of the Parisian Bohemian artist, the disaffected idealist kicking at the shins of tradition.

The term Impressionism also implies the pinning down of movement, of the ephemeral. This was to find its most successful expression in the exquisite paintings and sculpture of Degas (1834–1917) and the weighty sculpture of Rodin (1840–1917). A similar end was also achieved in music by the composers Debussy (1862–1918) and Ravel (1875–1937), who sought to capture mood and resonance rather than narrative development.

If the middle of the 19th century saw the dissolution of form—which, in pictorial terms, had been a sine qua non from the Renaissance onwards—in the work of the Impressionists, it also saw the introduction of new solid forms in the environment. Baron Haussmann (1809–91), under the direction of Napoleon III, continued the re-shaping of Paris as a modern, planned city, opening large boulevards connecting strategic *places*. Much of his planning was dominated by new considerations: a large, industrial population, modern materials, modern communications, especially railways—and the need for mob control, which, though not new, was now tackled on a large scale. The French ability to adapt to modernism was underlined by a series of World Exhibitions held in Paris, and it was the experience of these which propelled the nation so forcibly into the 20th century. The most potent symbol of this startling progress was the Eiffel Tower, built for the Paris Exhibition of 1889, and a work in which industrial engineer, architect and sculptor suddenly and radically unite.

The Twentieth Century

1914–18	World War I: north and northeastern France devastated by 52 months continuous fighting; industry and farms in ruins;

around a million-and-a-half Frenchmen killed, as many again injured; Armistice signed, Nov. 11, 1918 in a railway carriage in the Compiègne Forest

1919–39   Conference of Paris; the Treaty, signed at Versailles, demanded "restitution, reparation and guarantee," which included making France's eastern borders safe for the future as well as demanding financial help from Germany in rebuilding devastated areas; Alsace and Lorraine, lost to France since 1871, were regained; Presidents of the period were Poincaré 1913–20, Millerand 1920–24, Doumer 1931–32, Lebrun 1932–39; right-wing politics gave way to the rise of the left as the '20s and '30s progressed; 1934 Stavisky Affair, a shady financier's suicide was rumored to have been arranged by the police to prevent his revelations of high-life corruption; riots and demonstrations followed—the nadir of the Third Republic; government of National Union formed; 1936 elections brought in the Popular Front, government formed by Léon Blum, the Socialist leader; many advanced social measures were instituted but the regime was defeated finally by the looming German menace and its inability to cope with foreign affairs; 1939 appeasement, foolishly maintained by both France and Britain, resulted in World War II; 1940 French surrender to German army

1940–44   The French State (Vichy Government); France divided into the northern German-occupied zone and the southern zone, under the control of 84-year-old Marshall Pétain; 1944 June 6, D Day, successful Allied invasion of France

1944–46   Provisional Government under General de Gaulle; 1945 May 6, unconditional surrender of the Germans; American aid assists French recovery

1947–58   Fourth Republic: 1946–54 Indochinese War, trouble in Africa leading to independence for Morocco and Tunisia; 1949 France joins NATO; 1954 Algerian struggle for independence gets underway; it, the Suez debacle and other crises eventually destroy the Fourth Republic; 1957 Treaty of Rome and formation of the Common Market

1958–present Fifth Republic: de Gaulle returns to head country; he proposes new constitution with presidential form of government, is determined to make France once more an international power; 1960 nuclear device exploded in the Sahara; 1962 new constitution approved; Algeria granted independence; 1967 France leaves NATO; 1968 widespread disturbances begun by student uprisings in Paris ("The Events of May 1968") bring the country to a standstill; de Gaulle reasserts his authority; 1969 April referendum against de Gaulle's methods and programs; he resigns and Georges Pompidou becomes President; 1974 on Pompidou's death Giscard d'Estaing takes over, a right-wing politician, though not a Gaullist; 1981 the socialist François Mitterrand wins the presidency

The diffusion of Romanticism in the second half of the 19th century led to a splintering of cultural direction. The avant garde of the mid-century had become the Establishment of the *fin de siècle,* while younger artists on the other hand were dominated by one concept—modernism. In painting the many implications of Impressionism are illustrated by the developments that led from it, ranging from the broad color fields of Gauguin (1848–1903), the technical detail and structural contrivance of Seurat (1859–91), and most influentially in the flat modulations of Cézanne (1839–1906). The most controlled assessment of the ferment, and probably the greatest masterpiece of Post-Impressionism, was Proust's novel *Remembrance of Things Past* (from 1913), which, in combining a dissolution of subject matter with a restructuring of material in an equally convincing and yet artificial manner, pointed towards the future.

The ferocious flat colors used by the Fauves, led by Matisse (1869–1954) and Derain (1880–1954), caused an outrage in 1905. But barely two years later the development of Cubism by Braque (1882–1963) and the Spaniard Picasso (1881–1973)—which rejected all established notions of the relationship between object, artist and audience—heralded a valid and frightening view of the world, adapted to 20th century needs. Similar trends were developed by the poet Apollinaire (1880–1918) and in the novel by Gide (1869–1951). However, the assurance and confidence of this generation of artists was shattered by the experience of the Great War.

For four years French soil soaked up the blood of Europe's youth, and France suffered almost more than her foe in bearing the brunt of subsequent economic and moral disaster in this, the second of three German invasions within 80 years. The Romantic dream of a modern Europe turned into a senseless nightmare. However, during the Great War young men from all over the Western world had a taste of French culture, which, in its wake, they were keen to renew. Paris and its environs were to attract painters, writers and dilettantes as a result of its role both as a cultural center and as a resort of liberalism. Russian artists such as Kandinsky (1866–1944) and Chagall (1887–1985), the composer Stravinsky (1882–1971), the Romanian sculptor Brancusi (1876–1957), and various writers including Gertrude Stein (champion of the Cubists), Anaïs Nin, Hemingway and Joyce only formed the vanguard of a creative torrent.

Paris was to form a focal point and context for most of the major inter-war artistic movements; Constructivism, Dadaism and Surrealism each found their French spokesmen, notably in the writers André Breton (1896–1966) and Aragon (1897–1966). There was a great fecundity and cross-fertilization of ideas, so well brought to life in the novels and stories of Colette (1873–1954). The career of say, Picasso, reflects the wealth of influences of the time.

Nonetheless, French culture itself remained somewhat directionless, and at best eclectic. The work of the so-called School of Paris emphasizes this; it is difficult to envisage the high Expressionist Soutine sharing a Montmartre studio with the delicate Modigliani, but he did. It was a time when monumental classical works could be created side by side with Cubist-inspired constructions. Perhaps the most consistent vision of the time was that of the Swiss-born architect Le Corbusier (1887–1966) whose chapel at Ronchamp (1950–54) and Unité d'Habitation at Marseille (1947–52) are high points in a career dedicated to the combination of esthetically satisfying form and a theoretical social utility.

Overall, the most important aspect of inter-war French culture was the development of the doctrine of Existentialism by Jean-Paul Sartre (1905–80). In his novel *Nausea,* and in *The Roads to Freeedom* trilogy, he underlined the individual's need to abstract himself from his immediate surroundings, and in doing so to develop his own moral and ethical code. Sartre's example was taken up by Albert Camus, the criminal poet Jean Genet and Simone de Beauvoir, each of whom modified the doctrine by introducing broader moral and critical questions. The age of the creative individual, rather than the member of a "movement," had arrived.

A foil to Sartre's vision can be found in the writings of the historian and Gaullist Minister for Culture André Malraux (1901–76); his ability to digest and redefine the national cultural heritage from a world view provided a vital central vortex about which the strands of modern French creative thought could orbit. This motion was most characteristically expressed in an urge towards art as experiment. The novels of Robbe-Grillet and Marguerite Duras embody this in their enigmatic structure. A similarly radical move occurred in the theatrical work of Ionesco, Anouilh and the Irish expatriate Samuel Beckett, musically in the structural preoccupations of Messiaen (b. 1908) and his pupil Pierre Boulez (b. 1925).

However, it was probably the cinema which realized the greatest steps. An ideal existential medium, the form also fascinated the Surrealists. France has often been regarded as the birthplace of the cinema; the popular trickeries of the Lumière brothers in the early years of the century enjoyed international success, and were the outcome of a long-standing French fascination with photography. The portraits by Nadar (1820–1910) are among the first masterpieces of photography, and the mechanical imagery of the camera had fascinated the painters Manet, Degas and Toulouse-Lautrec.

Between the wars the cinema industry boomed, and by 1930 had reached a remarkable maturity in the work of Jean Renoir (1894–1979) —*Une Partie de Campagne* (1936) and *La Règle du Jeu* (1939) represent the 20th-century flowering of a humorous and humane tradition stretching back to Montaigne and Molière. The work of Marcel Carné (b. 1903) and his collaborator Jacques Prévert—especially the magical *Les Enfants du Paradis* (1944), made illicitly in German-occupied Paris—represents the modernization of another French tradition, the *opéra comédie*. A strong Romantic sense permeates the films of the Surrealist poet Jean Cocteau (1889–1963), from the lyrical *Beauty and the Beast* (1946) to the masterly *Orphée* (1950), (yet another example of France's empathy with classical themes).

The 1950s saw a truly remarkable development, initially through the auspices of the critical journal *Cahiers du Cinema*. Its editors, including Godard (b. 1930), Truffaut (1932–1982) and Chabrol (b. 1930) inaugurated a new wave of self-conscious cinema, based on the immediacy of American B-movies, and a commitment to the unique political and expressive qualities of film. Truffaut's *Four Hundred Blows* (1959) and *Jules et Jim* (1961), and Godard's *Breathless* (1960) and *Weekend* (1967) remain dominant masterpieces of modern French cinema. In their wake, the six "Moral Tales" of Rohmer (b. 1920) and the playful narrative games of Rivette (b. 1928) are outstanding.

Modern France has sloughed off many of its traditional bohemian associations, and has adopted rather the lofty role of *maîtresse* of Euro-culture; its position is one of conservatism. Even the vigorously modern Pompidou complex in Paris represents primarily an ambitious (and successful) assertion of France's place at the heart of European creativity. The annual Cannes film and television festivals in early summer inexplicably remain the major world marketplace and arbiters of good taste in each medium. In contrast to the serious work of Boulez, French popular musical taste remains distinctly old hat. Nonetheless, France does remain the most enriched of European countries—with the possible exception of Italy—and the maintenance of local museums, galleries and folk festivals put the rest of Europe to shame.

THE FOOD OF FRANCE

The Noble Art

by
ANNE WILLAN

Anne Willan is President and founder of the Ecole de Cuisine La Varenne *in Paris. Her food column in the* Washington Post *is widely syndicated and her books include* French Regional Cooking *and* La Varenne's Cooking Course.

Born British, naturalized American, I am an unabashed chauvinist about French food. To wander through a French open market, the vegetables overflowing from their crates, the fruits cascading in casual heaps on the counter, is a sensual pleasure. To linger outside a bakery in the early morning, watching the fresh breads and croissants being lined up in regimental rows, must awaken the most fickle appetite. Just to read the menu posted outside a modest café alerts the imagination to pleasures to come.

Best of all, the French are happy to share their enthusiasm for good food with others. There are more good restaurants and eating places in France than in any other European country; the streets are lined with delicatessens, butchers, cheese shops, bakeries and pastry shops selling food. And I have yet to find a Frenchman, cantankerous though he may be, who does not warm to anyone who shows an interest in his national passion for wines and fine cuisine.

Fine cuisine does not necessarily mean fancy cuisine. Masters though French chefs are of the soufflé and the butter sauce, the salmon in aspic and the strawberry *feuilleté,* such delicacies are reserved for celebration. Everyday fare is much more likely to be roast chicken, steak and *frites,* omelette, or pork chop. Bread, eaten without butter, is mandatory at main meals, while the bottle of mineral water is almost as common as wine.

Where the French do score is in the variety and quality of their ingredients. Part of the credit must go to climate and geography—just look at the length of the French coastline and the part seafood plays in the cooking of Normandy, Brittany and Provence. Count the number of rivers with fertile valleys for cattle and crops. Olives and fruits flourish in the Mediterranean sun, while from southwest of Paris running up north to the Belgian border, is one of the great bread-baskets of Europe.

These resources have been exploited to the full. It was in the vegetable garden of Louis XIV at Versailles that many of our familiar fruit trees were propagated. The 365 cheeses credited to France (there are probably more) are not just an accident of nature. The French are the most fussy, critical and appreciative buyers I know; the most insistent among them demand, and get, the finest raw materials for cooking in the world.

Styles of Cooking

No one but the French identifies three basic styles of cuisine—classical, *nouvelle* and regional—not to mention offshoots like diet cooking *(cuisine minceur),* women's cooking *(cuisine de femme)* and even *cuisine de concierge.* No other European nation pays so much attention to menus and recipes.

Most sophisticated are the sauces and soufflés, the *mousselines* and *macédoines* of classical cuisine. Starting in the 17th century, successive generations of chefs have lovingly documented their dishes, developing an intellectual discipline from what is an essentially practical art. As a style, classical cuisine is now outmoded—scarcely a restaurant claims still to serve it—but its techniques form the basis of rigorous professional training in French cooking. In some measure, all other styles of cooking are based on its principles.

Nouvelle cuisine, for instance, is directly descended from the classics. Launched with great fanfare 20 years ago, *nouvelle cuisine* takes a fresh, lighter approach, with simpler sauces and a colorful, almost oriental view of presentation. First-course salads, often with hot additions of shellfish, chicken liver, or bacon, have become routine. For a while cooks experimented with way-out combinations like vanilla with lobster and chicken with raspberries, but now new-style cooking has settled down, establishing its own classics. Typical are *magrets de canard* (boned duck breast) sautéd like beefsteak and served with a brown sauce of wine or green peppercorns, *pot au feu* made of fish rather than the usual beef, and flans of vegetables like spinach and zucchini (courgettes).

New-style cooking has swept French restaurants, with somewhat mixed results. When scouting out a place to dine, I'm always wary of flowery adjectives like "fresh-culled" and I avoid wilfully odd combinations such as scallops with mango and saffron. The shorter the menu, the more likely the dishes are to be fresh. The use of local ingredients is a good sign, but imported caviar is not.

Just recently, cooks have made a refreshing return towards the third, grassroots style of French cooking, that of the countryside. Indeed, many cooks never left it, for classical and *nouvelle* cuisines are almost exclusively the concern of professionals, and are dominated by men. However, regional dishes are cooked by everyone—chefs, housewives, grandma, and the café on the corner. Here women come into their own, for the best country cooking has an earthy warmth that the French prize as typical of *cuisine de femme*.

The city of Lyon exemplifies the best of regional cuisine. Restaurants are often run by women known as *mères* (mothers), featuring such local specialties as poached eggs in *meurette* (red wine sauce), *quenelles* (fish dumplings) in crayfish sauce, sausage with pistachios, and chocolate gâteau. Lyon hotly disputes Paris's title as gastronomic capital of France, pointing to the cluster of starred restaurants which surround the city. What is more, some of the world's finest wines are produced only 150 kilometers north, in Burgundy. Certainly the Lyonnais cooking style is different from Paris, less élitist and more robust.

Lyon may represent the best of French regional cooking, but there's plenty to look for elsewhere. Compare the sole of Normandy, cooked with mussels in cream sauce, with the sea bass of Provence, flamed with dried fennel or baked with tomatoes and thyme. Contrast the butter cakes of Brittany with the yeast breads of Alsace, the braised endive of Picardy with the gratin of cardoons found in the south. An excellent hunting ground are *charcuteries,* pastry shops and, best of all, open markets where locals do their shopping.

Authentic regional specialties are based on local products. They have a character that may depend on climate (cream cakes survive in Normandy but not in Provence) or geography (each mountain area has its own dried sausages and hams). History has brought spice bread to Dijon, legacy of the days when the Dukes of Burgundy controlled Flanders and the spice trade. Ethnic heritage explains ravioli around Nice on the Italian border, waffles in the north near Belgium, and dumplings close to Germany. Modern ethnic influences show up in cities, with many an Arab pastry shop started by Algerian immigrants, and many a restaurant run by Vietnamese.

Regional food is inseparable from regional wine. Even the simplest meal is incomplete without a companion glass, and wine is used extensively in cooking. *Coq au vin* made with a hearty red Burgundy is a totally different dish from *coq au reisling* using a fruity white from Alsace. Nor is it coincidence that the great wine-growing areas—Bordeaux, Burgundy and Alsace—are also famous for their cooking. Even less prestigious wine areas like Provence and the Loire have good food to match their lighter wines.

There's no denying that eating well is a French preoccupation. But so is a balanced diet. Health food stores and fitness centers are no longer a rarity. The rich patronize luxury spas such as Eugénie-les-Bains, where Michel Guérard, creator of *cuisine minceur* offers a double slate of health food and gourmet cuisine. The less favored repair, as they have for 300 years, to old-fashioned spas like Vichy, home of the mineral water. Here *curistes,* often subsidized by the government's Social Security program, drink their daily doses of water while taking a promenade under leafy trees.

Cooking Training

Training is an important factor in maintaining the standards of French cooking. Professional chefs begin their three-year apprenticeship at age 16, starting in baking, pastry or cuisine, and later branching into specialties like aspic work and sugar sculpture. To be a *chocolatier* is a career in itself. Much more than a manual trade, cooking in France aspires to an art, and its exponents achieve celebrity status. In the 1800s it was Carême; in the 1900s it was Escoffier; and today it is Paul Bocuse and his *nouvelle cuisine* cohorts. Each decade has its stars, their rise and fall a constant source of eager speculation in the press and at the table.

The different cooking disciplines call for different characteristics. A *cuisinier*, for instance, is likely to be flamboyant and autocratic; he tastes and adjusts as he goes, relying on instinct and flair for the right result. A pastry chef must have more patience, following exact measurements and forming precise, even shapes. He needs visual talent as he decorates his creations, knowing he sells them as much by their appearance as by their taste.

These are the élite. To enjoy a meal or a dish cooked by them is an event, not to be missed but not to be contemplated on a regular basis. Far more important in everyday eating are the army of down-to-earth cooks who make food in France such an adventure.

Food Shops

Fundamental to French existence is the baker, the *boulanger*. From medieval times, legislation has governed the weight and content of loaves of bread, with stringent penalties for such crimes as adulteration with sand or sawdust. Today the government pegs the price of white bread and you'll find the famous long loaves a bargain compared with the price of brioche, croissants, wholewheat *(pain complet),* rye *(pain de seigle)* or bran loaves *(pain de son).* White bread can be bought as thin *flûtes* to slice for soup, as *baguettes,* or as the common, thicker loaves known simply as *pains.*

As French bread stays fresh only a few hours it is baked in the morning for midday, with another session in the afternoon. A baker's day starts at 4 A.M. to give the dough time to rise. Sadly, but understandably, there is a lack of recruits so more and more French bread is industrially produced, lacking the right nutty flavor and chew to the crisp crust. The clue to bread baked on the spot is the heady smell of fermenting yeast, so sniff out a neighborhood bakery before you buy.

A good many bakers still resist modernization, led by Lionel Poilâne in Paris, whose name has become synonymous with stoneground, wholewheat bread baked in the traditional brick oven. Parisian cafés often feature sandwiches made with his huge, coarse-textured loaves, and you can go to the original Poilâne bakery at 8 rue du Cherche-midi (6th arrondissement) to see the classic wood-fired ovens which the wily Poilâne still maintains with an eye to publicity.

If bread is the staff of French life, pastry is the sugar icing. The window of a city pastry shop (in the country, bakery and pastry shop are often combined) is a wonder-world of éclairs and meringues, madeleines, petits fours, tartlets and puff pastry, spun sugar and caramel. You'll find open pies, laden with seasonal fruits, pound cakes, nut cakes, chocolate cakes, plus the chef's specialty, for he is certain to have one. Survey them with a sharp eye: they should be small (good ingredients are expensive) and impeccably alike in color and size (the sign of an expert craftsman). Lastly the window should not be overflowing; because of the high cost, the temptation to cram the shelves with leftovers from the day before is strong.

The *charcuterie* is almost as French an institution as the bakery. *Chair cuite* means cooked meat and a charcuterie is a kind of delicatessen, specializing in pâtés, terrines, ham, sausages, and all kinds of cooked and raw pork. A charcuterie also sells long-lasting salads like cucumber, tomato, or grated carrot vinaigrette, and root celery (celeriac) *remoulade* (with mustard mayonnaise). Cooked "dishes of the day" may include *coq au vin, choucroute alsacienne* with smoked pork hock and a variety of sausages, cassoulet, or stuffed cabbage. Often you'll also find condiments like pickles, plus a modest selection of wines, cheeses and desserts such as rice pudding or baked apple. Only bread is needed to complete the meal, and you're set for the world's best picnic!

French cheese deserves, and gets, close attention. Sometimes whole shops are devoted to this branch of gastronomy. Take a whiff of the pungent odor, brace yourself, and plunge into a complex display of goat, sheep and cow's milk cheeses, of fresh and aged cheeses, low fat and high fat, soft, hard and blue cheeses. You can admire cheeses wrapped prettily in vineleaves or trapped in wooden boxes to prevent their running away; you can be tempted by wheels of Gruyère and smile at the suggestive little *bouton de culotte* (underpants button).

Choosing a cheese is as delicate a matter as wine. In a good cheese shop you will be welcome to sample any of the cut cheeses and assistants will help with advice. One cardinal rule is to look for *fromage fermier* (farmer's cheese), a rough equivalent of château-bottled wine. If the label says *lait cru* (raw milk) even better—only when milk is unpasteurized does the flavor of some cheeses, Camembert for example, develop properly. Lastly try to keep a cheese cool without refrigeration and eat it as soon as you can. The delicate soft cheeses like Brie can become overripe in a matter of hours, which is one reason why a wide-ranging selection of cheese is a rarity in a restaurant.

All kinds of other specialty stores exist, often for local craft products. In Dijon, for instance, you'll find shops selling mustards in ornamental pots; in Gascony (near Bordeaux) it's *foie gras* and canned *confit* (preserved duck or goose). The Provençal hill town of Apt goes in for preserves, and Montélimar, close to the almond orchards of the sheltered Rhône valley, makes nougat.

The most famous concentration of food shops in the world must be clustered around the place de la Madeleine in Paris. On one corner stands Fauchon, dean of luxury food emporiums. (When an arsonist set fire to the place in 1977, the intense blaze was reportedly fed by the cognac casks in the cellar.) Fauchon sells everything from wild mushrooms to hand-made candies and the most recherché of game pâtés, all wrapped in those gift packages at which the French excel. Just across the square stands Hédiard, specialist in spices, exotic fruits and preserves. Next door is La Maison de la Truffe and Caviar Kaspia, while for cheese it's a step around the corner to La Ferme Saint-Hubert.

Market Forces

The Madeleine crossroads may be unique, but with a bit of persistence a more modest version can be found in most French towns in the weekly market, often held in a picturesque open hall which may be centuries old. Markets start early, typically around 8 A.M., and often disband at noon. In Paris, street markets continue to thrive in almost every quarter, and although the main wholesale market of Les Halles has moved to the suburbs, the area around the rue Coquillière is still worth exploring for its maze of truffle vendors, game purveyors and professional kitchen equipment outlets.

A market is not just somewhere to absorb local color. You'll see what fish is available and what produce is at its best. Often you'll find little old ladies offering rabbits and herbs, honey and spice bread baked at home. You'll come across local cheeses and, with luck, find a few specialties like the *pissaladière* onion tart of Provence and the candied chestnuts of Privas, near Lyon.

French markets are still dominated by the season—there is little or no sign of frozen produce and meats. The first baby lamb heralds Christmas, little chickens arrive around Easter, together with kid and asparagus. Autumn excitement comes with wild game—venison, pheasant and wild boar. Even cheeses look and taste different with the time of year, depending on whether the animals have been fed in or out of doors.

Many country festivals also revolve around a seasonal specialty. Best known are the *vendange* (grape-picking) feasts held in wine areas, but lesser gatherings may celebrate garlic, apples, walnuts or honey. Many a vineyard village holds a snail festival with a prize for the foolhardy person who can eat the most snails in record time.

Alas, France is no longer impervious to supermarkets. As everywhere, they exist for convenience, but are of little gastronomic interest. The serious housewife still does most of her food shopping by going from butcher to baker to fruit and vegetable shop five or six days a week. Time-consuming, but time well spent, think the French.

Eating like the French

The French light breakfast can come as no surprise: its unbeatable wakeup combination of croissant, brioche or crusty roll with coffee has swept much of the world. Tourists may be offered a glass of orange juice as well. Traditionally the coffee comes as *café au lait,* milky and steaming in a wide two-handled bowl for dipping the bread—these bowls, patterned with flowers or costumed figures and inscribed with a first name, make charming gifts to take home.

If you're an early riser there's a long wait until lunch, for snacks are not a French habit. The structure of a meal, its timing and its content are taken seriously. The American "grazing" phenomenon of mini-meals snatched here and there throughout the day is almost unheard of, and snacks are regarded as spoiling the appetite, not to mention being nutritionally unsound.

However at noon you'll be rewarded by what, for most Frenchmen, remains the main meal of the day. In much of the country everything still stops for two hours (including long-distance trucks on the roads, a useful tip for motorists); children return from school, museums lock their doors. The pattern is much the same in large provincial cities. Restaurants, bistrots, and cafes are crammed with diners, most tucking in to at least two and often three or more courses.

Fixed-price *menus* offer excellent value with such dishes as country terrine, egg mayonnaise, roast leg of lamb or *sole meunière,* with two or three choices for each course. Cheese or salad is followed by dessert, with bread and often a quarter liter of wine or mineral water thrown in. In the wake of a new tax on entertainment, many prestigious restaurants have battened down with fixed-price lunches which may even include a tasting of luxury dishes like a salad of hot *foie gras* and crayfish, or escalopes of salmon with wild mushrooms. It's an excellent way of controlling your outgoings, if not your intake.

Lunch keeps French adults going until evening, but you may want to follow the example of schoolchildren, who are allowed a treat on the way home. Often it is *pain au chocolat,* a stick of chocolate stuffed in a length of French bread or, more expensively, baked inside croissant dough. By 8 P.M. you'll be ready for dinner and for one of the greatest pleasures France has to offer.

Dining Out

The choice of restaurants in France is a feast in itself. At least once during your trip you may want to indulge in an outstanding occasion. But restaurants are just the beginning. You can also eat out in cafés, bistrots, brasseries, fast-food outlets (they, too, have reached France), or in *auberges* which range from staid country inns to sybaritic hideaways with helicopter pads and cooking to match.

Simplest is the café (where the expresso machine is king), offering drinks and snacks like *croque monsieur* (toasted ham and cheese sandwich), *oeuf au plat* (baked eggs), *le hot dog,* and foot-long sandwiches of French bread. Larger city cafés serve hot meals, dishes such as onion soup and braised beef with vegetables, consumed on marble-topped tables to a background of cheerful banter. Like English pubs, cafés are a way of life, a focal point for gossip and dominoes in practically every village.

The name *bistrot,* once interchangeable with café, has recently taken a fashionable turn. In cities, instead of sawdust on the floor and a zinc-topped counter, you may find a bistrot is designer-decorated, serving new-style cuisine to a trendy, chattering crowd. If you're lucky the food will be as witty and colorful as the clientele. Such spots can be great fun to visit, but watch out for the prices.

With few exceptions, brasseries remain unchanged, great bustling places with white-aproned waiters and hearty, masculine food. Go here for oysters on the half-shell and fine seafood, for garlic snails, *boudin* (black pudding), sauerkraut, and vast ice-cream desserts. Originally, a brasserie brewed beer and, as many brewers came from Alsace on the borders of Germany, the cooking reflects their origins.

As for fast food in France, I have to confess an almost total ignorance. On the *autoroute* I flee past chains with whimsical names like "Short Straw" and "Four-sided Roof". No doubt they serve unremarkable steak and caramel custard at standard prices (wherever you go in France, steak is a poor bet). Worst food of all is liable to be at airports, where you'll find microwaved *croque monsieur* and instant coffee at top rates.

The importance placed on food in France is echoed by the number of gastronomic societies, from the *Chevaliers du Tastevin* to the *Chaîne des Rôtisseurs* and the *Confrérie des Cordons Bleus,* to mention only three. The French believe that good eating, at whatever level, is an art that merits considerable time and attention. The French have done the hard work for you and as a traveler you can reap the benefit. Please don't let the opportunity go by!

FRENCH WINES

The Vine of Pleasure

by
PAMELA VANDYKE PRICE

Pamela Vandyke Price is a noted British writer on wine. She has published twenty-one books on the subject, her latest being The Penguin Wine Book. *Her writing, broadcasting and lecturing on wine and wine-related subjects have won her several awards, both British and French.*

France is the most important wine-growing country in the world. It may dispute with Italy over which country produces the greater quantity of wine, but it is the great French wines which have set standards for the others, the French vintages which always make headlines, and French traditions which seem to hold most fascination. The great French estates, renowned for centuries, continue to attract visits from royalty, heads of state, the rich and the famous . . . and from more ordinary travelers.

Whether you are a would-be connoisseur or are (so far) indifferent to wine you have much to gain from metaphorically whetting your palate in anticipation of one of the greatest pleasures France has to offer. The object of this chapter is to provide a brief introduction to a huge and endlessly absorbing subject to which countless books have been devoted, to help you discover for yourself what all the fuss is about. Wine is and always has been so important to the French that no one can claim to know France without some understanding of its role in the French way of life, of the characteristics of major wines and of the regions where they are grown. Further reading undertaken before you encounter French wine on its own soil will certainly stand you in good stead, as will a specialist pocket reference book (buy one in English to take with you) and a notebook to record your own finds.

A Taste of History

The vine came to France with the Romans. Their first vineyards were along the banks of the river Rhône, a great natural highway north from the Mediterranean. Soon, other areas were found ideal for its cultivation and, by medieval times, writers were recording the qualities of regional wines. For six centuries the kings of France were crowned at Reims, in Champagne country, and celebrated their coronations with the local wine (then only intermittently bubbly); but for everyday consumption they favored the wines of Burgundy. Kings and the powerful noble families owned vineyards, but the great religious houses were also significant proprietors. From 1152–1453 England owned the region extending from south of the Loire to the Pyrenees and eastwards almost to Burgundy. It was during this period that the light-toned wines shipped from the Bordeaux region became known as *clairet*— *clair* meaning light in color—to distinguish them from the deeper red wines of the hinterland, which also came to Bordeaux for shipment. This is why, in English, the wine is referred to as claret.

The nobles and religious houses lost their property in the French Revolution at the end of the 18th century, but the great wines survived this and other disasters, including the devastation of wars.

In 1878, the terrible parasite *phylloxera vastatrix* began to destroy the vineyards of France. The solution was found in importing resistant American stock on to which the local vines could be grafted. This huge undertaking, involving thousands of vineyards and millions of vines, got under way towards the end of the century, but was not completed until after World War I.

The Wine Trade

Today the importance of wine to the French economy is enormous. In modern times, exports to northern Europe and to English-speaking countries across the world have developed fairly steadily: in particular, the compatriots of Thomas Jefferson continue to share his appreciation of the wines of France. The business of the shippers *(négociants)* is big even by standards of international trade. A number of famous estates are now owned by foreigners, and interests in the big firms are developed by multinational business concerns.

Large sections of the French population are involved in wine-growing: from the great wine dynasties, with their turbulent histories, down to families working their small inherited vineyards in their spare time. Generations work in the vineyards where generations toiled before them. French growers today have adapted fully to the conditions and demands of the 20th century, marrying science with experience. Even the most traditional wine regions have taken advantage of modern discoveries to improve and protect their vines and wines.

Wine Terms

One important reason why French wine has such a high reputation is that it is subject to strict controls intended to maintain tradition and quality, thus serving both growers and consumers. The category of control is recorded on the label, giving the wine a sort of pedigree (though not a *guarantee* that the wine is fine or that you'll enjoy it).

Appellation d'Origine Contrôlée (Controlled Place Name), abbreviated to A.O.C. or A.C. This is the top category. It gives legal protection to the wine's name, specifies where the wine comes from, how the vines are grown and how the wine is made. The only A.C. wine not obliged to state its category on the label is Champagne.

Vin Délimité de Qualité Supérieur (Superior Quality Wine from a Specified Area), or V.D.Q.S. Like an A.C. wine, the wine will have come from a named area which is prescribed and protected by law; however, the conditions of production are less strict than for A.C. wines (for instance greater yields per hectare are permitted). Like *appellation* wines, V.D.Q.S. wines are officially tasted, and are certainly not to be despised.

Vin de Pays (Local Wine) comes from a specific region, some having pretty names, such as *Jardin de la France* or *Ile de Beauté*. Standards may vary, but wines in this category are good value for money. If you want a local wine, this is the sort to order.

Vin de Table (Table Wine) is a slightly lower category, but a *Vin de Pays* may also bear the words *Vin de Table* on its label. Wines in both categories must state where they came from and should be pleasant to drink. Ask for either if you want a local wine: the phrase is *un vin de la région.*

Vin de Consommation Courant (Wine for Drinking Currently), or V.C.C. is a non-vintage (i.e. undated) branded wine, usually drunk only locally. This is the lowest classification—your real *vin ordinaire.*

If you want a dry or dryish wine, order *un vin sec.* In a sparkling-wine region, however, the terms *demi-sec* and even *sec,* imply some degree of sweetness. There the term to use for a dry wine is *brut;* and if you ask for a *vin doux,* this should result in your getting a sweet wine. *Un vin doux naturel* is one of the wines made in the south and southeast, many of which are based on Muscat grapes and are slightly sweetish, higher in alcohol than an ordinary table wine. They are mostly drunk between times or as apéritifs. *Un vin de marque* is a branded wine.

Discovering New Wines

As wine is the everyday national drink of the French, any visit to France provides opportunities for trying wines you may not already know or are not readily available back home. The fact that such wines are not exported has nothing to do with their quality, but rather because not enough is made and also because, sadly, export customers often prefer the better-known names, even at astronomic prices. Be adventurous—try what the locals find enjoyable on special occasions. In a good restaurant modest wines should provide both quality and interest.

The French buy wines for everyday at the local grocery or supermarket or, in the vineyards, at "cellar door" sales from growers. You may find a wine shop, possible called a *vinothèque,* in a resort or wine region, but prices can be high and, as with other things, you need some knowhow or an experienced friend to be sure that you are getting quality.

Don't assume that everyone in France will have a wide knowledge of wine. You may meet a Burgundian who's never tasted Bordeaux, someone on the Côte d'Azur who may be ignorant of Alsace. Although huge supermarkets often have displays of wines from all over the world, the locals will probably just drink their own region's produce, maybe a non-vintage branded wine—a *vin de consommation courante.* Even in the main wine regions people do not regularly drink the wines that bear the great names. Indeed, you should avoid the very famous names unless you're prepared to pay high prices: many French classics can be nearly as expensive on their native soil as in the export markets. Your best bet is always to choose wines that are locally recommended.

Savoir Boire

Any smart bar or hotel will be able to serve a wide range of drinks, and it's worth while trying the local tipples. There are dozens of French apéritifs and liqueurs, but you should ask about them, and about any local casual drink, if venturing to sample something new. Vermouth will be available anywhere, but if you don't want a cocktail, you should specify *sans gin.* The vermouths of Marseille are famous, as are the very light vermouths of Chambéry, which are always drunk straight, and sometimes in a version flavored with Alpine strawberries.

Bars can usually provide wine by the glass, including sparkling wine if you're in an area that produces it. One drink that is definitely French and somewhat chic is *vin blanc cassis,* white wine spiked with *cassis* (blackcurrant) liqueur. Formerly a specialty of Burgundy, it has also become known as *un kir,* after Canon Félix Kir, Resistance hero and Mayor of Dijon. In sparkling wine regions a *Kir royale* is made with the local bubbly, and sometimes with *framboise* (raspberry) instead of *cassis.*

If you are fortunate enough to be invited to a French household for dinner, do not be surprised if you are not offered an apéritif. But you may be offered *un peu de porto,* for the French drink more port than the British—though admittedly of a somewhat more ordinary quality.

In France, wines are seldom decanted, except in very top-class eating-places. The French also tend to drink vintage wines younger than many people abroad. Try to shun the enormous "balloon" glasses that many French restaurants think impressive: they are clumsy and merely over-aerate the wine. Ask for a simple "Paris"-type goblet or tulip-shaped glass. Certain young red wines, such as Beaujolais and some of the Loire reds, are traditionally served cool, at cellar temperature.

At the end of a meal, you may be offered Marc (pronounced "ma")— a spirit distilled from the final pressings of the grapes—as a change from the more usual Cognac or Armagnac; or, perhaps, a slightly less expensive grape brandy or, of course, a liqueur. Don't drink any good brandy in a goldfish-bowl-sized glass and *never* let the wine waiter warm the brandy glass over a flame—this will mark you as someone who doesn't know how to appreciate a great spirit. Should you buy a cheap wine to drink on a picnic, the expression *une bouteille consignée* means that the bottle is returnable and you will get a few centimes on it.

Visiting the Vineyards

A certain amount of research before your trip can ensure maximum use of time and value for money, and that you don't miss that one fascinating place you would love to have seen. Personal interests will have a lot to do with where you go, but you will need detailed advice and up-to-date information, which you can get by writing to the information offices in the wine regions or the local tourist offices. When already in a vineyard area you might also ask your hotel or a restaurant you have enjoyed if they can recommend places for you to visit.

In the chief wine regions there are usually tours, arranged specifically for visitors, often with multi-lingual guides. It is as well to find one of these as, unless it is really big, a wine establishment may not employ an English-speaking guide.

Bear in mind that the bigger establishments in the classic regions are used to showing people around and providing information; some even have their own small museums or displays relating to their product. Not only will what you see in top establishments be likely to prove a rewarding experience in itself, but many of the great wine areas are also rich in works of art and architecture, as well as being near interesting towns for exploring and shopping—all a great boon for a family party which might well get bored with a succession of vineyards and wineries.

Vineyards are particularly beautiful in late spring and early summer when the vines are coming into leaf. The main French holiday season is from around mid-July to September, and in August many firms are run by a skeleton staff. Don't plan vineyard visits at harvest time (vendange): accommodations are difficult as the wine firms fill the hotels with their business visitors, people are busy and some establishments are closed to outsiders. The date of the grape harvest varies: in the south it may start around mid-September, but the further north you go, the later it will be, sometimes well into October. After the harvest in the fall, the vine leaves turn glorious shades of gold, crimson, amber and scarlet—a wonderful sight in sunny weather.

At any time of the year, you must bear in mind the sacred lunch hour—or rather lunch hours, for lunch may start at mid-day or one o'clock and go on until two or three; tours of wineries will stop before the installation closes.

The sign Dégustation gratuite (free tasting) may tempt you to visit a grower, but though the tasting may be free, you'll usually be expected to buy some wine. The official tasting rooms and those of the big houses won't pressurize you to buy, however.

If you are shown round a cellar and are asked to taste the wines from cask or vat, remember that you may be expected to spit them out. If you're shy and swallow lots of wine, possibly still fermenting, you risk an upset stomach.

Don't tip anyone showing you round unless it's obvious that you should. Usually a member of a firm will expect just a "Thank you" and a handshake.

The Main French Wine Regions

Alsace. This is possibly the most picturesque region in France and, despite being next to Germany (indeed, part of Germany for two periods this century), Alsace and its wines are definitely French. It

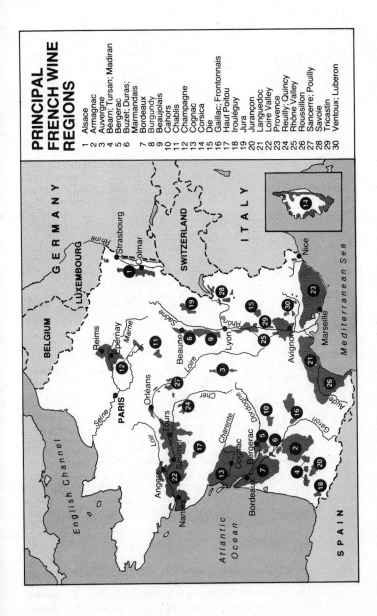

PRINCIPAL FRENCH WINE REGIONS

1. Alsace
2. Armagnac
3. Auvergne
4. Béarn; Tursan; Madiran
5. Bergerac
6. Buzet; Duras; Marmandais
7. Bordeaux
8. Burgundy
9. Beaujolais
10. Cahors
11. Chablis
12. Champagne
13. Cognac
14. Corsica
15. Die
16. Gaillac; Frontonnais
17. Haut Poitou
18. Irouléguy
19. Jura
20. Jurançon
21. Languedoc
22. Loire Valley
23. Provence
24. Reuilly; Quincy
25. Rhône Valley
26. Roussillon
27. Sancerre; Pouilly
28. Savoie
29. Tricastin
30. Ventoux; Luberon

produces one-third of all *Appellation Contrôlée* wines bought in France. The beautiful *Route du Vin* runs from north to south in the shadow of the Vosges Mountains, through fairy-tale villages garlanded with flowers, topped with storks' nests, elegant with fountains. A few of the many delightful towns worth visiting are Riquewihr, Eguisheim, Obernai and Hunawihr. Colmar and Strasbourg, the most important cities, have superb museums containing exhibits on wine.

The wines of Alsace are produced by several thousand small producers. You will find that each establishment makes individual wines, in different quality categories—try several, including the late-picked *vendange tardive* wines, and any that bear the names of individual vineyard sites. The wines are named after the grapes that go into them—Riesling, Sylvaner, Gewürztrammer, Pinot Gris or Tokay d'Alsace, Pinot Blanc, Muscat. Edelzwicker is a blend. All are white, except for a few rosy-red ones made from the Pinot Noir. The Crémants d'Alsace are fully sparkling wines, made by the Champagne method.

Detailed information may be obtained from the *Centre d'Information du Vin d'Alsace* (C.I.V.A.), 69004 Colmar.

Bordeaux. This is the largest area for quality wines and merits a stay of several days. Dry white and red wines are made, some rosé, very little sparkling wine, and the great sweet white wines. Some estates, such as certain ones in the Graves, make both red and white. The wines are kept above-ground in *chais,* or stores, as the water table prevents excavation of deep cellars. Bordeaux wines are put into square-shouldered bottles.

The Médoc, in the north, is the famous region where three of the "first-growth" clarets—Lafite, Latour, Mouton-Rothschild—come from. The museum at the latter estate is well worth a visit. If you have no time to linger in the Médoc, even a half-day tour will enable you to drive past some of the great estates. The Graves area, south of Bordeaux, is where the Haut Brion and other outstanding properties are situated. As the area is in the suburbs of Bordeaux itself, you can visit it in a couple of hours, if pressed for time. Further south, there's the wine circuit of the Sauternes and Barsac areas and, across the river, the pretty regions of the Entre-Deux-Mers and Premières Côtes de Bordeaux. St.-Émilion, very picturesque and worth several hours' exploration, is also across the river from Bordeaux and, to the north here, the regions of Bourg and Blaye are attractive and today make interesting red and white wine.

Information about estates open to visitors and tours may be obtained from the *Syndicat d'Initiative,* corner of the Allées de Tourny, Cours du XXX Juillet, in the center of Bordeaux; also at the local offices of the wine organizations—those of Pauillac and St.-Émilion are very helpful.

Burgundy. This is just about as far north as you can safely make good red wine. The region is quite small and the vineyards are often plot-sized, sometimes with many owners. The main Burgundian wine area, the Côte d'Or, is famous for both red and white wines; some rosé is made, as well as much sparkling wine, most of it white. The northern part of the Côte d'Or is the Côte de Nuits, and the southern part the Côte de Beaune. The wines of southern Burgundy, including the Côte Chalonnaise and the Mâconnais, are especially good value and not intimidatingly expensive. The area of Chablis lies apart from the main area, to the northwest of Côte d'Or, and produces white wine only.

The wines of Burgundy come in sloping-shouldered bottles, and are classified according to a fiendishly complicated system—there are several fat volumes on the topic. One point to bear in mind is that the wines of growers themselves may be more individual than those of the often blended wines of the *négociants* (shippers), although each great establishment will have its own house style.

Clos de Vougeot, in the north, headquarters of the *Confrérie des Chevaliers du Tastevin,* is worth a visit to see the characteristic Cistercian building and the huge wine press. In Beaune there are many fascinating places to explore, including the Hospices de Beaune, the great medieval foundation which, today, draws most of its revenue from bequests of vineyards, the wines of which are sold at the world-famous sale in November. The nearby Musée du Vin (Wine Museum) has a fine collection. The Tourist Office, opposite the Hotel Dieu (main building of the Hospices) can provide information on the many firms you can visit, and tours. The whole region is rich in works of art.

Beaujolais. This—the southern end of the Burgundy region, near Lyon—is the kind of archetypal hilly French countryside celebrated in innumerable movies. Each of the main communes or parishes has a tasting room, often decorated in a somewhat ebullient fashion celebrating the wine and open to all comers. Traditionally, most Beaujolais is red, but some white wine is made and there is even a sparkling white version. Its bottles have sloping shoulders. The very young wine, such as the *Nouveau,* is usually served cool.

Champagne. The most northerly region of the wine areas of France is spread out, its main centers being Reims, Épernay and Ay, with another area to the south around Sézanne and Troyes.

Each of the great Champagne establishments makes an individual style of wine, most being non-vintage (undated), but also including vintage wines and the "luxury cuvées," (blends) of which Moët's Dom Pérignon is among the best-known. The original Dom Pérignon, Cellarer of the Benedictine Abbey of Hautvillers, in the heart of the region, was a wine genius. In his lifetime (1639–1715) and long after, he enjoyed wide renown for his palate and incomparable expertise as a blender of wines from various Champagne vineyards. He did not invent bubbly, however,—it has existed in some shape or form as long as wine has been made, the bubbles in Champagne being a natural byproduct of fermentation.

There are several other "luxury cuvées," all magnificent to drink, and impressive in price. Most Champagne is made from a blend of black grapes, Pinot Noir and Pinot Meunier, and the white Chardonnay grape. But Blanc de Blancs is made solely from white grapes, and Blanc de Noirs only from black ones, but you won't often find them outside the region. Pink Champagne, Champagne *rosé,* which is mostly non-vintage, is made either with a mixture of white and black grapes (especially black) or is a blend with red wine, notably from Bouzy (that aptly-named region).

A fairly recent variation of Champagne is *crémant,* which is slightly less fizzy than the fully sparkling wines. The still wines of the Champagne region are called Coteaux Champenois and are mostly white, though a little red is made. Take advantage of being in the region to try *ratafia,* a slightly sweet apéritif: its odd name derives from the fact that it used to be the wine with which signatories to a contract settled or "ratified" their agreement. It is made of freshly-pressed grape juice combined with brandy and then aged.

Champagne is marketed in distinctively thick bottles to resist the pressure inside, though some of the luxury wines come in bottles with unusual shapes and decorations.

The Champagne area is well-organized for tourists. There are three routes shown on the tourist map, colored blue, red and green, which lead you through the region. At Hautvillers, stop and see the tombs of Dom Pérignon and Dom Ruinart in the church, and in Épernay the Musée du Vin de Champagne in the avenue du Champagne, where many great establishments are situated. The great window in the cathedral at Reims shows wine being made. The galleries under the Champagne houses are extensive, often many miles of levels, so take walking shoes—unless you visit one where a little train whisks visitors around—and wear a coat as it can be definitely cool. Try to see some of the Reims houses where the curious *crayères*, flask-shaped openings in the chalk, were cut out by the Romans.

The *Comité Interprofessionel du Vin de Champagne* (C.I.V.C.) is at 5 rue Henri-Martin, 51200 Épernay, and they or tourist offices can supply information, including the opening times and particulars of guides available in the various cellars.

Loire. The Loire is the longest river in France, and on its banks and those of its tributaries, a huge range of wines is made—from dry to sweet, red, white, semi-sparkling and fully sparkling. Poets have sung their praises since early times. Some are made in huge installations, as at Saumur, others, as in Muscadet, come from smaller estates or, as at Vouvray, from little plots in the pale-colored soil. The cellars where the wines are made and matured are often actually underneath the vineyards. Some wines bear estate names, but many are labeled merely according to their region and with the names of their makers. Remember that, for example, the Sancerre or Pouilly Fumé of one maker will be different from that made by even a next-door neighbor.

Many of the big establishments and the regional museums have interesting exhibits relating to the wines of the area—ask about these from the local syndicates and tourist bureaux. There is one such wine museum in Tours.

Rhône Valley. This region splits easily into two areas: the north—from south of Lyon down to the twin towns of Tain and Tournon; and the south—with Avignon at its center. Plenty of white wines are made here, aromatic and robust, although the reds are perhaps best known. One of the world's most loved rosés, Tavel, is made here in the south just above Avignon, and is not a pink wine to be drunk carelessly for it carries its own punch. The reputation of the sweet wines of Muscat-de-Beaumes-de-Venise is spreading; they are especially good when drunk chilled. The tiny estate of Château Grillet, in the northern Rhône near Vienne, which makes white wine, is the only vineyard in France to have its very own A.C. classification.

Particularly interesting these days are the "new" vineyard areas making good wines—the Ardèche, Côtes du Ventoux, Gigondas, Lirac and Cairanne are just a few of the southern ones. Don't disdain wines humbly labeled *Côtes du Rhone* either, especially if they bear the name of a reputable maker. It's said with truth that a good Rhône is better value than an indifferent Burgundy. The Rhône bottles have sloping shoulders.

In Avignon, the *Maison du Vin,* 41 cours Jean-Jaurès, can supply information about the wines, cellars and tasting rooms open to visitors. There are plenty of these and some include small museums and exhibits of wine equipment.

For the more specialized wine lover, the superb Université du Vin at Suze-la-Rousse in Provence runs courses on all aspects of wine and attracts students from all over the world.

Other regions. Huge quantities of wine are made in the south, in the Hérault, Aude, Gard and Languedoc-Roussillon regions. In the past much of the wine was used for blending, today such lesser-known areas are making individual wines well worth trying, such as many of the *vins de pays.*

The foothills of the Pyrenees, the Dordogne Valley, many of the central regions and the Jura along the Swiss border all produce wine, some of considerable quality. Interestingly, the Jura was the home of Louis Pasteur, the great 19th-century chemist, whose discovery of bacterial action was at least partly the result of his familiarity with the film of yeast cells, the *flor,* that grows on the surface of Jura wines while they are maturing.

With a final cry of *santé,* we should remind readers that in the northern regions where vines cannot grow well, there is a very good—and sometimes lethally strong—alternative in cider, which visitors to Normandy and Brittany should definitely try.

EXPLORING FRANCE

PARIS

A Voyage of Discovery

The problem of where to start your discovery of this fascinating city is easily solved by the convenient fact that the geographical center of Paris and its historic heart are one and the same: the boat-shaped Ile de la Cité. One of two islands in the middle of the Seine river as it flows through Paris, the Ile de la Cité is today crowned by the twin towers of the mighty Gothic cathedral of Notre Dame. But originally it was the place where the ancient Parisii first set up their primitive huts around 200 B.C.

Start your exploratory journey at the western tip of the island, at the place du Pont-Neuf. It's in the middle of Paris's oldest bridge, confusingly called the New Bridge, the Pont Neuf. The bridge dates from 1578 and a splendid annual fair in June celebrates its original opening. Facing you is an equestrian statue of Henri IV, the Protestant Bourbon king who converted to Catholicism and did much to shape the city we know today before falling victim to a fanatical assassin in 1610. Behind the king the peaceful tree-lined square du Vert-Galant (a nickname often used for him) is the starting-point for the Vedettes du Pont-Neuf, the glass-topped motorboats that will take you for a delightful and instructive ride along the Seine by day or by night.

Heading east you come to the lovely triangular place Dauphine, which still has a few 17th-century houses, as well as a couple of pleasant restaurants and good wine bars. At the far end looms the monumental facade of the law courts, the Palais de Justice, part of a huge complex of buildings that includes the Conciegerie and the Sainte Chapelle. It is built on the site where the Roman governors and earliest kings lived, later becoming the seat of Parliament. The Conciergerie was originally part of the royal palace, but is best known as the prison where Queen Marie Antoinette and many others were held before being led off for execution on the guillotine during the French Revolution. You'll recognize the building by its four imposing towers overlooking the Seine on the north side, one of which, the Tour de l'Horloge, or Clock Tower, on the corner of the boulevard du Palais, is adorned with a clock that has been ticking away since 1370. Inside you'll be shown the guardroom with its Gothic vaulting, the huge Salle des Gens d'Armes, the prisoner's gallery, various cells (including Marie Antoinette's), and the chapel, where exhibits connected with the ill-fated queen are displayed.

Head now for the Sainte Chapelle, one of the finest examples of Gothic architecture in France, with breathtakingly beautiful stained glass. The chapel was built to hold the reputed Crown of Thorns—bought by the French king Louis XI, St. Louis, from Emperor Baldwin I of Constantinople—and was consecrated in 1248. Two-thirds of the stained glass designed to create a fittingly sumptuous setting for the holy relic has survived. The Sainte Chapelle is a must on any visitor's itinerary, especially if you can combine a visit with one of the magical candlelit concerts held there.

A few steps away is the picturesque flower market, beside the Seine. It has been attracting shutter bugs for decades (on Sundays the flowers change into birds). From here, follow the rue de la Cité to the parvis de Notre Dame. This large traffic-free square affords a marvelous view of the magnificent Gothic cathedral.

Notre Dame

Work on Notre Dame began in 1163. The site of the church had previously seen a Roman temple, an early Christian basilica and a Romanesque church (beneath the square the interesting Archeological Crypt museum displays the results of excavations on this very spot). The choir and altar were consecrated 19 years later but the superb sculpture surrounding the main portals was not put into position until 1240. In spite of various 17th-century changes the cathedral remained basically the same until the French Revolution at the end of the 18th century, when the frenzied mob hacked down or stripped away everything inside and out they considered to be "counter to the spirit of the Revolution." Even the statues of the Kings of Judah on the facade were beheaded in the belief that they depicted the despised royal line of France! An interesting postscript to this vandalism occurred in 1977 when some of the severed heads were discovered buried beneath what was once a mansion owned by an ardent royalist; they are now on show in the Musée de Cluny. By the beginning of the 19th century the excesses of the revolutionary period had died away and the cathedral could fulfil its religious function once again, one of its most splendid ceremonies being the coronation as emperor of Napoleon Bonaparte in 1804.

The facade divides into three, with the three huge portals, or doors, at the base: the Portal of the Virgin on the left, the Portal of the Last Judgement in the center and the Portal of St. Anne on the right, all of them surrounded by magnificent biblical carvings adorned with foliage, fruit and other traditional motifs. The portals are surmounted by the

Galerie des Rois (the Kings' Gallery), then by the great rose window (best seen, of course, from inside) and by the Grande Galerie (Great Gallery) at the base of the twin towers—between which you can glimpse the spire crowning the chancel, which was added during restoration in the 19th century.

The interior, with its vast proportions, soaring nave and the multicolored light filtering in through the great stained-glass windows, manages to inspire awe in spite of the inevitable throngs of visitors. You'll find a mass here a memorable experience, as are the organ concerts. Standing by the massive 12th-century piers supporting the towers you can look down the nave to the crossing with a beautiful 14th-century statue of the Madonna and Child known simply as Notre Dame de Paris (Our Lady of Paris), on the south side at the entrance to the choir. The choir itself has some fine choir stalls, a *Pietà* by Nicolas Coustou and sculptures of Louis XIII and his new-born heir, the future Louis XIV, all the result of a vow the childless king had taken after 23 years of marriage—when he promised to dedicate his whole kingdom to the Virgin if his wife gave him a son. South of the choir is the former sacristy, now the treasury, where you can see chalices, manuscripts and other church heirlooms.

If you're feeling strong enough to tackle the famous towers, make your way to the entrance to the staircase in the north aisle. A mere 387 steps and a lot of breathlessness later you'll be rewarded by one of the best-known views in Paris, framed by the highly photogenic gargoyles that feature on so many postcards. For another lovely view, this time of the east end of the cathedral, ringed round by soaring flying buttresses, walk round to the pretty square Jean XXIII. Before leaving the Ile de la Cité, continue to its eastern tip, where the square de l'Ile de France houses a moving modern crypt dedicated to the memory of the many who were deported during the Nazi occupation of France and died in the concentration camps.

The Ile Saint-Louis

The narrow Pont Saint-Louis takes you across from the Ile de la Cité to the smaller Ile Saint-Louis, one of the most delightful parts of Paris. It was originally two separate islands, but these were joined together by an engineer called Christophe Marie in the 17th century (his name survives in the Pont Marie, leading to the mainland). He also had a series of classical mansions built on the island and this smart piece of speculation explains why the Ile Saint-Louis is all-of-a-piece with its narrow streets and quays full of nobly-proportioned buildings all dating from the same period.

The two finest mansions are the Hôtel Lambert at the eastern end of the rue Saint-Louis-en-L'Ile and the Hôtel de Lauzun, the only one open to the public. Quite apart from its magnificent painted ceilings, tapestries and gilded carvings it has interesting literary associations: in the 19th century the "Hashish-Eaters' Club," founded by the Romantic poet Théophile Gautier and frequented by Charles Baudelaire among many others, met here regularly. The island's only church, Saint-Louis-en-L'Ile, is also worth a visit for its exceptionally rich fittings and decoration. But you should also save time for a stroll through this oasis of calm in the heart of the city, which incidentally has a number of good restaurants.

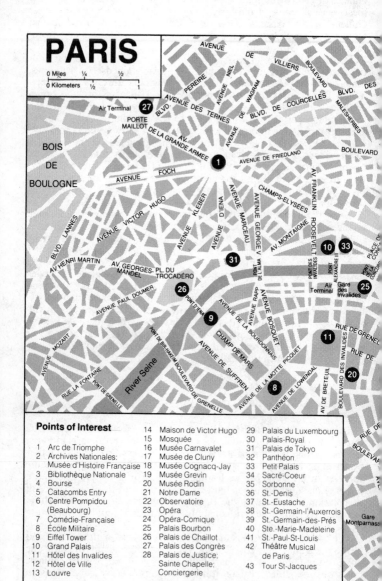

PARIS

0 Miles ¼ ½
0 Kilometers ½ 1

Points of Interest

1 Arc de Triomphe
2 Archives Nationales:
   Musée d'Histoire Française
3 Bibliothèque Nationale
4 Bourse
5 Catacombs Entry
6 Centre Pompidou
   (Beaubourg)
7 Comédie-Française
8 École Militaire
9 Eiffel Tower
10 Grand Palais
11 Hôtel des Invalides
12 Hôtel de Ville
13 Louvre

14 Maison de Victor Hugo
15 Mosquée
16 Musée Carnavalet
17 Musée de Cluny
18 Musée Cognacq-Jay
19 Musée Grevin
20 Musée Rodin
21 Notre Dame
22 Observatoire
23 Opéra
24 Opéra-Comique
25 Palais Bourbon
26 Palais de Chaillot
27 Palais des Congrès
28 Palais de Justice;
   Sainte Chapelle;
   Conciergerie

29 Palais du Luxembourg
30 Palais-Royal
31 Palais de Tokyo
32 Panthéon
33 Petit Palais
34 Sacré-Coeur
35 Sorbonne
36 St.-Denis
37 St.-Eustache
38 St.-Germain-l'Auxerrois
39 St.-Germain-des-Prés
40 Ste.-Marie-Madeleine
41 St.-Paul-St-Louis
42 Théâtre Musical
   de Paris
43 Tour St-Jacques

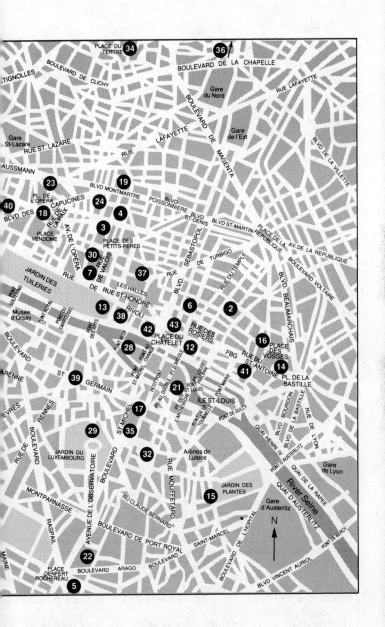

The Marais

Crossing by the Pont-Marie you reach the Right Bank (i.e. the north side of the river). From here, head up to the restored Marais district, a definite must for anyone interested in the history of Paris and its architecture.

The Marais, once a marsh (which is what the name means), first became a place of importance in the 14th century, when Charles V decided to leave the royal palace on the Ile de la Cité, which held so many unhappy memories after the bloody riots led by Etienne Marcel, a cloth merchant and provost of Paris. He opted instead for the Marais. However, the district didn't really become fashionable until the early-17th century, when Henri IV built a Royal Square and the rich and noble families of the time flocked to build their own mansions round about. Many of these splendid *hôtels particuliers,* as they are known in French, have today been restored after a long period of neglect, the result of an enlightened government decision in the early '60s to designate the Marais a "protected area." It is now the most delightful place to visit, with many attractive little shops and restaurants. The Marais Festival, held in June and July, stages concerts, drama and ballet in illuminated courtyards, mansions and churches throughout the district.

Your first sight will be the Hôtel de Sens, a fine medieval survival. With its pointed corner towers, Gothic porch and richly carved decorative details, this 15th- and 16th-century building is an interesting mixture of fairytale château and defensive stronghold. Once lived in by the archbishops of Sens, it was also the home of the worldly-wise first wife of Henri IV, Queen Margot, whose amorous exploits were a byword. It now houses a fine-arts library, the Bibliothèque Forney, which stages good temporary exhibits.

A short walk along the quai des Célestins brings you to the rue des Jardins Saint-Paul, where you'll find some good small antique shops and craft workshops, and also a fraction of Philippe Auguste's ramparts built to surround 12th-century Paris (which was only about an eighth the size of modern Paris). At the end of the street turn left and follow the rue de Jouy until you reach the Hôtel de Beauvais, where Mozart delighted Paris with his playing when he was only seven; the building has some superb vaulted cellars dating from the 13th century. If you walk along the rue Saint-Antoine you can visit the well-known church of Saint-Paul-Saint-Louis, built by the Jesuits in the 17th century and modeled on the church of the Gesù in Rome.

The busy rue Saint-Antoine is just the place for spotting ordinary Parisians going about their daily business, maybe even the descendants of the furious mob who stormed the nearby Bastille in 1789. But before reliving this world-shaking event, stop off at # 62, where the Hôtel de Béthune-Sully houses the excellent Caisse Nationale des Monuments Historiques, which organizes guided visits all over Paris as well as having a beautiful formal garden and mounting good architectural exhibits. You can buy an illustrated plan of the Marais from the porter's lodge inside the gates.

There is little left to see of the place de la Bastille, since on July 14, 1789, the furious mob utterly destroyed the Bastille prison, which had once held the mysterious Man in the Iron Mask, and which they saw as the hated symbol of the tyranny of the *ancien régime.* Ever since people all over France celebrate the date by dancing in the streets, staging firework displays and generally living it up on their *Fête Nationale* (National Holiday). The July Column in the center of the otherwise empty square was erected to commemorate the men and women who lost their lives during the 1830 uprising that put the "bourgeois monarch," Louis Philippe, on the throne. The "power to the people" theme is being continued with the building here of the Opéra de la Bastille, an opera house designed to bring this usually expensive art within the reach of ordinary folk.

After this historical pilgrimage make your way back along the rue Saint-Antoine to the rue de Birague, a narrow street leading to the lovely place des Vosges, Henri IV's former Royal Square or Place Royale. (It is now called after the Vosges Mountains in eastern France for the distinctly unromantic reason that it was the first region of France to cough up the taxes imposed by the revolutionaries in 1800!) The king's and queen's pavilions face each other on the north and south sides, while the equestrian statue in the middle is of Louis XIII. Also in the square is the home of that giant of 19th-century French literature Victor Hugo, which can be visited. Madame de Sévigné, whose letters paint such a vivid picture of 17th-century life, once lived at # 1, while Alphonse Daudet, author of the charming *Letters from My Windmill,* was another inhabitant.

The continuation of the north side of the place des Vosges, running westwards, is the rue des Francs-Bourgeois or Street of the Free Citizens (who were so poor when they lodged here in alms houses in the 14th century that they were allowed to be free of, or exempt from, taxes). The street's best-known mansion is the Hôtel Carnavalet, once lived in by Madame de Sévigné and now an enthralling museum of the history of Paris. The street running beside the Musée Carnavalet takes you past some fine restored mansions to the rue du Parc-Royal, lined by more imposing 17th-century buildings. Continue on and you come to the Hôtel Libéral-Bruand in the rue de la Perle, which again houses a museum, the Musée Bricard, or Musée de la Serrure, tracing the history of locks and locksmiths from Roman times down to the present. The nearby Hôtel Juigné, or Hôtel Salé (so called because it was built for the royal collector of the hated salt tax), has been redesigned to form a Picasso Museum, opened in 1985. This inspired museum offers a wide range of the artist's work, excellently displayed, but be prepared for huge crowds at any time of year.

The street running down the other side of the Musée Carnavalet, the rue de Payenne, has a little garden full of stone monuments and sculpture and, at # 11, the Swedish Cultural Center in a handsome former mansion. Well-designed art exhibits are often held here, as they are at the Marais Cultural Center, which you'll find if you turn right into the rue des Francs-Bourgeois once again (at # 26). Also in the rue des Francs-Bourgeois, at 36, is the Swiss Cultural Center, which has started staging some interesting art exhibits. Further along is the Palais Soubise, housing France's priceless National Archives and the Museum of French History, where you can see such precious exhibits as letters written by Joan of Arc. This was also once the home of the Cardinal de Rohan, a key figure in the story of the "Queen's Necklace."

There are far too many lovely mansions in the Marais for us to describe here (the Hôtel Guénégaud in the nearby rue des Archives, housing the Hunting Museum, is one of the finest), but we recommend that you try to find time to wander around, peering into courtyards to spot the wealth of elegant staircases, wrought-iron lamps and balustrades, carved doorways, intricately fashioned balconies and so on. We'll make just two more recommendations: visit the church of Notre-Dame-des-Blancs-Manteaux in the rue des Francs-Bourgeois to see its extraordinarily elaborate inlaid pulpit; and take a stroll in the picturesque Jewish district centered on the rue des Rosiers, with its many tiny synagogues and kosher shops and restaurants. Since the French withdrawal from North Africa the former predominantly East European atmosphere has been superseded by a more North African ambience as many Franco-Jewish families settled here.

The Hôtel de Ville and Beaubourg

The City Hall (Hôtel de Ville) and the area around it have undergone a sea change in recent years and are now most attractive. The square in front of the Hall is now traffic free and well lit for strolling and you may find an exhibit on during your visit, probably connected with the history of Paris. The building may look old, especially when it is illuminated at night, but it is actually an over-enthusiastic modern copy of its 16th-century predecessor, which was burned down during the savage Paris Commune in 1871. This was only one of the many dramatic events that have taken place here over the centuries. It was the scene of public executions for hundreds of years and in the 14th century the fierce uprising against royal authority led by Etienne Marcel resulted in the city's government being established here. During the French Revolution the revolutionaries did a fair amount of damage, and five years later their former hero, the tyrannical Robespierre, took shelter here before being dragged off to the very guillotine to which he had condemned so many "enemies of the people." When the short-lived Restoration period ended with the fall of Louis-Philippe, the City Hall became the temporary seat of government (1848) and again witnessed violent clashes. After the destructive fire of 1871, the building was completely restored (1874–84) in its present over-elaborate form. In 1944 the returned hero General de Gaulle calmly took over the city from the Resistance here and, ever since, it has been the scene of ceremonial events—particularly from 1977, when Paris elected its first mayor for over a hundred years. The mayor was—and still is at presstime—the Gaullist leader Jacques Chirac, now prime minister for the second time, who has done a great deal to enliven Paris, especially in the previously dead summer months.

Behind the City Hall you can see the three-tiered classical facade of the church of Saint-Gervais-Saint-Protais, well known for its organ music (the distinguished musical family of the composer François Couperin were organists here for generations). The church also has a lovely paneled Golden Chapel (Chapelle Dorée) and some good 16th-century stained glass.

This end of the rue de Rivoli is more popular than the Concorde end, with the vast department store Le Bazar de l'Hôtel-de-Ville (or B.H.V.) attracting huge numbers of shoppers. To the west stands the Gothic Tour Saint-Jacques, now used as a weather center but once the scene of experiments conducted by the great mathematician and philosopher Blaise Pascal, whose statue you can admire at its foot. The tower originally formed part of a church that was demolished shortly after the Revolution. The place du Châtelet, south of the tower, is dominated by two large theaters, the one on the west side offering opera, ballet and concerts, the one on the east, concerts, at reasonable prices.

Just north of the Tour Saint-Jacques you come to the "Plateau Beaubourg," the home of the famous Georges Pompidou Art and Culture Center since 1977. To get to it, cross the rue de Rivoli and take the rue Saint-Martin, where you'll find the interesting church of Saint-Merri, built in the late 16th century in the late-Gothic style of an earlier age and adorned with several fine paintings and a superb organ, used for concerts during the Ile de France Festival in the summer months. A little way further on and you'll find yourself confronted with the most popular building in Europe, not to mention one of the most controversial. The Italian and British architects whose design won the competition for President Pompidou's brainchild—an arts complex designed to restore Paris to its rightful place as the world's leading art capital—decided, preposterously or imaginatively, depending on your point of view, to allow the maximum amount of space inside the building by thrusting everything possible to the outside: stairs, escalators, elevators, ventilation shafts, gas and water pipes, the lot. The result is a vast, gaudily colored and brilliantly illuminated structure sometimes compared to an oil refinery or an ocean liner! Critics have blamed poor construction and materials for problems of wear and tear, and the huge numbers of visitors are a strain. Be prepared to stand in line for some time before being even allowed on to the escalator taking you up to the exhibit floors—safety regulations don't allow more than 4,300 persons at any one time. Refurbishment is underway to increase space for exhibitions by 25 percent and improve their presentation; work on the top floor is finished, on the third and fourth, in progress.

The Center, which is generally referred to as the Beaubourg Center, or just Beaubourg, is primarily the home of the National Museum of Modern Art, the largest collection of modern art in the world. It has a particularly fine range of Matisses and will give you a good overview of the various "-isms" of modern art (fauvism, cubism, expressionism and so on), as well as of more recent, and sometimes fairly way-out, developments. But Beaubourg has many other attractions beside this superb collection: an excellent reference library, a cinémathèque showing classics from all over the world, a children's painting studio, an acoustics and music research center, a reconstruction of the studio in which the great Romanian-French sculptor Constantin Brancusi worked, an industrial design center, and a large bookshop. On top of all that, it's constantly staging temporary exhibits, concerts, theater and ballet performances, and a series of lively "happenings" (check the huge noticeboard on the ground floor to see what's going on while you're there). The whole ambiance is still further enlivened by the many entertainers doing their thing on the piazza in front of the Center, invariably attracting throngs of onlookers.

Les Halles and the Bourse Area

The streets and squares around Beaubourg are full of fashion boutiques, art galleries, chic little restaurants, café-theaters and busy cafés ideal for people-watching. The general liveliness of this part of Paris is due in part to the proximity of Les Halles, Paris's famous food market for over 800 years but now a multi-faceted entertainment-and-shopping complex that offers a wide appeal to tourists and Parisians alike. To get there walk along the rue Aubry-le-Boucher, cross the busy boulevard Sebastopol and continue along the rue Berger to the attractive square des Innocents with its beautiful Renaissance fountain, the

Fontaine des Innocents, standing on the site of what was once Paris's largest cemetery. It was designed by Pierre Lescot and the graceful sculpted figures are the work of Jean Goujon, whose work can also be seen in the Louvre and the Musée Carnavalet.

The rue de la Ferronnerie, running parallel to the southern side of the square, has strong historical associations: it was here, outside # 11 to be precise, that the course of French history changed abruptly with the assassination in 1610 of King Henri IV, by a teacher and mystic called François Ravillac.

Les Halles Mark 2 came into being after the departure, in 1969, of the mammoth food market to Rungis near Orly airport. Two years later the famous 19th-century glass and cast iron market buildings were pulled down and 1979 saw the unveiling of the "Forum," a pedestrians-only shopping-and-leisure center in glass and concrete, built on several different levels. Here you'll find big-name fashion boutiques (Cardin, Saint-Laurent and co.), accessory and perfume stores, a huge branch of the FNAC, an upmarket discount house selling records, sports goods and audiovisual equipment at bargain prices, plus a very wide range of books at regular prices. The leisure scene is catered for by several movie houses, a children's theater, two museums (one devoted to holography, the other a branch of the famous Grévin waxworks museum) and a variety of restaurants to suit all pocketbooks.

Round and about the Forum are a number of other attractions, the major one being a popular "children's garden" full of delights, to which adults are refused admittance. And if you've heard nostalgic stories about finishing up an evening on the town with a visit to the all-night cafés and restaurants once frequented by the market porters, you'll be glad to know that many of them are still going strong and are still full of atmosphere.

Another landmark that has survived the changing fortunes of Les Halles unscathed is the lovely church of Saint-Eustache with its Gothic ground plan, Renaissance decoration and classical 18th-century facade. The church has long been associated with fine music—Berlioz's *Te Deum* and Liszt's *Missa Solemnis* were both given their first performance here—and still echoes to the sounds of superb concerts throughout the year. Among several interesting paintings inside, don't miss an early Rubens, *The Pilgrims of Emmaus.* Below Saint-Eustache is the last part of the Forum to be completed, in 1987: more shops and movie houses, a sports center and Olympic pool, concert halls, an art gallery, and even underground gardens with a tropical greenhouse.

The round building on the west side of Les Halles is the Bourse du Commerce or Commodities Exchange, a 19th-century structure on the site of a splendid mansion built for Queen Marie de Médicis (a tall column is the only surviving fragment of her home). The nearby rue du Louvre contains the city's only all-night post office; cross it and turn into the rue Jean-Jacques Rousseau (the great man lived here towards the end of his life) to reach the Galerie Véro-Dodat, one of several elegant 19th-century shopping arcades that are now back in fashion. At the far end turn right into the rue Croix des Petits-Champs, leading to the 17th-century place des Victoires. Here you can admire some elegant facades and an equestrian statue of Louis XIV. The circular "square" is a center of avant-garde fashion, with several boutiques, as well as a couple of good restaurants. To the north is the basilica of Notre-Dame-des-Victoires, of interest because of the thousands of votive offerings you'll find inside—it has been the goal of a pilgrimage to the Virgin Mary since the early 19th century.

The massive Banque de France, just south of the place des Victoires, was set up by Napoleon in 1800. Opposite you'll find another attractive old shopping arcade, the Galerie Vivienne, leading to France's best-known library, the monumental Bibliothèque Nationale, which underwent extensive renovation and extension in the mid-80s. Originally the royal library, its collection contains a copy of every single book or pamphlet printed in France since the early 16th century. The highly decorative Galerie Mazarine, once filled with the magnificent art collection of Cardinal Mazarin, is now used for excellent special exhibits on literary themes; the Cabinet des Médailles et Antiques displays coins, medals and cameos. Two other sights worth seeing in this area: the Bourse or Stock Exchange, reached via the rue Vivienne (you can visit it any weekday morning); and the nearby rue des Colonnes, with a long pillared arcade.

The Opéra and the Grands Boulevards

A short walk north from the Bourse along the rue Notre-Dame-des-Victoires and the rue Montmartre brings you to the boulevard Montmartre, almost opposite the famous Musée Grevin, Paris's major wax-works. This will be your first taste of the *Grands Boulevards,* a semicircle of broad streets running from the place de la République in the west and following the line of the city's former ramparts. The boulevards' heyday came in the late-18th and early-19th centuries, when all fashionable Paris came here to stroll and take the air, to dine in one of the many elegant restaurants and to see a show staged in the theaters and circuses at the eastern end of the semicircle. This is still a major entertainment area, with dozens of movie houses and theaters, and plenty of good traditional restaurants, some serving seafood until late at night. But it is no longer chic and is too jammed with automobiles to be a pleasant spot for strolling.

Following the boulevards east you come across two triumphal arches, the Porte Saint-Denis and the Porte Saint-Martin, erected in the 1670s to commemorate military victories and adorned with allegorical sculpture. The place de la République at the far end of the boulevards has been the setting for many stirring events, especially during the Paris Commune, but has little of interest now. Better work your way westwards, past the Passage des Panoramas, where Robert Fulton, the American inventor of the steamship, attracted huge crowds to his "cycloramas," an early version of Vistavision. The next boulevard, the boulevard des Italiens, is "opera land": here you'll find the Opéra Comique (also called the Salle Favart), the home of light opera, and at the far end the majestic 19th-century Opéra, one of the world's best-known houses for grand opera. This grandiose building, literally covered with opulent decorative detail, houses an interesting small museum; inside, high above the marble and gilt, the auditorium ceiling is the work of the Russian painter Marc Chagall, who lived in France for over sixty years.

The famous Café de la Paix on the corner of the place de l'Opéra is a favorite haunt of wealthy foreign visitors, while keen shoppers should make their way behind the Opéra to the boulevard Haussmann, with its upmarket department stores Au Printemps and Galeries Lafayette. The boulevard des Capucines has another well-known department store, the somewhat staid Trois-Quartiers. But you'll also spot the famous Olympia music hall, which once echoed to the powerful voice of Edith Piaf and is still a key venue for the top entertainers, and the Cognacq-Jay Museum, specializing in the paintings and furniture of the 18th century. Look out too for two historic landmarks: at # 14 a commemorative plaque tells you that the Lumière brothers staged the first performance of their new invention, the forerunner of the modern movie, in 1895; and at # 11 on the last of the boulevards, the boulevard de la Madeleine, Alphonsine Duplessis, lived and died. She was the model for the heroine of Alexandre Dumas *fils'* play, *La Dame aux camélias,* later to be turned into an opera by Verdi—*La Traviata.*

The Madeleine area

The boulevards end in a flourish with one of Paris's best-known churches, Sainte-Marie-Madeleine, always known simply as La Madeleine. Modeled on a Roman temple, it was begun by Napoleon as a monument to the glory of his *Grande Armée* but was not finished until long after the Restoration. Louis XVIII then decreed that it was to be a church after all, dedicated to Mary Magdalen. There is nothing of special interest inside, but the Corinthian columns surmounted by a carved frieze running around the outside are most impressive and the symmetrical effect created by the Palais Bourbon beyond the rue Royale, the place de la Concorde and the Seine easily explains why this is one of the city's best-known vistas.

Beside the church you'll find an attractive flower market and a kiosk housing one of two tourist offices run by the Paris transport system (RATP). Then take the rue Royale, best known for Maxim's restaurant at # 3, which incidentally is now owned by couturier Pierre Cardin. Leading west off this street is the elegant faubourg Saint-Honoré, a mecca for fashion freaks with its many fashion houses and expensive boutiques. Here too are the British Embassy (at # 35), St. Michael's English church in the rue d'Aguesseau just opposite, and further along the Elysée Palace, the official residence of the French president. The inevitable security precautions mean that you can't do more than peer from a distance into the courtyard of this splendid building in which Madame de Pompadour, the Empress Josephine and the future Napoleon III all lived at one time.

Continuing along the same street you come to the church of Saint-Philippe-du Roule, with a fine fresco of the *Deposition.* A short walk from here along the rue de Courcelles and you can visit the Musée Jacqemart-André on the boulevard Haussmann; it has a permanent collection of 18th-century paintings and furniture plus some Italian Renaissance rooms, and also stages special exhibits.

The Place Vendôme and the Palais Royal

If instead of taking the rue du faubourg Saint-Honoré you turn left off the rue Royale into the rue Saint-Honoré, full of expensive little shops with hand-made accessories, you will soon come to the place Vendôme (turn north into the rue de Castiglione). The octagonal *place* with its discreetly opulent buildings forms the most perfect group of 17th-century buildings to have survived down to our own day, and is also the home of the fabulous Ritz Hotel. It is dominated by a huge stone column covered with bronze melted down from guns captured at the Battle of Austerlitz, one of Napoleon's most famous victories. So it's only right that the figure perched on the top should be Napoleon himself—though it's not the original, which was replaced first by one of Henri IV (hastily substituted when the emperor went into exile), then by a huge *fleur-de-lys,* and eventually by another, less grandiose figure of Napoleon.

The *place* and the deluxe rue de la Paix leading northwards are well known for their jewelry stores: Cartier, Chaumet and Van Cleef & Arpels are all old-established inhabitants. But this area is also the home of many of the world's major airlines. The same applies to the nearby avenue de l'Opéra, leading up to the Opéra, which is nowhere near as fashionable as it used to be. And even the rue de Rivoli, just south of the place Vendôme—take the rue de Castiglione to reach it—has more souvenir shops than elegant boutiques these days. Yet it's still very pleasant to walk along the covered arcade, and you may find this a good place for a restful tea or coffee in one of the many tearooms here, including the famous "English tearooms" above Smith's English bookshop.

A walk eastwards will offer you the pleasure of seeing the dashing bronze-gilt statue of Joan of Arc in the place des Pyramides, close to the spot where she fell wounded in 1429 when the English held Paris and she launched an attack against the gate that once stood here. The square is the starting-point for many of the excursion buses taking tourists around Paris and the Ile de France. Continuing along the rue de Rivoli your next landmark will be the Musée des Arts décoratifs, on the right-hand side. This excellent applied arts museum has famous collections of furniture and jewelry, but is perhaps best known for its imaginatively staged temporary exhibits and excellent boutique selling the best in French design and art books. The Finance Ministry building next door will eventually house items from the Louvre's vast collections that cannot now be shown through lack of space. Next door is the new fashion museum, the Musée des Arts de la Mode.

The next port of call is the place du Palais-Royal, with its chic antique emporium, Le Louvre des Antiquaires. The Palais Royal (Royal Palace) itself is on the north side of the square. It was built by Cardinal Richelieu, Louis XIII's chief minister, but after his death became the home of Anne of Austria, Louis' widow, and her small son Louis XIV. It continued to be lived in by various members of the royal family, including Louis-Philippe's father, known as Philippe Egalité (Philip Equality) because of his democratic views.

It soon became ultra-chic to go for a stroll in the Palais Royal gardens, to drink coffee in the many coffeehouses round about or gamble in one of the gaming clubs. There were even a circus and dance hall at one time, not to mention the theater Philippe had built next door, which soon became France's most famous playhouse. But not everyone who visited the Palais Royal was bent on pleasure: in 1793 a determined young woman called Charlotte Corday called at one of the shops to buy the knife with which she murdered Marat in his bath.

The gardens are a peaceful oasis in the heart of a busy district and may well tempt you into a stroll there yourself. In appreciating the peace and quiet you'll be in good company, as such well-known literary figures as Jean Cocteau and Colette chose to live here. So did General de Gaulle's Arts Minister André Malraux, a staunch advocate of the need to restore Paris's decaying buildings to their former splendor. His name lives on in the typically Parisian square, adorned with fountains and white globe lamps, in front of Philippe Egalité's theater, the world-famous Comédie Française or Théâtre Français. If you're a theater buff you should make sure to see a performance here, particularly of a play by one of the trio of *Grand Siècle* playwrights, Corneille, Molière or Racine.

The Louvre and the Tuileries

The short rue de Rohan will take you back to the rue de Rivoli, which you should cross to take you into the place du Carrousel, centered on the Arc de Triomphe du Carrousel; this was modeled on the arch of Septimus Severus in Rome and built to celebrate Napoleon's 1805 victories, though the name "Carrousel" comes from an elaborate equestrian display held here to celebrate the birth of Louis XIV's first child in 1662. The extraordinary view from this spot is one of Paris's finest: look west and you can admire the huge Louvre Palace; look east and, set off against the typically French formal gardens laid out by the great landscape artist Le Nôtre, you are treated to a breathtaking vista through the Tuileries Gardens to the place de la Concorde with its obelisk, on up the Champs-Elysées to the much bigger triumphal arch known the world over simply as the Arc de Triomphe, with a glimpse behind it of the skyscrapers of the Défense business and residential district on the western outskirts of the city. Open-air concerts are sometimes held in the place du Carrousel and are a definite must—the little arch's pink pillars look superb when floodlit.

But the major sight here must of course be the majestic Louvre, once the palace of the French kings, now one of the world's major museums. It was first built in the early 13th century, as a fortress complete with towers and high walls for Philippe Auguste. But it was François I who had it transformed into a palace three hundred years later. In spite of later changes and additions, the Louvre still looks basically as it did when François's architect Pierre Lescot designed it. At the end of the 16th century the widowed Queen Marie de Médicis had another palace built to stand close to the Louvre: called the Tuileries Palace (the name means "tile kilns", a reference to the fact that the clay soil was once used for tile-making), it was burnt to the ground during the Paris Commune leaving only the beautiful Tuileries Gardens stretching from the Louvre to the place de la Concorde.

Today the whole complex of buildings including the Louvre Museum forms a letter "A" widening from east to west, the south side running along beside the Seine, and the bar of the "A" formed by the grandiose and harmonious Cour Carrée, probably the most interesting part of the building architecturally (parts date back to François I's palace). A major transformation is taking place in front of the Louvre: a controversial pyramid-shaped structure made of glass and concrete and designed by the Chinese-American architect I.M. Pei is going up, its main purpose being to provide good natural lighting for a series of new underground galleries and exhibition areas. An underground passage will link the two wings of the Louvre once the Finance Ministry building in the rue de Rivoli has been converted into new exhibition rooms. Above ground, on the west side facing the Tuileries Gardens, the Tuileries terraces are being reconstructed.

Before visiting the Louvre's collections, step outside the Cour Carrée to admire the colonnade designed by Claude Perrault, a 17th-century architect who also designed the Paris Observatory—he was incidentally the brother of Charles Perrault, who wrote the original versions of *Cinderella* and many other well-loved fairy stories. Opposite is the church of Saint-Germain-l'Auxerrois, whose bell gave the signal for the slaughter of thousands of Protestants during the terrible Massacre of St. Bartholomew in 1572.

The Louvre Museum is made up of seven separate departments: Oriental Antiquities, Egyptian Antiquities, Greek and Roman, Sculpture, Paintings, Prints and Drawings, and Furniture and *Objets d'art.* We advise you to buy a plan or guidebook from the busy publications department inside the museum and work out what you want to see. You might like to take one of the regular guided tours in English, or follow a set itinerary with an English cassette. We have no space here to describe the collections in detail, but should like to recommend a few highlights which most visitors wouldn't want to miss. Top of the list must be Leonardo's famous *Mona Lisa,* though you may be surprised at how small the lady with the enigmatic smile seems; and sad to say, she has had to be encased in a glass box, as she's already been subject to attacks by various madmen or vandals. If you have trouble finding her, bear in mind that she is known in French as *La Joconde* (from the Italian *La Gioconda*) and look out for signs leading you to her. The paintings department contains so many masterpieces it's impossible to pick out any other highlights, but the Rembrandts and much of the Italian school generally draw the biggest crowds.

In the sculpture department the best-known exhibit is Michelangelo's rough-hewn *Slaves* for the tomb of Pope Julius II, while no one would want to miss the stunning Apollo Gallery, with the magnificent crown jewels of France. The *Victory of Samothrace,* generally known as the *Winged Victory,* and the famous *Venus de Milo* are the major attractions in the Greek and Roman department. Among the Egyptian antiquities don't miss the *Seated Scribe,* and the enthralling Crypt of Osiris in the basement, designed to recreate the atmosphere of an embalmer's workshop, complete with animal mummies.

If weather permits, what better to follow your visit to the Louvre than a rest in the lovely Tuileries Gardens before venturing on to the place de la Concorde? Although they can be crowded and dusty in summer, they're a good place to admire the symmetry of what is technically known as a "French-style garden," a *jardin à la française* (as opposed to an "English-style garden," which is much less formal). You'll find the same type of fountains and ornamental ponds and statues and little bits of lawn fenced off with low box hedges surrounding neat flowerbeds in the grounds of châteaux all over France. At the western end are twin pavilions, the Jeu de Paume and the Orangerie. The Jeu de Paume, to the north, gets its name from an early version of tennis that was popular in 17th- and 18th-century France. It was long famous as the Impressionist Museum but after extensive renovation and redecoration it will be used to house temporary art exhibits, while the fabled Impressionist collection has been transferred to the brand new Musée d'Orsay on the other side of the river.

The Orangerie, the twin pavilion on the Seine side of the gardens, houses a fine collection of Impressionist and modern art bequeathed to the French nation by a private collector, as well as the superb *Waterlilies* series of paintings by Manet, in a specially built semicircular gallery. Between the two pavilions an ornamental gate flanked by a pair of winged horses carved from a single block of marble for the one-time royal château at Marly will make you reach for your camera. They are the work of 17th-century sculptor Antoine Coysevox, while their twins on the other side of the place de la Concorde are by his nephew Guillaume Coustou.

The Champs-Elysées

The place de la Concorde, scene of so many momentous events, is your introduction to the majestic avenue des Champs-Elysées, sweeping ahead of you as you emerge from the Tuileries. Quite apart from its elegance—still undimmed in spite of the surging traffic—the Concorde is a perfect place for enjoying superb vistas full of the symmetry for which much of Paris is famous. To the east you can look back through the Tuileries Gardens to the Louvre. To the south, you can take in the Pont de la Concorde spanning the Seine to the imposing classical facade of the Palais Bourbon, seat of the Assemblée Nationale, France's parliament. Turn to face north and—symmetry once again—there appears the classical facade of the Madeleine, framed by a pair of huge colonnaded 18th-century mansions built by Gabriel, who also designed the Petit Trianon at Versailles. One of these mansions is the deluxe Hôtel Crillon, the other the headquarters of the French navy. And of course to the west lies the most famous vista of all, the broad and tree-lined Champs-Elysées.

Before setting off along it, a word about the obelisk towering above you. It is well over three-thousand-years old and was once at Luxor in Egypt, before being offered to France by Mahommed Ali, the Turkish Viceroy of Egypt, at a particularly opportune moment. The square was originally built to honor Louis XV and bore his name, with a statue of this much-loved king in the center. But in 1792 the revolutionary mob toppled the king's statue and renamed the square the "Square of the Revolution." Less than a year later another king was toppled, but Louis XVI's fate was worse than that of his predecessor: he was one of over a thousand victims whose heads were sliced off by Madame Guillotine's dreaded blade. The guillotine stood where the fountain now is on the river side of the square. When all the blood had been washed away, the Revolution and the Empire had come and gone and a more peacable age had been ushered in, sensible Louis-Philippe decided that the center of the optimistically renamed "Square of Concord" should be adorned with a strictly non-controversial monument. Which is why the gift of the obelisk came at the right time!

As you start the long walk up the Champs-Elysées (the name, by the way, means Elysian Fields) bear in mind that they were originally designed as a magnificent garden, by Le Nôtre once again. Although the fashionable ladies and their escorts who once paraded up and down here in their carriages, especially during the Second Empire, vanished long ago, you'll still enjoy a stroll through the slightly dusty gardens at the Concorde end of the avenue. Incidentally, the building to your right as you enter the gardens, on the corner of the avenue Gabriel, is the United States Embassy. The gardens are dotted with theaters and expensive restaurants, while to the right can be glimpsed the elaborate gates leading into the gardens of the Elysée Palace and the British Embassy. At the first crossroads on the right-hand side you can visit the open-air stamp and coin market, which also has stands selling interesting old postcards. On the left-hand side the avenue Winston Churchill, leading to the Pont Alexandre III over the Seine and the Invalides, is flanked by two "palaces" built for the Great Exhibition of 1900. The Petit Palais on the left has a permanent collection of furniture and applied art, plus the 19th-century paintings belonging to the City of Paris, while the huge Grand Palais stages only special exhibits, many of them major shows devoted to a single painter. With its glass roofs it is one of Paris's landmarks and the inside, full of twirling art nouveau staircases, is no less striking; it is due for refurbishment after which a magnificent new concert hall will open here. The west side of the Grand Palais houses the Palais de la Découverte, a science museum with an excellent planetarium.

Beyond the palace, on the same side of the Champs-Elysées, is a deluxe district forming a triangle bordered by the avenue Montaigne and the avenue George-V, where you'll find many of the world's top couture houses, including Dior and Nina Ricci. This whole area is attractively illuminated over the Christmas and New Year period, especially the avenue Montaigne, which has several big theaters.

After the Rond-Point des Champs-Elysées the avenue widens and the gardens give way to broad sidewalks lined by cafés with open-air terraces, shops, movie houses and offices. This is the best-known section of the avenue and you'll soon see why it's still a name to conjure with, though many aspects have changed in recent years. The crowds are foreign rather than Parisian these days (and incidentally muggers and car thieves are legion, especially in the evenings, so *en garde!*), airline offices and car showrooms easily outnumber fashionable boutiques, and gastronomically the Champs-Elysées have definitely gone downhill, with fast-food outfits everywhere. But you can still enjoy a cup of coffee or a drink in one of the many cafés, watching the cosmopolitan crowds stroll by, and the elegant shopping arcades leading off the right-hand side still have some chic stores and a couple of good restaurants tucked away out of sight. The famous Lido nightclub, at the Arc de Triomphe end on the right-hand side, is easily identified by the number of tourist buses parked outside, while another important landmark for visitors to Paris—the city's tourist office—is on the other side at # 127.

If you're in Paris on July 14 you won't want to miss the impressive military parade staged here to celebrate the fall of the Bastille, and shortly after the avenue is packed by equally dense crowds when the winner of the Tour de France, the world's major cycling event, flashes past to the frenzied acclaim of thousands of fans. In fact the Champs-Elysées is a favorite place for staging victory processions of all kinds: two major ones were after World War I, and then when Paris was liberated in 1944, with General de Gaulle leading his followers down the avenue before the triumphal mass in Notre Dame cathedral. When great men die the nation tends to do processional homage to them here too—Victor Hugo in 1885, General de Gaulle in 1970.

All these parades start at the top of the Champs-Elysées, where the massive Arc de Triomphe towers over the place Charles-de-Gaulle, still better known by its old name of the Etoile or the Star—the 12 broad avenues radiating out from it do indeed form a star. The arch was built in classical style to celebrate Napoleon's victorious armies and commissioned by the emperor himself, though by the time it was completed, in 1836, the days of imperial glory had vanished and so had he. Indeed the first of many elaborate and emotional ceremonies to be staged here was the arrival of the carriage bearing Napoleon's remains to their last resting place beneath the dome of the Invalides. Under the huge arch lies the tomb of the unknown soldier, topped by a flame ceremonially rekindled every evening at 6.30 by members of one of the French army's regiments, and on Armistice (November 11) or V.E. Day by the president in person.

The superb groups of reliefs carved on the arch (best seen at close quarters—take the underpass from the top of the Champs-Elysées) include François Rude's masterpiece called the *Departure of the Volunteers in 1792,* generally known as *La Marseillaise* after France's national anthem, a stirring symbol of patriotism with the Motherland, the wings outspread, exhorting the volunteers to fight for France. The other sculptures depict Napoleon's greatest battles, or allegorical subjects with resounding names such as "Resistance" or "Peace," while the names of Napoleon's many campaigns are carved into the arch. The little museum at the top now has an audiovisual presentation of its history, but you should make sure to carry on to the topmost platform, which affords glorious views over Paris.

The Trocadéro, Passy and the Bois

One of the twelve avenues, the avenue Kléber, will take you to the Trocadéro, dominated by the vast Palais de Chaillot, dating from 1937. It has two curving wings separated by a vast terrace lined by glittering gilded statues and offering another splendid view, this time through formal gardens to the Seine and on to the Eiffel Tower and the Ecole Militaire, with the bulky Tour Montparnasse in the distance. The Palais houses Paris's maritime and anthropological museums, the Musée de la Marine and the Musée de l'Homme, in the west wing, and in the east wing the Musée des Monuments français, with life-size reproductions of some of France's major historic buildings, and the little Cinema Museum, with the famous *Cinémathèque,* created by Langlois, which has daily showings (and a branch at the Pompidou Center). Also in this building is one of Paris's state-subsidized theaters, the Théâtre National de Chaillot.

The avenue du Président-Wilson, leading from the Trocadéro to the place de l'Alma, houses several more museums: the Palais de Tokyo, with various collections, including the National Photographic Center, though its post-Impressionist collection has now moved to the Musée d'Orsay; the Museum of Modern Art of the City of Paris, devoted to 20th-century painting; the Musée Guimet, specializing in Far Eastern art; and the Fashion and Costume Museum in the Palais Galliéra.

If you take the rue Franklin on the other side of the place du Trocadéro you come to the rue de Passy, a chic shopping street in the heart of one of two pleasant and prosperous residential districts in western Paris near the Bois de Boulogne. Passy and Auteuil did not officially become part of Paris until the second half of the 19th century and they still have a feeling of separateness, with their peaceful cul-de-sacs known as *"villas,"* and their villagey squares surrounded by trees and gardens. The western end of the rue de Passy leads to the Ranelagh Gardens. Here you can visit the Musée Marmottan, a private collection of Renaissance tapestries and sculpture plus mementoes of the Napoleonic era, greatly enriched by a superb collection of paintings by Claude Monet and some of his Impressionist contemporaries, donated by Monet's son.

Close to the museum are the buildings of the O.E.C.D., originally built by a member of the Rothschild family. On the far side of the place de Colombie, with its statue of King Peter I of Serbia and his son Alexander I of Yugoslavia, stretches the Bois de Boulogne, still in Paris but the perfect place for taking a break from urban surroundings. This appropriately lung-shaped oasis of greenery covering 900 hectares (nearly 2,250 acres) on the western edge of the city is surprisingly relaxing, and even more surprisingly full of wildlife, considering the traffic thundering through. We should warn you that it isn't wise to wander alone here, except around the lakes, the Pré-Catelan or Bagatelle, where there are always plenty of strollers; and even couples should steer clear of the place at night.

The Bois, as it is generally called, was laid out on the instructions of Napoleon III and during the Belle Epoque was an ultra-fashionable place to see and be seen. Nowadays it is best known for its sports and leisure opportunities, with its famous race courses—Auteuil and Longchamp—tennis courts, boating lakes, bikes for rent, pigeon-shooting, fishing, riding stables, even a polo ground. It also has several good but expensive restaurants. One of the pleasantest spots is Bagatelle, a delightful little château set in grounds famous for their displays of flowers. It was built in the 18th century at lightning speed for a wager and has now been magnificently restored; the City of Paris holds good art exhibits here. The Bois also has a full-scale museum, the Musée des Arts et Traditions populaires, a well-displayed folk art and traditional customs collection. This can be found near the Les Sablons metro station, next door to the Jardin d'Acclimatation—a children's menagerie and amusement park that can also be reached by a little train running from the Porte Maillot. From here you may go for a stroll in once-aristocratic Neuilly, an "inner suburb" that is still an expensive residential area though its main streets are increasingly dominated by modern office buildings; the capital's American Hospital is sited here.

The Eiffel Tower and the Invalides

After a wander in the Bois, you can continue your exploration of central Paris by walking from the Palais de Chaillot across the river to the Eiffel Tower, built in the 1880s and *the* symbol of Paris for people the world over who have never even set foot in France. Gustave Eiffel's iron lady 320 meters (1,050 feet) high can be seen from all over Paris, though its top may be wreathed in clouds or mist. When it was built it was the world's tallest monument and it still has no rivals for the impression of simultaneous lightness and solidity it creates. After refurbishment in the early eighties the Tower now has a huge range of amenities, including an excellent restaurant, for which you must reserve well ahead. The views from all three floors are superb, but be prepared to stand in line for some considerable time at Easter and during the summer months, as this is one of the most popular sights in Paris.

At the foot of the Eiffel Tower stretches the Champ de Mars, once used for military maneuvers and later for elaborate national festivals, but now just a pleasant place for strolling, with a children's playground, donkey rides and Punch and Judy shows. At the far end rises the imposing Ecole Militaire, a fine 18th-century building where France's army officers are trained, as Napoleon Bonaparte was before them. On the other side of the avenue de Suffren near here you might like to visit the Village Suisse, an antique market now housing a series of small upmarket shops and galleries in place of the former stalls.

Behind the Ecole Militaire the U.N.E.S.C.O. building, a good example of bombastic, empty mid-20th-century architecture, is multinationally decorated with paintings by Picasso, a statue by Henry Moore and one of Alexander Calder's mobiles. Now take the avenue de Tourville, leading from the place de l'Ecole Militaire straight to the Hôtel des Invalides and the majestic Eglise du Dôme, where Napoleon's remains lie in a series of six coffins within a tomb of red porphyry beneath the tallest dome in Paris, a gilded masterpiece by the 18th-century architect Jules Hardouin-Mansart. There is an instructive *son-et-lumière* performance here. The church contains many other important tombs and monuments, as well as magnificent architectural and sculptural decorations. The other church in the Invalides complex, Saint-Louis-des-Invalides, might seem bare by comparison if it weren't for the tattered enemy flags hanging from the cornice, a shadowy reminder of the many battles fought by Napoleon's armies.

The Invalides was built to house wounded (or "invalid") veterans, 4,000 of whom were given a magnificent home by Louis XIV. Fewer than a hundred old soldiers live there today, but the building has retained its connection with the army and now houses the well-planned Musée de l'Armée or Army Museum, with many enthralling historical exhibits; the Musée des Plans-Reliefs, with models of French fortifications; and the Musée de l'Ordre de la Libération, an important source of information if you're at all interested in the French Resistance to the enemy during World War II. For a fine view of the 18th-century complex make your way to the north facade overlooking the Esplanade des Invalides, which is nearly 200 meters (over an eighth-of-a-mile!) long and is dominated by a fine equestrian statue of Louis XIV flanked by reliefs of Justice and Prudence. The esplanade, sweeping down to the Seine and now planted with lawns and trees, contains one of Paris's two air terminals, opposite the imposing foreign ministry. The British Council and the Canadian Cultural Center are also here.

Opposite the eastern side of Les Invalides is the Hôtel Biron, housing the superb Rodin Museum, with many masterpieces by the 19th century's greatest sculptor, plus preliminary drawings; it also has some furniture and paintings once belonging to Rodin, who was allowed to use part of this beautiful 18th-century mansion with its delightful garden as a studio in return for leaving his painting collection to the nation. South and east of the Rodin Museum lies the district known as the Faubourg Saint-Germain, full of palatial mansions now mostly housing ministries or embassies. A walk along the rue de Grenelle or the rue de Varenne will give you a few glimpses of the facades and courtyards of these magnificent buildings, only one of which can be visited: the Hôtel de Salm containing the Legion of Honor Museum, which presents the history of this major French decoration and a collection of medals and other insignia.

Opposite here is the new Musée d'Orsay, a huge building overlooking the Seine that once housed a major rail station, the Gare d'Orsay, together with the grandest of "station hotels," complete with superb Salle de Fêtes adorned with chandeliers and ornamentation of all kinds, now restored to its former glory. The magnificent station building, designed by Victor Laloux (who also designed the City Hall), was started in 1898 on the site of the Palais d'Orsay which was burnt down in 1871 at the end of the Paris Commune, at the same time as the Tuileries Palace the other side of the Seine vanished for ever. The station was ready in time for a grand opening on Bastille Day 1900 to coincide with the opening of the Great Exhibition. But it had a short life, as the advent of electrification led to larger trains that could no longer be fitted into the station and in 1939 the Gare d'Austerlitz took over mainline traffic, leaving only suburban lines. The ghost station was put to various uses over the next forty years and narrowly escaped total demolition by being classified as a "historical monument" in 1973 (the façades and decoration) and 1978 (the whole complex). This paved the way for its transformation into a museum to house fine and applied art dating from the period 1848–1914, a particularly rich period in French art, but one that suffered from lack of space in the city's other major museums.

The new museum was finally opened to the public in 1987 and immediately became enormously popular. The imaginative conversion of the vast interior was the work of an Italian architect, Gae Aulenti, who created a building within a building by constructing inside the soaring, elegant structure of the old station what looks like the bottom half of a de Mille film set made from Burgundian limestone. The result is a spacious labyrinth of rooms and levels, exciting in itself, but not always kind to the works of art on view. In such a setting it is the more massive pieces that come off best—and some of them are very massive indeed. There are plenty of refreshment facilities, and an endless variety of views across the vast space. For an unusual panorama over Paris, find the clock room on the upper level, close to the Impressionist galleries—containing a major part of the museum's treasures—and look out over the Seine to the Tuileries through the glass face of the great timepiece.

If you follow the river to the west you come to the Palais Bourbon, home of France's parliament, which you have already seen from the other side of the Seine.

Saint-Germain-des-Prés and Montparnasse

A short bus ride, if your legs are feeling the strain by this time, will take you from the Palais Bourbon to Saint-Germain-des-Prés, long the mecca of intellectuals and would-be intellectuals after enjoying a firmly aristocratic past. The new artistic prominence of the Les Halles and Beaubourg areas has drawn the avant-garde away to the Right Bank, but this is still a center of French publishing, with many fascinating specialist bookshops, and art and antiques—tiny art galleries and narrow little antique shops are to be found in all the streets running down to the Seine. The fashionable candlelit restaurants and jazz cellars are still a great magnet.

The district centers on the church of Saint-Germain-des-Prés, part of a Benedictine abbey that was destroyed during the French Revolution. It has a Romanesque bell tower and the east end, too, is still basically as it was in the 12th century. Beside the church, the rue de l'Abbaye will take you to one of the most delightful spots in the whole of Paris: the enchanting place Fürstemberg (turn left into the rue Fürstemberg), where the painter Eugène Delacroix had his studio (you can visit the pleasant little museum that has been opened there). With its white globe lamps and catalpa trees this peaceful square looks almost like a stage set, and you'll find many other delights in the area if you allow yourself time to wander around the narrow old streets, a paradise for shutter bugs.

Opposite the church, the famous Deux-Magots café (the name comes from a pair of grotesque Chinese figures inside, called *magots* in French) is still busy at all times of day and most of the night, though you won't rub shoulders with the intellectual giants of France these days, as you might have done in the heyday of existentialism when Jean-Paul Sartre and his followers virtually lived here. The Café de

Flore next door tends to be a gay mecca nowadays (especially upstairs), while on the other side of the boulevard the Brasserie Lipp is still the haunt of politicians and movie people—you won't get a table on the ground floor unless you've got influential friends!

Before visiting the area close to the Seine, take the rue Bonaparte southwards to the huge place Saint-Sulpice which boasts an elaborate fountain with statues of four great bishops and preachers dating from 1844 and fronting the church of the same name. Originally the parish church of Saint-Germain-des-Prés, it is best known for its beautiful wall paintings by Delacroix, in the first chapel on the right, and its fine organ.

At the river end of the rue Bonaparte the Ecole Nationale des Beaux-Arts, Paris's fine arts academy, now stages good art exhibits. From here a short walk along the quai Malaquais brings you to the place de l'Institut, and the majestic Institut de France, a 17th-century building with a gleaming cupola built with funds left by Cardinal Mazarin in his will and housing five academies, including the world-famous Académie Française: to be elected to this prestige-laden institution with only 40 "immortal" members is the highest literary honor that can be bestowed on a Frenchman—or a Frenchwoman since the election of Marguerite Yourcenar in the early 80's. A little further along the 18th-century Monnaie or Mint includes a coin museum, and workshops that can occasionally be visited.

On the way back to the boulevard Saint-Germain you might like to stop off at the rue de Buci to buy the ingredients for a superb picnic from the mouthwatering open-air market there. The nearby rue de l'Ancienne Comédie houses the Café Procope, once the haunt of Encyclopedists Diderot, d'Alembert and the great Voltaire (you can still see the table he used to sit at) and later of poets Paul Verlaine and Stéphane Mallarmé; originally a coffeehouse, it is now a busy restaurant. Behind the Procope the picturesque Cour du Commerce Saint-André has many historical associations, as well as being a pleasant place for a light lunch or tea: Marat printed his revolutionary newspaper *L'Ami du peuple* here, and Dr. Guillotin conducted experiments on sheep to perfect the "humane" new method of execution that was to be such in demand during the Revolution and remained France's method of execution right down to its abolition in 1981.

The bustling Odéon crossroads is set off by the Odéon Theater, surrounded by streets named after major French playwrights and authors. Some of the most interesting French theater is still performed in this 18th-century classical building, one of Paris's state-subsidized theaters. The south side of the theater overlooks the Luxembourg Gardens, an oasis of greenery with its ornamental ponds and dozens of statues. This is a particularly relaxed place for strolling, but you might also care to visit the Luxembourg Palace, built by Queen Marie de Médicis to look like the Pitti Palace in Florence. After serving as a prison during the Revolution, and then housing first the Directory and later the Consulate, it is now the seat of the Senate (France's parliamentary Upper House). Its major point of interest is the wall paintings by Delacroix in the former library.

South of the Luxembourg Gardens the avenue de l'Observatoire, laid out with lawns and flowerbeds, leads to the Observatory. Before reaching it you come to the boulevard du Port Royal with the convent church of Val-de-Grâce, built by Queen Anne of Austria in thanksgiving for the birth of the future Louis XIV.

From here you can either visit the Latin Quarter to the east or Montparnasse to the west. If you start with Montparnasse you should take the boulevard Montparnasse, the best place to begin your visit being the place du 18 juin 1940 (the date of General de Gaulle's famous appeal from London after the fall of France during World War II). We suggest you visit this area in the evening, as Montparnasse, once a district of poets and painters but now full of towering skyscrapers and modern hotels, is a major entertainment district, with movies, theaters and café-theaters galore, and has several well-known restaurants, including the Coupole, once frequented by Ernest Hemingway. The square is overshadowed by the huge 59-story Tour Maine-Montparnasse, the tallest skyscraper in Europe with the fastest elevator on the continent whisking you up to enjoy a magical view over Paris. The foot of the tower is a modern shopping center, including a branch of the upmarket Galeries Lafayette department store, while behind it you'll find the Montparnasse rail station, the terminus for trains to Chartres and Versailles. At # 34 in the boulevard de Vaugirard beside the station is the well-designed Postal Museum, while the nearby rue Antoine-Bourdelle (reached via the avenue du Maine) is named after the sculptor whose home, at # 16, has been turned by the city into a museum of his work (don't miss his fine studies of Beethoven).

The rue de la Gaîté, full of theaters and the famous Bobino music hall, is as "gay" (in the old sense of the word) as it has been for centuries. Turn into the boulevard Edgar-Quinet to reach the Cimetière Montparnasse, where many celebrated artists and writers are buried, including Charles Baudelaire, the Dadaist Tristan Tzara, Guy de Maupassant and the sculptors Bourdelle, Rude and Ossip Zadkine. Not far away, in the rue d'Assas, is the Zadkine Museum in the house where he lived and worked.

The Latin Quarter

The Latin Quarter, Paris's student district since the days of the great scholar Pierre Abelard in the 12th century, can either be visited from the eastern edge of the Luxembourg Gardens and the Val de Grâce, or from the river end of the boulevard Saint-Michel. The "boul' Mich'," as it is generally known, is the main thoroughfare of the Latin Quarter —so called because Latin was the students' *lingua franca* in the Middle Ages and remained the university's official language down to the Revolution. It is still thronged with students at all times of the day and night and the surrounding streets are full of jazz cellars, experimental movies and crowded little restaurants.

The rue de la Harpe, lined with Tunisian and Greek restaurants (and incidentally a haunt of pickpockets at night, so watch your purse), leads off the place Saint-Michel eastwards to the rue Saint-Séverin and the church of the same name, a fine example of the Gothic style as it changed and developed, with a beautiful double ambulatory and a charnel house next door dating from the 15th century. The same street takes you on to another church, Saint-Julien-le-Pauvre, belonging to a Greek Orthodox order and decorated with dozens of icons. The view from the garden to the north of it, which is said to possess the oldest tree in Paris, a false acacia, is striking—a close-up of Notre Dame just the other side of the Petit Pont.

Behind Saint-Séverin the rue Saint-Jacques and the rue de Cluny will bring you to the place Paul-Painlevé, facing the entrance to the Musée de Cluny. This 15th-century mansion, which once belonged to the monks of Cluny Abbey in Burgundy, was built on the site of the city's Roman baths, the ruins of which can be seen in and just outside the museum. The collection of medieval art and craftwork is particularly famous for its tapestries, the undoubted jewel being the superb *Dame à la Licorne* (Lady with a Unicorn) series. Here, too, you can see the heads of the Kings of Judah hacked off the facade of Notre Dame.

On the other side of the rue des Ecoles runs the north wing of the Sorbonne, Paris's main university building. Its name comes from Robert de Sorbon, a medieval canon who founded a theological college here. When you've had a look at the splendid staircase and, if a lecture isn't in progress, at the Puvis de Chavannes mural in the main lecture hall, continue round the building and up the boulevard Saint-Michel to the Sorbonne church, a good example of French classical architecture. Behind the Sorbonne are various élite academic institutions and the mighty Panthéon, at the end of the rue Soufflot; beneath its huge dome are buried such illustrious Frenchmen as Victor Hugo, Jean-Jacques Rousseau and Voltaire. This rather cold and gloomy building also has some interesting murals, the most famous illustrating the story of St. Geneviève, patron saint of Paris, on whose hill (the Montagne Sainte-Geneviève) the Panthéon stands. Behind the Panthéon the church of Saint-Etienne du Mont has a magnificent shrine containing relics of the saint, as well as a 16th-century rood screen.

The rue Clovis behind the church leads to the Ecole Polytechnique, where France's most brilliant students are educated, though many of its activities and departments have been moved out to the suburbs. The rue Descartes on the right will take you to the pretty place de la Contrescarpe, a lively center of Parisian nightlife. This whole area has retained something of a medieval feel, with picturesque inn signs swinging from iron hooks. The continuation of the rue Descartes, the rue Mouffetard, is famous for the highly colorful street market that has been held there for centuries; don't miss the old houses and the tiny little alleyways leading off it.

From the place de la Contrescarpe the rue Lacépède takes you to the rue Monge; turn left into it, then right to reach the entrance to the Arènes de Lutèce, the ruins of Paris's Roman arena and all that is left of the powerful Roman city of Lutetia, the forerunner of Paris, apart from the remains of its baths in the Musée de Cluny. The arena was destroyed by Barbarian invaders in 280 and not rediscovered until the late 19th century.

Close to here, in the place Jussieu, you'll see the modern buildings of the Pierre et Marie Curie University, on the site of the old Halle aux Vins, where millions of gallons of wine were stored from Napoleonic times right down to the 1970s. The new Arab Institute building is most attractive. The university has a good mineral collection but it can be visited only during term-time. If you follow the rue de Jussieu you can relax in the Jardin des Plantes, the city's peaceful botanical gardens, which also house a small zoo and menagerie, an aquarium, a reptile house and the city's Natural History Museum. Behind the gardens, in the place du Puits-de-l'Hermite, an unexpected sight is the tall minaret of the Mosquée (Mosque), the center of Moslem life in Paris, with a good tearoom and bath-house.

Montmartre and Pigalle

High up on a hill in the north of Paris and best visited as a separate excursion is lively Montmartre, a name conjuring up a delightfully free-and-easy bohemian life with a typically French flavor, though the presence of so many foreign tourists means that the atmosphere is more cosmopolitan than French these days. If you can close your eyes to the worst excesses of tourist exploitation you'll find that even the best-known spots still have considerable charm, and in the narrow side streets you'll still find ordinary Parisians going about their daily business away from the beaten tourist track.

The name Montmartre is said to come from a corruption of *mont des martyres,* the martyr's mountain, because it was here that St. Denis and two of his priests were beheaded in A.D. 272. According to the legend the redoubtable saint promptly picked up his head and set off northwards to the spot where the town and cathedral of Saint-Denis stand today. He is said to have suffered martyrdom in the rue Yvonne-le-Tac, leading off the place des Abbesses, which is the best place to start your tour of Montmartre. Strangely enough, the very same spot in this picturesque street (where a chapel can now be seen at # 9) has another historic association: nearly 1300 years later, in 1534, Ignatius Loyola and his companions took the vows that eventually led to the founding of the powerful order of the Jesuits.

A climb up the rue Ravignan brings you to the delightful place Emile Goudeau, a good illustration of Montmartre's appeal to painters. Here, at # 13, Picasso, Braque and other giants of modern painting had their studios, in a building picturesquely called "Le Bateau-Lavoir," the "Ship Wash-house." Sadly, this picturesque building burned down in 1970, just after a decision had been taken to restore it and turn it into a museum or gallery. It's been replaced by an innocuous concrete structure—still happily divided into artists' studios—so to see how it looked you must walk around the corner to the rue d'Orchampt with its wooden buildings lit by tall windows.

The rue Orchampt leads to the winding rue Lepic, where Vincent Van Gogh and his brother Theo lived (at # 54). Around the corner in the rue Girardon the centuries-old Moulin de la Galette, immortalized in one of Renoir's paintings, was originally used for grinding flour to make the flat waffles or biscuits known as *galettes.* In the 19th century the mill was a popular dance hall and cabaret frequented by painters and lovers of the bohemian life for which Montmartre was so famous. Appropriately enough, you can visit the grave of Henri Murger, whose *Scenes of Bohemian Life* was the inspiration for Puccini's opera *La Bohème,* in the nearby Montmartre Cemetery, easily reached from the bottom of rue Lepic via the rue Joseph-de-Maistre. Other literary and artistic figures who lie buried here include Stendhal and the Goncourts, Fragonard, Greuze and Degas, and musicians Berlioz and Offenbach.

If you follow the rue Caulaincourt up past another little cemetery to the rue des Saules you can visit the interesting Museum of Jewish Art at # 42, and in the rue Cortot on the left, # 12 houses the Montmartre Museum, with hundreds of exhibits painting a vivid picture of old Montmartre. Near the museum, you'll be surprised to hear, is a genuine vineyard, still producing enough wine to keep the local bars and restaurants merry at grape harvest time in October. One well-known bar-cabaret is the Lapin Agile, where you can soak up the atmosphere of Montmartre as you perch on wooden benches listening to lively French songs, while another cabaret with a colorful past is La Bonne Franquette, at the bottom of the rue des Saules.

Cross the rue Norvins and you come to the rue Poulbot (called after an artist whose drawings of cheeky urchins you'll see everywhere) and a little waxworks museum, the Historial, illustrating the history of Montmartre. The tiny place du Calvaire offers marvelous views over Paris and leads into the picturesque but tourist-packed place du Tertre, surrounded by restaurants and cabarets and dotted about with artists who're sure to offer to paint your portrait, so be warned.

Just off the place du Tertre is the church of Saint-Pierre, one of the oldest in the city and once part of a mighty abbey. But your main goal hereabouts must be the huge wedding cake of a church you'll surely have seen gleaming white in the distance during your travels around Paris. The Sacré Coeur was built by public subscription as a symbol of national revival after the disastrous Franco-Prussian War in 1870 and remains a symbol of Paris for many tourists. The view from the top of the cupola is fantastic, but you should also make sure to see the mosaic decoration inside and the fine modern stained glass. The little funicular will take you down to the bottom of the gardens fronting the Sacré Coeur, or you can saunter slowly down the many flights of steps.

You might like to combine your visit to Montmartre with an evening in one of the nightclubs in Pigalle or Clichy, where you'll land up after your downwards journey: from the rue Steinkerque turn right into the boulevard Rochechouart and walk along to place Pigalle. This is a major center of Parisian nightlife, though little frequented by Parisians themselves. By daylight it's all rather seedy and tawdry, but at night it does still have something of the romantic glamor so grippingly captured on canvas by Toulouse-Lautrec, and such well-known names as the Moulin Rouge or the Folies-Bergère are still going strong.

Fringe Pursuits

Here are a few places on the edges of the city that will tempt you if you're feeling like a spot of greenery.

The Bois de Vincennes is the eastern counterpart to the Bois de Boulogne and though less famous has plenty to interest the visitor with a yen for the wide-open spaces. Its trotting racecourse and zoo are major attractions, but it also has two museums, one of African and Australasian art, the other of transport, two lakes, a magnificent flower garden and, yes really, a full-scale royal castle! The château de Vincennes has a 14th-century keep housing a museum illustrating its history, a Gothic chapel and twin royal pavilions, not to mention many royal associations: Louis XIV spent his honeymoon here, while Henry V of England died in the keep in 1422.

Then, on the southern edge of the city, you'll find the lovely Parc Montsouris, close to the student campus known as the Cité Universitaire, with very superior hostels, some of them designed by the great Le Corbusier. You may like to continue from here along the avenue René-Coty to the place Denfert-Rochereau where you can visit the famous Catacombs, Roman quarries used as an ossuary from the end of the 18th century.

In the northwest you'll find the Parc Monceau, full of artistically arranged ruins, statues, pyramids and pagodas, even a little windmill;

it was masterminded by the same Philippe Egalité who planned the Palais-Royal gardens. While you're up here you should try to visit two good museums nearby, the Nissim-de-Camondo, a former mansion filled with 18th-century furniture and furnishings, and the Cernuschi, specializing in Far Eastern Art.

In the northeast the main spot of greenery is the much larger Parc des Buttes-Chaumont, full of little hills and with a suspension bridge taking you across to an island crowned by a little temple. Near the Buttes-Chaumont is the beautiful Père Lachaise cemetery with the tombs of Bizet, Rossini, Chopin, Cherubini, David, Molière, La Fontaine, Beaumarchais, Modigliani, Oscar Wilde and Edith Piaf.

A new attraction in northern Paris is the huge La Villette park, on the site of the old slaughterhouse. The hub of this complex is a vast new science museum, including the Géode movie hall with a dazzling curved screen covering 1,000 square meters, a library and a science bookshop. It is surrounded by all sorts of structures and play areas that will keep children happy for hours.

PRACTICAL INFORMATION FOR PARIS

 SECURITY WARNING. Paris is being plagued by a wave of violence and crime that is affecting tourists as well as residents. The police warn that even such famous tourist areas as the Champs-Elysées are infested with thugs after 10 at night—literally thousands of incidents of mugging, bag-snatching, and violent thefts from cars are reported to them each month. Other danger spots to avoid late at night are the Esplanade des Invalides, the Halles/Beaubourg area, the place and boulevard St.-Michel and surrounding streets and the rue du faubourg Montmartre.

Security in the métro has improved, but pickpocketing is still rife, as it is in any large city. Best wear your purse slung across you, as most Frenchwomen do, rather than over one shoulder, where it is easy prey to bag-snatchers on foot or on mopeds. And beware of small groups of children—most of them Gipsies and too young to prosecute—who, police say, are the worst offenders.

 GETTING TO TOWN FROM THE AIRPORTS. You have various methods of traveling to and from Paris's two airports to the city center. If you have heavy bags, you'd best get a taxi or the special airport buses, but be sure to allow plenty of time during rush hours (especially Friday evenings) as the roads to the airports get traffic-clogged. The other alternatives are train/express, métro and ordinary city buses.

By Bus. Buses leave from both termini at Roissy/Charles-de-Gaulle airport every 15 minutes between 5.30 A.M. and 11 P.M. for the air terminal at the Porte Maillot on the western edge of Paris. From here you can travel on by métro or taxi. Fare is around 35 frs. and journey time outside rush hours is around 45 minutes. From Orly-Ouest and Orly-Sud airports buses leave every 15 minutes during the day, less often in the evening, for the Les Invalides city terminal in the 7th *arrondissement* south of the River Seine. Fare is again around 35 frs. and journey time around 35–40 minutes, longer during rush hours. Special buses also operate between the two airports (around 65 frs.), taking at least an hour.

By Train. Free shuttle buses leave from Gate 30 (arrivals floor) at Terminal 1, and Gates A5 and B6 at Terminal 2 at Roissy/CDG airport for the rail station called Roissy-Aéroport CDG, from where you can take the *Roissy-Rail* service into Paris's Gare du Nord mainline station, which enables you to get off at any station on line B of the RER (express métro) network. This line is slotted into the ordinary métro system, so connections are easy, and at our presstime it was about to have direct connections with RER line C. Trains now operate at 7-minute intervals.

Fares. 24 frs. to the Gare du Nord, 28 frs. through to any métro or inner-circle RER station. This service is fast and efficient, but it involves a fair amount of walking, as does *Orly-Rail,* the sister service from Orly airport. Here trains leave at 15-minute intervals (30-minute in the evening) from Gate F (arrivals floor) at Orly-Ouest and Gate H at Orly-Sud and take you to Pont-de-Rungis-Aéroport d'Orly station. From here the C line of the RER takes you into the Gare d'Austerlitz, the Gare des Invalides and many other stops, with connections to métro lines from most stations.

Fares. To Paris-Austerlitz, around 19 frs.; to any métro or inner-circle RER station, around 21 frs.

By City Bus. The regular 351 bus will take you from Roissy rail station (take the shuttle bus there from the airport) to the Nation or Vincennes métro stops.

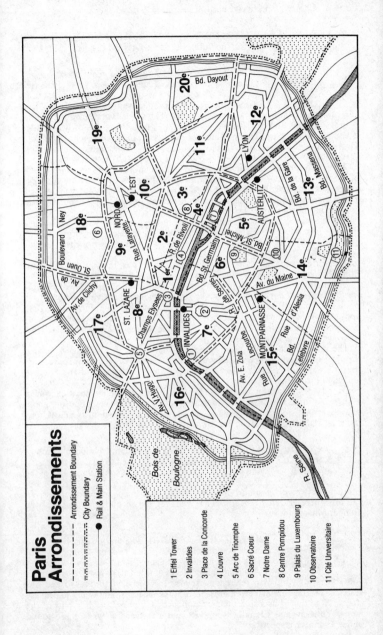

Paris Arrondissements

- - - Arrondissement Boundary
.... City Boundary
● Rail & Main Station

1 Eiffel Tower
2 Invalides
3 Place de la Concorde
4 Louvre
5 Arc de Triomphe
6 Sacré Coeur
7 Notre Dame
8 Centre Pompidou
9 Palais du Luxembourg
10 Observatoire
11 Cité Unversitaire

From Orly regular buses 215 and 183A will take you to Denfert-Rochereau and Porte de Choisy respectively, both in southern Paris.

By Taxi. A taxi from Roissy/CDG airport to a spot in central Paris will cost in the region of 160–200 frs. including tip; from Orly a little less.

TOURIST INFORMATION. The main Paris Tourist Office is at 127 av. des Champs-Elysées, 75008 Paris (tel. 47-23-61-72). Open 9 A.M. to 9 P.M. Mon.–Sat. 9 A.M. to 8 P.M. Sun. and public holidays in summer; 9 A.M. to 8 P.M. Mon.–Sat., 9 A.M. to 6 P.M. Sun. in winter. This office is crammed with information on Paris and can also supply brochures for other parts of the country if you're traveling on. The multilingual hostesses can make hotel reservations for a small charge (not more than five days in advance) and in the same building you'll find the main office of the S.N.C.F. (French Rail) tourist service.

There is a special recorded-message telephone information service for details of the week's events—concerts, ballet, exhibits, parades, son-et-lumière, special events of all kinds; called *Sélection Loisirs,* it offers a version in English, reached by dialing 47-20-88-98 (though you may need to listen to it twice round, as the pronunciation sometimes leaves a lot to be desired).

There is also a tourist information office in the *Mairie* or City Hall in Paris (just by Hôtel-de-Ville métro stop). And the City of Paris puts up posters all over the city giving details of one-off events—parades, firework displays, you name it, they organize it.

There are branch offices at Austerlitz, Lyon and Nord rail stations and at the Eiffel Tower, but these may be closed on Sun. and public holidays.

Information on what's on in Paris during your stay is best gleaned from the weekly *L'Officiel des Spectacles* or the slightly more expensive *Pariscope,* both available from all newsstands and drugstores and full of information. Both appear on Weds., the day the movie programs change. Your hotel will probably have a copy of the free weekly *Paris-Sélection,* which is also obtainable from some travel agencies and from tourist offices.

The national dailies *Le Figaro* and *Le Monde* give full details of movies, theaters, opera and ballet, exhibits and other events. Other useful sources are the *International Herald Tribune,* published daily in Paris, and the English-language fortnightly *Passion.*

Over 50 of Paris's top hotels have installed an electronic information system known as *Cititel,* which will provide answers to a huge range of questions about cultural events in Paris and the whole of the Ile de France region, as well as hotel room availability, airline and rail timetables and so on.

TELEPHONES. All Paris and inner-suburb numbers now have eight digits—as opposed to seven in the past—and always begin with a 4. If you come across one of the old seven-digit numbers, merely add a 4 to it. To call another Paris or inner-suburb number, simply dial the eight-digit number. To call anywhere else in France, dial 16, wait for the second tone and dial the number you want.

HOW TO GET AROUND. The first essential step is to buy a booklet called *Plan de Paris par Arrondissement.* This contains maps of each district, or *arrondissement,* as well as listing places of interest, post offices, churches and so on, all with map references. It also has maps of the métro and bus systems. It's on sale at newsstands, in most bookstores, stationers and drugstores. Note that it lists street names alphabetically under the *first* part of the name. Thus avenue Franklin-Roosevelt and rue General-Leclerc are found under F and G respectively.

Paris is a small city as capitals go, and you may well want to walk to many of the sights. But public transport is good: fast, efficient and frequent, and good value too.

By Métro. Paris's subway, the métro, is one of the world's best. Trains run at 90-second intervals during the day, and only a little less frequently at night. Our map on pages 112–13 will help you get your bearings, but in general the system is easy to understand and use.

There are large, clear maps in every station of the whole system. Many stations also have push-button maps that show the quickest way to your destination at a glance. Some stations also have machines that print out cards explaining the way to museums, historic buildings, and so on.

Each métro line has a number, but they are normally known by the names of the stations at either end. Thus, line 1 is known as Vincennes–Neuilly because it goes east to west from the Château de Vincennes to the Pont de Neuilly. Look for these names when changing lines—connections are called *correspondances*. They are clearly visible on the orange illuminated signs on platforms.

A flat fare system operates throughout the métro. Tickets can be bought singly or in packs *(carnets)* of ten. 1st.-class *carnets* cost 42 frs., 2nd. class 27.50 frs. You can use 2nd.-class tickets in 1st.-class cars at certain times of day, but check locally as these times vary. You may make as many changes of lines as you like on one ticket. Tickets can be bought from all métro stations, some rail stations, and at *Tabac* cafes. There are also a few slot machines in streets. Once you have your ticket, feed it into the machine at the platform entrance, which will then open automatically. You should hold on to your ticket as inspectors sometimes come through trains, though you don't need to show it on leaving the métro.

By Express Métro (R.E.R.). The express métro—the *Réseau Express Régional*, or R.E.R.—is basically a commuter service operating to nearby towns like Versailles or St.-Germain-en-Laye. But it is also useful for getting around Paris itself, being fully integrated with the ordinary métro. And you can use métro tickets for all R.E.R. trips that do not extend beyond the city limits. There are three lines—A, B, and C—and routes are clearly marked on métro maps.

For trips outside the city limits, buy your ticket from one of the machines inside stations, pressing the relevant buttons to indicate your destinations, whether you want a round-trip or one-way ticket, and so on. As in the métro, then feed your ticket into the machine to get onto the right platform. Unlike the métro, however, you *must* keep your ticket with you, as you need to feed it into another machine to enable you to leave the system, or if you want to change to the métro from the R.E.R., or vice versa. If you're continuing on your journey the machine will light up with the words *Reprenez Votre Ticket* (Take your ticket back), and you should do just that, as you'll need it later to leave the system.

By Bus. Paris has a good daytime bus network, but only a few lines run in the evenings, and even fewer on Sundays and public holidays. Services are fairly speedy, except during the rush hour, though naturally not as quick as the métro. On the other hand, they are a much better way of seeing the city. They are also easy to use, with maps of each route clearly shown at bus stops and in every bus, with every stop marked. Ring the bell to make the driver stop if the red sign *Arrêt Demandé (stop requested)* isn't already lit up.

Second-class métro tickets are used on the buses. For short trips, one ticket is enough, but for longer journeys you'll need two. In the case of the circular P.C. *(Petite Ceinture)* line, you'll need four. Route maps at all bus stops show how many tickets you need for each trip.

Ticket Bargains. A good bargain is the *Formule 1* pass, good for unlimited travel on the métro, R.E.R. and buses within the city limits for one 24-hour period. Other, more expensive, passes are good for unlimited travel into the suburbs as well as central Paris. Prices change frequently so check locally. In the métro and R.E.R., slot the pass into the machine as usual. But on buses you must show it to the driver as you enter. Do *not* slot it into the machine or it will be canceled for good.

The *Paris Sesame* pass also entitles you to unlimited travel on the métro, R.E.R. and buses within the city, plus a few suburban lines. Unlike the Formule

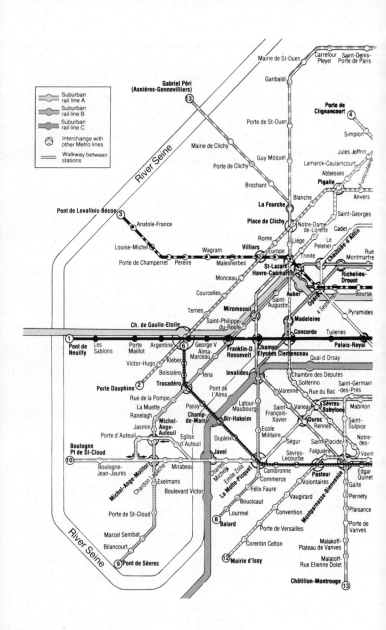

PARIS METRO

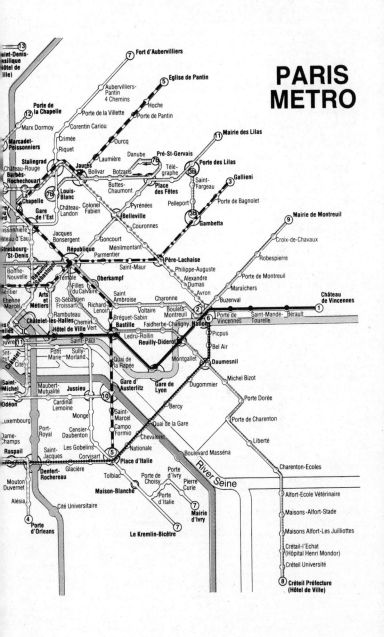

1 pass, however, it is valid for two, four or seven consecutive days. It can be bought at French National Tourist Offices overseas as well as in Paris at any of the following: R.A.T.P's tourist offices (53bis quai des Grands-Augustins, 6e, or 20 pl. de la Madeleine, 1er); any one of 50 métro stations (lists are posted in métro stations); main rail stations; Roissy/C.D.G. airport (terminal 1, gate 28); Orly airport (both Ouest and Sud); Banque Nationale de Paris (2 blvd. des Italiens, 2e, or pl. Clichy, 18e); Crédit Commercial de France (115 av. des Champs-Elysées, 8e). Take your passport. If you're staying longer, a monthly pass, a *Carte-Orange,* is a good buy.

By Taxi. Taxis are numerous and relatively inexpensive. The best way to get one is either via your hotel porter, who will expect a small tip, or from a taxi rank with the blue-and-white taxi sign. Few taxis, regardless of whether their roof-top "for hire" sign is lit, will stop in the street. You can also get cabs at rail stations and airports, but they will add an extra charge of 4–6 frs. (There are also small additional charges for luggage). Most taxis will refuse to take more than three passengers.

There are three fare zones—inner-city, inner-suburbs and outer-suburbs—with fares determined by distance. Daytime (6.30 A.M.–8 P.M.) rates at our presstime were 2.44 frs., 3.80 frs. and 5.10 frs., per kilometer respectively. Night-time rates were 3.80 frs., 5.10 frs. and 5.10 frs. respectively. Lower rates are charged for trips to the outer suburbs if you keep the driver for the return trip, but waiting time is charged at 65 frs. per hour. Tip about 15 per cent.

There are a good many unofficial cabs as well, without meters, normally found waiting outside stations, nightclubs and hotels. Many are not insured and will charge anything they think they can get away with. If you do take one, make sure you agree the fare before starting. But you're better off avoiding them.

By Car. Paris traffic can make New York seem like a deserted country lane. Some bizarre personality change overcomes even the most placid Parisian behind the wheel, a situation not helped by the almost total absence of road signs. Rules and regulations, in as much as they can be said to exist at all, are theoretically the same as in the rest of the country. But the most important point to remember is the "priority from the right" ruling, a right Parisians are prepared to die for, as they have no hesitation in proving.

Parking is practically impossible. Your best bet is to head for an underground lot. Maps pinpointing them are available from tourist offices.

 HOTELS. Paris has a vast number of hotels, ranging from the Superdeluxe to the very modest. Despite this, accommodations can still be hard to come by, a result not only of the enduring popularity of Paris as a tourist destination, but, especially in the fall, an abundance of trade fairs, congresses, conventions and the like that fill hotels to bursting. French National Tourist Offices abroad issue a helpful calendar of the busiest periods, but you should nonetheless make sure to book as far in advance as possible, especially if your preference is for smaller and more traditional hotels.

Standards vary widely. In the very top hotels you'll find services, amenities and furnishings the equal of those anywhere in the world. Many hotels have undertaken modernization work recently which has inevitably led to higher prices—some previously featured in our Inexpensive category have shot right up to Expensive. But problems remain. For instance, service in the large modern hotels may be at best impersonal, at worst downright sloppy. You should also be aware that many of the picturesque little spots on the Left Bank may well be long on charm but short on decent plumbing and electricity. And where modern bathrooms have been installed, the bedrooms themselves have naturally shrunk appreciably. This does not mean that good service and comfort as well as atmosphere is a thing of the past, just that it is harder to find.

Noise can also be a problem in Paris hotels. A growing number have double glazing, but very few, outside the most expensive, have airconditioning. So in humid summer weather you may find yourself forced to choose between sweltering in your room with the window shut or lying awake because of the noise. If at all possible, specify that you want a room overlooking the courtyard *(sur cour)* rather than on the street *(sur rue)*. If you've booked one, insist on getting it when you arrive.

The good news is that one or two areas, such as popular Montmartre, are acquiring some new or newly-renovated hotels. They are generally run as groups (the Timhôtels, for example), and offer modern amenities and bright attractive rooms at reasonable prices. Most are also small enough to make more likely the prospect of a friendly welcome.

Only a few hotels have restaurants, and most of them are in the more expensive categories. But this is in no sense a problem. One of the main delights in Paris is eating out and you will almost always be better off eating away from your hotel, unless it has a particularly fine restaurant. As we say, this almost certainly means it will be expensive.

Prices and Grades. We have divided the hotels in our lists first by *arrondissement* and then into five grades, determined solely by price. These are: (S), meaning Superdeluxe, (L) Luxury, (E) Expensive, (M) Moderate and (I) Inexpensive. You should expect to pay around 1,700 frs. per night for a double room with bathroom in a Superdeluxe hotel, around 1,000–1,600 frs. in a Luxury hotel, 600–900 frs. in an Expensive hotel, 350–550 frs. in a Moderate hotel and 170–300 frs. in an Inexpensive hotel. These figures do not include breakfast, which will range upwards from around 25 frs. per person for a Continental breakfast (coffee or tea, plus croissant, rolls and jelly). Top rates in a Superdeluxe hotel may be as much as 95–100 frs.

The initials AE, DC, MC and V in the listings indicate the credit cards accepted by each establishment, standing respectively for American Express, Diners Club, MasterCard (incorporating Access) and Visa.

First Arrondissement

Inter-Continental-Paris (S), 3 rue de Castiglione (tel. 42-60-37-80). 460 rooms and suites. Wonderfully comfortable, with excellent service. Offers an assortment of pleasant restaurants, cafeterias and grill-rooms, with openair lunchtime dining in summer. Well-placed near Tuileries Gardens; belongs to British Grand Metropolitan group; airconditioned. AE, DC, MC, V.

Meurice (S), 228 rue de Rivoli (tel. 42-60-38-60). 161 rooms. Halfway between the *Ritz* and the *Crillon*, this is one of the top-notchers. With grill and small bar; airconditioned. AE, DC, MC, V.

Ritz (S), 15 pl. Vendôme (tel. 42-60-38-30). 164 rooms and suites. Situated midway between the Opéra and Tuileries Gardens, the Ritz underwent a facelift in the early '80s after being bought by the same Egyptian family who now own London's Harrods. It has lost none of its old-world charm, however; the two restaurants, the *Espadon Grill* and the *Vendôme*, are both good, with delicious *haute cuisine* and fabulous wines. Some suites are named after famous guests, such as Coco Chanel, Marcel Proust, and King Edward VII. Two small but renowned bars, pool, pretty courtyard garden, and secretarial service complete the facilities; airconditioned. AE, DC, MC, V.

Castille (L), 37 rue Cambon (tel 42-61-55-20). 76 rooms, all with bath. Just off pl. de la Madeleine. Bar and restaurant. AE, DC, MC, V.

Duminy-Vendôme (E), 3 rue du Mont-Thabor (tel. 42-60-32-80). 79 rooms, all with bath or shower. Renovated and expanded. AE, DC, MC, V.

Normandy (E), 7 rue de l'Echelle (tel. 42-60-30-21). 138 rooms, 123 with bath. Comfortable, renovated. Restaurant and relaxing, wood-paneled bar. AE, DC, MC, V.

Novotel Paris Les Halles (E), pl. Marguerite-de-Navarre (tel. 42-21-31-31). 285 rooms, all with bath. Opened in 1985 in the heart of the renovated market district. Modern, efficient, well-run, but little ambiance. Restaurant, bar. AE, DC, MC, V.

Régina (E), 2 pl. des Pyramides (tel. 42-60-31-10). 130 rooms, all with bath. Facing Tuileries Gardens. Restaurant and bar. AE, MC, V.

Royal St.-Honoré (M), 13 rue d'Alger (tel. 42-60-32-79). 80 rooms. Comfortable, some rooms with balconies. Restaurant. Just off the Tuileries. AE, DC, MC, V.

Timhôtel Le Louvre (M), 4 rue Croix-des-Petits-Champs (tel. 42-60-34-86). 56 rooms, all with bath or shower. Member of good new moderately priced chain. AE, DC, MC, V.

Family (I), 35 rue Cambon (tel. 42-61-54-84). 25 rooms, 22 with bath or shower. Friendly—has long-established clientele. A few rooms at (M) prices.

Palais (I), 2 quai de la Mégisserie (tel. 42-36-98-25). 19 rooms, a few with bath or shower. Close to Seine and opposite Ste.-Chapelle. Adequate.

Second Arrondissement

Westminster (S), 13 rue de la Paix (tel. 42-61-57-46). 102 rooms, all with bath or shower. Restaurant, bar, airconditioned. AE, DC, MC, V.

Edouard-VII (E), 39 av. de l'Opéra (tel. 42-61-56-90). 100 rooms, all with bath or shower. Close to the Opéra. Good restaurant, *Delmonico*. AE, DC, V.

Opéra d'Antin l'Horset (E), 18 rue d'Antin (tel. 47-42-13-01). 60 rooms, 52 with shower. A member of well-run Horset chain, well-located for Opéra and big department stores. AE, DC, MC, V.

Choiseul-Opéra (M), 1 rue Daunou (tel. 42-61-70-41). 43 rooms, all with bath or shower. On same street, near Opéra, as Harry's Bar. AE, DC, MC.

Gaillon Opéra (M), 9 rue Gaillon (tel. 47-42-47-74). 26 rooms, all with bath or shower. Refined decor, near the Opéra. AE, DC, V.

Esmeralda (I), 4 rue St.-Julien-le-Pauvre (tel. 43-54-19-20). 19 rooms, 16 with bath or shower. Just by pretty square Viviani opposite Notre–Dame; 17th-century building with smallish rooms but pleasantly furnished.

Third Arrondissement

Pavillon de la Reine (L), 28 pl. des Vosges (tel. 42-77-96-40). 49 rooms, all with bath or shower. Newly opened on the famous square; peaceful patio. AE, DC, MC, V.

Marais (M), 2bis rue Commines (tel. 48-87-78-27). 38 rooms, all with bath or shower. Rooms small but comfortable, communicating for parents with children. AE, V.

Fourth Arrondissement

Deux-Iles (E), 59 rue St.-Louis-en-l'Ile (tel. 43-26-13-35). 17 rooms, all with bath or shower. Attractive small hotel in 17th-century house on Ile St.-Louis, with bar and sitting-room in old cellars.

Lutèce (E), 65 rue St.-Louis-en-L'Ile (tel. 43-26-23-52). 23 rooms, all with bath or shower; some rooms are duplexes. Small, peaceful and delightful hotel, also on Ile St.-Louis.

Bretonnerie (M), 22 rue Ste.-Croix-de-la-Bretonnerie (tel. 48-87-77-63). 30 rooms, all with bath or shower. 17th-century building near Hôtel de Ville, Pompidou Center and the Marais; some rooms with antiques.

St.-Louis (M), 75 rue St.-Louis-en-l'Ile (tel. 46-34-04-80). 21 rooms, all with bath or shower. Attractive rooms on five floors—the top story has marvelous view—with good modern bathrooms; good value.

Place des Vosges (I), 12 rue Birague (tel. 42-72-60-46). 16 rooms, all with bath or shower. Just by pl. des Vosges, small and pleasant. AE, DC, MC, V.

Fifth Arrondissement

Colbert (E), 7 rue de l'Hôtel Colbert (tel. 43-25-85-65). 40 rooms, all with bath or shower. By the river, just opposite Notre-Dame, an 18th-century building with attractive, smallish rooms. AE, V.

Collège-de-France (M), 7 rue Thénard (tel. 43-26-78-36). 29 rooms, all with bath or shower. In heart of Latin Quarter; some rooms have oak beams. AE.

Avenir (I), 52 rue Gay-Lussac (tel. 43-54-76-60). 44 rooms, only 7 with bath or shower. Modest budget hotel; very low prices; 6 floors, no elevator.

Nevers-Luxembourg (I), 3 rue Abbé-de-l'Epée (tel. 43-26-81-83). 26 rooms, only 8 with bath or shower. Attractively decorated; modest, but good value.

Sixth Arrondissement

L'Hôtel Guy-Louis-Duboucheron (S), 13 rue des Beaux-Arts (tel. 43-25-27-22). 27 rooms, all with bath. Attractive and very fashionable, furnished with antiques, including Mistinguett's mirror-lined bed (you can also sleep in the room where Oscar Wilde died). Bar, restaurant; airconditioned. AE.

Lutétia-Concorde (L), 45 blvd. Raspail (tel. 45-44-38-10). 293 rooms, all with bath or shower. Near Bon Marché department store, with pleasant atmosphere and good, old-fashioned service. Renovated from top to toe under the eagle eye of famous fashion-designer Sonia Rykiel. Restaurant and bar. Airconditioned; some (S) rooms. AE, DC, MC, V.

Relais Christine (L), 3 rue Christine (tel. 43-26-71-80). 51 rooms, all with bath. 16th-century cloisters converted into a delightful hotel in a reasonably quiet side street in St.-Germain-des-Prés. Good service. Bar. AE, DC, MC, V.

L'Abbaye St.-Germain (E), 10 rue Cassette (tel. 45-44-38-11). 45 rooms, all with bath or shower. Quiet and attractive hotel in what was once a monastery building.

Angleterre (E), 44 rue Jacob (tel. 42-60-34-72). 30 rooms, all with bath or shower. Once the home of the British Ambassador, and Hemingway used to live here too. Excellent service, traditional and atmospheric; highly recommended. AE. DC, V.

Odéon (E), 3 rue de l'Odéon (tel. 43-25-90-67). 34 rooms, all with bath or shower. Apparently this mansion once belonged to Mme. de Pompadour. AE, V.

Fleurie (M), 32 rue Grégoire-de-Tours (tel. 43-29-59-81). 30 rooms, all with bath or shower. Just off blvd. St.-Germain. Pretty facade adorned with illuminated statues set in niches. AE, DC, V.

Madison (M), 143 blvd. St.-Germain (tel. 43-29-72-50). 55 rooms, all with bath or shower. Set back from the blvd., in tiny square facing the church. Front rooms have delightful view but are rather noisy. Fully renovated in 1986. Bar. AE, MC, V.

Marronniers (M), 21 rue Jacob (tel. 43-25-30-60). 37 rooms, all with bath or shower. Quiet, with delightful courtyard garden. Light lunches served in bar or garden.

Pas-de-Calais (M), 59 rue des Sts.-Pères (tel. 45-48-78-74). 41 rooms, all with bath or shower. Here since the early 19th century and remains popular. Built around tiny courtyard, but try to get a room away from the street.

Seine (M), 52 rue de Seine (tel. 46-34-22-80). 30 rooms, all with bath or shower. Well-placed, in heart of St.-Germain-des-Prés. Some rooms a bit run down, but particularly helpful staff. AE, DC, V.

St.-André-des-Arts (I), 66 rue St.-André-des-Arts (tel. 43-26-96-16). 32 rooms, 28 with bath or shower. Close to pl. St.-Michel, on pedestrian street.

Vieux Paris (I), 9 rue Gît-le-Coeur (tel. 43-54-41-66). 21 rooms, 14 with bath or shower. On picturesque street close to Seine and pl. St.-Michel; very old building, charming though a bit run down, with friendly service. A few (M) doubles.

Seventh Arrondissement

Pont-Royal (L), 7 rue Montalembert (tel. 45-44-38-27). 80 rooms, 75 with bath or shower. Near the new Orsay Museum; some rooms rather cramped for this category, but pleasant atmosphere, attractive bar, and restaurant; airconditioned. AE, DC, MC, V.

Sofitel-Bourbon (L), 32 rue St.-Dominique (tel. 45-55-91-80). 112 rooms, all with bath. Near Les Invalides, modern, well-run, with good restaurant and bar. Airconditioned. AE, DC, MC, V.

Montalembert (E), 3 rue Montalembert (tel. 45-48-68-11). 61 rooms, 60 with bath. Next door to Pont Royal, but considerably less expensive. MC, V.

St.-Simon (E), 14 rue St.-Simon (tel. 45-48-35-66). 34 rooms, all with bath or shower. Quiet, between two gardens. Pleasant cellar bar.

Résidence Elysées-Maubourg (E), 35 blvd. de Latour-Maubourg (tel. 45-56-10-78). 30 rooms, all with bath or shower. Close to Les Invalides and the Eiffel Tower, with comfortable rooms and pleasant atmosphere. Extensively renovated in mid-'80s. Bar. AE, DC, MC, V.

Bellechasse (M), 8 rue de Bellechasse (tel. 45-51-52-36). 32 rooms, all with bath or shower. On quiet street close to Seine and Orsay Museum; small, modern rooms, a few with old beams. AE, DC, MC, V.

Bourdonnais (M), 111 av. de la Bourdonnais (tel. 47-05-45-42). 60 rooms, all with bath or shower. Restaurant (closed weekends and Aug.) and quiet, cheerful bar. DC, V.

St. Germain (M), 88 rue du Bac (tel. 45-48-62-92). 29 rooms, all with bath or shower. Well managed. Near St. Germain des Prés. AE.

Varenne (M), 44 rue de Bourgogne (tel. 45-51-45-55). 24 rooms, all with bath or shower. Converted mansion, peaceful and friendly, with pretty little patio; good value. AE.

Verneuil St.-Germain (M), 8 rue de Verneuil (tel. 42-60-82-14). 26 rooms, all with bath or shower. On quiet street, with pleasant atmosphere; small, very attractive rooms, with beams and stylish décor. AE, MC, V.

Empereur (I), 2 rue Chevert (tel. 45-55-88-02). 40 rooms, 23 with bath or shower. Close to Les Invalides with Napoleon's tomb, as its name suggests.

Palais Bourbon (I), 49 rue de Bourgogne (tel. 47-05-29-26). 34 rooms, 26 with bath or shower. Near Rodin Museum. Small rooms, modernized. Bar.

Eighth Arrondissement

Bristol (S), 112 fbg. St.-Honoré (tel. 42-66-91-45). 200 rooms and suites. One of the most elegant hotels in Paris, close to British Embassy and a stone's throw from the Elysée Palace; chic clientele includes many diplomats; pool and good restaurant. Airconditioned. AE, DC, MC, V.

Crillon (S), 10 pl. de la Concorde (tel. 42-65-24-24). 189 rooms. Grandiose site, with views across to National Assembly building on far side of Seine; popular with wealthy Americans (since the time of Benjamin Franklin and Thomas Jefferson, when they visited it as a private palace). Completely refurbished in early '80s; with one of the best hotel restaurants in Paris; airconditioned. AE, DC, MC, V.

George V (S), 31 av. George V (tel. 47-23-54-00). 292 rooms. Off Champs-Elysées, fashionable hotel often used by rich Arab businessmen; its bar is almost a club for visiting U.S. impresarios, starlets, businessmen and the press. Reception halls and some rooms furnished with antiques; restaurant has modern art displays; airconditioned. Restaurant. AE, DC, MC, V.

Lancaster (S), 7 rue de Berri (tel. 43-59-90-43). 67 rooms, all with bath. Quiet, a bit over-priced, but charmingly furnished suites overlook courtyard; with restaurant, bar, airconditioning. AE, DC, MC, V.

Plaza-Athénée (S), 25 av. Montaigne (tel. 47-23-78-33). 218 soundproofed rooms and suites. Just far enough from Champs Elysées to escape noise and glitter; *Régence* restaurant, plus *Relais-Plaza*, chic for an expensive after-theater supper; on winter evenings the downstairs bar becomes an intimate disco; airconditioned. Great brunch on Sun. AE, DC, MC, V.

Le Prince de Galles (S), 33 av. de George V (tel. 47-23-55-11). 171 rooms. Friendly, attractive place under same management as the *Meurice* (1st arrondissement); restaurant. AE, DC, MC, V.

Royal Monceau (S), 37 av. Hoche (tel. 45-61-98-00). 220 rooms, all with bath. Not far from the Etoile and near the chic Parc Monceau. Good restaurant serving Paris's most popular brunch on Sun.; also bar and pool; airconditioned. AE, DC, MC, V.

Residences Maxim's (S), 42 av. Gabriel (tel. 45-61-96-33). Couturier Pierre Cardin's latest venture. Lovely old building refurbished. AE, DC, V.

San Regis (S), 12 rue Jean Goujon (tel. 43-59-41-90). 32 rooms. Luxurious palace hotel near the *grands couturiers*. Restaurant. DC, V.

Balzac (L), 6 rue Balzac (tel. 45-61-97-22). 70 rooms, all with bath or shower. Previously the old-established *Celtic* but has been luxuriously renovated and renamed. Airconditioned. Deluxe restaurant, bar. AE, DC, MC, V.

Napoleon (L), 40 av. de Friedland (tel. 47-66-02-02). 140 rooms, 100 with bath. Has a charm you don't get in most newer hotels; some less expensive rooms; elegant restaurant and pleasant bar. AE, DC, MC, V.

Pullman-Windsor (L), 14 rue Beaujon (tel. 45-63-04-04). 135 rooms, all with bath or shower. Close to Etoile, quiet, elegant; good facilities for businessmen; good restaurant (closed weekends and Aug.); airconditioned. AE, DC, V.

Résidence Maxim's (L), 42 av. Gabriel (tel. 45-61-19-92). Couturier Pierre Cardin's latest venture—a lovely old building refurbished from top to toe to make a luxury hotel. Not yet open at our presstime.

La Trémoïlle (L), 14 rue de la Trémoïlle (tel. 47-23-34-20). 112 rooms, all with bath or shower. Run by same management as *Plaza-Athénée*. Close to Champs-Elysées and couture houses; with good service, all modern facilities and period furnishings; restaurant and bar; airconditioned. AE, DC, MC, V.

Warwick-Champs-Elysées (L), 5 rue de Berri (tel. 45-63-14-11). 147 rooms, all with bath or shower. A stone's throw from the Champs-Elysées; good restaurant—*La Couronne*—and bar; airconditioned. AE, DC, MC, V.

Astor l'Horset (E), 11 rue d'Astorg (tel. 42-66-56-56). 128 rooms, all with bath or shower. Belongs to the well-run Horset chain; restaurant and bar. AE, DC, MC, V.

Powers (E), 52 rue François 1er (tel. 46-23-91-05). 56 rooms, all with bath or shower. Close to Champs-Elysées; pleasant atmosphere; bar; AE, V.

Résidence Lord Byron (E), 5 rue Chateaubriand (tel. 43-59-89-98). 30 rooms, all with bath or shower. Pleasant and small, close to Etoile.

Roblin (E), 6 rue Chauveau-Lagarde (tel. 42-65-57-00). 70 rooms, all with bath or shower. Well-located near the Madeleine and good for serious shoppers, within walking distance of fbg. St.-Honoré and big department stores; restaurant and bar. AE, DC, MC, V.

Alison (M), 21 rue de Surène (tel. 42-65-54-00). 35 rooms, all with bath or shower. Modern rooms. Just off La Madeleine. AE, DC, MC, V.

Chambiges (M), 8 rue Chambiges (tel. 46-23-80-49). 30 rooms, 25 with bath or shower. Pleasant little hotel, close to Seine and av. Montaigne; a few doubles in (E) price range.

Madeleine-Plaza (M), 33 pl. de la Madeleine (tel. 42-65-20-63). 53 rooms, 48 with bath or shower. Just by the Madeleine church. AE, MC, V.

Mayflower (M), 3 rue Chateaubriand (tel. 45-62-57-46). 24 rooms, all with bath or shower. Small and cozy, close to Etoile. V.

Tronchet (M), 22 rue Tronchet (tel. 47-42-26-14). 34 rooms, all with bath or shower. Just by the Madeleine and convenient for main department stores. AE, DC, MC, V.

Bellevue (I), 46 rue Pasquier (tel. 43-87-50-68). 48 rooms, 16 with bath or shower. Near St. Lazare station; very low prices.

Champs-Elysées (I), 2 rue d'Artois (tel. 43-59-11-42). 40 rooms, 19 with bath or shower. One of the very few modestly-priced hotels in the ritzy Champs–Elysées area. Adequate.

Wilson (I), 10 rue de Stockholm (tel. 45-22-10-85). 37 rooms, only 8 with bath or shower. Modest, but convenient for St. Lazare station.

Ninth Arrondissement

Ambassador-Concorde (L), 16 blvd. Haussmann (tel. 42-46-92-63). 300 rooms, all with bath. Rather impersonal and commercial atmosphere, but convenient for major department stores and Opéra; with restaurant and bar. Airconditioned. AE, DC, MC, V.

Grand (L), 2 rue Scribe (tel. 42-68-12-13). 588 rooms, all with bath or shower. Close to Opéra; well run by same management as *Inter-Continental*, with old-fashioned service; restaurant and very good bar. AE, DC, V.

Commodore (E), 12 blvd. Haussmann (tel. 42-46-72-82). 160 rooms, all with bath. Two restaurants, one a convenient bar-cum-grill room. AE, DC, MC, V.

Bergère-Mapotel (M), 34 rue Bergère (tel. 47-70-34-34). 135 rooms, all with bath or shower. Quiet, appears slightly off the beaten track but is in fact near the Opéra and Bourse; good service; some (M) rooms. AE, DC, MC, V.

Central Monty (M), 5 rue de Montyon (tel. 47-70-26-10). 66 rooms, all with bath or shower. Near the *grands boulevards* and Bourse; bar. AE, DC, MC, V.

Excelsior-Opéra (M), 5 rue Lafayette (tel. 48-74-99-30). 53 rooms, all with bath or shower. Almost next door to Galeries Lafayette. AE, DC, MC, V.

London Palace (M), 32 blvd. des Italiens (tel. 48-24-54-64). 49 rooms, 47 with bath or shower. This well-run hotel is unusual in having reduced rates in July and Aug. MC, V.

Moulin Rouge (M), 39 rue La Fontaine (tel. 42-81-93-25). 50 rooms, all with bath or shower. New, very good rooms and breakfast. AE, DC, V.

Tenth Arrondissement

Pavillon-L'Horset (E), 38 rue de l'Echiquier (tel. 42-46-92-75). 91 rooms, all with bath or shower. A bit out of the way, but close by the rue de Paradis, where the finest china and porcelain showrooms are. AE, DC, MC, V.

Modern'Est (M), 91 blvd. de Strasbourg (tel. 46-07-24-72). 30 rooms, all with bath. Right opposite Gare de l'Est.

Europe (I), 98 blvd. Magenta (tel. 46-07-25-82). 36 rooms, 26 with bath or shower. Convenient for Gare du Nord and Gare de l'Est; bar. MC, V.

Londres et Anvers (I), 133 blvd. Magenta (tel. 42-85-28-26). 43 rooms, 13 with bath or shower. Near Gare du Nord and Gare de l'Est. AE, DC, V.

Eleventh Arrondissement

Holiday Inn (L), 10 pl. de la République (tel. 43-55-44-34). 333 rooms, all with bath or shower. Modernized reincarnation of grand, traditional hotel; comfortable, though not very central; with '20s-style restaurant; bar; airconditioned. AE, DC, MC, V.

Twelfth Arrondissement

Paris-Lyon Palace (M), 11 rue de Lyon (tel. 43-07-29-49). 128 rooms, all with bath or shower. Near Gare de Lyon; restaurant. AE, DC, MC, V.

Terminus Lyon (M), 19 blvd. Diderot (tel. 43-43-24-03). 61 rooms, 60 with bath or shower. Also close to Gare de Lyon; bar. AE, MC, V.

Thirteenth Arrondissement

Timhôtel Italie (I), 22 rue Barrault (tel. 45-80-67-67). 73 rooms, 68 with bath or shower. One of group of new, well-run hotels with contemporary furnishings and pleasant service; restaurant and bar. AE, DC, MC, V.

Timhôtel Tolbiac (I), 35 rue de Tolbiac (tel. 45-83-74-94). 54 rooms, all with bath. Another member of the new group; a little out of the way, but useful for Austerlitz station and Orly airport.

Fourteenth Arrondissement

Meridien Montparnasse (L), 19 rue Commandant-Mouchotte (tel. 43-20-15-51). 950 rooms, all with bath. Large, rather impersonal hotel near Tour Montparnasse; wonderful view from top floors; free bus link with Porte Maillot air terminal; has restaurants, bars, shops; airconditioned. AE, DC, MC, V.

PLM-St.-Jacques (L), 17 blvd. St.-Jacques (tel. 45-89-89-80). 797 rooms, all with bath. Not on usual tourist track, but convenient for Orly airport (airport bus stops here). You get a free night when you've spent 12 days in a year in any PLM hotel. Restaurants and bars to suit all tastes and purposes; airconditioned. AE, DC, MC, V.

Lenox (M), 15 rue Delambre (tel. 43-35-34-50). 52 rooms, all with bath. New hotel in Montparnasse. Well equipped rooms; light dinners served at bar until 2 A.M. AE, DC, V.

Delambre (I), 35 rue Delambre (tel. 43-20-66-31). 36 rooms, 34 with bath or shower. Close to Tour Montparnasse.

Idéal (I), 108 blvd. Jourdan (tel. 45-40-45-16). 69 rooms, 67 with bath or shower. Close to Cité Universitaire. AE, V.

Parc Montsouris (I), 4 rue du Parc (tel. 45-89-09-72). 35 rooms, all with bath or shower. Near pretty Parc Montsouris and Cité Universitaire. V.

Fifteenth Arrondissement

Hilton (L), 18 av. de Suffren (tel. 42-73-92-00). 479 rooms, all with bath and balcony: some rooms at (S) rates; two restaurants (rooftop one is closed Aug.), coffee shop, boutiques, hairdresser, bank; airconditioned. AE, DC, MC, V.

Nikko de Paris (L), 61 quai de Grenelle (tel. 45-75-62-62). 777 rooms, all with bath. Ultra-modern hotel owned by Japan Airlines, overlooking Seine, to west of Eiffel Tower; mixture of Japanese and French décor; has Japanese and French restaurants, pool, sauna, shops; airconditioned. AE, DC, MC, V.

Sofitel-Paris (L), 8–12 rue Louis-Armand (tel. 45-54-95-00). 635 rooms, all with bath. Near Exhibit Center at Porte de Versailles, a bit out of the way unless you're motorized; conference rooms, restaurants (good chef), pool, nursery, gym, sauna; airconditioned. AE, DC, MC, V.

Holiday Inn (E), 69 blvd. Victor (tel. 45-33-74-63). 90 rooms, all with bath. Also close to Exhibit Center at Porte de Versailles; restaurant and bar; airconditioned. AE, DC, MC, V.

Suffren-La Tour (M), 20 rue Jean-Rey (tel. 45-78-61-08). 407 rooms, all with bath. Just by Eiffel Tower; restaurant, bar, garden; airconditioned. AE, DC, MC, V.

Timhôtel Montparnasse (I), 22 rue de l'Arrivée (tel. 45-48-96-92). 33 rooms, 31 with bath or shower. Just by Montparnasse station; another of the new group of well-run, attractive small hotels, with contemporary furnishings, good modern bathrooms and pleasant service. The 11th night you stay at a Timhôtel in a year is free. AE, DC, MC, V.

Sixteenth Arrondissement

Raphaël (L), 17 av. Kléber (tel. 45-02-16-00). 93 rooms, all with bath and balcony. Close to Etoile; exclusive, comfortable and very quiet; well-decorated with period furniture; restaurant and bar. AE, DC, MC, V.

Résidence du Bois (L), 16 rue Chalgrin (tel. 45-00-50-59). 20 rooms, all with bath. Near Etoile; belongs to Relais et Châteaux group; quiet and attractive, with some rooms overlooking peaceful garden; must reserve well ahead.

Kléber (M), 7 rue de Belloy (tel. 47-23-80-22). 22 rooms, all with bath. Halfway between Etoile and Trocadéro. Very well-run. AE, DC, MC.

Queen's (M), 4 rue Bastien-Lepage (tel. 42-88-89-85). 22 rooms, all with bath or shower. Amenities are modern, but prices still reasonable. V.

Sévigné (M), 6 rue de Belloy (tel. 47-20-88-90). 30 rooms, all with bath or shower. Same management and good service as *Kléber;* close to Etoile. Has a few (E) rooms. AE, DC, MC.

Poussin (I), 52 rue Poussin (tel. 46-51-30-46). 28 rooms, all with bath or shower. Close to Auteuil racecourse; a few doubles are in (M) range.

Ranelagh (I), 56 rue de l'Assomption (tel. 42-88-31-63). 29 rooms, only 9 with bath. A rarity in this chic part of Paris—a modest spot for budget travelers.

Seventeenth Arrondissement

Concorde-Lafayette (L), 3 pl. due Général-Koenig (tel. 47-58-12-84). 1,027 rooms, all with bath. Convenient for Roissy/Charles-de-Gaulle air terminal, but rather impersonal, vast complex with conference rooms, secretarial services, restaurants for all tastes and most pocketbooks, chic and expensive shopping arcade, nightclub, movies; service can be indifferent; airconditioned. AE, DC, MC, V.

Meridien-Paris (L), 81 blvd. Gouvion-St.-Cyr (tel. 47-58-12-30). 1,027 rooms, all with bath. Huge, U.S.-style hotel with several restaurants, boutiques, and bar with jazz after 10 P.M. Convenient for air terminal and generally well-run, though service can be impersonal and even slapdash. Airconditioned. AE, DC, MC, V.

Regent's Garden (E), 6 rue Pierre-Demours (tel. 45-74-07-30). 41 rooms, all with bath. In 19th-century mansion near Etoile, with pretty garden; extensively modernized; excellent service. AE, DC, MC, V.

Banville (M), 166 blvd. Berthier (tel. 42-67-70-16). 40 rooms, all with bath. A little far out, but quiet and friendly, with attractive wallpaper and furnishings. MC, V.

Etoile (M), 3 rue de l'Etoile (tel. 43-80-36-94). 25 rooms, all with bath or shower. Close to Etoile. Very modern rooms; bar. AE, DC, MC, V.

Mercure Paris-Etoile (M), 27 av. des Ternes (tel. 47-66-49-18). 56 rooms, all with bath or shower. Second inner-city hotel opened by this well-known medium-priced chain. Well-run but little ambiance. Airconditioned. Bar. AE, DC, MC, V.

Médéric (I), 4 rue Médéric (tel. 47-63-69-13). 29 rooms, all with bath or shower. Close to the Parc Monceau. V.

Eighteenth Arrondissement

Mercure Paris Montmartre (E), 3 rue Caulaincourt (tel. 42-94-17-17). 308 rooms, all with bath. The first venture into the capital by this well-known chain; airconditioned. AE, DC, MC, V.

Terrass (E), 12–14 rue Joseph-de-Maistre (46-06-72-85). 108 rooms, all with bath. Close to Montmartre cemetery; delightful, surprisingly quiet for this rackety area of Paris; restaurant and bar. AE, DC, MC, V.

Regyn's Montmartre (M), 18 pl. des Abbesses (tel. 42-54-45-21). 22 rooms, all with bath or shower. Recent (1984), much-needed addition to Montmartre's hotels; small, attractive, with modern amenities. AE, DC, V.

Timhôtel Montmartre (I), 11 pl. Emile-Goudeau (tel. 42-55-74-79). 61 rooms, 50 with bath. Perched high up on atmospheric square where Picasso used to live—completely renovated, now one of the well-run Timhôtel group. AE, DC, MC, V.

Neuilly

Club Méditerranée (L), 58 blvd. Victor-Hugo (tel. 47-58-11-00). 330 rooms, all with bath. Run in the typically friendly Club Med style, pleasant atmosphere, excellent buffet, though a bit overpriced; garden. Airconditioned. AE, DC, V.

Maillot (I), 46 rue de Sablonville (tel. 46-24-23-45). 30 rooms, 23 with shower. Small, friendly hotel close to air terminal at Porte Maillot; very reasonable for this expensive area; breakfast at any time.

Suburbs and Airports

With old Paris bursting out of city limits, there has been a frenzy of building in nearby suburbs, now well connected to Paris by good transportation facilities. If central accommodations are scarce, and particularly if you have a car, the suburban hotels might be a good bet. However, they can be impersonal, not to say cold, and they tend to be geared more to business visitors than to tourists. Check also our *Ile de France* chapter.

Bagnolet. **Novotel Paris-Bagnolet** (E), 1 av. République (tel. 43-60-02-10). 611 rooms, all with bath. Two restaurants, bar, pool. Airconditioned. AE, DC, MC, V.

Ibis Paris Bagnolet (M), (tel. 43-60-02-76). 414 rooms, all with bath. Restaurant. MC, V.

Courbevole. Novotel Paris-La Défense (E), 2 blvd. Neuilly (tel. 47-78-16-68). 276 rooms, all with bath. Restaurant, bar; airconditioned. AE, DC, MC, V.

Orly Airport. Frantel Paris Orly (E), at nearby Rungis (tel. 46-87-36-36). 206 rooms, all with bath. Restaurant and pool; airconditioned. AE, DC, MC, V.

Hilton International Orly (E), (tel. 46-87-33-88). 380 soundproofed rooms. *Louisiane* restaurant; coffee shop; airconditioned. AE, DC, M, V.

Holiday Inn Orly (E), at nearby Rungis (tel. 46-87-26-66). 168 rooms, all with bath. Restaurant and pool. Airconditioned. AE, DC, MC, V.

Motel PLM Orly (M), at Orly-Ouest (tel. 46-87-23-37). 200 rooms. Restaurant; airconditioned. AE, DC, MC, V.

Paris Penta (M), (tel. 47-88-50-51). 494 rooms. Same management as *Lotti* and *Scribe* in central Paris; restaurant. AE, DC, MC, V.

Arcade Orly-Aéroport (I), at Orly-Sud (tel. 46-87-33-50). 203 rooms, all with bath. Restaurant. V.

Roissy/Charles-de-Gaulle Airport. Holiday Inn (E), (tel. 39-88-00-22). 250 rooms. Restaurant; airconditioned. AE, DC, V.

Sofitel (E), (tel. 38-62-23-23). 352 rooms. Restaurant and pool; airconditioned. AE, DC, MC, V.

Arcade (I), (tel. 38-62-49-49). 356 rooms, all with bath. Modern, well-run, right by rail station (direct service to the Gare du Nord); free bus service at regular intervals to airport building; good value. Restaurant. Airconditioned. V.

 RESTAURANTS. It is almost certainly fair to claim that Paris has more restaurants to the square mile, certainly more good restaurants, than any other city in the world. Eating out here is a constant pleasure and delight. The reasons for this are many and varied. But they can be summed up by saying that not only are the French excessively discriminating about where and what they eat, they also eat out much more regularly than most other people, especially in Paris. The happy result of this is that, catering to such a discerning public that enjoys the added advantage of a positive embarrassment of riches from which to choose, Parisian restaurants are in the main both extremely good value and reasonably priced. Indeed there is a quite staggering number of modest restaurants frequented principally by the locals that offer excellent value *and* excellent food.

True, this is in part the result of the competition provided by fast food restaurants, which, despite the odds, have enjoyed considerable success in Paris (tourism has played its part in this). Thus, many smaller restaurants today offer "formula" meals that offer little choice but amazing value for money. Yet at the same time, the demand for more traditional restaurants has remained strong, with new places constantly opening. It's no exaggeration to say that you could eat out twice a day for a good many years at a different restaurant every time and still not exhaust the possibilities.

Intriguingly, however, apart from the "formula" meals, fixed-priced *menus* are less common in Paris than in the rest of the country. And you're more likely to find them in expensive restaurants than in the lower price ranges. The reason for this is that even top executive expense-accounters have had to slim down their budgets these days so that in order to woo them back inside the hallowed portals many top restaurants, including some of the world-famous ones, have begun offering fixed-priced meals that are usually half the price of the *à la carte* menu. But, underlining the fact that they are aimed foursquare at the business man, it is rare to find a fixed-priced *menu* in a top restaurant outside weekday lunchtimes.

In fact weekends are a problem. In spite of the huge numbers of tourists in Paris, most restaurateurs still basically cater to Parisians, who in turn flee the city at weekends whenever they get the chance. Plus, legislation now obliges owners and managers to give staff two consecutive days off a week. Added to which, most of the top fish restaurants, as in a number of other countries, tend to close Sunday and Monday. The net result is that weekend closures make sense for many Parisian restaurants. Sunday in particular is a bad day for dining out in Paris, though this is less true of inexpensive places.

Annual closures are another problem. Many restaurants close for at least four weeks in the year. Those with a predominantly Parisian clientele will usually shut up in July and/or August, while those popular with tourists are more more likely to shut in the "dead months" of January or February, though the mid-semester vacations in November are another popular closing time. Public holidays are also a problem. In the main, restaurants that close on weekends generally also close on public holidays, though smaller neighborhood places are more likely to stay open. But check locally to be sure, as decisions are often made at the last minute, especially in family-run establishments.

Mealtimes are rigid. Lunch starts between 12 and 1.15—very rarely later—while it's hard to get dinner before 8, except in places catering mainly to tourists. Evening last order times vary widely. Neighborhood restaurants mostly won't take you after 9.30 or 10, but the chic places stay open later, a number into the small hours (we specify in our lists if they stay open after 11.30). But there are few 24-hour places, not surprising perhaps in a country where the ritual of eating is of such significance. We give details of a few in our lists, however.

Reservations pose problems at both ends of the price scale. Many inexpensive restaurants are not keen to take telephone reservations. Instead try stopping by earlier in the day or a day or two ahead. As for the expensive spots, though of course they accept telephone reservations, a number also will not accept more than a certain proportion of foreign diners—generally around 30 per cent of their total capacity—arguing that they depend on French customers year round and that it is not fair to turn away these regular customers during the peak summer months. If you're set on a top restaurant and can't get in, the concierge at your hotel may be able to get you a table; alternatively, if you have French friends they may be able to call for you. The fact remains, however, that the gastronomic temples of Paris have far more business than they need and can afford to pick and choose.

Prices and Grades. As with hotels, we have listed restaurants by *arron-dissements,* and then by price within each *arrondissement.* We have divided our restaurants into three categories, determined solely by price. These are (E), meaning Expensive, (M) Moderate and (I) Inexpensive. Even within one category prices can vary a great deal, depending on what you eat and, as important, what you drink. As a rough guide, however, a three-course *à la carte* meal will cost around 300–350 frs. in an Expensive restaurant (and around 600–700 frs. in one of the gastronomic highspots), around 150–300 frs. in a Moderate restaurant and 100–150 frs. in an Inexpensive restaurant. Note that these prices are *per person* and do *not* include wine. And remember also that if you choose either a fixed-priced *menu* or a "formula" menu that you can expect to pay a great deal less, often up to 50 per cent in the top places.

The initials AE, DC, MC, and V in the listings indicate the credit cards accepted by each establishment, standing respectively for American Express, Diners Club, MasterCard (incorporating Access) and Visa.

First Arrondissement

Le Carré des Feuillants (E), 14 rue Castiglione (tel. 42-61-39-44). A new arrival on the Paris gastronomic scene, opened in 1985 by Alain Dutournier, longtime chef of the *Trou Gascon* in the 12th arrondissement. Gascony specialties cooked new-style, superb armagnacs to round off your meal. Closed weekends. V.

L'Escargot Montorgueil (E), 38 rue Montorgueil, in the middle of what used to be Les Halles food market (tel. 42-36-83-51). Opened in the 1830s and still going strong, with delightful 19th-century decor of mirrors and traditional wall sofas. Chic clientele. Snails, of course, but other well-cooked dishes too. Closed Mon., Tues. and most of Aug. Good-value lunch *menu.* AE, DC, MC, V.

Le Grand Véfour (E), 17 rue de Beaujolais, behind the Palais-Royal gardens (tel. 42-96-56-27). Still one of Paris's finest restaurants, though no longer owned by the great Raymond Oliver. Now belongs to Jean Taittinger who runs the world-famous Concorde hotels and is keeping up the long-standing tradition of excellent food and superb service. Closed weekends and Aug. AE, DC, V.

Mercure Galant (E), 15 rue des Petits-Champs (tel. 42-96-98-89). Fashionable restaurant with turn-of-the-century decor. Good mixture of traditional and new cooking. Very good *foie gras de canard*. Closed Sat. lunch and Sun.

L'Absinthe (M), 24 pl. du Marché-St.-Honoré (tel. 42-60-02-45). Friendly service in this chic little restaurant near the pl. Vendome and the av. de l'Opéra. The cooking is mostly "new" with delectably fresh ingredients from the market opposite. Attractive decor with *art nouveau* bits and pieces. Closed Sat. lunch and Sun. Open till 11.30 P.M. AE, DC, V.

Armand (M), 6 rue du Beaujolais (tel. 42-60-05-11). Very good, *nouvelle cuisine;* near Palais Royal gardens. Closed Sat. for lunch, Sun. and last 3 weeks in Aug. AE, DC, V.

Barrière Poquelin (M), 17 rue Molière, near the Comédie Française (tel. 42-96-22-19). Small, intimate and chic. New-style cuisine (particularly good fish) and excellent game in season. Good value *menu.* Closed Sat., for dinner on Sun. and most of Aug. AE, DC, V.

Le Caveau du Palais (M), 19 pl. Dauphine (tel. 43-26-04-28). Attractive place on a summer's evening, when you can sit outside in the peace and quiet of this leafy square. Good classical cooking. Closed weekends. AE, V.

A la Grille (M), 15 pl. du Marche Saint-Honoré (tel. 42-61-00-93). Pleasant decor; good *menu.* Near Tuileries. Closed Sat. and Sun. AE, DC, V.

Le Pharamond (M), 24 rue de la Grande Truanderie, in the Les Halles area (tel. 42-33-06-72). Specializes in tripe, but has plenty of other good dishes to tempt you, too. Turn-of-the-century decor. Closed Sun., Mon. lunchtime and July. AE, DC, V.

Au Pied de Cochon (M), 6 rue Coquillière. Never closes, though it has inevitably lost some of its charm now that the food market has disappeared to the suburbs. But you can still enjoy the grilled pig's trotters and onion soup that made it famous. Nostalgic musical accompaniment too. Renovated from top to toe in mid-'80s. AE, DC, V.

La Tour de Montlhéry (M), 5 rue des Prouvaires. Crowded, bustling bistrot specializing in steaks and good, home-style cooking. Lively atmosphere, redolent of the old days of Les Halles food market. Closed Sun. and mid-July to mid-Aug., but otherwise open 24-hours a day.

André Faure (I), 40 rue du Mont-Thabor, near the Tuileries and the pl. de la Concorde (tel. 42-60-74-28). Good place for a simple, home-style lunch or a special "farmhouse dinner." Good value. Closed Sun.

Bistro de la Gare (I), 30 rue St.-Denis (tel. 42-60-84-92). Fashionable *art nouveau*-style decor and "formula" meals to which you can add delicious desserts and reasonable wines.

Chez Paul (I), 15 pl. Dauphine (tel. 43-54-21-48). In a delightful little square behind the law courts and the Ste.-Chapelle. Charming, crowded, unpretentious bistrot with genuine marble counter and straightforward home cooking, presided over by a very Parisienne *patronne.* A few tables outside. Closed Mon., Tues. and Aug.

Second Arrondissement

La Corbeille (E), 154 rue Montmartre (tel. 42-61-30-87). Close to Bourse. Reasonable prices, Provencal cooking. Closed Sat. except for dinner Sept. through May.

Le Petit Coin de la Bourse (M), 16 rue Feydeau (tel. 45-08-00-08). Owned by well-known restaurateur Claude Verger. Lively atmosphere, some "new" cuisine. Closed weekends. AE, V.

Pile ou Face (M), 52bis rue Notre-Dame-des-Victoires (tel. 42-33-64-33). Tiny upstairs dining room popular with brokers from nearby Bourse at lunchtime, with couples seeking romance in the evening. Closed weekends and Aug. Airconditioned. Good-value *menu.*

Le Vaudeville (M), 29 rue Vivienne (tel. 42-33-39-31). Beautiful 1930s room with great atmosphere especially at dinner; good shellfish. Open daily to 2 A.M. AE, DC, MC.

L'Amanguier (I), 110 rue de Richelieu (tel. 42-96-37-79). Near the Bourse and quite close to the Opéra. Delightful green-and-white decor—with parasols and garden chairs. Short but imaginative menu, very reasonably priced, with particularly good desserts. Open to 11.30 P.M. AE, DC, V.

Third Arrondissement

L'Ambroisie (E), 9 pl. des Vosges (tel. 42-78-51-45). Formerly *Quaie des Tournelles*. Very inventive cuisine, especially fish. Closed Sun., Mon. and Aug. MC, V.

Guirlande de Julie (E), 25 pl. des Vosges (tel. 48-87-94-07). Pleasant atmosphere in this flower-filled restaurant in the lovely pl. des Vosges in the heart of the Marais. Good-value lunch *menus*. Closed Mon., Tues., Feb. AE, V.

L'Ambassade d'Auvergne (M), 22 rue du Grenier-St.-Lazare (tel. 42-72-31-22). Hearty country-style dishes from the Auvergne in central France, in a spacious tavern near the Centre Beaubourg/Pompidou. Open to 12.30 A.M. Closed Sun.

Taverne des Templiers (M), 106 rue Vieille du Temple (tel. 42-78-74-67). Don't be put off by the somewhat overdone medieval decor, as the food, cooked mostly in the classical style, is really good. Close to Picasso Museum. Closed weekends and Aug. AE, V.

Fourth Arrondissement

Quai des Ormes (E), 72 quai de l'Hôtel-de-Ville (tel. 42-74-72-22). Nice setting close to the Hôtel de Ville. Rather chic, mostly "new" cuisine. Closed weekends and Aug. V.

Bofinger (M), 7 rue de la Bastille (tel. 42-72-87-82). Probably the most genuine *brasserie* in town, though it tends to be expensive. Splendid *art nouveau* decor. Good for after-theater suppers as it's open to 1 A.M. AE, DC, MC, V.

Chez Julien (M), 1 rue du Pont-Louis-Philippe. Attractive, one-time bakery, hence the beautiful old ceramic tiles. Now serves excellent *nouvelle cuisine*, though portions are apt to be small. Closed Sat. for lunch, Sun. and Mon. for lunch. AE, DC, V.

Coconnas (M), 2bis pl. des Vosges (tel. 42-78-58-16). Delightful setting in the heart of the Marais. Good-value, interesting cuisine. Under same management as the famous Tour d'Argent. Closed Mon., Tues. and mid-Dec. to mid-Jan. AE, DC, V.

Le Coin du Caviar (M), 2 rue de la Bastille (tel. 48-04-82-93). Just off pl. de la Bastille. Good spot for smoked fish, salmon and caviar. Wine by the glass. Open daily to 12.30 A.M.

Le Domarais (M), 53bis rue des Francs-Bourgeois (tel. 42-74-54-17). Worth coming for the decor alone; once the annexe of the Crédit Municipal pawn-brokers—red-velvet seats and intimate atmosphere make it truly special. Good food too, at reasonable prices. Closed Sat. for lunch, Sun. and Mon. for lunch. AE, DC, V.

L'Excuse (M), 14 rue Charles-V (tel. 42-77-98-97). Small, quiet and elegant in the southern section of the Marais near the Seine. Good newish cuisine, pleasant ambiance. Open till midnight. Closed Sun. V.

Le Tourtour (M), 20 rue Quincampoix (tel. 48-87-82-48). Fashionable restaurant near the Centre Beaubourg/Pompidou. Charming 17th-century building, now designed to look like a sidewalk cafe, with genuine Parisian paving stones underfoot. Goodish food, reasonable prices. Open to 1 A.M. AE, DC, V.

La Brasserie de l'Ile (I), 55 quai Bourbon, Ile St-Louis (no telephone reservations). Crowded *brasserie* with cheerful, lively waiters who manage to keep smiling in spite of the crush. Traditional Alsatian dishes and fruity Alsatian wines. Popular for Sunday lunch but you must get there early. A good place to go after visiting Notre-Dame. Closed Wed., also Thurs. for lunch and Aug. Open to 1.30 A.M.

Au Gourmet de l'Ile (I), 42 rue St.-Louis-en-l'Ile (tel. 43-26-79-27). Delightful and good-value little restaurant on the Ile St.-Louis. Must reserve. 17th-century cellar setting, country-style dishes. Closed Mon., Thurs. and Aug.

Petit Gavroche (I), 15 rue Ste.-Croix-de-la-Bretonnerie. Typically Parisian bistrot with amazingly low prices and cheerfully casual atmosphere. Closed Sun. and Aug.

Au Tibourg (I), 31 rue du Bourg-Tibourg (tel. 42-78-57-44). Excellent, Greek-inspired cuisine; lively atmosphere. Closed Sun. AE, DC, MC, V.

Fifth Arrondissement

Auberge des Deux Signes (E), 46 rue Galande (tel. 43-25-46-56). Wonderful medieval setting with views of Notre-Dame. The cooking is good too, with some Auvergnat dishes. Closed Sun. AE, DC, MC, V.

Jacques Cagna (E), 14 rue des Grands Augustins (tel. 43-26-49-39). Some of the most elegant cuisine in Paris; reserve well ahead for dinner. Genuine 16th-century house. Closed Sat., Sun. and Aug. AE, DC, V.

La Tour d'Argent (E), 15 quai de la Tournelle (tel. 43-54-23-31). A world-famous restaurant that is once again living up to its reputation. Extremely expensive, but worth it if you can afford it, for the elegant decor and service, the views of Notre-Dame, the attention to detail at every level, the magnificent wines (don't forget to have an old Armagnac in the cellar, too) and not least the cooking which is French *haute cuisine* at its best with some *nouvelle cuisine* too. Good news is that La Tour d'Argent offers a fixed-price *menu*, Tues. to Sat. lunchtime; it works out at less than half the price of an *à la carte* meal. Closed Mon. AE, DC, V.

Villars-Palace (E), 8 rue Descartes (tel. 43-26-39-08). In the rue Mouffetard area and fashionable, with garden. Mostly fish cooked new-style (i.e. very lightly poached or steamed) and shellfish. Closed Sat. for lunch. AE, DC, MC, V.

La Bûcherie (M), 41 rue da la Bûcherie (tel. 43-54-78-06). An old favorite, with log fires, classical music and relaxed atmosphere. Good "new" cooking though some people find the portions rather small. Lovely view of Notre-Dame from tables by the window. Located in the section of the rue de la Bûcherie near the Petit Pont. Open to 1 A.M. Closed Mon. for lunch. AE, DC, V.

Au Pactole (M), 44 blvd. St.-Germain (tel. 46-33-31-31). Careful cooking blends new and classical cuisine. Discreet atmosphere. Good value lunchtime *menu*. Closed Sat. lunch and Sun. V.

Balzar (I), 49 rue des Ecoles (tel. 43-54-13-67). A genuine *brasserie* with waiters in long white aprons and traditional home-style cooking. Open to 12.30 A.M. Closed Tues. and Aug.

La Marée Verte (I), 9 rue de Pointoise (tel. 43-25-89-41). Excellent address for a good and generous meal. Good-value *menu*. Closed Sun., Mon. and Aug. V.

Le Petit Prince (I), 12 rue Lanneau (tel. 43-54-77-26). Attractive little place in the Contrescarpe area, excellent value. Airconditioned. Open to 12.30 A.M. AE.

Sixth Arrondissement

Le Paris (E), 23 rue de Sevres (tel. 45-48-74-34). Newly opened in the same building as the *Lutétia* hotel. Wonderful 1930s decor; good-value *menu* (lunch only) and dinner. Closed Sun., Mon. and Aug. AE, DC, MC, V.

La Petite Cour (E), 8 rue Mabillon (tel. 45-26-52-26). Delightful little court-yard set below sidewalk level on a narrow street a bit away from the bustle of blvd. St.-Germain makes for perfect summer meals. Mostly "new" cuisine. Good value (M) *menu* at lunch. Closed Sun. and for lunch on Mon. Also mid-Dec. to mid-Jan. V.

Relais Louis XIII (E), 8 rue des Grands-Augustins (tel. 43-26-75-96). Wonderful old building near the Seine but very modern cuisine. Closed Sun. and for lunch on Mon. AE, DC, V.

L'Echaudé St. Germain (M), 2 rue de l'Echaudé (tel. 42-22-92-50). Old decor with beams. Simple food. Open daily to 1 A.M. AE, DC, MC, V.

Grégoire (M), 80 rue du Cherche Midi (tel. 45-44-72-72). Very small bistrot with short and interesting menu and good wines. Good-value *menu*. Closed Sat. for lunch, Sun. and Aug. AE, V.

Chez Hansi (M), 3 pl. du 18-juin-1940 (tel. 45-48-96-42). Large, bustling Alsatian *brasserie* opposite the Tour Montparnasse. Open till 3 A.M. daily. AE, DC, V.

Joséphine (M), 117 rue du Cherche-Midi (tel. 45-48-52-40). Good atmosphere and friendly service in rather chic bistrot. Mostly classical cuisine from the southwest of France. Good house wine. Closed weekends, July and Christmas period. V.

Lipp (M), 151 blvd. St.-Germain (tel. 45-48-53-91). A Parisian institution, always crowded and a favorite haunt of politicians, writers and film people. Fair home-style cooking (marvelous *pot-au-feu*). No reservations. Open till 12.45 A.M. Closed Mon., Easter, first week in Nov., July and Christmas period.

Le Muniche (M), 27 rue de Buci (tel. 46-33-62-09). Another crowded spot, but the patrons are more Bohemian than *chez* Lipp. Much more French than German, despite its name. Some tables outside in summer. Open to 3 A.M. AE, DC, MC, V.

Le Petit Zinc (M), 25 rue de Buci (tel. 43-54-79-34). An old favorite, ever-popular, ever-crowded. Tables outside in summer. Traditional home-style cooking, plus excellent oysters. Open till 3 A.M. AE, DC, MC, V.

Tante Madée (M), 11 rue Dupin (tel. 42-22-64-56). Another old favorite, now back on form, for home-style cuisine. Good value. Closed Sat. for lunch and Sun. AE, DC.

Vagénende (M), 142 blvd. St.-Germain (tel. 43-26-68-18). Charming turn-of-the-century decor in this popular restaurant which is a favorite with our readers. It boasts old-fashioned fare and portions are generous. Good game in season. Open till 2 A.M. AE, DC, MC, V.

Aux Charpentiers (I), 10 rue Mabillon (tel. 43-26-30-05). Typical Parisian bistrot, unpretentious and altogether delightful. Used to be the headquarters of the Carpenter's Guild (the walls are covered with fascinating period photographs of the guild members at their get-togethers). The food is good too—plain straightforward homely dishes, very reasonably priced. Open till 11.30 P.M. Closed Sun., Christmas and New Year period. AE, DC.

Les Classiques (I), passage Dauphine. In attractive little, traffic-free street of the rue Dauphine in the heart of St.-Germain-des-Prés, this is just the place for that light lunch that can be so hard to find in Paris. Good salads, a few hot dishes; good range of teas as well as wines.

Petit St.-Benoît (I), 4 rue St.-Benoît (no telephone reservations). Amazingly low prices in this popular bistrot in the heart of St.-Germain-des-Prés. Closed weekends and Aug.

Polidor (I), 41 rue Monsieur-le-Prince (tel. 43-26-75-34). Old-established genuine Paris bistrot with literary associations (André Gide and Paul Valéry used to come here, among many others). Good home cooking, in generous helpings. Closed Sun., Mon. and Aug.

Le Procope (I), 13 rue de l'Ancienne Comédie (tel. 43-26-99-20). Large, crowded, bustling café-restaurant with a famous past (Voltaire and Balzac knew it as a coffee house). Adequate food, plenty of atmosphere. Open till 1.30 A.M. Closed July. AE, DC, V.

Seventh Arrondissement

Alain Perrard (E), 84 rue de Varenne (tel. 45-51-47-33). Newly opened restaurant with chef well known for nouvelle cuisine. Closed Sun. and Sun.

Chez les Anges (E), 54 blvd. de Latour-Maubourg (tel. 47-05-89-86). Spacious and comfortable; near the Invalides with a judicious mixture of classical, mostly from Burgundy, and "new" dishes. Closed Sun. evening and Mon. AE, DC, MC, V.

Le Bellecour (E), 22 rue Surcouf (tel. 45-55-68-38). Mostly classical Lyonnaise cuisine. Closed Sat. for lunch in winter, all day Sat. in summer, Sun. and most of Aug. AE, DC, MC, V.

Divellec (E), 107 rue de l'Université (tel. 45-51-91-96). One of Paris's greatest eating places, specializing in mouthwateringly fresh fish. Good-value *menu* for lunch. Closed Sun., Mon., Aug. and Christmas period. AE, DC, V.

Le Jules Verne (E), on the 2nd floor of the Eiffel Tower (tel. 45-55-61-44). A restaurant that's worthy of Paris's most famous landmark. Very popular so reserve well ahead. Lovely views, of course, but good, stylish cuisine too, and live piano music at times. AE, V.

Au Quai d'Orsay (E), 49 quai d'Orsay (tel. 45-51-58-58). This pleasant spot has long been fashionable. Chef specializes in imaginative potato and mushroom dishes. Closed Sun. and Aug. AE, DC, MC, V.

Chez Françoise (M), in the Invalides Air Terminal (tel. 47-05-49-03). Popular with diplomats and politicians from the nearby Foreign Ministry and National Assembly. Good cuisine and excellent wine list. Very Parisian, old-style. Closed Sun. for dinner, Mon. and Aug. AE, DC, V.

Ferme St.-Simon (M), 6 rue St.-Simon (tel. 45-48-35-74). Excellent *nouvelle cuisine;* light and delicious. Closed Sat. for lunch, Sun. and part of Aug. V.

Le Petit Niçois (M), 10 rue Amélie (tel. 45-51-83-65). An old favorite near the Eiffel Tower and Les Invalides, but the Mediterranean cuisine has recently taken on a new lease of life. Closed Sun., Mon. for lunch and Aug. Airconditioned. AE, V.

La Sologne (M), 8 rue de Bellechasse (tel. 47-05-98-66). Convenient for new Orsay Museum, this reliable spot specializes in game from the Sologne forest and marshland in central France. Closed weekends. AE, DC, V.

Chez l'Ami Jean (I), 27 rue Malar (tel. 47-05-86-89). Good hearty cuisine from the Pays Basque. Very good value. Closed Sun. and Aug.

La Fontaine de Mars (I), 129 rue St.-Dominique (tel. 47-05-46-44). Typically French little restaurant near the Eiffel Tower, plain and popular with local residents in this chic area. No frills, but straightforward home cooking and friendly service. Tables outside in summer beside a delightful fountain set in a little square. Closed Sat. evening, Sun. and Aug.

La Petite Chaise (I), 36 rue de Grenelle (tel. 42-22-13-35). One of the oldest restaurants in Paris. Charming, slightly shabby and traditional, and always full. Excellent value.

Thoumieux (I), 79 rue St.-Dominique (tel. 47-05-49-75). French home-style cooking, with specialties from southwestern France, in typically Parisian bistrot. Closed Mon. and mid-July to mid-Aug. AE, V.

Eighth Arrondissement

Chiberta (E), 3 rue Arsène-Houssaye (tel. 45-63-77-90). Wonderfully fresh ingredients, stylish decor, chic dinners make this a must if you can afford it. Closed weekends, Aug. and Christmas period. AE, DC, V.

Fouquet's (E), 99 av. des Champs-Elysées (tel. 47-23-70-60). Overpriced, but the food is basically good in this eternal landmark. A place to be seen. Open to midnight. AE, DC, MC, V.

Lamazère (E), 23 rue de Ponthieu (tel. 43-59-66-66). Chic and expensive, with particularly good dishes from the southwest of France, including splendid *cassoulet* and *foie gras.* Open till midnight. Closed Sun. and Aug. AE, DC, MC, V.

Lucas-Carton (E), 9 pl. de la Madeleine (tel. 42-65-22-90). One of the major events of the mid-'80s for French and other gastronomes was the news that the brilliantly inventive Alain Senderens had closed his world-famous restaurant L'Archestrate in the 7th *arrondissement* and was presiding instead over the old-established Lucas-Carton, with its splendid *art nouveau* decor and turn-of-the-century aura. Extremely expensive *nouvelle cuisine* at its subtle best, definitely for aficionados. Closed weekends, most of August and over Christmas-New Year period. V.

Le Marcande (E), 52 rue Miromesnil (tel. 42-65-19-14). Elegant and spacious with pleasant service and newish cuisine. Closed weekends and for most of Aug. AE, DC, V.

La Marée (E), 1 rue Daru (tel. 47-63-52-42). One of Paris's top restaurants for superbly cooked traditional dishes, especially fish and shellfish. Closed weekends and Aug. AE, DC.

Marius et Janette (E), 4 av. George-V (tel. 47-23-41-88). Excellent fish restaurant, recently renovated and now rather fashionable. Specializes in Mediterranean dishes like *bouillabaisse* and *bourride*. Closed weekends, Christmas and New Year period. AE, V.

Maxim's (E), 3 rue Royale (tel. 42-65-27-94). Turn-of-the-century and world-famous. This ultra-chic restaurant has been revitalized from top to toe. Prices are very high but (M) meals are served on the second floor and there are also fixed-price after-theater suppers served from 11 P.M. Open to 1 A.M. Closed Sun. AE, DC, V.

Pavillon de l'Elysée (E), 10 av. des Champs-Elysées (tel. 42-65-85-10). Set in a delightful 19th-century "pavilion" in the gardens bordering the Champs-Elysées and now run by the famous Gaston Lenôtre. Marvelous cuisine, but very high prices. However, less expensive meals can be had at *Les Jardins* on the ground floor. Airconditioned. Closed weekends and Aug. (but *Jardins* stays open). AE, DC, V.

Au Petit Montmorency (E), 5 rue Rabelais (tel. 42-25-11-19). Very imaginative cuisine, though not yet well known—awaits discovery. (M) *menu.* Closed Sat., Sun. and Aug. V.

Taillevent (E), 15 rue Lamennais (tel. 45-63-39-94). One of France's top restaurants, now specializing in *nouvelle cuisine* with amazing choice of wine (500 vintages no less!). In what was once an elegant private mansion. Airconditioned. Very expensive, but also very memorable. Closed weekends and Aug.

Androuët (M), 41 rue d'Amsterdam (tel. 48-74-26-93). There are no fewer than 300 cheeses and cheese dishes on offer in this restaurant attached to a celebrated cheesemonger's. Excellent wines to bring out their full flavor. Good-value *menu.* Closed Sun. AE, DC, V.

Chez Edgard (M), 4 rue Marbeuf (tel. 47-20-51-15). Always crowded, popular with the after-theater crowd. Specializes in fish and shellfish. Open to 1 A.M. Closed Sun. AE, DC, MC, V.

La Fermette-Marbeuf (M), 5 rue Marbeuf. Another useful address if you're going to the theater or the movies. Good-value set *menu,* and one room with genuine *art nouveau* decor discovered during renovations (the other is a copy). Open till 11.30 P.M. AE, DC, MC, V.

Moulin du Village (M), 25 rue Royale (tel. 42-65-08-47). Owned by British wine expert Steven Spurrier. Newish cuisine, excellent wines and peaceful setting. Closed Sat. for dinner and Sun. V.

La Cour St. Germain (I), 19 rue Marbeuf (tel. 47-23-84-25). Specializes in *menu-carte;* pleasant decor. Open daily to midnight. AE, DC, MC, V.

L'Hippopotamus (I), 6 av. Franklin-Roosevelt (no telephone reservations). One of a menagerie of four beasts known for their good meat, ridiculously low prices and cheerful atmosphere. Not a gastronomic experience, but fun. Open to 1 A.M.

Théâtre du Rond-Point (I), av. Franklin-Roosevelt (tel. 42-56-22-01). Even if you're not attending a performance at Jean-Louis Barrault's famous theater you can enjoy a meal in the very pleasant foyer-restaurant with its theatrical decor and busy waiters. Good teas too. Closed for dinner on Sun. Open to midnight. V.

Ninth Arrondissement

Opéra (Café de la Paix) (E), 3 pl. de l'Opéra (tel. 47-42-97-02). Superb Napoleon III decor. Refined *nouvelle cuisine* and very good wines and desserts. Closed Aug. AE, DC, MC, V.

Auberge Landaise (M), 23 rue Clauzel. Specializes in cooking from the Bordeaux region and does it beautifully. One of the best cassoulets in Paris. Rustic decor to go with the food, though the cooking's full of subtlety too. Closed Sun. and Aug. AE, DC, V.

La Table d'Anvers (M), 2 pl. d'Anvers (tel. 48–78–35–21). New restaurant near Montmartre, with noted chef (Conticini) and good-value *menu.* Open daily to 10.30 P.M. V.

Ty-Coz (M), 35 rue St.-Georges (tel. 48-78-42-95). Well-known Breton fish restaurant. Closed Sun., Mon. and part of Aug. AE, DC, V.

Chartier (I), 7 rue du Faubourg-Montmartre (tel. 47-70-86-29). Turn-of-the-century decor and ludicrously low prices.

Le Roi du Pot-au-Feu (I), 34 rue Vignon (tel. 47-42-37-10). Plain but hearty *pot-au-feu* makes a welcome change if you've been indulging in rich cuisine. Closed Sun. and July. v.

Tenth Arrondissement

Brasserie Flo (M), 7 cour des Petites-Ecuries (tel. 47-70-13-59). A genuine 19th-century Alsatian *brasserie* set in a courtyard. Always full so reservations are essential, especially for late-evening dining. Open till 1.30 A.M. AE, DC, V.

Casimir (M), 6 rue de Belzunce (tel. 48-78-32-53). Cuisine half modern and half regional, with good-value *menu*. Closed Sat. for lunch and Sun. AE, DC, V.

Julien (M), 16 rue du Faubourg St.-Denis (tel. 47-70-12-06). Fashionable, *art nouveau* decor and traditional French cuisine. Clientele is fashionable too, particularly in the evening, when it stays open till 1.30 A.M. AE, DC, V.

Terminus-Nord (M), 23 rue de Dunkerque (tel. 42-85-05-15). Large and very lively bistrot, opposite the Gare du Nord. Decorated in outrageous *art nouveau* style and under the same ownership as the Brasserie Flo and Julien. Good value, but you may have to wait for your table. Open to 12.30 A.M. AE, DC, V.

Eleventh Arrondissement

Chez Philippe (Auberge Pyrénées-Cévennes) (M), 106 rue de la Folie-Méricourt (tel. 43-57-33-78). Old cafe with exquisite food from the southwest of France. Serves until 10.30 P.M. Closed Sat., Sun. and Aug.

Sousceyrac (M), 35 rue Faidherbe (tel. 43-71-65-30). Bustling family-run restaurant serving specialties from the Périgord region with wonderful *foie gras.* Generous portions and good service. Closed weekends. v.

Twelfth Arrondissement

Au Trou Gascon (E), 40 rue Taine (tel. 43-44-34-26). Genuine turn-of-the-century bistrot with inventive "new" cuisine versions of regional cooking from Gascony, plus superb wines. Closed weekends, mid-July to mid-Aug. and Christmas.

La Gourmandise (M), 271 av. Daumesnil (tel. 43-43-94-41). Simple decor for generous and refined cuisine. Good-value *menu* for lunch (I) and dinner (M). Closed Sat. for lunch, Sun., one week in Apr. and most of Aug. AE, DC, V.

Thirteenth Arrondissement

Les Vieux Métiers de France (E), 13 blvd. Auguste-Blanqui (tel. 45-88-90-03). Light and modern cuisine (mainly fish), served by candlelight in 17th-century decor. Closed Sun. and Mon. AE, DC, MC, V.

Fourteenth Arrondissement

Le Duc (E), 243 blvd. Raspail (tel. 43-20-96-30). One of Paris's finest seafood restaurants, firmly anchored in the "new" cuisine so don't come here if you're against the idea of raw scallops or underdone *loup de mer.* But we are willing to bet that chef Jean Minchelli will convert you if you're prepared to try. Anyway, *nouvelle cuisine* addicts will adore it, but make sure to reserve. Closed Sat. to Mon.

Auberge de l'Argoat (M), 27 av. Reille (tel. 45-89-17-05). Inventive cooking dedicated to fish and shellfish; great *terrines de poisson.* Cider from Britanny, of course. Closed Sun., Mon. and Aug.

La Coupole (M), 102 blvd. Montparnasse (tel. 43-20-14-20). Large, famous and long-standing *brasserie* that looks like an arty railway station. Fun people, sound classical cooking. Open all day from 8 A.M. to 2 A.M. with dancing too. Closed Aug. v.

Le Dôme (M), 108 blvd. du Montparnasse (tel. 43-35-34-82). Large and bustling restaurant in the heart of Montparnasse, now specializes in fish. Airconditioned. Open to 1 A.M. Closed Mon. AE, DC, V.

Fifteenth Arrondissement

Bistro 121 (E), 121 rue de la Convention (tel. 45-57-52-90). Bistrot with a mixture of traditional and new cooking. Closed Sun. evening, Mon. and mid-July to mid-Aug.; Christmas and New Year period. AE, DC, V.

Olympe (E), 8 rue Nicolas-Charlet (tel. 47-34-86-08). Run by well-known young female chef. Inventive cuisine, rather small portions. Closed Mon., Aug. and Christmas. AE, DC, V.

La Maison Blanche (M), 82 blvd. Lefebvre (tel. 48-28-38-83). Very plain decor for simple and short menu, giving some of the best value in Paris. Closed Sat. for lunch, Sun., Mon. and 2 weeks in Sept. AE.

Aux Senteurs de Provence (M), 295 rue Lecourbe (tel. 45-57-11-98). Charming old bistrot specializing in wonderfully aromatic Mediterranean dishes—mostly fish. Closed Sun., Mon., Easter period and Aug. V.

Sixteenth Arrondissement

Faugeron (E), 52 rue de Longchamp (tel. 47-04-24-53). One of the very best restaurants in Paris serving delicious "new" cuisine. Smart and popular, so do reserve. Good wine list. Closed weekends, Aug. and Christmas. Airconditioned.

La Grande Cascade (E), in the Bois de Boulogne (tel. 45-27-33-51). Attractive leafy setting near the famous Longchamp racecourse, with the refreshing sound of the nearby waterfall that gives it its name. Built like a spacious garden pavilion, it seems to belong to a more leisurely era. Classical cuisine, but also a good place for a delicious ice cream after the races or a stroll in the Bois. Popular for society weddings, so excellent for people-watching. Closed from just before Christmas to the end of Jan. AE, DC, V.

Jean-Claude Ferrero (E), 38 rue Vital (tel. 45-04-42-42). In the charming *Hotel Particulier* with tiny garden. Excellent *nouvelle cuisine* and extremely fresh seasonal products. Closed Sat., Sun., Christmas period and last 2 weeks of Aug. AE, DC, V.

Michel Pasquet (E), 59 rue la Fontaine (tel. 42-88-50-01). Chic and tiny, so you must reserve ahead. Stylish cuisine, with some "new" touches. Good value menu. Closed weekends. AE, DC, V.

Pré Catalan (E), rte. de Suresnes, Bois de Boulogne (tel. 45-24-55-58). One of Paris's best and most sought-after restaurants. Very expensive, but very beautiful, especially if it's fine enough to sit out 'neath the spreading chestnut trees. Wonderfully ingenious, mainly "new," cuisine. Closed Sun. evenings, Mon. and most of Feb. AE, DC, V.

Prunier-Traktir (E), 16 av. Victor-Hugo (tel. 45-00-89-12). Long-established seafood restaurant with elegant clientele and '20s decor. Outdoor meals in summer. Closed Sun., Mon., July and Aug. AE, DC, V.

Robuchon (E), 32 rue de Longchamp (tel. 47-27-12-27). Young chef-owner Joël Robuchon is an excellent practitioner of the *nouvelle cuisine* and a worthy successor to the great Jamin. Good value *menus*. Must reserve well ahead. Air conditioned. Closed weekends and July. AE, DC, V.

Au Clocher du Village (M), 8 rue Verderet (tel. 42-88-35-87). Home-style cooking, chic bistrot ambiance. Closed Sat. for lunch, Sun., Aug. V.

Relais d'Auteuil (M), 31 blvd. Murat (tel. 46-51-09-54). Attractive bistrot near the Bois de Boulogne; good traditional cuisine. Closed Sat. for lunch, Sun. AE, DC, V.

Brasserie Stella (I), 133 av. Victor-Hugo (tel. 47-27-60-54). The favorite meeting place for residents of this well-heeled neighborhood. Particularly lively after-theater crowd, but be prepared to be rather cramped. Open to 1.30 A.M. Closed Aug.

Seventeenth Arrondissement

La Coquille (E), 6 rue du Débarcardère (tel. 45-72-10-73). Ultra-traditional cooking, beautifully done, specializing in game in season. Rather elegant. Closed Sun., Mon., Aug. and Christmas. Aug. V.

Le Manoir de Paris (E), 6 rue Pierre-Demours (tel. 45-72-25-25). Run by the same chef-owner as the excellent *Ferme St.-Simon* in the 7th arrondissement. Delicious *nouvelle cuisine*, fashionable clientele. Closed weekends and July. AE, DC, V.

Michel Rostang (E), 20 rue Rennequin (tel. 47-63-40-77). Well-known for *nouvelle cuisine* versions of home-cooked dishes, so must reserve. Airconditioned. Closed Sat. (but open for Sat. lunch May to Sept.), Sun. and Aug. V.

Petrus (E), 12 pl. du Maréchal-Juin (tel. 43-80-15-95). Specializes in *nouvelle* seafood. Twenties decor. Closed Sun., Mon. and mid-Aug. to mid-Sept. AE, DC, MC, V.

Baumann (M), 64 av. des Ternes (tel. 45-74-16-66). A lively crowd patronizes this cheerful restaurant busily eating *choucroute* till 1 A.M. So many different versions you won't know which to choose. Other Alsatian dishes too, plus modish *art nouveau*-style decor. AE, DC, V.

Brasserie Lorraine (M), pl. des Ternes (tel. 42-27-80-04). Long-standing and popular with literary and artistic crowd for its excellent oysters and other shellfish, plus good game in season. Open till 2 A.M. AE, DC, V.

Chez Georges (M), 273 blvd. Pereire (tel. 45-74-31-00). Huge portions of traditional French home-cooking, very popular with the habitués of this distinguished part of Paris. Good for Sunday lunch. Closed Sat. and Aug. AE, DC, V.

La Toque (M), 16 rue de Tocqueville (tel. 42-27-97-75). Tiny but comfortable bistrot serving excellent food (chef worked with Michel Guérard). Good-value *menu*. Closed Sat., Sun., Aug. and Christmas period. V.

La Grosse Tartine (I), 91 blvd. Gouvion-St.-Cyr (tel. 45-74-02-77). Convenient for Porte Maillot hotels and the Bois de Boulogne. Family-type cuisine, with specialties from southwestern France. Good wine list, tables outside in summer. Closed Sun., Mon., Tues. for dinner and Aug. AE, DC, V.

L'Amanguier (I), 43 av. des Ternes (tel. 43-80-19-28). Another version of the good-value restaurant in the 2e. AE, DC, V.

Eighteenth Arrondissement

Beauvilliers (E), 52 rue Lamarck (tel. 42-54-54-42). New chef for this charming, well known restaurant just behind Montmartre. Little terrace for sunny days. Closed Mon. for lunch, Sun. and first 2 weeks in Sept. V.

Au Cadet de Gascogne, L'Auberge du Village (M), 4 pl. du Tertre (tel. 46-06-71-73). Quite elegant and less "villagey" than some Montmartre restaurants, but still open late (2 A.M.) and with live accordion music in the evenings; a few tables outside, if you don't mind being jostled by the crowds in the square. Closed part of Jan. and Feb.

Chez ma Cousine (M), 12 rue Norvins (tel. 46-06-49-35). Small and friendly, with cabaret in the evening. You can also enjoy a pancake here during the afternoon. AE, DC, MC, V.

La Crémaillère 1900 (M), 15 pl. du Tertre (tel. 46-06-58-59). Very pretty *art-nouveau*-style decor, tiny garden, delicious *nouvelle cuisine* (specializing in fish), live pianist in the evening. Open daily, but closed Mon. and Tues. from Nov. to Easter. AE, DC, MC, V.

Da Graziano (M), 83 rue Lepic (tel. 46-06-84-77). Charming little Italian restaurant, overshadowed by the huge arms of the Moulin de la Galette and with an adorable tiny garden. And the food's good too. Open till 12.30. Airconditioned. V.

Marie Louise (M), 52 rue Championnet (tel. 46-06-86-55). Long-standing bistrot, off the beaten track but worth it for good value traditional French cuisine. Closed Sun., Mon., July and Aug. V.

Wepler (M), 14 pl. Clichy (tel. 45-22-53-24). Large, long-standing restaurant which makes a change from the more trendy places in Montmartre. Particularly good for seafood. Open daily to 1.30 A.M. AE, DC, MC, V.

Le Bateau-Lavoir (I), 8 rue Garreau (tel. 46-06-02-00). Little restaurant on the top of Montmartre. Good, hearty simple cooking and very cheap. Closed in June.

La Bonne Table (I), 5 rue Seveste (tel. 46-06-96-40). Authentic *restaurant montmartrois* with good simple menus. Closed Sun.

Chez Toi ou Chez Moi (I), 8 rue du Marche Ordener (tel. 42-29-58-24). Generous and charming cooking—good soups and unusual main courses. You'll feel at home. Must reserve. Open daily.

Au Pichet du Tertre (I), 10 rue Norvins (tel. 46-06-24-19). Good choice of *menus* at reasonable prices. Villagey atmosphere. Open to 11.30 P.M. at weekends. Closed Tues. V.

Le Tournant de la Butte (I), 46 rue Caulaincourt (tel. 46-06-39-86). Very inexpensive fixed-price *menu,* cheerful atmosphere and live music at times. Crowded, even though this isn't the touristy part of Montmartre. Closed Mon. and Sept.

Le Verger-Pereire (I), 275 blvd. Pereire (tel. 45-74-33-32). Incredibly cheap good restaurant in this rather expensive district. Wine in carafe. Open daily to midnight. V.

Nineteenth Arrondissement

The **av. Jean-Jaurès,** close to where the slaughterhouses used to be has several fine restaurants close together and all specialize, of course, in meat. Among them are:

Au Cochon d'Or (E), at no. 192 (tel. 46-07-23-13). Huge portions of traditional French meat dishes and is generally thought to be the best of these restaurants; offal dishes are a specialty. Open all week. AE, DC, MC, V.

Au Boeuf Couronné (M), at no. 188 (tel. 46-07-89-52). Large and cheerful with equally large portions and particularly delicious tripe. Closed Sun. AE, DC, MC, V.

Aux Deux Taureaux (M), at no. 206. Traditional meat and offal dishes. Closed weekends. AE, DC, V.

Ferme de la Villette (M), at no. 184 (tel. 46-07-60-96). Long-established. Serves shellfish as well as meat specialties. Open till midnight. Closed Sun. and Aug. AE, DC, MC, V.

Twentieth Arrondissement

You are really off the beaten track here, but here are two suggestions in case you find yourself stranded in the far east:

Le Relais des Pyrénées (E), 1 rue de Jourdain (tel. 46-36-65-81). Traditional fare from southwestern France, which means *confit d'oie, foie gras,* etc. Closed Sat. and Aug. AE, DC, MC, V.

Le Bistrot du XXe (I), 44 rue du Surmelin (tel. 48-97-20-30). Generous cooking under former *charcuterie* ceiling. A good address in this part of Paris. Closed Sat., Sun., public hols., and Aug. AE, V.

Neuilly

Bourrier (M), 1 pl. Parmentier (tel. 46-24-11-19). Set in a pretty square well away from the traffic at the Porte Maillot. Fine "new" cuisine served by the chefs as there are no waiters. Rather elegant. Closed weekends, but open for Sat. lunch May through Sept., most of Aug., Christmas and New Year. V.

Café de la Jatte (M), 67 blvd. de Levallois (tel. 47-45-04-20). Pleasant lunching or dining on the huge terrace of this new restaurant on the île de la Jatte—trendy, to see and be seen. Serves until midnight. Closed Sat. for lunch. AE, V.

Sébillon-Paris-Bar (M), 20 av. Charles-de-Gaulle, just by Porte Maillot (tel. 46-24-71-31). Long-standing and always busy restaurant. Good traditional cooking. Has been extensively redecorated and is now airconditioned too. Open to 1 A.M. AE, DC, MC, V.

L'Amanguier (I), 12 av. de Madrid (tel. 47-45-79-73). Yet another offshoot of this very popular and good-value group of restaurants. Open till 11.30 daily. AE, DC, V.

La Boutarde (I), 4 rue Boutard (tel. 47-45-34-55). This might look like a modest provincial café, but in fact it has a very unprovincial clientele. Crowded with expense-accounters at lunchtime. Straightforward home-style cooking;

very tasty though portions can be small. You can eat outside in summer. Cheerful waiters. Closed Sat. for lunch and Sun. DC, V.

Drugstore de Neuilly (I), pl. du Marche (tel. 46-37-58-88). Very popular and well-run, with plain but good home-style dishes and a delightful little courtyard garden for summer meals. Open to 1 A.M. Also has takeaway counter.

Boulogne-Billancourt

Au Comte de Gascogne (E), 89 av. Jean-Baptiste-Clément (tel. 46-03-47-27). One of the best restaurants in the Paris area. Specialties from southwestern France and some "new" cuisine. Closed weekends and Aug. AE, DC, V.

Laux à la Bouche (M), 117 av. Jean-Baptiste-Clément (tel. 48-25-43-88). Despite its punning name (the chef-owner is Monsieur Laux), this is a serious little restaurant with carefully cooked traditional French dishes, and particularly fine fish. V.

La Petite Auberge Franc-Comtoise (M), 86 av. Jean-Baptiste-Clément (tel. 46-05-67-19). Typical 19th-century inn decor, with outdoor service in fine weather. Specialties from the Franche-Comté region, of course, plus some *nouvelle cuisine* dishes. Closed Sun. and Aug. AE, DC, V.

Le Poivre Vert (I), 1 pl. Bernard Palissy (tel. 46-03-01-63). High quality cuisine at low prices; the hungry can order *grandes portions*. Terrace. Open daily. V.

 BARS, WINE BARS AND CAFÉS. With the predominance of sidewalk cafés, bars in Paris are less common and less frequented than in many other capitals. However, among the more attractive are those in skyscrapers, where you can enjoy fabulous views.

Wine bars, where you can get a glass of vino and a tasty light meal such as pâté, a plate of cold cuts, or a delicious cheese dish, are becoming a welcome feature of some parts of the city, and are a great boon to visitors—but note that the old-style *bistrot à vin* rarely offers anything much in the way of food, being more a place for hardened local drinkers. The majority of the new-style wine bars close fairly early, so don't rely on them for an evening meal, and many shut all weekend.

People-watching from a sidewalk café is one of the traditional delights savored by generations of visitors to Paris. There are hundreds—maybe thousands —of cafés all over the city, ranging from chic places on the Champs-Elysées or near the Opéra, to intellectual haunts in Saint-Germain-des-Prés or Montparnasse, to neighborhood corner cafés where the locals gather to exchange gossip, play cards, and watch television. The prices vary according to the location, but as no one will stop you lingering over a single cup of coffee or a drink, (except in some student places in the Latin Quarter where you'll be expected to reorder every hour or so), even the more expensive spots won't break the bank. Prices are lower if you stand at the bar than if a waiter or waitress serves you at a table. Don't do as you would in a British pub and pay for your drinks at the bar and then go and sit down—the manager will certainly come over and rebuke you.

Blue Fox, 25 rue Royale, 8e. Wine bar run by Steven Spurrier, who also presides over the *Moulin du Village* and the *Académie du Vin.* Closed Sat. evening and Sun.

Café Costes, 4 rue Berger, 1er. A bar rather than a café, in the Les Halles area. Trendy; designed by Philippe Stark.

Café de la Paix, 12 blvd. des Capucines, 9e, just by the Opéra. Popular with wealthy foreign visitors.

La Calvados, 40 av. Pierre-Ier-de-Serbie, 8e. Bar frequented by Paris's smart set. Drink until the early hours or later—it stays open all night. Good pianist.

Ciel de Paris, on top of the Tour Montparnasse, 14e. Superb views from this bar.

La Closerie des Lilas, 171 blvd. du Montparnasse, 6e. Haunt of writers and painters since the '30s, though some claim it's overrated. Popular for a late-night drink; pianist plays sometimes.

La Coupole, 102 blvd. du Montparnasse, 14e. Café; an old favorite.

Deux Magots, 170 blvd. St.-Germain, 6e. Not the intellectual's mecca it used to be in the heyday of Sartre and Co., but this café is still fairly fashionable and good for people-watching. You even get street entertainment thrown in at times—fire-eaters, acrobats, mimes and the like.

Le Dôme, 108 blvd. du Montparnasse, 14e. Another well-known Montparnasse café, but the new (fake *art nouveau*) décor is a bit overdone.

L'Ecluse, 15 quai des Grands-Augustins, 6e. Once a typical Left Bank cabaret, now a slick wine bar with converted gas lamps, art nouveau posters, and a distinctly upmarket clientele. It's been such a success that it's spawned a mini-chain: on rue Mondétour, 1er; rue du Pont-de-Lodi, 6e; 15 pl. de la Madeleine, 8e; 64 rue François-Ier, 8e; 2 rue du Général-Bertier, Neuilly. All are open to 1.30 A.M. (last orders at 1) and closed Sun. v.

Le Flore, 172 blvd. St.-Germain, 6e. Next door to *Deux Magots,* though it doesn't share the unbeatable corner location. Upstairs a traditional gay meeting place, but the sidewalk tables are for all-comers. Changed hands in the mid-'80s, but the new owners had to sign an undertaking to leave it just as it is!

Fouquet's, 99 av. des Champs-Elysées, 8e, on corner of av. George-V. A place to be seen—very chic and expensive. A good bar as well as a café.

Harry's Bar, 5 rue Daunou, 2e. Dating from 1911, it has never looked back, even though the Hemingway era is well and truly over. Popular with Parisians as well as expatriate and visiting Americans, there are now *Harry's Bars* all over Europe. Open year-round until the wee hours.

Lipp, 151 blvd. St.-Germain, 6e. Officially a brasserie (see *Restaurants*), but has a few tables out front.

Montgolfier, Sofitel-Paris Hotel. An outside elevator whisks you up to this panoramic bar. Even has a swimming pool!

Pacific Palisades, 51 rue Quincampoix, 4e. In the Beaubourg area, a bar frequented by genuine Parisians. Very chic, art deco; good simple meals.

Le Petit Bacchus, 13 rue du Cherche-Midi, 6e. Wine to go as well as to imbibe on the premises. Closes 7.15, also Sun. and Mon.

Petit-Opportun, 15 rue Lavandières-Ste.-Opportune, 1er. Bar in the Châtelet area, above a well-known jazz spot of the same name. Open late.

Plein-Ciel, Concorde-Lafayette Hotel, 17e, at the Porte Maillot. Lovely views from this bar over the Bois de Boulogne.

La Rhumerie, 166 blvd. St.-Germain, 6e. Another favorite St.-Germain café, always crowded. Specializes in a huge range of punches.

Rosebud, 11bis rue Delambre, 14e. Long-established bar in Montparnasse, open daily to around 2 A.M.

Le Rubis, 10 rue du Marché St.-Honoré, 1er. Extensive choice of wines, good lunchtime food. Closed weekends and most of Aug.

Le Sélect, 99 blvd. du Montparnasse, 6e. Café retaining something of the old Montparnasse atmosphere despite the rebuilding that has transformed this area. Open late.

La Tartine, 24 rue de Rivoli, 4e. Typical Parisian spot, with a regular clientele enjoying the good range of wines and the friendly atmosphere. Closes 10 P.M. and all-day Tuesday, lunch on Wed.

Taverne Henri-IV, 13 pl. Pont-Neuf. Pleasant wine bar on edge of pretty square.

CITY TOURS. The *R.A.T.P.* (Paris Transport Authority) Tourist Service, on the pl. de la Madeleine, 8e and at 53 quai des Grands-Augustins, 6e, organizes various guided excursions in and around Paris. Both offices are open daily, including public holidays.

Bus Tours. The starting point for bus tours of the city is the pl. des Pyramides, 1er, at the Palais-Royal end of the Tuileries Gardens. Tours generally are in double-deckers, either accompanied by a guide or with a taped commentary (many in English), and last around three hours. "Paris-by-Night" tours usually finish up at the Lido on the Champs-Elysées for the floor show.

Contact *American Express,* 11 rue Scribe, 9e (tel. 42-66-09-99); *Cityrama,* 4 pl. des Pyramides, 1er (tel. 42-60-30-14); or *Paris Vision,* 214 rue de Rivoli, 1er (tel. 42-60-30-01), for details.

Limo Tours. *Hans Forster's Limousine Guide Service,* 202 rue de Rivoli, 1er (tel. 42-96-40-02) for answering machine with message in English), have guided limo-tours carrying up to seven passengers, and exploring either central Paris or the surrounding area for a minimum of three hours. Around $25–30 an hour all told—no additional mileage charge. *Must reserve.*

Walking Tours. There is a wealth of guided tours to such places as the Marais, the Ile St.-Louis, and St.-Germain-des-Prés. Generally, these concentrate on a particular topic—for example, private walled gardens in St.-Germain, synagogues or restored mansions in the Marais—or a specific historic building, such as the Hôtel de Lauzun on the Ile St.-Louis. The great majority of tours are accompanied by French-speaking guides, for they are popular with French visitors as well as foreign tourists, but as such a tour can be the only way to get to see certain private buildings and gardens, you may nevertheless think it worth while. Tours usually start at 2 P.M. and last about two hours. Charges vary, but are in the region of 20–35 frs. per person.

Details are given in *Pariscope* and *L'Officiel des Spectacles* or in dailies such as *Le Figaro* and *Le Monde.* Tours are often restricted to about 30 people, so it is a good idea to turn up early at the appointed rendezvous. You can sometimes reserve ahead for tours organized by the *Caisse Nationale des Monuments Historiques* (Bureau des Visites-Conférences, Hôtel de Sully, 62 rue St.-Antoine, 4e, tel. 42-74-22-22), which publishes a small booklet every two months listing all tours planned for the next two months. For visits to some private mansions you may be asked to show identification, so be sure to have your passport on you.

River Tours. *Bateaux Mouches* (tel. 42-25-96-10) start from the Right Bank (i.e. north) end of the Pont de l'Alma, 8e; *Bateaux Parisiens-Tour Eiffel* (tel. 45-51-46-45) from the Port-La Bourdonnais, 7e, and also from Quai Montebello near Notre-Dame. *Vedettes Paris Ile-de-France* (tel. 47-05-71-29) from the Port de Suffren, 7e; and *Vedettes du Pont Neuf* (tel. 46-33-93-38) from the Square du Vert Galant, in the middle of the Pont-Neuf. Departures daily, generally every half-hour between 9.30 or 10 and 5 or 6. Price 25–30 frs. Special lunch and dinner cruises, (casual dress should be avoided), about 250 frs. and 400–450 frs. respectively, including meal.

Tours in flat-bottomed barges along the Canal St.-Martin to the Villette in northeastern Paris are available from *Canauxrama* (tel. 46-24-86-16). Departures from either 5bis quai de la Loire (métro: Jaurès) or Port de l'Arsenal (métro: Bastille). Times vary depending on river traffic: best to check beforehand. Prices 55–70 frs. Day cruises on the Canal de l'Ourcq depart from Bassin de la Villette, 19e, at 8.45 (return in special bus). 120 frs. *Quiztour,* 19 rue des Athènes (tel. 48-74-75-30), runs the famous "Patache Eautobus" that plies Paris's St.-Martin Canal. Check schedules and prices locally.

Air Tours. *Hélicap* (tel. 45-57-75-51) offer helicopter trips over Paris, or the Défense on the western edge of the city, or Versailles; or you can have a long panoramic flight. From 270 frs. for Versailles, to 1,100 for the panoramic (discounts for groups of ten or more). *Reservations essential. Chainair* (tel. 43-59-20-20) run tours over Paris, and will also take you down to the Loire Valley to fly over the fabulous châteaux or to Mont St.-Michel.

 MUSEUMS AND GALLERIES. Museums in Paris split into three basic groups: those belonging to the City of Paris—indicated by the initials CP in our lists—national or state-owned—shown by the initial N—and private collections. Opening times change frequently, so always double check.

City of Paris museums close Monday, but otherwise open 10 to 5.40. Children under 7 and anyone over 65 enter free at any time. Sundays it's gratis for one and all to permanent collections—though you may still have to pay to visit special temporary exhibits.

State-owned museums close Tuesday (except for the Musée d'Orsay, Monday). Otherwise, opening times vary considerably, some places still closing over lunch. There's no admission charge for under-18s, or for professional artists, journalists, or teachers with documentation to prove their status. Half-price is the general rule on Sundays for all-comers, and on other days for 18–25s, over-65s, and those attending (and therefore paying for) lecture tours.

Private museums, too, have widely differing opening hours. In the case of a special exhibit, times may be quite different from those applying to the main collection. Check in *Pariscope* or *L'Officiel des Spectacles*. Those eligible for free or reduced admission to State-owned museums can sometimes obtain concessions in private establishments—it is worth a polite enquiry. Proffering a student card may also result in a reduced charge.

Admission rates vary enormously, but the *Direction des Musées de France*, Palais du Louvre, Cour Visconti, 34 quai du Louvre, 75001, publishes a brochure every two months with details of all Paris museums, including admission charges. Both *Pariscope* and *L'Officiel des Spectacles* publish lists of museums open on public holidays. Beware particularly of May, which has a public holiday every week most years: May 1, May 8, Ascension Day and Whit Monday.

Commercial galleries may well not open until 10 A.M., but there's a good chance they'll be open till 7 P.M., though smaller ones may close between around 12.30 and 2. They are normally closed Sunday and public holidays; some also close Monday mornings, or even all day Monday. Usually there's no admission charge, as most galleries aim to sell what they have on display. The best hunting ground is in the Saint-Germain-des-Prés area, particularly the little streets between the boulevard and the Seine.

Archives Nationales (Museum of the History of France), Hôtel Soubise, 60 rue des Francs-Bourgeois, 3e (tel. 42-77-11-30). Open 2–5; closed Tues. and public hols. Half-price on Sun.; no admission charge for students and teachers. *Métro:* Hôtel-de-Ville, Rambuteau.

Bibliothèque Forney, Hôtel des Archevêques de Sens, 1 rue du Figuier, 4e (tel. 42-78-14-60). Open Tues. to Sat., 1.30–8. No admission charge. *Métro:* Pont-Maries, St.-Paul.

Bibliothèque Nationale, 58 rue de Richelieu, 2e (tel. 47-03-81-26). Open daily except public holidays, 12–6. *Métro:* Bourse, Pyramides, 4-Septembre.

Centre National d'Art et de Culture Georges Pompidou, Plateau Beaubourg, 4e (tel. 42-77-12-33). Open 12–10 weekdays except Tues.; weekends and public hols., 10–10. No admission charge to the Center itself, but you must pay to visit the National Museum of Modern Art (except Sun.) and special exhibits. Special one-day pass *(laissez-passer un jour)* costs around 25 frs. Guided tours at 3.30 on weekdays, 11 on weekends. Frequent guided tours of individual exhibits. *Métro:* Châtelet, Hôtel-de-Ville, Rambuteau.

Crypte du Parvis de Notre-Dame, pl. du Parvis Notre-Dame, 4e (tel. 43-29-83-51). Open daily 10–5, 5.30 in summer. Half-price Sun. and public holidays. *Métro:* Cité.

Ecole Nationale Supérieure des Beaux-Arts, 17 quai Malaquais, 6e (tel. 42-60-34-57). Special exhibits only; open daily except Tues., 1–7. *Métro:* St.-Germain-des-Prés.

Galeries Nationales du Luxembourg, 19 rue de Vaugirard, 6e (tel. 42-34-25-95). Open daily exc. Mon., 11–6; Thurs. 11–10. Reduced admission charge on Sat. *Métro:* St.-Sulpice. *RER:* Luxembourg.

Grand Palais, av. du Général-Eisenhower, 8e (tel. 42-89-54-10). N. Open Mon., and Thurs. to Sun., 10–8; Wed. 10–10; closed Tues. Reduced admission charge on Sat. Special exhibits only, no permanent collection. *Métro:* Champs-Elysées-Clemenceau.

Historial de Montmartre (Historical Waxworks), rue Poulbot, 18e (tel. 46-06-78-92). Open, Easter to Nov. 12, daily 10.30–12.30, 2.30–5.30; same times on Wed., Sat., Sun. and public holidays only the rest of the year. *Métro:* Abbesses.

Hôtel de Ville, pl. Hôtel de Ville, 4e (entrance may be in the rue de Rivoli). Special exhibits generally open 10–6 or 6.30; closed Tues. *Métro:* Hôtel de Ville.

Invalides, Esplanade des Invalides, 7e. *Musée de l'Armée* (tel. 45-55-92-30). Open daily 10–5; 10–6 April through Sept. Half-price for foreign students. Film on the two World Wars shown between 2 and 5. *Musée des Plans-Reliefs* (tel. 47-05-11-07). Open daily 10–12.30, 2–5.30. No extra admission charge if you have a ticket for the Army Museum. *Son et Lumière* (sound-and-light show), "Ombres de Gloire" ("Shadows of Glory") at 10.30 P.M. in French and 11 P.M. in English; additional show in English at 9.30 P.M. mid-Aug. through April only. *Métro:* Latour-Maubourg, Varenne.

Jeu de Paume, pl. de la Concorde, 1er (tel. 42-60-12-07 or 42-96-42-73). N. Currently closed for renovations. *Métro:* Concorde.

Note: All the Impressionists and Post-Impressionists are now in the new Musée d'Orsay (see below).

Maison de Balzac, 47 rue Raynouard, 16e (tel. 42-24-56-38). CP. Open 10–5.40; closed Mon. No admission charge on Sun. (except for temporary exhibits). *Métro:* La Muette, Passy.

Maison de Victor Hugo, 6 pl. des Vosges, 4e (tel. 42-72-16-65). CP. Open 10–5.40; closed Mon. No admission charge on Sun. *Métro:* Bastille, St.-Paul.

Marais Cultural Center, 28 rue des Francs-Bourgeois, 3e (tel. 42-72-73-52). Special exhibits only, no permanent collection. Opening hours generally 10–7 daily, except Tues., but check locally. *Métro:* St.-Paul.

Monnaie de Paris (The Mint), 11 quai de Conti, 6e (tel. 43-29-12-48). Open 11–5, except Sun. No admission charge. Workshops can be visited Mon. and Wed. at 2.15. Special exhibits generally open same times. *Métro and RER:* St.-Michel.

Musée Bricard de la Serrure (Lock Museum), 1 rue de la Perle, 3e (tel. 42-77-79-62). Open 10–12, 2–5; closed Sun., Mon., and public holidays. *Métro:* St.-Paul.

Musée Carnavalet (History of Paris Museum), 23 rue de Sévigné, 3e (tel. 42-72-21-13). CP. Open Tues. to Sun., 10–5.40. Prints, drawings and photographs section open only Mon. to Fri., 2–7, Sat. 10–12. *Métro:* Chemin Vert, St.-Paul.

Musée Cernuschi, 7 av. Velasquez, 8e (tel. 45-63-50-75). Open usually 10–5.40; closed Mon. and public holidays. Opening times sometimes change when temporary exhibits are on, so check locally. Half-price for students. No admission charge for permanent collections on Sun. *Métro:* Monceau, Villiers.

Musée Cognac-Jay, 25 blvd. des Capucines, 2e (tel. 42-61-94-54). Open Tues. to Sun., 10–5.40. No admission charge on Sun. *Métro:* Opéra.

Musée d'Art et d'Essai (Palais de Tokyo), 13 av. du Président-Wilson, 16e (tel. 47-23-36-53). N. Open 9.45–5.15; closed Tues. Some rooms close between 12 and 2. Half-price on Sun. *Métro:* Alma-Marceau, Iéna.

Musée d'Art Juif (Museum of Jewish Art), 42 rue des Saules, 18e (tel. 42-57-84-15). Open 3–6; closed Fri. and Sat. *Métro:* Lamarck-Caulaincourt.

Musée d'Art Moderne de la Ville de Paris, 11 av. du Président-Wilson, 16e (tel. 47-23-61-27). Open Tues., and Thurs. to Sun., 10–5.0; Weds. 10–8.30; closed Mon. No admission charge on Sun. *Métro:* Alma-Marceau, Iéna.

Musée de Cluny (Musée National des Thermes), 6 pl. Paul-Painlevé, 5e (tel. 43-25-62-00). Open daily except Tues. and public hols., 9.45–12.30, 2–5.15 (no admittance after 11.45 and 4.30). Half-price on Sun. *Métro:* Odéon, St.-Michel. *RER:* Pont-St. Michel.

Musée de la Chasse et de la Nature (Hunting Museum), Hôtel Guénégaud des Brosses, 60 rue des Archives, 3e (tel. 42-72-86-43). Open 10–5.30; closed Tues and public holidays. Half-price for children under 10. *Métro:* Rambuteau.

Musée Delacroix, 6 pl. de Furstemberg, 6e (tel. 43-54-04-87). N. Open 9.45–5.15; closed Tues. Half-price admission on Sun. *Métro:* St.-Germain-des-Prés.

Musée de la Légion d'Honneur et des Ordres de Chevalerie, 2 rue de Bellechasse, 7e (tel. 45-55-95-16). Open daily except Mon., 2–5. No admission charge on Sun. *Métro:* Solférino. *RER:* Quai d'Orsay.

Musée de la Marine, Palais de Chaillot, pl. du Trocadéro, 16e (tel. 45-53-31-70). Open 10–6; closed Tues. and public holidays. Half-price for children under 12. *Métro:* Trocadéro.

Musée de la Poste, 34 blvd. de Vaugirard, 15e (tel. 43-20-15-30). Open 10–5; closed Sun. and public holidays. No admission charge for under-18s; half-price for those between 18 and 25 and over-65s. *Métro:* Falguière, Montparnasse-Bienvenue, Pasteur.

Musée de l'Holographie (Holography Museum), Grand Balcon, Forum des Halles, 3e (tel. 42-96-96-83). Open Tues. to Sat., 10.30–7; Sun. and public holidays, 1–7. *Métro and RER:* Châtelet.

Musée de l'Homme, Palais de Chaillot, pl. du Trocadéro, 16e (tel. 45-53-70-60). Open daily 9.45–5.15; closed Tues. Films shown at 3 daily, except Tues. and Sun. (no extra charge). *Métro:* Trocadéro.

Musée de l'Opéra, pl. de l'Opéra, 9e (tel. 42-66-50-22). Open daily 10–5; closed Sun., public holidays, and the two weeks before Easter. *Métro:* Opéra.

Musée de Montmartre, 12 rue Cortot, 18e (tel. 46-06-61-11). Open Tues. to Sat., 2.30–5.30; Sun. 11–5.30; closed Mon. Half-price admission for students and over-60s. *Métro:* Anvers, Lamarck-Caulaincourt.

Musée des Arts-Décoratifs, 107 rue de Rivoli, 1er (tel. 42-60-32-14). Has been extensively renovated and modernized, offering excellent presentation of exhibits. Open Wed. to Sat. 12.30–6.30; Sun. 11–6; closed Mon. and Tues. Reductions for those below 25 and over 65. *Métro:* Palais-Royal, Tuileries.

Musée des Arts de la Mode, 109–11 rue de Rivoli, 1 er (tel. 42-60-32-14). Open same times as Arts Decoratifs (see above).

Musée des Arts et Traditions Populaires, 6 av. du Mahatma-Gandi, 16e (tel. 47-47-69-80). N. Open daily 10–5.15; closed Tues. Half-price on Sun. *Métro:* Les Sablons.

Musée des Monuments Français, Palais de Chaillot, pl. du Trocadéro, 16e (tel. 47-27-35-74). Open daily 9.45–12.30, 2–5.15; closed Tues. Half-price on Sun. *Métro:* Trocadéro.

Musée d'Orsay, 1 rue de Bellechasse, 7e (tel. 45-44-41-85). Main entrance opposite *Legion d'Honneur* museum. Closed Mon. *Métro:* Solférino. *RER:* Quai d'Orsay.

Musée du Cinéma, Palais de Chaillot, pl. du Trocadéro, (tel. 45-53-21-86). Open daily except Tues. and public hols. Guided tours only at 10, 11, 2, 3 and 4. *Métro:* Trocadéro.

Musée du Louvre, Palais du Louvre, 1er (tel. 42-60-39-26). Open 9.45–6.30; closed Tues. Half-price on Sun.

Main entrance via the ground floor in the Egyptian Antiquities section. Special exhibits in the Pavillon de Flore open 9.45–5 daily except Tues. Entrance hall houses an information bureau, an exchange counter, art bookshop and counters selling postcards and reproductions.

Cassette guides in French or English are available for hire with players (deposit payable); also special lecture tours on specific themes (check program locally). *Métro:* Louvre, Palais-Royal.

Musée Grévin (Waxworks Museum), 10 blvd. Montmartre, 9e (tel. 47-70-85-05). Open daily 1–7 (no admittance after 6). *Métro:* Montmartre. Also on Grand Balcon, Forum des Halles, 3e (tel. 42-61-28-50). 10.30–7.30 weekdays; 1–8 Sun. and public hols. "Sound and Light" show illustrating turn-of-the-century Paris included in admission charge. *Métro and RER:* Châtelet.

Musée Guimet, 6 pl. d'Iéna, 16e (tel. 47-23-61-65). N. Open 9.45–12, 1.30–5.15; closed Tues. Half-price on Sun. *Métro:* Alma-Marceau, Iéna.

Musée Gustave Moreau, 14 rue de la Rochefoucauld, 9e (tel. 48-74-38-50). N. Open 10–12.45, 2–5.15; closed Tues. Half-price for students and on Sun. *Métro:* Trinité.

Musée Jacquemart-André, 158 blvd. Haussmann, 8e (tel. 45-62-39-94). Open 1.30–5.30; closed Mon. and Tues. *Métro:* Miromesnil, St.-Philippe-du-Roule.

Musée Marmottan, 2 rue Louis-Boilly, 16e (tel. 42-24-07-02). Open daily 10–5.30; closed Mon. Half-price admission for students. *Métro:* La Muette.

Musée National des Arts Africains et Océaniens (Museum of African and Australasian Art), 293 av. Daumesnil, 12e (tel. 43-43-14-54). Open daily 10–12, 1.30–5.15; closed Tues. Half-price on Sun. *Métro:* Porte Dorée.

Musée Nissim-de-Camondo, 63 rue de Monceau, 8e (tel. 45-63-26-32). Open 10–12, 2–5; closed Mon., Tues., and public holidays. Half-price admission for students and over 65s. *Métro:* Villiers.

Musée Notre-Dame de Paris, 10 rue du Cloître Notre-Dame, 4e (tel. 43-25-42-92). Open Wed., Sat., and Sun., 2.30–6. *Métro:* Cité.

Musée Ossip Zadkine, 100bis rue d'Assas, 6e (tel. 43-26-91-90). CP. Open daily 10–5.40; closed Mon. *Métro:* Notre-Dame-des-Champs, Port-Royal, Vavin.

Musée Picasso, Hôtel Salé, 5 rue de Thorigny, 3e (tel. 42-71-25-21). Open daily 10–5.15, Wed. 10–10, closed Tues. *Métro:* Chemin Vert.

Musée Rodin, 77 rue de Varenne, 7e (tel. 47-05-01-34). N. Open daily 10–4.30 (5.45 in summer); closed Tues. Half-price on Sun. *Métro:* Varenne.

Musée National d'Histoire Naturelle, 57 rue Cuvier, 5e (tel. 43-36-54-26). Open daily except Tues. and public hols. Anatomy and Mineralogy departments, 1.30–4.50; 10–4.50 on Sun. Entomology department 2–5. Temporary exhibits 10–5.30. Menagerie open daily 9–5 (9–7 in summer). *Métro:* Censier, Gare d'Austerlitz, Jussieu, Monge.

Orangerie des Tuileries, pl. de la Concorde, 1er (tel. 42-97-48-16). Open daily 9.45–5.15; closed Tues. Half-price on Sun. *Note:* Monet's *Waterlilies* cannot be visited between 12 and 2. *Métro:* Concorde.

Palais de la Découverte, av. Franklin-Roosevelt, 8e (tel. 43-59-16-65). Open daily 10–6; closed Mon. Extra charge for Planetarium. Half-price for under-18s, and over-65s. *Métro:* Champs-Elysées-Clemenceau, Franklin-Roosevelt.

Petit Palais, av. Winston-Churchill, 8e (tel. 42-65-12-73). CP. Open daily 10–5.40; closed Mon. No admission charge on Sun. *Métro:* Champs-Elysées-Clemenceau.

Swedish Cultural Center, 11 rue Payenne, 3e (tel. 42-71-82-20). Special exhibits only, no permanent collection. Opening hours generally 12–6 weekdays; 2–6 weekends; but check locally. No admission charge. *Métro:* St.-Paul.

Swiss Cultural Center, 36 rue des Francs-Bourgeois, 3e (tel. 42-71-44-50). Open Tues.–Sat. 2–7; Sun. 2–5; closed Mon. and public hols. No admission charge.

 HISTORIC BUILDINGS AND SIGHTS. With its crucial role throughout much of European history, the city of Paris is predictably chock-full of buildings and other sights of historic interest. Many of the former have been turned into museums, and appear by our *Museums* section. The initials CP indicate that the property is owned by the City of Paris.

American Cemetery, 190 blvd. Washington, Suresnes, just outside Paris. Go to the *RER* station at La Défense then take the 360 bus.

Arc de Triomphe, pl. Charles-de-Gaulle-Etoile, 8e (tel. 43-80-31-31). Open daily 10–5 or 5.30. Small extra charge to use the elevator and for the audio-visual presentation of major events in the Arch's history. Half-price on Sun.; closed most public holidays. *Métro:* Charles-de-Gaulle-Etoile.

Arènes de Lutèce (Lutetia Arena), rue des Arènes, 5e. Permanently open. *Métro:* Jussieu.

Bagatelle, route de Sèvres-à-Neuilly. Château open for special exhibits only, usually May to Oct. Check locally. Gardens open on a seasonal basis, with admission charge depending on the flower displays currently available. *Métro:* Les Sablons, Pont de Neuilly, then a 10–15 minute walk; or Porte Maillot, then bus 244.

Bourse, rue Vivienne, 2e (tel. 42-33-99-83). Guided tours every half-hour, 11–1, exc. Sat., Sun., and public holidays. Also public gallery. *Métro:* Bourse.

Catacombs, pl. Denfert-Rochereau, 14e (tel. 43-22-47-63). CP. Open Tues. to Fri., 2–4; weekends 9–11 and 2–4; closed Mon. and public hols. Guided tours Wed. at 2.45. *Bring a flashlight. Métro and RER:* Denfert-Rochereau.

Château de Vincennes, av. de Paris, Vincennes (tel. 43-28-15-48). Guided tours 10–5.30 in summer; 10–5 in winter. *Métro:* Château de Vincennes.

Conciergerie, 1 quai de l'Horloge, 4e (tel. 42-74-22-22). Open daily 10–5; 10–6 in summer. Half-price on Sun. and public holidays. *Métro:* Châtelet, Cité.

Eiffel Tower, Champ-de-Mars, 7e (tel. 45-55-91-11). 1st and 2nd floors open daily 10 A.M. to 11 P.M. (9.30–midnight in high summer); 3rd floor daily 10 A.M. to 10.30 P.M. (9.30–11.30 in high summer). Audio-visual show illustrating the history of the Tower is given on 1st floor, open daily 10.30 A.M. to 11 P.M.

(9.30–midnight in high summer). Post office open 10–7 only. *Métro:* Bir-Hakeim. *RER:* Champ-de-Mars.

Hôtel de Béthune-Sully, 62 rue St.-Antoine, 4e (tel. 48-87-24-14). Open Mon. to Fri. 10–12, 2–5. *Métro:* St.-Paul.

Hôtel de Lauzun, 17 quai d'Anjou, 4e. CP. Guided tours only, generally on Tues. at 3. Check dates with the *Caisse Nationale des Monuments Historiques,* 62 rue St.-Antoine, 4e (tel. 48-87-24-14), or look at lists in the *Caisse's* bimonthly bulletin or one of the weekly "What's On In Paris" publications. Get there early as tours are restricted to 30 people. *Métro:* Pont-Marie.

Madeleine, pl. de la Madeleine, 8e. *Métro:* Madeleine.

Mémorial de la Déportation, sq. de l'Ile de France, at the tip of the island. Permanently open. *Métro:* Cité.

Montmartre Cemetery, av. Rachel, 18e. Open daily 7.30–4.30 (7.30–6 in summer). *Métro:* Blanche, pl. de Clichy.

Montparnasse Cemetery, 3 blvd. Edgar-Quinet, 14e. *Métro:* Edgar Quinet.

Notre-Dame, pl. du Parvis de Notre-Dame, 4e (tel. 43-54-22-63). Cathedral open daily but visits not allowed during masses. Organ recitals Sun. at 5 (free). You can climb up the towers daily 10–4.30 or 5.30. Half-price on Sun. and public holidays. *Métro:* Cité.

Observatoire, rue du Faubourg-St.-Jacques, 14e (tel. 43-20-12-10). Guided tours on 1st Sat. of the month at 2.30, or on application. *Métro:* Denfert Rochereau. *RER:* Port Royal.

Panthéon, pl. du Panthéon, 5e (tel. 43-54-34-51). Open daily 10–5 (10–6.30 June through Sept.). Half-price on Sun. and public holidays. *RER:* Luxembourg.

Père-Lachaise Cemetery, blvd. de Menilmontant, 20e. Open Mon. to Sat., 7.30–6, 16 Mar. to 5 Nov.; 8.30–5.30, 6 Nov. to 15 Mar.; Sun. 9.–5.30 (winter), 9–6 (summer). *Métro:* Père-Lachaise, Philippe-Auguste.

Sainte-Chapelle, blvd. du Palais, 4e (tel. 43-54-30-09). Open daily 10–5. Half-price on Sun. and public holidays. *Métro:* Cité.

Tour Montparnasse, pl. R. Dautry, 15e (tel. 45-38-52-56). Open daily, 9.30 A.M.–11.30 P.M. Apr. to Sept., 10–10 Oct. to Mar. *Métro:* Montparnasse-Bienvenue.

 PARKS AND GARDENS. The parks and gardens of Paris are both varied and beautiful—whether they be of the large, rambling, wooded variety, or the formally laid-out open spaces in the center of the city. Those that are enclosed usually shut at dusk; however, the Bois de Boulogne and Bois de Vincennes are always open, though they should be avoided at night, particularly if you are alone.

Bois de Boulogne, on western edge of city. Includes seven lakes, the Grande Cascade (waterfall), the Longchamp and Auteuil racetracks, the Roland-Garros tennis stadium, a polo field, a children's zoo and amusement park (the Jardin d'Acclimatation—see below), camping grounds, the Bagatelle Park, which exhibits spring flowers, roses (June, July) and water lilies, and a Shakespeare Garden, where openair theater is staged in summer and fall. *Métro:* Les Sablons, Porte Dauphine, Port d'Auteuil.

Bois de Vincennes, on southeastern edge of city. Includes Paris' principal zoo, a racetrack, three lakes, two museums. *Métro:* Porte de Charenton, Porte Dorée.

Jardin d'Acclimatation, Porte des Sablons, 16e (tel. 46-24-10-80). Open daily 9–5.30. Activities available Wed., Sat., Sun., only. *Métro:* Les Sablons.

Jardin des Plantes, on the Left Bank, near Austerlitz rail station. Includes botanical gardens, a small zoo, an Alpine garden, greenhouses, and the Natural History Museum. Each section is open at various times; check locally. *Métro:* Gare d'Austerlitz.

Jardin des Tuileries, on east of pl. de la Concorde, 1er. *Métro:* Tuileries.

Jardin du Musée Rodin, rue de Varenne, 7e. Open 10–5.45 (4.30 in winter, closed Tues. *Métro:* Varenne.

Luxembourg Garden, on the Left Bank, off blvd. St.-Michel. Puppet shows, generally around 3 P.M., Wed., Sat., Sun., in term time, daily in school holidays. *Métro:* Luxembourg.

Moorish Gardens, in Paris Mosque, 1 pl. du Puits de l'Ermité, 5e. Open daily 2–5; closed Fri. *Métro:* Monge.

Parc des Buttes-Chaumont, 9e. *Métro:* Buttes-Chaumont.

Parc Floral, Château de Vincennes, av. de Paris, Vincennes (tel. 43-43-92-95). Open Jun. to Sept., 9.30–8; other months it closes roughly at dusk: Apr. and May, 7; Mar. and Oct., 6; Nov. and Dec., 5.30; Jan. and Feb., 5. *Métro:* Château de Vincennes.

Parc Monceau, off blvd. de Courcelles, 8e. *Métro:* Monceau.

Parc Montsouris, blvd. Jourdan, 14e. *Métro:* Porte d'Orléans or *RER* Cité Universitaire.

 NIGHTLIFE. The nightlife in Paris is rightly world-renowned. Other things may change, but this most vivacious of cities can still be relied upon for an exciting—though not inexpensive—evening out. Whether it's a traditional show, complete with *Les Girls,* or for the very latest in disco pyrotechnics, you will not be disappointed.

Shows. Dinner plus a floor show is one of the traditional ways of spending a night on the town in Paris. It doesn't come cheap—you'll usually find you're expected to drink champagne, though this doesn't seem to put people off. You'd do best to reserve several days ahead to make sure of getting a good table, and don't be surprised if your fellow guests are mostly other tourists.

Alcazar de Paris, 62 rue Mazarine, 6e (tel. 43-29-25-46). Dinner at 8, show around 9.30.

La Belle Epoque, 36 rue des Petits-Champs, 2e (tel. 45-62-05-67). Dinner and dancing at 9, show at 10.30.

Cabaret des Champs-Elysées, 78 av. des Champs-Elysées, 8e (tel. 43-59-09-99). Dinner and dancing at 8, show at 10, with extra show at 12.30 on Fri. and Sat. Closed Sun.

Le Don Camilo, 10 rue des Sts.-Pères, 6e (tel. 42-60-20-31). Dinner and show from around 8.30. Prices more reasonable than most.

L'Eléphant Bleu, 49 rue de Ponthieu, 8e (43-59-58-64). Dinner and dancing at 9, show around 10.30.

Folies-Bergère, 32 rue Richer, 9e (tel. 32-46-77-11). Show at around 8.45.

Chez Hippolyte, 23 av. du Maine, 6e (tel. 45-44-64-13).

Lido, 116 av. des Champs-Elysées, 8e (tel. 45-63-11-61). Dinner and dancing at 8, shows at around 10.15 and 12.30.

Moulin Rouge, pl. Blanche, 9e (tel. 46-06-00-19). Dinner and dancing at 8, shows at around 10 and midnight.

Le Paradis Latin, 28 rue du Cardinal-Lemoine, 5e (tel. 43-25-28-28). Dinner and show at about 8, "Champagne revue" at about 10.30.

Raspoutine, 58 rue Bassano, 8e (tel. 47-20-04-31). Dinner and show from about 9; stays open until dawn.

Les Girls. A lot of the shows in this category that were once merely titillating are frankly pornographic nowadays, but these two strip shows have proved their worth and can be safely recommended:

Crazy Horse Saloon, 12 av. George-V, 8e (tel. 47-23-32-32). Two slick shows at around 9.25 and 11.45, Sun. to Thurs., and three on Fri. and Sat.—at 8.20, 10.35 and 12.50. Airconditioned.

Le Milliardaire, 68 rue Pierre-Charron, 8e (tel. 42-25-25-17). Shows at around 10.30 and 12.30; "night show" at 2 A.M.

Private Clubs. These are both very expensive and notoriously hard to get in to. The best entrée is, inevitably, knowing the right people. Failing that, do your best to look interesting yet also respectable, and see how you do.

L'Apocalypse, 40 rue du Colisée, 8e (tel. 42-25-11-68).

L'Atmosphere, 45 rue François-Ier, 8e (tel. 47-20-49-37).
Castel's, 15 rue Princesse, 6e (tel. 43-26-90-22).
Elysées-Matignon, 2 av. Matignon, 8e (tel. 42-25-73-13).
Le Garage, 41 rue Washington, 8e (tel. 42-25-53-20).
Régine's, 49 rue de Ponthieu, 8e (tel. 43-59-21-60).

Just A Fun Evening Out. If you don't feel the urge to rub shoulders with the ultra-fashionable set, and don't want to spend a fortune on a slick show either, but just want a pleasant evening out, here are some places that might fit the bill. Many close on Sundays, but closing days change frequently, so check in *Pariscope* or *L'Officiel des Spectacles* when you are in Paris.
La Canne à Sucre, 4 rue Ste.-Beuve, 6e (tel. 42-22-23-25).
Le Caveau de la Bolée, 25 rue de l'Hirondelle, 6e (tel. 46-33-33-64).
Le Caveau des Oubliettes, 1 rue St.-Julien-le-Pauvre, 5e.
Chapelle des Lombards, 19 rue de Lappe, 11e (tel. 43-57-24-24).
Chez ma Cousine, 12 rue Norvins, 18e. (tel. 46-06-49-35). (See also "Restaurants" section.)
Club des Poètes, 30 rue de Bourgogne, 7e (tel. 47-05-06-03). Two shows nightly, except Sun.
Félix, 23 rue Mouffetard, 5e (tel. 47-07-68-78).
Le Lapin Agile, 22 rue des Saules, 18e (tel. 46-06-85-87).
La Rôtisserie de l'Abbaye, 22 rue Jacob, 6e (tel. 45-62-68-04). Closed Aug.
Villa d'Este, 4 rue Arsène-Houssaye, 8e (tel. 43-59-78-44). Closed Aug.

Jazz Clubs. Paris is one of the great jazz centers of the world—whether it be the stolidly traditional form, classic bebop, jazz-rock, or, increasingly, South American and African offshoots. For exact details of who's playing when, and where, see either of the excellent specialist magazines, *Jazz Hot* or *Jazz Magazine,* or listen to the jazz programs on *France Musique.* The clubs come and go, or change their identity, and remember that nothing gets going before 10 or 11 at night. Credit cards are almost never accepted, and though prices are generally reasonable, they do vary depending on the attraction.
Le Caméléon, 57 rue St.-André-des-Arts, 5e (tel. 43-26-64-40). Inexpensive. Record bar and live music in cellar.
Le Caveau de la Huchette, 5 rue de la Huchette, 5e (tel. 43-26-65-05). Live music in cellar. Open late Fri. and Sat. Entrance 40–50 frs.
Le Montana, 28 rue St.-Benoît, 6e (tel. 45-48-62-15). Live piano sometimes in the bar.
New Morning, 7–9 rue des Petites Ecuries, 10e (tel. 45-23-51-41). The best in Paris. Entrance 80–100 frs. (including reduction on first drink).
Le Petit Journal, 71 blvd. St.-Michel, 5e (tel. 43-26-28-59). Closed Sun. and Aug. Entrance and first drink 60–65 frs, second drink 35–40 frs.
Le Petit Opportun, 15 rue des Lavandières-Ste.-Opportune, 1e (tel. 42-36-01-36). Record bar and live music in basement. Entrance and first drink, up to 100 frs.
Slow Club, 130 rue de Rivoli, 1e (tel. 42-33-84-30). Open late at weekends. Entrance 45–55 frs.
Le Sunset, 60 rue des Lombards, 1e (tel. 42-61-46-60). Live music in cellar. Open very late. Entrance and first drink, about 70 frs., second drink 40–50 frs.

Rock. You can get to sample the best of what the capital has to offer at the following. Entrance, including the first drink, will be in the region of 70–100 frs.—around 35–45 frs. for subsequent libations. Most don't get in the groove until 11.30 or midnight, but they carry on till about dawn. Prices often rise on weekends, when the crowds flock in.
Les Bains, 7 rue du Bourg-l'Abbé, 3e (tel. 48-87-01-80). Live rock Wed. nights.
Bus Palladium, 6 rue Fontaine, 9e (tel. 48-74-54-99). Mostly live rock, some discs.
Gibus, 18 rue fbg. du Temple, 10e (tel. 47-00-78-88). *The* place to rock.

Le Palace, 1 Cité Bergère, 9e (tel. 42-46-10-87). Also disco—check for when there's live rock.

Rose Bonbon, 34 rue de la Roquette, 11e (tel. 48-06-69-58). Live rock most nights.

Gay's The Word. Paris seems to be full of gay locales these days, some fairly rough. Here are two of the more respectable:

Chez Moune, 54 rue Pigalle, 9e (tel. 45-26-64-64). Opens around 10 P.M., except Sun. and public holidays, when it starts about 4.30 P.M.

Madame Arthur, 75bis rue des Martyrs, 18e (tel. 42-64-48-27). An enduring gay favorite with a good cabaret at around 250 frs.

Discos. Paris is full of discos, but, as is the nature of such places, they come and go—some enjoying a meteoric rise to fame before dying a quick death, others carrying on as fashions wax and wane about them. Those we list here *should* still be in business by the time you arrive in Paris, but don't be surprised if one or two have changed at least their name. Discos usually open about 10 or 10.30 at night, and stay on the boil till around dawn. Some close on Mondays but a fair number open Sunday afternoons; virtually all of them stay open during the summer, but check locally to be on the safe side. Quite a few let girls in free during the week.

La Main Jaune, pl. Porte-de-Champerret, 17e (tel. 47-63-26-47).

Navy-Club, 58 blvd. de l'Hôpital, 13e (tel. 45-35-91-94). Open Sun. afternoons too. Some live music on Tues. and Wed.

La Paillote, 45 rue Monsieur-le-Prince, 6e (tel. 43-26-45-69).

Le Riverside, 7 rue Grégoire-de-Tours, 6e (tel. 43-54-46-33).

Whisky à Gogo, 57 rue de Seine, 6e (tel. 43-29-60-01).

Who's, 13 rue du Petit-Pont, 5e (tel. 43-25-13-14). Closed Mon. and Tues.

Zed Club, 2 rue des Anglais, 5e (tel. 43-54-93-78). Closed Mon., Tues. and Aug.

 MUSIC, MOVIES AND THEATER. For the lowdown on the very latest, buy one of the weekly "What's On" publications, *Pariscope,* or *L'Officiel des Spectacles,* both of which appear on Wednesday—the day the movie programs change. They list everything you can think of in the way of entertainment, cultural or otherwise. Your hotel may have a copy of *Paris Sélection,* a free publication produced by the Paris Tourist Office. Another useful aid is the *Sélection Loisirs* telephone service—call 47-20-88-98 for the English-language version. The recorded message covers the week's happenings in the capital. Keep an eye open, too, for posters displayed by the City Hall all over Paris; they'll tell you about one-off events such as firework displays, openair dances, etc.

Music and Ballet. Performances of classical and contemporary music can be enjoyed at **La Maison de la Radio, Théâtre des Champs Elysées,** the **Salle Pleyel, Salle Gaveau** and the **Centre Beaubourg.** Check *Pariscope* for details. Orchestras include the Orchestre National de France, Nouvel Orchestre Philarmonique, and the Orchestre de Paris. Combine the delights of sightseeing with the joy of music and attend one of the numerous concerts held within Paris' historic churches—such as Notre-Dame, St.-Louis-des-Invalides, St.-Germain-l'Auxerrois, St.-Merri and Ste.-Chapelle, all of which provide the most stunning settings, especially the last-named. Leaflets covering six months of programs can be obtained from Ste.-Chapelle itself or from the Paris Tourist Office, and you'd be well advised to reserve well ahead if possible.

During the summer, the excellent *Festival de l'Ile-de-France* stages marvelous concerts of classical music in churches, abbeys, châteaux and town halls all over the Ile de France, while the *Festival du Marais* includes concerts given in the courtyards of the area's beautifully restored mansions.

You won't need a knowledge of French to enjoy the excellent productions at the Paris **Opéra,** but you'll likely have a lot of trouble getting tickets. The **Opéra**

Comique (also known as the Salle Favart) is Paris' second opera house, specializing in opera with spoken dialogue (which is what the term *opéra comique* means in French).

The Opéra is also the home of the state-subsidized ballet company, which, under Rudolf Nureyev, has a fairly high reputation. But you'll find that much of the most interesting ballet in Paris comes during the annual November–December Ballet Festival, held in the **Théâtre des Champs-Elysées** on the avenue Montaigne. Other venues include the **Théâtre de la Ville**, the huge **Palais des Congres,** and the **Palais des Sports** at the Porte de Versailles. The gigantic **Théâtre Musical de Paris,** on the place du Châtelet, offers opera and ballet aimed at a more popular audience, with correspondingly lower seat prices than those at the Opéra. You may also find productions at the ultra-modern **Palais Omnisports de Bercy** in eastern Paris.

The *Festival du Marais* also includes ballet performances, as does the *Festival Estival* (Summer Festival), which runs from mid-July to around mid-September. Outside Paris, opera—and occasionally ballet—is staged in the pretty opera house in Versailles.

Movies. Paris has hundreds of movie houses, some huge and palatial, some tiny and uncomfortable. Programs change on Wednesdays—you'll find details of what's showing in the "What's On" publications or in the daily press. The standard program has movies showing at two-hourly intervals between around 2 P.M. and midnight (later on Fri. and Sat.). Prices are 30% lower on Mondays. The letters "v.f." (*version française*) beside a foreign film in a newspaper or magazine listing mean that it has been dubbed into French; the letters "v.o." (*version originale*), that it is showing in the original language with French subtitles.

The bigger and more expensive movie houses are mostly on the Champs-Elysées or around the Opéra, the smaller art houses in the Latin Quarter or St.-Germain-des-Prés. Paris has two *cinémathèques,* showing classics from all over the world, one in the Beaubourg/Pompidou Center, the other at the Palais de Chaillot on the place du Trocadéro, 16e.

Theater. Productions are naturally in French, so if your command of the language isn't great, you may find them heavy going. Among Paris' best-known "national" (i.e. state-subsidized) theaters is the **Comédie Française,** near the Opéra and beside the Palais-Royal on the place André-Malraux. The company specializes in performances of the great dramatists of the 17th century, but also ranges well beyond the classical repertoire, staging works by modern playwrights from France and all over the world. Seats can be reserved in person a maximum of one week ahead, or you can queue for at least an hour before a performance.

The **Théâtre de Chaillot,** on the place du Trocadéro, has some interesting experimental shows from time to time. The **Odéon,** on the place de l'Odéon, in the Latin Quarter, is used mainly as an overspill for the Comédie Française, but also houses visiting companies, including major foreign troupes (such as Britain's Royal Shakespeare Company) playing in their native language.

The **Théâtre de la Ville,** on the place du Châtelet, stages a major international theater festival, plus opera and ballet at times.

Most commercial theaters are located in the Opéra and Montparnasse areas. A surprising number of plays turn out to be translations of American or British hits, but you may also find works by such well-known French dramatists as Jean Anouilh, Henri de Montherlant, or the evergreen Ionesco.

Experimental theater hovers mainly on the fringes of Paris. One of the best-known names is the **Lucernaire,** 53 rue Notre-Dame-des-Champs (tel. 45-44-57-34).

SHOPPING. Many visitors to Paris find that shopping is one of the highlights of their trip. Specialist retailing has long been a feature of the Paris scene and you'll be delighted by the many little shops so typical of the city, selling anything from the latest fashion accessories to household goods or charming handmade gift items. Department stores also exist of course, the best-known being the old-established *Galeries Lafayette* and *Au Printemps* in the boulevard Haussmann near the Opéra. *Trois-Quartiers* in the boulevard de la Madeleine, just by the Madeleine church, is staider, but very good for accessories.

These big stores are open all day, from around 9.30 to 6.30, and stay open year-round. But smaller shops keep very erratic hours. As a rough rule of thumb, ordinary non-food shops are open 9 or 9.30 to around 7 P.M. but may well shut for lunch (generally 12–2). Fashion boutiques generally open later, around 10, but stay open during the lunch hour, as do large bookshops, shoe shops and the like. Small food shops open early (8 or 8.30) and don't close till late (7.30 to 8.30), but they take a long break in the middle of the day: 12.30 or 1 to 3.30 or 4. Most small food shops are open Sunday mornings, but many close Monday. Many small stores, such as antique shops or print shops, that are open all day Saturday will be shut Monday morning, or even Monday all day.

If you're resident outside France, take advantage of the V.A.T. refunds available to all visitors. See "Leaving France" in *Facts at Your Fingertips.* Many of the best discounts and savings are to be had from perfume shops.

Fashion. Here your pocketbook will be the deciding factor. If you can afford the most expensive *haute couture,* the avenue de Montaigne, 8e, where you'll find such hardy perennials as *Christian Dior, Guy Laroche, Nina Ricci* and *Ungaro,* or the rue du fbg. St.-Honoré, 8e (*Louis Feraud, Lanvin, Torrente,* to name but a few), are the best bets. Most of the other big names are in the adjoining streets: *Balmain, Courrèges* and *Ted Lapidus* in the rue François-Ier; *Givenchy* in the av. George-V; *Yves Saint-Laurent* in the av. Marceau; *Chloé,* av. Franklin-Roosevelt; *Chanel,* rue Cambon. The more avant-garde couture designers are in St.-Germain-des-Prés: *Sonia Rykiel* (6 rue de Grenelle) and *Chantal Thomass* (5 rue du Vieux-Colombier), for instance. Here too are the long-famous boutiques for beautiful ready-to-wear: *Dorothée Bis* (33 rue de Sèvres), *Anastasia* (18 rue de l'Ancienne-Comédie), *Gudule* (72 rue St.-André-des-Arts) and *Tiffany* (12 rue de Sèvres). There are plenty of other good boutiques here with a mixture of top ready-to-wear and less rarefied, but still fashionable outfits: try *Eve* or *La Gaminerie* (137 blvd. St.-Germain).

The renovated Les Halles area is another happy hunting-ground for fashion aficionados. The *Forum* is crammed with designer and other boutiques and accessory stores. *Agnès B* (rue du Jour) is a favorite for sophisticated yet not too way-out outfits, while the punningly-named *Halles Capone* (rue Turbigo) is the place for superbly cut jeans. Not far away the round place des Victoires is another home of with-it fashion, with the great *Kenzo,* plus *Victoire.*

The chic department stores near the Opéra, *Galeries Lafayette* and *Au Printemps,* have a whole series of "shops-within-shops," and the nearby rue Tronchet is worth visiting for the ever-classic *Cacharel, Erès* for sleek swimwear and beach outfits, or the long-popular *Madd.*

Accessories. The rue Tronchet is also good for accessories: *La Bagagerie* for bags and purses; *Carel* and *Renast* for fabulous shoes; *Hélion* for gloves. A short walk away you'll find the city's best-known leather-goods stores: *Hermès* (24 rue du fbg. St.-Honoré), *Sellerie de la Cour* and *Sellerie de France* (265 and 271 rue St.-Honoré). *Lancel* (pl. de l'Opéra) also has good bags and purses.

If you're on the Left Bank, *La Bagagerie* is also in the rue de Rennes, or try for shoes at *Carel* or *Tilbury* (rue du Four), *Cassandre, Céline* and *Charles-Jourdan* (rue de Rennes), *François Villon* (rue Bonaparte), *Robert Clergeric* (rue due Cherche-Midi) and trendy *Maud Frizon* (rue des Sts.-Pères).

Jewelry. Frenchwomen wear a great deal of jewelry and you'll find Paris a good place for choosing something really special. The top jewelers are conveniently found grouped together in or around the place Vendôme near the Tuileries. In the square itself are *Boucheron, Chaumet* and *Van Cleef & Arpels,* while the great *Cartier* is just around the corner at 13 rue de la Paix and the stylish *Jean Dinh Van* at 7 rue de la Paix. *Fred,* in the rue Royale by the Madeleine church, has been attracting visitors to Paris for generations and also has a branch in the Galerie du Claridge off the Champs-Elysées. *La Boutique du Crillon* in the Hôtel Crillon in the place de la Concorde has a good selection of expensive pieces and is conveniently open till 8 P.M. daily.

But buying jewelry needn't break the bank. You can pop into a chain store and come out with the current style in costume jewelry, maybe even in plastic, that will give an added zing to your new Paris outfit. In between the two extremes there are a number of middle-range stores specializing in well-designed pieces at affordable prices. Try *Fleurmay,* 204 rue de Rivoli, 1er, or *Fabrice,* 33 and 54 rue Bonaparte, 6e. Fashion-conscious youngsters should make sure not to miss *Agatha,* 97 rue de Rennes, 6e, and in the Forum des Halles.

Perfume. The big department stores near the Opéra (who will give you discounts of up to 20 per cent on well-known brand names) and *Sephora,* 50 rue de Passy, 16e, and in the Forum des Halles, all have a wide range of perfumes, including all the big names. Sephora claims to be the world's largest perfume store and offers good prices on beauty products as well as perfumes. If you're aiming for a particular scent, make instead for one of the upmarket discount stores, such as *Liz* at 194 rue de Rivoli, 1er, Galerie Elysées 26, 26 av. des Champs-Elysées, 8e, and 112 rue du fbg. St.-Honoré, 8e, or *Michel Swiss,* 16 rue de la Paix, 16e. *Paris Look,* 13 av. de l'Opéra, 1er, advertises 25 per cent off major names, *Patchouli,* 3 and 5 rue du Cherche-Midi, 6e (also a beauty salon), 20% off. Two reliable family-run discount places are *Catherine,* 6 rue de Castiglione, 1er, and *Maréchal,* 232 rue de Rivoli, 1er. For a *Guerlain* scent you are restricted to one of their own boutiques: 2 pl. Vendôme, 1er; 29 rue de Sèvres, 6e; 68 av. des Champs-Elysées, 8e; or 93 rue de Passy, 16e.

Antiques. The cream of the antique dealers are to be found in St.-Germain-des-Prés, especially in four streets that are referred to as "the antiques square:" Bonaparte, Jacob, Bac, Sts.-Pères. The *Cour des Sts.-Pères,* off the street of the same name, 7e, is full of little antique shops, or you might try the *Jardins St.-Paul,* again off the street of the same name. The *Louvre des Antiquaires* antique emporium in the pl. du Palais-Royal, 1er, and the *Village Suisse,* 52 av. de la Motte-Piquet, 15e, are other good places for visiting a lot of small shops or booths under one roof.

You'll surely have heard of Paris's unbeatable flea market or *marché aux puces,* which celebrated its centenary in 1985. Its hundreds of little shops and stalls covering a staggering 6½ kms. (4 miles) in the area round the Porte de St.-Ouen, 17e, and the Porte de Clignancourt, 18e, on the northern edge of Paris offer marvelous opportunities for browsing, and you may even find a genuine antique at a bargain price if you get there early enough. (Open Mon. and weekends only.)

Markets. Talking of markets, whether or not you want to buy, you should try to take in the famous flower market on the Ile de la Cité near Notre Dame. There are other good flower markets beside the Madeleine church and in the place des Ternes, 17e, while the Ile de la Cité one is transformed into a bird market on Sundays. Then the city has another old-established specialist market: the stamp market held on Thurs. and weekends on the av. Marigny and the av. Gabriel off the southern end of the Champs-Elysées. Many of the stalls also sell a good range of old postcards: a view of one of your favorite parts of France as it looked decades ago makes a good souvenir of your visit.

Souvenirs and Gift Shops. For more traditional souvenirs try the Tuileries end of the rue de Rivoli, 1er. Here you'll spot headscarves with pictures of the

Eiffel Tower, the Sacré-Coeur, the Arc de Triomphe, the Louvre or the Beaubourg/Pompidou Center—or even all five at once. All the stores have miniature Eiffel Towers and everything under the sun decorated with the spindly landmark: ashtrays, keyrings, charm bracelets, earrings, pendants, you name it. Miniature busts of Napoleon are another popular buy, often to be found on stalls or barrows near Les Invalides too. Illustrated books on France make good mementoes or presents to take home. Try the rue de Rivoli again, with two well-known English-language bookshops, *Galignani* and *W.H. Smith,* at nos. 224 and 248, and *Brentano's* at no. 37 in the nearby av. de l'Opéra. All of these also have good books on French art and architecture but you'll find even bigger selections in the museum bookshops (especially those in the Centre Pompidou/Beaubourg and the Musée des Arts Décoratifs, as well as in the huge Publications Department in the Louvre). *La Hune,* 170 blvd. St.-Germain, 7e (conveniently open till midnight Mon.–Fri.) is excellent for books in French and English on every aspect of French art and culture, including movies, music, dance, theater and applied art. *Artcurial,* 9 av. Matignon, 8e, is an art gallery with a good bookshop and the nearby *Jullien-Cornic,* at 29 on the same street, also has a good range of French fashion and costume titles. Lovers of French cuisine should call in at Paris's food-and-wine bookshop, *Le Verre et l'Assiette,* 1 rue du Val-de-Grâce, 5e, when visiting the Latin Quarter.

As for gift shops, St.-Germain-des-Prés is a happy hunting ground. Here you'll find, among many others, *La Rose des Vents,* 65 rue de Seine, 6e, for pots pourris, dried flowers, scented soaps and the like; *Monsieur Renard,* 6 rue de l'Echaudé, 6e, for antique dolls and automata; *Françoise Thibault,* 1 rue Jacob, 6e, and 1 rue Bourbon-le-Château, an old favorite for pretty handpainted items —all within a few minutes' walk of one another. On the Right Bank we doubt you'll be able to resist the temptations of *Léon,* 222 rue de Rivoli, 1er, which has been selling exquisite thimbles and paperweights, and magical porcelain boxes decorated with flowers and copies of Sèvres designs, for over 100 years.

Food and Drink. If you prefer to take home food or drink itself, rather than books about it, there's plenty of choice. Every little corner grocery will have tempting displays on offer, but for Paris's top groceries you must go to the pl. de la Madeleine, to *Fauchon* and *Hédiard.* A good range of regional candy specialties can be found at *Aux Douceurs de France,* 70 blvd. de Strasbourg, 10e. Dried herbs make usefully lightweight presents: look in the openair food markets or try *L'Herbier de Provence* in the Forum des Halles. If cheese is your thing, the biggest choice is at *Androuët,* 41 rue d'Amsterdam, 8e, and to go with the cheese, what better than a special bottle of wine? Corner groceries or the *Nicolas* chain of wine shops will have a wide range, but for a large selection of the country's most famous wines in rare vintages, don't miss *Vins Rares et de Collection,* 3 rue Laugier, 17e, where prices range from around 20 frs. up to 10,000 frs. (free tastings in the cellar).

 EXCURSIONS FROM PARIS. Trips out of Paris to the countryside surrounding the city are organized by the *R.A.T.P.* (Paris Transport Authority), 53 quai des Grands-Augustins, 6e, and pl. de la Madeleine, 8e. Guides are normally French-speaking only, but a number speak English.
In addition, the following trips are also available:

By Luxury Bus. For guided tours in luxury buses with English commentary you have a choice: *American Express,* 11 rue Scribe, 9e (tel. 42-66-09-99); *Cityrama,* 4 pl. des Pyramides, 1er (tel. 42-60-30-14); or *Paris Vision,* 214 rue de Rivoli, 1er (tel. 42-60-30-01). All three organize half- and whole-day excursions to such places as Chartres, Giverny (sometimes combined with Rouen), Fontainebleau, Malmaison, Versailles, or to two destinations combined (Versailles with Chartres, Fontainebleau or Malmaison; Fontainebleau and Barbizon with Malmaison); Cityrama also offers Chantilly. *Europabus,* 214 rue de Rivoli, 1er (tel. 42-96-14-99), runs half-day excursions to Chantilly, Chartres, Fontainebleau, Giverny and Versailles; hostesses usually speak English.

By Bus. The very full program of lecture tours organized by the *Caisse Nationale des Monuments Historiques,* Hotel de Sully, 62 rue St.-Antoine, 4e (tel. 42-74-22-22), includes a few bus tours to lesser-known museums and historic buildings, some of them not normally open to the public. The commentary is usually in French and presumes a fairly detailed knowledge of art history and architectural terms.

By Train. Paris has six mainline rail termini:

Gare d'Austerlitz: for trains to the southwest, going to Bordeaux and on to Spain via Orléans, Tours and Poitiers, to Bourges and Montluçon, and to Toulouse via Limoges.

Gare de l'Est: for trains to the east to Nancy and Strasbourg and on to Germany.

Gare de Lyon: for trains to the southeast, including the T.G.V. (high-speed train) to Lyon, Grenoble, Marseille, Nice and Montpellier.

Gare de Montparnasse: for trains to the west (especially Brittany) via Chartres, Angers and Le Mans.

Gare du Nord: for trains to the north (and on to Britain, Belgium, Holland and the Scandinavian countries.

Gare St.-Lazare: for trains to Normandy, and to Britain via Dieppe.

For passenger enquiries in English, call 43-80-50-50 for all destinations.

By Express Métro. The RER (*Réseau Régional Exprès*) has fast trains slotted into the ordinary métro inner-city network, and going out to such places as Versailles, St.-Germain-en-Laye and St.-Rémy-les-Chevreuse, as well as to the two Paris airports, Orly and Roissy/Charles de Gaulle.

By Car. Roads out of Paris are far too numerous to list here. Note, however, that the main highways or motorways (*autoroutes*), marked with blue signs, are the A1 northward; the A4 eastward to Metz and Strasbourg; the A6 southward through Dijon and Lyon to the Riviera (by which time it has become the A7); the A10 southwestward to Bordeaux via Orléans and Tours; and the A13 westward to Normandy.

USEFUL ADDRESSES. Embassies and Consulates. *U.S. Embassy,* 2 av. Gabriel, 8e (tel. 42-96-12-02); *U.S. Consulate,* rue St.-Florentin, 1er (tel. 42-60-14-88). *British Embassy,* 35 rue du fbg. St.-Honoré, 8e (tel. 42-66-91-42); *British Consulate,* 2 Cité du Retiro (3rd Floor), 8e (tel. 42-66-91-42). *Australian Embassy,* 4 rue Jean Rey, 15e (tel. 45-75-62-00). *Canadian Embassy,* 35 av. Montaigne, 8e (tel. 42-25-99-55). *New Zealand Embassy,* 9 rue Léonard-de-Vinci, 16e (tel. 45-00-24-11).

Medical Emergencies. Hospitals with English-speaking staff: *American Hospital,* 63 blvd. Victor-Hugo, Neuilly (tel. 47-47-53-00); *British Hospital,* 48 rue de Villiers, Levallois-Perret (tel. 47-58-13-12). Pharmacies or chemists open long hours: *Dhéry,* galerie des Champs, 84 av. des Champs-Elysées, 8e (tel. 45-62-02-41), open nonstop; *Drugstore,* on the corner of blvd. St.-Germain and the rue de Rennes, 6e, has a pharmacy counter open daily to 2 A.M.; *Pharmacie des Arts,* 106 blvd. Montparnasse, 6e, is open Mon. to Sat. to midnight and Sun. 8 P.M. to midnight.

Note: Any prescription you need outside normal opening hours will generally have to be stamped by the police first (this is to prevent drug addicts taking up doctors' and pharmacists' time at night); contact the nearest *Commissariat de Police* for details.

Emergency Telephone Numbers. *Ambulance,* 43-78-26-26; *Medical,* 47-07-77-77; *Dentists* 8 P.M. to 8 A.M. weekdays, all-day weekends and public holidays, 47-37-51-00. Automatic call boxes are to be found at main intersections for use in emergencies requiring police help (*Police-Secours*) or medical help (*Services Médicaux*).

An *SOS Service* for English-speakers is available after 7 P.M. on 47-23-80-80. They'll do their best to help, whatever the problem. The U.S. Embassy has a

Welfare Service and the American Aid Society (open mornings only). The British Embassy will do their best to help too. However, in the case of a lost pocketbook, passport, or other such papers, you *must* first go to the nearest *commissariat de police* and get them to sign and stamp a form giving details of the theft.

NORTHWEST FRANCE

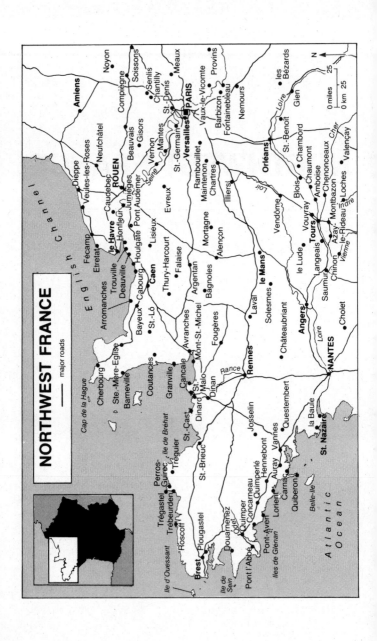

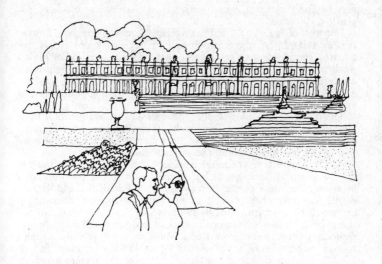

THE ILE DE FRANCE

A Foretaste of Riches to Come

The Ile de France, or Island of France, is the general, rather poetic name for the area surrounding Paris. It provides a magnificent foretaste of what the whole of this fascinating country has to offer: there are lovely buildings, many of them with historic associations, and old, attractive towns and villages. But many visitors remember the Ile de France best for its superb landscapes of winding river valleys and peaceful lanes bordered by sunny meadows, dotted with a wealth of little churches containing no special treasures but seeming to fit perfectly into their setting. Many of the villages are surprisingly rural in spite of the number of Parisians who have bought second homes here for holidays and weekends. It is their presence, in fact, that has largely preserved the charm of these villages for, in contrast to the sophisticated, bustling metropolitan life of the capital, they like to renovate picturesque mills or rebuild ruined barns and imagine that they are the country dwellers that their parents or grandparents may genuinely have been.

No wonder that this is pre-eminently a land of painters. Do your homework by visiting the Impressionists' galleries in the Musée d'Orsay, in Paris, the Monets in the Orangerie and the Musée Marmottan. After that, as you travel around the Ile de France, you can't fail to spot the riverside vistas, undulating meadows and rural scenes that seem to have been taken straight out of the impressionist canvasses and, indeed, may be the very spots chosen, scarcely altered by our modern, less gentle civilization.

Just west of Paris you'll find the riverside towns of Bougival, Louveciennes and Marly, where Renoir and Monet, Sisley and Degas frequented the *guingettes,* or taverns, that offered openair dancing to weekending Parisians, and where they painted many of their light-filled masterpieces. In and around Fontainebleau and Barbizon was the haunt of Corot and of Millet and Théodore Rousseau, whose studios you can visit.

The region is full of forests too. Make sure to allow time for a walk in the beautiful forests of Fontainebleau or Rambouillet, Sénart or Coye, Marly or St.-Germain—the list is surprisingly long for an area so close to one of the world's major capital cities.

As for architecture, the range is huge: wonderful Gothic cathedrals at Chartres and Beauvais; elaborate palaces at Versailles, Fontainebleau and Vaux-le-Vicomte; historic abbeys at Port-Royal and Royaumont, and tiny chapels such as St.-Blaise-les-Simples, charmingly decorated by Cocteau, at Milly-la-Forêt. At Senlis you can still see traces of the Gallo-Roman civilization; at Provins you'll find yourself wandering through medieval streets. Museums are in plentiful supply, too. At Sceaux there is the official Ile de France Museum, full of exhibits connected with the art and history of the region; a superb museum devoted entirely to the Renaissance is housed in the Château d'Ecouen; St.-Germain-en-Laye has the country's National Antiquities Museum, with famous prehistoric and later collections. Then you can gain insight into the lives of famous men by visiting their former homes, now turned into intimate museums—Rodin in Meudon, Maurice Denis in St.-Germain-en-Laye, Chateaubriand near Sceaux. Or you may prefer specialized museums—photography in Bièvres, cars and carriages in Compiègne, horses in Chantilly, china and porcelain in Sèvres, or urban transport in St.-Mandé.

If you are traveling with children, you'll find much to keep them entertained, and, better still, you can combine their pleasures with your own at Thoiry and Breteuil, where the dynamic owners have worked hard to provide all you could want for a family day out combining culture and outdoor pursuits.

Visiting the Ile de France

Many visitors see the region in terms of a series of days out from their base in Paris, and this is clearly a good solution for those without cars. On the other hand, you might like to base yourself in one of the attractive towns and visit both Paris and the Ile de France from there. You thus get the best of both worlds if you choose somewhere with good train connections such as Versailles, or on the express métro line such as St.-Germain-en-Laye or St.-Rémy-lès-Chevreuse. Motorists can enjoy any number of attractive tours, stopping off at lesser-known châteaux as well as visiting the major sights.

St.-Cloud, Sèvres and Versailles

Just west of Paris and easily reached by public transport is the pleasant town of St.-Cloud, perched above the river Seine. Its magnificent château, once Napoleon's favorite residence and where he was married—his nephew Louis-Napoleon was proclaimed emperor here,

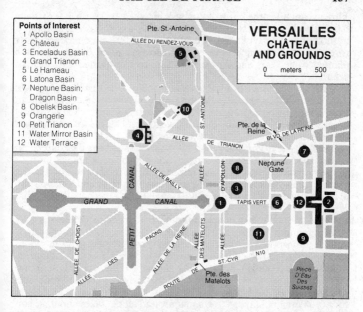

Points of Interest
1 Apollo Basin
2 Château
3 Enceladus Basin
4 Grand Trianon
5 Le Hameau
6 Latona Basin
7 Neptune Basin;
  Dragon Basin
8 Obelisk Basin
9 Orangerie
10 Petit Trianon
11 Water Mirror Basin
12 Water Terrace

VERSAILLES
CHÂTEAU AND GROUNDS

0   meters   500

too, in 1852—was burnt down during the Franco-Prussian War in 1870. The ruins were razed to the ground a decade or so later, and all that now remains are lovely terraced gardens known as the Parc de St.-Cloud and backed by a small forest. This is a pleasant place for strolling and enjoying the views over the Seine, with perhaps a light lunch or tea. There is a small museum beside the main entrance devoted to the history of the château from the time of Henri III down to its destruction. On the other side of the river is the world-famous Sèvres National Porcelain Manufactory, where fine china has been made since the 18th century. You can visit the workshops and the National Ceramics Museum.

But the greatest attraction on this western edge of Paris must be the Palace of Versailles, which, with the Mont St.-Michel, is the most-visited place in France outside the capital. Versailles marked the end of feudalism in France, and, in its insensate glory, foreshadowed the French Revolution a century later. Psychologically and historically, Versailles may be regarded as the result of a childhood shock suffered by the young king Louis XIV. With his mother, Anne of Austria, he was forced to flee Paris, and was captured temporarily by a group of nobles known as the *Frondeurs.* Louis came to hate Paris and the Parisians, who had sided with the conspirators. His distaste was such that he visited his country's capital only a few times once he had come of age.

In 1661, at the age of 23, just after the blow to his pride received at Vaux-le-Vicomte, where Louis discovered that his finance minister lived in greater luxury than he did himself, the young monarch began to work on his tremendous palace at Versailles. The problems of nature did not daunt him—hills were razed, marshes were drained, and water for the magnificent fountains was channeled from the Seine several miles away. Work on Versailles continued over a period of 50 years.

Three years after the entire court was installed there, 36,000 men and 6,000 Percheron horses were still laboring away. The Orangerie, as hothouses were then called, was filled with 3,000 almond trees, laurel roses, pomegranate and orange trees. More than 150,000 flowers were planted each year, and entire forests were transported to adorn the grounds.

With over 1,000 of France's greatest nobles living in the palace with him, Louis XIV began to substitute royal privileges and sinecures for local power and feudal rights. Holding the king's shirt when he dressed became a more important source of wealth and status than the possession of an entire county in the provinces.

The next king, Louis XV, and his mistress, Madame de Pompadour, embellished the château still further, and added a new note of intimacy to their private apartments—an inside staircase linked their two sitting-rooms. Louis XV also built the Petit Trianon (the Grand Trianon with a terrace overlooking the Grand Canal having been built by Louis XIV).

Louis XVI, the last of the Bourbon monarchs to live in the great palace, found it too like a prison for his taste. He took refuge from its stifling atmosphere in the Petit Trianon, while Marie-Antoinette, his queen, disported herself in the pastoral village her husband indulgently built for her. You can still visit the *Hameau* (Hamlet) as it is known, where she played at being a milkmaid with Sèvres porcelain milk pails!

If you are short of time, above all visit the main palace. The guided tour (you are not allowed to wander around alone) takes about an hour and gives you at least a glimpse of the way the Bourbons lived. It also helps you appreciate why, more than two centuries later, the French still speak of *grandeur*. If you have more time to spare, you can continue to the Trianons, and stroll through the gardens of the main palace. The views are stupendous, but the fall, when the leaves change color, is probably the most spectacular time of year to visit. Unfortunately, the popularity of the palace has given rise to ever longer lines and delays as vast numbers of visitors crowd into the buildings and grounds.

Before entering the château, stop for a glance at the exterior. Appropriately in the middle are the rooms in which the king lived; on his left, the queen and later Madame de Maintenon. The two wings were occupied by the royal children and the princes of the blood. The courtiers lived in the attics.

Among the major sights of your tour will be the solemn Mansart-designed chapel where king and queen attended mass daily in their gilt boxes. Of the reception rooms, the most famous and loveliest is the Galerie des Glaces, the Hall of Mirrors, where the Treaty of Versailles ending World War I was signed in 1919—and where the German Empire was proclaimed in 1871. The gallery, which was empty for decades, has been beautifully restored, regilded and furnished; on a few special occasions it is still lit by the blaze of candles reflected in the shimmering mirrors.

The royal bedrooms are properly ceremonious, but even more interesting are the *petits appartments* where the king and queen lived in the company of their close friends and servants. The miniature opera house, built by Gabriel for Louis XV, is equally delightful.

In the last couple of decades many of the once sadly empty state rooms have been furnished with period furniture painstakingly collected, purchased and donated from all over France and other countries, particularly the United States. This long task of restoration and renovation reached an important stage in 1980 when President Giscard d'Estaing ceremonially opened the refurbished bedroom of Louis XIV. In 1985 the work was nearing completion, and it is now possible to enjoy Versailles in something approaching its original splendor.

The grounds, covering some 250 acres, were designed originally by Le Nôtre and are adorned with many sculptures. Parisians love the lawns, formal flowerbeds and ornamental lakes, and go there time and time again, particularly in fall. But the most breathtaking sight is the playing of the fountains. Their operation costs a fortune in our democratic days, so they play only on a few Sundays in the summer months. Also not to be missed, if you happen to be there at the right time, are the magnificent *fêtes de nuit,* with floodlighting and fireworks, held on a couple of evenings in July and September.

In the mid-'80s, several smaller fountains were refurbished and the formal gardens replenished to create an even more attractive circuit that is accompanied by magnificent music echoing the hunting horns of the court enjoying *la chasse.* The best place to start your fountain tour is, as Louis XIV himself advised, on the main terrace: "Leave the palace by the entrance hall to the marble courtyard (*Cour de Marbre*), then stop at the top of the steps to take in the view of the flowerbeds, pools and fountains. Then continue straight on to the top of the Latona Parterre, and pause to gaze at Latona, the amphibians, the grassy slopes and statues, the Royal Avenue, Apollo and the Canal, before turning round to view the Parterre and the Palace." In restoring Louis' beloved fountain displays to something approaching their former glory, the designers have followed his instructions as closely as possible. A well-illustrated plan will guide you as you visit such delights as the Dragon Fountain, the Apollo Pool, the Colonnade, the Water Avenue or the Bathing Nymphs. The largest ornamental pool of all is the Pool of Neptune, which has a huge sculptured group depicting Neptune and Amphitrite and no fewer than 99 different fountains and spraying jets of water. This is where the "Evening Festivities in the Pool of Neptune" and "Triumph of Neptune" are held, enhanced by lighting effects, music and fireworks.

The Grand Trianon is a pink marble pleasure palace, one of the most delightful Baroque buildings in France. It was designed by Mansart in 1687. It has long been used as a "guest house", with such illustrious visitors as Peter the Great down to modern-day heads of state such as the Queen of England.

The Petit Trianon, commissioned by Louis XV and designed by Gabriel, the architect of the place de la Concorde in Paris, in 1768, owes its fame to its last owner, the hapless Marie-Antoinette. She came to this gray stone mansion nearly every day to flee the noxious atmosphere of the court. Close by she built the village, with dairy and mill, where, dressed as shepherdesses, she and her companions lived a make-believe bucolic life. Between the two Trianons is a Carriage Museum, housed in a former guard house.

There are guided tours of the old town of Versailles, which has some beautiful houses and gardens. Try also to visit the cathedral, St.-Louis, the Lambinet Museum in a lovely 18th-century mansion, and the Potager du Roi, or Royal Kitchen Garden, where fruit, vegetables and flowers were grown for the Court (it is now a horticultural college).

The Chevreuse Valley and Rambouillet

About halfway between Versailles and Rambouillet is the Chevreuse valley, once very rural but now a popular spot for Parisians' weekend cottages. On the way you might like to visit the excellent photographic museum at Bièvres, with its 15,000 cameras and more than 800,000 photographs. Dampierre château, home of the duc de Luynes and dating from the Middle Ages, was rebuilt in the 17th century and has a fine library, a good family collection of paintings, and gardens designed by Le Nôtre. Not far away is the château of Breteuil, which has been owned and lived in by the same family since it was built in the early 17th century. It has many lovely pieces of furniture, the most famous of which is the "Teschen table," a gift from Empress Maria Theresa of Austria and inlaid with jewels and precious stones. The lifesize wax figures dressed in period costume in many of the rooms (including the novelist Marcel Proust, who stayed here) bring the château's past to life successfully. The young marquis de Breteuil and his wife have reacted energetically to the problem of the cost of upkeep (they have won an award for their dynamism) and organize all sorts of concerts, plays and other events to attract visitors.

Nearby are the ruins of the Jansenist abbey of Port-Royal-des-Champs, where the great 17th-century dramatist Jean Racine received much of his education, with a museum close by.

Rambouillet is a small town with some impressive buildings, including the town hall and the château, surrounded by a river-laced forest. The 14th-century château was one of the homes of Catherine de Médicis and Henry IV, and although it is one of the French president's official homes, you may visit it except on the rare occasions that he is in residence. There is a good deal to see, including Marie-Antoinette's prettily decorated "dairy," a "shell pavilion," and the room in which Napoleon spent his final night before he was sent off to his lonely exile on St. Helena.

At one end of the attractive grounds is the National Sheepfold, founded by Louis XVI with a flock of 376 sheep imported from Spain. The Forest of Rambouillet is a good place for walking.

Chartres

Although Chartres is chiefly visited for its magnificent Gothic cathedral with its world-famous stained glass, it is a pleasant town well worth exploring further, with many old houses and picturesque streets. It's best to devote a whole day to a visit here, though if you're short on time it's perfectly possible to visit the cathedral alone in half a day.

The cathedral of Our Lady at Chartres is generally considered a supreme example of medieval architecture. But worship on this spot goes right back to before the Gallo-Roman period—if you visit the immense crypt you'll be shown a well that was the focus of ceremonies held by the Druids. As so often happened the original cult of a fertility goddess merged into that of the Virgin Mary with the arrival of Christianity, but in the case of Chartres there was a particularly strong reason for this. In the late 9th century Charles the Bold presented Chartres with what was believed to be the tunic, or chemise, of the Virgin Mary. This precious relic attracted huge numbers of pilgrims to Chartres, which is indeed still a pilgrimage center. Every year thousands of students still make the pilgrimage to Chartres on foot from Paris and other pilgrimages are held at regular intervals.

And the modern visitor can still share a curious experience that has instilled a sense of awe in pilgrims through the ages. If you look towards the horizon just after Ablis as you cross the rich plain of the Beauce, you will seem to see the twin spires of Chartres cathedral rising out of the wheatfields.

The Gothic cathedral that is so widely revered today is in fact the sixth Christian building on the same site. Most of it was built at the end of the 12th century, after the Romanesque cathedral, dating from the early 11th century, had burned down in a disastrous fire in 1194. An outburst of religious fervour followed the discovery that the priceless relic had miraculously survived and in a moving communal effort uniting rich and poor alike the new Gothic cathedral took only 25 years to build, which helps to explain why it presents such a harmonious whole. It has remained substantially the same to this day, except that the wooden rafters were destroyed in yet another fire, this time in the early 19th century, and replaced by a metal frame.

Before going inside the cathedral, examine the west front with the famous Portail Royal with its twin towers and statue columns. The portal (it has borne the prefix "royal" since the 12th century) is a survival from the Romanesque cathedral and is in fact made up of three separate portals. Taken together their carvings depict the life of Christ, including glimpses of his Old Testament ancestors, with as a counterpoint scenes from the everyday life of the period. Both towers are Romanesque. The left-hand one is the earlier of the two but is misleadingly known as the "New Tower" because its slender Gothic spire dates from the early 16th century, when it was built to replace the earlier wooden one. The right-hand tower still has a fine Romanesque spire, contrasting interestingly with its taller and slimmer twin.

The rose window above the portal dates from the 13th century, while the three windows below it, among the finest examples of medieval stained glass, are 12th century. But you must naturally go inside the cathedral to understand why Chartres is so famous for its stained glass. Even in dull weather the glass glows with jewel-like richness, the famous "Chartres blue" predominating—a magnificent deep blue made to a special formula that has apparently never been repeated. You will notice that in some of the windows, mainly the three magnificent ones above the Royal Portal, the coloring seems lighter. This is the result of recent cleaning and, though the purists complain, there is no doubt that it gives a better idea of how the windows originally looked. Only one other 12th-century window, the celebrated "Notre Dame de la Belle Verrière" in the south choir aisle, survived the fire; the others are virtually all 13th-century and miraculously emerged unscathed from the Revolution and from two world wars (though they were taken down and stored in a place of safety during World War II).

It is well worth taking a pair of binoculars with you to pick out the details of these splendid windows, which include some particularly interesting scenes depicting local craftsmen at work. If you want to know more about the technique of stained glass and the medieval trades depicted at Chartres, visit the gallery opposite the north porch of the cathedral, which shows good audio-visual documentaries.

A reminder of the cathedral's role as a place of pilgrimage is the huge marble labyrinth in the floor of the nave (unfortunately it's hard to see beneath the chairs used for services)—pilgrims were apparently expected to travel along its entire length (almost 300 meters) on their knees.

The screen surrounding the choir is decorated with groups of sculptures depicting the life of Christ and the Virgin Mary; the earliest carved in the late-Gothic period while the most recent date from the 18th century. Opinion is divided as to their artistic merit, whereas the 18th-century group above the high altar, depicting the Assumption, has few admirers.

Guided tours of the crypt, the largest in France, start from the Maison des Clercs opposite the south front of the cathedral. The Romanesque and Gothic chapels running round the crypt have recently been stripped of the 19th-century paintings that used to disfigure them and can now be seen in all their purity. You will also be shown part of a 4th-century Gallo-Roman wall and 12th-century wall paintings.

Chartres is an ideal town to wander in as it has many picturesque streets and attractive buildings illustrating the city's development over the centuries. For instance the Museum, to the north of the cathedral, is housed in an 18th-century building that was once the bishop's palace. Its varied collection includes some fine Renaissance enamel plaques (in the chapel), a splendid painting of Erasmus by Holbein, tapestries, arms and armor, and a large number of paintings, mostly French and Flemish, from the 17th and 18th centuries, as well as a room devoted to the history of Chartres. In the summer months chamber music concerts are held here on weekends.

If you stroll through the narrow streets, clambering up and down the many steps, you'll see any number of interesting old houses, especially in the rue Chantault, the rue aux Herbes, the rue des Ecuyers and the rue de la Tannerie on the other side of the river Eure. And you'll discover that the cathedral doesn't have a monopoly of fine stained glass—the windows in the church of Saint-Pierre date from the early 14th century, those in Saint-Aignan from the 17th. Chartres also has a Romanesque church in Saint-André, but it is now partly in ruins.

And finally—a striking contrast with the city's medieval sculpture—near the station you'll see the powerful monument to Jean Moulin, the prefect of Chartres who became a Resistance hero in World War II and died under torture.

Maintenon, Dreux and Mantes

The château of Maintenon, with its Renaissance façade, 17th-century wing, and vast gardens designed by Le Nôtre, is flanked on the right by a branch of the Eure, and on the left by a late-Gothic chapel. The unusually interesting interior is still furnished as it was in the days of its most famous occupant, Madame de Maintenon, the morganatic wife of Louis XIV. In 1984 the 300th anniversary of their marriage was celebrated, and in 1985 a permanent exhibition and audiovisual show were set up.

Farther along the charming Eure valley lies the ancient town of Dreux. In its center is a belfry, whose 142 steps will give you a good opportunity to stretch your legs. The cathedral of St.-Pierre on the square dates from the 13th–16th centuries and has three beautiful stained glass windows. Stroll along the Grande-Rue for a glimpse of some unusual wooden houses dating from the 15th and 16th centuries. On a bluff northwest of the town, set in a park surrounded by the fortified walls of a ruined château, is the royal chapel of St.-Louis. Built by Louis-Philippe, it contains the tombs of the Dukes of Orléans.

Beyond the forest of Dreux on the Mantes road is the lovely château of Anet, designed by Philibert Delorme for Diane de Poitiers, Henri II's favorite, and destroyed by fire during the Revolution. All that remains is the entrance gate, the exquisitely furnished left wing, and the chapel decorated with Jean Goujon's delightful bas-reliefs.

The most interesting part of Mantes was demolished during World War II, but the collegiate church of Notre-Dame is worth a visit. It was built at the same time as its famous namesake in Paris, and the two are similar in many details.

Near Mantes, and also easily visited from Paris, is the 16th-century château of Thoiry, which has some beautiful furniture and tapestries, marvelous archives full of treasures (including papal bulls, letters from Napoleon, Thomas Jefferson and Benjamin Franklin, even two manuscript waltzes by Chopin, discovered in a trunk labeled "old clothes" in an attic by the American pianist Byron Janis), and a fascinating Museum of Gastronomy with a collection of elaborate *pièces montées,* those uniquely French table centerpieces beloved of pastrycooks and specially designed in this case to honor the bicentenary of the great chef Antonin Carême. Thoiry is also famous for its safari park, in which hundreds of animals are allowed to roam freely in conditions as close as possible to their natural habitats. The young Viscount and his energetic American wife have worked hard to create an enjoyable and instructive day out for all the family, with marked itineraries and audiovisual presentations for children. They were the first people to breed the "ligron"—a cross between a lion and a tiger—that has since become world-famous.

Malmaison, Bougival and St.-Germain-en-Laye

Just outside Paris on the way to Normandy, at Rueil, is the château of Malmaison, the country house where Napoleon and his beloved Joséphine lived during the early 19th century. Although Napoleon lived in later years at both Compiègne and Fontainebleau, it was at Malmaison that he spent his happiest years. There is something enchanting yet absurd about this pretty house with its rose gardens and stone basins, making it the most moving of all the Napoleonic museums. All the rooms are furnished as they were in the time of Napoleon. Joséphine's bedroom on the second floor is especially beautiful, not least its tent-draped ceiling. Fascinating also are the library, games room and dining room, all with handsome furnishings, as well as Joséphine's gowns and jewels. She spent her remaining years following her divorce from Napoleon at Malmaison.

Right beside Malmaison is the château of Bois-Préau, which Joséphine bought in 1810. It was bequeathed to the French state by its American owners and now houses another Napoleonic museum full of exhibits connected with the "little corporal," including his famous gray coat and his triangular hat.

Bougival, farther along the river Seine, was once the haunt of the Impressionists. The river views are still lovely, and one of the taverns, whose lively scenes they often painted, is being restored in homage to them. This is one of the pleasantest places close to Paris for a riverside lunch or dinner, as are nearby Louveciennes or Port-Marly. Marly-le-Roi once boasted a château with pavilions designed by Mansart as signs of the zodiac wheeling round the Sun King. All that is left today is a pleasant park and forest, and even the famous *Machine de Marly,* a series of 14 giant waterwheels intended to pump water from the Seine to the château's pools and fountains (some of it was pumped as far as Versailles), vanished for ever in the '60s.

Beyond Marly lies St.-Germain-en-Laye, attractively set on a hill and surrounded by a small forest. It is one of the prettiest towns close to Paris, well worth a visit for its lovely views, its tempting shops and historic buildings. Since the arrival of the express métro, the town has become a popular place to live for wealthy Parisians tired of the noise and bustle of central Paris.

The Renaissance château in the center of town was built by François I as a royal residence, and Le Nôtre designed the long terrace offering lovely views over the Seine valley. Mary, Queen of Scots, lived there until the age of 16, when she married her childhood playmate, the French dauphin. Louis XIV was born in this château, and James II spent the last years of his exile here. Today it is the National Museum of Antiquities, specializing in the prehistoric period. A museum devoted to the painter Maurice Denis, a member of the Nabis group, is housed in an old priory where he once lived. A new museum in the center of town is devoted to the composer Claude Debussy, who lived here. St.-Germain is also famous for the *Fête des Loges,* a centuries-old funfair held in August in the forest.

To the north at Maisons-Laffitte, a water sports and horseracing center, is the château of Maisons, Mansart's masterpiece. Marking the transition between the Baroque and the classicism of Louis XIV, it was once occupied by the 19th-century banker Jacques Laffitte, who added his name to that of the château. Also worth visiting is the town of Conflans-Ste.-Honorine, right on the confluence of the Oise and the Seine. It has an interesting museum and is well known for its annual "Boatmen's *Pardon*" in June.

Etampes, Fontainebleau and Provins

South of Paris, beyond L'Hay-les-Roses, where you can see what are probably the finest rose gardens in the world, lies the magnificent park of Sceaux, designed, yet again, by Le Nôtre. Nothing is left of the original château, built by Colbert and made famous by the Duchesse de Maine, except the outbuildings. The interesting Museum of the Ile de France is housed in a modern château, and between mid-July and early-October, France's major chamber music festival is held in the Orangerie designed by Mansart. Near Sceaux, a most attractive small château in the Vallée-aux-Loups, at Châtenay-Malabry, was the home of the writer Chateaubriand and an important center of the Romantic movement in French literature. It is made up of three "pavilions" or wings, the Pavillon de la Rochefoucauld, the central Pavillon Chateaubriand (the earliest, dating from the late-18th century), and the Pavillon Montmorency. The lovely grounds, designed by Chateaubriand himself and pleasantly informal by French standards, include a small brick tower, the Tour Velléda, where he wrote part of *Martyrs* and the opening of the book that made him a household name throughout Europe and North America, the *Mémoires d'Outre-Tombe.*

South of Sceaux is Montlhéry, noted for its 13th–15th-century tower and its automobile racetrack. Nearby Ste.-Geneviève-des-Bois has a beautifully kept Russian cemetery and a picturesque Russian Orthodox

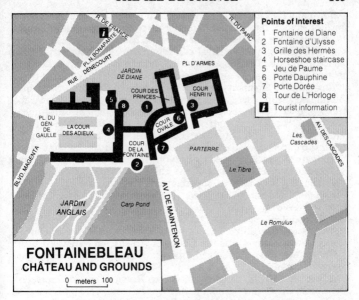

Points of Interest
1. Fontaine de Diane
2. Fontaine d'Ulysse
3. Grille des Hermès
4. Horseshoe staircase
5. Jeu de Paume
6. Porte Dauphine
7. Porte Dorée
8. Tour de L'Horloge
i Tourist information

FONTAINEBLEAU
CHÂTEAU AND GROUNDS
0 meters 100

church called Notre-Dame-de-l'Assomption, where a particularly love-ly Easter mass is held: a colony of White Russians came to live here in the 1920s.

Etampes is pleasantly situated on the banks of the river Chalouette, and has a wealth of lovely old buildings. In the rue Louis Moreau the church of St.-Basile has an interesting Romanesque portal, the rest of the church dating from the 12th through to the 16th centuries. Behind St.-Basile, the rue de la Cordonnerie leads to the Gothic church of Notre-Dame-du-Fort, with its 60-meter (200-ft.) steeple and a southern façade reminiscent of the Royal Portal at Chartres. Nearby is the house of Diane de Poitiers, who keeps popping up in our wanderings through the Ile de France and the neighboring Loire Valley. The rue du Château Guinette brings you to the oddly shaped Guinette Tower, a royal lookout dating from the 12th century. A bit farther on is a Gothic church, St.-Martin, with a curious Renaissance leaning tower.

East of Etampes is the forest of Fontainebleau, covering some 16,200 hectares (40,000 acres) and delightfully and typically French. Wild it is, yet the roads and alleys that wind through it are well-marked on Touring Club maps that show every meander, including short cuts. They are named, of course, and so are individual oaks and beeches noted for their age and beauty, among them the Jupiter, the Washing-ton, and the La Fayette. Highway signs point out stag and boar cross-ings, and all winter long you may meet hunts with hounds and horns. The rocks are celebrated, and also have names: the best known, Plutus and Gargantua, are used as training schools by the French Alpine Club. Two of the most interesting spots are the Hauteurs de la Solle, which cross magnificent groves and then drop down to the Seine valley, and the road from Barbizon to the Gorges d'Apremont with the best view of the rocks.

For many the château of Fontainebleau is even more redolent of the spirit of France than Versailles. Louis VII seems to have started building it, but it was the flamboyant François I in the early-16th century who transformed the medieval castle into a magnificent Renaissance palace, importing Primaticcio and Rosso from Italy to direct the flock of decorators, painters and mosaic and stucco experts in creating a setting suitable for his mistress, the Duchesse d'Etampes. Benvenuto Cellini had a studio here while he worked for François, and Leonardo's *Mona Lisa* first came to France because François bought it for one of his rooms. His successor, Henri II, ornamented the palace with his initial interlaced with D for Diane de Poitiers, his lady love. After his death the queen, Catherine de Médicis, continued the building work.

The gardens were designed by Le Nôtre under the patronage of Louis XIV, who also rebuilt parts of the château in the classical style. It remained for Napoleon to appreciate its full potential. He had the estate completed and redecorated. He also used it as a prison for Pope Pius VII. And it was at Fontainebleau, in the spring of 1814, that Napoleon called together his Old Guard and bade them farewell before he was escorted to Elba. Then it was known as the Cour du Cheval-Blanc; now it is known as the Cour des Adieux, or Farewell Court.

Unlike Versailles, Fontainebleau has a feeling of intimacy, perhaps because each monarch added a wing of his own. The guided tour will lead you through the Empire-period Red Room, scene of Napoleon's abdication, the Council Room dating from Charles IX and Louis XV, the Throne Room, and the Queen's Bedroom—beautifully redecorated for Marie-Antoinette. In the royal apartments you'll see famous Gobelin tapestries and a magnificent mantelpiece by Primaticcio. The Oval Court, which you reach after descending the King's Staircase, occupies the site of the original castle.

You can also visit the private apartments of Napoleon and Joséphine and the Galerie des Cerfs, where Queen Christina of Sweden, a guest at the château, ordered the assassination of her favorite courtier, Monaldeschi. You can see his coat-of-mail hanging there.

Around Fontainebleau

Close to Fontainebleau is the village of Barbizon, now no more than a single street lined with restaurants and hotels for visitors who come in search of the beauty found there by painters since 1830. Corot was the first Barbizon enthusiast, followed by Millet and Daubigny. If you want to get an idea of how Barbizon looked when Corot was there, stroll down the rue de Fleury with its quaint village look. Millet's and Rousseau's houses have become small museums, and so has the Auberge du Père Ganne, where the artists used to spend merry evenings.

Another village popular with the Impressionists was Bourron-Marlotte, located midway between Fontainebleau and Nemours in the forest of Fontainebleau. In the mid-'80s the village's château opened to the public for the first time. It was built on the foundations of a feudal castle and its elegant brick and stone wings date from the late -16th or early-17th centuries. Louis XV's father-in-law, the exiled King of Poland Stanislas Leczinski, who built the fabulous place Stanislas in Nancy, lived here for a while. Among other treasures, the château has some magnificent 17th- and 18th-century paneling, perfectly preserved, and Directoire furniture once belonging to the elegant Madame Récamier.

Also close to Fontainebleau is the delightful village of Milly-la-Forêt, a favorite with wealthy Parisians in search of a weekend retreat. Its best-known inhabitant was the poet and playwright Jean Cocteau, whose pretty turreted château can be glimpsed in the middle of the village. And Milly's main claim to fame is the lovely little 12th-century chapel he decorated called St.-Blaise-des-Simples, well worth a visit for his bold frescoes of medicinal plants or *"simples,"* many of which are grown in and around the village, plus a superb head of Christ wearing the Crown of Thorns, as well as a Resurrection. The chapel also has a bust of Cocteau, who is buried here. A stroll around the village will enable you to see the magnificent wooden market building with a lofty beamed roof worthy of a church.

On the banks of the Loing nestles the charming village of Moret-sur-Loing, another favorite weekend haunt of Parisians. Moret was immortalized by the painter Sisley, who lived here for 20 years. You can also see a number of Renaissance houses here and visit Clemenceau's house. The local people stage a magnificent show on summer evenings, a mixture of *son-et-lumière* and pageant, with spectacular costumes and special effects, illustrating the history of their ancient town.

South of Fontainebleau, and also on the Loing river, the pleasant town of Nemours is best known for its museum specializing in the prehistory of Paris and the Paris region. The area around the town has some strangely shaped rocks called "Rocher de Beauregard," "Rocher Soulès" and so on, which provide some interesting walks.

Provins

Provins is one of the most interesting towns in the whole of the Paris area. It grew up on the site of a Roman camp, and under the influence of the counts of Champagne became the economic capital of that province. Famous for rose-growing ever since the time of the Crusades, it was the third most important city in France, after Paris and Rouen, during the Middle Ages. In the 13th century the red rose of Provins was introduced into the arms of the English House of Lancaster by a member of that house who was by marriage a count of Provins.

You will want to visit Caesar's Tower, a magnificent keep of the early 12th century, the Grange aux Dîmes, or Tithe Barn, housing an interesting collection of precious stones, and the church of St.-Quiriace. In the lower city, walk along the ramparts, and stop for a look at the 12th-century abbey of St.-Ayoul.

Vaux-le-Vicomte

Vaux-le-Vicomte is one of the great monuments of French 17th-century architecture, built by Le Vau and decorated by Le Brun for Louis XIV's Superintendent of Finances, the great Fouquet. When the château was finished, its owner decided to give a party in honor of his king. There were 80 tables, 30 buffets, 6,400 pieces of solid gold plate, and a new play by Molière set in a garden rustling with 1,200 fountains and cascades. The king, wild with rage at being outshone, banished Fouquet and confiscated his wealth.

The approach to the château is relatively unimpressive: a stroll in the grounds is needed to appreciate the whole spectacular creation. The gardens, designed by Le Nôtre, offer a foretaste of his brilliant achievements at Versailles, with Grand Canal, terraces, cascades and avenues of carefully trimmed trees.

Nearer Paris is the town of Brie-Comte-Robert, with a Gothic church and arcades in the rue des Halles. The 16th-century château of Gros Bois belonged at one time to the Count of Provence, later to be Louis XVIII. It has a fine collection of furniture and works of art dating from the end of the 18th century. Nearby, at Condé-en-Brie, is a 17th–18th-century château that once belonged to the Prince de Condé. Sumptuously furnished, with many of the pieces originally designed for the Condés, it now belongs to the Sade family, who possess a great many unpublished manuscripts written by the present marquis's great-great-great-grandfather, the original marquis de Sade. A short detour brings you to the charming château of Ormesson, encircled by a mirror of water and beautiful grounds designed by—you guessed it—Le Nôtre. It is said to have been built by Henri IV for Gabrielle de Santény.

Vincennes, Champs and Guermantes

On the eastern edge of Paris is the suburb of Vincennes, with a large and rambling woody park, the Bois de Vincennes, and an interesting castle. Today, inspite of its Royal past, the Bois de Vincennes has a rather dowdy reputation. But don't let this put you off. There's plenty to see and do here: a large zoo, an excellent museum of African and Australasian art, a Transport Museum, two artificial lakes, a magnificent flower garden, a cycle track, plus many restaurants and cafés. What's more, there's a full scale royal castle, the château de Vincennes.

A guided visit to the castle includes the 14th-century keep, with a museum illustrating its history; the Gothic chapel with beautiful stained glass; and the twin royal pavilions in the imposing Cour d'Honneur (Louis XIV spent his honeymoon in the king's pavilion); Henry V of England, victor at the battle of Agincourt and Shakespeare's King Hal, died in the castle in 1422. Next to the château is the Parc Floral de Paris (Floral Garden), which will be fascinating to the dedicated gardener, specializing as it does in dahlias, irises, water plants, orchids, rhododendrons and azaleas—each in their correct season. There are also exhibits, a children's garden and some modern sculpture.

East of Vincennes the Marne Valley area is worth exploration that will awaken memories of famous battlefields down the centuries. One of the most dramatic moments came on September 7, 1914 when Marshal Joffre ordered his troops: "Advance, and if you cannot, hold your positions and be killed." To support the British entrenched in the Grand Morin valley, the French brought 6,000 men from Paris in 600 ordinary taxis, each of which made the perilous trip twice.

Other famous battles were fought at Château-Thierry, on the edge of the Champagne region. It has an ancient castle built by Charles Martel in 720 and has always been the cynosure of invaders' eyes. American troops gained glory there on Hill 204 and at Belleau Wood in World War I. For the French, Château-Thierry is chiefly celebrated as the birthplace of witty fabulist La Fontaine, whose 16th-century mansion, appropriately located on rue Jean de La Fontaine, can be visited.

Nearer Paris are two lovely Marne Valley châteaux. One is Guermantes, with attractive grounds and a charming 17th-century interior, whose name so appealed to Marcel Proust that he borrowed it for his great multi-volume novel *Remembrance of Things Past.* The other is Champs, which may be used by the French president or premier as a summer residence. Built in the early-18th century, its most celebrated tenant was Madame de Pompadour. Champs is a model of comfortable living in the old style. Each suite was equipped with its own dressing-room and bath, a novelty for the times, as was the basement kitchen. The gardens with sweeping vistas and ornamental pools are very attractive; so are Madame de Pompadour's bedroom and the sitting room decorated with *chinoiseries* by Huët.

Senlis and Compiègne

On the way to Senlis you might like to visit Mortefontaine, Ermenonville, and Chaâlis. Just outside Mortefontaine is the Parc de Valliéra, which inspired many of Corot's paintings, particularly *Souvenir de Mortefontaine,* and may also have been the inspiration for Watteau's famous *Embarquement pour Cythère.* A short distance beyond is the 18th-century château of Ermenonville, set in lovely gardens—designed by the Marquis de Girardin—and one of the first examples in France of the informal *jardin a l'anglaise.* Jean Jacques Rousseau, who died while a guest of the Marquis de Girardin at Ermenonville, was buried on the tiny Island of Poplars. The grave is still marked, although his remains were later moved to the Panthéon in Paris. In town there is an interesting 16th-century church with a 13th-century choir.

The 18th-century abbey at Chaâlis—the work of Jean Aubert, the architect of the stables at Chantilly and the Rodin Museum in Paris—is notable for the simplicity of its design and its perfect proportions. Beyond the abbey gate stretches the strange *Mer de Sable,* a "Sea of Sand," whose glistening whiteness contrasts with the lush greenery surrounding it. Children will enjoy a visit to the amusement park, where camels carry them across the dunes and Indians attack a mail train, and to a small zoo.

Between the twin forests of Chantilly and Ermenonville lies one of the brightest stars in the Ile de France firmament, Senlis, surrounded by a splendid beech forest. Senlis has a Gothic cathedral older than those of Paris and Chartres, and nearby stand the remains of the royal palace that housed French rulers from the time of Charlemagne to Henri IV. In an 18th-century addition to this château you will find a hunting museum. Fragments of the Gallo-Roman walls of Senlis can still be seen. West of the town are remains of a Roman arena that once seated more than 10,000 spectators. A conducted tour of the old town provides an excellent introduction.

Farther along the same road is the stunning castle of Pierrefonds, perched on a promontory with fairytale towers soaring to the sky. The original building was dismantled by Louis XIII, so the present château is a 19th-century fascimile painstakingly restored by Viollet-le-Duc.

Historic Compiègne

Route Eugénie, crossing the majestic oak and beech forest of Compiègne, leads to the town of Compiègne, whose history, dating from Charlemagne, has included many moments of great drama. Joan of Arc was finally captured in the Battle of Compiègne in 1430; in the 18th century Corsica was ceded to France in a treaty that was signed here. Louis XV built the impressive but rather lifeless château, which ranks after Versailles and Fontainebleau as one of the palaces of the French monarchs. Napoleon married Marie-Louise of Austria here. The Empress Eugénie and her Bonaparte husband made it the scene of some of their greatest weekend parties. The château houses a fine collection of First Empire furniture and a series of paintings illustrating the story of Don Quixote. In another building in the grounds is a Vehicle Museum, with carriages, bicycles and automobiles of all periods.

The beautiful 16th-century Hôtel de Ville was built by Louis XII; in its bell tower the quarter-hours are marked by carved wooden figures moving into view and then disappearing. It houses two museums that specialists will find exciting: the Musée Vivenel, displaying a fine collection of Greek vases, and the Musée de la Figurine Historique, with 85,000 lead, tin and wooden soldiers from Vercingetorix to de Gaulle. Visit also the 13th-century churches of St.-Jacques and St.-Antoine, the abbey built by Charles the Bald, and the 12th-century tower from which Joan of Arc is alleged to have set out before her capture by the Burgundian and English armies.

A short distance from Compiègne, near Rethondes, is the Clairière de l'Armistice, where a railway car was run out on a spur line especially for the occasion. In it the Armistice of 1918, marking the Allied victory, and the French surrender of 1940, were signed—the latter accompanied by Hitler's jig for joy. The car now is a replica of the original.

Not far from here is the Museum of Franco-American Cooperation at Blérancourt. Housed in two wings of the château, the collection traces the history of Franco-American friendship from the days of the American Revolution to the present.

Noyon and Soissons

Farther northeast along the river Oise is Noyon, an ancient village which, in spite of damage in both world wars, still proudly displays treasures dating from the Middle Ages. The cathedral was built in the late-12th century and the early part of the 13th. Its transitional character, combining the simplicity and strength of the Romanesque style with the grace and daring of the Gothic, makes the cathedral one of the most interesting in this region. South of it is the 16th–17th-century bishopric housing the municipal museum. The Hôtel de Ville, or Town Hall built during the same era, was largely destroyed in World War I, but it has been restored, as has the birthplace of John Calvin.

Close to Noyon, on the edge of the forest, is the ruined Cistercian Abbaye d'Ourscamps, begun during the 12th century. Most striking is the infirmary, dating from the middle of the 13th century.

Its geographical location has made Soissons, east of Compiègne, a predestined battleground. Both the town and its handsome 13th-century cathedral of St.-Gervais suffered heavy damage during World War I. The cathedral lost one of its towers and the nave was split in two, but it has been restored. At the end of the choir may be seen Ruben's *Adoration of the Shepherds.* Also worth seeing are the 13th-century church of St.-Léger, the beautiful façade of the abbey of St.-Jean-des-Vignes, the abbey of St.-Médard and its 9th-century crypt and, in the rue de la Bannière, the memorial to the British soldiers who fell during the battles of the Aisne and the Marne in World War I.

A short detour after leaving Soissons will enable you to visit the château of Villers-Cotterêts, begun by François I, decorated by Philibert Delorme, and enlarged to include grounds landscaped by Le Nôtre.

The vast forest of Villers-Cotterêts was a royal hunting ground until 1789, and stag hunts are still held here. In the town you can see the house where Alexandre Dumas *père* was born, at no. 54 in the street of the same name. There is also a museum dedicated to the two Dumas, father and son. At La Ferté Milon is the birthplace of Jean Racine, the great classical dramatist, but the house cannot be visited.

Enghien, Ecouen and Beauvais

St.-Denis, an otherwise unattractive industrial suburb six km. (four miles) north of Paris, houses the famous basilica (officially now a cathedral) where most of the French monarchs were crowned and where, since Dagobert in 638, they were buried. The first sanctuary was built in 475, to be replaced in 630 and again in 775, but the present church was begun in 1140. Inside are the celebrated *gisants,* tombs bearing recumbent statues of such illustrious personages as François I, Catherine de Médicis and Henri II. St.-Denis also has an interesting and attractively arranged art and history museum in a newly restored Carmelite monastery.

Beyond St.-Denis is Enghien, noted not only for its casino and racetrack, but for a small lake and thermal springs with sulphurous water. North of both St.-Denis and Enghien is the beautiful 16th-century château of Ecouen, well worth visiting for its excellent Museum of the Renaissance, displaying marvelous bronzes, enamels and tapestries as well as furniture.

Beauvais is crowned with the tallest, as well as one of the most beautiful, cathedrals in Europe. After the usual early history of destruction by fire, the Beauvais religious authorities decided in 1225 to build the largest and highest cathedral in the world. Their ambitions were inflated—the height of the vaulted roof (43 meters/141 ft.) is greater than that of Notre Dame in Paris. From then on, Beauvais' history was an unfortunate sequence of faith, miscalculation and collapse. Forty years of labor were required to prevent the choir from falling down. Then after finishing the transept, the bold Beauvasians unwisely topped it with a steeple. Inadequately buttressed, it crashed to the ground in 1573, and with it the last hope that the cathedral could ever be completed.

Even in its unfinished state, the cathedral is fascinating. The pillars that sweep to the sky give a marvelous impression of lightness and are a thrilling sight, as are the Beauvais and Flemish tapestries and the stained-glass windows dating from the 13th, 14th and 16th centuries. The cathedral also has a famous astronomical clock.

Between St.-Denis and Beauvais lies the Château de Nointel, with famous 17th-century gardens now superbly restored (Fragonard painted some lovely views of them). The château was opened to the public in the mid-'80s and is well worth a visit for its collections of Empire furniture and modern graphic art.

Chantilly

South of Beauvais is Chantilly, celebrated for cream, lace, horse-races, a forest and a supremely romantic Renaissance château built on two islands in the middle of a small lake. Chantilly's real story begins in the 16th century with the Connétable de Montmorency, who held power under six successive kings. Even Catherine de Médicis liked him—he found the cure for her barrenness. To kill him off at the age of 75 in the battle of St.-Denis, the Protestants found that it required five sword thrusts, two pike blows, and a cannonball in the spine.

As you come up to the château gate, stop to visit on the left the 18th-century stone stable built by the Duc de Condé to house 240 horses and 420 dogs for stag and boar hunts in the nearby forest. The stables, with their indoor and outdoor paddocks, are still used today. In the attractive grounds, designed (of course) by Le Nôtre, are the maison de Sylvie and the *hameau,* Chantilly's version of a Marie-Antoinette village for play. The nearby racetrack is one of the prettiest in Europe.

The château itself is made up of two separate buildings, the 16th-century Petit-Château and the 19th-century Grand-Château, mirrored in the ornamental ponds that surround them. Inside is the Musée Condé, containing magnificent paintings and tapestries hung in paneled halls, as well as one of France's finest 15th-century illuminated manuscripts, the *Très Riches Heures du Duc de Berry,* depicting the 12 months of the year. The collection of miniatures by the first great French painter, Jehan Fouquet, is outstanding. In the Jewel Room is the enormous pink diamond known as Le Grand Condé.

Nearby is another architectural treasure, the Gothic abbey of Royaumont. The dormitory, chapter hall and library are now occupied by the International Center of Culture, and concerts are held here in the summer months.

PRACTICAL INFORMATION FOR THE ILE DE FRANCE

TOURIST OFFICES. The regional tourist office for the Ile de France—written enquiries only—is the *Comité Régional de Tourisme d'Ile-de-France,* 101 rue de Vaugirard, 75006 Paris (tel. 42-22-74-43). In addition, the *départements* of the Ile de France also have their own tourist offices (again, written enquiries only): **Essonne,** 4 rue d l'Arche, 91000 Corbeil-Essones (tel. 60-89-31-32); **Eure-et-Loir,** 7 pl. J-Moulin, 28000 Chartres (tel. 37-21-37-22); **Hauts-de-Seine,** 1 rue Troay, 92140 Clamart (tel. 46-42-17-95); **Seine-et-Marne,** 2 av. Gallieni, 77000 Melun (tel. 64-37-19-36); **Seine-St.-Denis,** 2 av. Gabriel Péri, 93100 Montreuil (tel. 42-87-38-09); **Val-de-Marne,** 11 av. de Nogent, 94130 **Vincennes** (tel. 48-08-13-00); **Val d'Oise,** 23 l'Isle-Adam 95290 (tel. 34-69-09-76); **Yvelines,** préfecture 78101 Versailles (tel. 39-51-82-00).

There are local tourist offices in the following towns: **Beauvais,** 6 rue Malherbe (tel. 44-45-08-18) (closed Aug.); **Chantilly,** av. Maréchal-Joffre (tel. 44-57-08-58) (closed mid-Nov. through Feb.); **Chartres,** 7 cloître Notre-Dame (tel. 37-21-54-03); **Compiègne,** pl. Hôtel-de-Ville (tel. 44-40-01-00); **Fontainebleau,** 31 pl. Napoléon-Bonaparte (tel. 64-22-25-68); **Mantes-la-Jolie,** pl. Jean-XXIII (tel. 34-77-10-30); **Rambouillet,** pl. Libération (tel. 34-83-11-91); **St.-Germain-en-Laye,** 1 bis rue République (tel. 34-51-05-12); **Senlis,** pl. Parvis Notre-Dame (tel. 44-53-06-40); **Versailles,** 7 rue Réservoirs (tel. 39-50-36-22).

REGIONAL FOOD. The cooking of the Ile de France is inseparable from Paris. You'll find specialties like onion soup, *matelote* fish stew (once made with fish from the many local rivers), grilled pigs' feet, little pork *pâtés de Pantin* wrapped in pastry in all manner of shapes. Led by the sophisticated pastrycooks of the capital, brioches, croissants and butter pastries are particularly good.

Game such as hare, deer, pheasant, and the modest rabbit, is popular—incredibly, wild boar still survive in the forest of Fontainebleau only 65 kms. (40 miles) from Notre Dame. Country *auberges* featuring such treats an hour or so's drive from the capital are much-advertised but can be high-priced traps for the unwary.

Most importantly, the Ile de France acts as Paris' vegetable garden. A dish *à la parisienne* has button mushrooms, once cultivated in caves along the Seine river valley. Look out for cherries with duck in *canard montmorency*, for strawberries and peaches in charlottes and gâteaux. Artichokes, turnips, peas and green beans appear in dishes like *potage cultivateur* vegetable soup and *navarin* lamb stew with baby vegetables. The cream soups like *potage argenteuil* with asparagus, and *potage germiny* with sorrel are particularly fine.

 HOTELS AND RESTAURANTS. Accommodations in the Ile de France are rarely outstanding—perhaps because thousands of French families have purchased little farms, cottages, manors and châteaux in the area and consequently rarely have need of hotels. Nonetheless, with prices in Paris getting higher all the time, many visitors take advantage of the lower prices found in some of the inner suburbs—Malmaison, St.-Germain-en-Laye, St.-Rémy-les-Chevreuse—where the express métro, the RER, operates and where a number of good hotels have now been built. The area has numerous excellent restaurants, however, many in hotels.

For general notes on hotels and restaurants, see "Hotels" and "Restaurants" in *Facts at Your Fingertips*.

ANET. Restaurant. *Manoir d'Anet* (M), 3 pl. château (tel. 37-41-91-05). Closed Feb. and first half Nov., Tues. and Wed. Right opposite château; good-value classical dishes; must reserve for lunch.

BEAUVAIS. *Chenal* (M), 63 blvd. Général-de-Gaulle (tel. 44-45-03-55). 25 rooms. Well run, good service but no restaurant. AE, DC, MC, V. *Palais* (I), rue St. Nicolas (tel. 44-45-12-58). 14 rooms. Very close to cathedral; well managed; no restaurant. V.

Restaurants. *Crémaillère* (M), 1 rue G.-Patin (tel. 44-45-03-13). Closed Tues. evening, Wed. Old favorite for well-prepared regional dishes and cosy atmosphere. V. *À La Côtelette* (M), 8 rue Jacobins (tel. 44-45-04-42). Closed July, Sun. evening, and Mon. (except hols.). Near cathedral, with some good regional specialties. AE, V. *Marignan* (I), 1 rue Malherbe (tel. 44-48-15-15). Closed Feb., Sun. for dinner, Mon. Snacks on ground floor, attractive full-scale restaurant upstairs with good traditional dishes and wide range of fixed-price meals. MC, V.

BOUGIVAL. *Château de la Jonchère* (E), 10 côte Jonchère (tel. 39-18-57-03). 6 rooms. Closed Wed. Once a private château bought by Napoleon for one of Joséphine's brothers; now converted with no expense spared into hotel-restaurant with startling colorful décor; lots of style, good *nouvelle cuisine,* lovely grounds. AE, DC, MC, V. *Forest Hill* (M), 12 rue Yvan-Tourgueneff (tel. 39-18-17-16). 175 rooms. Attractive modern hotel overlooking Seine, with openair pool and pleasant restaurant. AE, DC, MC, V.

Restaurants. *Camélia* (E), 7 quai Georges-Clemenceau (tel. 39-69-03-02). Closed Sun. evening and Mon. Smart roadside inn near river serving superb *nouvelle cuisine* in delightful setting; popular with well-heeled Parisians, so must reserve. AE, DC, V. *Huitre et Tarte* (M), 6 quai G. Clémenceau (tel. 39-18-45-55). Newly opened; creativity and good value. Closed Sun. for dinner, Mon. and Aug. V.

At **Louveciennes**, *Aux Chandelles* (M), 12 pl. Eglise (tel. 39-69-08-40). Closed Sat. for lunch, Sun. for dinner and Wed. Pretty setting on village square up hill from river; garden and *nouvelle cuisine* versions of good home cooking.

v. *Tilleuls* (M), 2 quai Conti (tel. 39-69-00-97). Closed Feb., Mon. and Tues. Delightful terrace overlooking river; reliable classical cuisine. v.

At **Port-Marly,** 2 km. (1¼ miles) west, of Bougival, *Lion d'Or* (M), 7 rue Paris (tel. 39-58-44-56). Closed first half Mar., first half Sept., Tues. and Wed. Attractive village setting as in the Impressionists' day; good newish cuisine. AE, v.

BRETEUIL. Restaurants. *Crêperie* (I), in château grounds. Closed Oct. through Apr.; open Sun. and public hols. only. Convenient pancake place.

At **Chevreuse,** *Auberge du Moulin* (M), 56 rue Porte-de-Paris (tel. 30-52-16-45). Closed mid-Aug. to mid-Sept., and Tues. Attractive, creeper-covered building; adequate food. v. *Puszta* (M), Carrefour St.-Laurent (tel. 34-61-18-35). Closed Tues. Good-value *menu* made up of Hungarian specialties; ambiance is Hungarian; attractive garden for eating out on fine days. v. *Loubasque* (I), 18 rte. de la Madeleine (tel. 30-52-15-77). Closed mid-Aug. to mid-Sept., and Thurs. Specialties from the Basque country.

At **St.-Rémy-les-Chevreuse,** *Cressonnière* (E), 46 rte. de Port-Royal (tel. 30-52-00-41). Closed part of Feb., Tues. and Wed. Looks like a country inn but serves very chic *nouvelle cuisine,* plus a few classical dishes. Outdoor meals in summer. AE, DC, v.

CHANTILLY. *Campanile* (M), rte. Creil (tel. 44-57-39-24). 50 rooms. Modern motel-type; no atmosphere but quiet and well run; grillroom for basic meals. v.

At **Chaumontel,** 9 km. (5 miles) away, *Château de Chaumontel* (E), (tel. 34-71-00-30). 20 rooms. Closed mid-July for 3 weeks. Once the Prince de Condé's hunting lodge, now a peaceful and elegant château-hotel with moat and gardens.

At **Gouvieux-Chantilly,** 3 km. (2 miles) west, *Château de la Tour* (M), chemin de la Chaussée (tel. 44-57-07-39). Beautiful country house in the middle of a park; with tennis and restaurant. AE, v.

At **Lys-Chantilly,** 7 km. (4½ miles) south, *Hostellerie du Lys* (M), (tel. 44-21-26-19). 35 rooms. Closed Christmas and New Year period. Secluded and delightful, with garden and terrace for summer meals. AE, DC, MC.

Restaurants. *Relais Condé* (M), 42 av. Joffre (tel. 44-57-05-75). Closed second halves of both Jan. and July, also Mon. (except public hols.). Converted chapel conveniently close to racecourse; classical, and also more modern cuisine. AE, DC, v. *Relais du Coq Chantant* (M), 21 rte. Creil (tel. 44-57-01-28). Upmarket version of a road-house, with mixture of classical and *nouvelle cuisine.* AE, DC, MC. *Capitainerie du Château* (I), (tel. 44-57-15-89). Closed Mon. and Tues. Welcome new find actually in the medieval basement of the château, complete with period kitchen equipment; handy help-yourself buffet available non-stop 10.30–6.30, followed by cheese and dessert, with a couple of hot dishes too; good value menus. *Quatre Saisons* (I), 9 av. Général-Leclerc (tel. 44-57-04-65). Closed most of Feb., and Mon. (except public hols.). Attractive, with flowery terrace for openair meals. Some Danish specialties; dishes deliciously light, *menus* good value. AE, DC, v.

CHARTRES. *Grand Monarque* (M), 22 pl. des Épars (tel. 37-21-00-72). 47 rooms. Good mixture of classical and more modern cuisine in this pleasant converted coaching inn; belongs to Mapotel group. AE, DC, MC, v. *Mercure* (M), 6 av. Jehan-de-Beauce (tel. 37-21-78-00). 49 rooms. Central, modern and well run; restaurant. AE, DC, MC, v.

Restaurants. *Estocade* (E), rue Porte Guillaume (tel. 37-34-27-17). In beautiful setting along the river; good classical cuisine. Closed Sun. for dinner and Mon. AE, DC, MC, v. *Henri IV* (E), 31 rue du Soleil d'Or (tel. 37-36-01-55). Closed Jan., Feb., Mon. evening and Tues. (except public hols.). Old favorite close to cathedral; classical cuisine with a few *nouvelle cuisine* touches. DC. *Buisson Ardent* (M), 10 rue au Lait (tel. 37-34-04-66). Closed most of Aug., Wed. and Sun. for dinner. Another long-time favorite; attractive old building with beams and good-value *menus.* AE, DC. *Vieille Maison* (M), 5 rue au Lait (tel. 37-34-10-67). Closed first halves of both Jan. and July, both Sun. and Mon. for dinner. Another attractive old place near cathedral; *nouvelle cuisine.* AE, DC, MC, V.

CHÂTEAU-THIERRY. *Ile de France* (M), rte. de Soissons (tel. 23-69-10-12). 56 rooms. Closed one week at Christmas. Overlooking Marne river, just outside town; well run and comfortable; restaurant. AE, DC, MC, V.

Restaurant. *Auberge Jean de la Fontaine* (M), 10 rue des Filoirs (tel. 23-83-63-89). Good, generous cooking. Good-value *menus* at weekend. Closed Sun. for dinner, Mon. and Aug. V.

COMPIÈGNE. *Residence de la Forêt* (M), 112 rue St. Lazare (tel. 44-20-22-86). 19 rooms. Nice new hotel near golf course and race track. Restaurant overlooking garden. DC, V. *France* (I), 17 rue Eugène-Floquet (tel. 44-40-02-74). 20 rooms. 17th-cent. inn still going strong, with restaurant (M) delightfully called "The Rôtisserie of the Spinning Cat." AE, DC.

Restaurants. *Hostellerie Royal-Lieu* (E), 9 rue Senlis (tel. 44-20-10-24). Closed part of Feb. Deluxe dining room with attractive openair terrace; mostly *nouvelle cuisine;* also a comfortable hotel. 17 rooms. AE, DC, V.

At **Choisy-au-Bac,** 3 km. (2 miles) northeast, *Auberge des Etangs du Buissonnet* (M), (tel. 44-40-17-41). Closed both Sun. and Mon. for dinner. Attractive inn on edge of forest with nice garden and good classical cuisine including a few regional dishes. V.

At **St.-Jean-aux-Bois,** 11 km. (7 miles) away, *Bonne Idée* (M), 3 rue Meuniers (tel. 44-42-84-09). Closed mid-Jan. to mid-Feb., 2 weeks from end Aug., Tues., Wed. for lunch. Pleasant inn in forest setting; mostly classical cuisine; also has 14 attractive rooms. AE, V.

CONFLANS-STE.-HONORINE. Restaurant. *Au Bord de l'Eau* (M), 15 quai Martyrs-de-la-Résistance (tel. 39-72-86-51). Closed one week early Mar., Aug. and Mon. Lunches only, but is open Sat. for dinner too. Right beside river; straightforward grills and good fresh fish.

ENGHIEN. Restaurant. *Duc d'Enghien* (E), Enghien Casino (tel. 34-12-80-00). Closed Jan., Sun. for dinner, Mon. Excellent *nouvelle cuisine;* elegant decor, clientele to match. AE, DC, V.

ETAMPES. At **Court-Pain,** 9 km. (5 miles) south, *Auberge de Courpain* (M), (tel. 64-95-67-04). Attractive, peaceful spot with big garden; good classical cuisine and lovely antique furniture. AE, DC.

Restaurant. *Grand Monarque* (I), 1 pl. Romanet (tel. 64-94-29-90). Closed most of Feb., Sun. eve., Mon. Near Notre-Dame-du-Fort church; good value. AE, DC, MC, V.

FONTAINEBLEAU. *Aigle Noir* (E), 27 pl. Napoléon (tel. 64-22-32-65). 30 rooms. Grand hotel overlooking palace gardens; period furniture plus all modern comforts; two restaurants (see below). AE, DC, MC, V. *Ile de France* (M), 128 rue France (tel. 64-22-21-17). 29 rooms. Attractive, typically French provincial building, but the restaurant (I) in this pleasant hotel serves Chinese cuisine. AE, DC, V. *Toulouse* (I), 183 rue Grande (tel. 64-22-22-73). 18 rooms. Closed mid-Dec.to mid-Jan. Small and cozy, in town center; no restaurant. V.

At **Barbizon,** 9½ km. (6 miles) away, *Bas-Bréau* (E), 22 rue Grande (tel. 60-66-40-05). 12 rooms and 7 apartments. Closed Jan. to mid-Feb. Beautiful garden, tables outside in summer; excellent food, specialty is game with wild mushrooms in season. AE, DC, V. *Alouettes* (I), 4 rue Antoine-Barye (tel. 60-66-41-98). 30 rooms. Closed Sun. for dinner. Comfortable Logis de France; good restaurant. AE, DC, V.

At **Recloses,** 10 km. (6 miles) away, *Casa del Sol* (M), (tel. 64-24-20-35). 8 rooms. Closed Jan. and Tues. (except July and Aug.). Relais du Silence on edge of forest; home-style cuisine. AE, DC.

Restaurants. *Beauharnais* (E), in *Aigle Noir* hotel, 27 rue Bonaparte (tel. 64-22-32-65). Grand restaurant in grand hotel, but cuisine is far from stuffy, with *nouvelle cuisine* specialties as well as light versions of classical cuisine. AE, DC, MC, V. *Bivouac* (M), also in *Aigle Noir* hotel. More modest, with good-value newish cuisine. AE, DC, V. *François Ier* (M), 3 rue Royale (tel. 64-22-24-68). Closed Jan. and Thurs. (except in summer). Opposite the Cour des Adieux. Fast service for good food; game in season. AE, DC, V. *Filet de Sole* (I), 5 rue du Coq-Gris (tel. 64-22-25-05). Closed July, Tues. and Wed. Attractive old building, good-value cuisine.

At **Barbizon,** 9½ km. (6 miles) away. *Relais* (M), 2 av. Charles-de-Gaulle (tel. 60-66-40-28). Closed last half Aug., Christmas and New Year, Tues. and Wed. Good home cooking, outdoor meals in summer. v. *Flambée* (I), 26 rue Grande (tel. 60-66-40-78). Closed for dinner Mon. through Thurs. Unusual and good-value *menu*.

ILLIERS-COMBRAY. *Moulin de Montjouvin* (I), rte. Brou (tel. 37-24-32-32). 14 rooms. Closed mid-Dec. to mid-Jan., first half Aug. and Wed. Good place for lunch if visiting Proust museum or as a base for visiting Chartres (25 km., 15 miles, away); country inn with big garden, tennis and miniature lake. DC, MC.

MAINTENON. *Château d'Esclimont* (E), at St.-Symphorien-le-Château (tel. 37-31-15-15). 50 rooms. Lovely 16th-century Relais et Châteaux member surrounded by grounds with tennis courts, pool, angling; rooms and apartments in château itself and also in converted stables, keep and hunting lodge; pleasant restaurant. AE, DC, V.

Restaurant. *Aqueduc* (M), pl. Gare (tel. 37-27-60-05). Closed Feb., Sun. for dinner, Mon. (except public hols.). Good classical cuisine; also has 18 rooms. AE, DC, V.

MAISONS-LAFFITTE. Restaurants. *Premier de Manon* (M), 8 av. Grétry (tel. 39-62-03-94). Closed Sun., Mon. and Aug. Pleasant *menu-carte* with home cooking; good value. Garden. AE, DC, V. *Tastevin* (M), 9 av. Eglé (tel. 39-62-11-67). Closed first half Feb., mid-Aug. to mid-Sept., Mon. for dinner, and Tues. In the public gardens, with terrace for outdoor meals; good *nouvelle cuisine*. AE, DC, V. *Laffitte* (M), 5 av. St.-Germain (tel. 39-62-01-53). Closed Aug., Tues. for dinner, and Wed. Good classical dishes, with a lot of fish. AE, V.

MALMAISON. Restaurants. *El Chiquito* (E), 126 av. Paul-Doumer (tel. 47-51-00-53). Closed Aug. Expensive but attractive, with lovely garden; specializes in fish. v. *Pavillon Joséphine* (M), 191 av. Napoléon-Bonaparte (tel. 47-51-01-62). Closed two weeks in Aug., Sun. for dinner and Mon. Good-value *menus*, interesting *nouvelle cuisine*; just by château entrance. AE, DC, V. *Relais de St.-Cucufa* (M), 114 rue Général-de-Miribel (tel. 47-49-79-05). Closed two weeks in Aug., both Sun. and Mon. for dinner. Attractive terrace for summer meals; particularly good fish. AE, DC, V.

MANTES. At **La Roche-Guyon,** 16 km. (10 miles) away, *St.-Georges* (I), (tel. 34-79-70-16). 15 rooms. Quiet hotel with riverside terrace and home-style cooking; also convenient for visiting Giverny (see Normandy chapter).

MEAUX. *Sirène* (M), 33 rue Général-Leclerc (tel. 64-34-07-80). 16 rooms. Closed Feb.; restaurant closed Sun. for dinner. 18th-century building with garden and good restaurant. AE, DC, V. *Richemont* (I), quai Grande-Ile (tel. 60-25-12-10). 42 rooms. Restaurant closed Sun. and public hols. On banks of Marne and a good base for visiting the region; modern and well run; garden; grillroom. MC, V.

Restaurants. *Relais St.-Etienne* (M), 1 pl. Charles-de-Gaulle (tel. 64-34-00-26). Good local specialties served in this long-standing restaurant opposite cathedral; good-value (I) *menus*. AE, DC, V.

At **Condé-Ste.-Libiaire,** 11 km. (7 miles) away, *Vallée de la Marne* (M), 2 quai Marne (tel. 60-04-31-01). Closed mid-July to mid-Aug., Tues. for dinner, Wed. Attractive riverside inn, ideal for lunch or dinner when visiting Marne valley; outdoor meals in lovely garden in summer; reliable classical cuisine. v.

At **La Ferté-sous-Jouarre,** 20 km. (12½ miles) away, *Auberge de Condé* (E), 1 av. de Montmirail (tel. 60-22-00-07). Closed most of Feb., Mon. for dinner, and Tues. Rich classical cuisine with occasional "new" touches in this elegant inn; good place for lunch if visiting Marne valley. AE, DC, MC, v.

MILLY-LA-FORÊT. Restaurant. *Moustier* (E), 41 bis rue Langlois (tel. 64-98-92-52). Closed mid-Aug. to mid-Sept., Christmas and New Year, Mon. and Tues. except public hols. Converted 12th-century crypt, elegant, with light and subtle *nouvelle cuisine*. Convenient for visitors to Cocteau's chapel. AE, v.

NEMOURS. *Roches* (I), av. L.-Pelletier in St.-Pierre district (tel. 64-28-01-43). Closed two weeks in Feb. On edge of forest, with good restaurant; (also closed Sun. evening and Mon. for lunch); ideal for a peaceful night or two or an al fresco lunch when visiting the Fontainebleau/Moret region. AE, DC, MC, v.

Restaurant. *Ecu de France* (M), 3 rue Paris (tel. 64-28-11-54). Closed Christmas and New Year. Delightful addition; classical cuisine; also a hotel with 28 rooms. AE, DC, MC, v.

PROVINS. Restaurant. *Vieux Remparts* (M), 3 rue Couverte (tel. 64-00-02-89). Closed end of Feb. to mid-Mar., last 2 weeks of Sept., Tues. for dinner, Wed. Attractive old building in Ville Haute. Good hearty cuisine and good-value (I) *menu.* AE, v.

RAMBOUILLET. *St.-Charles* (M), 15 rue Groussay (tel. 34-83-06-34). 14 rooms. Closed last half Dec. to early Jan. and first half of Aug. On edge of forest, no restaurant.

At **Senlisse,** 15 km. (10 miles) away, *Gros Marronnier* (M), (tel. 30-52-51-69). Closed Dec. to Feb. 15. 14 rooms. Typically Ile-de-France village setting for this 12th-century building; good home-style cooking. AE, DC, v.

Restaurants. *Poste* (I), 101 rue Général-de-Gaulle (tel. 34-83-03-01). Closed mid-Aug. to mid-Sept., mid-Feb. to mid-Mar., Mon., and Sun. eve. Good value spot near château. AE, v.

At **Senlisse,** 15 km. (10 miles) away, *Pont-Hardi* (M), (tel. 30-52-50-78). Closed half of Aug., part of Feb., Wed., and Tues. eve. Attractive country inn with newish cuisine and 5 charming rooms. DC, v.

At **Dampierre,** 12 km. (7½ miles) northeast, *Auberge du Château* (M), 1 Grande-Rue (tel. 30-52-52-89). Closed first halves of Jan. and Aug., Sun. evening and Mon. Opposite château; rich classical cuisine. DC, v.

ST.-DENIS. *Melody* (M), 15 rue Gabriel-Péri (tel. 48-20-87-73). Closed Aug., Sun., Mon. for dinner. Generous and imaginative cooking and nice selection of wines. v. *Mets du Roy* (M), 4 rue Boulangerie (tel. 48-20-89-74). Closed Easter period, second half July, and at weekends. Right opposite cathedral; reliable cuisine. AE, DC, v.

ST.-GERMAIN-EN-LAYE. *La Forestière* (E), 1 av. Président-Kennedy (tel. 39-73-36-60). 24 rooms. Closed Mon. (except if public hol.). Deluxe Relais et Châteaux member on edge of forest with good restaurant (*Cazaudehore*) serving cuisine from southwest France. v.

At **Orgeval,** 11 km. (7 miles) away, *Moulin d'Orgeval* (M), (tel. 39-75-95-74). 13 rooms. Closed mid-Dec. to mid-Feb. Pleasant riverside terrace for outdoor meals; classical cuisine; comfortable rooms; garden and tennis. v.

Restaurants. *Pavillon de la Croix de Noailles* (E), carrefour de Noailles (39-62-53-46). Closed Mon. Converted 18th-century hunting lodge outside town; delicious *nouvelle cuisine*. AE, DC. *Pavillon Henri IV* (E), 19–20 rue Thiers (tel. 34-51-62-62). Lovely views will whet your appetite for excellent classical cuisine served in luxuriously converted little château where Louis XIV was born. AE, DC, MC, V. *Petite Auberge* (M), 119 rue Léon-Désoyer (tel. 34-51-03-99). Closed second half Mar., July, Tues. for dinner, Wed. Home-style cooking, including meat grilled over open fire; good value. *Au Sept rue des Coches* (M), 7 rue Coches (tel. 39-73-66-40). Closed most of Aug., Sun. for dinner and Mon. Fashionable décor and equally fashionable *nouvelle cuisine*. AE, DC, MC, V.

SENLIS. *Hostellerie Porte-Bellon* (I), 51 rue Bellon (tel. 44-53-03-05). 20 rooms. Closed mid-Dec. to mid-Jan., Friday (except in high season). Close to town center and bus station; with restaurant. V.

Restaurants. *Rôtisserie de Formanoir* (M), 17 rue Châtel (tel. 44-53-04-39). Converted 16th-century monastery near cathedral; mostly "new" cuisine. V. *Vert Galant* (I), 15 pl. Henri IV (tel. 44-53-60-15). Closed Sun. for dinner, Mon. and last 2 weeks of Aug. Beautiful 13th-century vaulted restaurant, with lovely garden. Excellent and good-value *menu-carte*. AE, V.

THOIRY. *Etoile* (I), (tel. 34-87-40-21). 12 rooms. Closed Jan. and Mon. Modest hotel-restaurant across village green from château; good value. AE, DC, MC, V.

At **Douains,** near Pacy-sur-Eure, *Château de Brécourt* (M), (tel. 32-52-40-50). 24 rooms. Closed Wed. Relais et Châteaux member, 17th-century building in huge grounds; goodish food and particularly pleasant atmosphere; must reserve for lunch as this is a popular spot for visitors to Giverny and Anet as well as Thoiry. AE, DC, MC, V.

Restaurants. At **Montfort-l'Amaury,** *Préjugés* (E), 18 pl. Robert-Brault (tel. 34-86-92-65). Closed Jan. and Tues. Elegantly converted old building serving equally elegant *nouvelle cuisine*. AE, DC, V. *Chez Nous* (M), 22 rue Paris (tel. 34-86-01-62). Closed first half March, Oct., Fri. evening in winter, Sun. eve. and Mon. Old favorite for rural atmosphere; mostly classical cuisine. AE, DC, V.

At **Les Mousseaux-Pontchartrain,** *Auberge Dauberie* (M), 53 rue Dauberie (tel. 34-87-80-57). Closed Feb., Mon. and Tues. Delightful village spot with good *nouvelle cuisine*. AE, DC, V.

VERSAILLES. *Trianon Palace* (L), 1 blvd. Reine (tel. 39-50-34-12). 120 rooms. Deluxe, close to château; huge garden; excellent restaurant (some classical, some *nouvelle* cuisine). AE, DC, MC, V. *Versailles* (M), rue Ste.-Anne (tel. 39-50-64-65). 48 rooms. Modern, near château; no restaurant. AE, V. *Home St.-Louis* (I), 28 rue St. Louis (tel. 39-50-23-55). 27 rooms. Good little hotel, recently modernized; close to château; no restaurant.

Restaurants. *Trois Marches* (E), 3 rue Colbert (tel. 39-50-13-21). Closed Sun. and Mon. Very close to château and a wonderful experience! One of the best in France for *nouvelle cuisine*. AE, DC, MC, V. *Boule d'Or* (M), 25 rue Maréchal-Foch (tel. 39-50-22-97). Closed Sun. eve. and Mon. Boasts of being the oldest inn in Versailles (dates from 1696) and offers interesting dishes to recipes by France's greatest chefs of the last six centuries. AE, DC, V. *Brasserie du Théâtre* (M), 15 rue des Réservoirs (tel. 39-50-03-21). Open daily to 1 A.M. Fine decor. V. *Rescatore* (M), 27 av. St.-Cloud (tel. 39-50-23-60). Closed Sat. for lunch and Sun. Delicious fish, near château. *Potager du Roy* (I), 1 rue Maréchal-Joffre (tel. 39-50-35-34). Under same ownership as *Trois Marches* but considerably less expensive; good-value *menus*. V.

TOURS AND EXCURSIONS. By Bus. There are excellent guided tours from Paris in luxury buses to Versailles, Chantilly, Compiègne, Fontainebleau and Chartres. Companies running tours are *American Express*, 11 rue Scribe, 9e (to Chantilly, Fontainebleau, Malmaison, Versailles); *Cityrama*, 4 pl. des Pyramides, 1er (to Fontainebleau, Malmaison, Versailles); *Europabus* (Chartres, Fontainebleau and Barbizon, Versailles); *Paris Vision*, 214 rue de Rivoli, 1er (Chantilly, Chartres, Fontainebleau, Versailles). French-speaking visitors will enjoy excursions to lesser-known châteaux and churches, run by the *Régie Autonome des Transports Parisiens* (tickets at pl. de la Madeleine or 53 quai des Grands Augustins, Paris).

On Foot. Guided tours of towns such as Senlis or Versailles are to be recommended, and take place generally from Mar. or Easter through Sept., often weekends only, at around 3 P.M. Check with local tourist offices, which are the usual starting points. Tours are conducted by official guide-lecturers from the National Historical Monuments Commission, though in some cases you can hire a cassette and cassette player in English and follow a marked itinerary.

 SIGHTSEEING DATA. Note that many places have reduced admission charges for children, students, senior citizens and the disabled. For general hints on visiting French museums and historic buildings, and an important warning, see "Sightseeing" in *Facts at Your Fingertips.*

ANET. Château (tel. 37-41-90-07). Open March through Oct., daily except Tues., 2.30–6.30; on Sun. and public hols. also 10–11.30. Winter, weekends and public hols. only 10–11.30, 2–5.

BARBIZON. Auberge du Père Ganne, rue Grande (tel. 60-66-46-73). Open daily except Tues., 10–6. Closed Mon., Tues., Thurs., Sat. in winter and Jan.
Millet's Studio, rue Grande. Open daily except Tues., 10.15–12, 2–6.
Rousseau Museum, rue Grande (tel. 60-66-22-38). Open daily except Tues., 10–12, 2–6. Closed Christmas and New Year.

BEAUVAIS. Galerie Nationale de Tapisseries. Next to cathedral. Open daily except Mon., 10–12, 2.30–5 (to 6.30 in summer).

BIÈVRES. Musée Français de la Photographie (French Museum of Photography), 78 rue Paris (tel. 69-41-10-60). Open daily 10–12, 2–6.

BLÉRANCOURT. Musée National de la Coopération Franco-Américaine, Château de Blérancourt, Chaumy (tel. 23-39-60-16). Open daily except Tues., 10–12, 2–4.

BRETEUIL. Château (tel. 30-52-05-11 or 30-52-05-02). Open daily 2.30–5.30 or 6; Sun., public hols. and in July and Aug., also open 11–12.30. English-speaking guides available; grounds open daily 10–5.30 or 6; concerts and theater shows held Easter through Oct., Sun. at 5 P.M.

CHAÂLIS. Château and **Abbaye** (abbey), (tel. 44-54-00-01). Open Mar. through Oct. only, Mon., Wed. and Sat., 1.30–6; Sun. and public hols., 10–12, 1.30–6, except May 1.

CHAMPS-SUR-MARNE. Château (tel. 60-05-24-43). Open daily except Tues., Wed. and public holidays, 10–12, 1.30–5.30; in winter closes at 4 or 5.

CHANTILLY. Château housing **Musée Condé** (tel. 44-57-03-62). Open daily except Tues., Apr. through Sept., 10–6; winter, 10.30–5.
Musée Vivant du Cheval (Horse Museum), Grandes Ecuries (château stables), (tel. 44-57-13-13). Open daily except Tues., Apr. through Oct., 10.30–6; winter, Mon. to Sat. 1–5, Sun. and public hols. 10.30–6. Equestrian displays with commentary, Apr. through Oct., daily at 11.45, 3.15 and 5.15 (inquire locally for further details).

CHARTRES. Cathédrale (Cathedral). *Crypt:* guided visits start out from Maison des Clercs, 18 cloître Notre-Dame, at 10.30, 11.30, 2.30 and 4.30, plus

5.30 in summer; no visits allowed during pilgrimages. *Towers:* 9.30–12, 2–6, winter 10–12, 2–5. *Treasury:* 10–12, 2–6, winter 10–12, 3–5 (except Jan.); closed Jan., public hols. and Sun. A.M.

Maison de Picassiette, 22 rue de Repos. Open daily, Sept. through June, 10–12, 2–6; closed Tues. in July and Aug.

Musée des Beaux-Arts (Fine Arts Museum), Jardins de l'Evêché. Open daily except Tues., 10–12, 2–5; summer until 6 P.M. Closed on public hols.

CHÂTEAU-THIERRY. Maison Natale de Jean de La Fontaine (Birthplace of Jean de La Fontaine), 12 rue Jean de La Fontaine (tel. 23-69-05-60). Open daily except Tues., Apr. through Sept., 10–12, 2–6 or 2.30–6.30; winter 2–5 only.

COMPIÈGNE. Château, pl. Général-de-Gaulle (tel. 44-40-02-02). Open daily except Tues. and public hols., 10–12, 1.30–6 (to 5 in winter). Audio-visual presentation available, as are combined tickets for château, *Musée National de la Voiture et du Tourisme* and *Musée du Second Empire.*

Clairière de l'Armistice (Armistice Clearing and Museum), in Forêt de Compiègne near Rethondes (tel. 44-40-09-27). Open daily, Mar. to Nov. 11, 8–12, 1.30–6.30; rest of year, daily except Tues., 9–12, 2–5.30.

CONDÉ-EN-BRIE. Château. Open July and Aug., daily 10–12, 2.30–6.30; other months open Sun. and public hols. only, 2.30–6.30, but closed Nov. to Easter.

CONFLANS-STE.-HONORINE. Musée de la Batellerie (Barge Museum), Château du Prieuré, 3 pl. Gérelot (tel. 39-72-58-05). Open March through Aug. 9–12, 2–6. Other months open weekends only 2–5. Closed weekends, Tues. A.M. and public hols.

COURANCES. Château. Open from first Sun. in Apr. to Nov. 2, weekends and public hols., 2.30–6.30.

ECOUEN. Musée National de la Renaissance, Château (tel. 49-90-04-04). Open daily except Tues. and public hols., 9.45–12.30, 2–5.15.

ERMENONVILLE. Parc Jean-Jacques Rousseau (tel. 44-54-00-08). Open daily except Tues., 9–12, 2–7.

FONTAINEBLEAU. Château and Musée National (tel. 64-22-27-40 or 64-22-34-39). Open daily except Tues., and public hols., 9.30–12.30, 2–5. Combined tickets available for *grands appartements* and *petits appartements.*

MAINTENON. Château (tel. 37-23-00-09). Open Apr. through Oct., daily except Tues., 2–6; Sun. and public hols. 10–12, 2–6; winter, weekends, Sun. A.M. and public hols. only, 2–5; closed Jan. Helicopter flights on request; frequent concerts.

MAISONS-LAFFITTE. Château (tel. 39-62-01-49). Open daily, except Tues.

MALMAISON AND BOIS-PRÉAU. Châteaux (tel. 47-49-20-07). Open daily except Tues., 10–12, 1.30–4.30 or 5 (last visits ½ hr. before closing).

MEAUX. Palais Épiscopal (Bishop's Palace) housing **Musée Bossuet** (tel. 64-34-84-45). Open daily, except Tues. and public hols., 2–6. Guided tours May through Dec., Sun. at 3.30.

Jardin de l'Évêché (Bishop's Palace Garden). Open daily 9–6 (tours as for *Palais épiscopal*).

MONTLHÉRY. Tour de Montlhéry (Montlhéry Castle Keep). Open Mon. to Wed., 10–12, 2–4; weekends and public hols., 2.30–5.30; closed Thurs. and Fri.

MORET-SUR-LOING. Donjon (Keep), (tel. 60-70-50-39). Open March through Sept., Sun. and public hols. 3–6; also Sat. when festival is on, 3–7; Summer Festival late June to early Sept., Sat. 10 or 10.30.
   Maison de Clemenceau (Clemenceau's House), (tel. 60-70-51-21). Open daily 2.30–6; closed Dec. to Palm Sun.

NEMOURS. Château, rue Gauthier ler. Open daily except Tues. and public hols., 2–5.30, Sat., Sun. and Mon.
   Musée de Préhistoire d'Ile de France (Regional Prehistory Museum), av. Stalingrad (tel. 64-28-40-37). Open daily except Tues and public hols., 10–12, 2–5.

NOYON. Musée Calvin. Open daily except Tues. (check times locally).
   Musée du Noyonnais, Palais Épiscopal. Open daily except Tues., 10–12, 2–5 or 6.

OURSCAMPS. Abbaye (Abbey), (tel. 44-76-98-08). Open daily 8–6. Infirmary closed 9.30–12 on Sun. and religious hols. for masses. Frequent concerts and organ recitals.

PORT-ROYAL-DES-CHAMPS. Abbaye (Abbey), Magny-les-Hameaux. Open daily, except Tues. and Fri. A.M., 10–12, 2–6; winter weekends and public hols., 10–12, 2.30–5.
   Musée National des Granges de Port-Royal (Barn Museum), Magny-les-Hameaux (tel. 30-43-73-05). Open Wed. to Sun. 10–11.30, 2–5 or 5.30. Closed certain public hols.

PROVINS. Grange aux Dîmes (tithe barn), housing *Musée du Moyen-Age* (medieval museum); *Porte St.-Jean* and *Tour de César* are all open Apr. to Sept., 10–12, 2–5 or 6, and 2–4.30 only in winter.

RAMBOUILLET. Château (tel. 34-83-34-54). Open daily except Tues., public hols. and Presidential occasions. 10–12, 2–4. Admission charge includes *Laiterie de la Reine* (Queen Marie-Antoinette's "Dairy") and the *Pavillon des Coquillages* (Shell-decorated Pavilion).

ST.-CLOUD. Domaine National de St.-Cloud (park). Open daily 7 A.M. to 8 P.M.; no admission charge for those on foot; small charge for cars.
   Musée Historique (tel. 46-02-70-01), beside entrance to Parc de St.-Cloud. Open Wed., weekends and public hols. only, 2–5. Audiovisual presentation at regular intervals.

ST.-DENIS. Basilique (Cathedral), pl. Hôtel-de-Ville (tel. 42-43-00-71). Open daily 10–4; no visits during Sun. morning masses and public hols.
   Musée d'Art et d'Histoire de la Ville de St.-Denis (town art and history museum), 22 bis rue Gabriel-Péri (tel. 42-43-05-10). Open daily except Tues., 10–5.30 (Sun. 2–6.30) and public hols. Guided visits weekends (tel. 42-43-33-55).

STE.-GENEVIÈVE-DES-BOIS. Eglise Notre-Dame de l'Assomption (Church of Our Lady of the Assumption). Open Sun. and public hols. 2–5 (3–7 in winter).

ST.-GERMAIN-EN-LAYE. Musée des Antiquités Nationales (National Museum of Antiquities), Château de St.-Germain (tel. 34-51-53-65). Open daily except Tues. and public hols., 9.45–12, 1.30–5.15.

Musée Départemental du Prieuré-Maurice Denis, 2 bis rue Maurice-Denis (tel. 39-73-77-87). Open Wed. to Sun., 10.30–5.30; closed public hols.

Musée Claude Debussy, no details at presstime, please check locally.

ST.-MANDÉ. Musée des Transports Urbains (Museum of Urban Transport), 60 av. Ste.-Marie (tel. 43-28-37-12). Open Apr. through Oct., weekends only, 2.30–6.

SCEAUX. Musée de l'Ile-de-France (Regional Museum), Château de Sceaux (tel. 46-61-06-71). Open Wed., Thurs., Fri. P.M., Sat. and Sun., 10–12, 2–6 or 7.

SENLIS. Jardin du Roy (King's Garden). Open Wed. afternoon through Mon., 10–12, 2–6 (to 5 in winter).

SÈVRES. Musée National de Céramique de Sèvres (National Ceramics Museum), pl. Manufacture (tel. 45-34-99-05). Open daily except Tues., 9.30–12, 1.30–5.15. For visits to workshops check locally (no children under 14).

SOISSONS. Abbaye St.-Jean-des-Vignes (Abbey of St. John of the Vineyards). Visits to cloisters, refectory and wine cellars and *Logis Abbatial* (abbot's house). Open Mar. through Oct., daily except Tues., 10–12, 2–5 (or 6); winter, Wed. and weekends only, same times.

THOIRY. Château et Réserve Africaine de Thoiry (Château and Safari Park), (tel. 34-87-40-67). Open daily Apr. through Oct., 9.45–6 (6.30 Sun.); winter 10–5 (5.30 Sun.). Reservation essential for guided tour of château; explanatory leaflets provided for state rooms, Archive and Gastronomy Museums, etc. Explanatory cassettes available free for Safari Park; two itineraries (8 km., 5 miles, by car or 3 km., 2 miles, on foot).

VAUX-LE-VICOMTE. Château (tel. 60-66-97-09). Open daily Apr. through Oct., 10–6; winter, weekends only, 2–6; closed mid-Dec. through Jan. Fountains play 2nd and 4th Sat. in month, around 3–6; candlelit evening visits 1st and 3rd Sat. (check time locally).

VINCENNES. Château, entrance in av. Vincennes (tel. 43-28-15-48). Tours of *Donjon* (keep) daily except Tues. and public hols., 10–5.

VERSAILLES. Musée National des Châteaux de Versailles et de Trianon, Château de Versailles (tel. 39-50-58-32). Open daily except Mon. and public hols. Basic entry fee (around 20 fr.) entitles you to visit the *grands appartements* and the *Galerie des Glaces* (Hall of Mirrors) without a guide. For the private apartments and the Royal Opera House you must buy a special ticket in the second hall and be accompanied by a guide; guided tours in English available at intervals. For the *Chambre du Roi* (King's Bedroom) you must again have a guide and it is open only 10.15–11.30 and 2–4.20. Expect enormous lines and delays in summer.

The *Grand Trianon* (open 9.45–5, no admission after 4.30) requires an extra admission fee of about 10 fr., as does the *Petit Trianon* (open 2–5 only, closed weekends, Mon. and public hols.). Combined tickets for the two Trianons cost around 15 fr.

Half-price for everyone on Sun. Under-18s are free at all times, 18–25s plus the over-60s pay half price at all times. The grounds are free from sunrise to sunset.

The fountains play with musical accompaniment (*Grandes Eaux Musicales*) two or three Sun. per month from May to early Oct., usually at 3.30 for 1 to

1½ hours. Check schedule with Paris or Versailles Tourist Offices (tel. 39-50-36-22). Admission around 15 fr. For further events see under *Son et Lumière.*

Musée Lambinet, 54 blvd. Reine. Guided tours July through Sept. only, open Tues. to Sun. except public hols. 2–6.

VILLERS-COTTERÊTS. Musée Alexandre-Dumas, rue des Moutiers. Open daily except Tues. and third Sun. of each month, 2–5; also open Sun. and public hols., 9–12.

 SON-ET-LUMIÈRE. Meaux. *Spectacles Historiques et Nocturnes* (pageants with *son-et-lumière*) are presented in summer, generally mid-June through July, on Fri. and Sat. evenings.

Moret-sur-Loing. *Son-et-lumière* and a pageant with local actors is put on from late June to early Sept., Sat. evenings.

Versailles. *Fête de Nuit et Feu d'Artifice* is a pageant combining theater, *son-et-lumière,* fountain display, fireworks, music and so on, lasting around 2 hours and performed at the Bassin de Neptune at about 9 P.M. on a couple of Sats. in July and late Aug./early Sept. Tickets around 20 fr.; reservations essential (tel. 39-50-36-22). *Le Triomphe de Neptune,* Neptune's Triumph, with fireworks, fountain displays and music and light effects, lasting around 1 hour, can be seen most Sats. from late June to early Sept.

THE LOIRE VALLEY

Château Country

The Loire Valley region southwest of Paris, with its broad meandering rivers—the Cher, Indre, the Loir and the Vienne, as well as the Loire itself—its lush green meadows, acres of vineyards, pearly skies and generally mild climate is known to Frenchmen as the Garden of France, but foreign tourists rightly think of it as "Château Country." Here you'll find no fewer than 1,000 châteaux gracing almost every town and village, from imposing feudal castles to intricately decorated pleasure palaces and tiny manorhouses.

Of those 1,000 lovely buildings, around 30 regularly attract large numbers of visitors and we refer to the finest of them in the following pages. But this is a part of France that repays leisurely exploration, and wherever you go you'll find lesser-known châteaux that anywhere else in the world would be star attractions.

You may like to follow one of the tourist routes planned by the local tourist authorities: you can concentrate on the Ladies of Touraine—Eleanor of Aquitaine, Agnès Sorel, Diane de Poitiers, Marguerite of Navarre—or revive memories of your schooldays by retracing the careers of the turbulent Plantagenet dynasty. Likewise, the *Route Jacques Coeur* offers many delights, or you can follow in the footsteps of Rabelais, Ronsard or King Louis XI. Alternatively, you may prefer to take one of the well-planned excursions in comfortable buses and then return your favorite châteaux for a more extended visit. But whichever way you choose to explore the region, you'll have the added delight of sampling the deliciously light and fruity local wines, tasting the plump fish from the region's many rivers and reveling in the wonderfully fresh produce of the fields and farms in this exceptionally fertile valley.

Tours

The pleasant and lively city of Tours, only two hours by train or car from Paris, makes a good base from which to explore the rich and fertile region the majestic Loire. Although many tourists hurry off every day to visit the châteaux and attractive towns nearby, Tours itself deserves an extended visit. It has been a prosperous city down the centuries, yet has managed, in spite of postwar expansion, to retain the charm of a peaceful provincial center. An imaginative development and restoration scheme has left the heart of the old city intact, banishing tower blocks and industrial buildings to the outskirts, so that as you wander the picturesque streets of the Old Town—le Vieux Tours—or the elegant district around the cathedral where the clergy once lived, you'll find it hard to remember that you're in one of France's major cities.

Everything of interest in Tours is conveniently within walking distance of the center and you should allow time to ramble at leisure. The splendid Saint-Gatien cathedral makes a good starting-point, its soaring west front illustrating late-Gothic craftsmanship at its finest. The view of the east end from the attractive place Grégoire de Tours is particularly fine. Inside, there's some magnificent stained glass, some dating from the 13th century, and miraculously still intact in spite of wartime bombing. The area behind the cathedral has been restored and is most picturesque; this was once the heart of the Roman town, and the semicircular street leading off from the southeastern corner of the cathedral follows the line of the long-vanished Roman amphitheater. Beside the cathedral is the Fine Arts Museum, housed in the former bishop's palace, a graceful building with a lovely garden. Close by, towards the river, is Tours Castle, now a historic waxworks museum.

The rue Colbert, a narrow and attractive street with some picturesque old houses, including one on the site of a work-shop where Joan of Arc bought her suit of armor before setting out for Orléans in April 1429, leads to the Old Town. On the way you'll come to one of Tours's most interesting museums: the small Wine Museum, devoted to the craft of wine making through the ages. It's in the cellars of a now-vanished abbey. Behind it you can see two wine presses, one dating from the Gallo-Roman period, the other from the Middle Ages. Almost next door is the Musée du Compagnonnage, which offers a fascinating picture of craftsmanship illustrated by intricate "masterpieces" made by members of an association of *compagnons,* a sort of alternative guild which started as early as the 15th century. The Old Town nearby suffered badly from wartime bombing and subsequent neglect, but has now come into its own again after patient restoration. Many of the narrow streets and squares are banned to cars and are ideal territory for lovers of old buildings.

The Environs of Tours

Places of interest close to Tours include the Grange de Meslay, a medieval tithe barn which makes a superb setting for summer concerts, and also offers an audiovisual presentation of local history; the wine village of Vouvray; and the priory at Saint-Cosme, where the poet Ronsard lived and died. But most tourists head for Touraine's splendid châteaux, all of which are in easy reach of Tours.

Amboise's château first became a royal residence in the Gothic period, but the dominant feature now is the Renaissance wing built by François I in the early 16th century. Don't miss the graceful Saint-Hubert chapel built for Anne of Brittany by her first husband Charles VIII in 1493. An interesting Renaissance Show called "At the Court of King François" is held here on summer evenings, with 16th-century music, hundreds of actors, fireworks, light effects and marvelous costumes. As you watch this entirely local show, planned and staged by inhabitants of Amboise, you'll find it hard to believe that the château was the setting in 1560 of a hideous massacre in which over 1,000 Protestant Huguenots, who had been involved in a plot to abduct the young François I and his queen Mary Stuart, later Mary Queen of Scots, were strung up from every available hook, pole and balcony—including what is now known as the Conspirators' Balcony on the Logis du Roi. Before leaving Amboise don't miss the attractive manor house of Clos de Lucé, where Leonardo da Vinci spent the last few years of his life under the patronage of the young François I. The museum in the basement is filled with models made to Leonardo's detailed plans by the IBM company.

Whereas the château of Amboise is perched up above the Loire, lovely Chenonceau, only a few miles away, sits astride this region's other major river, the peaceful Cher. With its formal gardens, its beautiful gallery spanning the river filled with the sparkling reflections of sunlight on water, and its associations with two remarkable women, it is one of the few major châteaux to have enjoyed a relatively peaceful history. Built in 1515, Henry II presented the château to Diane de Poitiers, his mistress, on his accession in 1547 much to the chagrin of his queen, Catherine de Médicis. She was to have her revenge in due course, however, for when Henri died in 1559 she confiscated Chenonceau (which was after all royal property) and offered Diane the much less attractive Chaumont instead. Chenonceau is one of very few châteaux in which you are allowed to ramble at will without a guide, so leave yourself plenty of time to enjoy it and to admire the lovely gardens. The son-et-lumière show staged here is also planned to let you roam through the grounds, rather than sitting on reserved seats. It's a magical experience as well-known actors declaim poetry and prose connected with the château and the major periods in its history and the woods are filled with birdsong and music. The village of Chenonceaux (oddly, the spelling differs from that of the château) is small and attractive.

South of Chenonceau are the châteaux of Montpoupon and Montrésor, both well worth a visit, but the major attraction here is the delightful town of Loches, set peacefully by the meandering river Indre. Much of it has changed little since the Middle Ages and to step inside the citadel perched above the town is to step back many centuries in time. This impression will be heightened if you can be there over the July weekend when Loches stages its Craft Fair, with local craftsmen and shopkeepers dressed in medieval costume as they demonstrate their skills or cry their wares. But at any time of year you'll be enchanted by the picturesque streets (most of them now restored), the interesting little Folklore Museum in the Porte Royale, the Lansyer Museum beside it, once the home of a painter friend of Delacroix and containing some of the great painter's sketchbooks, the curious Saint-Ours church crowned by twin pyramids, and by the château, part castle and part Renaissance pleasure palace. In one of the rooms you can see the recumbent statue of Agnès Sorel, Charles VII's beautiful favorite, who lived here in the 16th century. Far gloomier are the barred cells in the massive keep, parts of which date from the 11th century.

Villandry and Langeais

The closest major château to the west of Tours is Villandry, the last of the great Renaissance châteaux to be built in the Loire Valley and best known for its magnificent terraced gardens. In the early years of this century the owner decided to restore the gardens to their former formal splendor and the result is unique in Europe: Renaissance gardens faithfully modeled on the original plans, with a superb geometric kitchen garden on the lower level, in which carefully nurtured vegetables are complemented by fruit and flower borders to create formal patterns of great beauty. The higher levels consist of a herb garden, an ornamental water garden with a small lake shaped like those splendid gilt mirrors you'll so often have seen in French châteaux, and best of all, a "Garden of Love" planted with little box- and yew hedges surrounding beds of red or yellow flowers and trimmed into shapes symbolizing four types of love: Tragic Love, with swords and daggers and red flowers representing spilt blood; Adulterous Love, with horns and fans and *billets doux* and the yellow flowers of jealousy; Tender Love, adorned with hearts and flames and secret masks; and Passionate Love, whose symbolic hearts are broken by passion.

The château has some fine paintings, many of them by Goya and other Spanish artists (the present owner's family, who live in the château, originally came from Spain) but do also try to leave time to wander in the woods high up above the gardens. From here you can see across the Loire Valley and on a clear day may catch a glimpse of another much-visited château close to Tours, Langeais.

Feudal Langeais, built at lightning speed in the mid-15th century on the orders of Louis XI, is still very much complete, with its drawbridge, fortress towers and machicolated *chemin de ronde* for the watch. It has an even earlier keep, dating from as early as 990 and is unusual in this part of France in being right in the center of the little town. The inside of the castle is a fascinating museum of 15th- and 16th-century furniture, tapestries and paintings, often crowded but not to be missed.

Château le Breil de Foin, south of Le Lude, is a charming place dating from the 16th century; the château of Alexandre Dumas's *Lady of Montsoreau.*

Azay-le-Rideau, Ussé and Chinon

Fairy-tale châteaux mirrored in still waters will be one of the abiding memories you take back with you from this beautiful part of France, and none seems more magical than Azay-le-Rideau, a jewel-like Renaissance structure built partly over the Indre downstream from Loches. There is little of interest inside, apart from a famous portrait of Henri IV's striking mistress Gabrielle d'Estrées, but the outside seems sheer perfection, with its corner turrets and Great Staircase.

Nearby Ussé, built in the 15th century, has an even truer claim to the description of fairy-tale château. Charles Perrault, the 17th-century writer who produced numerous fairy tales, is said to have been inspired by it for the setting of *The Sleeping Beauty*. Its shimmering whitish blocks of stone and romantic turrets set against the dark trees of the Forest of Chinon certainly fit the legend perfectly. A lovely Gothic chapel with Renaissance decorative details can also be visited in the grounds. But its major treasure—a series of magnificent Aubusson tapestries depicting the life of Joan or Arc—was stolen in 1975 and has never been recovered.

The city of Chinon is reflected in yet another river, this time the Vienne, which flows into the Loire at nearby Candes. Like Loches, Chinon still has a maze of narrow medieval streets, with overhanging houses that have mostly now been restored. During its famous Medieval Market in August you can see tumblers and acrobats performing in medieval dress, listen to concerts of medieval music and even gorge yourself on a medieval banquet with the local citizens dressed as serving wenches or jesters. You will of course drink the red wine of Chinon, one of this region's two famous red wines (the other comes from nearby Bourgeuil on the other side of the Loire). Chinon's château is a real castle for once, but little of it is left now. It was at Chinon in 1429 that Joan of Arc first recognized the Dauphin as he lurked among his courtiers. The city's *son-et-lumière* show is appropriately devoted to her.

A few miles from Chinon you can visit La Devinière, the house where François Rabelais was born and lived as a child, describing it in his rumbustious novel *Gargantua*. At Saché is the delightful manor house where Balzac wrote some of his best-loved novels; in the Balzac Museum inside the château you can pore over his proofs and manuscripts.

Fontevraud and Saumur

Near Chinon—one of the delights of this region is that distances are not great—is the 12th-century abbey of Fontevraud, a must for English-speaking visitors because it contains the recumbent statues of four English kings and queens: Richard the Lionheart, Henry II, Eleanor of Aquitaine and Isabel of Angoulême, wife of King John. They were all buried here too, along with other members of the Plantagenet dynasty, but their tombs were broken open and their bones scattered during the French Revolution. Thereafter, the building was used as a prison until as recently as 1964, when it passed into the care of the Historic Monuments Department. The fine Romanesque abbey seems a little stark now but the huge nave, with finely carved capitals, and the light filled choir are most impressive, and make a splendid setting for concerts staged by the Cultural Center that is now housed here. You will also be shown a most unexpected building: the octagonal kitchens, topped by a series of conical turrets disguising the chimneys. The strange appearance of this Romanesque building was caused by an over-zealous 19th-century restorer who believed it to be a chapel; it was a British visitor, originally dismissed as a lunatic by the French authorities, who proved that it was designed as a purely functional building used chiefly for smoking meat and fish.

Further downriver lies the pleasant town of Saumur, the home of France's best-known cavalry school. It was once a major Huguenot center and it has never entirely recovered from the revocation of the Edict of Nantes in 1685, which caused a very large number of its inhabitants to flee into exile. Nearer our own time it was the scene of a heroic stand by a group of officers and cadets from the cavalry school, who managed to hold up the German advance in 1940 for a few days, though many of them died in the attempt.

The château, dating from the late-14th century, is said to have inspired one of the miniatures in the famous *Book of Hours* painted for the Duc de Berry. It now houses a Horse Museum and a Decorative Arts Museum with a particularly fine ceramics collection. If you're in the area in late-July, try to get tickets for the famous Black Squadron *(Cadre Noir)* cavalry display and military tattoo. But at any time of year take children (and adults) fascinated by war to the impressive Tank Museum, filled with French, German, US and British tanks, and even a few Soviet ones. Apart from horses, the other specialties of the Saumur area are mushrooms, most of them grown in cliff caves that were originally quarries (you can visit an interesting Mushroom Museum in just such a cave in Chênehutte-les-Tuffeaux near Saumur), and the famous sparkling white wine known as *Saumur champenoise*—a great deal cheaper than Champagne, but many think it just as good.

A delightful excursion from here will take you along the river to the graceful church at Cunault, which once formed part of a Benedictine Abbey and dates from the 11th and 12th centuries. Cunault is a particularly pleasant little town that has retained something of the aura of its days as a river port before the Loire became un-navigable, with its slate-roofed waterfront bars once frequented by bargees and rather reminiscent of an English pub. It is a center of local craftsmanship, with a good shop selling beautifully made craft pieces, and occasionally stages craft fairs on Sundays *(les dimanches animés de Cunault)*.

Angers

Further west still is the town of Angers, once a busy port but now better known as the center of production for the celebrated Anjou wines. The outside of its mighty château seems very much a fortress, with its curtain wall, massive towers and drawbridge, though once inside you'll be surprised by the peaceful elegance of the hibiscus-filled garden. It was originally put up by the violent Foulques Nerra, one of the Counts of Anjou, but was rebuilt by Saint Louis (Louis IX) in the 13th century, and is a splendid example of feudal architecture. The finest exhibit inside the château is the magnificent *Apocalypse* tapestry, displayed in a specially built gallery. It was made in the 14th century for Louis I of Anjou and was originally nearly 530 feet (170 meters) long. As so often in France, it suffered at the hands of the Revolutionaries, but 330 feet (107 meters) were recovered during a 19th-century reconstruction.

Other splendid tapestries can be seen in the Governor's Lodge (Logis du Gouverneur) and the Logis Royal, but be sure to visit Angers's beautiful Saint-Maurice cathedral too. With its Romanesque facade, the original stained glass windows and wonderfully carved doorway it is perhaps the finest cathedral in this part of France. The former Saint-Jean Hospital—an interesting illustration of medieval health care —houses another remarkable set of tapestries, dating this time from the mid-20th century and known as *Le Chant du Monde*. And a new treat in Angers is the museum housed in the Gothic Toussaint church, until recently a romantic ruin but now ingeniously restored with a glassed-over roof replacing the ruined vaulting. This unusual method of restoration has proved very successful in displaying the work of Angers's major artist, the 19th-century sculptor David d'Angers.

East of Tours

The attractive little town of Blois is a good center for visiting more of the region's châteaux, and for excursions into the strange Sologne area to the south, with its wild and sometimes desolate landscapes, much-favored by hunters.

Blois itself is dominated by its château, much of it built by François I, in the early 16th century, including the superb Renaissance staircase. You are allowed to wander freely, though if you choose the guided tour you'll be regaled by details of the bloodiest deed committed here—the assassination of the powerful Duc de Guise in 1588 by men in the pay of Henri III. For lovers of architecture Blois is a right royal feast, with its three separate wings dating from the late-Middle Ages, the Renaissance and the neo-Classical period under Gaston d'Orléans.

The church of Saint-Nicolas is the most interesting of Blois's many churches. Once part of a Benedictine abbey, it is just below the château and close to the Loire. The old streets of the area round the rue Haute and the cathedral of Saint-Louis are gradually being restored and are well worth exploring.

Very close to Blois and set in lawn-filled grounds is the little-known Renaissance château of Beauregard, originally built as a hunting lodge for François I and still a private home. The 16th-century kitchens, which can be visited, were still used by the grandparents of the present owners. But Beauregard's chief interest lies in its superb Galerie d'Illustres, a beautiful long room with a Delft-tiled floor and adorned with over 350 17th-century portraits of 15 French monarchs, accompanied by their queens and children, and of many by the major personalities alive during their reigns in the then known world: kings of other lands, popes, prelates, political figures. A more enjoyable and painless history lesson would be hard to imagine!

The best-known château near Blois is huge Chambord, standing in vast grounds that are said to be as large as Paris. This somewhat forbidding royal palace was a favorite residence of François I, who from 1519 had it almost entirely rebuilt and who loved hunting in the woods surrounding it. Except for the great double stairway to the terrace where the ladies could watch the royal hunting parties there is little to see inside Chambord. Cheverny, with its beautiful furnishings, is more like a stately home (it is still lived in in fact). It also houses an interesting Hunting Museum and you can even see hunts setting out from here with packs of hounds; on some summer evenings splendid shows using hunting horns and fireworks are staged here. The other major château near Blois, Chaumont, is another feudal castle with towers and battlements, but on a less massive scale than Chambord.

An excursion from Blois into the Sologne can easily be combined with a visit to the the delightful 15th-century château of Moulin, on the edge of the typically Sologne village of Lassay-sur-Croisne. This little red-brick turreted manor house surrounded by a moat provides an interesting contrast to some of the grander châteaux in the area, feeling like a house you might actually live in yourself, with its pleasing kitchen and small and elegantly furnished 15th- and 16th-century rooms.

Further south (you may prefer to visit it from Loches) lies the château of Valençay, which is often said to resemble Chambord but on a smaller scale. Its most famous inhabitant was the great French diplomat, one-time bishop and politician, Talleyrand, who bought it after the French Revolution on the orders of Napoleon, whose Foreign Minister he was at the time. A must for architecture-lovers, the château was modified and added to over 200 years and illustrates a variety of different styles, all of which seem somehow to blend to create a particularly pleasing and harmonious whole. Inside you'll find many mementoes of Talleyrand and some fine Louis XVI and Empire furniture. The grounds are a haven for an amazing number of birds, ranging from preening peacocks to unusual species of ducks and even parrots, as well as a mini-zoo with all sorts of exotic creatures. The carriage house has been turned into a small museum of veteran cars.

Orléans

Further east still, and only an hour's train ride from Paris, is the city of Orléans, which suffered badly from wartime bombing but has now been extensively restored. Orléans's heroine is Joan of Arc, who saved the city from the besieging English and Burgundian armies in 1429. On May 7 and 8 every year she is celebrated in the brilliant Joan of Arc Festival. Unfortunately, the wartime devastation has left little of major interest to see in Orléans, but the cathedral of Sainte-Croix, a majestic structure built at intervals over the centuries (it was begun in the late-13th century), should certainly be visited. The carved choir stalls are perhaps its greatest treasure; they were designed by no less a trio than Mansart, Gabriel and Lebrun in the early-18th century.

The city also has a good Fine Arts Museum, a graceful Renaissance town hall and many interesting old streets, though a good number of the buildings are inevitably reconstructions. Ask for a map at the Tourist Office and explore in the best possible way—on foot.

Upstream from Orleans, undoubtedly the finest building is the Benedictine abbey at Saint-Benoît-sur-Loire, one of the most beautiful Romanesque buildings in France and a fit resting place for the saintly founder of the Benedictine order. St. Benedict had originally been buried in the monastery at Monte Cassino in Italy in the 6th century, but an enterprising abbot decided during the following century that his remains, and those of his sister St. Scholastica, must be brought back to France. He sent a raiding party of monks to Italy and, their mission successfully accomplished, renamed the abbey Saint-Benoît (it had originally been known as Fleury). To attend a mass when the Gregorian chant is being sung is a most moving experience, not least because you are following in the footsteps of Joan of Arc, who visited the church in 1429. At Germigny des Prés nearby is a ninth-century church with fine mosaics.

Beyond the Loire Region—Le Mans and Vendôme

Although they are some way from the Loire, the towns of Le Mans and Vendôme are often visited from one of the Loire centers. Le Mans' pride is its largely Romanesque cathedral of Saint-Julien, with its wonderful Gothic east end supported by soaring flying buttresses and a superbly sculpted Romanesque porch. Inside you can see some fine Renaissance tombs, Romanesque stained glass and 16th-century tapestries. The most interesting building in the Old Town—the Vieux Mans —is the Maison de la Reine Bérangère, dating from the early-16th century and now housing a small museum devoted to the history and ethnography of Le Mans and the whole of the Sarthe region. Incidentally, Queen Bérengère was Richard the Lionheart's wife in the 13th century and had nothing to do with the house renamed after her, though she did found a convent close to Le Mans. The Old Town, surrounded by the city's Gallo-Roman ramparts, is a pleasant place for strolling. The high point of life in Le Mans is of course the famous "24 Hours" motor race, which draws huge crowds.

Not far from Le Mans and a definite must if you're interested in the revival of Gregorian plainsong or chant is the Benedictine abbey of Solesmes, rebuilt in about 1830, where you can attend the Gregorian mass at any time of the year, as well as admiring the lovely sculpted saints' figures in the transept known as Les Saints de Solesmes. The village, too, set on the banks of the Sarthe river, is one of the prettiest in the whole area.

Vendôme, attractively set on the river Loir (not to be confused with the Loire with an "e"), seems to be surrounded on all sides by water, and you'll find that you're constantly crossing little bridges over canals and streams as you stroll through its pleasant streets. The view of the beautiful Gothic abbey church from the old heart of the city (known as the Quartier Ancien) is particularly fine. Vendôme also has a picturesque ruined château.

PRACTICAL INFORMATION FOR THE LOIRE

VALLEY

TOURIST OFFICES. The regional tourist office for the Loire region—written enquiries only—is the *Comité Regional du Tourisme,* 10 rue du Colombier, BP 2412, 45000 Orléans (tel. 38-62-68-48). In addition, there are departmental tourist offices (again, written enquires only) at: **Indre-et-Loire,** 16 rue de Buffon, 37032 Tours (tel. 47-61-61-23); **Loiret,** 3 rue de la Bretonnerie, 45000 Orléans (tel. 38-66-24-10); **Loir-et-Cher,** 11 pl. du Château, 41000 Blois (tel. 54-78-55-50).

There are local tourist offices in the following towns: **Amboise,** 1 quai Général-de-Gaulle (tel. 47-57-09-28); **Angers,** cour Gare (tel. 41-87-72-50), and pl. Kennedy (tel. 41-88-69-93); **Blois,** 3 av. Jean-Laigret (tel. 54-74-06-49); **Le Mans,** 40 pl. République (tel. 43-28-17-22); **Orléans,** pl. Albert-ler (tel. 38-53-05-95); **Saumur,** 5 rue Beaurepaire (tel. 41-51-03-06); **Tours,** pl. Maréchal-Leclerc (tel. 47-05-58-08); **Vendôme,** tour St.-Martin, rue Poterie (tel. 54-77-05-07).

REGIONAL FOOD AND DRINK. Simple and refreshing, the cooking of the Loire valley is easy to enjoy. Specialties include: Orléans and Blois: *pâté de Pâques* (Easter pie made of veal and pork), *andouillettes* (chitterlings), *saucisses* (sausages), *volailles du Gâtinais* (poultry), *canard à la solognote* (duck), *civet de lièvre de Sologne* (jugged hare), *gâteau d'amande* (almond cake), and *cotignac* (quince spread).

Tours and Angers: *rillettes de Tours* (pork or goose seasoned, cooked, and served in earthenware dishes), *coques* (black pudding spiced with herbs), *boudins blancs* (white sausage of pork). Among the fried Loire fish are: *sandre* or *brochet au beurre blanc* (perch or pike with white butter sauce), *saumon de la*

Loire (salmon), *alose farcie* (stuffed shad), *truite au Vouvray* (trout with a wine sauce), *pêche au Chinon* (peaches poached in red wine), and *tarte aux pruneaux* (prune tart).

In general you cannot go wrong with salads and fruit desserts, for the Loire is lush soil for most produce. Local cheeses include the fresh *cremets,* at its best with fruit, and goat cheeses in innumerable guises.

The local wines are mostly white, including the delicious sparkling Saumur champenoise, best in its very dry *(brut)* version. Others you will come across are Touraine Sauvignon (very grapey), Vouvray and the famous light and dry Muscadet. Two very fine red wines are Chinon and Bourgueil (the wines of Rabelais); and the sweetish rosé d'Anjou is well known. Touraine has some dry rosé wines, and the sweetish local rosés make a popular chilled apéritif.

Specialties to take home as gifts include pretty boxes of marzipan, stuffed prunes *(pruneaux fourrés),* and barley sugar *(sucre d'orge).*

 HOTELS AND RESTAURANTS. A wide range of accommodations is on offer in this very popular region. Hotels get very full in summer, however, so reserve ahead. A brochure is published annually by *Château-Accueil,* c/o Chateau de Thaumiers, Thaumiers, 18210, Charenton-du-Cher (tel. 48-60-87-62), giving details of châteaux where you can be sure of a friendly welcome and learn about the history and cuisine of the region.

For general notes on hotels and restaurants, see "Hotels and Restaurants" in the *Facts at Your Fingertips.*

AMBOISE. *Choiseul* (E), (tel. 47-30-45-45). Old hotel completely renovated; modern comforts including pool. Closed Jan. and Feb. v. *Château de Pray* (M), just outside town at Chargé (tel. 47-57-23-67). 16 rooms. Closed Jan. to early Feb. Attractive small 18th-cent. château set in own grounds, with restaurant. AE, DC, MC, V. *Lion d'Or* (M), 17 quai Guinot (tel. 47-57-00-23). 22 rooms. Closed Nov. to first half of Mar. Comfortable, typical provincial hotel-restaurant. *France et Cheval Blanc* (I), quai Général-de-Gaulle (tel. 47-57-02-44). 24 rooms. Closed Nov. to Mar. Close to river; good value and good cuisine. v.

Restaurants. *Mail Saint-Thomas* (M), pl. Richelieu (tel. 47-57-22-52). New, with imaginative cooking and beautiful garden. Open daily to 9.30. AE, v. *Crêperie dans un jardin* (I), in grounds of Clos de Lucé manor house. Open Easter and May to mid-Sept., during château opening hours. Friendly little pancake parlor also serving salads and teas.

ANGERS. *Concorde* (E), 18 blvd. Foch (tel. 41-87-37-20). 73 rooms. Modern, central, with brasserie-style restaurant. AE, DC, MC, V. *Anjou* (M), 1 blvd. Foch (tel. 41-88-24-82). 51 rooms. Very comfortable, with good (M) restaurant *(Salamandre).* AE, DC, MC, V. *Croix de Guerre* (I), 23 rue Château-Gontier (tel. 41-88-66-59). 30 rooms. Quiet hotel in true provincial style. AE, V.

Restaurants. *Logis* (M), 17 rue St.-Laud (tel. 41-87-44-15). Closed mid-July to mid-Aug. Specializes in seafood. AE, DC, V. *Toussaint* (M), 7 rue Toussaint (tel. 41-87-46-20). Closed Aug., over Christmas and New Year, ten days in Feb, Sun. and Mon. Close to château and cathedral; excellent *nouvelle cuisine* versions of regional specialties. AE, DC, V. *Amandier* (I), 7 rue Cordelle (tel. 41-88-22-78). Closed part of July and Sun. for lunch. Small, family-run spot in little street close to main square; excellent value.

At **St.-Sylvain-d'Anjou,** 5 km. (3 miles) north via N23, *Auberge Eventard* (M), tel. 41-43-74-25). Closed Jan., Sun. for dinner and Mon. Good choice, *nouvelle cuisine* as well as traditional dishes, served in elegant surroundings. AE, DC, V.

AZAY-LE-RIDEAU. *Grand Monarque* (M), pl. République (tel. 47-45-40-08). 30 rooms. Old-established, family run, close to château. Restaurant, closed second half Nov. through Feb., (M) has tables outside in summer. AE, MC, V. *Biencourt* (I), rue Balzac (tel. 47-45-20-75). 8 rooms. Typical *tourangelle* (Tours-style) house near château; no restaurant.

Restaurants. *Muscadin* (M), rue Adélaïde-Riché (tel. 47-43-23-96). Closed part of Jan., Nov., Tues. for dinner and Wed. (except July and Aug.). Tiny, good service, nice atmosphere. AE, V. *Aigle d'Or* (I), 10 rue Adélaïde-Riché (tel. 47-45-24-58). New restaurant with chef from château d'Artigny; garden.

LES BEZARDS. **Restaurant.** *Auberge des Templiers* (E), (tel. 38-31-80-01). Closed mid-Jan. to mid-Feb. One of the best in France, with good mixture of classical and new cuisine. Also a deluxe hotel with 22 rooms. AE, DC, MC, V.

BLOIS. *Anne de Bretagne* (M), 31 av. Jean-Laigret (tel. 54-78-05-38). 29 rooms. Closed ten days in Feb. Between station and château; no restaurant. MC, V. *Ibis* (M), 15 rue Vallée Maillard (tel. 54-74-60-60). 40 rooms. Modern; restaurant. MC, V. *Gerbe d'Or* (I), 1 rue Bourg-Neuf (tel. 54-74-26-45). 25 rooms. Good value; with restaurant. V. *St.-Jacques* (I), pl. Gare (tel. 54-78-04-15). 32 rooms. Logis de France right opposite station; no restaurant.
Restaurants. *Hostellerie Loire* (M), 8 rue Maréchal-de-Lattre-de-Tassigny (tel. 54-74-26-60). Closed mid-Jan. to mid-Feb., part of June and Sun. Well-known and reliable town-center restaurant; mainly classical cuisine. Also has 17 rooms. AE, DC, V. *Péniche* (I), quai St.-Jean (tel. 54-74-37-23). Unusual converted barge on river with good *nouvelle cuisine* and particularly pleasant atmosphere. AE, MC, V.
At **Ménars**, 8 km. (5 miles) northeast, and convenient for visitors to that pretty château, is *Epoque* (M), 23 rue Charron (N152), (tel. 54-46-81-07). Closed first half of Jan., Tues. for dinner and Wed. (except July and Aug.). Elegant classical cuisine in delightful village setting. V.

CHAMBORD. *St.-Michel* (M), opposite château (tel. 54-20-31-31). 38 rooms. Closed mid-Nov. to mid-Dec.; restaurant also closed Mon. for dinner and Tues. in winter. Well-run Logis de France; garden, tennis, good restaurant. V.
Restaurant. At **Bracieux**, 8 km. (5 miles) away, *Relais* (E), 1 av. Chambord (tel. 54-46-41-22). Closed over Christmas and Jan., Tues. for dinner, and Wed. Converted coaching inn on edge of forest, serving excellent *nouvelle cuisine*. Good-value (M) *menus.* AE, DC, V.

CHAUMONT-SUR-LOIRE. *Château* (M), 2 rue Maréchal-de-Lattre-de-Tassigny (tel. 54-20-98-04). Closed Dec. through Feb.; restaurant also closed Mon. Long-standing, well-run establishment close to château, with pool, garden, large comfortable rooms—a few are (E)—and (I) restaurant. AE, DC, MC, V.
At **Onzain**, 2 km. (1¼ miles) away, *Domaine des Hauts de Loire* (E), rte. d'Herbault (tel. 54-20-72-57). 22 rooms and 6 apartments. Closed Dec. to mid-Mar. Delightful restored manor house in large grounds, with tennis and angling; very fine classical cuisine; Relais et Châteaux member. AE, DC, MC, V.

CHENONCEAUX. *Bon Laboureur et Château* (M), 6 rue Dr.-Bretonneau (tel. 47-23-90-02). 29 rooms. Closed mid-Dec. to mid-Feb., Wed. for lunch and Tues. mid-Nov. to mid-Mar. An old favorite right by château, attractive and comfortable, with good classical cuisine. AE, DC, MC, V. *Château de Chissay* (I), 5½ km. (2½ miles) east via N76 (tel. 54-32-32-01). 7 rooms. Closed Nov. through Mar. Genuine 15th and 16th-century château with good views and pleasant restaurant (M). AE, V. *Renaudière* (I), 24 rue Dr.-Bretonneau (tel. 47-23-90-04). 12 rooms. Closed mid-Nov. through Feb.; restaurant also closed Sun. for dinner and Mon. for lunch. Small and good value, with peacful garden. MC, V.

CHINON. *Boule d'Or* (M), 66 quai Jeanne d'Arc (tel. 47-93-36-92). 19 rooms. Closed Dec. and Jan. Old-established Logis de France overlooking river in town center, with restaurant. AE, DC, MC, V. *Hostellerie Gargantua* (M), 73 rue Voltaire (tel. 47-93-04-71). 11 rooms. Closed Dec. through Feb. In picturesque heart of old town. Friendly service, regional classical cuisine in elegant ambiance. AE, DC, MC, V. *France* (I), 47 pl. Général-de-Gaulle (tel. 47-93-33-91). 25 rooms.

Closed Dec. to mid-March, Sat. and Sun. (except summer). Very French façade overlooking leafy square at entrance to old town; no restaurant. AE, V.

At **Beaumont-en-Véron,** 5 km. (3 miles) by D749, *Giraudière* (M), route Bourgueil et Savigny (tel. 47-58-40-36). 25 rooms. 17th-century house in woods and meadows. Family-style; no restaurant. AE, DC, MC, V.

At **Marçay,** 7 km. (4 miles) south, *Château de Marçay* (E), (tel. 47-93-03-47). Chic Relais et Châteaux member; dates from 15th century. Country location, with pool, good restaurant with superb local wines, and elegant service. Closed mid-Jan. to mid-March. AE, MC, V.

Restaurants. *Plaisir Gourmand* (M), 2 rue Parmentier (tel. 47-93-20-48). Closed part of Feb., part of Nov., Sun. for dinner and Mon. A welcome new find in heart of old town, with inventive cuisine complemented by delicious local wines. V. *Ste.-Maxime* (M), 31 pl. Général-de-Gaulle (tel. 47-93-05-04). Closed mid-Dec. to mid-Jan. and first half of Mar. Very central, good value. V.

COUR-CHEVERNY. *St.-Hubert* (I), rue Nationale (tel. 54-79-96-60). 20 rooms. Closed Dec. to mid-Jan. and Tues. (except April 15 to Sept. 15); restaurant closed Tues. all year around. Old-established hotel with excellent service and good regional cuisine. MC, V.

FONTEVRAUD. Restaurants. *Licorne* (M), rue Arbrissel (tel. 41-51-72-49). Closed end Nov. to mid-Jan., Sun. for dinner, Mon. and two weeks end-May/early June. Close to abbey, small and elegant with marvelous *nouvelle cuisine.* AE, V. *Auberge Abbaye* (I), 8 av. Roches (tel. 41-51-71-04). Good-value home cooking with good regional wines.

GIEN. *Rivage* (I), 1 quai Nice (tel. 38-67-20-53). 29 rooms. Closed Feb. Overlooking Loire; spacious rooms, good (M) restaurant. AE, DC, MC, V.

LANGEAIS. *Hosten* (M), 2 rue Gambetta (tel. 47-96-82-12). 11 rooms. Closed second half of Jan., mid-June to mid-July; restaurant also closed Mon. for dinner and Tues. Traditional Logis de France with very good restaurant serving classical dishes. AE, DC.

Restaurant. *Langeais* (M), 2 rue Gambetta (tel. 47-96-70-63). Close to château; good cooking. Also has 12 (M) rooms. AE, DC.

LOCHES. *George Sand* (M), 39 rue Quintefol (tel. 47-59-39-74). 18 rooms. 17th-century building overlooking river, with good restaurant. MC, V. *Château* (I), 18 rue Château (tel. 47-59-07-35). 12 rooms. Opposite château, friendly, with lovely terrace overlooking town and flower-filled courtyard; no restaurant. *France* (I), 6 rue Picois (tel. 47-59-00-32). 22 rooms. Closed Jan.; restaurant also closed Sun. for dinner and Mon. for lunch. Modest, but central and good-value cuisine, with attractive courtyard for summer meals. V.

LE LUDE. *Maine* (I), 24 av. Saumur (tel. 43-94-60-54). 24 rooms. Closed mid-Dec. to mid-Jan.; restaurant also closed Sat., Sun. for dinner (in winter) and second half of Sept. Attractive creeper-covered building with modernized rooms and good restaurant. MC, V.

At **Port-des-Roches,** 10 km. (6½ miles) northwest, *Auberge Port des Roches* (M), (tel. 43-94-43-23). Attractive setting on Loir river, with pool, sailing, fishing, tennis, and good restaurant.

Restaurant. *Renaissance* (I), 2 av. Libération (tel. 43-94-63-10). Closed last half Apr., Oct., Sun. for dinner and Mon. Small, cheerful dining room; good food. DC, V.

LUYNES. *Domaine de Beauvois* (E), 4 km. (2½ miles) northwest via D49 (tel. 47-55-50-11). 35 rooms and 6 apartments. Closed mid-Jan. to mid-Mar. Relais et Châteaux member, 15th and 16th-century building furnished with antiques, set in wooded grounds, with pool, tennis, angling and riding; excellent restaurant. V.

LE MANS. *Concorde* (E), 16 av. Général-Leclerc (tel. 43-24-12-30). 64 rooms and 3 apartments. Comfortable and close to old town, with good restaurant. AE, DC, MC, V. *Central* (M), 5 blvd. René-Levasseur (tel. 43-24-08-93). 38 rooms. Newly modernized, with very quiet rooms on courtyard. AE, DC, MC, V.

Restaurants. *Grenier à Sel* (M), 26 pl. Eperon (tel. 43-23-26-30). Good simple cooking with fresh produce. Closed Sun. for dinner and Mon. AE, V. *Grillade* (M), 1 rue Blondeau (tel. 43-24-21-87). Closed end July and Sun. (except April through Sept.). Near cathedral. AE, V.

At **Arnage,** 9 km. (5½ miles) south via N23, *Auberge des Matfeux* (M), rte. d'Angers (tel. 43-21-10-71). Closed Jan., last half of July, Sun. for dinner, Mon. and dinner on public hols. Very chic, in attractive leafy setting, with excellent light cuisine. AE, DC, MC, V.

MONTBAZON. *Château d'Artigny* (E), 2 km. (1¼ miles) out of town via D17, (tel. 47-26-24-24). 48 rooms and 7 apartments. Closed Dec. to mid-Jan. Built in early-20th century in Louis XV style by the Coty perfume family. Now a Relais et Châteaux member with spacious and luxurious rooms, excellent *nouvelle cuisine* and distinctly upmarket atmosphere. Tennis courts, pool, golf course, riding; "musical weekends," mostly in winter. V. *Domaine Tortinière* (E), (tel. 47-26-00-19). 14 rooms and 7 apartments. Closed mid-Nov. through Feb. Across the valley, with huge garden and pool, very comfortable rooms and good restaurant; closed Tues. for lunch and Mon. in March. MC, V.

At **Veigné,** via route de Monts, *Moulin Fleuri* (M), (tel. 47-26-01-12). 10 rooms. Closed last half Oct., most of Feb., Sun. for dinner and Mon. (except July and Aug.). Attractive converted mill beside Indre river, with pleasant restaurant and terrace. AE, V.

Restaurant. *Chancelière* (E), 1 pl. Marronniers (tel. 47-26-00-67). Closed mid-Nov. to first week in Dec., Feb., Sun. for dinner, Mon. High reputation; serves *nouvelle cuisine* regional dishes; lovely antique furniture. Also has 14 rooms. AE, V.

MUR-DE-SOLOGNE. **Restaurant.** *Croix Blanche* (I), (tel. 54-83-81-11). Closed Mon. Busy restaurant, typical of Sologne region, specializing in game. Also has rooms and private stretch of river for anglers; close to Moulins château.

ORLÉANS. *Sofitel* (E), 44 quai Barentin (tel. 38-62-17-39). 108 rooms. Overlooking Loire, modern, with pool and popular restaurant. AE, DC, MC, V. *Orléans* (M), 6 rue Crespin (tel. 38-53-35-34). 18 rooms. Closed late July to late Aug., second half Dec., Sat. (Oct. to May). Central; well-planned, modern rooms, no restaurant. *Terminus* (M), 40 rue République (tel. 38-53-24-64). 26 rooms. Closed Christmas and New Year. Good service, central. AE, MC, V.

Out of town: *Auberge Montespan* (M), 2 km. (1¼ miles) on Blois road (tel. 38-88-12-07). 10 rooms. Closed mid-Dec. to end Jan. Attractive converted manor house with lovely garden overlooking Loire and excellent classical cuisine. V.

At **Olivet,** 4 km. (2½ miles) from town, *Reine Blanche Frantel* (E), 643 rue Reine Blanche (tel. 38-66-40-51). 65 rooms. Modern, very comfortable and well-run, with grill room. Closed Sat. for lunch. AE, DC, MC, V. *Rivage* (M), (tel. 38-66-02-93). 29 rooms. Closed Feb.; restaurant also closed Sun. for dinner and Mon. (in winter). Pleasant setting overlooking river; good restaurant. AE, DC, MC, V.

Restaurants. *Crémaillière* (E), 34 rue Notre-Dame-de-Recouvrance (tel. 38-53-49-17). Closed Aug., Sun. for dinner and Mon. One of the very best in region for *nouvelle cuisine,* excellent service too. AE, DC, V. *Antiquaires* (M), 2 rue au Lin (tel. 38-53-52-35). Closed Aug., Sun. and Mon. Lovely old beams, stylish cuisine, and good wine list at reasonable prices. AE, DC, V. *Bigorneau* (M), 54 rue Turcies (tel. 38-68-01-10). Closed part of Feb., part of July, Sun., Mon. and public hols. Very attractive place in old town specializing in fish. AE, DC, V. *Etoile d'Or* (I), 25 pl. Vieux-Marché (tel. 38-53-49-20). Central, good value; also has a few rooms.

LES-ROSIERS-SUR-LOIRE. Restaurant. *Jeanne de Laval* (E), on road to Angers (tel. 41-51-80-17). Closed first half Mar., end Nov. to Jan., and Mon., except public hols. One of best in Loire Valley for regional cuisine cooked in classical style. Also has 11 rooms. AE, DC, V.

SACHÉ. Restaurant. *Auberge XIIe Siècle* (M), (tel. 47-26-86-58). Closed Tues., Feb. Very attractive old inn with local wines and imaginative cuisine. AE, DC, V.

SAUMUR. *Campanile* (M), côte de Bournan à Bagneux (tel. 41-50-14-40). 43 rooms. Large comfortable rooms with country views; good breakfast. V. *Roi René* (M), 94 av. Général-de-Gaulle (tel. 41-67-45-30). Overlooking river on island in middle of Loire, well run and friendly, much liked by readers; pleasant restaurant. Closed Christmas to Jan. 15, and Sat. for lunch Easter through Oct. AE, DC, MC, V.

At **Chênehutte-les-Tuffeaux,** 8 km. (5 miles) from Saumur, *Prieuré* (E), via D751 (tel. 41-67-90-14). 36 rooms and 12 less expensive bungalow rooms. Closed Jan. and Feb. Converted priory in enormous grounds with glorious views over Loire; pool, mini-golf and good *nouvelle cuisine.* V.

Restaurants. *Auberge-St.-Pierre* (I), 6 pl. St.-Pierre (tel. 41-51-26-25). Friendly family-style restaurant in old part of town. *Gambetta* (I), 12 rue Gambetta (tel. 41-51-11-13). Closed Christmas and New Year period., Easter period, Sun. for dinner and Mon. Traditional cooking; garden. AE, DC, V.

SOLESMES. *Grand Hôtel* (M), (tel. 43-95-45-10). 40 rooms. Closed Feb.; restaurant also closed Sun. for dinner (Nov. through Jan.). Opposite abbey, with well-planned modern rooms, friendly service and delicious meals. AE, DC, MC, V.

TOURS. *Univers* (E), 5 blvd. Heurteloup (tel. 47-05-37-12). 88 rooms and 3 apartments. Close to station, with well-known restaurant. AE, DC, MC, V. *Bordeaux* (M), 3 pl. Maréchal-Leclerc (tel. 47-05-40-32). 53 rooms. Old-established, well-run hotel just by station, with good restaurant serving local specialties and fine wines from own cellar near Vouvray. AE, DC, MC, V. *Châteaux de la Loire* (M), 12 rue Gambetta (tel. 47-05-10-05). 32 rooms. Closed mid-Dec. to mid-Jan. and weekends (except March 15 through Oct.). Small and friendly, in central yet quiet street; no restaurant. AE, DC, MC, V. *France* (M), 38 rue Bordeaux (tel. 47-05-35-32). 36 rooms. Modernized, sauna; no restaurant. Near station. DC, MC, V. *Royal* (M), 65 av. Grammont (tel. 47-64-71-78). 32 rooms. Comfortable, good service; garage for each room. AE, DC, V. *Colbert* (I), 78 rue Colbert (tel. 47-66-61-56). 16 rooms. Near cathedral, with tiny garden, friendly service; no restaurant. AE, DC, MC, V.

In **Rochecorbon,** *Fontaines* (M), 6 quai Loire (tel. 47-52-52-86). 15 rooms. Logis de France beside Loire, with well-decorated rooms but no restaurant. AE, DC, MC, V.

Restaurants. *Poivrière* (M), 13 rue Change (tel. 47-20-85-41). Closed most of Aug., Sun. and Mon. Attractive old building in heart of old town, serving mostly *nouvelle cuisine* and offering a warm welcome. AE, V. *Tuffeaux* (M), 19 rue Lavoisier (tel. 47-47-19-89). Closed Sun., Mon., Jan. and most of Aug. Near cathedral and Loire; chic ambiance and excellent *nouvelle cuisine* based on regional fish specialties. V. *Ecuelle* (I), 5 rue Grand-Marché (tel. 47-66-49-10). Closed Mon. for lunch. Hearty, generous cooking; terrace. V. *Rûche* (I), 105 rue Colbert (tel. 47-66-69-83). Closed Sun., Mon. for lunch. Elegant yet friendly atmosphere; carefully cooked local specialties, excellent value, must reserve. AE, DC, MC, V.

VALENÇAY. *Espagne* (E), 9 rue Château (tel. 54-00-00-02). 12 rooms and 6 suites. Closed mid-Nov. to mid-March. Delightful Relais et Châteaux member, run by same family for generations. Garden and terrace, marvelous service in the grand manner, excellent classical cuisine. AE, V.

VENDÔME. *St.-Georges* (M), 14 rue Poterie (tel. 54-77-25-42). 37 rooms. Restaurant closed Sat. for lunch, Sun. for dinner and second half Jan. Central and comfortable, with good restaurant. AE, DC, MC, V. *Vendôme* (M), 15 fbg. Chartrain (tel. 54-77-02-88). 35 rooms. Closed for Christmas and New Year period. Well-renovated Logis de France close to Loir river; good classical cuisine in *Cloche Rouge* (M) restaurant. MC, V.

Restaurant. *Daumier* (I), 17 pl. République (tel. 54-77-10-15). Closed Sun. for dinner, Mon. and Jan. Mostly fish; good value; terrace. AE, DC, MC, V.

VERETZ. *St.-Honoré* (I), (tel. 47-50-30-06). 9 rooms. Closed Feb.; restaurant closed Sun. for dinner and Mon. (except mid-June to mid-Sept.). Pleasant Logis de France overlooking peaceful Cher river, with popular restaurant. AE, DC, V.

VILLANDRY. *Cheval Rouge* (M), (tel. 47-50-02-07). 20 rooms. Closed Nov. through Feb.; restaurant closed Mon., except May through Aug. Right beside château. Modern building, slightly stuffy atmosphere, but good service and pleasant restaurant serving mostly classical cuisine. V.

VOUVRAY. At **Vernou-sur-Brenne**, 4 km. (2½ miles) east, *Perce-Neige* (M), rue Anatole-France (tel. 47-52-10-04). 15 rooms. Closed Feb.; restaurant closed Sun. for dinner and Mon., except summer. Attractive regional architecture and big garden; restaurant serves well-prepared dishes. AE, MC, V.

Restaurant. *Grand Vatel* (I), rue Brûlé (tel. 47-52-70-32). Closed Dec., Sun. for dinner (except May through Sept.) and Mon. Elegant dining room with colorful frescos and adequate classical cuisine. Also has 7 (I) rooms. AE, DC, V.

 TOURS AND EXCURSIONS. By Air. Viewing the chateaux from the air is a marvelous experience. An hour-long flight from Tours airport, covering 200 km. (125 miles) gives you a bird's eye view of 10 châteaux as well as panoramas of the Cher and Loire rivers. Cost in 1987 was 500 fr. per person (minimum of three); departures on Wed., Fri. and Sun. Shorter circuits of about 20 minutes cost about 200 fr. There are also flights from Amboise and Blois. Reservations are essential: call 47-64-27-14 or contact the tourist office in Tours (tel. 47-05-58-08) or the Loir-et-Cher departmental office in Blois (tel. 54-78-55-50).

Various helicopter excursions are on offer from Blois, in July and Aug. only, from 220 fr. per person for 10 minutes to 1,300 fr. for an hour (minimum of four people). Reservations are essential: call 54-74-06-49 or 54-78-23-21, or reserve in person at Blois tourist office or at the *Hélistation* (heliport), at Pont-Charles-de-Gaulle just outside Blois on D 951 road (open 10–1, 2–7).

A new venture organized by the tourist office in Blois and *Agence Wagons-Lits,* 46 rue Denis-Papin, BP 44, 41003 Blois (tel. 54-78-92-00) are helicopter trips from the Paris heliport to one of four Relais et Châteaux hotels in the Loire. Gourmet dinners, flights over some of the Loire châteaux and a car are part of the package, but individual requirements can be catered for. As a rough guide, the 1987 price for four people with two nights in a château-hotel was 11,000 frs. per person. Book well ahead.

Balloon flights over the Loire and Cher valleys are the latest variation on the château-visiting theme. Arrangements can be made direct at some of the Relais et Châteaux hotels; otherwise contact M. Jacquelin d'Assigny (tel. 47-41-12-99). 1987 cost for an hour's flight for two was 2,000 frs. All trips are dependant on reasonable weather.

By Car. The regional tourist offices have devised a number of routes with a theme, for example the *Route Jacques-Coeur,* which takes in the towns of Bourges and Gien and some attractive châteaux, several of which welcome visitors for bed and breakfast. Other routes are: *Route des Dames de Touraine, Sur les Pas de Ronsard en Touraine, A la Recherche des Plantagenets* and *La Rabelaisie en Touraine.* Leaflets and maps are available in French or English from tourist offices.

By Bus. All the major bus companies have tours of the Loire Valley and its châteaux from Paris, some combined with tours of Normandy and/or Brittany, and lasting two to four days.

A comprehensive château-visiting service is provided Easter through Sept. by the SNCF (French Rail) and Europabus from Tours. Whole-day and half-day tours are available, visiting three or more châteaux, and often including wine-tasting; also trips to sound-and-light shows, evenings, July to early-Sept. Tours are popular so book ahead if possible: detailed schedules and prices from special reservations office in Tours station (tel. 47-05-46-09).

From Blois, *STD Autocars,* 6 pl. Victor-Hugo (tel. 54-78-15-66), run excursions to Chambord, Cheverny, Amboise and Chenonceau, mid-Apr. to mid-Sept., with English-speaking guides. During May and Oct. there are twice-weekly trips to Chambord where you are left free to wander at will. Information and reservations also at city tourist office; departures from rail station.

Less frequent excursions are run from other centers such as Angers, Loches, Orléans and Saumur. Inquire at tourist offices for details.

By Boat. A boat departs from Chinon for Montsoreau every morning and afternoon. The boat is accessible to disabled people, and lunch or dancing aboard may be arranged. Contact: *Val de Loire Croisières,* pl. Liberté, Thure, 86140 Lencloître (tel. 49-93-89-46).

On Foot. Walking tours of cities are organized in all major centers, generally from mid-June to mid-Sept. Some have official guide-lecturers (usually bilingual in French and English), as at Bourges and Loches, and some hire you a cassette in English with a city plan to follow, as at Tours. Details from local tourist offices.

 SIGHTSEEING DATA. For general information about visiting France's museums and historic buildings, and an important warning, see "Sightseeing" in *Facts at Your Fingertips.* Note that many châteaux and museums have reduced admission charges for children, students, senior citizens and the disabled: please check locally.

A special pass called a *Passeport Loisirs* (Leisure Passport) is available from *Crédit Agricole* banks for around 40 frs. a month or 60 frs. a year. This entitles you to reductions of at least 20–25 per cent on admission charges to many museums and châteaux, as well as reductions at many festivals, fairs, concerts, movies and tourist events.

AMBOISE. Château, including St.-Hubert Chapel. Open daily, Palm Sun. through Oct., 9–12, 2–7; winter, 9–12, 2–5.30.

Clos-Lucé (tel. 47-57-62-88). Open daily 9–12, 2–7 (no lunchtime closure June through Aug.). Closed Jan.

ANGERS. Ancien Hôpital St.-Jean. Jean Lurçat tapestries. Open 10–12, 2–6; closed Mon. and public hols.

Château du Roi René, promenade du Bout du Monde (tel. 41-87-43-47). Open 9.30–12, 2–6 in summer; 10–12, 2–5 in winter. Half price on Sun.

Logis Barrault, *Musée des Beaux-Arts* (Fine Arts Museum), 10 rue Musée (tel. 41-88-64-65). Open daily except Mon., and public hols., 10–12, 2–6.

Musée David d'Angers, Eglise Toussaint, 33 rue Toussaint (tel. 41-88-64-65). Open daily except Mon., 10–12, 2–6.

AZAY-LE-RIDEAU. Château. Open Apr. through Sept., daily 9.15–12, 2–6.30; winter, closes at 4.45 or 5. Closed certain public hols.

BEAUGENCY. Château. Open daily except Tues., 9–12, 2–6; to 4 in winter.

BEAUREGARD. Château (tel. 47-47-05-41). Open Apr. through Sept., daily 9.30–12, 2–6.30; winter, to 5 P.M. and closed Wed., Jan. 15 to Feb. 15. Guided tours only.

BLOIS. Château (tel. 54-78-06-62). Open mid-Mar. through Sept., daily 9–12, 2–6.30 (no lunchtime closure June through Aug.); winter, 9–12, 2–5.
Eglise St.-Nicolas. Open daily; guided tours obligatory Nov. to mid-Mar.

LE BREIL DE FOIN. Château, Genneteil (tel. 41-82-25-13). Open mid-July through Aug., 3–7.

CHAMBORD. Château, Bracieux (tel. 54-20-31-32). Open daily, mid-June through Aug., 9.30–12, 2–7; other periods to 6, or 5 in winter. Closed certain public hols.

CHAUMONT-SUR-LOIRE. Château (tel. 54-46-98-03). Open daily (except Tues.), Apr. through Sept., 9.30–11.45, 2.15–5.45; winter (except Tues. and Wed.), 9.45–12.30, 2–4.30.

CHENONCEAU. Château (tel. 47-29-90-07). Open daily, mid-Mar. to mid-Sept., 9–7; sometimes to 8 on weekends in July and Aug. Winter times vary—check locally. Extra charge for *Musée de Cire* (Waxworks).

CHEVERNY. Château (including *Musée de la Chasse*—Hunting Museum), (tel. 54-79-96-29). Open daily, Apr. to mid-June, 9–12, 2.15–6 or 6.30; mid-June to mid-Sept., 9.30–6.30. Winter times vary—check locally.

CHINON. Château (tel. 47-93-13-45). Open daily, mid-Mar. through Sept., 9–12, 2–6 (no lunchtime closure July and Aug.); in winter, daily except Wed., 9–12, 2–5, but closed Jan. and Dec.

LA DEVINIÈRE. Maison de Rabelais (Rabelais' House); (tel. 47-95-91-18). Open daily, mid-Mar. through Sept., 9–12, 2–6; winter, except Wed., to 5, but closed Jan. and Dec.

FONTEVRAUD. Abbaye (Abbey). Open Apr. through Sept., 9–12, 2–6; winter, 10–12, 2–4. Closed Tues. and certain public hols.

GIEN. Château, housing *Musée International de la Chasse* (International Hunting Museum), (tel. 38-67-24-11). Open daily, Palm Sun. through Oct., 9.15–12.15, 2.15–6.30; winter, to 5.

LANGEAIS. Château (tel. 47-96-72-60). Open mid-Mar. through Sept., daily except Mon., 9–12, 2–6.30 (no lunchtime closure July and Aug.); winter to 5.30.

LOCHES. Château. *Logis Royal* (Royal Lodge), (tel. 47-59-01-32). Open daily, mid-Mar. through Sept., 9–12, 2–6; winter, to 5, but closed Wed., Dec. and Jan. *Donjon* (Keep), (tel. 47-59-07-86). Opening periods as for *Logis Royal,* but times 9.30–12.30, 2.30–6.30; winter to 5.30. One ticket for both; guided tours available.
Musée Lansyer (Art Museum). Open daily (except Fri. and Christmas period), 9–11.45, 2–6; winter, to 4 or 5.
Musée de Terroir (Folklore Museum), in Porte Royale. Open as *Musée Lansyer* above.

LE LUDE. Château (tel. 43-94-60-09). Open Apr. through Oct., daily: gardens 9–12, 3–6; château 3–6.

LE MANS. Maison de la Reine Bérangère (Museum of History and Ethnography). Open daily except Mon., Tues. and public hols. 9–12, 2–6.

MONTPOUPON. Château (tel. 47-94-23-62). Open mid-June through Sept., daily 10–12, 2–7; otherwise open weekends and public hols. only, but closed Nov. to Easter. Guided tours only.

MONTRÉSOR. Château (tel. 47-94-20-04). Open Apr. through Oct. only, 9–12, 2–6.30.

MOULIN. Château, Lassay-sur-Croisne (tel. 54-83-83-51). Open Mar. to mid-Nov., daily 9–11.30, 2–6.30.

ORLÉANS. Musée des Beaux-Arts (Fine Arts Museum), pl. Cathédrale. **Musée Historique** (Gallo-Roman exhibits), Hotel Cabu. Open daily except Tues., 10–12, 2–5.

SACHE. Château (tel. 47-26-86-50). Open daily except Wed., mid-Mar. through Sept., 9–12, 2–6 (no lunchtime closure July and Aug.); winter to 5, but closed Jan. and Dec.

SAINT-BENOÎT-SUR-LOIRE. Abbaye Bénédictine (Benedictine Abbey: church and crypt). Open daily, 7 A.M.–10 P.M. (except during masses). Guided tour upon written request. Mass with Gregorian chant on Sun. and some religious festivals, at 10.45, weekdays at 11.45.

SAUMUR. Château des Ducs d'Anjou (tel. 41-51-30-46). Open daily, Apr. through Oct., 9–11.30, 2–6 (no lunchtime closure July through Sept.); evening visits in July and Aug., 8.30–10.30; winter, daily except Tues., 9.30–11.30, 2–5. Admission ticket covers: *Musée des Arts Décoratifs* (Decorative Arts Museum) and *Musée du Cheval* (Horse Museum).
  Musée des Blindés (Tank Museum). Open 9–11.30, 2–5.30.
  Musée du Champignon (Mushroom Museum), at St.-Hilaire-St.-Florent, via D751, 3 km. (2 miles) from town center (tel. 41-50-31-55). Open mid-Mar. to mid-Nov., 10–12, 2–6.

SOLESMES. Abbaye St.-Pierre (Abbey), (tel. 43-95-03-08). Masses with Gregorian plainsong at 9.45 weekdays and 10 on Sun. and public hols.; arrive early to secure a seat.

TOURS. Historiale de Touraine (Waxworks Museum), Château de Tours, quai d'Orléans (tel. 47-61-02-95). Open daily, July through Sept., 9–9; other months, generally 9–12.30, 2–7, except winter 2–6 only.
  Hôtel Gouin, 25 rue Commerce (tel. 47-66-22-32), housing *Musée Archéologique de Touraine* (Archeological Museum). Open daily, mid-Mar. through Sept., 9–12, 2–6; winter, daily (except Fri.), 9–12, 2–5, but closed Jan. and Dec.
  Hôtel Mame, 19 rue Emile-Zola (tel. 47-05-60-87). Open Apr. through Oct. only, 2.30–7.
  Musée des Beaux-Arts (Fine Arts Museum), rue Lavoisier (tel. 47-05-68-73). Open daily except Tues. and public hols., 9–12.45, 2–6.
  Musée du Compagnonnage (Craft Masterpieces Museum), rue Nationale (tel. 47-61-81-24). Open daily except Tues., 9–12, 2–6.
  Musée des Vins de Touraine (Wine Museum), rue Nationale (tel. 47-61-07-93). Open daily except Tues., 9–12, 2–6.
  Prieuré de St.-Cosme (Ronsard's Home), (tel. 47-20-99-29). Open mid-Mar. through Sept., daily except Wed., 9–12, 2–6 (no lunchtime closure July and Aug.); winter, to 5, but closed Jan. and Dec.

USSE. Château (tel. 47-95-54-05). Open mid-Mar. through Oct., daily 9–12, 2–7; Oct., to 6; closed rest of year.

VENDÔME. Cloître de la Trinité (tel. 54-77-26-13). Open daily except Tues., 10–12, 2–6.

VILLANDRY. Château. Open Palm Sun. to Nov. 11 only, 9–6. Gardens open year-round, 9–sunset or 8, whichever is earlier.

VILLESAVIN. Château. Open summer 10–11.30, 2–6.30; Oct. through Dec., afternoons only; closed Christmas through Feb.

SON-ET-LUMIÈRE. The "sound and light" presentations illustrating the history of famous buildings that are now staged the world over were pioneered in the famous châteaux of the Loire Valley. They still offer some of the best performances of their kind anywhere and we highly recommend attendance at at least one of them. Shows are generally given May through September. Details from tourist offices.

WINE. Wine Tasting. There are many cellars *(caves)* open to tourists for visits and tasting. For information contact *Conseil Interprofessionel des Vins d'Anjou et de Saumur,* 21 blvd. Foch, 49000 Angers or *Comité Interprofessionel des Vins de Touraine,* 19 sq. P.-Mérimée, 37000 Tours.

Wine Fairs. Every year wine fairs are held at the following times: *Jan.,* Angers and Vouvray; *Feb.,* Azay-le-Rideau, Bourgueil, Montlouis and Tours (Fondettes); *Mar.,* Chinon; *Apr.,* Amboise and Bourgueil; *Aug.,* Amboise, Montlouis and Vouvray; *Nov.,* Luynes (feast of *bernache,* the greenish fermented juice left after the grapes are pressed).

SHOPPING. For **regional craftwork** the best place is *Maison de la Touraine,* 4 blvd. Heurteloup in Tours. **Basketwork** is made in the village of Villaines-les-Rochers near Azay-le-Rideau and Saché, though it can be found throughout the area. **Lace** is another local specialty: try *Le Prieuré* in Beaulieu-les-Loches on the outskirts of Loches (open every day except Tues.). Charming **old prints** of the châteaux and other historic buildings are on sale at *Béatrix Hocq,* 74 rue des Halles, Tours, which also sells copies of marvelous old **tapestries** with historic details. **Modern sketches** of the medieval buildings of Tours may be found at *Atelier du Change,* rue du Change, Tours (open afternoons only). Most châteaux have a good range of well illustrated books on the region, as well as items connected with their history.

You can choose from a good range of local **wines** at *Maison de l'Anjou,* opposite the château in Angers (closed Tues.), the *Maison des Vins de Touraine,* 19 sq. P.-Mérimée, Tours, and at *Vinothèques* in Chinon and Tours. Round red tins of **barley sugar** *(sucre d'orge)* and **marzipan-stuffed prunes** *(pruneaux fourrés)* packed in miniature wooden crates, are local specialties that make good presents.

BRITTANY

Land's End with Celtic Folklore

Except perhaps for Alsace, no other mainland province is more different from the rest of France, or at any rate feels itself to be more different, than Brittany. This is because, alone among Frenchmen, the Bretons are of Celtic origin. Their land was colonized in the 5th and 6th centuries by Celtic emigrés from Britain, and to this day Bretons have more in common in some ways with the Welsh, Irish or Scots than with other Frenchmen. Like the Irish, they are passionate, whimsical, witty and high-spirited; but they are also tenacious and hard-working, like the Scots. And they have a truly Celtic sense of mystery and love of legend. Their vast windswept granite peninsula is still haunted by distant echoes of a magical past, of Tristan and Isolde, of Merlin and King Arthur.

Brittany was not annexed to the French crown till 1532, and today most of its people still feel a sense of Breton nationhood. Few desire secession from France, but they do want more autonomy and are keen to keep alive the old Breton culture. Until recently the Breton language, akin to Welsh, was dying out as a vehicle of daily speech except among some older people in remoter areas; but some eager young patriots are now seeking to revive it, and all-Breton schools, state examinations in Breton and an increasing amount of Breton-language publishing are all helping to realize their goal. The young have also led a renaissance of Breton folklore, music and dance. Alas, the picturesque old Breton costumes are no longer a part of daily wear, but they are readily brought out of mothballs for the numerous summer festivals in towns and villages, and for the typically Breton religious ceremonies known as *pardons,* when costumed villagers parade through the streets, carrying banners, statues and candles, to pay homage to their local saint (Brittany has hundreds of its own saints, few of them recognized by Rome). It is then that you will see women wearing the famous Breton *coiffes*—white lace head-dresses whose style varies from area to area.

Bretons today may be losing some of their old piety, but they remain more devoutly Catholic than most other French people. In the 16th century they developed their own special religious architecture, which survives today around the churches of some villages—stone crucifixes and ossuaries (sarcophagi) with elaborate carvings depicting local saints, the life of Christ and the Passion. Some of them stand alone by the sea where drowned sailors are commemorated. Many sons of this seafaring race lost their lives in storms off these treacherous coasts. Today, with Europe's fishing industries declining, only some 10,000 Bretons are fishermen: but many others still man France's Navy and merchant fleets, and the sea continues to play a big part in Breton life—above all through tourism.

The 2,000-mile coastline is heavily indented and richly varied: awesome rocky headlands, where the waves burst into spray, alternate with secretive sandy coves or wide pristine beaches, and idyllic forest-lined creeks and estuaries. This is ideal territory for a family seaside holiday or for sight-seeing. All along the coast and just inland are scores of handsome abbeys and tall churches, ancient shrines, turreted castles, and towns enclosed by medieval ramparts. Nearly all the buildings are in grey local granite, which gives an austere beauty different from the styles of much of the rest of France.

Culturally, the province is divided into two parts: Upper Brittany to the east, around the capital Rennes; and, to the west, Lower Brittany *(la Bretagne bretonnante),* the more interesting and typically Breton of the two. Here traditions and the Breton language survive more strongly than in the eastern area, which has long been more exposed to French influences. The dividing line is roughly from St.-Brieuc in the north to a point east of Vannes in the south. Scenically, however, the contrasts in Brittany are less between east and west than between north and south, between the coast and the interior. The north and west coasts are more rugged and grandiose, the south is more open and gentle, and warmer. But even in the north there are fertile plains close to the sea where farming is rich. The coastal area is quite thickly populated, while the interior is emptier, poorer and more desolate.

St.-Malo and the Rugged North Coast

A journey anti-clockwise round the coast begins in the northeast corner, across the Norman border from the abbey of Mont-St.-Michel. The first Breton town you come to is Dol, with a 13th-century granite cathedral. For a good view of the area, go to the top of nearby Mont-Dol, where St. Michael is said to have done battle with Satan. Round the bay is the pretty fishing-port of Cancale, and just beyond it the rugged rocky headland of the Pointe du Grouin. To the west, at Rothéneuf, do not miss the bizarre sculptures carved on the rocks by Abbé Fouré—a good example of *l'art brut.*

St.-Malo is one of the best-loved of Breton towns. The ancient walled city stands on a peninsula within massive 13th-century ramparts; there is a broad walk along the top, with fine views of the coast. The old city was badly bombed during the Allied siege of this Nazi redoubt in August 1944, but has been carefully restored and is still very picturesque. The castle is worth a visit, also the Quic-en-Groigne waxworks museum of local history and—just offshore—the tomb of Chateaubriand on the islet of Le Grand Bé. Two miles up the Rance estuary is the world's first tidal powered hydro-electric dam. There are four tides a day here, instead of the usual two. The dam is open to visits.

Further up the Rance, the charming old town of Dinan also has fine ramparts, as well as half-timbered houses and an old castle with a towering keep. Dinard, on a headland facing St.-Malo, is a large, sedate family resort, not as fashionable as it once was. Westwards from here there stretches a magnificent succession of craggy capes and sandy beaches backed by pine-forests. Of the many lively bathing-resorts, St.-Cast, Sables-d'Or and Le Val-André are the best. The fortress of La Latte stands majestically on a headland, while Cap Fréhel has grandiose scenery of red and black cliffs.

Inland from here, east of the pleasant market town of Lamballe, are the massive ruins of the 13th-century castle of La Hunaudaie. Going west, you pass through the cathedral city of St-Brieuc, capital of this part of Brittany. You then enter the wild country of Goëlo, where l'Arouest is another wild and lovely headland, facing the rocky, romantic island of Bréhat (accessible by boat). The fishing-port of Paimpol was the setting of Pierre Loti's novel *Pêcheur d'Islande*. Tréguier is noted for its glorious Gothic cathedral, with a fine cloister and Renaissance choir-stalls.

Perros-Guirec, a lively little town on a promontory, is Brittany's largest resort after Dinard and La Baule. West of here there stretches the strange and lovely Coast of Pink Granite, noted for its profusion of pink, bizarrely-shaped rocks. At the resort of Trégastel they stand scattered on the beach as well as spilling out over the sea in a myriad of tiny islands. This area is ideal for children who like climbing, shrimping and playing in rock lagoons. The more scientifically-minded can go just inland, to Pleumeur-Bodou, to visit France's leading space-communications center with its big white balloon-like dome. History-lovers can go beyond Lannion to explore the ruins of the hilltop castle of Tonquédec.

The Romantic West, Around Brest and Quimper

At Morlaix you enter Finistère, the most typical and truly Breton part of Brittany. Morlaix is the capital of a rich market-gardening region that exports artichokes and cauliflowers. To its southwest are two villages with some of the finest religious stone sculptures in Brittany, dating from the 16th and 17th centuries—St.-Thégonnec with its triumphal arch, ossuary, richly-carved crucifix, and ornate pulpit in the church; and Guimiliau where the baptistry in the church vies in splendor with the vivid sculptures of its crucifix.

To the north is the modern port of Roscoff, where ferries sail for England and Ireland, and nearby is the market town of St.-Pol-de-Léon whose streets are dominated by the tower of its 13th-century cathedral and the 250-foot steeple of the Kreisker chapel, the prototype of the many tall churches in this part of Brittany: another, as fine, is at Le Folgoët, to the west. Further on lies the mysterious open landscape of the Pays de Léon, stretching to the "Coast of Legends" by the Atlantic, where lush pastures slope to lovely river valleys known as *abers:* l'A-berWrac'h, a fashionable yachting center, is the most typical. From the port of Le Conquet, or from Brest, you can take a two-hour boat trip to the island of Ouessant where the waves dash against jagged rocks and thousands of migrating birds nest in the ledges of the cliffs.

Brest, the leading French naval base on the Atlantic coast, stands on the north side of a magnificent natural harbor. The town was heavily bombed during World War II, and rebuilt in an ugly rectangular style; what's more, the heyday of its naval glory is past, though it is still a major repair center for tankers and other big ships. You can visit the dockyards, or get a good view of them from the Cours Dajot. To the east, the village of Plougastel-Daoulas has a remarkable crucifix. It is also the center of a strawberry-growing district.

The Crozon peninsula, south of Brest harbor, has several attractive fishing-ports, such as Camaret whose ladies misbehaved in France's best-known lewd drinking-song. For a good view of the whole area, you should drive to the summit of the Menez-Hom hill. Then go south to Ste.-Anne-la-Palud, venue for one of Brittany's most famous *pardons;* then on to the picturesque village of Locronan, with a fine church and Renaissance houses round a square.

Douarnenez, France's leading sardine-fishing port, has not much of interest. To the west, the Cap Sizun peninsula points a long finger into the Atlantic, ending in the Pointe du Raz, the most westerly tip of France. On this towering headland you can scramble amid the rocks—preferably led by a local guide—and watch the waves lashing the rocks far below. Cap Sizun has a bird sanctuary, best visited in the spring. Some eight km. (five miles) out at sea is the bleak Ile de Sein whose 600 inhabitants, mostly fisherfolk, live in tiny houses furnished partly from shipwrecks. The island is an hour's boat trip from Audierne. It covered itself in glory in June 1940 when the entire male population sailed to Britain to fight with the Free French.

Southwest of Quimper, around Pont l'Abbé, is the Pays Bigouden, where Breton traditions survive most strongly: here on special days women still wear their tall distinctive white *coifs,* and here Per-Jakez Hélias set his famous best-selling study of Breton rural life, *The Horse of Pride.* Worth a visit are the Eckmühl lighthouse, the prehistory museum at St.-Guénolé, and the crucifix by the lonely seaside chapel of Notre-Dame-de-Trenoën. Next you will come to Quimper, a grace-ful city with quaint old streets, a fine cathedral, and a good art museum. From here a delightful boat trip can be made down the lovely river Odet to the sea at Benodet.

Concarneau to Nantes: the Gentle South Coast

Southern Brittany has a gentle, open coast of wide sandy beaches backed by dunes and pinewoods. It is less rugged than the north or west and the climate is warmer. Bénodet and Beg-Meil, south of Quimper, are two smart and lively bathing-resorts with echoes of the Riviera. Going east, you come to the big tuna-fishing port of Concarneau whose walled island citadel in the harbor, the Ville Close, is highly pic-turesque. You can wander in its old streets and visit its museum of fishing.

East again is Pont-Aven, a pretty little town which the Post-Impres-sionist painters loved: Gauguin was one of those who lived and worked there. Nearby are the lovely wooded estuaries of the Aven and Belon, the latter famous for its oysters. At Quimperlé, the apse of the 12th-century church of Ste.-Croix is Brittany's finest Romanesque building. Lorient, a naval base and major fishing port, was the main German submarine base on the Atlantic during the war and was subsequently badly damaged. It has since been rebuilt in spacious rectangular style.

The Carnac/Vannes sector of the south coast is of exceptional and varied interest. The resort of Carnac draws archeologists from the world over because of its strange prehistoric remains—notably the thousands of stone menhirs (standing stones) and megaliths in long straight rows, and the big Tumulus of St.-Michel with its funeral chambers. There is a good archeological museum here. You should visit, too, the curious church of St.-Cornély (local patron saint of horned cattle!). On its facade are figures of the saint and two bulls. At the nearby abbeys of St.-Michel and Ste.-Anne you can hear superb Gregorian plainsong.

The big resort of Quiberon stands on a peninsula south of Carnac, wild and rocky on its west side. Here at the Hôtel de la Plage, St.-Pierre, Jacques Tati shot parts of his hilarious movie *M. Hulot's Holiday.* Offshore, easily reached by boat, is lovely Belle-Ile, with many coves and grottoes and a fine rugged coastline. Back on the mainland, just east of Carnac, you come to La Trinité, a training center for ocean-going yachtsmen, and then to Locmariaquer, which has more megaliths. The village faces on to the Gulf of Morbihan, an inland sea of great beauty, studded with small islands and rich in birdlife. On one islet is the remarkable Tumulus of Gavrinis, probably the ancient tomb of a Celtic king. On the Rhuys peninsula south of the gulf, the village of St.-Gildas used to contain a monastery where Abelard nursed his grief after parting from Héloïse. To the east is the 13th-century castle of Suscinio, formerly a ruin, now partially restored.

Vannes is a graceful old town of character, with massive ramparts, a fine 13th-century cathedral and quaint gabled houses. Auray is also attractive, while Ste.-Anne d'Auray is Brittany's leading pilgrimage center, with a big annual *pardon.* Southeast from here you come to the marshy salt lagoons of the Guérande peninsula, between the lively fishing-port of Le Croisic and the large and more sophisticated resort of La Baule. There is little of interest at St.-Nazaire, a shipbuilding town that has seen better days; but just inland lies the strange marshy lagoon of La Grande Brière, with a bird sanctuary and an outdoor museum of rural life.

Finally to Nantes, which is not typically Breton nor today officially part of Brittany, but has historic associations with the province nonetheless. Today it is a large, busy industrial city and port, with much also to interest the lover of art and history—notably the massive ducal palace, the Gothic cathedral (superb interior), and a number of museums, including one devoted to regional folk arts. Strolling along its broad avenues, or *cours,* which were once watercourses, is particularly pleasant. At Nantes in 1598 Henri IV signed the Edict giving protection to France's Protestants.

Rennes and the Wild Interior

Brittany's interior may be less exciting than its coast, but it has much to offer the discerning traveler. To the east, around Rennes, it is un-dulating pastoral country; to the west it is more wild and remote, a region of forests and rock-strewn moorlands where many farms and villages have scarcely been touched by modern prosperity.

Rennes, Brittany's capital, is a dignified, friendly town with two universities. The main sights are the cathedral (fine altar piece), the Palais de Justice, and the Musée des Beaux-Arts. There are quaint medieval streets round the cathedral. Combourg, to the north, is a charming old town by a lake with a feudal castle that was the home of the writer Chateaubriand. Fougères, to the east, has an even more splendid castle, with towers and massive ramparts: Balzac set his novel *Les Chouans* in this area. The little town of Vitré has preserved its medieval character almost intact and also boasts a romantic many-turreted castle.

The forest of Paimpont, west of Rennes, lies at the heart of Celtic legend, for this was the original "Brocéliande," the home of Merlin the Enchanter according to the Arthurian tales. Today the forest's character is somewhat different: Coëtquidan, on its southern fringe, is the site of France's leading military academy, St.-Cyr, recently transferred from Versailles. The lovely town of Josselin, to the west, has a majestic towered château that rivals Fougères' as one of the two finest in Brittany. It stands by a river, with old houses stretching up the hill to the basilica of Notre-Dame-du-Roncier, site of a major *pardon*.

A beauty spot of the western hinterland is the long, curving lake of Guerlédan, created artificially and used as a reservoir and for sailing. The village of Kernascléden has an old church with remarkable 15th-century frescos (restored), while at Pleyben lies the most impressive of all Breton crucifixes. Pleyben is at the heart of a strange, austere upland region where great rocks stand as lonely sentinels on hilltops. To its east lies the Montagne Noire, and to its north the Monts d'Arrée, where on a fine day the Roc Trévezel offers a stunning panorama over northwest Brittany as far as the coast at Brest and at Roscoff.

PRACTICAL INFORMATION FOR BRITTANY

TOURIST OFFICES. The regional tourist office for the whole of Brittany—written enquiries only—is the *Délégation Régionale de Tourisme,* 3 rue d'Espagne, BP 4175, 35041 Rennes cedex. Brittany also has a tourist office in Paris: *Maison de la Bretagne,* Centre Maine-Montparnasse, 17 rue de l'Arrivée 15e (tel. 45-38-73-15). In addition, the five *départements* of Brittany also have their own tourist offices (again, written enquiries only): **Côtes du Nord,** 1 rue Chateaubriand, 2200 St.-Brieuc; **Finistère,** 6 rue René-Madec, 29000 Quimper; **Ile-et-Vilaine,** Préfecture, 1 rue Martenot, 35032 Rennes cedex; **Morbihan,** Préfecture, BP 400, 56009 Vannes cedex; **Loire Atlantique,** 34 rue de Strasbourg, 44000 Nantes.

There are local tourist offices in the following towns: **La Baule,** 8 pl. Victoire (tel. 40-24-34-44); **Carnac,** 74 av. Druides (tel. 97-52-13-52); **Concarneau,** quai d'Aiguillon (tel. 98-97-01-44); **Le Croisic,** pl. Gare (tel. 40-23-00-70); **Dinan,** 6 rue Horloge (tel. 96-39-75-40); **Dinard,** 2 blvd. Féart (tel. 99-46-94-12); **Lorient,** pl. Jules-Ferry (tel. 97-21-07-84); **Morlaix,** pl. Otages (tel. 98-62-14-94); **Nantes,** pl. Change (tel. 40-47-04-51); **Perros-Guirec,** 21 pl. Hôtel-de-Ville (tel. 96-23-21-15); **Quiberon,** 7 rue Verdun (tel. 97-50-07-84); **Quimper,** 3 rue Roi-Gradlon (tel. 98-95-04-69); **Rennes,** pont de Nemours (tel. 99-79-01-98); **Roscoff,** squ. Le Jeune (tel. 98-69-70-70), (Closed Oct. to mid-Apr.); **St.-Brieuc,** rue St.-Gouéno (tel. 96-33-32-50); **St.-Malo,** esplanade St.-Vincent (tel. 99-56-64-48); **Vannes,** 29 rue Thiers (tel. 97-47-24-34).

REGIONAL FOOD AND DRINK. Brittany is well-known for its excellent fish and shellfish. Oysters from Belon, the Bay of Morlaix and Cancale; scallops from the bay of St.-Brieuc and Quiberon; grilled or stuffed clams; and of course the king of the sea, the lobster, served grilled or in a rich sauce *à l'armoricaine* (not *à l'américaine,* American-style, as many people suppose, but deriving from the *Armorici,* the ancient name for the Bretons). Inland there is excellent salmon from the Aulne and trout from the Black Mountains, while the Loire provides pike and its estuary, young eel *(civelles)* which served fried are a specialty of Nantes.

Pork products are good, with ham from Morlaix and *andouillette* (small chitterling sausage) from Quimperlé. A special treat is lamb that has grazed on the salt-water marshes around the coast *(agneau pré-salé).* The region is also well-known for its vegetables, especially artichokes and cauliflowers, grown around St.-Pol-de-Léon, while if you go to Plougastel try the excellent strawberries. Throughout the province are *crêperies* where you can sample the famous Breton pancakes: *galettes de sarrasin* (buckwheat pancakes), savoury pancakes topped with egg or ham; or *galettes de froment* (wheat-flour pancakes), eaten with jam or sugar. If you're still hungry, try a *far breton,* a rich cake made with butter.

The traditional Breton drink is cider. The only local wines are *Muscadet* and *Gros-Plant* from around Nantes, both of which are white and delicious with fish and shellfish.

HOTELS AND RESTAURANTS. During high season (July–Aug.) prices rise by about 20%. You must reserve ahead for these months, especially if bringing a family. Rooms in chic resorts (Dinard, La Baule) are about 25% less than in Paris, while tiny ports or resorts may be 50% cheaper or more, but hotels here can be spartan and old-fashioned, though normally friendly. Many hotels are closed in the winter months, except in large cities.

For general notes on hotels and restaurants, see "Hotels and Restaurants" in *Facts at Your Fingertips.*

LA BAULE. *Hermitage* (L), esplanade François-André (tel. 40-60-37-00). 230 rooms. Closed mid-Oct. to mid-Apr. Luxurious hotel from another era, now completely modernized with private beach, sauna, pool, and three excellent restaurants. AE, DC, MC, V. *Castel Marie-Louise* (E), esplanade Casino (tel. 40-60-20-60). 28 rooms. Very comfortable small hotel, set in its own peaceful garden; fine traditional cuisine. AE, DC, MC, V. *Royal* (E), esplanade François-André (tel. 40-60-33-06). 115 rooms. Closed Oct. through Mar. Elegant hotel not far from casino and beach. AE, DC, MC, V. *Christina* (M), 26 blvd. Hennecart (tel. 40-60-22-44). 36 rooms. On beach; open all year; restaurant. MC, V. *Palmeraie* (M), 7 allée Cormorans (tel. 40-60-24-41). 23 rooms. Closed Oct. through Mar. Quiet hotel set in pinewoods near sea, with pretty garden; good home-style cooking. AE, DC, MC, V.

Restaurants. *Espadon* (E), 2 av. Plage (tel. 40-60-05-63). Closed Sun. for dinner and Mon. in winter (except public hols.), and mid-Nov. to mid-Jan. (except Christmas). Magnificent view over sea from this 5th-floor restaurant; excellent *nouvelle cuisine.* AE, DC, V. *Ankou* (M), 38 av. de l'Etoile (tel. 40-60-22-47). Closed Tues. for lunch, Mon. (except July and Aug.) and Jan. Classical cuisine with good fish. AE, V.

At **Pouliguen,** 3 km. (2 miles) west. **Restaurant.** *Voile d'Or* (M), av. Plage (tel. 40-42-31-68). Closed Nov. through Jan., Tues. for dinner and Wed. except in summer. Go for the little *menu* (I) served weekdays for lunch in summer. AE, V.

BELLE-ILE. At **Port Goulphar:** *Castel Clara* (E), (tel. 97-31-84-21). 41 rooms. Closed Nov. through Feb. Large, well-decorated rooms overlooking sea, with pool and tennis courts; good *nouvelle cuisine.* AE, V.

At **Sauzon:** *Cardinal* (M), pointe du Cardinal (tel. 97-31-61-60). 80 rooms. Closed Oct. to mid-June. Quiet, modern hotel with sea views. Restaurant.

At **Port-Goulphar.** *Grand Large* (I), (tel. 97-31-80-92). 20 rooms. Very well situated with great views.

BÉNODET. *Gwel-Kaër* (M), av. Plage (tel. 98-57-04-38). 24 rooms. Closed Jan.; restaurant closed Mon. and Sun. for dinner (except public hols.). Well-equipped rooms near beach with views of sea or garden. v. *Kastel Moor* (M), av. Plage (tel. 98-57-05-01). 23 rooms. Closed Oct. to Easter. Modern hotel near sea, with tennis court and pool; restaurant in *Ker Moor* hotel next door (tel. 98-57-04-48). MC.

Restaurant. At **Ste.-Marine** (on opposite bank of Odet estuary via toll bridge), *Jeanne d'Arc* (M), 52 rue Plage (tel. 98-56-32-70). Closed Mon. for dinner (except July and Aug.), Tues. and Nov. through Mar. Good mixture of Burgundian and Breton cuisine; has a few rooms (half-board obligatory in summer).

BILLIERS-PENLAN. *Château de Rochevilaine* (E), pointe Pen-Lan (tel. 97-41-69-27). Closed mid-Nov. to mid-Mar. Restored Breton manor house right by sea, with beautiful gardens and heated sea-water pool. Excellent cuisine. AE, DC, MC, V.

BREST. *Sofitel Océania* (E), 82 rue Siam (tel. 98-80-66-66). 82 rooms. Modernized, well-equipped, stylish rooms. AE, DC, MC, V. *Continental* (M), squ. Tour d'Auvergne (tel. 98-80-50-40). 75 rooms. Restaurant closed Sat. for lunch, Sun. Well-placed for station and harbor, a bit old-fashioned but comfortable. AE, DC, MC, V. *Voyageurs* (M), 15 av. Clemenceau (tel. 98-80-25-73). 40 rooms. Closed first half of Jan., last week in July and first half of Aug.; restaurant closed Sun. for dinner and Mon. Central but quiet; excellent restaurant offers traditional cuisine with emphasis on fish dishes. AE, DC, MC, V.

Restaurants. *Frère Jacques* (M), 15bis rue Lyon (tel. 98-44-38-65). Closed Sat. for lunch and first half of Aug. Inventive cuisine in elegant surroundings. AC, DC, MC, V. *Poulbot* (M), 26 rue Aiguillon (tel. 98-44-19-08). Closed Sat. for lunch, Sun., last half of Aug., first week Sept. Pleasant bistrot-style restaurant with good-value *menu*. AE, DC, MC, V.

CANCALE. *Continental* (M), quai Administrateur-Thomas (tel. 99-89-60-16). 20 rooms. Closed Oct. through March; restaurant closed Mon. Traditional hotel on harbor's edge; restaurant has some tables outside in summer. MC, V.

At **La Pointe-du-Grouin,** 3 km. (2 miles) north via St.-Jouan: *Pointe du Grouin* (M), (tel. 99-89-60-55). 16 rooms. Closed Oct. through Mar.; restaurant closed Tues. (except mid-July through Aug.). Quiet, family hotel with spectacular views of Mont St.-Michel bay. V.

Restaurants. *Bricourt* (M), 1 rue Duguesclin (tel. 99-89-64-76). Closed Tues. and Wed. through Feb. In beautiful old house full of antique furniture. Good *nouvelle cuisine* with inventive use of local produce; good-value *menu*. MC, V. *Cancalais* (M-I), quai Gambetta (tel. 99-89-61-93). Closed mid-end Nov. through Feb. Small harbor-side restaurant with excellent fish and seafood. Also has 8 (I) rooms. MC, V.

CARNAC. *Diana* (E), 21 blvd. Plage (tel. 97-52-05-38). 32 rooms. Closed Oct. through Apr. Modern hotel beside beach; some rooms have sea view. V. *Novotel Tal Ar Mor* (E-M), av. Atlantique (tel. 97-52-16-66). 106 rooms. Closed Jan. Large, well-equipped rooms; not far from harbor with direct access to salt-water cure center; pool. AE, DC, MC, V.

At **Plouharnel.** *Birvideaux* (M), Kerhueno (tel. 97-52-35-35). Small, modern hotel with pool, garden, restaurant.

Restaurants. *Lann-Roz* (M-E), 35 av. Poste (tel. 97-52-10-48). Closed Jan.; restaurant closed Wed. (except June through Sept.). Good inventive cooking with emphasis on fish dishes. Also has some (M) rooms overlooking garden.

CONCARNEAU. *Sables Blancs* (M), plage des Sables Blancs (tel. 98-97-01-39). 48 rooms. Closed Nov. through Mar. Quiet hotel near beach; some rooms with sea view. AE, DC, MC, V. *Modern* (I), 5 rue Lin (tel. 98-97-03-36). 19 rooms. Small hotel close to fishing harbor.

At **Cabellou plage,** 5½ km. (3½ miles) away on road to Quimperlé, *Belle Etoile* (E), (tel. 98-97-05-73). 29 rooms. Closed Dec. through Feb.; restaurant closed Tues. in winter and also Dec. through March. Large old house set in pine forest close to beach; comfortable rooms; garden and tennis court. AE, DC, V.

Restaurants. *Galion* (E), 15 rue St.-Guénolé in the Ville Close (Walled Town) (tel. 98-97-30-16). Closed Sun. for dinner and Mon., Feb. to mid-Mar. and first half of Dec. Excellent *nouvelle cuisine* in fine old Breton building. AE, DC, MC, v. *Coquille* (M), 1 rue Moros (tel. 98-97-08-52). Closed Sun. for dinner (except July and Aug.), Mon., last week in April, first week in May, and Christmas and New Year period. Right on the harbor; traditional cooking with good fresh fish. AE, MC, V. *Chez Armande* (M-I), 15bis av. Dr.-Nicolas (tel. 98-97-00-76). Closed Sun. for dinner, Mon. and mid-Nov. to mid-Dec. Small restaurant near yacht harbor; attractive dining-room; good-value *menu*. v.

LE CROISIC. At **Port Lin.** *Océan* (M), pl. Charles-de-Gaulle (tel. 40-42-90-03). 20 rooms. Closed mid-Nov. through Jan. Lovely sea views; good seafood. v.

Restaurant. *Bretagne* (M), 11 quai Petite Chambre (tel. 40-23-00-51). Closed Tues. for dinner, Wed. (except July and Aug.), and Nov. through Feb. Small, beside harbor; good fish. v.

DINAN. *Avaugour* (M), 1 pl. du Champ Clos (tel. 96-39-07-49). 27 rooms. Comfortable rooms, some overlooking ramparts and garden; good *nouvelle cuisine* with good-value *menus*. AE, DC, MC, V. *Bretagne* (M), 1 pl. Duclos (tel. 96-39-46-15). 45 rooms. Well-situated, modernized hotel. AE, DC, MC, V. *Marguerite* (I), 29 pl. Du-Guesclin (tel. 96-39-47-65). 19 rooms. Modest, traditional hotel. AE, DC, V.

Restaurants. *Caravelle* (E), 14 pl. Duclos (tel. 96-39-00-11). Closed Wed. (Nov. through June), mid-Oct. to mid-Nov., two weeks in Feb. Excellent *nouvelle cuisine* with some regional dishes. Also has 11 (M) rooms. *Relais des Corsaires* (I), 5 rue Quais (tel. 96-39-40-17). Nice old decor, interesting fish and shellfish dishes, well-priced *menu*.

DINARD. *Reine Hortense* (L), 19 rue Malouine (tel. 99-46-54-31). 10 rooms. Closed mid-Nov. through Mar. Large, luxurious rooms in a villa overlooking the sea; no restaurant. AE, DC, V. *Grand Hôtel* (E), 46 av. George-V (tel. 96-46-10-28). 100 rooms. Closed Oct. through Mar. Palatial old hotel, now completely modernized; good traditional cooking. AE, DC, MC, V. *Printania* (M), 5 av. George-V (tel. 99-46-13-07). 77 rooms. Closed Oct. to Easter. Marvelous views over Baie du Prieuré. AE, V. *Altaïr* (I), 18 blvd. Féart (tel. 99-46-13-58). 22 rooms. Closed mid-Dec. to mid-Jan.; restaurant closed Sun. for dinner (in winter) and Wed. (except school holidays). Well-known for its restaurant: good *nouvelle cuisine;* inventive fish dishes. AE, DC, V.

At **la Richardais,** 3 km. (2 miles) southeast by D114. **Restaurant.** *Petit Robinson* (M), 38 rue des Fougeonnais (tel. 99-46-14-82). Great for shellfish; (I) *menus*. AE, DC, MC, V.

HENNEBONT. 4 km. (2½ miles) south via D781, *Château de Locguénolé* (E), rte. de Port-Louis (tel. 97-76-29-04). 33 rooms. Closed mid-Nov. through Feb.; restaurant closed Mon. (except in summer and public hols.). Small Breton château set in grounds, with very comfortable rooms, pool, and one of the best restaurants in Brittany, serving fine *nouvelle cuisine*. AE, DC, MC, V.

LAMBALLE. *Tour d'Argent* (M), 2 rue Dr.-Lavergne (tel. 96-31-01-37). 30 rooms. Closed Sat. (except July and Aug.), mid–end June and part of Oct. Attractive old hotel with pleasant rooms. Restaurant is (I), closed Sat. AE, DC, MC, V.

At **La Poterie,** 4 km. (2½ miles) out of town via D28, *Auberge Manoir des Portes* (M), (tel. 96-31-13-62). 16 rooms. Closed Jan. through Feb., restaurant closed Mon. (except July and Aug.) and Sun. for dinner. Lovely 16th-century building in peaceful countryside. Good restaurant. AE, DC, V.

LEZARDRIEUX. *Relais Brenner* (E), au Pont (tel. 96-20-11-05). 27 rooms. Closed Nov. through Mar. Quiet, large rooms overlooking garden; traditional cooking with emphasis on seafood. AE, DC, MC, V.

LORIENT. *Bretagne* (M), 6 pl. Libération (tel. 97-64-34-65). Near station. Good facilities; restaurant. AE, DC, MC, V.
Restaurants. *Arcades* (M-I), 11 blvd. Franchet-d'Espérey (tel. 97-21-17-42). Closed Sun. Near station; good fish. AE, DC, V. *Poisson d'Or* (M-I), 1 rue Maître-Esvelin (tel. 97-21-57-06). Closed Sat. for lunch, Sun. (but open for dinner July and Aug.), and first half of Feb. Elegant restaurant serving classical cuisine. AE, DC, MC, V. *Pic* (I), 2 blvd. Franchet-d'Espérey (tel. 97-21-18-29). Closed Sat. for lunch, Thurs., first week in Mar., two weeks in June, two weeks in Dec. Good *nouvelle cuisine* with emphasis on fresh produce, particularly fish. V.

MOELAN-SUR-MER. *Manoir de Kertalg* (E), (tel. 98-39-77-77). 10 rooms. Newly opened with very good service. By river, in own huge grounds. No restaurant.

NANTES. *Sofitel* (E), île Beaulieu (tel. 40-47-61-03). 97 rooms. Restaurant closed for dinner and at weekends. Quiet hotel, not very central, on island in the Loire. Good restaurant; pool, tennis court. AE, DC, MC, V. *Astoria* (M) 11 rue Richebourg (tel. 40-74-39-90). 45 rooms. Closed Aug. In quiet street near station; no restaurant. *Colonies* (M), 5 rue Chapeau Rouge (tel. 40-48-79-76). 39 rooms. Ask for the rooms at the back *(a l'arrière)* as they're quieter. No restaurant. AE, DC, V. *Hôtel* (M), 6 pl. Duchesse Anne (tel. 40-29-30-31). 31 rooms. Comfortable, modern hotel; some quiet rooms overlooking garden; no restaurant. AE, MC, V.
At **Orvault,** 6½ km. (4 miles) northwest via N137 and D42, *Domaine d'Orvault* (E), chemin Marais-du-Cens (tel. 40-76-84-02). 30 rooms. Delightful rooms overlooking large, peaceful garden; tennis court; excellent *nouvelle cuisine;* closed school hols. in Feb. and Mon. for lunch. AE, DC, V.
At **Sorinières,** 10½ km. (6½ miles) towards Sables d'Olonne (via D178), *Abbaye de Villeneuve* (E), (tel. 40-04-40-25). 14 rooms. Luxurious hotel in restored 18th-century abbey in beautiful grounds; pool and excellent restaurant. AE, DC, MC, V.
Restaurants. *Maraîchers* (E), 21 rue Fouré (tel. 40-47-06-51). Closed Sat. for lunch, Sun., Mon. and Aug. Imaginative *nouvelle cuisine* served in pleasant surroundings. AE, DC, V. *Sirène* (M), 4 rue Kervégan (tel. 40-47-00-17). Closed Sat. for lunch, Sun. and over Christmas and New Year. Good classical cuisine, excellent fresh fish. AE, DC, V. *Café Marché* (I), 1 rue Mayence (tel. 40-47-63-50). Old bistrot serving good hearty food. Good-value *menu.* Open for lunch only; closed weekends and Aug. *Voyageurs* (I), 16 allée du Commandant-Charcot (tel. 40-74-02-41). Closed first half of Jan. Close to station; good fresh produce, particularly fish. V.
At **Bellevue,** 8 km. (5 miles) out of town via All motorway, *Delphin* (E), 3 promenade Bellevue (tel. 40-25-60-30). Closed Sun. for dinner, Mon., most of Aug., and Christmas and New Year. Well-situated beside the Loire; distinguished, mainly *nouvelle cuisine.* AE, DC, MC, V.

PAIMPOL. Restaurants. *Repaire de Kerroc'h* (M), 29 quai Morand (tel. 96-20-50-13). Closed Mon. for dinner and Tues. and most of Jan. Restored 18th-century house overlooking harbor. Good fresh fish and seafood; also has 7 smallish but elegant rooms. AE, DC, MC, V. *Vieille Tour* (M), 13 rue de l'Eglise (tel. 96-20-83-18). Closed Tues. for dinner, Wed. (except school hols.), Nov. to mid-Dec. Traditional dishes with delicious fish. Good-value *menu.* V.

PERROS-GUIREC. *Grand Hôtel de Trestraou* (M), blvd. Joseph Le Bihan (tel. 96-23-24-05). 68 rooms. Well-modernized hotel, overlooking beach and beside salt-water cure center. Good restaurant. AE, DC, MC, V. *Printania* (M), 12 rue Bons-Enfants (tel. 96-23-21-00). 38 rooms. Closed Sun. and Mon. (in winter), and mid-Dec. to mid-Jan. Elegant hotel with marvelous sea views, close to beach. Tennis court. AE, DC, MC, V. *St. Yves* (I), blvd. Aristide Briand (tel. 96-23-21-31). 20 rooms. Closed Nov. Close to Trestraou beach. MC, V.

Restaurant. *Feux des Iles* (M), 53 blvd. Clemenceau (tel. 96-23-22-94). Closed Sun. for dinner and Mon. for lunch (in winter, except public hols.), mid-Oct. to mid-Nov. and most of Jan. Attractive garden overlooking sea. Good-value *menu*. Also has 15 rooms. DC, V.

PLEHEDEL. *Château de Coatguélen* (E), on D7 between Paimpol and Lanvollon (tel. 96-22-31-24). 16 rooms. Closed Jan. through Mar., Tues. for lunch and Wed. Small château set in grounds with tennis court, pool and 9-hole golf course. Delightful rooms and excellent restaurant. AE, DC, MC, V.

PLÉNEUF-VAL-ANDRÉ. **Restaurant.** *Cotriade* (M), Port de Piégu (tel. 96-72-20-26). Closed Mon. for dinner, Tues., end of May and mid-Dec. to mid-Jan. Small restaurant overlooking harbor; beautifully cooked fish. V.

PLOUGASTEL. **Restaurant.** *Chevalier de l'Auberlac'h* (M), 5 rue Mathurin Thomas (tel. 98-40-54-56). Closed Sat. for lunch, for dinner, Mon. and first half of Oct. Delightful old inn with good *nouvelle cuisine*. AE, DC, MC, V.

PONT-AVEN. **Restaurants.** *Moulin de Rosmadec* (M), near bridge in town center (tel. 98-06-00-22). Closed Sun. for dinner (in winter), Wed., part of Feb. and mid-Oct. to mid-Nov. Charming 15th-century mill with terrace overlooking river; good traditional dishes. *Taupinière* (M), 4 km. (2½ miles) towards Concarneau (tel. 98-06-03-12). Closed Mon. for dinner (except July and Aug.), Tues, mid-Sept. to mid-Oct, first half of March. Imaginative "new" dishes served in thatched cottage. AE, DC, MC, V.

PONT L'ABBÉ. *Château Kernuz* (M), (tel. 98-87-01-59). 2½ km. (1½ miles) by RN785. Beautiful 16th-century château. Comfortable; pension compulsory in summer; pool; restaurant.

PONTS-NEUFS. **Restaurant.** *Lorand-Barre* (E), (tel. 96-32-78-71). Closed Sun. for dinner, Mon. and Dec. through Feb. Magnificent classical cooking in old house full of antique furniture; must reserve. AE, DC.

QUESTEMBERT. **Restaurant.** *Bretagne* (E), 13 rue St.-Michel (tel. 97-26-11-12). Closed Sun. for dinner (except July and Aug.), Mon. and Jan. to mid-Mar. Excellent, inventive *nouvelle cuisine*. Also has 5 quiet and comfortable rooms. AE, DC, V.

QUIBERON. *Sofitel Thalassa* (L), pointe du Goulvars (tel. 97-50-20-00). 108 rooms. Closed Jan. Quiet, modern hotel with comfortable rooms and excellent restaurant. Linked by corridor to salt-water cure center; pool. AE, DC, MC, V. *Ker Noyal* (E), rte. St.-Clément, chemin des Dunes (tel. 97-50-08-41). Closed Nov. through Feb. Large, luxurious hotel set in attractive garden. AE, V. *Bellevue* (M), rue Tiviec (tel. 97-50-16-28). 41 rooms. Closed Oct. through Mar. Rooms comfortable with lovely views. Pool. AE, MC, V.

At **Port Haliguen,** 2½ km. (1½ miles) via D200, *Navirotel* (M), 10 pl. Port-Haliguen (tel. 97-50-16-52). 21 rooms. Closed Jan. to mid-Feb. Small hotel overlooking harbor and bay, with excellent fish restaurant. AE, DC, MC, V.

Restaurants. *Pêcheurs* (M), 1 rue Kervozes (tel. 97-50-12-75). Closed Sun. for dinner, Mon. and Jan. Great shellfish on the terrace by the harbor and good wines. Very good (I) *menus*. AE, DC, MC, V.

QUIMPER. *Griffon* (M), 131 rte. de Bénodet (tel. 98-90-33-33). 50 rooms. Restaurant closed Sat. for dinner and Sun. (in winter). Modern hotel (also closed for Christmas and New Year) on outskirts with well-equipped rooms, pool and sauna. AE, DC, MC, V. *Tour d'Auvergne* (M), 13 rue Réguaires (tel. 98-95-08-70). 45 rooms. Closed mid-Dec. to mid-Jan.; restaurant also closed Sat. for dinner and Sun. (except Easter, July and Aug.). Traditional hotel with good regional cooking. MC, V. *Terminus* (I), 15 av. Gare (tel. 98-90-00-63). 25 rooms. Closed Sun. (Nov. through Feb.) and Oct. Near station; no restaurant. MC, V.

Restaurants. *Capucin Gourmand* (M), 29 rue Réguaires (tel. 98-95-43-12). Closed Sun. for dinner, Mon., part of Feb. and last half of Aug. Good traditional cuisine in elegant setting. AE, DC, V. *Tritons* (I), allées Locmaria (tel. 98-90-61-78). Closed for lunch, Mon. and Sept. Good-value fish dishes. Open late.

QUIMPERLÉ. *Hermitage* (M), 2½ km. (1½ miles) via D49 (tel. 98-96-04-66). 24 rooms. Closed Nov. through Mar. Quiet, delightful hotel set in own grounds with pool. V.

Restaurant. *Bistro Tour* (M), rue Dom-Morice (tel. 98-39-29-58). Closed Sat. for lunch, Sun. for dinner, Mon.; last two weeks of June and one week in Dec. Good wines. Good-value (I) *menus.* V.

RENNES. *Altea* (E), 1 rue Cap-Maignan (tel. 99-31-54-54). 140 rooms. Restaurant closed Sat. for lunch, Sun. and over Christmas and New Year period. Not very central, but near station; all modern comforts; good restaurant. AE, DC, MC, V. *Garden* (M), 3 rue Duhamel (tel. 99–65–45–06). 22 rooms. Very good little hotel; patio; simple food can be served. V. *Du Guesclin* (M), 5 pl. Gare (tel. 99-31-47-47). 66 rooms. Traditional hotel near station, now completely modernized. AE, DC, MC, V. *Angelina* (I), 1 quai Lamennais (tel. 99-79-29-66). 25 rooms. Close to old part of city; no restaurant. AE, DC, MC, V.

Restaurants. *Escu de Runfaô* (E), 5 rue Chapitre (tel. 99-79-13-10). Closed Sun. all day and Mon. for lunch. Classical but imaginative cuisine in beautiful old building. AE, V. *Corsaire* (M), 52 rue Antrain (tel. 99-36-33-69). Closed Sun. (except for lunch Sept. through June) and Aug. Traditional cuisine with special emphasis on fish. AE, DC, MC, V. *Piré* (M), 18 rue Maréchal-Joffre (tel. 99-79-31-41). Closed Sat. for lunch and public hols. High-standard *nouvelle cuisine;* delightful garden for outdoor meals. AE, DC, V. *Ti-Koz* (M), 3 rue St.-Guillaume (tel. 99-79-33-89). Closed Sun., Sat. in July and Aug. Classical cuisine served in beautiful 16th-century house with fine Breton furniture. DC, MC, V.

RIEC-SUR-BÉLON. Restaurants. 3 km. (2 miles) south via D24, *Kerland* (M), Pont-du-Guilly (tel. 98-06-42-98). Closed mid-Feb. to mid-Mar., Sun. for dinner, Mon. for lunch (except May through Sept.). Charming country inn with view of Bélon valley; *nouvelle cuisine.* V. *Mélanie* (M), pl. Eglise (tel. 98-06-91-05). Closed Tues. and Nov. through Jan. Typical Breton house with fine furniture and pictures, well-known for its seafood. Also has 7 rooms. AE, DC.

ROSCOFF. *Brittany* (M), blvd. Ste. Barbe (tel. 98-69-70-78). 19 rooms. Closed Oct. to Easter. Good location facing sea. Pool. V. *Gulf Stream* (M), rue Marquise de Kergariou (tel. 98-69-73-19). 32 rooms. Closed Oct. through Mar. Quiet, modern hotel; most rooms have sea view. MC, V. *Bellevue* (I-M), rue Jeanne d'Arc (tel. 98-61-23-38). 23 rooms. Closed Oct. to mid-May (but hotel open over Easter). Quiet, well-situated, with suitably marvelous view. Restaurant.

STE.-ANNE-D'AURAY. Restaurant. *Auberge* (I), 56 rte. de Vannes (tel. 97-57-61-55). Closed Tues. for dinner and Wed. (except July and Aug.), Feb. and first half of Oct. Good plain food. Also has 9 rooms. V.

ST.-ANNE-LA-PALUD. *Plage* (E), right beside beach (tel. 98-92-50-12). 32 rooms. Closed mid-Oct. through Mar. Perfect, secluded hotel, with pool, sauna and excellent cooking. AE, DC, MC, V.

ST.-BRIEUC. *Griffon* (M), rue Guernesey (tel. 96-94-57-62). 45 rooms. Rooms simple but comfortable. Pool, tennis, restaurant. AE, DC, V. *Théâtre* (I), pl. Théâtre et Poste (tel. 96-33-23-18). 10 rooms. Right in town center, pretty rooms overlooking market square; no restaurant. Closed Sun. evening and public hols. AE, MC, V.

Restaurants. *Aiguade* (M), 46 rue de Gouët (tel. 96-33-56-44). Closed Sun. all day and Mon. for lunch. Pleasant atmosphere, quite elegant, traditional cooking with imaginative touches. AE, DC, V. *Quatre Saisons* (M), 61 chemin des Courses (tel. 96-33-20-38). Closed part of Feb., second half of Aug. and Sun. Attractive restaurant with first-rate *nouvelle cuisine;* tables outside when fine; good-value *menus.* AE, DC, MC, V. *Pesked* (I), 59 rue du Légué (tel. 96-33-34-65). Closed Sun. for dinner, Mon., Mar. and first half of Oct. Small restaurant with traditional cooking and good fish dishes.

At **Plérin,** 3 km. (2 miles) NE via D24, *Vieille Tour* (M), 75 rue Tour (tel. 96-33-10-30). Closed Sat. for lunch, Sun., second half of June and over Christmas and New Year. Inventive cuisine with good use of fresh local produce, especially fish. AE, DC, V.

ST.-CAST. *Ar Vro* (M), 10 blvd. Plage (tel. 96-41-85-01). 47 rooms. Closed mid-Sept. through May. Quiet, by beach among pines; some rooms overlook sea. AE, DC, MC, V. *Dunes* (I), rue Primauguet (tel. 96-41-80-31). 27 rooms. Closed Nov. through Mar. Very close to sandy beach; tennis; restaurant. Full board compulsory in season. V.

Restaurant. *Biniou* (M-I), Pen-Guen beach (tel. 96-41-94-53). Closed Wed. in April and May, mid-Sept. to mid-Mar. Good local fish; terrace for open-air meals. MC.

ST.-GUÉNOLÉ. *Mer* (M), 184 rue François-Péron (tel. 98-58-62-22). 17 rooms. Closed first half of Feb. and mid-Oct. through Nov.; restaurant closed Sun. for dinner and Mon. (in winter). Comfortable rooms overlooking sea. Classical cuisine with emphasis on seafood. AE, DC, MC, V.

ST.-MALO. *Korrigane* (E), 39 rue Pommellec (tel. 99-81-65-85). 10 rooms. Closed mid-Nov. to Easter. Central, very comfortable, beautifully furnished, with pleasant atmosphere. AE, DC, V. *Thermes* (E), 100 blvd. Hébert (tel. 99-56-02-56). 98 rooms. Modern rooms; heated seawater pool. AE, DC, MC, V. *Elisabeth* (M), 2 rue Cordiers (tel. 99-56-24-98). 17 rooms. In 16th-century building inside walls, no restaurant. AE, DC, V.

At **St.-Servan,** 6½ km. (4 miles) out on road to Dol, *Valmarin* (E), 7 rue Jean-XXIII (tel. 99-81-94-76). 10 rooms. Closed Sun. for dinner (in winter), Jan. and Feb. 18th-cent. house set in lovely garden. Large, comfortable rooms; no restaurant. AE, V.

Restaurants. *Cap Horn* (M), 100 blvd. Hébert (tel. 99-56-02-56). Very good *nouvelle cuisine* served in lovely room with sea view. AE, DC, MC, V.

At **St.-Servan,** 6½ km. (4 miles) out on road to Dol, *Métairie de Beauregard* (M-E), St.-Etienne (tel. 99-81-37-06). Closed Sept. to mid-June. Manor house in country setting; excellent traditional dishes. AE, DC, V. *Atre* (I), 7 esplanade Commandant-Menguy (tel. 99-81-68-39). Closed Tues. for dinner, (except July and Aug.), Wed. and mid-Dec. to mid-Jan. Small, pleasant restaurant serving good seafood. AE.

TRÉBEURDEN. *Manoir Lan-Kerellec* (E), pointe Kerellec (tel. 96-23-50-09). 10 rooms. Closed mid-Nov. to mid-Mar.; restaurant also closed Mon. (except mid-June to mid-Sept.). Small, luxurious manor house with rooms overlooking sea; tennis courts. Good, imaginative cuisine. AE, DC, V. *Ti al-Lannec* (M), allée Mézo-Guen (tel. 96-23-57-26). 23 rooms. Closed mid-Nov. to mid-Mar.; restaurant also closed Mon. for lunch. Peaceful hotel overlooking bay of Lannion. Pleasant rooms and good restaurant. AE, V.

Restaurant. *Glann Ar Mor* (M), 12 rue Kerariou (tel. 96-23-50-81). Closed Wed., part of Mar. and Oct. Good-value, traditional cuisine. Also has 8 (I) rooms.

TRÉBOUL. Restaurant. *Arcades* (M-I), 67 rue Commandant-Fernand (tel. 98-74-00-64). Closed Mon. (except July and Aug.), and Feb. Large, bustling restaurant with good seafood. Also has 20 (I) rooms.

TRÉGASTEL. *Belle Vue* (M), 20 rue Calculots (tel. 96-23-88-18). 33 rooms. Closed Oct. through April (but open at Easter). Large, comfortable house near beach in pleasant garden. Restaurant open for dinner only. MC, V. *Beau Séjour* (M-I), plage Coz-Pors (tel. 96-23-88-02). 20 rooms. Closed Oct. through Mar. Pleasant family hotel overlooking sea, with lovely view from restaurant. AE, DC, V.

TRÉGUIER. *Kastell Dinec'h* (M), rte. Lannion (tel. 96-92-49-39). 15 rooms. Closed Tues. for dinner, Wed. (except July and Aug.), Jan., Feb. and second half of Oct. Beautiful old Breton house with large peaceful garden. V.

VANNES. *Marébaudière* (M), 4 rue Aristide-Briand (tel. 97-47-34-29). Closed mid-Dec. to mid-Jan.; restaurant closed Sun. for dinner (in winter). Quiet, central hotel with good restaurant (see below). AE, DC, MC, V. *Image Ste.-Anne* (M-I), 8 pl. Libération (tel. 97-63-27-36). 33 rooms. Friendly, with good traditional restaurant. MC, V.

Restaurants. *Lys* (M), 51 rue Maréchal-Leclerc (tel. 97-47-29-30). Closed Mon., Sun. for dinner (except in summer), first half of Oct. and first half of Mar. Excellent *nouvelle cuisine* with good use of fresh produce. AE, DC, MÇ, V.

At **Monterblanc,** 12 km. (7½ miles) northeast by D126, *Auberge Petit Verger* (I), (tel. 97-45-95-57). Very good *menu* at low price.

 TOURS AND EXCURSIONS. By Train. The SNCF (French railways) organize weekend excursions to Brittany from Paris in June, July and Sept., for around 1,000 to 1,600 fr. Inquire at main-line rail stations for brochure or write: *Tourisme SNCF,* BP 62.08, 75362 Paris cedex 08.

By Car. Excursions with a planned itinerary and overnight stops in the splendid *Relais et Châteaux* hotels, or alternatively in 2- or 3-star hotels, are organized by the regional tourist office in Rennes.

By Bus. Europabus has a two-day tour from Paris to St.-Malo and Mont St.-Michel from Apr. through Oct., around 1,600 fr.; and a seven-day "Best of Brittany" tour from Paris (or six days from Rennes), mid-May to mid-Sept., around 4,000 fr. Cityrama has a selection of two-, three- and four-day tours from Paris combining Brittany with Normandy and the Loire Valley, Apr. to Nov., around 3,000 fr. Paris Vision has a two-day tour from Paris to St.-Malo and Mont St.-Michel, Apr. to Nov., around 1,600 fr.

By Boat. The offshore islands are an outstanding attraction. The Ile de Bréhat (Côtes du Nord), the Iles Glénan, the Ile de Sein and the Ile d'Ouessant in Finistère, as well as Belle-Ile, the Ile d'Houat and the Ile d'Hoedie in Morbihan, are all easily reached by regular boat trips. Services reach a peak in the summer, but continue through the winter as well. Details from local tourist offices. In addition there are regular trips along the rivers Rance and Odet, and excursions around the gulf of Morbihan. For the latter contact *Les Vedettes Vertes,* Gare Maritime, 56000 Vannes.

Brittany is criss-crossed by 600 km. (375 miles) of canals and navigable waterways which you can explore in boats ranging from a fully-equipped cabin cruiser to a traditional longboat or converted barge. Prices are from 1,800 fr. for a weekend out of season to 7,000–8,000 fr. for a week in the height of summer. For information write: *Comité de Promotion Touristique des Canaux Bretons,* 3 rue des Portes-Mordelaises, 35000 Rennes.

By Bike. This is a perfect area for biking. You can choose an organized round trip in a group with a guide (full-board terms) or set off on your own with the help of a planned itinerary (half-board terms). Prices range from 800–1500 fr. for the group trip, to 550–1000 fr. for the solo trip. Write: *Association pour le Développement de la Randonnée en Massif Armoricain,* 3 rue des Portes-Mordelaises, 35000 Rennes.

 SIGHTSEEING DATA. For general hints on visiting museums and historic buildings, and for an important warning, see "Sightseeing" in *Facts at Your Fingertips.*

AURAY. Chartreuse (Carthusian Monastery). Open morning and afternoon. Closed 10 days in Sept. and Oct. Guided tours every 20 min.

BREST **Musée Naval.** Open daily except Tues.

BRIÈRE (LA GRANDE). Parc Animalier (Animal Sanctuary). Open June through Oct., daily.

CARNAC. Musée Préhistorique. Open daily Easter to mid-Oct., 10–12, 2–4.
Tumulus St.-Michel. Guided tours, Easter through Sept. Open all day mid-June through Sept.

COMBOURG. Château. Open early Apr. through Sept., afternoons only. Guided tours every 20 min. Park open mornings.

CONCARNEAU. Musée de la Pêche (Fishing Museum). Open daily July and Aug. 9.30–8.30; rest of the year 10–12.30, 2–6.30.

DINAN. Château de la Duchesse Anne. Open daily June through Aug., 9–12, 2–7; rest of year, daily except Tues. and mornings Nov. through Feb. Check locally for times.

DINARD. Aquarium and **Musée de la Mer** (Marine Museum). Open Whitsun through Sept., daily 10–12, 2–6 (7 on Sun.).

FOUGÈRES. Château. Opening times generally 9–6; closed Nov. through Feb. except Sun. in Feb. and weekends in Nov. Guided tours hourly (in English, summer only).

JOSSELIN. Château. Open June to mid-Sept. 2–6. Also open 10–12 in July and Aug.

NANTES. Château des Ducs de Bretagne, 1 pl. Marc-Elder (tel. 40-47-18-15), housing *Musée d'Art Populaire Breton* (Museum of Breton Folk Art), *Musée des Arts Decoratifs* (Decorative Arts Museum) and *Musée des Salorges* (Maritime Museum). Open Feb. through Dec., daily (except Tues. and public hols.) 10–12, 2–6; July and Aug. also open Tues. No admission charge at weekends.
Musée des Beaux-Arts (Museum of Fine Arts). Open daily (except Tues. and public hols.) 9.15–12, 2–6 (5 in winter). No admission charge at weekends.

PLOUBALAY. Château d'Eau. Open daily mid-May to mid-Sept.; stays open lunchtimes. Winter, weekends all day, weekdays afternoons only.

QUIMPER. Musée Départmental Breton (Brittany Museum), pl. St.-Corentin. Open May to mid-Sept. daily 10–12, 2–6. Closed Tues. and public hols.

RENNES. Cathédrale St.-Pierre. Closed Sun. P.M. in July and Aug. Have 1 fr. coins ready to operate illumination of altarpiece.

Musée des Beaux Arts (Museum of Fine Arts). Open daily (except Tues. and public hols.).

ST.-MALO. Donjon St.-Malo (St. Malo's Keep), housing **Musée d'Histoire de la Ville** (History of St.-Malo Museum). Open daily except Tues., 9.30–12, 2–6; closed Jan.

Quic-en-Groigne (Waxworks Museum). Open Apr. through Sept., daily 9–12, 2–6.30. Guided tours (commentary in English on request) every 5–10 min.

VANNES. Musée Archéologique (Archeological Museum). Open daily, except Sun. and public hols., 9.30–12, 2–6.

Trésor de la Cathédrale St. Pierre (Cathedral Treasury). Open daily, except Sun., July to mid-Sept., mornings and afternoons.

VITRÉ. Château (tel. 99-75-04-54). Open daily except Tues., generally 10–12, 2–5.30; Sat. and Sun. 2–5.30. Nov. to Easter, 2–5.30 only. Children under 7 free, those aged 7–15, students and over-65s pay half price.

SPORTS. Sailing and **windsurfing** are well catered for. Most seaside resorts have sailing schools (inquire at local tourist offices on arrival or write to the regional tourist office in Rennes for a list). The minimum age is normally eight. **Golf:** Brittany has ten courses, seven of which are 18-hole courses. Many are beautifully situated by the sea, as at Dinard and Pen Guen. Green fees are around 100 fr. a day, 400–500 fr. a week. **Riding** and **pony-trekking** are among the wealth of sporting activities provided inland in Brittany, as is **fishing** for salmon or trout in the hills of the Monts d'Arée. An excellent booklet, *Stages et Randonnées Organisées,* giving prices and dates, is produced by the *Association pour le développement de la Randonnée en Massif armoricain,* 3 rue des Portes-Mordelaises, 35000 Rennes.

SPECIAL EVENTS. A peculiarity of Brittany is its religious processions or *pardons,* so-called because on certain saints' days the Church would pardon the sins of the faithful. Each town, village or hamlet has its own colorful processions, winding through the streets, the participants dressed in Breton costume.

In addition, many towns and villages also have various colorful events celebrating aspects of Breton or Celtic culture. Most *pardons* and other special events take place in the summer. Full details of all are available from local tourist offices.

NORMANDY

Beach-heads and Abbeys

William the Conqueror and Joan of Arc, the Bayeux Tapestry and Norman architecture, the Canadian Jubilee raid and the D-Day landings—Normandy probably has more associations for English-speaking visitors than any other part of France. Easily reached from Paris and Britain, it offers varied scenery ranging from the wild granite cliffs in the west to the long sandy beaches along the Channel coast, from the wooded valleys of the south to the lush green meadows and apple orchards in its heart. Its rich butter, cheese and cream, cider and calvados have also made it one of the finest gastronomic regions of a country famed for fine eating. It contains many historic cities and a wealth of fine buildings and museums. And here too is Mont St.-Michel, the glorious Gothic abbey perched on a rocky mound in the sea and one of the country's most dramatic and wonderful sights.

For many people today, though, Normandy is chiefly remembered for the key role it played in World War II. Here, on the long Channel beaches, the D-Day landings took place in June 1944, beginning the long process that led to the final victory of the Allies. Normandy paid a terrible price in the war, suffering twice over—first when the Germans invaded in 1940 and again during the Battle of Normandy in 1944. But restoration and reconstruction followed soon afterwards and the region today is prosperous and hard working. It is ideal for either short one- or two-day visits or for longer vacations.

Rouen—Old and New

Rouen, an ancient city that was once the capital of the old province of Normandy, now has a splendid modern "monument," a fitting symbol of the invigorating blend of old and new in this attractive and important city. This is the dazzling modern church and monument dedicated to France's patron saint, Joan of Arc, in the place du Vieux-Marché, the ancient market place where she met her death. The stylish new buildings are a conscious attempt to ensure that the 20th century will leave as lasting an architectural memorial in Rouen as previous centuries. Everywhere you see the contrast of old and new—the glass and concrete conference center beside the Gothic cathedral, the traditional Théâtre des Arts and the ultra-modern Espace Duchamp-Villon and, set in the windows of the brand-new Joan of Arc church, gorgeous 16th-century stained-glass panels thankfully removed from a nearby church before it was destroyed in the devastation of 1944.

Other sights you won't want to miss include the great cathedral of Notre Dame. Its richly carved façade is flanked by the early Gothic St.-Romain Tower on the left and the Butter Tower on the right, so called because it was built with money donated by wealthy citizens for the privilege of eating butter during Lent. Inside, the beautiful 13th-century choir has an ambulatory enriched by the tombs of the earliest dukes of Normandy. Much superb restoration has been accomplished, as it also has at the nearby church of St.-Maclou, which has an extraordinary façade with five gables. Its lacy intricacy will soon make clear why this type of late-Gothic architecture is known as Flamboyant. The abbey church of St.-Ouen, reopened after long restoration, has a fine Gothic nave. Both churches are used for concerts and recitals.

One historic building that survived the bombing unscathed is the strange Aître St.-Maclou. It was once a cemetery for people who had died of the plague and is said to have inspired the French composer Saint-Saëns' *Danse Macabre*. Its timber-frame buildings are carved with skulls, bones and gravediggers' implements, though they are now set around a pretty flower-filled courtyard.

Rouen's liveliest street is the rue du Gros-Horloge, bridged by a Renaissance clock house containing an ornate clock. Near here are the early-Renaissance law courts with a stunningly intricate façade. Beneath the courtyard is a mysterious Romanesque building with Jewish inscriptions that has excited and puzzled scholars the world over. It is undoubtedly the earliest surviving Jewish building in France. Harder to find, as it is now part of a bank, is the Hôtel de Bourgthéroulde, an elaborate Gothic and Renaissance mansion with a carved frieze depicting the meeting in 1520 of the French and English kings on the Field of the Cloth of Gold. In the city center, you'll also find the Tour Jeanne d'Arc, where the Maid was threatened with torture. Near here, watch out for the pretty chapel of St.-Louis and the Lycée Corneille, where the great 17th-century dramatist studied.

In many ways, the whole of old Rouen is a museum, but before leaving try to visit at least two of the city's museums. The Fine Arts Museum has some magnificent paintings plus a wonderful ceramics collection. The other "must" is the Secq-des-Tournelles Museum, which has the world's finest collection of wrought iron. The city is a major cultural center, so you may like to round off your day by attending a concert in the Théâtre des Arts, the fine new music academy or one of the ancient churches.

The Seine Valley and Its Abbeys

Between Rouen and the English Channel, the meandering Seine valley is full of interest. Among its sights are the soaring ruins of the abbey of Jumièges, the imposing church at St.-Martin-de-Boscherville and the no less monumental Pont de Brotonne, a new toll bridge spanning the Seine just upriver from Caudebec-en-Caux. This dramatic modern structure sounded the death knell for a couple of little ferries that used to cross the river, but there are a few other car ferries still in business that add color to a leisurely exploration of the broad river.

Due west of Rouen at St.-Martin-de-Boscherville is the mighty Romanesque abbey church of St.-Georges. Amazingly, this huge building never served more than 35 to 40 monks in its heyday. Beyond the little town of Duclair, you come first to Jumièges, consecrated in 1067, the year after the Battle of Hastings, in the presence of William the Conqueror. Allow plenty of time to wander among the highly romantic ruins. A few miles further on, the abbey of St.-Wandrille, founded in the 7th century, still houses a community of Benedictine monks. The conducted tour by one of the monks includes the ruined Gothic church, the cloisters and the splendid "new" church, erected in 1969. Actually it's a huge 13th-century tithe barn brought here from southern Normandy.

Nearby is Caudebec, rebuilt after extensive damage in World War II, though the fine Gothic church, which Henri IV believed the most beautiful in his kingdom, escaped destruction. The little resort of Villequier is further on. It is chiefly known for the Victor Hugo Museum, opened because the author's favorite daughter was drowned here while boating with her husband only six months after their wedding. The cause of the tragedy was the *mascaret,* a dramatic tidal wave that used to be one of the sights of Caudebec and Villequier before damming work lessened its effect.

Before heading for the coast, cross the river and take a look at the imposing ruins of the castle of Robert le Diable and at another abbey, Bec-Hellouin near Brionne. It is set in a pretty, rather English-looking village with an interesting church. One of its abbots, Lanfranc, became adviser to William the Conqueror and Archbishop of Canterbury, an office later held by his successor at Bec-Hellouin, St.-Anselm. A community of Benedictine monks took over the abbey again in 1948 and the 15th-century St. Nicholas tower, the cloisters and other monastic buildings can all be visited. Next to the abbey is a popular vintage automobile museum.

Other historic buildings in this area are the château of Harcourt, with its tree museum, and the château of Champ-de-Bataille, the seat of the Harcourts, one of France's most famous families. They are both in the département of the Eure, the capital of which is Evreux. This too was a war casualty, but still has several buildings worth visiting, notably the belfry, the bishops' palace and the beautifully-restored cathedral with its marvelous stained glass.

The Alabaster Coast and Dieppe

At the mouth of the Seine, beyond Lillebonne with its Roman ruins, lies the busy port of Le Havre, much of which was flattened in World War II. Today it is a thriving port and has been extensively rebuilt in what is generally agreed to be a less than inspired style. But it does have an excellent modern museum with paintings by Dufy, Boudin, Monet and Pissarro.

East of Le Havre, the coast is best known for its spectacular white cliffs (hence the name Alabaster Coast). The most famous spot is the resort of Etretat, where you can admire the extraordinary shapes into which the sea has carved the chalk. Beyond Etretat is Fécamp, a fishing port and yacht harbor with a fine abbey church that for centuries was a major pilgrimage center. The pilgrims were drawn by a priceless relic, a lead vessel allegedly containing a few drops of Christ's blood. Pilgrimages are still made here, but many tourists prefer to visit the distillery producing Benedictine liqueur.

A string of modest resorts follows, such as St.-Valéry-en-Caux and Veulette-sur-Mer. The biggest town on this coast is Dieppe, a pleasing mixture of seaside resort—it has a casino, good hotels and the usual amenities—and busy fishing and trading port. On Saturdays, there is a colorful market beside the church. Towering over the eastern end of the shingle beach, beyond the memorials to the many Canadians who died here during the Jubilee raid in 1942, is Dieppe castle. It contains a marvelous collection of ivories and some good paintings, including a group by the British painter Walter Sickert, who lived and worked here.

Inland from Dieppe you can make many pleasant excursions into the delightful Norman countryside, full of green fields, half-timbered barns and orchards. You may like to visit the château of Miromesnil or the little spa town of Forges-les-Eaux, well known to Parisian gamblers as the nearest spot where they can indulge their passion for roulette. Under an old law, this allegedly wicked game cannot be played within 100 km. (62 miles) of the capital and Forges is just outside that limit.

Other trips from Dieppe include the War Museum on the road to Pourville, and leafy Varengeville, where there is a tiny church perched on the cliff top and surrounded by a graveyard in which Georges Braque is buried. He lived here and designed some of the stained glass in the church. Another attraction here is the enchanting Moutiers garden surrounding a house built by the British archtitect Sir Edwin Lutyens in 1898. Also worth a visit is the Manoir d'Ango, once the country house of Jean Ango, a 16th-century shipping magnate whose profiteering (with royal approval) resulted in the sinking and capture of over three hundred Portuguese ships.

The Côte Fleurie and the Pays d'Auge

To learn more about the colorful Ango, you should visit Honfleur, one of Normandy's most picturesque harbors on the other side of the Seine from Le Havre. In the Ethnographic Museum there are many exhibits connected with Ango and other Norman seafarers, including those who founded Quebec in the 17th century. Although long a haunt of painters, Honfleur is still a busy working harbor, which explains why the attractive waterfront with its tall slate-hung houses is relatively untouristy. Don't miss the wooden church of Ste.-Catherine and the little Eugène Boudin Museum. He was born in Honfleur and later worked here with his pupil, Claude Monet. Just outside the town is the Ferme St.-Siméon, now a chic hotel and restaurant, but visited by Monet and other painters when it was still a farm. Above the town you can visit the chapel on the Côte de Grace where a special sailor's mass is said on Whit Monday.

Following the coast westward, we come to Trouville, the first of the resorts on the Côte Fleurie, or Flowery Coast. Originally a tiny fishing village, Trouville is the oldest seaside resort in France, having started to become fashionable during the Second Empire. This fairly elegant bathing place has a long sandy beach, many hotels, a huge swimming pool and an aquarium. There is also a casino which is now enlivened by backgammon king Omar Sharif, one of the organizers of the galas and other attractions staged here. In spite of this sophistication, Trouville still has a fishing harbor, while its grander neighbor and rival, aristocratic Deauville, though not as chic as it was before the advent of air travel sent the jet-set off to more distant parts, is nothing but a pleasure ground for the well-heeled. Deauville's life centers around its glittering white summer casino (the winter casino is smaller and less opulent), its two race courses and its fine sandy beach dotted with brightly colored tents and sun umbrellas. The beach is bordered by the famous *plancues,* wooden walkways along which anybody who is anybody parades up and down to see and be seen.

West of Deauville, the resorts are more modest. Cabourg, with its curious fan-shaped pattern of streets and avenues radiating out from the casino, was one inspiration for Marcel Proust's imaginary resort of Balbec in his novel *Remembrance of Things Past.* It has taken on a new lease of life in recent years, and its sedate turn-of-the-century aura is disappearing. It has a good yacht harbor and several swinging discos.

Other pleasant resorts beckon, such as Houlgate and Villers-sur-Mer, but don't neglect the delightful inland area known as the Pays d'Auge. This is cheese, cider and calvados country. It is from here that Camembert, among the most famous cheeses in the world, comes. Another cheese, Pont l'Evêque, is named after a pleasant little town that still has a few old timbered houses in spite of wartime bombing, as does Lisieux, larger and further inland. But Lisieux is best known as a place of pilgrimage. It was here in the Carmelite convent that St. Teresa of Lisieux lived and died at the end of the 19th century. The vast basilica dedicated to her in 1954 is such a notable Catholic pilgrimage center that it was the only place outside Paris visited by the Pope during his visit to France in 1980. Lisieux also has an elegant 12th-century cathedral.

Caen, Bayeux and the Landing Beaches

West of Lisieux is the important town of Caen. It suffered appallingly during the war, but has been very successfully rebuilt and is now a lively modern city with an active cultural life. Ironically, the war damage was a good thing in one sense: William the Conqueror's castle, surrounded by buildings and virtually invisible before the war, can now be seen to full advantage perched on its low hill in the city center behind the richly-carved Gothic church of St.-Pierre. Within its ramparts are an excellent modern museum containing fine paintings and the interesting Normandy Museum, devoted to regional crafts and traditions.

You should also visit the twin abbeys, the Abbaye aux Hommes and Abbaye aux Dames, built by William and his wife Matilda of Flanders as a condition of the pope's raising the excommunication he had served on them—they were cousins and so should have obtained papal dispensation before marrying. The church of St.-Etienne in the Abbaye aux Hommes is the finest building in Caen, a magnificently austere Romanesque building with Gothic additions.

From Caen you can visit the charming little Romanesque church of Thaon, set in an idyllic valley, and the Renaissance château of Fontaine-Henry. And it is only a short journey to Bayeux, the first town in France to be liberated by the Allies. Its most famous possession is the Bayeux Tapestry (in fact an embroidered scroll), which illustrates the Norman Conquest. This miraculous survival from the Middle Ages is now housed in a converted 18th-century seminary near the cathedral, where you can first watch a good audiovisual introduction to its history and then study the tapestry itself, with cassette mini-guides to help you spot the details. Both introduction and cassettes are available in English. Do also visit the fine cathedral, a harmonious blend of Romanesque and Gothic. And a new point of interest in Bayeux is the Memorial Museum of the Battle of Normandy, opened in 1984.

But the main goal for visitors to this part of Normandy is the D-Day landing beaches, a few miles away on the coast. They were a focus of interest in 1984, when thousands of visitors, headed by the Queen of England and President Reagan, flocked here to celebrate the 40th anniversary of the landings. To obtain a graphic impression of those dramatic days in June 1944, you must visit the museum on the seafront at Arromanches. It is impressive even when it is swarming with visitors. To the east lie Gold, Juno and Sword Beaches, where the British landed, and the pleasant little resorts of Courseulles (known for its oysters), Ouistreham and Riva-Bella. Inland from Ouistreham you can visit Pegasus Bridge, taken by British parachutists on the night of June 5/6. West of Arromanches, beyond the little fishing port of Port-en-Bessin, is the enormously impressive American Cemetery. Its moving rows of white marble crosses and stars of David stretch neverendingly toward the cliff edge overlooking Omaha Beach, where so many young Americans lost their lives.

You may also like to follow Liberty Way, with special kilometer posts marking out the route taken by the liberating forces from Ste.-Mère-Eglise through St.-Lô and Avranches to Bastogne.

The Cotentin Peninsula and Mont St.-Michel,

The coast continues to the Pointe du Hoc, which offers splendid views of the Cotentin Peninsula, the curious finger of land thrusting out into the sea at the northwestern tip of Normandy. The east coast, where much of the American force was concentrated during the Normandy landings—Utah Beach is here—is one long stretch of sand. The west coast is wilder and more varied with small resorts such as Barneville-Carteret and Granville, a picturesque old town dominated by its fortress. This part of the coast is known as "The Coast with the Big Tides" and the tides are indeed spectacular, especially at Mont St.-Michel. But the wild northwest coast is also worth visiting for its magnificent scenery, particularly the granite promontory of the Nez de Jobourg and the Cap de la Hague.

The port of Cherbourg on the north coast has an important naval dockyard where France's atomic submarines are built, an art gallery and a museum devoted to World War II in general and the liberation of France in particular. Inland is Valognes, sometimes referred to as Normandy's Versailles because of the fashionable life it enjoyed in the 18th century and which still has many fine mansions in spite of wartime damage. Further south, Coutances has one of the country's purest Gothic cathedrals. Other places worth visiting are Villedieu-les-Poëles, famous for its beautiful wrought copper articles, and the nearby abbey of Hambye.

Most of the peninsula is relatively undeveloped and is a good place for a holiday if you like to be off the beaten track. But when you come right down to the south, near the border with Brittany, you are back in tourist territory. From Avranches, where the U.S. forces achieved a major breakthrough in 1944 (the town has a memorial to General Patton), you have a magnificent view of Mont St.-Michel, which, except for Paris and Versailles, attracts more visitors than any other place in France.

It has been called the *Merveille de l'Occident,* the Wonder of the West, and the name is apt enough. You may have seen dozens of pictures of this strange granite offshore mount, surmounted by a Gothic abbey with a tall spire, but nothing can prepare you for the breathtaking sight when you reach it.

Don't be put off by the hordes—and we really do mean *hordes*—of tourists and souvenir sellers. The Mount has been a popular pilgrimage center since the first chapel was built in the 8th century and medieval pilgrims were as eager for souvenirs as today's tourists. Not all the people who visit the Mount climb up the many steps to visit the marvelous Gothic abbey, so you shouldn't find it too crowded. Conducted tours of the abbey in English take place at frequent intervals and include the pre-Romanesque and Romanesque churches as well as the Gothic abbey with its many rooms and chambers and airy cloisters. Don't miss walking round the ramparts and visiting the terraced gardens with their glorious view of the abbey and the bay. But be careful if you walk round the Mount—the tide comes in at a dangerous speed, especially at the equinoxes, and there are nasty patches of quicksand. The bay itself is silting up and conditions are changing rapidly. It would be wise to pay close attention to any advice available locally.

Southern Normandy—Spas, Woods and Horses

East of Mont St.-Michel, the southern stretch of Normandy has many pleasant towns, such as Mortain, Domfront and Normandy's main spa, pretty Bagnoles-de-l'Orne. Further east lies Alençon, a lace-making center (you can visit the lacemaking academy and museum) with a dazzling Flamboyant Gothic church. This delightfully wooded area is known as the Normandie-Maine nature reserve. North of Alençon, try to visit the Haras du Pin, France's national stud founded in the early 18th century. Southeast of here, the Perche region is also renowned for its horses, while to the west lies the area described rather misleadingly as Norman Switzerland. Its wooded river valleys make it ideal walking country. A good center is Falaise, which boasts the huge château in which William the Conqueror was born.

Giverny

Before we leave Normandy, there is one last pilgrimage to be made, not to an abbey this time but to view the results of a rescue operation completed in 1980. In the little village of Giverny near Vernon, on the southeast edge of the region and easily reached from Paris, you can now visit the house where Impressionist painter Claude Monet lived and worked. And better still, you can wander in the beautiful gardens he captured so brilliantly on canvas. All has been lovingly restored and the waterlilies now bloom on the lily pond again.

PRACTICAL INFORMATION FOR NORMANDY

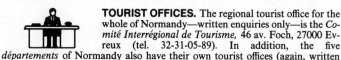

TOURIST OFFICES. The regional tourist office for the whole of Normandy—written enquiries only—is the *Comité Interrégional de Tourisme,* 46 av. Foch, 27000 Evreux (tel. 32-31-05-89). In addition, the five *départements* of Normandy also have their own tourist offices (again, written enquiries only): **Calvados,** pl. du Canada, 14000 Caen; **Eure,** BP 187, 27001 Evreux cedex (tel. 32-38-21-61); **Manche,** BP F2, 50009 St.-Lô cedex (tel. 33-57-52-80); **Orne,** BP 50, 61002 Alençon cedex (tel. 33-26-18-71); **Seine-Maritime,** BP 666, 76008 Rouen cedex (tel. 35-88-61-32).

There are local tourist offices in the following towns: **Alençon,** pl. Lamagdelaine (tel. 33-26-11-36); **Bayeux,** 1 rue Cuisiniers (tel. 31-92-16-26); **Cabourg,** Jardins du Casino (tel. 31-91-01-09); **Caen,** pl. St.-Pierre (tel. 31-86-27-65); **Cherbourg,** 2 quai Alexandre-III (tel. 33-44-39-92), additional office at Gare Maritime (mid-May to mid-Sept. only); **Deauville,** pl. Mairie (tel. 31-88-21-43); **Dieppe,** blvd. Général-de-Gaulle (tel. 35-84-11-77); **Evreux,** 35 rue Docteur-Oursel (tel. 32-38-21-61); **Le Havre,** pl. Hôtel-de-Ville (tel. 35-21-22-88); **Honfleur,** 33 cours Fossés (tel. 31-89-23-30); **Lisieux,** 11 rue Alençon (tel. 31-62-08-41); **Mont St.-Michel,** Corps de Garde des Bourgeois (tel. 33-60-14-30) (closed Nov. through Feb.); **Rouen,** 25 pl. Cathédrale (tel. 35-71-41-77); **Trouville,** pl. Maréchal-Foch (tel. 31-88-36-19).

REGIONAL FOOD AND DRINK. Normandy is the land of butter, cream, cheese and *calvados,* a powerful apple brandy. In the old days on festive occasions the Normans would bring 24 courses to table. Between the *entrée*—starter—and the main meat dish there was a *trou* (hole), often lasting several hours, when it was the custom to drink *calvados;* hence the expression *le trou normand.*

Many dishes are cooked with rich cream sauces; in fact the description *à la normande* usually means with a cream sauce. The richness of the milk makes excellent cheeses: *Pont-l'Évêque* (known since the 13th century) is made in the Pays d'Auge with milk that is still warm and creamy; *Livarot* (also produced for centuries) is made with milk that has stood for a while. Do not be put off by its strong smell. Then there are the excellent *Pavé d'Auge* and the best known of them all, *Camembert,* a relative newcomer, invented by a farmer's wife in the 19th century. Now so popular that it is produced all over France, the best *Camembert* is still made in Normandy (known as *Camembert au lait cru*).

There are many local specialties. Rouen is famous for its *canard à la Rouennaise* (duck in blood sauce), Caen for its *tripes à la mode de Caen* (tripe), and Mont St.-Michel for *omelette Mère Poulard.* Then there are *sole dieppoise* (sole poached in a sauce with cream and mussels), excellent chicken from the vallée d'Auge and lamb from the salt marshes. For those who like *boudin noir* (blood sausage), this is the region, and for lovers of seafood the coast provides oysters, lobsters and shrimps.

Normandy is not a wine-growing area but produces excellent cider. The best known comes from the vallée d'Auge and is 100 per cent apple juice. When it is poured into the glass it should fizz a little but not froth.

HOTELS AND RESTAURANTS. There are accommodations to suit every taste in Normandy. Even in the plush resort of Deauville, it is possible to find delightful and inexpensive little hotels. Both Honfleur and Pont-Audemer hotels are crowded most weekends, with an influx of Paris weekenders and the British yachting set, on top of the usual holiday makers. In the beach resorts the season is very short, July-Aug. only, but weekends are busy for much of the year; in June and Sept., accommodations are usually available at short notice. But dates vary, as with closing days and months for restaurants, so best check in advance. Many restaurants have a wide range of prices—look out for a fixed-price *menu.*

For general notes on hotels and restaurants, see "Hotels" and "Restaurants" in *Facts at Your Fingertips.*

ALENÇON. *Grand Cerf* (M), 21 rue St.-Blaise (tel. 33-26-00-51). 33 rooms. Closed mid-Dec. to mid-Mar.; restaurant closed Sun., Oct. through Mar. Centrally located. AE, DC, MC, V. *Chapeau Rouge* (I), 117 rue Bretagne (tel. 33-26-20-23). 16 rooms. Newly renovated; no restaurant.

Restaurants. *Petit Vatel* (M), 72 pl. Commandant-Desmeulles (tel. 33-26-23-78). Closed Sun. for dinner and Wed., last half of Aug. and part of Feb. *Nouvelle cuisine* with regional touches. AE, DC, MC, V. *Escargot Doré* (M), 183 av. Général-Leclerc (tel. 33-26-05-40). Closed Sun. for dinner, Mon. and Aug. Attractive setting, good grills, particularly fish. V.

ARROMANCHES. *Marine* (I), quai Canada (tel. 31-22-34-19). 22 rooms. Closed mid-Nov. through Feb. Near the sea, with restaurant. AE, V.

AVRANCHES. *Auberge St.-Michel* (M), 7 pl. Général-Patton (tel. 33-58-01-91). 22 rooms. Closed mid-Nov. to mid-March, Sun. night, Mon., and restaurant closed Mon. for lunch (except June through Aug.). Pleasant rooms with some looking on to garden. MC, V. *Croix d'Or* (M), 83 rue Constitution (tel. 33-58-04-88). 30 rooms. Closed mid-Nov. to mid-Mar. Genuine old inn with furniture to match. V.

BAGNOLES-DE-L'ORNE. *Bois Joli* (M), av. Rozier (tel. 33-37-92-77). 20 rooms. Closed mid-Oct. through Mar. Attractive Norman architecture; set in large garden near lake. Rich regional cooking in restaurant. Closed Sun. for dinner and Wed. AE, DC, MC, V. *Capricorne* (M), allée Montjoie (tel. 33-37-96-99). Modern and quiet, by forest. Restaurant for dinner only. AE, DC, MC, V. *Lutétia* (M), blvd. Paul Chalvet (tel. 33-37-94-77). 33 rooms. Closed mid-Oct. through Mar. Comfortable hotel surrounded by garden. AE, DC, V.

Restaurant. *Café de Paris* (M), av. R.-Cousin (tel. 33-37-81-76). Closed Oct. through Mar., Mon. (except public hols.) and for lunch on weekdays. Overlooking lake; mainly Italian specialties. AE, DC, MC, V.

BARNEVILLE-CARTERET. *Isles* (M), blvd. Maritime, Barneville Plage (tel. 33-04-90-76). 35 rooms. Closed mid-Nov. to mid-Jan. Typical Norman architecture, with some rooms overlooking sea; pleasant garden and (I) restaurant. AE, DC, MC, V. *Marine* (M), 11 rue Paris (tel. 33-53-83-31). 33 rooms. Closed mid-Nov. through Feb.; Sun. dinner and Mon., during Oct., Nov. and March. Well situated; restaurant serves good *nouvelle cuisine,* with excellent fish. DC, V. *Jersey* (I), 4 rue Sablière, Barneville Plage (tel. 33-04-91-23). 20 rooms. Beside beach, with view of Channel Islands on fine days; no restaurant.

Restaurant. *Hermitage* (M), promenade Abbé-Lebouteiller (tel. 33-04-96-29). Closed Dec. through Feb., but open for Christmas hols. and Wed. Beside harbor, serving excellent seafood. Also has some (I) rooms. DC, MC, V.

BAYEUX. *Argouges* (M), 21 rue St.-Patrice (tel. 31-92-88-86). 22 rooms. Beautiful rooms in 18th-century house with attractive garden; no restaurant. AE, MC, V. *Lion D'Or* (M), 71 rue St.-Jean (tel. 31-92-06-90). 30 rooms. Comfortable and quiet, yet in town center, closed mid-Dec. to mid-Jan.; good restaurant. AE, DC, V. *Pacary* (M), 117 rue Saint-Patrice (tel. 31-92-16-11). 30 rooms. Simple, modern, with nice pool. Restaurant. V.

Restaurant. *Gourmets* (I), pl. St.-Patrice (tel. 31-92-02-02). Closed last half of Oct., last half of Feb. and first week in Mar., Wed. for dinner and Thurs. Convenient for *Argouges* hotel. MC.

LE BEC-HELLOUIN. *Auberge de l'Abbaye* (M), pl. Eglise (tel. 32-44-86-02). 8 rooms. Closed Jan. and Feb.; restaurant closed Mon. for dinner and Tues. but open in summer. Quiet, comfortable rooms. Well-known restaurant serving classical Norman cuisine. V.

CABOURG. *Grand Hôtel* (E), promenade Marcel-Proust (tel. 31-91-01-79). 70 rooms. Old-established luxury hotel, now modernized throughout. Restaurant *Balbec: menu* is best value. AE, DC, MC, V. *Paris* (M), 39 av. Mer (tel. 31-91-31-34). 23 rooms. Closed Sun. night and Mon. Oct. through May. Pleasant, unpretentious rooms; no restaurant. *L'Oie Qui Fume* (I), av. Brèche-Buhot (tel. 31-91-27-79). 19 rooms. Closed Jan. Overlooking harbor.

At **Bavant.** *Hostellerie Moulin du Pré* (I), route de Gonneville-en-Auge (tel. 31-78-83-68). 10 rooms. Closed Oct., and Mon. and Tues. except in summer. Rural, with good restaurant (M). AE, DC, V.

CAEN. *Moderne* (M), 116 blvd. Maréchal-Leclerc (tel. 31-86-04-23). 56 rooms. Restaurant closed Sun. for dinner (mid-Oct. through Mar.). Central but quiet as in pedestrian street; good restaurant. AE, DC, MC, V. *Relais des Gourmets* (M), 15 rue Geôle (tel. 31-86-06-01). 32 rooms. Restaurant closed Sun. for dinner. Comfortable, staid hotel overlooking William the Conqueror's castle; good restaurant. AE, DC, MC, V. *Le Dauphin* (M), 29 rue Gemare (tel. 31-86-22-26). 21 rooms. Closed mid-July to mid-Aug. Nice little rooms. Very good restaurant (closed Sat.). AE, DC, MC, V.

Restaurants. *Bourride* (E), 15 rue Vaugueux (tel. 31-93-50-76). Closed most of Jan., first week in May, second half of Aug., Sun. and Mon. Excellent *nouvelle cuisine* using local produce. AE, DC, V. *Dauphin* (M), 29 rue Gemare (tel. 31-86-22-26). Closed mid-July to mid-Aug., school hols. in Feb., and Sat. Near castle; delicious regional cuisine. *Chalut* (I), 3 rue Vaucelles (tel. 31-52-01-06). Closed mid-Aug. to mid-Sept., Mon. and Tues. Not far from station; good value. V.

At **Bénouville,** 10 km. (6½ miles) northeast, *Manoir d'Hastings* (E), 18 av. Côte de Nacre (tel. 31-44-62-43). Closed first half of Feb., first half of Oct., Sun. for dinner and Mon. (except summer). Converted rural 17th-century priory. Inventive cuisine with fresh local produce. Also has 11 (E) rooms. AE, DC, V.

CAUDEBEC-EN-CAUX. *Manoir de Retival* (E), 2 rue St.-Clair (tel. 35-96-11-22). 10 rooms. Closed Nov. through Jan. and Sun. night (except public hols.). Old manorhouse with beautiful views; no restaurant. AE, DC. *Marine* (M), quai Guilbaud (tel. 35-96-20-11). 33 rooms. Comfortable hotel beside Seine serving excellent *nouvelle cuisine.* Closed Sun. for dinner. AE, V. *Normandie* (I), quai Guilbaud (tel. 35-96-25-11). 16 rooms. Closed Feb. and Sun. for dinner. Beside river; good-value restaurant. AE, V.

CHERBOURG. *Mercure* (M), gare maritime (tel. 33-44-01-11). 79 rooms. Near car-ferry terminal, quiet and comfortable. AE, DC, MC, V. *Louvre* (I), 2 rue Henri-Dunant (tel. 33-53-02-28). 42 rooms. In pedestrian street and close to beach. Very friendly atmosphere. Closed Christmas hols. V.

Restaurant. *Plouc* (M), 59 rue Blé (tel. 33-53-67-64). Closed Sat. for lunch, Sun. and most of Aug. Friendly atmosphere, good fish dishes and good-value *menus.* MC, V.

COURSEULLES-SUR-MER. *Belle Aurore* (M), 32 quai Est (tel. 31-37-46-23). 7 rooms. Closed Oct. through March, Mon. (except mid-June to mid-Sept.). Comfortable rooms overlooking harbor, good restaurant with emphasis on fish. AE, DC, V. *La Crémaillère* (I), av. Combattante (tel. 31-37-46-73). 20 rooms. Nice sea views; quietest rooms are in annex. AE, DC, MC, V.

COUTANCES. *Moderne* (M), 25 blvd. Alsace-Lorraine (tel. 33-45-13-77). 17 rooms. Closed mid-Dec. to mid-Jan. Restaurant closed Sun. Oct. through June. MC, V.

At **Trelly,** 11 km. (7 miles) away, *Verte Campagne* (M), Hameau Chevallier (tel. 33-47-65-33). 8 rooms. Closed mid-Nov. to mid-Dec., part of Feb., Sun. for dinner and Mon. (except mid-April to mid-Sept.). Comfortable rooms in converted 18th-century farmhouse complete with walled garden. Good restaurant (I). V.

Restaurant. At **Gratot,** 4 km. (2½ miles) northwest, *Tourne-Bride* (I), (tel. 33-45-11-00). Closed Christmas and New Year hols., Sun. for dinner. Old inn serving genuine local dishes.

DEAUVILLE. *Normandy* (L), 38 rue Jean-Mermoz (tel. 31-88-09-21). 300 rooms. Restaurant closed Jan. and first half of Feb. Old-established luxury hotel, extensively modernized. Near casino, facing sea. AE, DC, MC, V. *Royal* (L), blvd. Cornuché (tel. 31-88-16-41). 305 rooms. Closed Oct. to Easter. Deluxe hotel in the grand manner, with pool, tennis courts and excellent restaurant. AE, DC, V. *PLM Deauville* (E), blvd. Cornuché (tel. 31-88-62-62). 73 rooms. Comfortable modern hotel looking on to marina; no restaurant. AE, DC, MC, V. *Helios* (M), 10 rue Fossorier (tel. 31-88-28-26). 44 rooms. New hotel in the Norman style; pool; no restaurant. AE, V. *Patio* (I), 180 av. République (tel. 31-88-25-07). 11 rooms. Pleasant rooms, garden, no restaurant.

At **Mont Canisy,** 3 km. (2 miles) south, *Golf* (L), tel. 31-88-19-01). 165 rooms. Closed Oct. to mid-May. Peaceful luxury hotel overlooking golf course. AE, DC, MC, V.

At **Touques,** 2½ km. (1½ miles) southeast, *Amirauté* (E), (tel. 31-88-90-62). 114 rooms. In country setting; all modern comforts. AE, DC, V.

Restaurants. *Ambassadeurs* (E), in the casino, rue Edmond-Blanc (tel. 31-88-29-55). Closed mid-Sept. to mid-Mar. and for lunch. Excellent fish and shellfish. AE, DC, MC, V. *Augusto* (E), 27 rue Désiré-le-Hoc (tel. 31-88-34-49). Closed Mon., Tues. (except July, Aug. and Sept.). Chic clientèle; good seafood, specializes in lobster. AE, DC, V. *Chez Camillo* (M), 13 rue Désiré-le-Hoc (tel. 31-88-79-78). Closed Wed. (except July and Aug.), Feb. Good classic cuisine. AE, DC, MC, V. *Ferme* (M), le Bois-Lauret (tel. 31-87-42-62). Closed Jan., Wed. and Thurs. except in summer. Good fresh produce and interesting wines; good-value *menu.* *Yearling* (I), 38 av. Hocquart-de-Turtot (tel. 31-88-33-37). Closed Jan. to mid-Feb. and Tues. (except July and Aug.). Not far from racecourse. AE, V.

DIEPPE. *Présidence* (E), 1 blvd. Verdun (tel. 35-84-31-31). 88 rooms. Modern hotel with comfortable rooms, some overlooking sea. Restaurant *Queiros* on 4th floor; views. AE, DC, MC, V. *Univers* (E), 10 blvd. Verdun (tel. 35-84-12-55). 30 rooms. Closed Jan. Old-fashioned comfort; faces sea. AE, DC, MC, V. *Aguado* (I), 30 blvd. Verdun (tel. 35-84-27-00). 56 rooms. Good rooms overlooking sea; generous breakfast. No restaurant.

Restaurants. *Marmite Dieppoise* (M), 8 rue St.-Jean (tel. 35-84-24-26). Closed last week in June and first in July, Christmas and New Year period, Mon., and Sun. and Thurs. for dinner. Old favorite with British visitors. AE, DC, MC, V. *La Mélie* (M), 2 Grande-rue Pollet (tel. 35-84-21-19). Closed Feb., Sun. for dinner and Mon. New, good chef; mostly fish and shellfish. MC, V. *Port* (I), 99 quai Henri-IV (tel. 35-84-36-64). Closed over Christmas and New Year, Jan. and

Thurs. Quayside restaurant with good fish cooked in the classic manner. AE, MC, V.

DIVES-SUR-MER. Restaurant. *Guillaume le Conquérant* (M), 2 rue Hastings (tel. 31-91-07-26). Closed second half of Nov., Sun. for dinner and Mon. (except July and Aug.). 17th-cent. coaching inn. AE, DC, MC, V.

DUCLAIR. *Poste* (I), 286 quai Libération (tel. 35-37-50-04). 20 rooms. Closed Feb., first half of July, and restaurant closed Sun. for dinner and Mon. Pleasant rooms; restaurant overlooks Seine. AE, MC, V.
Restaurant. *Parc* (I), 712 av. Président-Coty (tel. 35-37-50-31). Closed mid-Dec. to mid-Jan., Sun. for dinner and Mon. Good traditional cuisine. Garden leading down to Seine. AE, DC, MC, V.

ETRETAT. *Dormy House* (M), rte. du Havre (tel. 35-27-07-88). 27 rooms. Closed Nov. through Mar. Quiet, with views of sea and famous cliffs. *Falaises* (M), blvd. René-Coty (tel. 35-27-02-77). 24 rooms. Central, not far from casino and beach; no restaurant. *Escale* (I), pl. Maréchal-Foch (tel. 35-27-03-69). 11 rooms. Closed Dec. and Jan.; restaurant closed Tues. for dinner and Wed. Pleasant rooms and good-value restaurant.
Restaurant. *Roches Blanches* (I), rue Abbé-Cochet (tel. 35-27-07-34). Closed mid-Jan. to mid.-Feb., Oct., Tues. and Thurs. (except July and Aug.). Near the beach. Good value. MC, V.
At **Saint-Jouin,** 11 km. (7 miles) south. *Belvédère* (I), (tel. 35-20-13-76). On top of hill overlooking Cap d'Antifer. Very good-value *menu*.

EVREUX. *France* (M), 29 rue St.-Thomas (tel. 32-39-09-25). 15 rooms. Closed last half of Feb. and most of Aug.; restaurant closed Sun. for dinner and Mon. Old house with beautiful garden; excellent restaurant. AE, DC, V. *Normandy* (M), 37 rue Edouard-Feray (tel. 32-33-14-40). 26 rooms. Closed Aug.; restaurant closed Sun. Pleasant rooms; traditional cooking served in country-style dining-room. AE, DC, MC, V. *Orme* (I), 13 rue Lombards (tel. 32-39-34-12). 27 rooms. Central, no restaurant. AE, V.
Restaurant. *Vieille Gabelle* (M), 3 rue Vieille-Gabelle (tel. 32-39-38-54). Closed second half July, Sun. for dinner, and Mon. Noted for its apple tarts. AE, V.

FÉCAMP. *Angleterre* (M), 93 rue Plage (tel. 35-28-01-60). 30 rooms. Closed Nov. through Dec. Modernized hotel near sea; no restaurant. AE, DC, V. *Mer* (M), 89 blvd. Albert-ler (tel. 35-28-24-64). 8 rooms. Closed Jan. Near sea and casino; no restaurant.
Restaurants. *Escalier* (M), 101 quai Bérigny (tel. 35-28-26-79). Closed Mon. (in winter months), last half of Nov. Overlooks harbor. Good fresh fish. DC, V. *Viking* (M–I), 63 blvd. Albert ler (tel. 35-29-22-92). Closed Mon. Rather impersonal building but good menus and fresh cooking. AE, DC, V.

GISORS. At **Bazincourt-sur-Epte,** 5½ km. (3½ miles) north via D14, *Château de la Rapée* (E), tel. 32-55-11-61). 10 rooms. Closed Feb., second half of Aug.; restaurant closed Tues. for dinner (except July and Aug.) and Wed. In the quiet of the Norman countryside; very comfortable; good traditional cuisine. AE, DC, V.

GRANVILLE. *Bains* (M), 19 rue Georges-Clemenceau (tel. 33-50-17-31). 55 rooms. Imposing old-style hotel, facing sea and near casino. Restaurant *Potinière* (closed Feb.) has good fish and some excellent (I) menus. AE, DC, MC, V. *Michelet* (I), 5 rue Jules Michelet (tel. 33-50-06-55). 20 rooms. Quiet and comfortable; no restaurant. MC, V.
Restaurant. *Phare* (M), 11 rue Port (tel. 33-50-12-94). Closed Wed. for dinner (except July and Aug.), Thurs., and mid-Dec. through Jan. Overlooks harbor; outdoor meals in fine weather. AE, DC, MC, V.

LE HAVRE. *Bordeaux* (E), 147 rue Louis-Brindeau (tel. 35-22-69-44). 31 rooms. Modern hotel in town center; no restaurant. AE, DC, MC, V. *Parisien* (M), 1 cours République (tel. 35-25-23-83). 22 rooms. Closed over Christmas and New Year period. Opposite station; well-equipped rooms; no restaurant. AE, DC, MC, V. *Marly* (M), 121 rue Paris (tel. 35-41-72-48). 36 rooms. Simple, useful for ferry passengers. AE, DC, MC, V.

Restaurants. *Manche* (M), 18 blvd. Albert-ler (tel. 35-41-20-13). Closed Sun. for dinner, Mon. and July. Overlooks sea; good fish. AE, DC, V. *Monaco* (M), 16 rue Paris (tel. 35-42-21-01). Closed Mon. (except July and Aug. and public hols.) Not far from car-ferry terminal. Good for fish; also has 11 rooms. AE, DC, MC, V.

HONFLEUR. *Ferme St.-Siméon et son Manoir* (L), rte. Adolphe-Marais, on the edge of town (tel. 31-89-23-61). 19 rooms. Delightful 17th-century farmhouse overlooking Seine estuary; additional rooms in nearby manor house. Relais et Châteaux member, with a mixture of modern and traditional cuisine in the popular restaurant. Closed Wed. for lunch (except public hols. Nov. through March). V. *Lechat* (M), 3 pl. Ste.-Catherine (tel. 31-89-23-85). 30 rooms. Closed mid-Nov. to mid-Dec.; restaurant closed Mon. Just behind harbor in pretty square. Good service. AE, DC, V. *Pélerins* (I), 6 rue Capucins (tel. 31-89-19-61). 12 rooms. Closed Jan.; restaurant closed Wed. Unpretentious, comfortable rooms, some (M). MC.

Restaurants. *Absinthe* (M), 10 quai Quarantaine (tel. 31-89-39-00). Closed Mon. for dinner, Tues. (except July and Aug.), and mid-Nov. to mid-Dec. Mixture of traditional and *nouvelle cuisine;* good service. AE, V. *Ancrage* (M), 12 rue Montpensier (tel. 31-89-00-70). Closed Tues. for dinner (except July and Aug.), Wed. and Jan. Overlooks harbor, excellent seafood. MC, V.

HOULGATE. *Ferme du Lieu Marot* (M), 21 rte. Vallée (outside town via D24), (tel. 31-91-19-44). 11 rooms. Closed Wed. (except mid-June through Aug.), mid-Nov. to mid-Dec., Jan. Peaceful setting among apple trees; pleasant rooms and homestyle cooking. *Hostellerie Normande* (M), 11 rue Deschanel (tel. 31-91-22-36). 10 rooms. Closed Tues. and Jan. Lovely garden, tables outside in fine weather. AE, DC, MC, V.

LISIEUX. *Place* (M), rue Henry-Chéron (tel. 31-31-17-44). 33 rooms. Closed Sun., Nov. to Easter. Close to cathedral, with large, well-appointed rooms; no restaurant. AE, DC, MC, V. *Espérance* (M), 16 blvd. Ste.-Anne (tel. 31-62-17-53). 100 rooms. Closed Oct. through Apr. Comfortable; restaurant. AE, DC, MC, V.

Restaurants. *Auberge du Pêcheur* (M), 2bis rue Verdun (tel. 31-31-16-85). Closed Wed., Thurs. and Oct. Excellent fish and shellfish. AE, DC, MC, V. *Ferme du Roy* (M), 2½ km. (1½ miles) outside town at 122 blvd. Herbert-Fournet (tel. 31-31-33-96). Closed Oct., and Thurs. In beautiful, restored farmhouse with garden. Traditional cuisine. V.

LE MONT ST.-MICHEL. *Mère Poulard* (E), (tel. 33-60-14-01). 27 rooms. Closed Oct. through Mar. Half-board terms compulsory in summer. Large quiet rooms, some with view over bay. Excellent restaurant, serving, of course, the famous omelet. AE, DC, MC, V. *Terrasses Poulard* (E), rue Principale (tel. 33-60-14-09). 30 rooms. New and fashionable, with perfect service and beautiful little garden. Full board compulsory in season. AE, DC, V. *St.-Aubert* (M), on mainland, on D976 (tel. 33-60-08-74). 27 rooms. Closed Nov. through Mar. Modern hotel, with large, well-decorated rooms; no restaurant. AE.

At **Beauvoir**, 4 km. (2½ miles) south via D976, *Gué de Beauvoir* (I), (tel. 33-60-09-23). 21 rooms. Closed Oct. to Easter. Modest hotel in large house; no restaurant.

Restaurant. *Mère Poulard* (E), in hotel of same name (see above). *Terrasses Poulard* (M), tel. (33-60-14-09). Closed Jan. Marvelous view; meals served outside in good weather; good traditional cooking. AE, DC, V.

NEUFCHÂTEL-EN-BRAY. *Lisieux* (I), 2 pl. Libération (tel. 35-93-00-88). 24 rooms. Closed Feb. and part of Nov.; restaurant closed Thurs. (except July and Aug.). Good location near Eawy Forest. AE, MC, V.

ORBEC. Restaurant. *Caneton* (E), 32 rue Grande (tel. 31-32-73-32). Closed Mon. for dinner, Tues., Feb. and Oct. In attractive 17th-century building; good Norman cuisine that has gained a high reputation; reservations essential.

OUISTREHAM. *Normandie* (M), 71 av. Michel-Cabieu (tel. 31-97-19-57). 14 rooms. Closed Sun. evening (except summer). Newly modernized hotel near Orne estuary, best known for its pleasant restaurant. AE, DC, V.
Restaurant. *Broche d'Argent* (M), in *Univers* hotel (tel. 31-97-12-16). Deliciously fresh seafood. Closed Sun. for dinner. AE, DC, V. *Roches* (I), route de Caen, 3 km. (2 miles) out (tel. 31-97-16-33). Good *menu*.

PONT AUDEMER. Restaurants. *Fregate* (M), 4 rue Seule (tel. 32-41-12-03). Closed mid-July through Aug., Tues. for lunch and Wed. Good cooking with regional produce. AE, DC, V. At **Couteville**, 10 km. (6 miles) northwest, *Auberge Vieux Puits* (M), 6 rue Notre-Dame-du-Pré (tel. 32-41-01-48). Closed Mon. for dinner, Tues., first half of July, and mid-Dec. to mid-Jan. Lovely 17th-century house with antique furniture and shining copper pots and pans. Also has 8 (M) rooms. V.
At **Campigny**, 6 km. (3½ miles) southeast via D810 and D29, *Petit Coq aux Champs* (E), La Pommeraye (tel. 32-41-04-19). Old thatched house in beautiful garden with pool. Classical cooking, though not too rich. Also has 10 quiet rooms (half-board compulsory in summer). AE, DC, MC, V.

ROUEN. *Dieppe* (E), pl. Bernard-Tissot (tel. 35-71-96-00). 44 rooms. Right by station, with comfortable, modernized rooms and good restaurant, serving mainly traditional cooking. AE, DC, MC, V. *Frantel* (E), rue Croix-de-Fer (tel. 35-98-06-98). 121 rooms. Modern hotel in center of old city. Well-equipped rooms and good restaurant serving *nouvelle cuisine*, closed Sun. and public hols. AE, DC, MC, V. *Normandie* (M), 19 rue Bec (tel. 35-71-55-77). 23 rooms. Quiet, in pedestrian street in old town. No restaurant. AE, DC, MC, V. *Cathédrale* (I), 12 rue St.-Romain (tel. 35-71-57-95). 23 rooms. In pedestrian street right beside cathedral, with old-fashioned rooms but pretty courtyard garden and lots of charm. No restaurant.
Restaurants. *Bertrand Warin* (E), 9 rue Pie (tel. 35-89-26-69). Closed Sun. for dinner, Mon., Aug. and Christmas. Excellent *nouvelle cuisine,* elegant ambience. Good-value *menu* at lunchtime. AE, DC, V. *Couronne* (E), 31 pl. Vieux-Marché (tel. 35-71-40-90). Closed Sun. for dinner. Said to be the oldest inn in France (dates from 1345). Mainly classical cuisine. AE, DC, V. *Beffroy* (M), 15 rue Beffroy (tel. 35-71-55-27). Closed Sun., Mon., most of Feb. and most of Aug. In attractive old building in old town. *Nouvelle cuisine* based on fresh Norman produce. AE, MC, V. *P'tits Parapluies* (M), 46 rue du Bourg-l'Abbé (tel. 35-88-55-26). Closed one week in Feb., Aug., Sat. for lunch and Sun. Very good; interesting lunch *menu*. AE, V. *Vieux Marché* (I), 2 pl. Vieux-Marché (tel. 35-71-59-09). Bustling bistrot in old town, with tables outside in summer. Huge menu, good fish specialties. AE, DC, V.

THURY-HARCOURT. Restaurant. *Relais de la Poste* (M), rte. de Caen (tel. 31-79-72-12). Closed mid-Dec. through Feb. Delicious regional cooking in restored coaching inn. Also has 11 peaceful rooms (half-board obligatory in summer). AE, DC, MC, V.

TROUVILLE-SUR-MER. *Carmen* (M), 24 rue Carnot (tel. 31-88-35-43). 16 rooms. Closed Jan.; restaurant closed Mon. for dinner and Tues. Small hotel close to beach with well-modernized rooms. AE, DC, MC, V. *St.-James* (M), 16 rue Plage (tel. 31-88-05-23). 14 rooms. Well situated near beach and casino. DC.

Restaurants. *Galatée* (M), right on the beach (tel. 31-88-15-04). Deliciously fresh seafood in definitely nautical ambience. AE, MC, V. *Vapeurs* (M), 160 blvd. Fernand-Moureaux (tel. 35-88-15-24). Closed Tues. for dinner, Wed., Jan. and last half of Nov. Lively brasserie overlooking harbor. Good choice of fish.

VERNON. At **Douains,** 10 km. (6 miles) away near Pacy-sur-Eure, *Château de Brécourt* (E), tel. (32-52-40-50). 24 rooms. Delightful Relais et Châteaux member in lovely grounds; pool and tennis. 17th-century décor, good restaurant, particularly pleasant atmosphere. Convenient for visiting Anet and Thoiry (see *Ile de France* chapter) as well as Giverny. Reservations essential. AE, DC, MC, V.

Restaurant. *Fleurs* (I), 71 rue Carnot (tel. 32-51-16-80). Unusual cooking at very reasonable prices. To be discovered.

VEULES-LES-ROSES. Restaurant. *Galets* (E), 3 rue Victor-Hugo (tel. 35-97-61-33). Closed Tues. for dinner, Wed. and Feb. Excellent *nouvelle cuisine* with particularly good fish. Popular with Britons arriving at Dieppe or Le Havre. V.

VILLEQUIER. Restaurant. *Grand Sapin* (I), rue Louis-le-Gaffric (tel. 35-56-78-73). Closed Wed. (except May through Sept.), Tues. mid-Jan. to mid-Feb. and second half of Nov. Terrace for outdoor dining overlooking Seine. Good traditional cooking. V.

TOURS AND EXCURSIONS. By Train. The SNCF (French Rail) organize a day trip from Paris to the D-day landing beaches on three Saturdays in summer, around 400 fr.; inquire at mainline stations for brochure.

By Car. The tourist authorities have organized several signposted routes in Normandy, such as the "Cheese Road," the "Cider Road," the "Abbey Road" and so on. Tourist attractions are pointed out along the way and you can buy local produce from signposted farms. Leaflets detailing the various routes are available from local tourist offices.

By Bus. Europabus, Cityrama, Paris Vision and RATP (Paris Transport Service) all offer numerous one-, two- or three-day bus tours to Normandy from Paris taking in all the major places of interest. Details from all tourist offices.

SIGHTSEEING DATA. For general hints on visiting museums and historic buildings, and for an important warning, see "Sightseeing" in *Facts at Your Fingertips.*

ALENÇON. Musée des Beaux Arts et de la Dentelle (Museum of Fine Arts and Lace). Open daily, except Mon., (Oct.through April), 10–12.30 and 2–5.30.

ANDELYS, LES. Château Gaillard, Open daily, except Tues., mid-Mar. through Oct., 9–12 and 2–6.

ARGENTAN. Abbaye Bénédictine, Church of St.-Germain, 2 rue de l'Abbaye. Open daily except Sun. and public hols., 2–4.

ARROMANCHES. Musée du Débarquement (D-day Landings Museum). Open daily 9–12 and 2–6 (mid-Sept. through Dec. 2–7); no lunchtime closure mid-June to mid-Sept.

BAYEUX. Centre Culturel Guillaume le Conquérant (William the Conqueror Cultural Center). Home of the *Tapisserie de la Reine Mathilde* (Bayeux

Tapestry). Open June through Sept., daily 9–7; Oct. through May, daily 9–12, 2–7.

Musée de la Bataille de Normandie (Battle of Normandy Museum). Open Nov. through Mar., weekends only, 10.30–12.30 and 2–6.30; Apr. through June and Sept. through Oct., daily 10–12.30 and 2–6.30; July and Aug., daily 9.30–7.

LE BEC-HELLOUIN. Abbaye (Abbey). Guided tours weekdays (except Tues. and certain public hols.) at 10, 11, 3, 3.45, 4.30, 5.15; Sun. and public hols. at 9.30, 12, 2.45, 3, 4.15 and 6.

Musée Automobile (Motor Museum). Open daily, 9–12 and 2–7.

CAEN. Château (William the Conqueror's Castle). Houses the *Normandy Museum.* Open daily except Tues. and public hols., 10–12, 2–6. Guided tours if requested; and the **Musée des Beaux-Arts** (Fine Arts Museum). Open daily except Tues. and public hols., 10–12, 2–6.

CHERBOURG. Musée des Beaux-Arts (Fine Arts Museum). Open daily except Tues. and public hols., 10–12 and 2–6.

Musée de la Guerre et de la Libération (World War II and Liberation of France Museum). Open daily in summer, 9–12 and 2–6; closed Tues. in winter.

DIEPPE. Musée Municipal (Town Museum), in the castle. Open daily in summer, 10–12 and 2–6; closed Tues. in winter.

Musée de la Guerre et du Raid du 19 Août 1942 (Jubilee Raid Museum), 2½ km. (1½ miles) out of town. Open Easter through Sept., daily except Mon., 10–12 and 2–6.

Château de Miromesnil, 13 km. (8 miles) outside town. Open May to mid-Oct., daily except Tues., 2–6.

EVREUX. Ancien Evêché (Bishop's Palace). Open daily except Mon., 10–12 and 2–5 (Sun. 2–6).

FALAISE. Château. Open daily except Tues., 9–12 and 2–6. Closed Oct. and Sun. in winter. Guided tours only.

FÉCAMP. Musée de la Bénédictine, 110 rue Alexandre-le-Grand. Guided tours (including tasting in distillery) daily from Easter to mid-Nov., 9–11.30 and 2–5.30.

GIVERNY. Maison de Claude Monet (Monet's House). Open Apr. through Oct., daily except Mon., 10–12 and 2–6.

LE HAVRE. Musée des Beaux-Arts André Malraux. Open daily 10–12 and 2–6; closed Tues. and public hols.

HONFLEUR. Musée Eugène Boudin. Open Easter through Sept., daily except Tues., 10–12 and 2–6; rest of the year, weekdays 2.30–5, weekends 10–12 and 2–6.

JUMIÈGES. Abbaye. Open May through Sept., daily except Tues., and public hols., 9–12 and 2–6; Oct. through Apr. 10–12 and 2–5.

LISIEUX. Les Buissonnets, 56 blvd. Herbert-Fournet (home of St. Theresa). Open daily 9–12 and 2–6, 4 or 5 in winter.

MONT ST.-MICHEL. Abbaye. Guided tours mid-May through Sept., daily 9–11.30 and 1.30–6; Oct. to mid-May, daily except Tues., Jan. 1, May 1 and Christmas Day, 9–11.30 and 1.30–4.

Haras du Pin (Stud Farm). Guided tours daily 9–12 and 2–6.

PLAGES DU DÉBARQUEMENT (D-day Landing Beaches), section of the coast between Ouistreham and St.-Marcouf. British section, comprising: Sword Beach, Juno Beach and Gold Beach. American section, comprising: Omaha Beach and Utah Beach.

ROUEN. Musée des Beaux-Arts (Fine Arts Museum). Open daily 10–12, 2–6, except Tues. and Wed. morning.
Musée Le Secq des Tournelles (Museum of Wrought Iron). Open daily 10–12, 2–6; closed Tues. and Wed. A.M. Same ticket as Fine Art Museum.

ST.-LÔ. Haras (Stud Farm). Guided tours daily, mid-July to mid-Feb., 10–11 and 2.30–4.30.

ST.-WANDRILLE. Abbaye. Guided tours daily at 10.30 (not on Sun.), 11.15, (11.30 on Sun.), 3 and 4.

STE.-MARIE-DU-MONT (Utah Beach). **Musée du Débarquement** (D-Day Landing Museum). Guided tours Easter through Oct., daily, 9–12 and 2–7; rest of the year only at weekends, 10–12 and 2–6.

STE.-MÈRE-ÉGLISE. Musée des Troupes Aéroportés (Museum of Airborne Troops). Open Easter through Oct., daily 9–12 and 2–7 (July and Aug. 9–7); Nov. to Easter during the week on request only, Sun. and public hols., 10–12 and 2–6. Closed mid-Nov. to Feb.

VARENGEVILLE-SUR-MER. Eglise de St.-Manoir d'Ango. Site of Braque's grave. Guided tours daily 10–12 and 2–6.30.
Parc des Moustiers. Open Easter through Oct., 10–12 and 2–7.

VILLEQUIER. Musée Victor Hugo (Victor Hugo Museum). Open Feb. through Oct., daily except Tues. (in summer), also closed Mon. in winter. 10–12 and 2–7.

SPECIAL INTEREST ACTIVITIES. Cooking. The *Dieppe Cookery Course* offers classes in English, Tues. through Fri., with rates based on half-board in one of three hotels from Mon. evening to Sat. morning. Two programs are offered, one of four lessons and one of six. You must be with a group of at least 15 people. 1500–2000 fr. Secrétariat, 18 blvd. de Verdun, 76200 Dieppe. The Marie-Blanche de Broglie cookery school in Paris run a one-week Cuisine au Château course in her family home near Rouen. The classes, with the emphasis on classic French and Norman cookery, take place in the mornings, in Aug. and Sept., Mon. through Fri. Accommodation is in a guesthouse in the grounds. Rates 5000 fr. for accommodation plus 6500 fr. for classes. Marie-Blanche de Broglie, 18 av. de la Motte-Picquet, 75007 Paris.

SPORTS. Riding. Normandy has a large number of riding centers offering a variety of holidays—pony trekking, beginners' classes, jumping and so on. Or you can meander through the countryside in a horse-drawn carriage or gipsy caravan. Details from tourist office in Evreux. **Golf.** Normandy has 14 golf courses, including 18-hole courses at Cabourg, Deauville and Dieppe. **Sailing.** Numerous sailing clubs as well as sailing schools along the coast; contact local tourist offices or write to tourist office in Evreux. **Windsurfing** is also very popular and the long sandy beaches are ideal for **sand sailing.** Fresh-water fishing is particularly good in the Orne *département* with its numerous rivers and lakes where you can try your luck with carp, pike or trout.

NORTHEAST FRANCE

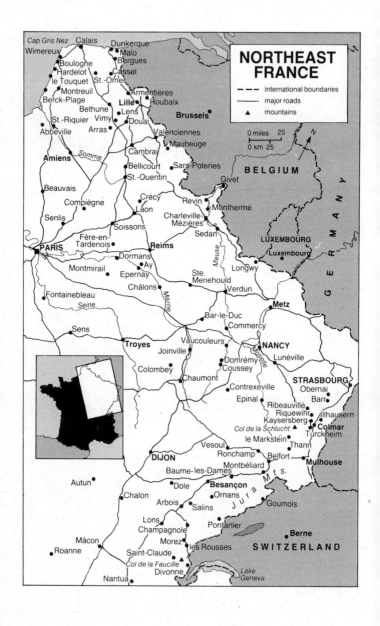

NORTHEAST FRANCE

- - - - international boundaries
——— major roads
▲ mountains

0 miles 25
0 km 25

N

Cap Gris Nez Calais Dunkerque
Wimereux Malo
Bergues
Boulogne Cassel
Hardelot St.-Omer
le Touquet
Montreuil Armentières
Berck-Plage **Lille** Roubaix
Bethune Lens
St.-Riquier Vimy Douai
Abbeville Arras
Valenciennes
Maubeuge
Amiens Somme
Cambrai
Bellicourt Sars-Poteries
Beauvais St.-Quentin **BELGIUM**
Givet
Compiègne Crécy
Léon Revin
Senlis Charleville- Montthermé
Soissons Mézières
Fère-en- Sedan **LUXEMBOURG**
Tardenois **Reims** Luxembourg
PARIS Dormans Longwy
Montmirail Ay Ste.
Epernay Menehould **GERMANY**
Fontainebleau Châlons Verdun
Seine Marne Meuse
Bar-le-Duc **Metz**
Sens Commercy
Vaucouleurs **NANCY**
Troyes Joinville Lunéville
Domrémy
Colombey Coussey
Chaumont **STRASBOURG**
Contrexéville Obernai
Epinal Barr
Ribeauvillé
Riquewihr Ilhausern
Kaysersberg **Colmar**
Col de la Schlucht ▲ Turckheim
le Markstein
Vesoul Thann
Ronchamp Belfort **Mulhouse**
DIJON Montbéliard
Baume-les-Dames
Autun Dole **Besançon**
Chalon Ornans J
Arbois Salins u
Lons Goumois r
Champagnole Pontarlier a
Mâcon Morez les Rousses M
Roanne Saint-Claude t
Col de la Faucille s
Nantua Divonne **Berne**
SWITZERLAND
Lake
Geneva

Brussels

THE NORTH

Ferry Boats and Flanders' Fields

The northern regions, officially known as Picardie and Nord-Pas-de-Calais, are the gateway to France for hordes of visitors on their way to Paris and the south from northern Europe. They seldom linger long in these industrial lowlands, which at first sight may not seem promising tourist country but in fact are full of interest—mighty cathedrals (such as Amiens), famous battlefields (the Somme), historic ports (Boulogne and Calais), elegant resorts (Le Touquet), and much besides.

Skies are often gray, and the landscape is mainly flat, broken here and there by isolated hills and giant slag heaps. From Valenciennes via Lille to the coast at Dunkerque, the sector beside the Belgian border remains one of the major industrial areas of France, but its pattern is changing as traditional industries (coal, textiles, steel) decline and new ones arrive (automobiles, electronics, petrochemicals). The government has been making a special effort to help this change-over by providing new infrastructure—hence the area has a better network of motorways and wide canals than any other part of France.

A crossroads of invasions across the centuries, the north abounds with battle memorials, from Crécy where England defeated France in 1346, to Vimy where the Canadians fought so heroically in 1917, and Dunkerque with its epic souvenirs of 1940. Used to visitors of all kinds—armed or unarmed—the people of the north are warm-hearted and open-minded, and they compensate for their tough industrial slog by a social and club life of unusual variety. Carnivals and parades fill the calendar, while the passion for unusual sports and hobbies (archery, darts, puppetry, pigeon fancying) seems more British than French. An even closer affinity is with Belgium, for the district around Lille forms the French part of Flanders: the towns with their giant belfries and stepped house façades are strikingly similar to Belgium's Flemish cities.

The Channel Ports: Dunkerque, Calais, Boulogne

Dunkerque, an old fortified seaport, was in the 17th century a stronghold of pirates, led by Jean Bart. They destroyed or captured 3,000 ships and took 30,000 prisoners. But the town's finest hour, as the world knows, came in May/June 1940, when an impromptu armada of little boats of every kind set out from England and rescued 350,000 men, two-thirds of them British, from the encircling *Wehrmacht.* The town was 80 percent destroyed in the war. But it has since expanded into a major industrial center and its commercial port is the foremost in France in terms of tonnage handled.

Calais, to the west, is France's most important passenger port, handling a large part of the traffic with Britain (Dover is a mere 45 km./28 miles away). Small wonder that the town's history has long been bound up with the English, who owned it from 1347 to 1558 (Queen Mary Tudor said, "When I am dead and opened, you shall find 'Calais' lying in my heart"). The local places of interest are mostly connected with England: near the town hall is Rodin's famous sculpture, *The Burghers of Calais,* the six citizens who offered themselves as hostages to save the city from the English in 1347; and five km. (three miles) away are the preliminary earthworks for the Channel Tunnel—the on-again-off-again project that has been marked by endless delays. In the mid–1980s, the chances of it being built look rather better than for many a decade.

Calais was rebuilt after massive World War II destruction. Today it has a variety of industries, notably chemicals and fabrics. The traditional lace manufacture has largely disappeared.

Boulogne, to the southwest, is Calais' rival for the cross-Channel traffic with Britain. It is also the leading fishing port of the Common Market, and a major cold-storage center. Boulogne was a town in Roman days, starting-point both of Caesar's successful invasion of Britain in 54 B.C. and of Bonaparte's abortive bid in 1803. The main feature of interest today is the old part of the town on a hilltop (*la ville haute),* girt by a great medieval wall. At weekends the town is invaded by day-trippers from England, very often drunk and rowdy.

Le Touquet and Other Beach Resorts

Along the coast from Cap Gris Nez to the Somme estuary, the sandy beaches are among the best in France. Hardelot-Plage, just south of Boulogne, has become *à la mode,* and its pine forests have filled up with the modern weekend villas of the well-to-do. South again lies Le Touquet-Paris-Plage, a shining name in the history of tourism. Its golden age of chic was in the railroad's heyday, when the rich and fashionable from Paris and London found it so relatively accessible. Today, such people prefer to jet away to the sunnier south, and Le Touquet has moved a bit down market. But it still fills to bursting in summer with holiday-makers, attracted by long beaches of fine sand, a racetrack, riding and yachting, and a local specialty, sand-sailing, as well as tennis and golf, nightclubs, concerts, two casinos, and the Palais de l'Europe for congresses and festivals.

Further south is another noted beach resort, Berck-Plage, frequented year-round because it is also a medical center for the treatment of bone diseases. Nearby, the Marquenterre bird sanctuary, open to visitors, protects over 300 species. Inland from the beaches, two towns are especially worth a visit: Montreuil, with a 16th-century fortress, and ramparts dating from the 12th century; and St.-Omer, southeast of Calais, where the magnificent 13th-century cathedral of Notre-Dame has a range of beautiful sculptures and carvings.

The Battlefields of 1914–18

Many of the fiercest battles of that long, cruel war of the trenches were fought in the Artois district, north of Arras, and in the rolling country above the Somme valley, northeast of Amiens. These areas are dotted with poignant war memorials, and with scores of Allied and German cemeteries, still neatly tended and carefully signposted. To visit them is a sobering, instructive kind of tourism.

The most majestic memorial is at Vimy Ridge, dominating the valley north of Arras—two mighty stelae of stone, flanked by sculptures of weeping, pensive women, "erected by the people of Canada, in memory of its 60,000 dead." The Canadian army seized this ridge in April 1917. Close by, the Canadian trenches and dug-outs have been preserved and can be visited. Just to the north is the French military mausoleum of Notre-Dame-de-Lorette, with a small war museum.

Much further south, the terrible casualties of the Somme battles of 1916 are commemorated by the giant British monument at Thiepval, the nearby Ulster Tower, and the Newfoundland Division's memorial park of Beaumont-Hamel, where the trenches are still clearly visible. Of likely interest to American visitors is the cenotaph at Bellicourt, just off the Cambrai-St.-Quentin road, paying tribute to the U.S. army's attack on the Hindenburg Line in 1918.

Industrial decay, as well as the sound of shellfire long silenced, haunts the plain of Artois around Lens and Béthune. Here the landscape is pitted with scores of conical coal tips, memorials to an industry that is fast dying. This was formerly one of the major coalmining regions of Europe, but the mines are nearing exhaustion and most have now closed. Flat landscapes, gray skies, decaying mines, long-buried soldiers—this is possibly the most melancholy part of France, but with its own sad beauty, like the war poems of Wilfred Owen.

The Inland Cities: Lille, Arras, St.-Quentin, Amiens

The metropolis of Lille is capital of the north, hub of a conurbation of over a million souls that includes the textile town of Roubaix, and Armentières where a Limey veteran today would be unlikely to find many girls unkissed for 40 years. Despite its dour exterior, Lille is a vibrant place, full of culture and night life, and a major center of commerce and industry. It has a brand-new subway system with easy access for the handicapped.

The Belgian frontier is on the back doorstep, and the architecture and ambience are so Flemish—cobbled streets, stepped façades, wood-paneled cafés—that you may feel you are in Belgium. Among Lille's many noted buildings, the art museum comes first: it is one of the richest in France, with works by Rubens, Van Dyck, Goya, Delacroix, Dufy and many other European masters. The old Bourse is a fine example of 17th-century Flemish architecture, while the church of Ste.-Catherine contains the beautiful *Martyrdom of St. Catherine* by Rubens. You should also visit the Paris Gate and the 15th-century Hospice Comtesse with its museum of popular art. In the old part of the town, the rue de la Monnaie is lined with graceful Flemish houses, which have recently been restored: through their windows you may be able to glimpse the delicacy of the brickwork.

Arras, 48 km. (30 miles) southwest of Lille, is well worth a visit. Despite wartime damage, its picturesque 17th-century Flemish architecture stands intact, notably in the Grand'-Place and the place des Héros, two impressive squares enclosed by brick houses with gables and arcades. The city hall with its belfry and the ancient abbey of St.-Vaast with its museum are other glories of Arras.

St.-Quentin, to the southeast, was the scene of a famous battle in 1557 when Philip II of Spain defeated the French. Today the town is worth a halt chiefly for its Lecuyer Museum, with a fine collection of 18th-century portraits by Quentin de la Tour, and its Gothic basilica, with stained-glass windows and sculptures of the 13th and 14th centuries. Valenciennes, a big town to the north, brings us back with a jolt into the late 20th century—here in 1979 there were violent riots against the planned closure of the local steelworks at Denain.

Finally to Amiens, capital of Picardy. Its great Gothic cathedral, begun in 1220, is one of the finest in France. Note especially the four-sided reliefs on the lower half of the west front, symbolizing the virtues and vices, local arts and crafts, and some fables; and the rich carvings of the 16th-century choir stalls. The 113-meter (373-ft.) steeple and the large rose window also date from the 16th century.

The Picardy Museum has an eclectic wealth of paintings by everyone, or almost, from Frans Hals to Fragonard, from Tiepolo to Renoir and Dali. And talking of Dali, modern culture in Amiens is also represented by the palatial Maison de la Culture, the first and one of the largest of the chain of arts centers foisted on France in the 1960s by de Gaulle's culture minister, author André Malraux. It survives to prove that even a white elephant can sometimes house interesting exhibits, concerts, plays and film shows. Lastly, on a fine day in spring or summer it might be worth taking a look at the curious *hortillonnages* in the eastern suburbs—a network of small canals enclosing market gardens. Till recently, this was a real market-on-the-water, with growers selling their wares from small barges, as in Bangkok. But the boats have now been replaced by unromantic trucks on *terra firma*. Such is progress.

PRACTICAL INFORMATION FOR THE NORTH

TOURIST OFFICES. The three *départements* of the North have their own tourist offices (written enquiries only). These are: **Nord,** 14 sq. Foch, 59000 Lille (tel. 20-57-00-61); **Pas-de-Calais,** 44 Grand Rue, 62200, Boulogne-sur-Mer (tel. 21-31-98-58); **Somme,** 21 rue Ernest-Cauvin, 80000 Amiens (tel. 22-92-26-39).

There are local tourist offices in the following towns: **Abbeville,** 26 pl. Libération (tel. 22-24-27-92); **Amiens,** rue Catelas (tel. 22-91-79-28); **Arras,** 7 pl. Maréchal-Foch (tel. 21-51-26-05); **Boulogne,** Pont Marquet (tel. 21-31-68-38); **Calais,** 12 blvd. Clemenceau (tel. 21-96-62-40); **Dunkerque,** rue Clemenceau (tel. 28-66-79-21); **Le Touquet,** Palais de l'Europe (tel. 21-05-21-65); **Lille,** Palais Rihour (tel. 20-30-81-00).

REGIONAL FOOD AND DRINK. Fish and shellfish are the star features in the menus of the region. North Sea herrings and oysters, *moules* (mussels), *coques* (cockles), *crevettes* (shrimps) are particularly succulent. Flanders has its own local dish, the *hochepot* (hotpot), as well as *veau* (veal) *à la Flamande, pâté de bécasse* (woodcock pâté) and *carbonnade,* beef braised in beer. In Picardy, duck pâtés and *ficelle picarde* (a ham and mushroom pancake) are popular. The region does not produce any wine, but brews beer in large quantities; cider is also made. *Genièvre* is a juniper-flavored fine-grain spirit.

The North is not so well known for its cheeses—*Maroilles, Mont des Cats* and *Goyère* —as for its pastries and confectionery. Among the latter are the *gaufres fourrées* (layered wafers) of Lille and Douai, *beignets* (fritters) of St.-Quentin, *chiques* (caramels) of Berck-sur-Mer, and macaroons of Amiens.

HOTELS AND RESTAURANTS. Some resort hotels are open only from Easter to September, so make a point of checking in advance. You will find that the regional specialties are excellent in even the most modest hotel restaurant and that in general fine food abounds.

For general notes on hotels and restaurants, see "Hotels" and "Restaurants" in *Facts at Your Fingertips.*

ABBEVILLE. *France* (I), 19 pl. Pilori (tel. 22-24-00-42). 77 rooms. Central and well-run, with good-value restaurant *(Pilori).* Closed mid-Dec. to mid-Jan. AE, DC, V.
Restaurants. *Escale en Picardie* (M), 15 rue Teinturiers (tel. 22-24-21-51). Closed Sun. for dinner, Mon., school hols. and Aug. Open to 8.45 P.M. Light *nouvelle cuisine;* go for the *menus.* AE, DC, MC, V.
At **Epagnette,** 3 km. (2 miles) south, *Picardière* (I), (tel. 22-24-15-28). Closed Tues. for dinner, Wed. Worth the short journey. AE, DC, MC, V.

AMIENS. *Nord-Sud* (M), 11 rue Gresset (tel. 22-91-59-03). 26 rooms. Restaurant closed Sun. for dinner. Comfortable, with rather elegant restaurant. AE, DC, MC, V. *L'Univers* (M), 2 rue Noyon (tel. 22-91-52-51). 41 rooms with balconies and patio. Between station and cathedral. AE, DC, MC, V.
Restaurants. *Couronne* (M), 64 rue St.-Leu (tel. 22-91-88-57). Closed mid-July to mid-Aug., and Sat. In old part of town and popular locally. V. *Marissons* (M), 66 rue Marissons (tel. 22-92-96-66). Closed Sat. for lunch, Sun. for dinner, Mon., week after Christmas, 4 weeks July–Aug. Modern cooking with good-value *menus* in 15th-century room with view of cathedral. *Mermoz* (M), 7 rue Jean-Mermoz (tel. 22-91-50-63). Closed mid–July to mid–Aug., Sat., and for dinner on Sun. Near station; good *menus* (try the special regional one). AE, DC, V.

ARRAS. *Astoria* (M), 12 pl. Foch (tel. 21-71-08-14). 32 rooms. Closed Christmas and New Year period; restaurant also closed Sun. for dinner and first half July. Opposite station, with quick-service brasserie as well as regular restaurant. AE, DC, MC, V. *Univers* (M), 3 pl. Croix-Rouge (tel. 21-71-34-01). 36 rooms. Converted monastery, stylish; pretty garden and elegant restaurant. AE, MC.
Restaurants. *La Faisanderie* (E), Grand-Place (tel. 21-48-20-76). Closed Sun. for dinner, Mon., school hols. and Aug. Open to 9 P.M. New, with good *nouvelle cuisine.* AE, DC, V. *Ambassadeur* (M), pl. Foch (tel. 21-23-29-80). Closed Sun. for dinner. Station buffet (entrance separate), serving delicious regional dishes plus classical cuisine. AE, DC, MC, V.

BERCK-PLAGE. *Comme Chez Soi* (I), 48 pl. Entonnoir (tel. 21-09-04-65). 19 rooms. Closed mid-Dec. to mid-Jan., part of Feb., Sun. for dinner, Mon. Close to beach, with good-value restaurant popular with locals.

BOULOGNE-SUR-MER. *Ibis* (M), blvd. Diderot (tel. 21-30-12-40). 79 rooms. Very convenient for ferries and also quite close to rail station; snackbar. MC, V. *Métropole* (M), 51 rue Thiers (tel. 21-31-54-30). 27 rooms. Closed mid-Dec. to early Jan. Small and central; no restaurant. V.
   Restaurants. *Liègoise* (M), 10 rue Monsigny (tel. 21-31-61-15). Closed Sun. for dinner and Fri. Good-value, delicious *nouvelle cuisine* in this old-established spot. AE, DC, MC, V. *Matelote* (M), 80 blvd. Ste.-Beuve (tel. 21-30-17-97). Closed mid-Dec. to mid-Jan. and second half June, Sun. for dinner and Tues. Overlooking beach and close to casino; popular with British foodies into *nouvelle cuisine.* MC, V. *Plage* (I), 124 blvd. Ste.-Beuve (tel. 21-31-45-35). Closed mid-Dec. to mid-Jan., Sun. for dinner (except July and Aug.), Mon. Close to harbor; also has 10 (I) rooms.

CALAIS. *Bellevue* (M), 23 pl. Armes (tel. 21-34-53-75). 42 rooms. Traditional, close to harbor; no restaurant. AE, DC, MC, V. *Meurice* (M), rue Edmond-Roche (tel. 21-34-57-03). 40 rooms. Quiet setting near public garden; restaurant under separate management. AE, DC, V.
   Restaurants. *Channel* (M), 3 blvd. Résistance (tel. 21-34-42-30). Closed Dec. through Jan., Sun. for dinner and Tues. Very popular place on seafront, home-style cooking. AE, DC, MC, V. *George V* (M), 36 rue Royale (tel. 21-97-68-00). Closed Sat. for lunch, Sun. for dinner and 2 weeks at New Year. Very welcoming atmosphere; popular for fish. AE, DC, V. *Sole Meunière* (M), 1 blvd. Résistance (tel. 21-34-43-01). Closed part of June and mid-Dec. to mid-Jan., Sun. for dinner and Mon. Well-known fish restaurant; good-value *menus.* AE, MC, V.

DOUAI. *Terrasse* (M), 8 terrasse St.-Pierre (tel. 27-88-70-04). 32 rooms. Traditional hostelry with interesting newish cuisine. AE, V.

DUNKERQUE. *Borel* (M), 6 rue Hermitte (tel. 28-66-51-80). 40 rooms. Very central and well-run; no restaurant. AE, DC, MC, V. *Europ* (M), 13 rue Leughenaer (tel. 28-66-29-07). 125 rooms. Restaurant closed Sun. for dinner and Mon. Modern and functional, with grillroom and good (M) restaurant *(Mareyeur).* AE, DC, MC, V.
   Restaurants. *Meunerie* (E), 174 rue Pierres (tel. 28-26-14-30). Closed Christmas through Jan., Sun. for dinner, Mon. Converted mill offering distinguished cooking (superb fish, "new"-style). AE, DC, V. *Métropole* (I), 28 rue Thiers (tel. 28-66-85-01). Closed mid-July to mid-Aug., Fri. for dinner, Sat. for lunch and Sun. for dinner; must reserve for meals on Sat. Near station; good classical dishes. AE, DC, MC, V.
   At **Malo les Bains,** *Bon Coin* (M), 49 av. Kléber. Closed New Year. Good shellfish; interesting menus. Also has 4 rooms. AE.

HARDELOT-PLAGE. *Ecusson* (M), 442 av. François-ler (tel. 21-83-71-52). 20 rooms. Closed mid-Jan. through Feb., Wed. (except mid-Jan. through Oct.). Comfortable modern rooms; classical restaurant (mostly fish). AE, DC, MC, V. *Pré-Catalan* (I), av. Blois (tel. 21-83-70-03). 12 rooms. Closed Oct. through Feb. Quiet and friendly; nice restaurant.
   Restaurant. *Golf* (M), av. Golf (tel. 21-83-71-04). Closed mid-Dec. through Jan., Sun. for dinner and Mon. Good-value *menus,* nice views over golf course. AE, DC, V.

LILLE. *Carlton* (E), 3 rue Paris (tel. 20-55-27-11). 68 rooms. Very central (close to opera house and station); well-modernized with soundproofed rooms; no restaurant. AE, DC, MC, V. *Bellevue* (E), 5 rue Roisin (tel. 20-57-45-64). 80 rooms. Very central and quite elegant; no restaurant. AE, V. *Royal Concorde* (E), 2 blvd. Carnot (tel. 20-51-05-11). 102 rooms. Very comfortable; no restaurant. AE, DC, MC, V. *Chagnot* (M), 24 pl. Gare (tel. 20-06-25-50). 75 rooms. Right by station; comfortable though not much atmosphere; grillroom. v. *Strasbourg* (I), 7 rue Roisin (tel. 20-57-05-46). 46 rooms. Small and modest, but gradually being renovated; no restaurant. AE, DC, V.

Restaurants. *Flambard* (E), 79 rue Angleterre (tel. 20-51-00-06). Closed Aug., Sun. for dinner, Mon. all day. 17th-century building, but cuisine very modern; one of best restaurants in France. AE, DC, V. *Huitrière* (E), 3 rue Chats-Bossus (tel. 20-55-43-41). Closed Aug., and Sun. for dinner. Old-established and still superb; marvelous fish. AE, DC, MC, V. *Paris* (E), 52 rue Esquermoise (tel. 20-55-29-41). Closed Aug., and Sun. for dinner. Elegant, very high standard of cuisine (mostly "new"). AE, DC.

Compostelle (M), 6 rue St.-Etienne (tel. 20-54-02-49). Closed Sun. for dinner. 16th-century building once used by pilgrims on way to Santiago de Compostela; newish cuisine and good-value *menus*. AE, DC, MC, V. *Devinière* (M), 61 blvd. Louis-XIV (tel. 20-52-74-64). Closed most of Aug., Sat. for lunch and Sun. Excellent, good-value *nouvelle cuisine;* must reserve. AE, DC, MC, V. *Provinciale en Ville* (M), 8 rue Ursulines (tel. 20-06-50-79). Closed Sun. for dinner and Mon. Good place for regional food. AE, V. *Brasserie André* (I), 71 rue Béthune (tel. 20-54-75-51). One of the few recommendable real (I) brasseries in Lille. Old decor; good *choucroutes* and wines. Open daily to midnight. V.

MONTREUIL-SUR-MER. *Château de Montreuil* (E), 4 chaussée Capucins (tel. 21-81-53-04). Closed mid-Dec. to mid-Feb.(except New Year period); restaurant—(I) *menus* during the week—closed for lunch on Thurs. (except July and Aug.). Elegant Relais et Châteaux member; attractive garden, lovely rooms, and superb cuisine; cookery classes held here. AE, DC, MC, V.

At **La Madeleine-sous-Montreuil,** 3 km. (2 miles) away, *Grenouillère* (E), (tel. 21-06-07-22). Closed Feb. and part of Nov., Tues. for dinner, Wed. (except July and Aug.). Rambling riverside inn; deliciously light cooking; also has 3 (M) rooms. AE, DC, V.

ROUBAIX. *PLM Grand* (M), 22 av. Lebas (tel. 20-73-40-00). 95 rooms. Central (near station), and very comfortable; no restaurant. AE, DC, MC, V. *Centre* (I), 1 rue Motte (tel. 20-73-13-14). 21 rooms. Modest, but central.

Restaurants. *Caribou* (E), 8 rue Mimerel (tel. 20-70-87-08). Closed mid-July through Aug., Easter hols., for dinner Sun., and all day Mon. Typically French traditional restaurant; gorgeous classical cuisine. V. *Charly* (M), 127 av. Lebas (tel. 20-70-78-58). Closed Aug. and Sat. Cheerful, always busy; home-style regional cooking. V.

St.-OMER. *Bretagne* (M), 2 pl. Vainquai (tel. 21-38-25-78). 33 rooms. Closed first half Jan.; restaurant also closed second half Aug., Sat., and Sun. for dinner. Known for its restaurant; also has convenient grillroom. AE, DC, V. *St.-Louis* (I), 25 rue Arras (tel. 21-38-35-21). 20 rooms. Closed Christmas and New Year period. Old building near basilica; well-modernized rooms; no restaurant. MC, V.

At **Tilques,** 6 km. (4 miles) northeast, *Vert-Mesnil* (E), (tel. 21-93-28-99). 40 rooms. 19th-century manor-house with nice grounds, pool, tennis courts and good (M) restaurant. Closed Sat. for lunch AE, DC, V.

Restaurants. *Cygne* (M), 8 rue Caventou (tel. 21-98-20-52). Closed Tues., Sat. for lunch, 3 weeks Dec. Pleasant; good chef. AE, MC, V.

At **Lumbres,** 13 km. (8 miles) away, *Moulin de Mombreux* (M), rte. Bayeng-hem (tel. 21-39-62-44). Closed mid-Dec. through Jan., Sun. for dinner, Mon. Pretty converted mill with inventive cooking and good wine list; also has 6 (I) rooms. AE, DC, MC, V.

ST.-QUENTIN. *France et Angleterre* (M), 28 rue Emile-Zola (tel. 23-62-13-10). 22 rooms. Closed Christmas and New Year hols. Central and well-modernized; no restaurant. AE, DC, V. *Grand* (M), 6 rue Dachery (tel. 23-62-69-77). 41 rooms. Best in town; well run and excellent restaurant (see below). AE, DC, MC, V.

Restaurants. *Président* (M), in *Grand Hôtel* (tel. 23-62-69-77). Closed first half Feb., most of Aug., Sun. for dinner, Mon. One of best in northern France; elegant décor and superb *nouvelle cuisine.* AE, DC, MC, V. *Riche* (M), 10 rue Toiles (tel. 23-64-12-12). Closed part of Jan., mid-July to mid-Aug., Sun. for dinner and Tues. Good café-restaurant with traditional food and good-value *menus.* MC, V. *Petit Chef* (I), 31 rue Emile-Zola (tel. 23-62-28-51). Closed Christmas and New Year period, first half July, and weekends. Unpretentious, traditional cuisine. AE, MC, V.

At **Neuville-St.-Amand,** 3 km. (2 miles) southeast, *Château* (M), (tel. 23-68-41-82). Closed part of Feb., part of Aug., Sun. and Wed. for dinner, Mon. Very attractive; fine classical cooking (especially fish). AE, DC, MC, V.

LE TOUQUET. *Novotel Thalamer* (E), Front-de-Mer (tel. 21-05-24-00). 104 rooms. Right beside sea and communicating directly with salt-water cure center; modern rooms, pool, tennis courts; light meals only. AE, DC, MC, V. *Westminster* (E), av. Verger (tel. 21-05-19-66). 145 rooms. Closed mid-Nov. to mid-Mar.; restaurant closed Mon. for dinner and Tues. "Grand hotel" in every sense; spacious rooms. AE, DC, MC, V.

Côte d'Opale (M), 99 blvd. Dr.-Pouget (tel. 21-05-08-11). 28 rooms. Closed mid-Nov. to mid-Mar. Lovely sea views and terrace; well-modernized rooms; good restaurant. AE, DC, V. *Manoir* (M), av. Golf (tel. 21-05-20-22). 46 rooms. Closed mid-Nov. to mid-Dec., Jan. to Easter, Tues., Wed. for lunch (except July and Aug.). Norman manor-house in country setting on edge of town, beside golf course; tennis, pool; restaurant. AE, V.

Restaurants. *Flavio* (E), 2 av. Verger (tel. 21-05-10-22). Closed Dec. through Feb., Wed. (except May through Sept.). Elegant, superb cuisine (mostly fish and shellfish). AE, DC, MC, V. *Chalut* (M), 7 blvd. Jules-Pouget (tel. 21-05-22-55). Closed mid-Dec. through Feb., Tues. for dinner (except July and Aug.) and Wed. Facing sea; good fresh fish and excellent wine list. V. *Pérard* (M), 67 rue Metz (tel. 21-05-13-33). Closed mid-Jan. to mid-Feb. Bustling spot with marvelous seafood from fishmonger next door. *Bistro Charlotte* (I), 36 rue St.-Jean (tel. 21-05-32-11). Closed Wed. and Jan. Charming little restaurant; good, simple cooking and good-value *menus.* MC, V.

At **Merlimont,** 10 km. (6½ miles) south, *Hostellerie Georges* (E), 139 rue Etaples (tel. 21-94-70-87). Closed Jan., Mon. for dinner, Tues. (except July and Aug.). Pretty garden; excellent fish dishes. MC, V.

VALENCIENNES. *Grand* (M), 8 pl. Gare (tel. 27-46-32-01). 96 rooms. Old-established but well renovated; opposite station; good service and classical cuisine. AE, DC, MC, V. *Notre-Dame* (I), 1 pl. Thellier-de-Poncheville (tel. 27-42-30-00). 40 rooms. Central; no restaurant.

Restaurant. *L'Alberoi* (M), in rail station. Excellent station buffet with good regional food and some good-value (I) *menus.* Closed Sun. for dinner and public hols. AE, DC, MC, V.

WIMEREUX. *Centre* (M), 78 rue Carnot (tel. 21-32-41-08). 25 rooms. Closed first half of June, Christmas and New Year period, Mon. Comfortable and friendly; good restaurant (I). Closed Mon. MC, V. *Aramis* (I), 1 rue Romain (tel. 21-32-40-15). 16 rooms. Closed Christmas and New Year period, Sun. (in winter). Modest, no restaurant. V.

Restaurant. *Atlantic* (E), Digue-de-Mer (tel. 21-32-41-01). Closed Feb., Sun. for dinner, Mon. (except Apr. through Sept.). Popular with British visitors arriving at Boulogne; delicious seafood; also has 11 (M) rooms.

 SIGHTSEEING DATA. For general notes on visiting museums and historic buildings in France, plus an important warning, see "Sightseeing" in *Facts at Your Fingertips.*

ABBEVILLE. Musée Boucher de Perthes (Local History Museum). Open 2–6 May through Sept., hols. in Feb., Easter; Wed. and Sun. Closed public hols.

AMIENS. Musée de la Picardie (Picardy Museum), 48 rue de la République. Open daily, 10–12, 2–6; closed Mon., Sun. afternoon and some public hols.

BAVAY. Musée Archéologique. Open daily, except Tues. and some public hols., 9–12, 2–5 (to 6 in summer).

ARRAS. Musée des Beaux Arts (Fine Arts Museum), in former abbey buildings next to the cathedral. Open daily, 12–2, 12–5.30; closed Tues. and public hols.

BERGUES. Musée Municipal (Municipal Museum), behind the Church of St.-Martin in 17th-century building (originally a pawn shop). Open daily, 10–12, 2–5; closed Fri. and public hols.

BOULOGNE. Musée des Beaux Arts (Fine Arts Museum), 34 Grand Rue. Open Wed. to Sun. and closed public hols., 9.30–12, 2–6.30.

CALAIS. Musée des Beaux Arts et de la Dentelle (Fine Arts and Lace Museum), (tel. 21-97-99-00). Open daily, 10–12, 2–5.30; closed Tues. and public hols.
Musée de la Guerre (War Museum), in one-time German blockhouse opposite the Hôtel de la Ville. Open daily June through Sept., 10.30–5.30.

CASSEL. Musée de la Histoire et de Folklore (History and Folklore Museum), Hotel de la Noble Cour. Open daily, June through Sept., 2–6; April and May, Sun. only.

DOUAI. Musée, in one-time chartreuse, or Charterhouse, west of town center. Open daily, 10–12, 2–5; closed Tues. and public hols.

DUNKERQUE. Musée d'Art Contemporain (Modern Art Museum), av. des Bains. Open daily, 10–12, 3–6; closed Tues. and public hols.
Musée Aquariophile (Marine Museum), av. Faidherbe. Open daily except Tues. and public hols. 10–12, 2–6.
Musée des Beaux Arts (Fine Arts Museum), pl. du Général de Gaulle. Open daily except Tues., 10–12, 3–6.

LILLE. Palais des Beaux Arts, pl. de la République. Open daily except Tues., 10–12.30, 2–5. Free Wed. and Sat. afternoons.
Musee Régional d'Arts et Tradition Populaires (Folk Art Museum), rue de la Monnai. Open daily, 10–12, 2–5; closed Tues.

MAUBEUGE. Musée Regional (Local Museum). Open daily, 2–4; closed Tues. and public hols.

ST.-OMER. Musée des Beaux Arts (Fine Arts Museum), pl. Victor Hugo. Open daily, 10–12, 2–5; closed Mon., Tues. and public hols.

ST.-RIQUIER. Musée de la Vie Rurale (Museum of Rural Life). Open daily, June through Sept., 10–12, 2–6; Apr., May, and Oct., Sat. and Sun. only, 2–6.

SARS POTERIES. Musée du Verre (Glass Museum). Open daily July and Aug., Sat. and Sun. only Sept. through June, 2–5.

VALENCIENNES. Musée Municipal (Municipal Museum), blvd. Watteau. Open daily, 10–12, 2–5; closed Tues. and public hols.

CHAMPAGNE

Sparkle from the Chalk

Champagne, a place name that has come to be a universal synonym for joy and festivity, is a word of humble origin. Like Campagna, its Italian counterpart, it is derived from the Latin *campus,* which means nothing more than an open field. In French, *campus* became *champ.* The old language extended it to *champaign,* meaning battlefield, and *champaine,* a district of plains.

Both "battlefield" and "plains" accurately describe the province. Lying between the Ile de France and Lorraine, with Belgium above it and Burgundy below it, Champagne is criss-crossed by Roman roads along which defenders and invaders have clashed for two millennia. In our own century, the history of World War I is dotted with the names of its towns and localities, such as Reims, Verdun, Soissons and the Chemin des Dames; more recently, the tiny village of Colombey-les-Deux-Eglises, home of Charles de Gaulle, has become a mecca; his fairly modest house, La Boisserie, is open to the public. The landscape of the area is sufficiently varied to include forests and flowers, hills and valleys, rivers and streams, and even several caves. But much of it consists of monotonous chalk plains, which Stendhal, who preferred mountains, called "the atrocious flat wretchedness of Champagne."

There is little flat wretchedness to be seen in the heartland of Champagne, where the grapes that go into its wine are grown. The 10,940 hectares (27,000 acres) of vineyards are scattered over beautiful countryside of rolling hills and valleys. There are three main grape-producing districts: the Montagne de Reims, lying like a lopsided horseshoe a few miles south of Reims; the lovely east–west Vallée de la Marne, a little farther south; and the picturesque Côte des Blancs, running due south from Epernay.

If you are visiting the region in the fall, plan to visit the Champagne Road through vineyards golden in the harvest sun. The views are enchanting and the prospect of one of France's storehouses of wealth is a pleasing sight for eyes and mind.

The deep chalk deposits left by a prehistoric inland sea may not embellish the topography, but they are the principal source of Champagne's glory. From blocks cut out of them, the great cathedral of Reims was built. The chalky subsoil is what makes Champagne grapes healthy and gives them their distinctive taste. Burrowing through solid chalk 30 meters (100 ft.) beneath Reims and Epernay are 193 km. (120 miles) of cellars where the sparkling wine is stored at an unvarying 10°C (50°F), exactly the temperature required to keep it continually at its best.

Just across the Marne lie the *hors classe* vineyards of Ay. About five km. (three miles) uphill to the west is the hilltop village of Hautvillers and the fine old Benedictine abbey where, in the 17th century, the learned Dom Pérignon discovered how to make champagne a blended sparkling wine, instead of the unblended still wine the abbey had produced up to that time.

The panorama from the abbey gardens is superb, but you will perhaps find the hilly region between Hautvillers and Ay even more visually satisfactory. Ten minutes from Epernay on the Reims bus will take you to a high point appropriately named Bellevue: the view over miles of vine-covered hills and valleys along the Marne is really spectacular. And if you walk back downhill for about three km. (two miles) to the village of Dizy, you will find that the beauty of the constantly changing view never diminishes.

The Cathedral City of Reims

Reims and its incomparable cathedral deserve a place on any tourist's itinerary. In 1918, after four years of pounding by German artillery, about all that remained of the beautiful old city were some hundred houses, a few churches and public buildings, and the battered cathedral. Present-day Reims is a new city, with wide, straight streets and modern buildings. Salvaged from its past are, besides the cathedral, the 3rd-century Porte de Mars; the church of St.-Rémi, which, with its curious mixture of Gothic and Romanesque styles, is of particular interest to students of architecture; and the dignified place Royale, which has been restored to look as it did when built under Louis XV. The Fine Arts Museum contains many fine tapestries and paintings, including the work of Delacroix, David, Daumier and Corot. And you shouldn't miss the Palais du Tau near the cathedral: once the bishop's palace, it dates from the beginning of the Christian era, and was used as a residence for the kings of France who were crowned in the cathedral. The Sainte-Chapelle, built in the early 13th century, is still intact, but much of the rest was modified in the late 17th century by the famous architects François Mansart and Robert de Cotte. The palace houses some fine tapestries and sculpture, but its chief pride is the Royal Treasure. The city itself, sharing the spotlight with Epernay, is the home of some well-known champagne firms. Some can be visited.

World War II bequeathed Reims a brand-new historical monument in the form of the room in the Modern and Technical College, where the German capitulation was signed on May 7, 1945. The room, its walls covered by the operational maps of General Eisenhower's headquarters, has been kept exactly as it was when the German army and navy chiefs sat down at its bar table to admit defeat to the Allies.

But the essential pride and glory of Reims is its cathedral, one of the greatest Gothic structures in France. It was here that France's kings were consecrated. Planned by Jean d'Orbais, the cathedral was begun in 1211 but not finished until a century later; its twin towers were completed at the end of the 15th century. Although work on it was not continuous, the entire cathedral is a marvel of unity and harmony. The western façade, with its three-pointed portals, its enormous rose window, its gallery of kings and its two towers, is a bewildering cascade of statuary and carved stone whose overall effect is one of unbelievable richness, grace and beauty. The interior is so simple it would be austere were it not for the majesty of its perfect proportions. The high vaulted nave and single chapel aisles on either side seem all the more impressive for being quite plain—no paintings or religious statuary. In one of the side chapels are six splendid stained glass windows by Marc Chagall, a moving link between the centuries.

After 700 years, Notre-Dame of Reims rises as an inspiring symbol of its city and province. Seemingly, especially from a distance, as fragile and airy as a glass of champagne the noble pile is in reality as solid as the deep chalk deposits from whose blocks its walls were built. Defaced during the French Revolution, shattered and burned during World War I, the cathedral stands today restored and almost as it was on the day in 1429 when Joan of Arc led Charles VII through its portals for his consecration.

An area of particular natural beauty and interest southeast of Reims is Les Faux de Verzy, a woodland of mutant beeches characterized by their peculiar umbrella-shaped tops. Some of them are over 500 years old, and they were first mentioned in the records of the abbey of St.-Basles in the 6th century.

Châlons and Troyes

South of Reims lie two major cities. First is Châlons-sur-Marne, crisscrossed by canals and possessing a fine Gothic cathedral (St.-Etienne) and the superb cloisters of Notre-Dame-en-Vaux, discovered by accident during restoration work. The church itself is part Romanesque and part early-Gothic (don't miss the magnificent stained glass). The Cloister Museum is the chief attraction, with its superb statuary depicting figures from the Old and New Testaments. The city has several other fine churches and a triumphal gateway, the Porte Ste.-Croix or Porte Dauphine, designed to enable Queen Marie-Antoinette to stage a triumphal entry in the 1770s.

Troyes, once the capital of the old province of Champagnole, is another "must." The most recent of its sights is the splendid Museum of Modern Art, opened in 1982 in the former bishop's palace, which has been skillfully converted to house a generously donated collection that includes paintings by Picasso and Braque. But it also has another of Champagne's magnificent cathedrals, St.-Pierre-et-St.-Paul, a huge structure whose building continued for centuries starting in the Gothic period. It again has wonderful stained glass: the elaborate west front has a glorious rose window in the Flamboyant Gothic style. The lovely 13th-century church of St.-Urbain is also worth visiting.

Troyes also has some fine old houses, many of them half-timbered, particularly in the picturesque rue des Chats and the rue Champeaux, and an interesting Tool and Craft Museum housed in a 16th-century mansion, the Hôtel de Mauroy. It has some fascinating exhibits connected with the various woodworking trades. The Fine Arts Museum has some good French paintings and a collection of enamels. If sightseeing has made you hungry, you should round off your visit by sampling an *andouillette de Troyes,* a tasty sausage made from pig's intestines that is the city's main culinary claim to fame.

The Ardennes

The little-visited Ardennes region of France lies mostly in Champagne, partly in Lorraine, yet is different from both of them. A land of water and forest, it is ideal for the fisherman, the camper or naturalist, or just for lazy motoring across its pleasant terrain. This is one of the few regions in France where boar and deer still roam naturally. The Ardennes forest is dark and somewhat gloomy, and the villages are often perched starkly between cliff and river.

The land of Rimbaud, it also inspired Victor Hugo, George Sand and Théophile Gautier, all of whom lived here and wrote of the Ardennes' beauty. It is bisected by the Meuse river, in and around whose wide valley lie its main tourist attractions: Charleville-Mezières, home of Rimbaud and boasting an impressive place Ducale; Sedan, with the largest castle in Europe (about three hectares/eight acres in area) and the château of Bellevue, where Napoleon III surrendered on September 2, 1870, to the Germans; and of course the Ardennes forest, where the Roches de Laifour and the Mont Malgré Tout offer magnificent views.

Also worth seeing are the little town of Revin, originally Spanish; the church of St.-Hilaire in Givet; the star-shaped town of Rocroi; and Monthermé, with its fortified church of St.-Léger (15th century).

PRACTICAL INFORMATION FOR CHAMPAGNE

 TOURIST OFFICES. The principal regional tourist office for the whole of Champagne (written enquiries only) is the *Comité Régional du Tourisme Champagne-Ardenne,* 2bis blvd. Vaubecourt, 51100 Châlons-sur-Marne (tel. 26-68-37-52). In addition, the *départements* of the region—again, written enquiries only—also have their own tourist offices. These are: **Aisne,** 1 rue St.-Martin, 02000 Laon (tel. 23-23-24-53); **Ardennes,** résidence Arduinna, 8 av. Georges-Corneau, 08000 Charleville-Mézières (tel. 24-56-06-08); **Aube,** Hôtel du Département, 10026 Troyes, (tel. 25-73-48-01); **Marne,** 2bis blvd. Vaubécourt, 51100 Châlons-sur-Marne (tel. 26-68-37-52); **Haute-Marne,** Hôtel de la Préfecture, 52000 Chaumont (tel. 25-03-65-00).

There are local tourist offices in the following towns: **Châlons-sur-Marne,** 3 quai des Arts (tel. 26-65-17-89); **Epernay,** pl. Mendes-France (tel. 26-55-33-00); **Reims,** 1 rue Jadart (tel. 26-47-25-69); **Troyes,** 16 blvd. Carnot (tel. 25-73-00-36).

REGIONAL FOOD AND DRINK. Not known for fine food, Champagne is best for simple specialties such as the hams of Reims and the Ardennes; for *andouillettes* sausages; the stuffed tongue of Troyes; for the celebrated *pieds de porc* (pigs' feet) of Sainte Ménehould; and for pâtés of pigeon, thrush *(grive)* and wild boar *(sanglier).* Fish dishes are concocted with *écrevisses* (crayfish) from the Meuse, *brochets* (pike) from the Aisne, and *truites* (trout) from Montmirail and the Argonne. Sample *poulet au champagne* and *coq au vin de Bouzy.*

Good cheese comes from southwest Champagne: *Brie,* its smaller cousin *Coulommiers,* full-bodied *Maroilles,* and cream cheeses such as *Boursin,* often flavored with garlic, herbs, or cracked pepper. If you're near Meaux, center of *Brie* production, visit the open market, full of cheeses at every stage from fresh to hard and dry.

Champagne, sometimes considered a dessert wine, is the French apéritif for special occasions. Purists regard it as the only wine which can be served throughout an entire meal, starting with the younger, lighter, and drier Champagnes and progressing gradually to the older, sweeter ones. With Champagne, the amount of *liqueur* (a solution of sugar and older, non-sparkling Champagne) added to each bottle determines its taste: *brut* (2–3%), *sec* (5%), or *demi-sec* (5–8%).

HOTELS AND RESTAURANTS. There is not much fancy about the hotels of the Champagne country, though they lack little in terms of solid comfort. Many are fairly new, the result of large scale rebuilding after the war.

For general notes on hotels and restaurants, see "Hotels" and "Restaurants" in *Facts at Your Fingertips.*

CHARLEVILLE-MÉZIÈRES. *Clèves* (M), 43 rue Arquebuse (tel. 24-33-10-75). 49 rooms. Modern hotel with good-sized rooms and good-value restaurant. AE, DC, MC, V. *Paris* (I), 24 av. Corneau (tel. 24-33-34-38). 29 rooms. Closed Christmas and New Year period. Opposite station; no restaurant. V. *Relais du Square* (I), 3 pl. Gare (tel. 24-33-38-76). 50 rooms. Close to station and old town; well-modernized; garden, restaurant. AE, DC, MC, V.

Restaurants. *Cigogne* (M), 40 rue Dubois-Crancé (tel. 24-33-25-39). Closed first half Aug., Sun. for dinner, Mon. Carefully-cooked classical dishes; popular with locals. V. *Buffet de la Gare* (I), in rail station (tel. 24-33-23-59). Very welcoming and good value: "eat as much as you like."

At **Montcy-Notre-Dame,** 2 km. (1¼ miles) north, *Auberge de la Forêt* (M), (tel. 24-33-37-55). Closed Sun. for dinner, Mon. Country setting; for good-value *menu* or more expensive classical *carte.* MC, V.

COLOMBEY-LES-DEUX-ÉGLISES. *Mapotel Dhuits* (M), on N19 road (tel. 25-01-50-10). 30 rooms. Closed mid-Dec. to mid-Jan. Modern, functional rooms in rural setting; good angling nearby; restaurant. AE, DC, MC.

Restaurant. *Montagne* (M), (tel. 25-01-51-69). Closed mid-Jan. through Feb., Mon. for dinner, and Tues. (except June through Aug.). Good-value classical cuisine; also has rooms (I).

EPERNAY. *Champagne* (M), 30 rue Mercier (tel. 26-55-30-22). 30 rooms. Modern and central; no restaurant. AE, DC, V. *Europe* (I), 18 porte Lucas (tel. 26-51-80-28). 26 rooms. Closed first half Aug.; restaurant closed Sun., Mon. Modest, a bit old-fashioned; pleasant atmosphere. AE, DC, MC, V.

At **Vinay,** 7 km. (4½ miles) east, *Briqueterie* (E), 4 rte. Sézanne (tel. 26-54-11-22). 42 rooms. Closed Christmas and New Year. Lovely setting—vineyards and garden; large, slightly old-fashioned rooms; good *nouvelle cuisine* and excellent wine list. AE, DC, MC, V.

At **Champillon**, 5 km. (3 miles) north, *Royal Champagne* (E), (tel. 26-51-11-51). 23 rooms. 18th-century coaching inn with splendid views of vineyards; Relais et Châteaux member with well-known restaurant. AE, DC, MC, V.

Restaurant. *Chapon Fin* (M), 2 pl. Mendès-France (tel. 26-51-40-03). Closed Sun. for dinner, Fri. Traditional home-style cooking; good-value *menus.*

FÈRE-EN-TARDENOIS. *Hostellerie du Château* (E), rte. de Fismes (tel. 23-82-21-13). 20 rooms. Closed Jan. and Feb. Relais et Châteaux member offering superb service in wonderful 16th-century château; excellent restaurant. MC, V.

Restaurant. *Auberge du Connétable* (M), on D967 (tel. 23-82-24-25). Closed Jan. to mid-Feb., Mon. Pleasant inn with newish cuisine; also has 4 (I) rooms; and swimming pool in grounds. AE.

GIVET. Restaurant. *Baudouin* (M), 2 pl. 148e R.I. (tel. 24-55-00-70). Closed part of Feb., mid-Aug. to mid-Sept., for dinner on Mon., Tues., Wed. 16th-century building close to Pont de Meuse; good mixture of regional dishes and *nouvelle cuisine;* reservations essential in evenings.

JOINVILLE. *Grand Point* (I), 7 rue Aristide-Briand (tel. 25-96-09-86). 27 rooms. Old-established, with restaurant. *Soleil d'Or* (I), 9 rue Capucins (tel. 25-96-15-66). 9 rooms. Closed Feb., Sun. for dinner, Mon. Friendly little place with good (M) restaurant. AE, DC, MC, V.

Restaurant. *Poste* (M), pl. Grève (tel. 25-96-12-63). Closed mid-Jan. to mid-Feb., Thurs. (except Apr. through Oct.). Good-value cuisine (mostly classical); also has 11 (I) rooms. AE, DC, MC, V.

LAON. *Angleterre* (M), 10 blvd. Lyon (tel. 23-23-04-62). 28 rooms. Closed Christmas and New Year period; part of Feb. Right by station; well-renovated; two restaurants. Closed Sun. in winter and Sat. for lunch. AE, DC, MC, V. *Chevaliers* (I), 3 rue Serurier (tel. 23-23-43-78). 15 rooms. Closed mid-Feb. to mid-March. Modest, well-run and friendly; near cathedral; no restaurant. AE, DC, MC, V.

Restaurants. *Bannière de France* (M), 11 rue Franklin-Roosevelt (tel. 23-23-21-44). Closed mid-Dec. to mid-Jan. 17th-century coaching inn; good classical cuisine; also has 18 rooms. AE, DC, MC, V. *Châteaubriand* (M), 7 pl. St.-Julien (tel. 23-20-46-77). Closed part of Mar., mid-Aug. to mid-Sept., Tues. Mostly local specialties; good-value *menu.* AE, DC, MC, V.

At **Urcel**, 13 km. (8 miles) south by RN2, *Hostellerie France* (M), (tel. 23-21-60-08). Welcoming and good value.

REIMS. *Boyer* (E), 64 blvd. Henri-Vasnier (tel. 26-82-80-80). 16 rooms. Closed Christmas through mid-Jan.; restaurant closed Mon. and for lunch on Tues. Splendid 19th-century mansion in town center surrounded by large gardens and with one of France's top restaurants (see below); Relais et Châteaux member. AE, DC, MC, V. *Frantel* (E), 31 blvd. Paul-Doumer (tel. 26-88-53-54). 125 rooms. Restaurant closed Sat. for lunch and Sun. (except hols.). Ultramodern and comfortable; close to motorway; good restaurant. AE, DC, MC, V.

Bristol (M), 76 pl. Drouet-d'Erlon (tel. 26-40-52-25). 40 rooms. Central and well-renovated; no restaurant. AE, DC, MC, V. *Paix* (M), 9 rue Buirette (tel. 26-40-04-08). Restaurant closed Sun. Modern and central; nice garden with pool; restaurant. MC, V.

Crystal (I), 86 pl. Drouet d'Erlon (tel. 26-88-44-44). 28 rooms. Peaceful yet near station; no restaurant. AE, MC, V. *Europa* (I), 8 blvd. Joffre (tel. 26-40-36-20). 32 rooms. Closed Christmas and New Year period. Central and well-sited opposite public garden; no restaurant. AE, DC, MC, V. *Gambetta* (I), 13 rue Gambetta (tel. 26-47-41-64). 14 rooms. Near cathedral; no restaurant. MC, V.

Restaurants. *Boyer-"Les Crayères"* (E), 64 blvd. Henri-Vasnier (tel. 26-82-80-80). Closed second half Dec. to mid-Jan., Mon., for lunch on Tues. Superb *nouvelle cuisine;* highly elegant setting; has over 120 different kinds of Champagne! Worth making a special journey to Reims, as many Parisians do, so must reserve. AE, DC, MC, V.

Chardonnay (M), 184 av. d'Epernay (tel. 26-06-08-60). Closed Aug., mid-Dec. to mid-Jan., Sat. for lunch, Sun. Owned by Boyer family and well-known for its regional cooking. AE, DC, MC, V. *Florence* (M), 43 blvd. Foch (tel. 26-47-12-70). Closed part of Feb., most of Aug., Mon. and Sun. for dinner (except Easter through Oct.). Elegant and well-run, in fine old mansion; wonderfully light versions of classical French repertoire. AE, DC, MC, V. *Foch* (M), 37 blvd. Foch (tel. 26-47-48-22). Closed most of Jan., second half July, to mid-Aug., Sun. for dinner, Tues. Old favorite in another attractive converted mansion; popular locally for newish cuisine. AE, DC, MC, V. *Vigneron* (M), pl. Jamot (tel. 26-47-00-71). Closed most of Aug., Sat. for lunch, Sun. A must for wine-lovers! 17th-century building full of wine labels, old posters, and tools for grape harvest; regional dishes accompanied by marvelous wines.

Boulingrin (I), 48 rue de Mars (tel. 26-40-63-44). Closed Aug., Sun. for supper. Genuine old-style brasserie, always busy; traditional home-cooking. MC, V. *Colbert* (I), 64 pl. Drouet-d'Erlon (tel. 26-47-55-79). Closed Mon. Typical little provincial restaurant; excellent value. AE, DC, MC, V.

At **Châlons-sur-Vesle**, 8 km. (5 miles) northwest, *Assiette Champenoise* (E), (tel. 26-03-14-94). Closed part of Feb., Sun. for dinner, Wed. Country inn in delightful village, with beautifully imaginative dishes. AE, DC, V.

At **Montchenot**, 11 km. (7 miles) south by RN51, *Auberge Grand Cerf* (M), (tel. 26-97-60-07). Closed Tues. for dinner, Wed., last 2 weeks of Aug., Christmas hols. Popular; *nouvelle cuisine* and great champagnes. Good-value *menu* weekdays. Terrace. AE, V.

SEDAN. *Univers* (M), 6 pl. Gare (tel. 24-27-04-35). 11 rooms. Closed Aug., Sun. Right by station, with popular (I) restaurant. DC, MC, V. *Europe* (I), 5 pl. Gare (tel. 24-27-18-71). 25 rooms. Closed Christmas and New Year period; restaurant closed Sun. Well-run, typically provincial hotel, opposite station; good-value restaurant (*Pierre Mouric*, closed Sun. for dinner, Mon. for lunch). AE, DC, MC, V.

Restaurants. *Bon Vieux Temps* (M), 3 pl. Halle (tel. 24-29-03-70). Closed Feb., Sun. for dinner, Mon. Classical cuisine, good ambience. AE, DC, MC, V. *Chariot d'Or* (I), 20 pl. Torcy (tel. 24-27-04-87). Closed Sun. for dinner, Mon. for dinner. Converted coaching inn; some regional specialties.

TROYES. *Grand* (M), 4 av. Maréchal-Joffre (tel. 25-79-90-90). 100 rooms. Opposite station. Has 3 restaurants: *Champagne* (M), for classical cuisine; *Jardin de la Louisiane* (I), for light meals; *Croco* (I), English-style pub. MC, V. *Poste* (M), 35 rue Zola (tel. 25-73-05-05). 33 rooms. Restaurant closed Sun. for dinner. Town-center hotel with very good restaurant, especially for fish, and pizzeria. AE, V. *Champenois* (I), 15 rue Gauthier (tel. 25-76-16-05). 26 rooms. Closed Aug., Christmas and New Year period, Sun. Quiet, a bit out of town; no restaurant. V.

Restaurants. *Bourgogne* (M), 40 rue Général-de-Gaulle (tel. 25-73-02-67). Closed Aug., Mon. for dinner, Sun. Excellent classical cuisine and fine wines. *Valentino* (M), cour Rencontre (tel. 25-73-14-14). Closed mid-Aug. to mid-Sept., first half Jan., Sun. for dinner, Mon. Attractive half-timbered building in pedestrian street; good fish. AE, DC, MC, V.

At **Bréviandes**, 5 km. (3 miles) south, *Pan de Bois* (I), 35 av. Général Leclerc (tel. 25-83-02-31). Closed Sun. for dinner (except in summer) and Mon. Beautiful country house; good-value *menus.* To be discovered. V.

VERDUN. *Bellevue* (M), rond-pont de-Lattre-de-Tassigny (tel. 29-84-39-41). 72 rooms. Closed mid-Oct. through Mar. Traditional spot with good old-fashioned service, large rooms and nice garden; (I) restaurant, dinner only. AE, DC, V. *Coq Hardi* (M), 8 av. Victoire (tel. 29-86-00-68). 42 rooms. Closed Christmas through Jan.; restaurant closed Wed. (except hols.). Very attractive; rooms furnished with antiques; close to river; newish cuisine. AE, DC. *Montaulbain* (I),

4 rue Vieille-Prison (tel. 29-86-00-47). 10 rooms. Closed mid-Dec. to mid-Jan. Peaceful little place near cathedral; no restaurant.

TOURS AND EXCURSIONS. By Bus. The S.N.C.F. and R.A.T.P., as well as the major Paris-based bus companies Cityrama and Paris Vision, have various excursions to Reims and/or Epernay. These usually include a visit to a champagne cellar and to one or more of the World War I battlefields. General de Gaulle's former home at Colombey-les-Deux-Eglises is visited by R.A.T.P., as is Troyes with its interesting modern art museum.

By Boat. Various opportunities for hiring boats or joining river cruises exist, ranging from the basic to luxurious gourmet holidays. Ask at tourist offices for their *Tourisme Fluvial* brochures.

By Car. The two most interesting car excursions are the along the "Champagne Route" and around the battlefields of World War I. The Champagne Route actually comprises three circuits through the main vine-growing areas, each circuit marked in a distinctive color (good maps are available from tourist offices).

The "Green Circuit" starts at Epernay and circles the Côtes des Blancs vineyards, famed for their white grapes, via the D40 and the D10. The "Red Circuit" follows the valley of the Marne, from Tours-sur-Marne to Dormans, via Hautvillers. The "Blue Circuit" starts from Reims and circles the celebrated Montagne de Reims district via the N31, D26 and N44. You may want to visit at least one of the *caves,* or cellars, along the route, some of which are over 24 km. (15 miles) long and date from Roman days. The leading champagne companies are happy to show you around on certain days. A full list, with visiting hours is available from the *Comité Interprofessional du Vin de Champagne,* 5 rue Henri-Martin, 51200 Epernay. English-speaking guides are normally available to take groups around.

Similarly, various marked routes allow you to visit the most famous of the World War I battlefields. The *Voie Sacrée* (Sacred Way) is the best known, and runs from Bar-le-Duc to Verdun. From Reims, it is a short drive to Dormans, site of both the Battles of the Marne, to Château-Thierry and nearby Hill 204 and Belleau Wood. A complete tour of the Battle of Verdun, fought in the heights surrounding the city, includes three itineraries. The first, about 29 km. (18 miles) long, is particularly recommended and includes visits to the forest of Vaux and Douaumont and the Trench of the Bayonets, where an entire infantry battalion was buried alive rather than surrender. The second circuit is longer—about 85 km. (53 miles)—and tours the Argonne, visiting Mt.-Homme, the Butte de Montfaucon, site of an American memorial, the American cemetery at Romagne-sous-Montfaucon and Varennes-en-Argonne. The third circuit is longer still—104 km. (65 miles)—and follows the banks of the Meuse to the crater of the Eparges, Hattonchatel, Apremont and St.-Michel.

Good maps are available from tourist offices of all three circuits.

SIGHTSEEING DATA. For general notes on visiting historic buildings and museums in France—and an important warning—see "Sightseeing" in *Facts at Your Fingertips.*

CHÂLONS-SUR-MARNE. Musée du Cloître Notre-Dame-en-Vaux, rue Nicolas-Durand (tel. 26-64-03-87). Open daily, except Tues. and some public hols., April through Sept., 10–12, 2–6; Oct. through Mar., 10–12, 2–5. Half-price for students and over 65s.

CHARLEVILLE-MÉZIÈRES. Vieux Moulin, housing **Musée Arthur-Rimbaud** and **Musée de l'Ardenne,** quai Rimbaud (tel. 24-33-31-64). Open daily, except Mon., 10–12, 2–6. Half-price for students and over 65s, and for everyone on Sun.

COLOMBEY-LES-DEUX-ÉGLISES. La Boisserie (General de Gaulle's former home), tel. 25-01-52-52. Open daily, except Tues., 10–12, 2–5. Closed one month in winter.

LAON. Musée. Open daily, except Tues. and May 1, 10–12, 2–6 (to 5 in winter).

REIMS. Musée Archeologique (Archeological Museum), 53 rue St.-Simon.
Musée du Tau, beside cathedral (tel. 27-47-74-39). Housed in former Bishop's Palace. Open daily 10–12, 2–6. Closed Tues. and some public hols. Half-price Sun. and public hols., and for those between 18 and 25 or over 60 at all times; quarter-price for children between 7 and 18; free below 7.
Musée-hôtel le Vergeur (Museum of Old Reims), rue Ceres. Open daily, except Mon., 2–6, some public hols., Christmas and New Year.
Salle de Guerre (War Room), 12 rue Franklin-Roosevelt (tel. 26-47-28-44). Open daily, except Tues., mid-March. to Nov. 11 (Armistice Day) only, 10–12, 2–6. No admission charge.

SEDAN. Château. Open daily, Apr. to mid-Sept., 10–6; daily, except Mon., mid-Sept. through Oct., 1.30–5.30; closed Nov. through March. Half-price for students and children under 16.

TROYES. Basilique St.-Urbain (church). Open Sun. 8.30–10, Mon. 8.30–10, 3–4.30, Tues. to Fri. 3–4.30, Sat. 3–6.30.
Musée d'Art Moderne and **Musée des Beaux-Arts.** Both open daily, except Tues. and public hols., 10–12 and 2–6.

ALSACE AND LORRAINE

Storks and Joan of Arc

You may get a shock when you first arrive in Alsace on France's eastern border, and wonder if you have strayed into Germany by mistake. The picturesque old houses with spotless façades enlivened by neatly-tended window boxes, their gabled roofs topped by storks from time to time, the stout women eating coffee and cakes in mid-afternoon, the German you'll often hear spoken, all seem far more German than French. None of this is surprising when you consider that both Alsace and neighboring Lorraine have frequently been under German domination, most recently for four years during World War II. Yet the Germans' attempt to annex the two provinces permanently merely seems to have stiffened the resolve of the Alsatians and Lorrainers, and they remain intensely French in spirit and outlook, as indeed they have always been. It's surely no coincidence that France's patron saint, Joan of Arc, was from Domrémy in Lorraine, or that France's national anthem, the highly patriotic *Marseillaise,* was written in Strasbourg, the capital of Alsace.

Both regions have much to offer visitors: lovely scenery in the Vosges mountains; picture-postcard villages along the Wine Road, where the deliciously grapey Alsatian wines can be savored in delightful half-timbered inns; the art cities of Colmar and Nancy; cosmopolitan Strasbourg, the home of Europe's Parliament; and one of France's most distinctive regional cuisines, too.

Strasbourg, Alsace's Capital

Lively Strasbourg makes a good center for exploring Alsace, with plenty of hotels and a wealth of restaurants to suit all tastes and pockets, though it's an expensive city on the whole thanks to the presence of so many of the new breed of "Eurocrats" on expense accounts. The dominant feature of the skyline is the pink sandstone Gothic cathedral topped by a lofty spire. The area round about is now, fortunately, traffic-free, so you can wander at you leisure, gazing up at the lovely façade and elaborate astronomical clock on the south front, which draws large crowds at noon. The hour is struck by a figure representing death, while the Apostles receive Christ's blessing and the cock crows to signal Peter's denial of his Savior.

Strasbourg is full of interest: medieval streets with carved timbered houses; the impressive château des Rohan (housing the museums of archeology, fine arts, and decorative arts), built in the 18th century for the cardinal, friend of Cagliostro, whose dissolute life shocked Queen Marie-Thérèse; the placid beauty of the district known as La Petite France, crisscrossed by the River Ill, which gave its name to the whole region once known as Ill-Sass; and the Bain-aux-Plantes, dominated by four massive 14th-century square towers, with old gabled houses reflected in the canals that serve as streets; the charming little square, delightfully named Marché-aux-Cochons-de-Lait (Suckling Pigs Market), in which there is a beautiful 17th-century house ornamented by carved wooden galleries.

At the end of the rue du Vieux-Marché-des-Poissons, where the old fish market used to stand, is the grimly named Pont du Corbeau—the Bridge of the Crow—for here it was, in medieval days, that malefactors were executed and their bodies exposed to the voracity of the crows. If you find this too grisly a spot in which to linger, go to the Alsatian Museum just on the right, where a beautiful collection of old Alsatian dresses, furniture and popular art will show you the lighter side of life in old Alsace.

The place Kléber is the liveliest spot in Strasbourg, and a pleasant place in which to sit with a cool tankard of beer, (France's best-known beers come from Alsace). In the nearby place Gutenberg is a statue to the inventor of movable type, Johann Gutenberg, who paved the way for our modern publishing industries by his work here in the 15th century. Not far distant is place Broglie, where, on the site of the present Bank of France, Rouget de Lisle composed the words and music of the *Marseillaise* in a fever of patriotic excitement following a public dinner in 1792. It is interesting to note that the song was first called *Chant de Guerre de l'Armée du Rhin* ("War Song of the Army of the Rhine"), but received its present title when it was adopted by the Provençal volunteers taking part in the storming of the Tuileries in Paris. The port of Strasbourg is one of the most important in France. You can also take boat trips along the Rhine starting from here.

Lying between Saverne, in the valley of the Zorn, and Strasbourg is the region of Dabo-Wangenbourg, which separates Alsace from Lorraine. This is splendidly picturesque country with forests, mountains, valleys, waterfalls and rocky promontories; a replica in miniature of all the natural beauties of both Alsace and Lorraine. Dabo and Wangenbourg, set high in the Vosges Mountains, are sheer delight for lovers of peace and quiet. From either you can see the lovely waterfalls of

Nideck and the tree-covered valley of the Zorn, climb the rock of Dabo and see the majestic panorama from the summit of its chapel dedicated to St.-Léon, or spend peaceful days angling.

Colmar

With its painted and carved old houses, and its Venetian Quarter crossed by the river Lauch, Colmar is one of the loveliest towns in Alsace. The Maison Pfister at the corner of the rue Mercière is a particularly beautiful house. In the Eglise des Dominicains (church of the Dominicans) is the exquisite *Madonna of the Rosebush* by Martin Schongauer, the 15th-century painter and engraver who was born and lived here; his house can also be visited. You will be entranced by the serenity of the 13th-century cloisters in the Unterlinden Museum, a former convent that is now one of the showplaces of Colmar, with a famous altarpiece (the *Isenheim Altar*) by Mathias Grünewald. And do not miss the Maison des Têtes (so called because of the variety of carved heads that ornament its façade). Also worth visiting is the Church of St. Martin, which has some lovely carvings and stained glass.

It is difficult to believe that this picturesque old town could have been the birthplace of Baron Haussmann, the energetic genius who demolished the old roads of Paris to make way for his magnificent boulevards. It is perhaps fortunate that he transferred his activities to Paris and left the wayward charm of Colmar intact.

The town is, incidentally, well known to historians of World War II because at the beginning of 1945 the Germans launched a large-scale offensive (the Battle of the Bulge) to recapture Alsace, forming the "pocket of Colmar" about halfway between Strasbourg and Colmar. The French General de Lattre de Tassigny, supported by several American divisions, reacted vigorously to this danger and forced the Germans to abandon their positions.

Mulhouse and the Crest Road

Mulhouse is a serious and industrial town. Although it can trace its origins to the 13th century, even its Hôtel de Ville, with its magnificent coffered ceiling and stained-glass windows, and St.-Etienne cathedral, again with lovely stained glass, offer little competition to the splendors of Colmar and Strasbourg. It is renowned for its weaving and spinning factories, which give a striking picture of the wealth of Alsace as their enormous chimneys belch forth the smoke that darkens the buildings. The richest deposits of potash in the region lie nearby.

For all this industrial activity, Mulhouse is surprisingly neat and tidy. Well-groomed parts and newly painted window boxes bursting with geraniums might be called the city's trademarks. One of the interesting features of its postwar housing developments is the circular apartment house. Mulhouse was once allied to the Swiss cantons, became an independent republic, and in 1798 voted to ally itself with France. Today it shares an airport with the Swiss city of Basel, and is connected by the Rhône-Rhine canal with Strasbourg, in northern Alsace. It has the National Motor Museum, as well as the Fire Brigade and Rail Museum.

From Mulhouse you can make a magnificent excursion up the superb Crest Road, or Route des Crêtes (built along the 1914 front), from

Thann to the Col de la Schlucht. This road, as its name suggests, links up some of the highest mountains in the Vosges. Two in particular are worth a visit, the Hohneck and the Grand Ballon. Both are accessible by mountain paths to their summits, and the views are truly breathtaking. From the Grand Ballon you can see the Black Forest, and, on a clear day, as far as the Bernese Alps. And, a few miles beyond the Col de la Schlucht, the Lac Vert, glowing like an emerald in its lonely mountain setting.

Markstein, near the Grand Ballon, is a popular winter sports resort. Kaysersberg, on the banks of the river Weiss, charming with its medieval houses, was the birthplace of Albert Schweitzer. The town has a museum commemorating the great humanitarian.

Along the Wine Road

Ribeauvillé, at the foot of the Vosges Mountains, has three ruined castles and vineyards that produce those most delectable of Alsatian wines, Riesling and Traminer. Nests of storks perch on its high towers, and during its delightful annual festival in September with music and dancing a procession proceeds to the place de l'Hôtel de Ville, and wine, flowing from the Fontaine du Vin, is served free.

Obernai, along with Riquewihr and Eguisheim, is very picturesque. Despite the usual summer invasion of tourists, it manages to retain a *gemütlich* charm. Ste.-Odile, patron saint of Alsace, was born here. The convent of Ste.-Odile is a place of pilgrimage as well as one of the most beautifully situated places in the whole of Alsace. The nuns of the convent have installed a guesthouse where visitors may stay as in an ordinary hotel, and this makes an ideal spot from which to visit the region. The tree-covered Mont Ste.-Odile, encircled by its Pagan Wall (nine km./six miles long), whose mysterious purpose and origins baffle archeologists, is a fitting setting for the saint of Alsace.

Picturesquely perched on a peak over 760 meters (2,500 ft.) high is the castle of Haut-Koenigsbourg. Dating from the end of the 15th century—with a 13th-century keep from which there is a magnificent view—it was somewhat over-conscientiously restored by Kaiser Wilhelm II between 1900 and 1908. Nearby Riquewihr is one of the most curious little towns in Alsace, with its ancient houses and medieval walls. The surrounding vineyards produce the famed Riesling wine.

Art Cities of Lorraine

The plateau of Lorraine, with its gentle undulating country watered by the Moselle and the Meurthe, offers a striking contrast to the wild scenery along the Route des Crêtes. But Lorraine has its own charm, and Nancy, its southern capital, with its harmoniously constructed squares and buildings, has the quiet elegance that is always associated with the best in French architecture.

Curiously enough it was a Pole, rather than a Frenchman, who was responsible for much of what is beautiful in Nancy. Stanislas Leszczynski, whose daughter Marie was married to Louis XV, through whom he was elected King of Poland, had to renounce the throne in 1737. As compensation he received the duchies of Lorraine and Bar, which at his death were to devolve on France. Stanislas settled in Nancy, and devoted himself to the embellishment of the city.

The place Stanislas, with its beautiful wrought-iron railings, its perfectly proportioned square and elaborate fountains, will remind you of Versailles. On one side of it is the Hôtel de Ville, with a magnificent staircase leading to the Salle des Fêtes from whose windows the full beauty of the place Stanislas may be appreciated. Opposite is the Arc de Triomphe erected by Stanislas to the glory of his son-in-law, Louis XV. See the ducal palace, built in the 13th century but unhappily much mutilated subsequently by wars and fire. Intelligent reconstruction has saved most of its beauty, and it now houses the fine Lorraine Museum.

The church of the Cordeliers was the traditional burial place of the dukes of Lorraine, and here the pomp and power of these feudal princes, once among the greatest in Europe, are evident in magnificently sculpted tombs in the old church. The tomb of the Duchess Philippa de Gueldre, with its realistic sculpture, is one of the most impressive in France.

From the place Stanislas, the Arc de Triomphe opens on to the superb place de la Carrière, lined with trees and elegant 18th-century houses leading to the Palais du Gouverneur, once the official residence of the governors of Lorraine; to the right is the enormous Pépinière, with its zoo and rose garden.

Little known to foreign tourists, but a definite "must" for lovers of *art nouveau,* is the marvelous Musée de l'Ecole de Nancy, in a quiet residential street. A comfortable turn-of-the-century house, its period décor and fittings still intact, has been converted into a monument to the artists who worked under the inspiration of Emile Gallé. The collection includes masterpieces by cabinetmaker Louis Majorelle and superb glass by the Daum brothers and by Gallé himself.

Lunéville, too, is reminiscent of Versailles. Here it was that Duke Léopold, at the beginning of the 18th century, built a small-scale replica of the château of Versailles, where he imitated on a more modest scale, the magnificence of the French court. The château and the beautiful Parc des Bosquets, with its gardens and fountains, owe much to this genial Polish prince, who was so sensitive to the spirit of 18th-century France.

The northern capital of Lorraine is Metz, a city little visited by tourists, but worth attention nevertheless. Its location, at the junction of the Seille and the Moselle, in which there are several islands, is pleasant. And there are many interesting buildings, especially a number of historic churches. Metz, in fact, has had a long and distinguished history becoming, successively, a great Roman city, the cradle and center of the Carolingian Empire, and an independent republic, before finally joining with France.

Of particular interest are the 7th-century church of St.-Pierreaux-Nonnains, the oldest in France, the 13th–15th-century Porte des Allemands, and the medieval Hôtel St.-Livier and city granary. The Gothic cathedral of St.-Etienne has been described as the "apotheosis of light." The nave, one of the masterpieces of Gothic art, and the stained-glass windows, are especially worth studying.

From the 18th century, when Metz became an important citadel, date the impressive buildings of the place d'Armes, the Porte Serpenoise, and the Esplanade, with its delightful walks along the banks of the Moselle. In the Museum of Fine Arts, part of which is in the Ancient Bath-house, are important Gallo-Roman collections, paintings by 17th-century Dutch masters, and by artists of the French School.

For the past century the region between Metz and Longwy, to the northwest, has been the principal center of the French steel industry.

But in recent years it has suffered increasingly from the world steel recession, and in the winding valleys the great blazing steel furnaces are closing down one after the other. Longwy, an austere, grimy town that lives entirely by steel, leapt into the world's headlines in 1979 when plans were announced for the closure of its main steelworks, and the workers replied with rioting that went on for weeks. New motor factories are arriving in northern Lorraine, but they are not enough to offset the very high unemployment levels in this depressed corner of France where the down-at-heel townlets have the look of having known better days.

Joan of Arc Country

Lorraine is the country of France's patron saint, Joan of Arc. It was in Domrémy that she was born in 1411 or a year later. You may visit her birthplace, and recall that it was in the garden that she heard her voices for the first time, at the age of 13. A single tower remains of the church in which she was baptized.

Near Coussey, Joan of Arc danced with the other children at country fairs attended by Pierre de Bourlémont, the local *seigneur,* and his wife Béatrice—the château of Bourlémont, may still be seen. Associated with Coussey and Brixey are St.-Mihiel and Ste.-Catherine, who, with the Archangel St. Michael, appeared to Joan. In the chapel of Notre-Dame at Bermont, where Joan vowed to save France, are the statues that existed in her time.

The small town of Vaucouleurs recalls Joan's arrival on May 13, 1428 to ask the help of the governor, Robert de Baudricourt. On February 23, 1429, clad in page's garb and her hair cut short, Joan of Arc rode out through the Porte de France to meet her destiny. Here you may visit the ruined château of Baudricourt, the church where Joan often worshipped and the house where she stayed.

PRACTICAL INFORMATION FOR ALSACE AND
LORRAINE

TOURIST OFFICES. The *départements* of both Alsace and Lorraine have regional tourist offices (written enquires only) at the following places: *Alsace*—**Bas-Rhin,** 9 rue du Dome, 67000 Strasbourg (tel. 88-22-01-02); **Haut-Rhin,** 68020 Colmar (tel. 89-23-21-11). *Lorraine*—**Meurthe-et-Moselle,** 4 rue Lyautey, BP 65, 54002 Nancy (tel. 83-35-61-20); **Meuse,** Préfecture, 55012 Bar-le-Duc (tel. 29-79-00-02): **Moselle,** Préfecture, 57000 Metz (tel. 87-30-81-00); **Vosges,** rue Gilbert, 88008 Epinal Cedex, BP 332 (tel. 29-82-48-93).

There are local tourist offices in the following towns: **Colmar,** 4 rue Unterlinden (tel. 89-41-02-29); **Contrexéville,** galeries Parc Thermal (tel. 29-08-08-68); **Gérardmer,** pl. Déportés (tel. 29-63-08-74); **Metz,** pl. Armes (tel. 87-75-65-21), with at the same address a Welcome Information office able to make hotel reservations; **Mulhouse,** 9 av. Foch (tel. 89-45-68-31); **Nancy,** 14 pl. Stanislas (tel. 83-56-50-50), with at the same address a Welcome Information office able to make hotel reservations; **Strasbourg,** pl. Gare (tel. 88-32-51-49), and 10 pl. Gutenberg (tel. 88-32-57-07), also at the conference center (Palais des Congrès), av. Schutzenberger (tel. 88-35-03-00), which has a Welcome Information office able to make hotel reservations.

REGIONAL FOOD AND DRINK. A happy marriage of German gusto and French finesse, Alsatian cooking ranks with the finest in France. *Choucroute alsacienne,* sauerkraut baked with smoked pork, bacon, pork hocks and Strasbourg sausages (very like frankfurters), leads a choice of *zewelwai* (onion quiche), *carpe à la juive* (carp baked with raisins, almonds and white wine), *coq au riesling* (braised chicken in white wine), *baekenoffe* (pork and potato casserole), and a variety of dishes with cabbage *(chou).* Game includes pheasant and wild boar, and their companion wild mushrooms—*girolles* and *cèpes* (boletus). Even the top Alsatian cheese has a German name, *munster,* a soft cow cheese, is notorious for its stunning smell. Noodles *(spaetzle)* and a type of dumpling are a favorite accompaniment. Alsatian fruit pies of plum, apple, billberry and apricot, are equally characteristic, with a custard filling in thick pastry to absorb the fruit juice. Sweet yeast breads are a breakfast favorite, particularly almond and raisin *kugelhopf* baked in a tall ring mold.

The food of Lorraine mirrors that of Alsace with notable local specialties such as quiche, both savory and sweet, roast goose with apples, rum babas, the *madeleines* of Commercy and the macaroons of Nancy (these last good gifts to take home).

The thing to drink with *choucroute* (sauerkraut) is, of course, beer, and it is in Alsace that the best beer in France is brewed. But it would be a mistake to neglect the excellent fruity white wines, particularly delicious in warm weather. Unlike other French wines, Alsatian wines take their names from the type of grape used in making them—Riesling, Traminer, Sylvaner, etc. The ordinary grades are sold under this name alone; the finer wines bear in addition the name of the locality from which they come—Riesling de Ribeauvillé for instance. The best come from Ribeauvillé, Barr, Riquewihr, Ammerschwihr and Turckheim.

Alsace also produces some of the finest liqueurs made from fruit to be found in France—*kirsch, quetsch, mirabelle, pruneau,* etc., and the delicate *framboise,* distilled from raspberries. Unfortunately, they are rather expensive these days.

Currant preserve *(confiture de Groseilles*) is a specialty in Bar-le-Duc. Don't miss the fabulous local dessert, *Duchesse-le-Duc,* consisting of vanilla ice-cream with currant preserve in generous quantities, topped with whipped cream and decorated with sugared violets.

HOTELS AND RESTAURANTS. Strasbourg has the biggest choice of both hotels and restaurants, but prices are high and accommodations can be hard to come by when the European Parliament is sitting. Elsewhere prices are generally reasonable; in fact Alsace has one or two top-notch restaurants known for their value-for-money meals. Motorists will find some attractive country inns offering good regional cuisine and peaceful rooms.

For general notes on hotels and restaurants, see "Hotels" and "Restaurants" in *Facts at Your Fingertips.*

AMMERSCHWIHR. Restaurant. *Armes de France* (E), 1 Grand-Rue (tel. 89-47-10-12). Closed most of Jan., Wed., for lunch on Thurs. One of the best restaurants in Alsace, serving both *nouvelle* and classical cuisine; also has 10 rooms. AE, DC, MC, V.

COLMAR. *Terminus-Bristol* (E), 7 pl. Gare (tel. 89-41-10-10). 85 rooms. *Auberge* restaurant closed mid-Dec. to mid-Jan. With two restaurants: *Auberge* for light meals; well-known *Rendezvous de Chasse* (see below). AE, DC, MC, V. *Colbert* (M), 2 rue Trois Epis (tel. 89-41-31-05). Ask for room on rue Taillandiers; near rail station. Bar-club; no restaurant. MC, V. *Turenne* (I), 10 rte. Bâle (tel. 89-41-12-26). 72 rooms. Modern and central; no restaurant. AE, DC, MC, V.

Out of town, 4½ km. (2½ miles) away, *Auberge Père Floranc* (M), (tel. 89-41-39-14). 13 rooms. Closed first half July, mid-Nov. to mid-Dec., Sun. (except July and Aug.), Mon. Friendly Relais du Silence with excellent restaurant (M), and good wine list. AE, DC, MC, V.

At **Kayserberg,** 11 km. (7 miles) away, *Chambard* (M), (tel. 89-47-10-17). Closed most of Mar., first half Dec., Sun. for dinner, Mon. (except hols.). Modern rooms in a picturesque old town; lovely views and excellent restaurant (mixture of classical and *nouvelle* cuisine). AE, DC, MC, V.

Restaurants. *Rendezvous de Chasse* (E), 7 pl. Gare (tel. 89-41-10-10). In *Terminus-Bristol* hotel, right opposite station; newish cuisine, good service. AE, DC, MC, V. *Fer Rouge* (E), 52 Grand'Rue (tel. 89-41-37-24). Closed first week in Aug., most of Jan., Sun. for dinner, Mon. Attractive old building, very modern cooking, one of the best in town. AE, DC, V. *Schillinger* (E), 16 rue Stanislas (tel. 89-41-43-17). Closed most of July, Sun. for dinner, Mon., except hols. Old favorite, one of the best in Alsace; mostly *nouvelle cuisine.* AE, DC, V. *Trois Poissons* (M), 15 quai Poissonnerie (tel. 89-41-25-21). Closed mid-June to mid-July, Christmas and New Year period, Tues. for dinner, Wed. Naturally enough, specializes in fish. MC, V. *Unterlinden* (M), 2 rue Unterlinden (tel 89-41-18-73). Closed Sun. for dinner, Tues. (except in summer), first 2 weeks Jan. Typical Alsatian cuisine; (I) *menus.*

CONTREXÉVILLE. *Cosmos* (M), rue Metz (tel. 29-08-15-90). 70 rooms. Closed Oct. through Apr. Very comfortable and quiet, in own grounds. Connected with spa building; restaurant. AE, DC, V. *Établissement et Souveraine* (M), (tel. 29-08-17-30). 29 rooms. Closed mid-Sept. to mid-May. Well-modernized old-style hotel, just by spa building, with 2 restaurants, one (M), one (I). AE, DC, V.

DOMRÉMY. Restaurant. *Basilique* (M), 1½ km. (1 mile) out of town (tel. 29-06-93-53). Closed Sun. for dinner and Mon. (except Apr. through Sept.). Good place for lunch when visiting Joan of Arc's birthplace; dishes from southwestern France. V.

EPINAL. *Mercure* (E), 13 pl. Stein (tel. 29-35-18-68). 50 rooms. Comfortable, with good restaurant, *Mouton Blanc* (M). AE, DC, MC, V.

Restaurants. *Ducs de Lorraine* (M), 16 quai Sérot (tel. 29-34-35-20). Closed mid-July to mid-Aug., Sun. for dinner and Mon. Attractive building beside Moselle river, well-known for classical cuisine; also has 10 comfortable rooms. AE, DC, MC, V.

ILLHAUSERN. Restaurant. *Auberge de l'Ill* (E), rue Collonges (tel. 89-71-83-23). Closed Feb. and first week July, Mon. (but open for lunch Apr. through Oct.) and Tues. One of France's very top restaurants, yet reasonable prices; lovely views over river; superb meals and excellent service. AE, DC.

ITTERSWILLER. *Arnold* (M), 98 rte. Vin (tel. 88-85-50-58). 27 rooms. Restaurant closed Sun. for dinner (except July and Aug.), and Mon. Old building with fine views of vineyards, very comfortable rooms and regional specialties in handsome dining room built into the rock face. AE, V.

LANDERSHEIM. Restaurant. *Auberge du Kochersberg* (M), rue Saessolsheim (tel. 88-69-91-58). Closed most of Feb., most of Aug., Sun. for dinner, Tues. and Wed. Luxury inn with excellent cuisine and marvelous wines from own cellar. AE, DC, MC, V.

METZ. *Frantel* (E), 29 pl. St.-Thiébaut (tel. 87-36-17-69). Restaurant closed Christmas and New Year period, Sat. for lunch and Sun. Near station, modern, with stylish airconditioned rooms and good restaurant *(Quatre Saisons).* AE, DC, MC, V. *Royal Concorde* (M), 23 av. Foch (tel. 87-66-81-11). 64 rooms. Closed Christmas and New Year. Comfortable hotel convenient for station; restaurant was closed for modernization at presstime. AE, DC, MC, V. *Cécil* (I), 14 rue Pasteur (tel. 87-66-66-13). 39 rooms. Well renovated rooms; friendly service; no restaurant. V. *Foch* (I), 8 av. Foch (tel. 87-74-40-75). 42 rooms. Simple hotel without restaurant. AE, V.

Restaurants. *Cambout* (M), 1 rue Cambout (tel. 87-74-56-16). Closed Sat. for lunch, Sun., school hols. in Feb. and mid-July to mid-Aug. The new venue in Metz for *nouvelle cuisine* and good fish. Modern decor. AE, DC, MC, V. *Dinanderie* (M), 2 rue Paris (tel. 87-30-14-40). Closed part of Feb., most of Aug., Christmas and New Year period, Sun. and Mon. Best in whole area; good-value *nouvelle cuisine*. V. *Ville de Lyon* (M), 7 rue Piques (tel. 87-36-07-01). Closed Aug., Sun. for dinner, Mon. Old-established and always busy; attractive décor and mostly regional cuisine. AE, DC, MC, V. *Gargouille* (I), 29 pl. Chambre (tel. 87-36-65-77). Closed Sun. and for lunch on Mon. Near cathedral; popular for good-value *menus*. V.

In **Borny suburb,** 3 km. (2 miles) east, *Belle-Vue* (E), 58 rue Pange (tel. 87-37-10-27). Closed mid-July to mid-Aug., most of Feb., Sun., Sat. for dinner and Mon. Old favorite, very popular with locals; newish cuisine. AE, V.

MULHOUSE. *Bourse* (M), 14 rue Bourse (tel. 89-56-18-44). 50 rooms. Closed Christmas and New Year. Central, yet quiet and elegant; no restaurant. MC, V. *Frantel* (M), 4 pl. Charles-de-Gaulle (tel. 89-46-01-23). 96 rooms. Modern and well run, with good restaurant; opposite rail station. AE, DC, MC, V. *Bâle* (I), 19 passage Central (tel 89-46-19-87). 31 rooms. Central, pleasant, with well-modernized rooms; no restaurant. V.

Restaurants. *Relais de la Tour* (M), 3 blvd. Europe (tel. 89-45-12-14). On 31st floor of Tour de l'Europe; revolves to offer superb views; good classical cuisine. AE, DC, MC, V. *Quai de la Cloche* (M), 5 quai Cloche (tel. 89-43-07-81). Closed mid-July to mid-Aug. and one week in Jan. Sun. for dinner, Mon. Delicious *nouvelle cuisine;* a welcome find. AE, DC, MC, V. *Wir* (M), 1 porte Bâle (tel. 89-56-13-22). Closed mid-June to mid-July, and Fri. Charming place with varied menu; also has 43 (I) rooms. DC, V.

At **Steinbrunn-le-Bas,** 8½ km. (5 miles) southeast, *Moulin du Kaegy* (M), (tel. 89-81-30-34). Closed Jan., Sun. for dinner, and Mon. In 16th–century mill, but cuisine is very modern. AE, DC, V.

At **Mulhouse-Sausheim,** by RN422A, 6 km. (4 miles) northeast, *Tissandière* (M), (tel. 89-61-85-85). Excellent menu, some regional food; good *pâtisseries*. Terrace, pool, tennis. Open daily to 10.30. AE, DC, MC, V.

NANCY. *Grand* (E), 2 pl. Stanislas (tel. 83-35-03-01). On lovely square; 18th–century building stylishly modernized; good classical restaurant *(Stanislas)*. AE, DC, MC, V. *Albert Ier et Astoria* (M), 3 rue Armée-Patton (tel. 83-40-31-24). 136 rooms. Central yet quiet twin hotels; sauna; no restaurant. AE, DC, MC, V. *Américain* (M), pl. André-Maginot (tel. 83-32-28-53). 51 rooms. Rooms well equipped. Central; no restaurant. AE, DC, MC, V.

Restaurants. *Capucin Gourmand* (E), 31 rue Gambetta (tel. 83-35-26-98). Closed first half Aug., Sun. for dinner and Mon. *Nouvelle cuisine,* with (M) *menus;* near pl. Stanislas, elegant décor, chic clientele. AE, V. *Gastrolâtre* (M), 39 rue Maréchaux (tel. 83-35-07-97). Closed April to mid-May, Christmas and New Year period, Sun. and Mon. Near pl. Stanislas; famous for regional cuisine cooked in *nouvelle cuisine* style; chic, good value. *Comptoir des Maréchaux* (I), 1 pl. Vaudémont (tel. 83-35-51-94). Closed Sun., Mon., early Jan., after Easter, 2 weeks end of Sept. New, by Grand Théâtre; simple, good-value *menus;* terrace. V. *Nouveaux Abattoirs* (I), 4 blvd. Austrasie (tel. 83-35-46-25). Closed Christmas and New Year hols., Aug. and weekends. Specializes in tasty meat dishes.

At **Liverdun,** 16 km. (10 miles) away, *Vannes* (M), (tel. 83-24-46-01). 11 rooms. Closed Feb., Mon., except public hols. Relais et Châteaux member overlooking Moselle river, and one of best hotels in region; with celebrated restaurant. AE, DC, V.

OBERNAI. *Diligence, Résidence Exquisit et Bel Air* (M), 23 pl. Mairie (tel. 88-95-55-69). Restaurant closed mid-Nov. to mid-Dec. Tues. (except June through Sept.), Wed. Three in one: rooms in three different buildings and all delightful. AE, MC, V. *Duc d'Alsace* (M), 6 rue Gare (tel. 88-95-55-34). 17 rooms.

No lunches; restaurant closed Mon. Friendly and comfortable, with restaurant and regional atmosphere. AE, DC, V.

At **Ottrott**, 4 km. (2½ miles) away, *Hostellerie des Châteaux* (I), (tel. 88-95-81-54). 14 rooms. Closed mid-Jan. to mid-Feb., and Tues. Delightful Relais du Silence on edge of forest; good restaurant (M). AE, MC, V.

Restaurants. *Gilg* (I), 1 rte. Vin (tel. 88-08-91-37). Closed mid-Jan. to mid-Feb., late June and early July, Tues. for dinner, Wed. Unpretentious *winstub*, very good value; also has 11 rooms.

At **Ottrott**, 4 km. (2½ miles) away, *Beau Site* (M), (tel. 88-95-80-61). Closed most of Jan., late June and early July. Mostly beautifully cooked regional cuisine, plus some more modern dishes; also has 14 delightful rooms. AE, MC, V.

RIBEAUVILLÉ. *Tour* (I), 1 rue Mairie (tel. 89-73-72-73). 32 rooms. Closed Jan. and Feb. Converted from a winery and quiet delightful; *winstub* but no proper restaurant. DC, MC, V.

Restaurants. *Clos St.-Vincent* (M), rte. Bergheim (tel. 89-73-67-65). Closed mid-Nov. through Feb., Tues. and Wed. Lovely setting, perched up overlooking vineyards; good classical cuisine; also a Relais et Châteaux hotel with peaceful rooms (E). V. *Zum Pfifferhüs* (I), 14 Grand-Rue (tel. 89-73-62-28). Closed mid-Feb. to mid-Mar., first week in July, Wed. and Thurs. Marvelous *winstub* in splendid 14th–century building; regional cuisine, intimate atmosphere.

RIQUEWIHR. Restaurants. *Auberge du Schoenenbourg* (M), 2 rue Piscine (tel. 89-47-92-28). Closed mid-Jan. to mid-Feb. Wed. for dinner and Thurs. Well-known place in vineyard setting; *nouvelle cuisine* versions of regional specialties. V. *Arbaletrier* (I), 12 rue Gal de Gaulle (tel. 89-49-01-21). Closed Wed. and Jan. Excellent simple and regional food. V.

STRASBOURG. *Hilton* (E), av. Herrenschmidt (tel. 88-37-10-10). 250 rooms. Restaurant *Maison du Boeuf* closed most of Aug., and Sat. for lunch. Deluxe standard; two restaurants, the good *Maison du Boeuf* is (E), *Le Jardin* (M). AE, DC, MC, V. *Kléber* (M), 29 pl. Kléber (tel. 88-32-09-53). 32 rooms. Central, newly renovated; no restaurant. AE, DC, MC, V.

Restaurants. *Buerehiesel* (E), 4 parc Orangerie (tel. 88-61-62-24). Closed part of Feb., most of Aug., over Christmas and New Year, Tues. for dinner, Wed. 17th–century building in lovely Orangerie park; inventive *nouvelle cuisine*. AE, DC, V. *Crocodile* (E), 10 rue Outre (tel. 88-32-13-02). Closed July to early Aug., also Christmas and New Year., Sun. and Mon. Well-known for traditional Alsatian specialties cooked new-style; superb local wines. AE, DC, MC. *Maison Kammerzell* (M), 16 pl. Cathédrale (tel. 88-32-42-14). Closed mid-Feb to mid-March and Wed. Marvelously photogenic building right by cathedral; good regional cuisine and, upstairs, a mixture of classical and "new" dishes; best reserve. AE, DC, MC, V. *Winstub Strissel* (I), 5 pl. Grande-Boucherie (tel. 88-32-14-73). Closed Sun., Mon. and July. Original *winstub* decor, great atmosphere; generous, regional cooking. *Baeckenoffe* Fri. V.

At **Marlenheim**, 20 km. (12½ miles) north, *Cerf* (M), 30 rue Général-de-Gaulle (tel. 88-87-73-73). Closed most of Jan., Mon. and Tues. At beginning of Alsace Wine Road and good for local dishes plus delicious seafood; also has rooms (M). AE, DC, V.

 TOURS AND EXCURSIONS. By Car. The scenic *Route du Vin* (Wine Road) between Mulhouse and Strasbourg was devised by wine producers and civic leaders to introduce tourists to the attractions of Alsace. The main towns are floodlit from May through Oct. There is a topnotch restaurant in Ammerschwihr, and picturesque Ribeauvillé makes a convenient stopover. For a map of the route, inquire at the tourist office in Strasbourg, Colmar or Mulhouse.

By Bus. The *S.N.C.F.* (French Railways) offers the following excursions by bus. From Epinal: *Route des Crêtes* (Crest/Mountain Ridge Road); from Gérardmer: Munster Valley, *Route des Cinq Châteaux* (Five Castles Road); from Lunéville: Baccarat; from Metz: Maginot Line, combined bus and boat excursion including cruise on Moselle river; from Mulhouse: Haut Koenigsbourg, the Rhine river; from Nancy: Lunéville and Baccarat, Domrémy; from Plombières: *Route des Cinq Chateaux;* from Strasbourg: "Flower-filled Villages of Alsace," Wine Road; and from Vittel: *Route des Crêtes et des Chaumes* (Crest/Mountain Ridge and Thatch Road).

Europabus has a day tour following the *Route du Vin* in Alsace. This coach starts from Strasbourg in July and Aug. only, stopping for lunch (with wine of course!). There is also a tour of Villages in Alsace. From Paris, the *RATP* organize a two-day excursion to Strasbourg and the Wine Road in Alsace.

 SIGHTSEEING DATA. For general notes on visiting museums and historic buildings in France, and an important warning, see "Sightseeing" in *Facts at Your Fingertips.*

COLMAR. City walking tours. June through Sept., 3 to 5 tours daily depending on demand. Details from tourist office.

Eglise des Dominicains (Dominican Church), tel. (89-24-46-57). Open daily, Apr. to mid-Nov., 10–6.

Musée Unterlinden, (tel. 89-41-89-23). Open daily, Apr. through Sept., 9–12, 2–6; Oct. through Mar, open daily, except Tues. and most public hols., 9–12, 2–5.

KAYSERSBERG. Maison Schweitzer, tel. (89-78-22-78). Open daily at Easter and May through Oct., 10–12, 2–6.

MULHOUSE. Musée National de l'Automobile (National Car Museum), (tel. 89-42-29-17). Open daily, 11–6; closed Tues.

Musée du Sapeur-Pompier et du Chemin-de-Fer (Fire Engine and Rail Museum), tel. (89-42-25-67). Open daily, Apr. through Sept., 9–6; Oct. through Mar. 10–5.

Verrières de St.-Etienne (Stained Glass museum), pl. de la Reunion. Open Mon. and Wed. to Fri. 10–12, 2–6; Sat. closes at 5; Sun. closed mornings; closed Tues.

NANCY. Hôtel de Ville (Town Hall), pl. Stanislas. *Grand Salons* (public rooms) can usually be visited on weekdays 9–12 and 2–5 but may be closed if meetings are in progress; also open some summer evenings (inquire at tourist office).

Musée des Beaux-Arts (Fine Arts Museum), 3 pl. Stanislas (tel. 83-37-65-01). Open daily except Mon. morning, Tues. and public hols., 10–12, 2–6.

Musée de l'Ecole de Nancy, 36 rue Sergent-Blandan (tel. 83-40-14-86). Open daily, 10–12, 2–5 (2–6 in July and Aug.); closed Tues.

Musée Lorrain, Palais Ducal, (tel. 83-32-18-74). Open daily, mid-June through Aug., 10–12, 2–6; closed Tues. and public hols.; rest of year closes at 5 (6 on Sun.).

STRASBOURG. Cathédrale (tel. 88-35-03-00). Astronomical clock, daily at 12.30 (small admission charge).

Château des Rohan, 2 pl. Chateau (tel. 88-32-48-95). Housing **Musé d'Archéologie, Musée des Arts Décoratifs,** and **Musée des Beaux Arts.** Open daily, Apr. through Sept., 10–12, 2–6; Oct. through Mar., 2–6 daily (except Tues.) and Sun. morning 10–12. Museums also closed on public hols.

Musée Alsacien, 23 quai St.-Nicolas. Same telephone number and hours as Château des Rohan.

Musée Historique, pont du Corbeau. Same telephone number and hours as Château des Rohan.

THE JURA AND
FRANCHE-COMTÉ

Forested Mountains, Eastern Bastion

The Jura Mountains form a huge natural barrier some 240 km. (150 miles) long and 40 to 80 km. (25 to 50 miles) wide that throws its curved length between France and Switzerland. The mountains were known to Caesar, who referred to them in his Commentaries as the Mons Jura. The name Jura is derived from *Juria,* meaning a forest, and no more fitting phrase could be found to describe this region than that of "the forested mountains." It is the name by which the region of Franche-Comté—the "free country"—is generally known to foreign visitors.

Approached from the French side, the Jura-Franche-Comté rises in a series of slopes from the valleys of the Saône and the Doubs to the sparkling, vineyard-covered uplands with the capital of which Arbois, and finally to the Jura Mountains. These fall away abruptly on the Swiss side as they descend to the lakes of Neuchâtel and Geneva.

It's a land where winter lingers long, where the mountain roads make driving hazardous, where wooden toys, clocks and pipes are still made by local craftsmen, a land enchanting and diverse in what it has to offer. Turbulent mountain streams full of trout; remote and beautiful lakes; cool, green valleys; solitary, winding mountain roads whose sides drop away abruptly into sheer precipices; all these you will find in the Jura as you journey from one unpretentious, picturesque little town to the next. Do not miss St.-Claude, famous for its pipes and for diamond cutting, lying amid its wild rugged mountains; Ornans, where the river Loue flows between old houses built on piles; the solitary splendor of the source of the river Lison; the magnificent Cascades du Hérisson in the Jura lake district (the name does not come from the French word for "hedgehog," as linguists might think, but from a Celtic term meaning "holy water"!); the deep Gorges de la Languouette crossed, high up, by a slender bridge; the unforgettable beauty of the source and valley of the Loue. Altogether, the region is ideal for a quiet, budget-priced vacation.

Besançon, Watchmaking Capital

At Besançon, the river Doubs forms a large loop, somewhat in the shape of a pear, completely encircling the old town. The narrow end of the loop is filled by an enormous rock, 120 meters (400 ft.) high, on which towers the ancient citadel. From its summit you can see the town and the river down below, as did the sentries in the citadel as they paced the heights centuries ago. Visit the ancient Roman Grande-Rue, which cuts right through the town, from the cathedral of St.-Jean, at the foot of the rock, to the Pont de Battant, at the other end. Nearly everything worth seeing in Besançon lies along or near this road.

Besançon has a curious mixture of architectural styles, for in addition to indigenous design there are, as in other towns in this district, traces of the Spanish occupation of the region that ended in 1674 when the French successfully reclaimed the Jura following a six-month seige of Besançon. Some of the old houses have beautiful wrought-iron grilles in front of the windows. The 12th-century cathedral of St.-Jean, with its 13th-century Gothic nave, and the subsequent additions and alterations made during the 15th, 16th and 18th centuries, houses the superb *Virgin with the Saints* by Fra Bartolomeo. Opposite is the Porte Noire, a 2nd-century Roman triumphal archway, through which you pass into the Grande-Rue.

Here you will find the Palais Granvelle, a magnificent Renaissance building with a delightful cloistered courtyard. Further on, in the place de la République, is the luxuriantly carved façade of the town hall, the Hôtel de Ville, while not far away, in the place de la Révolution, is the Musée des Beaux Arts, with a fine collection of French, Dutch, Italian, Spanish and English paintings, and an archeological section with Egyptian, Greek and Gallo-Roman remains. Victor Hugo was born in this old street, as were the brothers Lumière, pioneers of the movie camera.

But Besançon is not just a collection of antiquities. It is a busy town, with industries ranging from plastics and cheese processing to the making of the celebrated aperitif, Pernod. Far and away the most important, however, is the watch industry, established in 1893 by Swiss immigrants, though now in financial trouble. Besançon is also a lively town, and rich in the varied beauties of the surrounding countryside. Waterfalls, caves with fantastic grottoes, lakes and wooded hills, can be found within a short distance of the town.

It also has an interesting museum devoted to the Resistance movement in France during World War II and to the tragic deportation by the Germans of Jews and others.

South of Besançon

Nearby is the spa of Besançon-la-Mouillère, with baths for the treatment of bone and circulatory diseases. The salt springs of the region contain an unusually large percentage of iodine, sulphur and iron. Not far away is the Château de Moncley, which still has its original furnishings and some exceptionally fine 18th-century wallpapers.

Ornans, a most attractive village, has a Courbet Museum in the house where the great 19th-century painter and iconoclast was born.

Dôle, the birthplace of Pasteur, is an entrancing little town, halfway between Besançon and Dijon. With its houses clustered around the ancient church of Notre-Dame, its narrow, twisting, climbing streets, the charming place aux Fleurs (with a picturesque flower market), this is essentially a place in which you must *flâner* —stroll idly about. As in Besançon, you will find wrought-iron work reminiscent of Spain. You can visit the house where Pasteur was born and also the local art museum.

Arbois, a little town noted for its wine, has a Pasteur Museum in what was once the family home; among other things you will be shown the vine on which he conducted experiments into spontaneous generation. It also has a Wine Museum in the cellars of the City Hall. The whole area round about is noted for its strange, yellow-tinged wine *(vin jaune)* and for the local "straw wines" (known as such because the grapes are dried on straw)—pause when you sample one of them to remember that Pasteur's discovery of bacteria was helped along by the unusual wines made here! You may also like to visit Arbois's china museum, in an 18th-century mansion, and to plan an excursion to the Reculée des Planches, with fantastic waterfalls and caves.

North of Arbois lies Arc-et-Senans, where you can visit the former Royal Saltworks, built in the 18th century and originally planned to be the center of a most unusual circular "ideal town." The saltworks, which were turned in the early '80s into a cultural center specializing in exhibits and conferences on future studies, now house a Salt Museum; here you will find out about the huge deposits of salt in the nearby Forest of Chaux, a pleasant place to explore. You might even like to stay at Salins-les-Bains, a nice little spa closer to Arbois that again has some fascinating saltworks (the French word is *salines*), as well as a Gothic church and an attractive City Hall.

Lons-le-Saunier, where Rouget de Lisle, author of the *Marseillaise*, the French national anthem, was born, is a typical Jura community. A short distance away is Montaigu, a little village famous for the view it affords of the huge plain. Not far away are the extraordinary grottoes of Baume-les-Messieurs, enormous caves with grotesque rocks. The town has an abbey founded in the 6th century by the Irish monk St. Columban; if you are interested in local crafts make sure to visit the museum devoted to them in one wing of the abbey.

Nantua is attractively situated beside a lake, with mountains sheltering it to the north and south, and you can make relaxed excursions in its neighborhood. Motorboats tour the lake, while the restaurants are renowned for their cooking. *Sauce Nantua,* a delectable pale-pink sauce made with crayfish, is a local specialty that rates as one of the finest in classical French cuisine—don't miss it.

In the extreme southern corner and right on the border of Switzerland, only 13 km. (eight miles) from Geneva, is Divonne-les-Bains, a spa whose casino is popular with the Swiss; it also holds an international music festival each year in the Divonne theater.

Winter Sports Centers

Morez is the kind of resort you find only in the Jura. A long narrow town consisting virtually of only one street, stretching for over a mile in the deep valley of the Bienne, with mountains towering above on each side, it is an ideal winter sports center for those who really want exercise, or merely a rest. This and other Jura centers are family winter resorts par excellence, with plenty of inexpensive accommodations.

The combined facilities of Morez and Les Rousses comprise the Jura's leading winter sports center. Situated only about a mile from the Swiss frontier, it occupies a vast sunny plateau, interlaced with pine forest and dominated by La Dôle, one of the highest peaks in the Jura chain.

Pontarlier, while less spectacular in its setting, is still a splendid spot for winter sports and is becoming more popular yearly. Only 17 km. (11 miles) away is another of the important Jura centers: the Jougne–Les-Hôpitaux-Neufs–Métabief–Mont d'Or group of resorts, on a rolling plateau, with sunny slopes and a magnificent view of the Mont d'Or range. Near Pontarlier, the Château de Joux has an interesting Weapons Museum.

Belfort and Montbéliard

Belfort is not strictly in the Jura for it stands by the Trouée de Belfort, which separates the Jura from the Vosges. It is now a modernized industrial city whose chief interest for the visitor is the superb statue of the Lion of Belfort—22 meters (72 ft.) long and 10 meters (35 ft.) high—dramatically placed at the foot of the high rock upon which the citadel stands. Carved by Bartholdi, who also made the Statue of Liberty in New York, it symbolizes the heroic resistance of the town to the German siege in 1870, when, after much suffering, it surrendered on the orders of the French government. Inside the citadel, built by Vauban, is an art and history museum.

West of Belfort is one of the most famous modern buildings in Europe, built after another and later war. During the offensive to recapture Alsace in 1945 the chapel of Notre-Dame de Haut in the little town of Ronchamp was destroyed. To replace it, Swiss-born French architect Le Corbusier designed a beautiful and original building, which, with its rolled-back roof and "sun-breaker" windows, resembles nothing so much as a ship.

Montbéliard, not far from Belfort, has a castle housing a museum devoted to the famous zoologist and paleontologist Cuvier, and is also the birthplace of the founder of the Peugeot car firm, which can be visited. A few miles away you can see a ruined Roman amphitheater at Maneure; the Château de Belvoir, a well-furnished castle, is also worth a visit. Make sure to visit the Vallée du Doubs, southwest of Montbéliard.

Baume-les-Dames, a peaceful town with a fine abbey church lies halfway between Montbéliard and Besançon, and offers a fascinating excursion to the Grotte de la Glacière, a grotto with weird ice formations visible throughout the year, not just in winter.

PRACTICAL INFORMATION FOR THE JURA AND FRANCHE-COMTÉ

TOURIST OFFICES. The regional tourist office for the Jura and Franche-Comté—written enquiries only—is the *Comité Régional de Tourisme de Franche-Comté*, pl. de la 1ère-Armée-Française, 25041 Besançon Cedex (tel. 81-80-92-55). In addition, the three *départements* of the Franche-Comté also have their tourist offices (again, written enquiries only): **Doubs**, Préfecture de Doubs, 25000 Besançon (tel. 81-81-80-80); **Jura**, Préfecture du Jura, 39021 Lons-le-Saunier (tel. 84-24-19-64); **Haute-Saone**, BP 117, 70002 Vesoul Cedex (tel. 84-75-43-66).

There are local tourist offices in the following towns: **Arbois**, Mairie (City Hall) (tel. 84-66-07-45); **Belfort**, pl. Corbis (tel. 84-28-12-23); **Besançon**, pl. 1ère Armée-Française (tel. 81-80-92-55); **Divonne-les-Bains**, rue Bains (tel. 50-20-01-22); **Dole**, pl. Grévy (tel. 84-72-11-22); **Lons-le-Saunier**, 1 rue Pasteur (tel. 84-24-20-63); **Montbéliard**, 1 rue Mouhot (tel. 81-94-45-60); **Morez**, pl. Jean-Jaurès (tel. 84-33-08-73); **Pontarlier**, Mairie (City Hall), 56 rue République (tel. 81-46-48-33); **St.-Claude**, 1 av. Belfort (tel. 84-45-34-24).

REGIONAL FOOD AND DRINK. The finest local dishes make use of fish and shellfish from the region's lakes and streams, especially trout and crayfish, the game that can be shot in the local forests and mountains and, perhaps best of all, the amazing variety of edible fungi found everywhere in this part of France. *Morilles* (morels) are particularly delicious mushrooms.

Trout are often served with some sort of cream sauce *(truite à la crème)* and watch out for the beautiful pale pink *sauce nantua*, made from crayfish, which can be served with various dishes, including *quenelles de brochet* (a sort of paste or mousse of pike with cream, formed into sausage shapes). A similar dish of pike mousse with crayfish sauce will probably appear on the menu as *soufflé de brochet à la bisque d'écrevisses*. Poultry and pork products are also good, with special local sausages and a famous *pâté-en-croûte* made in Besançon. The local wine is used for several specialties, such as hare *(chaudronnée de Lièvre au vin d'Arbois)* or chicken *(coq au vin jaune)*.

Cheeses widely eaten here spill over from the Alps and include the hard Gruyère-type cheeses and round *Tommes*. Hot cheese fondue is popular, and *Cancoillotte*, a spread made with fresh cheese, white wine and garlic and often served on toast or spooned over potatoes.

The best-known wines are *Arbois, Château-Chalon, Etoile, Pupillin* and *Ménétru*, as well as the yellow wine *(vin jaune)* and straw wine *(vin de paille)* we've already referred to. Like most mountainous districts in France, Franche-Comté and the Jura produce some interesting fruit brandies or liqueurs. You'll find that the local plum and sloe brandies, kirsch and the unusual *gentiane*, distilled from gentians, will make a memorable end to a meal.

HOTELS AND RESTAURANTS. Hotels in this region are mostly small and fairly modest, with few luxury establishments. Most have restaurants and this is where the best meals are to be found. Consequently, the majority of our recommended restaurants are to be found in hotels.

For general notes on hotels and restaurants see "Hotels" and "Restaurants" in *Facts At Your Fingertips*.

ARBOIS. *Paris* (M), 9 rue Hôtel-de-Ville (tel. 84-66-05-67). 17 rooms. Closed mid-Nov. to mid-Mar. Cosy traditional spot with (E–M) restaurant serving inventive cuisine making good use of local produce. Restaurant also closed Mon. for dinner and Tues. AE, DC, MC, V. *Messageries* (I), 2 rue Courcelles (84-66-15-45). 26 rooms. Closed Dec. through Feb. Right by Pasteur's family home; no restaurant. V.

At **Monts-de-Vaux**, 15 km. (9 miles) out of town, *Monts de Vaux* (E), (tel. 84-37-12-50). 10 rooms. Closed Nov. and Dec.; restaurant closed Tues; Wed. for lunch, except in summer. Delightful Relais et Chateaux member on edge of forest; elegant diningroom serves good classical cuisine; half-board terms compulsory. AE.

At **Poligny**, 10 km. (6 miles) south, *Vallée Heureuse* (I), (tel. 84-37-12-13). 12 rooms. Closed second half of June and Oct.; restaurant closed Tues. P.M. and Wed. (except in July and Aug.). Peaceful spot beside trout river on road to Geneva; (I) restaurant.

ARC-ET-SENANS. At Port-Lesney, 7½ km. (5 miles) southeast, *Parc* (M), (tel. 84-73-81-41). 17 rooms. Closed Nov. to Easter. 18th–century manorhouse set in own grounds and now a friendly Logis de France, with restaurant.

Restaurant. *Relais* (M), Grande-Rue (tel. 81-86-40-60). Closed last half June and Nov.; Sun. Family-type meals in modest Logis de France; 11 (I) rooms.

BAUME-LES-DAMES. Restaurants. *Château d'As* (M), route Belfort (tel. 81-84-00-66). Closed mid-Dec. to mid-Feb.; Sun. P.M., Mon, except public hols. Excellent traditional cuisine, lovely garden; also has 10 (I) rooms. AE, V.

At **Pont-les-Moulins**, 6 km. (3½ miles) south, *Levant* (M), (tel. 81-84-09-99). Closed Nov. through Feb.; Sun. P.M. and Mon. Traditional food served in generous portions; very friendly service; also has 15 rooms. AE, DC, MC, V.

BAUME-LES-MESSIEURS. Restaurant. Near caves 3 km. (2 miles) south, *Grottes et Roches* (I), (tel. 84-44-61-59). Closed Oct. through March and Wed. (except July and Aug.). Pleasant spot right by caves and grottoes, with tables outside in good weather.

BELFORT. *Hostellerie du Château-Servin* (E), 9 rue Général-Négrier (tel. 84-21-41-85). 10 rooms. Closed part of Mar. and most of Aug.; restaurant closed Fri. Excellent *nouvelle cuisine;* popular with Swiss gourmets, which may explain the high prices!; rooms are beautifully furnished; big garden. AE, DC, V. *Grand Hôtel du Lion* (M), 2 rue Clemenceau (tel. 84-21-17-00). 54 rooms. Restaurant closed on Sat. from Nov. through Mar.; and for lunch on Sun. Close to old town; modern and comfortable rooms and restaurant. AE, DC, MC, V. *Capucins* (I), 20 fbg. Montbéliard (tel. 84-28-04-60). 35 rooms. Closed most of May, Christmas and New Year; weekends (except in July and Aug.). Halfway between station and Lion, with *brasserie* for light meals and fullscale (I) restaurant. V.

Restaurants. *Pot au Feu* (M), 27bis Grand-Rue (tel. 84-28-57-84). Closed Sun., Mon., Aug., early Jan. Good hearty cooking in old town. MC, V. At **Offemont**, 3 km. (2 miles) north, *Sabot d'Annie* (M), (tel. 84-26-01-71). Closed mid-semester vacations in Feb., Aug., Christmas and New Year; weekends. Small and friendly, with good mixture of classical and *nouvelle cuisine.* AE, DC, V.

BESANÇON. *Altea Parc Micaud* (E), av. Edouard-Droz (tel. 81-80-14-44). 96 rooms. Restaurant closed Sat. for lunch and Sun. Close to fortress and casino, modern, with restaurant, *Vesontio* (M), with good *menus.* AE, DC, MC, V. *Novotel* (M), 22 rue Trey (tel. 81-50-14-66). 107 rooms. Central but pleasantly leafy setting; restaurant for light meals. AE, DC, MC, V. *Moncey* (I), 6 rue Moncey (tel. 81-81-24-77). 25 rooms. Very central, but reasonably quiet; no restaurant. V. *Régina* (I), 91 Grande-Rue (tel. 81-81-50-22). 19 rooms. Closed Christmas to mid-Jan. Small family-type hotel near old town; no restaurant. V.

Restaurants. *Chaland* (M), promenade Micaud (tel. 81-80-61-61). Closed one week in Aug., school hols. in Feb., Sat. for lunch and Sun. On canal boat moored close to fortress; specializes in fish, cooked "new"-style. AE, MC, V. *Relais de la Mouillère* (M), av. Edouard-Droz (tel. 81-80-61-01). Closed Mon. In casino gardens, with open-air terrace for summer meals; mostly *nouvelle cuisine.* AE, DC, V. *Poker d'As* (M), 14 sq. St.-Amour (tel. 81-81-42-49). Closed July, Christmas and New Year; Sun. P.M., Mon. An old favorite; modest décor but good, mostly classical, cuisine. AE, DC, V.

CHAMPAGNOLE. *Vouivre* (M), 39bis rue Gédéon-David (tel. 84-52-10-44). 20 rooms. Comfortable rooms; own grounds, tennis, fishing. Restaurant in summer. AE, DC, MC, V.
Restaurant. *Belle Époque* (M), 54 rue Maréchal-Foch (tel. 84-52-28-86). Closed Nov. through Jan.; Wed, except July and Aug. Good classical cuisine, rather elegant; in *Ripotot Hotel,* but under different management. AE, DC, MC, V.

COL DE LA FAUCILLE. On N5 road, on Geneva side of Col *Mainaz* (E), (tel. 50-41-77-17). 25 rooms. Closed second half June, Nov. through Dec. Very comfortable chalet-style hotel with good classical (M) cuisine; wonderful views over Lake Geneva. AE, DC, V.

DIVONNE-LES-BAINS. *Château de Divonne* (E), route Gex (tel. 50-20-00-32). 28 rooms. Lovely views of Mont Blanc and Lake Geneva; very comfortable, with extensive grounds; excellent restaurant with mixture of classieal and "new" cuisine. V. *Grands Hôtels* (E), Parc des Grands-Hôtels (tel. 50-20-06-63). 145 rooms. Three hotels (called *Golf, Grand* and *Parc*) set in a huge garden with pool, tennis, casino and golf; close to Casino; various restaurants, (M). AE, DC, MC, V. *Bellevue Marquis* (I), av. Arbère (tel. 50-20-02-16). 17 rooms. Closed Dec. through Feb.; restaurant closed mid-Oct. through Apr.; Mon., and Tues. for lunch. Just outside town and very well run; good classical cuisine served in (M) restaurant. AE, DC, MC, V.

DOLE. *Chaumière* (M), 346 av. Genève (tel. 84-79-03-45). 18 rooms. Closed second half June, mid-Dec. to mid-Jan.; restaurant closed Fri. and Sun. P.M., Sat. for lunch. Converted farmhouse on edge of town and close to lovely Chaux forest; attractive dining room. AE, DC, MC, V. *Grand Hôtel Chandioux* (M), 2 rue Besançon (tel. 84-79-00-66). 32 rooms. Restaurant closed Sat. for lunch, Sun. P.M., Mon. for lunch. Well-modernized old building; good restaurant. AE, DC, MC, V.
At **Mont-Roland** 5 km. (3 miles) west, *Chalet du Mont-Roland* (I), (tel. 84-72-04-55). 16 rooms. Peaceful, with good-value restaurant. Closed Sun. for dinner. V.
Restaurant. *Buffet S.N.C.F.* (I), pl. Gare (tel. 84-82-00-48). Closed Thurs. P.M. Good-value meals in station buffet include some regional specialties.

GOUMOIS. *Taillard* (M), (tel. 81-44-20-75). 17 rooms. Closed Nov. through Feb.; restaurant closed Wed. in Mar. and Oct. Attractive country setting near Corniche des Goumois mountain road; restaurant serves good regional specialties. AE, DC, V.
Five km. (3 miles) north *Moulin du Plain* (I), (tel. 81-44-41-99). 22 rooms. Closed mid-Nov. through Feb. Very peaceful spot in lovely surroundings, with restaurant. MC.

LONS-LE-SAUNIER. *Cheval Rouge* (M), 47 rue Lecourbe (tel. 84-47-20-44). 18 rooms. Closed Nov.; restaurant closed Sat. P.M. (except in July and Aug.) and Tues. in July and Aug. Old building with attractive gardens and good restaurant serving *nouvelle cuisine* versions of traditional dishes. DC, MC, V. *Nouvel* (M), 50 rue Lecourbe (tel. 84-47-20-67). 25 rooms. Central, no restaurant. AE, V.
Restaurant. At **Courlans,** 6 km. (3½ miles) west, *Auberge de Chavannes* (M), (tel. 84-47-05-52). Closed second half June, Jan.; Tues. and Wed. One of best in Jura, so must book; picturesque country inn; regional cuisine with some very imaginative touches. AE, DC, V.

MONTBÉLIARD. *Grand Hôtel de Mulhouse* (I), 13 pl. Gare (tel. 81-94-46-35). 45 rooms. Closed Aug., Christmas and New Year. Right by station, an old building gradually being modernized, with restaurant. *Ibis* (I), rue Jacques-Foillet (tel. 81-90-21-58). 42 rooms. Closed Sun. for lunch. Modern and functional, with light meals available. MC, V.

Restaurant. *Tour Henriette* (M), 59 fbg. Besançon (tel. 81-91-03-24). Closed Aug., Sun. except for lunch Aug. through May. Mon. P.M. Very pleasant, with menu divided into classical dishes and some more inventive ones. AE, DC, MC, V.

MOREZ. *Europa* (I), 125 rue République (tel. 84-33-12-08). 30 rooms. Central, with restaurant. V. *Poste* (I), 165 rue République (tel. 84-33-11-03). 46 rooms. Closed mid-Nov. to mid-Dec.; restaurant closed Sun. P.M., Mon. Good value, with attractive garden and good regional cuisine. AE, DC, MC, V.

At **St.-Laurent-en-Grandvaux,** 12 km. (7½ miles) away, *Moulin des Truites Bleues* (E), (tel. 84-34-83-03). 20 rooms. Delightful converted watermill makes marvelous base for visiting Cascades du Hérisson; own forest, trout river, even waterfalls; excellent restaurant, too, serving regional specialties. AE, DC, MC, V.

NANTUA. *France* (M), 44 rue Docteur-Mercier (tel. 74-75-00-55). 19 rooms. Closed Nov. to Christmas; restaurant closed Fri. except Feb., July and Aug. Traditional and very comfortable; fine restaurant specializing in fairly elaborate classical cuisine. MC, V. *Embarcadère* (I), av. Sorbiers (tel. 74-75-22-88). 50 rooms. Closed mid-Dec. to mid-Jan.; restaurant closed Mon. Modern, overlooking lake, with delicious regional dishes, mostly cooked "new"-style; (M) restaurant. V. *Lyon* (I), 19 rue Docteur-Mercier (tel. 74-75-17-09). 18 rooms. Closed first half June, Nov.; restaurant closed Sun. p.m. (except in July and Aug.), Mon. Near lake, with (I) restaurant. V.

ORNANS. *France* (M), 51 rue Pierre-Vernier (tel. 81-62-24-44). 31 rooms. Closed Dec. to Jan. 15; restaurant closed Sun. P.M.; Mon. (except July and Aug.). Modern and comfortable, facing Courbet Museum; friendly atmosphere and good restaurant specializing in tasty wild mushrooms. DC, V.

Restaurant. At **Bonnevaux,** 6 km. (3½ miles) north, *Moulin du Prieuré* (M), (tel. 81-59-21-47). Closed mid-Dec. to mid-Mar.; Sun. P.M., Mon. (except June through Aug.). Lovely converted watermill in gorgeous river-valley setting; really good classical cuisine; also has 8 comfortable rooms in chalets in grounds. AE, DC, MC, V.

PONTARLIER. *Commerce* (M), 18 rue Dr.-Grenier (tel. 81-39-04-09). 30 rooms. Closed first 2 weeks Jan. Newly modernized; overlooks quiet public gardens; restaurant. V. *Grand Hôtel Poste* (M), 55 rue République (tel. 81-46-47-91). 55 rooms. Closed Nov.; restaurant closed Mon. (except July and Aug.); Sun. P.M. 18th-century coaching inn makes pleasant, typically provincial hotel in town center; with restaurant. V.

RONCHAMP. *Ronchamp* (I), rte de Belfort (tel. 84-20-60-35). 21 rooms. Closed Christmas through Jan., Sun. in winter. Modern, with garden; good value, helpful service; no restaurant. V.

LES ROUSSES. *France* (M), 323 rue Pasteur (tel. 84-60-01-45). 34 rooms. Closed mid-Nov. to mid-Dec. Comfortable and pleasant with good restaurant mostly serving *nouvelle cuisine*. AE, DC, V. *Parnet* (M), at Oye-et-Pallet (tel. 81-89-42-03). 18 rooms. On Lake St.-Point. Has good restaurant with regional specialties, great cheeses. (Closed Sun. for dinner, Mon. and Jan.) V. *Christiania* (I), route Porte de France (tel. 84-60-01-32). 25 rooms. Closed May and June, mid-Sept. to mid-Dec. Nice little family-type place, with restaurant.

At **la Cure,** on the Swiss border, *Arbez* (M), (tel. 84-60-02-20). Closed Mon. for dinner, Tues. and June. Good regional cooking; pleasant.

SAINT-CLAUDE. At **Le Martinet,** 3 km. (2 miles) south, *Joly* (I), (tel. 84-45-12-36). Closed Nov. through Jan.; restaurant closed Sun., Mon., (except in July and Aug.). Quiet country hotel beside river; traditional cuisine. v.

TOURS AND EXCURSIONS. By Bus. The S.N.C.F. operate various bus tours around the region from Belfort, Besançon and Divonne-les-Bains. Details are available from regional and local tourist offices and all rail stations.

By Car. A number of specially designated tourist routes have been developed in the Franch-Comté, some—the *Route Horlogère Franco-Suisse,* for example, (the French-Swiss Clock Road)—also extend into Switzerland. Check for details at the Besançon tourist office.

River Trips. There are numerous opportunities for water-borne trips in the Franche-Comté—canoeing, on barges, houseboats, etc.—many also offering a taste of local foods and wine. Details from tourist offices.

SIGHTSEEING DATA. In general, this region of France boasts more natural attractions than man-made ones. Nonetheless, the area has a fair sprinkling of châteaux, museums and other historic buildings. For general comments on visiting museums and historic buildings in France, see "Sightseeing" in *Facts at Your Fingertips.*

ARBOIS. Hôtel Sarret-de-Grozon, 9 Grande Rue (tel. 84-66-07-45). Open June, weekends only, 3–7; daily, July to mid-Sept., 3–7; closed Tues.
Maison Pasteur, rue Courcelles. Open daily, June through Sept., 10–11.30, 2–5.30; closed Tues. and second Sun. in April, May and Sept.
Musée de la Vigne et du Vin (Wine Museum), in City Hall cellars, rue Vieux-Château. Open June weekends only 3–7; daily, July and Aug., 3–7; closed Tues.
Reculée des Planches (Waterfalls and Caves), 4½ km. (2½ miles) east. Open daily, June through Aug., 9–12 and 2–6.30; school Easter vacations, May and Sept. 10–12 and 2–6; Apr. and Oct. open Sun. only 10–12 and 2–5.

ARC-ET-SENANS. Salines Royales (Saltworks), housing **Musée du Sel.** Open daily, May through Sept., 9–6; Oct. through Apr. 9–12 and 2–5.

ARLAY. Château, 12 km. (7½ miles) north of Lons-le-Saunier. Open 10–12, 2–6. Closed Sun. morning.

BAUME-LES-DAMES. Grotte de la Glacière, 19 km. (12 miles) south. Open daily, Easter through Nov., 9–7.

BAUME-LES-MESSIEURS. Musée de l'Artisanat Jurassien. Open daily, July to mid-Sept., 10.30–12.30 and 3–6.

BELFORT. Citadelle (Fortress). Open daily, May through Sept., 8–12 and 2–7. Closed Tues. in winter.
Lion. Open daily, Apr. through Sept., 8–7; Nov. through Mar., 12.30–5.
Musée d'Art et d'Histoire. In château inside fortress. Open daily, May through Sept., 8–12 and 2–7; Oct. through Apr., 10–12 and 2–5; closed Tues.

BELVOIR. Château (tel. 81-91-06-40). Open daily, July and Aug., 10–12 and 2–7; open Sun. and public holidays only, Easter through June, and Sept. through Oct., 10–12 and 2–7.

BESANÇON. Citadelle (Fortress) (tel. 81-82-16-22). Open daily, 9.30–6.

Musée des Beaux-Arts, 1 pl. Revolution. Open 9–12 and 2–6; closed Tues. and some public hols.

Musée Populaire Comtois (Regional Art and Crafts Museum), in citadelle. Open daily 9–1.30 and 1.30–5.30 or 6.30; closed Tues.

Musée de la Résistance et de la Déportation. Also in citadelle. Opening times as above.

Palais Granvelle (housing **Musée Historique**), (tel. 81-81-45-14). Open daily 9–12 and 2–6; closed Tues. and some public hols. Free admission on Weds. and Sun.

DOLE. Maison de Pasteur (Louis Pasteur's birthplace), 43 rue Pasteur. Open daily, Apr. through Sept., 10–12 and 2–6; closed Tues, May 1 and July 14.

Musée des Beaux-Arts, 85 rue Arènes. Open daily, Apr. through Sept., 10–12 and 2–6; closed Tues.; Oct. through Mar., 10–12 and 2–4; closed Mon.

GRAY. Musée Baron-Martin, northwest of Besançon. Open Apr. through Sept., daily except Tues., 9–12, 1–6; Oct. through Mar., 9–12, 2–5.

MONCLEY. Château, Moncley-Recologne (tel. 81-55-04-05). 16 km. (10 miles) northwest of Besançon. Open weekends, July and Aug., 2.30–6.30; open Sun. only, mid-May through June and first half Sept., 2.30–6.30; remainder of year call first for appointment.

MONTBÉLIARD. Château, housing Cuvier exhibit. Open daily, 10–12 and 2–6; closed Tues.

ORNANS. Musée Courbet, rue Froidière. Open daily, Apr. through Oct., 9.30–12 and 2–6; closed Tues.; Nov. through Mar., open weekends and public hols. only, 9.30–12 and 2–6.

PONTARLIER. Château de Joux (housing Weapons Museum), 8 km. (5 miles) southwest of town. Open daily, June through Aug., 9–12 and 2–5 or 6.30 (July and Aug.); weekends only, Apr. through May and Sept. through Oct., 9–12 and 2–5.

RONCHAMP. Chapelle Notre-Dame-du-Haut. Open daily, Apr. through Oct., 9–8; Nov. through Mar., 10–4.

ST.-CLAUDE. Musée du Diamant, 1 rue Gambetta. Open daily, mid-July to mid-Sept., 9.30–12 and 2–6.30.

Musée de la Pipe, beside Diamond Museum. Open daily, June through Sept., 9.30–11.30 and 2–6.30. Same ticket as Musée du Diamant.

 SHOPPING. The best-known local specialty is the pipes from St.-Claude, made in every conceivable shape and size. But other wooden articles are also good buys in this heavily-forested region—look out particularly for toys and elaborate cuckoo, and other, clocks. The watch industry has long been important in Besançon and in spite of current difficulties you may well find this a good place to buy a superbly handcrafted watch.

In the food line, the local wild mushrooms are famous; buy them preserved in tins or glass jars. The unusual "yellow" and "straw" wines of the region make good gifts for your connoisseur friends, or you may prefer one of the tall, slender bottles of fruit brandies or liqueurs. The famous pink *nantua* sauce can be bought too. And if you've enjoyed one of the local *fondues* you might like to choose a *fondue* set as a memento of your visit; various designs and materials available.

CENTRAL FRANCE

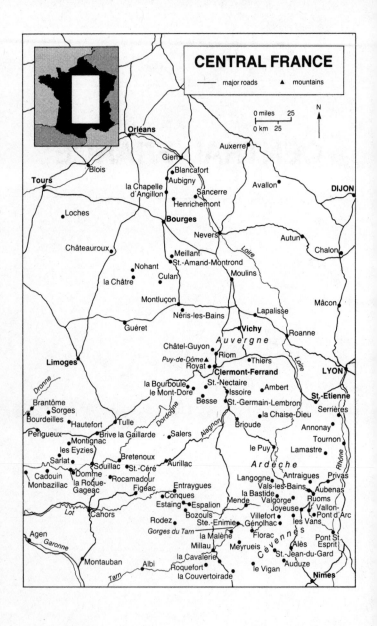

CENTRAL FRANCE

—— major roads ▲ mountains

0 miles 25
0 km 25

N

Orléans
Auxerre
Gien
Blois
Blancafort
Tours
Aubigny
la Chapelle
d'Angillon
Sancerre
Avallon
DIJON
Henrichemont
Loches
Bourges
Nevers
Autun
Châteauroux
Chalon
Meillant
St.-Amand-Montrond
Nohant
Culan
Moulins
la Châtre
Montluçon
Lapalisse
Mâcon
Néris-les-Bains
Guéret
Vichy
Roanne
Châtel-Guyon
Auvergne
Riom
Limoges
Puy-de-Dôme ▲
Thiers
Royat
Clermont-Ferrand
LYON
la Bourboule
St.-Nectaire
St.-Etienne
le Mont-Dore
Issoire
Ambert
Dronne
Besse
St.-Germain-Lembron
Serrières
Brantôme
la Chaise-Dieu
Sorges
Dordogne
Annonay
Bourdeilles
Hautefort
Tulle
Brioude
Tournon
Périgueux
Salers
le Puy
Montignac
Brive la Gaillarde
Lamastre
les Eyzies
Bretenoux
Alagnon
Ardèche
Sarlat
Souillac
Aurillac
Rhône
Cadouin
Domme
St.-Céré
Langogne
Antraigues
Privas
Monbazillac
la Roque-
Rocamadour
Vals-les-Bains
Aubenas
Gageac
Figéac
Entraygues
la Bastide
Joyeuse
Ruoms
Lot
Conques
Mende
Valgorge
Vallon-
Estaing
Espalion
Villefort
les Vans
Pont d'Arc
Cahors
Bozouls
Agen
Rodez
Ste.-Enimie
Génolhac
Garonne
Gorges du Tarn
Florac
Pont St.
la Malène
Esprit
Millau
Meyrueis
Alès
Montauban
Cévennes
Albi
la Cavalerie
St.-Jean-du-Gard
Tarn
Roquefort
le Vigan
Auduze
la Couvertoirade
Nîmes

THE BERRY AND THE
AUVERGNE

The Heart of France

If you tried to pinpoint the very center of France, you would soon find the pin hovering over the Berry and the Auvergne—in fact the villagers of Bruère-Allichamps in the Berry have even set up a Roman milestone to mark what is claimed to be the exact center of the country. Yet foreign tourists tend to skirt around these two central regions, concentrating on the Loire Valley or the Dordogne to the west, the Ile de France to the north, Burgundy and the Rhône Valley to the east or the Midi, the South of France. It's true that the châteaux in these provinces are smaller and often less imposing than those in the Loire Valley or the Paris area, and that the mountains of the Auvergne are less grandiose than the Alps or the Pyrenees. But this is precisely the attraction: everything is on a manageable scale and there is a strong feeling of this being the true France, what sociologists and pollsters like to call *la France profonde* (a term roughly equivalent to their U.S. counter-parts' references to "middle America" or the "silent majority"), the middle-of-the-road rural France where you can really get to know the country and its people, where age-old traditions and customs have been preserved more or less intact.

Exploring the Berry: Bourges

Nowhere is this sense of inherited traditions stronger than in the peaceful countryside of the Berry, an often mysterious region where sorcery and witchcraft are still said to be rife. Its chief city is Bourges, whose marvelous cathedral of St.-Etienne easily rivals those of Amiens, Chartres or Rouen, yet receives far fewer tourists. It makes an excellent base from which to visit the region, but make sure that you allow plenty of time to visit the city itself.

Once the Gallo-Roman capital of Aquitaine, Bourges enjoyed another period of glory in the 15th century, when Charles VII had to flee from the invading English armies and made the city the temporary capital of his kingdom. The most dashing figure in Bourges at that period was Jacques Coeur, a wealthy merchant who became Charles's treasurer, before eventually falling into disfavor leading to exile and death in a foreign land. His sumptuous Renaissance palace is still standing, however, and you will find that his name is always cropping up in and around Bourges, not least because his surname, which means "heart," makes a handy symbol for this region at the heart of France. But Bourges also owes a major debt to Jean, Duc de Berry, whose marvelous *Book of Hours,* the *Très Riches Heures de Berry,* is the glory of the Musée Condé in Chantilly Château. He turned Bourges, the capital of his dukedom, into an unrivaled center of the arts and culture in the late 14th and early 15th centuries.

Start by visiting the cathedral, with its wonderful stained glass and superbly intricate west front adorned with Romanesque and Gothic carvings. A recumbent statue of the Duc de Berry can be seen in the crypt. Next on the list comes Jacques Coeur's Palace, rightly acclaimed one of the finest secular buildings in France. The scene is nicely set by the carved figures that seemingly lean out of windows over the entrance to greet you, and the whole complex is richly adorned with carvings as befitted the residence of the wealthiest private citizen in the kingdom. Sadly, though, he had little time to enjoy it. The city has many other attractive old buildings, two of which also house museums: the Renaissance Hôtel Cujas is the home of the Berry Museum, with good local history and archeology collections, and the Hôtel Lallemant, again dating from the Renaissance, devoted to decorative or applied art.

The Route Jacques-Coeur

The colorful Jacques Coeur, with his conveniently symbolic name, has been pressed into service by some of the local château owners for the association they have founded to encourage tourists to visit their beautiful castles and manor houses and help in their struggle to preserve their heritage in an age of escalating costs. One of the many attractions of the Route Jacques-Coeur is that its privately-owned châteaux are still lived in. If, like many visitors, you have been a trifle disappointed by the coldness and emptiness of most of the great Loire châteaux, however breathtakingly lovely their architecture and setting, you will be delighted to spot such personal touches as family photographs and drinks trays in the reception rooms of the Berry châteaux.

This pleasant sense of visiting a private home, rather like the stately homes of England or Scotland, applies for instance to Menetou-Salon, a château just north of Bourges that was briefly the home of Jacques Coeur. It has a distinct Scottish baronial-hall quality to it, with its animal paintings and hunting trophies, and it seems appropriate, given her Scottish ancestry, that it is often visited by the Queen Mother of England—you can see her photograph in the drawing room. The château was initially inspired by the Palais Jacques-Coeur in Bourges, but was extensively rebuilt in the 19th century; it has some outstanding Flemish tapestries and a tiny chapel with some interesting examples of early-Italian art. In the grounds is an Automobile Museum, started by the grandfather of the present owner, a well-known racing driver.

The pride of nearby Château Maupas, built in the 15th century on Gallo-Roman foundations, is a superb collection of nearly 900 plates dating from the 17th to the 19th centuries—all the major French china workshops and styles are represented. Many other exhibits are connected with the celebrated Duchesse de Berry and her son the Comte de Chambord (one of the Marquis de Maupas was his tutor). Don't miss the pretty formal garden or the well-preserved kitchens. La Borne, a village close by, specializes in pottery, while Henrichemont is worth visiting for its unexpectedly large central square, which seems oddly like a stage set waiting in vain for the actors to arrive. The explanation is simple: the town was built by the energetic financier Sully and named for Henri IV (the name is a distortion of *Henrici Mons,* Henry's Hill), but was never completed due to the king's assassination.

East of Henrichemont lies Sancerre, an attractive town perched on a vine-covered hill with a 15th-century keep and some picturesque old houses, which gives its name to the excellent light white wine produced in this pleasantly hilly area. The village of Chavignol, a mile or so away, is another landmark on the gourmet map of France: the mouthwatering little round goat's cheeses called *crottins de Chavignol* are made here. Also nearby is the small but imposing Château of Boucard, pleasingly reflected in its moat. It is built round an elegant Renaissance courtyard and has one of the earliest staircases in France to be built with a landing. Concerts are held here in the summer months.

Another lovely courtyard is an attractive feature of La Verrerie, a château near Aubigny-sur-Nère, a small town worth visiting for its old gabled houses. Both the village and the château were long connected with the Stuart clan, one of whom built the present château in the 15th century. An Italianate Renaissance gallery and a chapel with interesting frescoes and decorated with the Scots thistle are among the delights of this château, one of several in the area where you can sample *la vie de château* by staying in one of the charming guest rooms or enjoying a meal in the tiny restaurant in the grounds presided over by the owners. Another historic château in this area is elegantly furnished pink-brick Blancafort, with a lovely formal garden and a very rare wooden spiral staircase.

Further north, the lively town of Gien, on the banks of the Loire, has a most attractive modern church devoted to France's patron saint, Joan of Arc, nestling up to the huge castle housing the International Hunting Museum. Even if hunting normally leaves you cold, you are bound to be fascinated by this well-planned museum, with its wonderful paintings of "the chase," still-lives, hunting trophies, weapons and tapestries. Gien is also famous for its faïence china, which you will see in many local shops; you can also buy it from the main workshops.

The Berry is a fitting place for a hunting museum, for it lies on the edge of the hunting-shooting-and-fishing region of the Sologne, whose desolate beauty is so memorably captured in Alain Fournier's magical novel *Le Grand Meaulnes*. If you are one of his admirers, don't miss La Chapelle d'Anguillon, where his parents' schoolhouse can still be seen, or the local château which houses a museum connected with him.

Literary associations are even stronger at Nohant, a delightful village where the Romantic novelist George Sand spent much of her time and received all the literary lions of her day. Her château can be visited. Nohant lies west of St.-Amand-Montrond, a pleasant market town around which the Route Jacques-Coeur châteaux south of Bourges are grouped. One of them is not in fact a château but an abbey, the stately Cistercian Abbaye de Noirlac, founded in 1137. This is one of the purest examples of the sober, unadorned Cistercian style as advocated by St. Bernard, with its graceful cloisters and the harmonious lines of its church and main rooms. As with many of the Jacques-Coeur buildings, temporary cultural exhibits are held here, as well as occasional concerts.

Close to Noirlac the Château de Meillant is a definite must for its richly-decorated Late Gothic/Early Renaissance façade dominated by the Tour du Lion, or Lion's Tower, a three-story staircase tower. The much plainer medieval eastern façade that faces you as you approach via the main gate does little to prepare you for the exuberance of the courtyard façade or the rich furnishings inside. Another surprise awaits you at Ainay-le-Vieil as you pass through the fortified gateway of a stern octagonal medieval fortress surrounded by a moat to enjoy the delights of a graceful Renaissance courtyard. The château has been owned and lived in by the same family since 1467 and is crammed with historical exhibits and mementoes. The main reception room, the Grand Salon, still has the decoration planned in honor of a visit by King Louis XII and Anne de Bretagne, and leads into a charming little Renaissance chapel.

The medieval fortress aspect predominates at Château Culan, a mighty stronghold with towers crowned by well-preserved wooden defensive hoardings; it is magnificently furnished with tapestries and furniture collected by its antique-dealer owner. Very different is Jussy-Champagne, another Route Jacques-Coeur château nearer to Bourges, whose harmonious brick-and-stone façade is most photogenically framed in lovely wrought-iron gates as you approach the drive. The impressive 17th-century stone fireplace encrusted with marble is well set off by 18th-century paneling and lovely painted overdoors. The pastoral landscape round the château is ideal for walking or picnicking before you return to Bourges or St.-Amand-Montrond. But on summer evenings one final treat lies in store: many of the châteaux stage magical evening visits lit solely by candlelight, sometimes accompanied by small-scale historical tableaux or pageants. Don't on any account miss this "illuminated fairyland" as the brochures poetically, but rightly, describe it.

Exploring the Auvergne

The Auvergne lies mainly in the Massif Central, France's mountainous heartland, with a rich geological heritage fashioned over the centuries by volcanic upheavals. It has six volcanoes as little—geologically speaking—as 10,000 years old, one of them, Sancy, ten times the size of Italy's Vesuvius. Yet the Auvergne's heritage, in spite of its lakes, and mountains, its lush green fields, its gorges and rivers, is not solely nature's responsibility. Few tourists realize that it has as many as 500 châteaux, ranging from imposing fortresses such as Murol to ruined 12th-century Tournoël, crushed by Richelieu, and majestic Parentignat, which has been owned by the same family since it was built during the reign of the Sun King. This part of France also has some particularly interesting Romanesque churches, with perhaps the finest at St.-Nectaire, Issoire and Orcival.

Yet the Auvergne has much else to offer, especially for those who like outdoor pursuits such as hiking and rambling, riding, fishing or canoeing—plus the sort of filling, rustic dishes that you need after a day in the open air! It is becoming an increasingly important skiing center, too, popular with those looking for energetic family holidays at reasonable prices, who prefer ski to *après-ski*.

But this is not solely a place for unsophisticated enjoyment, even if many of the French still persist, against all the evidence, in thinking of the sturdy Auvergnats as worthy but dull peasants. Spas are plentiful here (Vichy is the best-known, but La Bourboule, Châtel-Guyon and Royat are all major watering places too). Like spas all over the world, they have a full calendar of galas and concerts, golf championships and tennis tournaments. And, again like all spas, they have casinos. If you want grand hotels and smart restaurants you will obviously be better off here than in the more rural districts, but you won't necessarily eat better: the hard-working Auvergnats have a tradition of good eating and indeed run many of the best regional restaurants in Paris.

It should be remembered, however, that the Auvergne does have its modern aspect too. Clermont-Ferrand, its capital, has long been the capital of the tire industry as well: the great Michelin factory has been here since 1886. There are important hydro-electric plants, harnessing the region's mighty torrents, along with the metallurgical and chemical industries. These new industries have inevitably pushed into the background the region's traditional crafts, chief of which is lace-making, but a recent swing away from mass-produced goods to traditional craftsmanship is reviving some of them.

Montluçon, Moulins and Vichy

The Auvergne is usually approached from the west or the north. You may like to start in the northwest of the region with Montluçon, a delightful town dominated by the Ducs de Bourbons' château, built during the Hundred Years' War. The château houses two little museums, one devoted to the Bourbonnais region round about, tracing its history, natural history and art, the other, believe it or not, to the hurdy-gurdy, that apparently most humble of musical instruments, but here seen in marvelously elaborate and heavily ornamented versions. The view from the château's terrace takes in first the Vieux Montluçon, the Old Town, with its narrow streets coiling picturesquely round the château, then the distant hills that mark the beginning of the Massif Central.

After strolling through the old streets you might like to take in the nearby countryside. A few miles south is Néris-les Bains, an attractive spa town that has been attracting sufferers from various ailments since Roman times, while various pretty villages and manor houses can be visited within a radius of only a few miles round Montluçon.

Northeast of the town, old Moulins, with its narrow cobbled streets, has a famous triptych by the Maître de Moulins in its cathedral. To the south lies Vichy, one of the world's most famous watering places, with its well-kept flower beds and shady parks situated on the right bank of the Allier. The Romans were the first to appreciate the benefits of Vichy's nine springs. The famous Source des Célestins, whose bottled waters enjoy a worldwide reputation, produces over 204,570 liters (45,000 gallons) a day. The waters are strongly alkaline and are particularly recommended for digestive troubles. You can visit the Grand Etablissement Thermal.

The triangular Vieux Parc is the fashionable center of Vichy, a favorite promenade before the apéritif hour and during the evening. In the old part of the town is the striking church of St.-Blaise, a modern building of unconventional design built on to the old church. Inside, notice the glass and the murals of the cathedrals of France. At the 12th–16th-century Château Lapalisse, north of Vichy, you can watch an historical pageant on summer weekends.

Thiers and Riom

Thiers, 35 km. (22 miles) to the southeast and built on the crest of a rocky ravine, has been the cutlery capital of France since the Middle Ages. Every other shop displays knives of every shape and size at reasonable prices. But the town's many half-timbered houses are also a tourist attraction, as is the picturesque place Pirou dominated by the 15th-century Château Pirou.

Southwest of Vichy, on the road to Clermont-Ferrand, is the small town of Riom, with many Gothic and Renaissance art treasures, including lovely stained glass in the church of St.-Pierre and in the Palais de Justice. From the feudal ruins of the Château of Tournoël nearby there is a spectacular view over three plateaux. The Château of Chazeron, not far from Riom, was used as a prison during World War II and is now a cultural center where you can buy works of art; the views over the Lower Auvergne are superb.

Clermont-Ferrand and the Puy-de-Dôme

Lively Clermont-Ferrand, at the crossroads of the Massif Central, has a famous early Gothic cathedral, and its 12th-century basilica of Notre-Dame-du-Port, with its curious roof, is an admired example of the Auvergnat Romanesque style. Also worth visiting are the Ranquet Museum, displaying regional costumes and art, and the Fontaine d'Amboise.

The outstanding sights in this area are the ruins of the Roman Temple of Mercury and the view from the top of the Puy-de-Dôme. The panorama is really exceptional, with its succession of wooded *puys* (peaks of porous domite—a name derived from this area) rolling away before the eye. There are crater depressions on the summit of each, a reminder of the days when the volcanoes were active.

The Mont-Dore Region—Spas and Winter Sports

The spa town of St.-Nectaire, surrounded by wooded hills, boasts a beautiful Romanesque church. Nearby is the delightful resort of Murol with lovely Lake Chambon, a medieval château perched on a small hill, and a splendid view of Mont-Dore.

Excursions from here will take you to Orcival, with a beautiful church, and to Lake Guéry. Near Besse-en-Chandesse, in the heart of the region of ancient craters, lie the lovely lakes of Pavin, Chauvet, Contat-en-Féniers, St.-Amandin and Riom-ès-Montagne. Giving off reddish-brown reflections, they are surrounded by blue fir trees, villages of black lava, and enormous cattle farms with buildings made of lava and slate. Le Mont-Dore and La Bourboule are health resorts noted particularly for respiratory cures, and are starting points for many trips into the mountains.

The top winter sports resort in the Massif Central is Le Mont-Dore. The slopes are gentler than in the Alps or the Pyrenees, attracting beginners as well as those who prefer quieter places, smaller crowds, and lower prices.

To the south begins the ascent toward the Monts de Cantal, a popular region with skiers and hikers. Glacier valleys furrow out from the enormous bulk of the range and you can follow one of them straight toward the triangular pyramid of Puy Mary. The way down lies to the south, through the Mandaille Valley, a land of pastures and forests.

Salers is a well-preserved medieval village and the home of Cantal cheese. The fortified walls were designed by a Marshall Lafayette, an ancestor of the Lafayette who fought in the American Revolution.

Le Puy and the Southeast

Le Puy lies on the southeastern edge of the Auvergne, north of the wild Allier Valley, where the landscape suggests a Chinese painting with a high broad plateau broken by red humped domes or *puys.* In the fertile valley, cultivated yellow and tan squares lie like carpets spread over emerald hills.

The location of Le Puy is extraordinary. Four precipitous volcanic outcrops rise from the narrow plain: on the lowest, guarding the western approach, is a statue of St. Joseph and the Infant Jesus; the 11th-century chapel of St.-Michel balances precariously on the highest outcrop; on another peak dominating the town and the cathedral stands a huge statue of the Virgin, Notre-Dame-de-France, erected in 1860 from melted-down Russian cannon captured at Sebastopol during the Crimean War. Atop the fourth pinnacle sits an incredible Romanesque cathedral, Notre-Dame-du-Puy, built of polychrome lava. It is approached by a long flight of stone steps, affording a wonderful view of the narrow slanted street directly below, and the green landscape that rolls away into the distance. Its nave, also polychrome, is reminiscent of some Islamic mosque; the Black Virgin worshipped here recalls the ancient cult of Isis. Don't miss the elaborately penned bible of Théodulfe, one of the most precious specimens of Carolingian calligraphy, or the remarkable fresco of St.-Michael in the lovely cloisters, much influenced by the Moorish style, with their use of alternating black and white stones. (Note the beautiful Romanesque iron gate). The great medieval hilltop chateau of Polignac is 13 km. (eight miles) west of Le Puy.

Some 40 km. (25 miles) further north, in the middle of a high plateau covered with woods and pastures, lies the town of Chaise-Dieu, with a famous church, St.-Robert. Its frescoes of the *Danse Macabre,* splendidly drawn in red and black, represent Death dancing with the nobility, the bourgeoisie and the working folk. The huge Gothic cloisters and the choir with its beautiful early 16th-century Brussels and Arras tapestries and some 150 carved oak choirstalls are also worth seeing. A festival of sacred art is held here every summer.

Due north, some eight km. (five miles) from Ambert, is the Moulin Richard-de-Bas paper mill, with an interesting museum that illustrates both the history and method of manufacturing handmade paper. Ambert itself has given its name to a cheese, *fourme d'Ambert*, considered by connoisseurs to be one of France's finest blue cheeses. The small town has retained its 16th-century appearance and atmosphere centered on the circular town hall.

On the way from Le Puy to Clermont-Ferrand, at Brioude, where the Allier Valley and the fertile plain of Limagne meet, is another beautiful church. From here you can follow the winding green gorge of the river Alagnon north to St.-Germain-Lembron. On a nearby hill are the ruins of the Château of Nonette, dismantled by Richelieu.

Further north is the prosperous and cheerful town of Issoire with a remarkable 12th-century church, St.-Paul. It was almost completely razed to the ground in 1577, at the time of the Wars of Religion, by order of the Duc d'Alençon, son of Henri II. The work done, he ordered an inscription to be put up in the main square reading: "Here was Issoire."

PRACTICAL INFORMATION FOR THE BERRY
AND THE AUVERGNE

TOURIST OFFICES. The principal regional tourist office for both the Berry and the Auvergne—written enquiries only—is the *Comité Régional du Tourisme,* 45 av. Julien, BP 395, 63011 Clermont-Ferrand (tel. 73-93-04-03). In addition, the *départements* of both regions also have their own tourist offices (again, written enquiries only). These are: *Berry* —**Cher,** Préfecture, pl. M.-Plaisant, 18014 Bourges (tel. 48-24-14-95); **Indre,** rue Bourdillon, 36000 Chateauroux (tel. 54-22-91-20). *Auvergne* —**Cantal,** Préfecture, 15000 Aurillac (tel. 71-48-53-54); **Haute-Loire,** Hotel du Département, av. Charles-de-Gaulle, 43000 Le Puy (tel. 71-09-26-05); **Puy-de-Dome,** 69 blvd. Gergovia, 63038 Clermont-Ferrand (tel. 73-93-84-80).

There are local tourist offices in the following towns: **Basse-en-Chandesse,** Le Grand-Mèze (tel. 73-79-52-84); **La Bourboule,** pl. Hôtel-de-Ville (tel. 73-81-07-99); **Bourges,** rue Moyenne (tel. 48-24-75-33); **La Chaise-Dieu,** pl. Mairie (tel. 71-00-01-16); **Clermont-Ferrand,** 69 blvd. Gergovia (tel. 73-93-30-20), and another office at rail station; **Le Mont-Dore,** av. Général-Leclerc (tel. 73-65-20-21); **Montluçon,** 1 av. Marx-Dormoy (tel. 70-05-05-92); **Moulins,** pl. Hôtel-de-Ville (tel. 70-44-14-14); **Le Puy,** pl. Breuil (tel. 71-09-38-41); **St.-Amand-Montrond,** pl. République (tel. 48-96-16-86); **Salers,** pl. Tissandier d'Escous (tel. 71-40-70-68), (closed mid-Sept. through May); **Sancerre,** Mairie (town hall), (tel. 48-54-00-26); **Vichy,** 19 rue Parc (tel. 70-98-71-94).

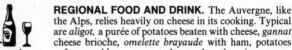

REGIONAL FOOD AND DRINK. The Auvergne, like the Alps, relies heavily on cheese in its cooking. Typical are *aligot,* a purée of potatoes beaten with cheese, *gannat* cheese brioche, *omelette brayaude* with ham, potatoes and cheese, and *tarte au fromage blanc,* a sweet cheesecake otherwise uncommon in France. But the Auvergne is also famous for charcuterie, particularly coarse-grained *saucissons secs* (dried salami sausages) and the local smoked raw hams.

Pork is the staple meat, appearing in stews like *potée* with ham, bacon, and cabbage, *petit salé aux lentilles* (salt pork with lentils) and *le pounti,* an egg flan with ham and Swiss chard or spinach. Puff pastry pies are popular, filled with anything from salmon to chicken, potatoes or pears. Fruit tarts, made with wild bilberries and raspberries, are a summer treat, while year-round pick-me-ups include liqueurs brewed from fruits and roots like *gentiane.* Try one with a *croquant* hazelnut biscuit cake for dipping, or a *cornet de Murat* rolled wafer.

The cheeses of Auvergne range widely from *Cantal,* a hard cheddar-type, to the blue *Fourme d'Ambert* and *Bleu d'Auvergne* to the creamy *St.-Nectaire,* and *St.-Marcellin,* plus a cluster of goat cheeses. Most famous of all is *Roquefort* from the Aveyron in southern Auvergne, a blue sheep's cheese which is aged in limestone caves to give it its unique mold. Genuine *Roquefort* has a little red sheep on the label. Although the Auvergne vineyards are not of the first rank, they do produce a number of acceptable wines, such as *Châteaugay, Corent, St.-Pourcain,* and *Chanturges.*

Berry's cuisine, or *cuisine berrichonne,* is mostly straightforward country fare based on slowly braised or stewed dishes, many using the game that is so plentiful in the local forests. The best-known recipe is *poulet en barbouille,* chicken served with a thick dark sauce made from its blood simmered gently with the crushed liver, cream, egg yolks, and sometimes wine and brandy too. *Pâté de Pâques,* an Easter meat pie made in various different ways, *sanciau,* a cross between an omelet and a pancake, which may be either savory or sweet, are other local specialties. Make sure to try the famous *crottin de Chavignol,* goat's cheese made near Sancerre, too. For dessert, a sweet *sanciau,* and black cherry tarts, are common.

Sancerre wines are among France's finest, with a light grapey flavor. Most are white, but there are a few reds. Try too the less well-known *Menetou-Salon,* which is becoming popular abroad.

 HOTELS AND RESTAURANTS. The Berry and Auvergne region has a number of top-notch "grand hotels" of the old school—now extensively modernized—in spa towns such as Vichy, but on the whole, however, the region is known for good-value modest inns and town-center hotel-restaurants, so delightfully typical of provincial France. It is significant that the France-Acceuil association of small, family-type hotels started in the Auvergne, though it has now spread all over France. This is also an area with many *gîtes* and other forms of self-catering accommodations: the Auvergne has well over 2,000 official *gîtes* and many other unofficial ones.

For general notes on hotels and restaurants, see "Hotels" and "Restaurants" in *Facts at Your Fingertips.*

Châteaux Accommodations. This part of France has several private historic châteaux offering delightful rooms, suites or even whole wings to guests, who will receive a warm personal welcome from the aristocratic owners, and all the information they require on excursions, sports facilities and cultural activities. In some cases, on advance request, guests can also enjoy a meal with the owners and their family. We give details of a few such private châteaux in our hotel lists, but be warned that it is advisable to reserve well in advance.

AUBIGNY-SUR-NÈRE. *Cheval Blanc* (I), 9 km. (5½ miles) west on D13 (tel. 48-58-06-92). 18 rooms. Traditional; good base. Pleasant, simple restaurant.

At **La Verrerie-Oizon,** 10 km. (6½ miles) southeast, *Château de la Verrerie* (E), (tel. 48-58-06-91). 6 rooms. Closed Oct. through Mar. Comfortable accommodations in historic private château once lived in by the Stuarts; large grounds with tennis, pool, canoeing, riding.

Restaurant. At **La Verrerie-Oizon,** 10 km. (6½ miles) southeast, *Maison d'Hélène* (M), château de la Verrerie (tel. 48-58-06-91). Closed mid-Oct. to mid-June, and Tues. In grounds of the lovely château, a tiny farmhouse converted into a charming restaurant supervised by the châtelaine. AE, DC.

BESSE-EN-CHANDESSE. *Mouflons* (M), rte. Super-Besse (tel. 73-79-51-31). 50 rooms. Closed Oct. through May, Sun. for dinner and Mon. (except in July and Aug.). Well-run modern hotel with large garden and good restaurant (lovely views). AE, V. *Gazelle* (I), rte. Compains (tel. 73-79-50-26). 29 rooms. Closed May and mid-Oct. to mid-Dec. Modest family hotel with restaurant and lovely views.

At **Super-Besse,** 7 km. (4½ miles) west, *Gergovia* (M), (tel. 73-79-60-15). 50 rooms. Closed mid-Apr. through June and Oct. to mid-Dec. Typical French ski resort hotel; well-planned rooms, glorious views, sauna; good-value restaurant (I).

LA BOURBOULE. *International* (M), av. Angleterre (tel. 73-81-05-82). 16 rooms. Closed second half Apr. and Nov. to Christmas. Close to the spa building, attractive hotel now modernized from top to toe; restaurant. AE, DC, MC, V. *Horizon* (I), 2 km. (1¼ miles) northeast via D996 (av. Maréchal-Leclerc), (tel. 73-81-08-40). 18 rooms. Closed mid-Nov. to mid-Dec. Welcome new find on way to Le Mont-Dore; good-value restaurant. V. *Parc* (I), quai Maréchal-Fayolle (tel. 73-81-01-77). 56 rooms. Closed Oct. to mid-May. Old-style establishment next to casino; nicely furnished, adequate restaurant. AE, DC, MC, V.

Restaurant. *Auberge Tournebride* (I), 1½ km. (1 mile) north via D88 (tel. 73-81-01-91). Closed second half Apr., Mon. (except in July and Aug., public hols. and all school hols.). Family-style restaurant in converted barn with good home cooking; also has 8 modest rooms.

BOURGES. *Central et Angleterre* (M), 1 pl. Quatre Piliers (tel. 48-24-68-51). 31 rooms. Restaurant closed mid-Dec. to mid-Jan. Modernized from top to toe, and now very comfortable, with good restaurant. AE, DC, MC, V. *Grand Argentier* (M), 9 rue Parerie (tel. 48-70-84-31). Closed Christmas through Jan.; restaurant also closed Sun. for dinner and Mon. AE, DC, V. Pretty rooms in 15th–century building; modest but pleasant restaurant. *Olympia* (I), 66 av. d'Orléans (tel. 48-70-49-84). 42 rooms. Traditional, simple rooms; no restaurant. AE, DC, MC, V.

Restaurants. *Jacques Coeur* (E), 3 pl. Jacques-Coeur (tel. 48-70-12-72). Closed mid-July to mid-Aug., over Christmas and New Year, Sat., and Sun. for dinner. Long famous for classical cuisine and superb Gothic décor. AE, DC, V. *Ile d'Or* (M), 39 blvd. Juranville (tel. 48-24-29-15). Closed second half of Feb. and first half of Sept., Sun., and Mon. for lunch. Good *nouvelle cuisine.* AE, DC, MC, V. *Marée* (I), 14 rue Prinal (tel. 48-24-41-45). Closed July, Sat. for lunch and Sun. Near Palais Jacques Coeur; modest, good value. V.

LA CHAISE-DIEU. *Echo et Abbaye* (M), pl. Echo (tel. 71-00-00-45). 11 rooms. Closed Nov. through Mar. Well known for good, reasonably-priced restaurant serving mostly regional cuisine; peaceful rooms. AE, MC, V. *Tremblant* (I), on D906 road (tel. 71-00-01-85). 28 rooms. Closed mid-Nov. through Mar. Pleasant rooms, garden and attractive terrace; good-value meals. V.

LA CHÂTRE. At **St.-Chartier,** *Château de la Vallée Bleue* (M), route de Verneuil. 15 rooms. Newly renovated; in large park; restaurant. MC, V.

Restaurant. *Tanneries* (I), Pont du Lyon d'Argent (tel. 54-48-06-82). New *auberge* with good chef and good-value *menus.* Also has 10 rooms. AE, DC, V.

CLERMONT-FERRAND. *Frantel* (M), 82 blvd. Gergovia (tel. 73-93-05-75). 124 rooms. Central and modern; good restaurant (see below). AE, DC, MC, V. *Gallieni* (M), 51 rue Bonnabaud (tel. 73-93-59-69). 80 rooms. Restaurant closed Sat. Central and well run; pleasant rooms with balconies; restaurant *Charade* (M). AE, MC, V. *Mercure Arverne* (M), 16 pl. Delille (tel. 73-91-92-06). 57 rooms. Newly renovated, very comfortable. Restaurant. AE, DC, MC, V. *Radio* (M), 43 av. Pierre-Curie (on the outskirts in Chamalières district), (tel. 73-30-87-83). 27 rooms. Closed mid-Nov. through Feb., for dinner and Mon. Comfortable, with elegant restaurant (E) offering lovely views and good cuisine; stylish twenties décor. AE, DC, MC, V. *Albert-Elisabeth* (I), 37 av. Albert-Elisabeth (tel. 73-92-47-41). 40 rooms. Convenient for station; no restaurant. AE, V.

At **Royat,** 3½ km. (2½ miles) north. *Métropole* (E), 2 blvd. Vaquez (tel. 73-35-80-18). 77 rooms. Closed Oct. through Apr. Typical "grand hotel" in spa town; very comfortable rooms and suites facing the spa building; restaurant is

(M). MC. *Royal St.-Mart* (M), 6 av. Gare (tel. 73-35-80-01). 63 rooms. Closed Oct. through Apr. Central, with nice garden and good old-fashioned service.

Restaurants. *Brezou* (I), 51 rue St.-Dominique (tel. 73-93-56-71). Closed Sat., Sun. and around Christmas. Warm and welcoming; good cooking. v. *Clavé* (M), 10 rue Adjutor (tel. 73-36-46-30). Closed Sat. for lunch, Sun. (May through Sept. only). Chic; stylish *nouvelle cuisine*. MC, V. *Retirade* (M), in *Frantel* hotel (tel. 73-93-05-75). Closed Sat. for lunch, Sun. Very good newish cuisine; elegant décor. AE, MC. *Truffe d'Argent* (M), 17 rue Lamartine (tel. 73-93-22-42). Closed Sat. for lunch. Attractive old building, newish cuisine and excellent service. AE, DC, MC, V.

At **Royat**, 3½ km. (2½ miles) north. *Belle-Meunière* (M), 25 av. Vallée (tel. 73-35-80-17). Closed Feb., Sun. for dinner, Wed. Rather chic with art nouveau décor and classical cuisine; also has 10 pleasant rooms. AE, DC, MC, V. *Royat-Restaurant* (M), blvd. J.B. Romeuf (tel. 73-35-82-72). Closed Sun. for dinner, Mon. (except in summer and mid-Jan. to mid-Feb.). Excellent chef; *nouvelle cuisine* and good desserts. Also has 14 rooms. AE, DC, MC, V.

ISSOIRE. *Pariou* (I), 18 av. Kennedy (tel. 73-89-22-11). 29 rooms. Closed mid-Sept. to mid-Oct., Christmas and New Year period, and weekends (except in July and Aug.). Modest but well-run modern hotel with good-value restaurant. MC, V.

Restaurants. *Relais* (M), 1 av. Gare (tel. 73-89-16-61). Closed second half Oct., Sun. for dinner, also Mon. (except June through Sept.). Central, popular with locals. v.

At **Sarpoil**, 11 km. (7 miles) southeast, *Bergerie* (M), (tel. 73-71-02-54). Closed Jan. and Feb., second half June, first half Sept., Sun. for dinner, Wed. Village atmosphere; well known for regional dishes served on openair terrace in fine weather; must reserve.

LE MONT-DORE. *Panorama* (M), av. Libération (tel. 73-65-11-12). 40 rooms. Closed Easter to mid-May, Oct. to Christmas. Well modernized, with great views, attractive garden and pleasant restaurant. v. *Puy Ferrand* (M), 4 km. (2½ miles) south via D983 road (tel. 73-65-18-99). Closed mid-Apr. to mid-May and Oct. to Christmas. Chalet-type building belonging to Relais du Silence association; well placed for ski slopes; good restaurant. AE, DC, MC, V.

Restaurants. *Belle Epoque* (M), rue Sauvagnat (tel. 73-65-07-68). Closed Nov., Wed. (except in July and Aug.). Small—must reserve—and stylish; mixture of classical and *nouvelle* cuisine. AE, DC, MC, V.

At **Le Genestoux**, 3½ km. (2 miles) north, *Pitsounet* (I), (tel. 73-65-00-67). Closed Oct. to mid-Dec., and Mon. (except July and Aug.). Very good value; home-style meals; must reserve.

MONTLUÇON. *Château St.-Jean* (M), on edge of town by Parc St.-Jean (on road to Clermont-Ferrand), (tel. 70-05-04-65). 8 rooms. Stylish and very comfortable, with big formal garden and excellent cuisine; once lived in by the head of the St. John's Hospitallers order. AE, DC, MC, V.

At **Néris-les-Bains**, 8 km. (5 miles) away, *Garden* (I), 12 av. Marx-Dormoy (tel. 70-03-21-16). 16 rooms. Closed Nov. Restaurant closed Fri. for dinner, Sun. for dinner (Dec. through Feb. only). Nice little spot popular with French families resting in this pleasant spa; pretty garden. MC, V.

Restaurants. *Ducs de Bourbon* (M), 47 av. Marx-Dormoy (tel. 70-05-22-79). Closed Mon. and Sun. for dinner. Typical provincial town-center restaurant with reliable classical cuisine and rather elegant dining room. AE, DC, MC, V. *Grenier à Sel* (M), 10 rue Notre-Dame (tel. 70-05-53-79). Closed mid-July to mid-Aug., Sun. for dinner, Mon. Attractive old building (former salt warehouse) in narrow street in Old Town; elegant, good service, mostly *nouvelle cuisine*. AE, DC, MC, V.

MONTMARAULT. *Château de Boussac* (E), 12 km. (7½ miles) southwest on D42 (tel. 70-56-63-20). 3 rooms. 17th–century moated château offering guest accommodations; personal welcome and assistance from owners, the Marquis et Marquise de Longeuil; meals available on advance request.

MOULINS. *Paris* (M), 21 rue Paris (tel. 70-44-00-58). 29 rooms. Restaurant closed Sun. for dinner and Mon. (except summer and public hols.). Charming Relais et Châteaux member near cathedral in Old Town; elegant restaurant serves some regional specialties. AE, DC, MC, V.
   At **Coulandon,** 6 km. (4 miles) west, *Chalet* (I), (tel. 70-44-50-08). 21 rooms. Closed mid-Nov. and Jan.; restaurant open for dinner only. Relais du Silence with family-style meals and huge garden. DC, MC, V.

LE PUY. *Chris'tel* (M), 15 blvd. Clair (tel. 71-02-24-44). 30 rooms. Restaurant closed mid-Dec. to mid-Jan., both Fri. and Sat. for lunch. Modern and comfortable; restaurant is (I). AE, V. *Licorn* (I), 25 av. Charles-Dupuy (tel. 71-02-46-22). 48 rooms. Simple, comfortable rooms; near station. V.
   Restaurants. *Bateau Ivre* (M), 5 rue Portail d'Avignon (tel. 71-09-67-20). Closed first half of July, Sun. and Mon. Classical cuisine and friendly ambiance; good-value fixed-price (I) lunches. DC, MC, V. *Cygne* (M), 47 blvd. Maréchal-Fayoule (tel. 71-09-32-36). Closed Dec. through Feb., and Fri. Good-value newish cuisine; also a hotel with 40 (I) rooms. AE, V.

RIOM. *Lyon* (I), 107 fbg. La-Bade (tel. 73-38-07-66). 15 rooms. Closed part of May and Sept. On edge of town, with garden but no restaurant.
   Restaurant. *Petits Ventres* (M), 6 rue Anne-Dubourg (tel. 73-38-21-65). Closed first half Jan., Sept., Sat. for lunch, Sun. for dinner, Mon. Friendly and good-value; mostly classical cuisine. AE, MC, V.

ST.-AMAND-MONTROND. *Poste* (I), 9 rue Dr.-Vallet (tel. 48-96-27-14). 24 rooms. Closed Dec.; restaurant closed Mon. Typical small-town hostelry; good cuisine, plenty of atmosphere, modest but comfortable rooms.
   At **Farges-Allichamps,** 10 km. (6½ miles) northwest, *Château de la Commanderie* (E), (tel. 48-61-04-19). 6 rooms. Charming accommodations in private château where the Count and Countess Jouffroy-Gonsans will give you a warm welcome; dinner available on advance request; meals also available for groups.
   At **Charenton-sur-Cher,** 14 km. (8½ miles) away, *Château de Thaumiers* (M), (tel. 48-60-87-62). 5 rooms. One of first private châteaux to offer guest accommodations (owner is head of the Château-Acceuil association); also has 2 (E) suites and self-catering accommodations; meals for small groups available on advance request.
   At **Bannegon,** 24 km. (15 miles) east, *Moulin du Chaméron* (M), (tel. 48-60-75-80). 10 rooms. Closed Nov. to mid-Mar., Thurs. for dinner. Delightful converted 18th–century watermill; pool, garden, angling and excellent restaurant. V.
   Restaurants. *Croix d'Or* (M), 28 rue 14-Juillet (tel. 48-96-09-41). Closed Fri. for dinner (except in July and Aug.). Good regional specialties; also has 16 (I) rooms. V. *Pont-du-Cher* (M), 2 av. Gare (tel. 48-96-00-51). Closed mid-Oct. to mid-Nov., and Mon. Good-value regional cuisine and lovely views over river valley; also has 13 (I) rooms.
   At **Ainay-le-Vieil,** 11 km. (7 miles) southeast, *Crémaillère* (I), (tel. 48-63-50-14). Closed mid-Jan. to mid-Feb., and Fri. Oct. through April. Logis de France right by château; family-style meals; also has 8 rooms. V.

SALERS. *Remparts* (I), esplanade Barrouze (tel. 71-40-70-33). 18 rooms. Closed mid-Oct. to mid-Dec. Large attractive rooms with lovely views; regional cuisine. V.
   At **Le Theil,** 6 km. (4 miles) southwest, *Hostellerie Maronne* (I), (tel. 71-69-20-33). Closed Nov. through Mar. Charming Relais du Silence with lovely garden and good food. MC, V.

SANCERRE. *Panoramic* (M), rempart Augustins (tel. 48-54-22-44). 56 rooms. Views over Sancerre vineyards are as panoramic as the name suggests; under same management as *Tasse d'Argent restaurant next door.* AE.

Restaurant. *Auberge Alphonse Mellot* (I), 16 pl. Halle (tel. 48-54-20-53). Closed Wed. and mid-Dec. to mid-Jan. Simple, hearty food and wines to take with you from the *propriétaire.* MC, V.

VICHY. *Aletti Thermal Palace* (E), 3 pl. Joseph-Aletti (tel. 70-31-78-77). 57 rooms. Closed Oct. through April. Particularly comfortable and pleasant but no restaurant. DC, MC. *Pavillon Sévigné* (E), 52 blvd. Kennedy (tel. 70-32-16-22). 48 rooms. Closed Oct. through Apr. Once lived in by the great Marquise herself; elegant, well-modernized; good restaurant. AE, DC, MC, V.

Albert ler (M), av. Doumer (tel. 70-31-92-45). 36 rooms. Closed mid-Nov. to Easter. Stylishly modernized turn-of-century building; no restaurant. AE, DC, MC, V. *Elysée-Palace* (M), 4 rue Paris (tel. 70-98-25-17). 68 rooms. Closed Oct. through Mar. (but restaurant stays open year-round). Forms part of complex including casino; airconditioned, sound-proofed rooms, disco, grillroom. AE, DC, MC, V. *Ermitage Pont-Neuf* (M), 5 sq. Albert-ler (tel. 70-32-09-22). 65 rooms. Closed Oct. through Apr. Central, good old-fashioned service; restaurant. *Novotel Thermalia* (M), 1 av. Thermale (tel. 70-31-04-39). 128 rooms. Comfortable impersonal rooms; direct access to spa building; grillroom for light meals; pool. AE, DC, MC, V.

Concordia (I), 15 rue Roovère (tel. 70-98-29-65). 34 rooms. Partly renovated. Restaurant. V. *Londres* (I), 7 blvd. Russie (tel. 70-98-28-27). 22 rooms. Closed Oct. through Mar. Central, good value; no restaurant.

Restaurants. *Violon d'Ingres* (E), rue Casino (tel. 70-98-97-70). Closed Tues. Very elegant, next to casino; delicious mostly "new" cuisine; popular with local gourmets, so must reserve. AE, DC, MC, V. *Grillade Strauss* (M), 5 pl. Joseph-Aletti (tel. 70-98-56-74). Closed mid-Jan. through Feb., Sun. for dinner, and Mon. (except Easter through Sept.). Old-established spot for classical cuisine; popular with spa visitors. AE, DC, MC, V. *Chez Mémère* (M), chemin de Halage (in Bellerive district on left bank of Allier river), (tel. 70-32-35-22). Closed mid-Sept. through Apr. No lunches except at weekends. Good place for summer evenings with its riverside garden; newish cuisine; also has 10 (I) rooms.

At **Abrest,** 5 km. (3 miles) southeast, *Colombière* (tel. 70-98-69-15). Closed mid-Jan. to mid-Feb., Sun. for dinner, and Mon. (except Easter through Sept.). Attractive, with pretty terraced garden; also has 4 (I) rooms. AE, DC, V.

At **Molles,** 14 km. (9 miles) east by D62, *Relais Fleuri* (I), route Mayet-de-Montagne (tel. 70-41-80-01). Closed Wed. and mid-Nov. through Dec. Open to 8.30 P.M. Run by two sisters; welcoming; hearty food; an experience not to be missed. Also has 10 rooms (half-board terms compulsory in season). DC.

TOURS AND EXCURSIONS. By Bus. S.N.C.F. (French railways) has a 3–day combined coach and train visit but it runs only two or three times a year. Local coach tours are organized from all main centers, with various excursions centered on the gastronomy of the Massif Central and the volcanoes in the Auvergne.

By Train. A "tourist train" runs from Dunières to St.-Agrève that has marvelous views of the granit uplands of Forez, the volcanic hills of the Velay and the Lignon gorges. The train runs from mid-May to mid-Oct. daily, and weekends and public holidays the rest of the year. For reservations call 77-25-45-01.

By Car. In the Berry, the major excursion follows the *Route Jacques-Coeur* around Bourges. Eleven privately-owned châteaux are featured on the route. Exhibits, concerts and special night-time visits by candle light are arranged in the summer. Further information is available at tourist office in Bourges.

The tourist authorities have also come up with five itineraries for visiting the *Routes des Châteaux d'Auvergne*. Details of them and of the 36 châteaux they cover are given in one fold-out brochure, available from any tourist office.

 SIGHTSEEING DATA. For general notes on visiting French museums and historic buildings—and an important warning—see "Sightseeing" in *Facts at Your Fingertips*.

AINAY-LE-VIEIL. Château. Open daily, Feb. through Nov., 10–12, 2–7 (or nightfall, whichever is earlier); closed Tues.

AMBERT. Moulin Richard-de-Bas (Paper Mill), 8 km., (5 miles) outside town. Open daily 9–11.30, 2–6, except July and Aug. 9–6.

BLANCAFORT. Château. Open daily, mid-Mar. to mid-Nov., except Tues., 10–12, 2–7; mid-Nov. to mid-Mar., Sun. and public hols. only, 10–12, 2–5.

BOURBON-l'ARCHAMBAULT. Château. Access by the Nevers road. Open mid-Apr. to mid-Oct., daily 2–6, Sun. 10–12, 2–6.

BOURGES. Cathédrale St.-Etienne. Crypt and towers open daily, except Tues., Sun. morning and some public hols., 10–12, 2–5; July and Aug. 9–12, 2–6.
  Hôtel Cujas, housing **Musée du Berry.** Open daily, except Tues. and public hols., 10–12, 2–6.
  Hôtel Lallemant (Applied Arts Museum). Open daily except Tues. and public hols., 10–12, 2–4; 2–6 Apr. to mid-Oct.
  Palais Jacques-Coeur. Open daily (except Tues. and public hols.), Easter through Oct., 9–11.15, 2–5.15; Nov. to Easter, 10–11.15, 2–4.15.

BOUSSAC. Château. Open daily, 9–12, 2–6; 2–7 in July and Aug.

LA BUSSIÈRE. Château. Open daily, except Tues., mid-Mar. to mid-Nov., 9–12, 2–6; mid-Nov. to mid-Mar., Sun. only, 9–12, 2–5.

LA CHAISE-DIEU. Eglise St.-Robert. Choir open daily, June through Sept., 10–12, 2–5; Oct. through Apr., closed Tues.
  Historical Waxworks Museum, (in monastery building next to cloisters). Open daily, May through Sept., only, 9–12, 2–7.

LA CHAPELLE d'ANGILLON. Château, housing **Musée Alain-Fournier.** Open daily, Easter through Nov., 9–12, 2–7; closed Sun. morning.

CLERMONT-FERRAND. Musée du Ranquet. Open daily, except Mon., Sun. morning and public hols., 10–12, 2–5.

CULAN. Château. Open daily, July through Sept., 9–11.45, 2–6.30; Nov. through June, same times but closed Wed.

GIEN. Château, housing **Musée International de la Chasse** (Hunting Museum). Open daily, 9.15–11.45, 2.15–5.30 (to 6.30 Easter through Oct.).
  Faïencerie (China Workshops), pl. Victoire (tel. 38-67-00-05). Open daily, except Sun. and public hols., 9.30–11.30, 2–5.30.

JUSSY-CHAMPAGNE. Château. Open daily, Apr. to mid-Nov., 9–11.45, 2–6.30.

LAPALISSE. Château la Palice (tel. 70-99-08-51). Open daily, Apr. through Oct., 9–12, 2–6; Apr., May and Oct. closed Tues.; Nov. through Mar. closed. Historical Pageant on Fri. and Sat. evenings July and Aug.

LEZOUX. Musée Archéologique. Open July, Aug., first 2 weeks of Sept., daily except Mon., 2.30–6.30; Sun. in June.

MAUPAS. Château. Open daily, Easter to mid-Oct., 2–7; mid-July through Aug., Sun. and public hols. only, also open 10–12.

MEILLANT. Château. Open daily, Mar. to mid.-Nov., 9–12, 2–7; mid-Nov. through Feb., closes at 5.

MONTLUÇON. Château des Ducs de Bourbon, housing **Musée de Montluçon,** and **Musée de la Vielle** (Hurdy-Gurdy Museum). Open daily, except Tues., mid-Mar. to mid-Oct., 10–12, 2–6; mid-Oct. to mid-Mar., daily, except Mon. and Tues., afternoons only.

MOULINS. Cathédrale. Treasury (containing Maître de Moulins triptych), open daily, July and Aug., 9–12, 2–6; Sept. through June, daily except Tues., same times.

MOUROL. Château. Open daily, June through Sept., 9–7; Oct. through May, Sun. and public hols. only, 2–7.

PARENTIGNAT. Château (tel. 73-89-06-55). Open Sun. and public hols. only, Easter and May to mid-June, 2–6; mid-June to mid-Sept., daily except Wed., 2–6.

SALERS. Hôtel de Bargues (tel. 71-40-73-42). Open daily, May through Oct., 10–12, 2–7 (closes at 5 in Oct.). A number of other houses in the Ville Haute are also open to the public; check times with tourist office.

THIERS. Maison des Couteliers (Cutlery Workshops and Museum), 58 rue des Couteliers. Open daily except Sun., June through Sept., 10–12, 2–6.30.

TOURNOËL. Château (tel. 73-33-53-06). Open daily except Tues., Easter through Oct., 9–12, 2–7; Nov. to Easter by appointment only.

VICHY. Grand Etablissement Thermal (Spa Buildings), av. General-Dwight-Eisenhower. Open June through Aug., Wed., Thurs. and Sat. only, 3.30–5. Occasionally open at other times; check with tourist office.

LA VERRERIE. Château. Open daily, mid-Feb. to mid-Nov., 10–12, 2–7.

WEST OF THE MASSIF CENTRAL

Rural Valleys and Prehistoric Paintings

Not so long ago this region of rural France could be referred to as undiscovered, but as increasing numbers of city dwellers react against the stresses and strains of urban living and head for places where they can adopt a more peaceful rhythm, at least for their holidays, these rural provinces and *départements* are changing rapidly. Yet although voices are constantly being raised to deplore the influx of holidaymakers, the region's new popularity is in many ways to the advantage of tourists, who find a wide range of festivals and events staged for their entertainment and pleasure.

The old provinces and regions of the Limousin and the Périgord, the Rouergue and the Quercy; the beautiful river valleys of the Dordogne, the Lot and the Tarn; all these are ideal holiday territory for those who do not insist on four-star hotels and the latest movies. They offer few internationally known buildings or sights, but their absence is easily compensated for by a wealth of picturesque villages, Romanesque churches, prehistoric remains and lonely castles perched high on sheer cliffs.

Limoges, City of Porcelain and Enamel

One of the chief cities of the region, Limoges lies directly on the rail and road route to and from Paris. Save a few hours to visit its cathedral of St. Etienne, the Adrien Dubouché Museum (ceramics), the Palais Episcopal or Municipal Museum with samples of Limoges china from the 12th century to the present, and some enchanting 13th-century houses.

In the mid-19th century, an American china retailer boarded a ship in New York, bound for France. His objective was to find a cup to match a broken one brought into his shop. Knowing only that the broken cup had come from France, he began his search, and finally came to Limoges, where he found china that matched the cup. For three-quarters of a century French craftsmen had been producing this delicate porcelain for the French market, using a pure white clay found in St.-Yriex, south of Limoges. This clay, called kaolin, had been known for centuries in China, but was discovered in Europe only in the 18th century.

This American, David Haviland, took a bold step—he moved to France, set up his own factory at Limoges and began to produce quality porcelain for the tables of American homes. Rapidly his fame spread, and china bearing the Haviland hallmark became synonymous with some of the finest produced in Europe.

Well worth your while is a tour of one of the porcelain factories and enamel workshops, which can be visited during the summer. Ask the tourist office for addresses and times when the public is admitted.

Périgord and the Dordogne Valley

Northeast of Bordeaux is the Périgord, known primarily for its prehistoric art and gourmet's cuisine. But there are rich, luxuriant valleys through which flow clear rivers: the Dordogne, the Vézère, the Auvézère, the Isle and the Dronne. Separating the valleys are rugged plateaus of granite and limestone, outcrops of rock and sheer cliffs.

The hilly country towards the Dronne valley has fortified châteaux perched on every slope and brown stone villages roofed in red tiles; you may occasionally see mule-drawn carts or fields being plowed by yoked oxen. You can also take slow-boat trips down the Lot or Dordogne rivers, looking up at the châteaux, or weave in a houseboat or flat-bottomed barge all the way up the Garonne from Bordeaux or Toulouse.

Brantôme on the banks of the Dronne is enchanting, with its crystal clear canal flanked by balustraded terraces and crossed by lovely old bridges. Interesting are its 11th-century bell tower, its white, 18th-century Benedictine abbey, a 15th-century church, and several fine grottoes. Nearby lies the Renaissance château of Bourdeilles, with a 14th-century fortress, open daily to the public.

Périgueux, capital of the Dordogne, is built on the site of an old Roman city, called Vésone after its protectress, the goddess Vesuna. Ruins of a pagan temple erected in her honor still stand. After the city was sacked by barbarians in the 3rd century, it was given back its Gallic name, Pétrocores, and the modern names of both the city and region developed from this word.

Starting with the ruins of a Roman arena that dates from the 3rd century, there is scarcely a period of architecture that is not represented in Périgueux. The cathedral of St.-Front, believed to have been built between 1125 and 1150, is one of the strangest in France. Built in the shape of a Greek cross, it is primarily Romanesque in style. Its five domes betray Byzantine influence, and understandably so, for Périgueux was on the trade route to the East. St.-Etienne, the other domed church in the city, is less ostentatiously restored than St.-Front.

A visit to the Périgueux Museum to look at the remarkable prehistoric collections makes a convenient preliminary to trips outside the city and gives you a chance to examine an unusual collection of Gallo-Roman mosaics, ceramics and bronzes. France's first-ever Truffle Museum opened at Sorges-en-Dordogne near Périgueux in 1981.

Prehistoric Art

Throughout the region are traces of Roman, medieval and Renaissance civilizations, but these are less striking attractions than the caves, caverns and grottoes of the countryside. It is in some of these that archeologists found the bones, utensils and paintings of Cro-Magnon man. The brown, gray and black paintings of racing horses and reindeer, of bison and cows, show a well-developed sense of form and movement. Unfortunately, most of the region's many caves are open very short hours, with a long lunch break, so don't reckon on visiting many in a day.

Forty-two km. (26 miles) southeast of Périgueux is Les Eyzies. It was here, at the confluence of the Beune and Vézère rivers, that Cro-Magnon skeletons were found in 1868. One skeleton remains, under glass. The village lies at the bottom of a 182-meter (600-ft.) cliff, and halfway up, under an impressive outcrop of rock, is a 16th-century château that now houses the National Prehistory Museum. On the terrace of the museum stands a statue of Cro-Magnon man as imagined by the sculptor Dardé in 1930.

In the vicinity of Les Eyzies, in the Beune valley, prehistoric paintings may be seen in the Font-de-Gaume grotto; engravings in the Combarelle grotto, and, at the Abri du Cap Blanc, a frieze in bold relief depicting a dozen animal figures.

Near Montignac-sur-Vézère are the Lascaux Caves, discovered in 1940 and containing what have been called the finest prehistoric paintings in Europe, possibly 30,000 years old. Despite precautions taken to preserve the paintings—including airconditioning—it was discovered in 1963 that they had begun to deteriorate, and the caves were closed permanently. An exact replica has now been built, and is well worth a visit. Other caves in the region include the particularly interesting one near Rouffignac.

Châteaux of Périgord

The surrounding countryside is liberally sprinkled with medieval châteaux. See Beynac-et-Cazenac, where the barons of Périgueux once met. From its ramparts the view over the meandering valley of the Dordogne is sensational. Then there's the heavily restored château of Fayrac situated near the impressive ruins of Castelnaud, which overlooks a picturesque village of narrow, winding streets and old houses with an admirable view of the Dordogne valley and the mighty castles of Beynac and Marqueyssac.

The charming village of La Roque-Gageac, wedged between rocky cliffs and the Dordogne, is dominated by the lofty castle of Marqueyssac, renowned for its magnificent terraced gardens, which afford a wide vista over the village to the château of Castelnaud across the river. Just west of La Bachellerie there's the beautiful 18th-century castle of Rastignac, reminiscent of the White House in Washington with its Ionic columns and rounded façade. The château of Biron, begun in the 12th century but including buildings of later periods, dominates the country for miles around.

The imposing château of Hautefort, with its crenellated walls, round towers and drawbridge, is worth visiting as is the 16th-century castle of Puyguilhem with its chubby tower topped by a peaked roof, its Renaissance staircase and carved windows; also Monbazillac famous for its wine as well as its grounds. At Thonac, the 16th-century château of Losse faces the river Vézère, its walls swathed in ivy. It was built by Jean de Losse, governor of the Périgord and a violent enemy of the Huguenots. Visit the massive ruins of the feudal castle of Commarque at Sireuil; also the macabre remains of the château de l'Herm, which was the scene of a family murder.

Climb up to the medieval town of Domme with a panoramic view of the valley from its ramparts; see Souillac with its interesting church, a fine 12th-century abbey in the Périgourdin–Romanesque style; and also the ancient abbey of Cadouin founded in 1115; then, St.-Céré, a picturesque little town with many 15th, 16th and 17th-century houses. Perched on a hillside nearby is the château of Montal, superbly restored at the beginning of this century. Don't miss the aristocratic old town of Sarlat with many fine houses, though unfortunately it is invaded by tourist hordes in the summer. One of the most spectacular feudal castles of the region is Castelnau-Bretenoux, surrounded by vineyards and commanding the river Lot from its high perch. Only the keep (an oriental-inspired tower built in 1080, with thin columned windows topped by a Moorish spindle), the main walls and corner towers remain of the original structure. A disaster occurred in 1850 when a bankrupt noble heir set fire to the castle hoping to collect the insurance. Later, it was bought and restored by Mouliérat, a famous tenor of the Opéra Comique who left it to the state, complete with tapestries, period furniture and knick-knacks of all kinds.

From St.-Céré you can make many pleasant excursions to the picturesque little towns and villages dotted about the surrounding countryside—Autuire and its nearby waterfall, Loubressac with its castle, Carennac, perched on the banks of the Dordogne with a Romanesque abbey and peaceful cloister, Martel, which still has many medieval buildings, or Gramat, a pleasant little market town.

A scenic route from St.-Céré to the industrial town of Tulle, set deep in the valley, winds high through wild, rugged, uninhabited lands. Tulle was the scene of one of the worst massacres of World War II.

Subterranean River

An excellent excursion from Brive, Périgueux or St.-Céré is to the Gouffre de Padirac, a well or abyss over 90 meters (300 ft.) deep, at the bottom of which is a subterranean river, reached by elevators and stairs. You can travel by boat for about 1 km. (½ mile), gliding in and out of vast chambers, one over 82 meters (270 ft.) high. The stalagmites and stalactites, the grotesque rock structures and the weird crystalline formations seen in the dimly lit underground passages have earned the Gouffre its reputation as one of the most interesting natural phenomena in France.

Not far from Padirac is Rocamadour, a village set in a narrow gorge of the river Alzou. According to tradition, Zacheus, a publican who had the honor of entertaining Jesus in his home, came to Gaul after the crucifixion and, under the name of Amadour, became a hermit and set up a shrine in the cliff overlooking the river. Since then, other chapels and shrines have been built in the cliff, one of them containing the crypt of St.-Amadour. The village consists of a single street of houses built in the Middle Ages to shelter pilgrims who came to honor St.-Amadour. Rocamadour is still the goal of pilgrimages. On top of the cliff is a 14th-century château, rebuilt during the 19th century, which houses the priests who are in charge of the shrines. There is a magnificent view from here over the village and its setting of spectacular cliffs.

The lively town of Cahors, once the capital of the province of Quercy, has a Romanesque cathedral in the domed style of Aquitaine, and the beautiful medieval bridge of Valentré, which spans the Lot. Some eight km. (five miles) away the château of the bishops of Cahors has been converted into a modern hotel, the towered château of Mercuès, overlooking the Lot valley. The Quercy has now been discovered, especially by British visitors, who appreciate the calm friendliness of the inhabitants, the lovely village architecture, the little-known historic monuments—and the fairly reasonable prices.

East to Conques

This damp limestone region, called the Châtaigneraie, was once so fertile that the area became over-populated, but the earth was soon impoverished by too intensive exploitation of its wealth. The men left, and today it consists mainly of a vast expanse covered with ferns and gorse, firs, pines and wild beeches, with the occasional poor hamlet.

Not far from Figeac (which has a good coin museum), but very different from it, is the partly abandoned village of Conques, a lovely place to lunch or stay. People come from afar to this wild valley, for here stands one of the most beautiful religious monuments in the south of France, Ste. Foy-de-Conques. It was begun some time near 1050 as one of the four major churches along the pilgrimage way to Santiago de Compostela in Spain.

From Conques delightful side trips can be made through the lovely Lot valley to Entraygues, with its 13th-century bridge and 16th-century houses (along the rue Basse), to the medieval town of Estaing, hugging the banks of the Lot, with a picturesque bridge and old castle; to nearby Espalion, beloved by fishermen, and by artists for its red stone bridge and Renaissance château built on the river's edge; to the tiny fortified village of St.-Côme on the Lot with its winding cobbled streets; to Bozouls precariously clinging to the edge of a deep canyon; to the medieval hill town of Rodez with its fortress-like cathedral commanding the main square and, beside it, a 16th-century bell tower of reddish-brown stone graced by late Gothic motifs. Rodez has recently given itself a face lift; the ramparts have been restored, pedestrian precincts have been built and the place is full of modern hotels and chic boutiques.

In the Causses region—high barren reaches, the realm of solitary winds—visit the near-deserted 14th-century village of La Couvertoirade, once a stop on the road to Santiago de Compostela, and also La Cavalerie, ancient seat of the Knights Templar. What makes the Causses appear even more like a wilderness is the infrequency of villages, but this loneliness is broken in the summer by huge herds of sheep coming up from the Camargue and the plains of Languedoc. The trek is made by tens of thousands of the animals, which come to graze on the short grass of the plateaux.

The Causses are limestone plateaux that were raised at the same time as the Pyrenees. Pressure caused fractures and cleavages that trapped the torrential autumn rains. Over thousands of years the swirling waters ate into the mass of stone, gouging out the canyons, caves, underground rivers and lakes that today delight the tourist, boatman and geologist. The most impressive of the Grands Causses are the Méjean (Aven Armand and Corniches), the large Causse du Larzac and the Causse Noir.

Gorges of the Tarn

The most famous and most impressive of these canyons, the Gorges of the Tarn, separating the Causse Sauveterre from the Causse Méjean, provides more than 48 km. (30 miles) of gorges, stretching from Millau, the headquarters for excursions into this strange part of France, all the way to Ste.-Enimie. The entire course of the canyon is a wilderness filled with sudden views of breathtaking silhouettes of the red and yellow cliffs, the rocky chaos of landslides that have tumbled into the river, routing the waters swirling around them. Various points along the gorges are floodlit on summer evenings. Though a highway winds its way the length of the canyon, you should also, if possible, go down the Tarn by boat.

Not far from Millau, at the foot of towering limestone cliffs, lies Roquefort-sur-Soulzon, famous for its ewes'-milk cheese since the time of the Romans. For a tour of Roquefort's caves, inquire at La Société des Caves, Caves de la Rue.

Now turn northward, away from the Gorges of the Tarn towards Mende, just before reaching Florac. Mende, town of the most sparsely populated region of France, is located at the base of a small foothill of the Causse. In July and August canoeists embark from under the old bridge of Notre-Dame-de-Peyrane for a cruise on the Lot, and hosts of campers pitch tents in the country around.

PRACTICAL INFORMATION FOR WEST OF THE
MASSIF CENTRAL

TOURIST OFFICES. The regional tourist office for the Dordogne—written enquiries only—is the *Comité Départemental de Tourisme,* 16 rue du President Wilson, 24000 Perigueux (tel. 53-53-44-35).

There are local tourist offices in the following towns: **Brive-la-Gaillarde,** pl. 14-Juillet (tel. 55-24-08-80); **Cahors,** pl. Aristide-Briand (tel. 65-35-09-56); **Les Eyzies-de-Tayac,** pl. Mairie (tel. 53-06-97-05), closed mid-Nov. to mid.-Mar.; **Limoges,** blvd. Fleurus (tel. 55-34-46-87); **Périgueux,** 1 av. Aquitaine (tel.

53-53-10-63); **Rocamadour,** Hôtel de Ville (tel. 65-33-62-59), June through Sept. only; **Rodez,** pl. Roch (tel. 65-68-02-27); **Sarlat,** pl. Liberté (tel. 53-59-27-67).

REGIONAL FOOD AND DRINK. Périgord cuisine is renowned throughout France. But not until you taste *cou d'oie farci* (stuffed goose neck), *galantine de dinde truffée* (boned, stuffed roll of turkey), and *pommes sar-ladaises* (potato cake fried in goose fat with truffles), will you really appreciate it. The specialty, and perhaps the secret, is truffles, often combined with foie gras (fattened goose liver). Recently, fattened duck liver, slightly more subtle and less rich, has become as popular as goose, together with the *magret* steaks made from duck breast. These can be cooked in a dozen ways, very like beef steak.

Confit is a way of preserving rich meats like goose, duck, pork, and innards like neck and gizzard, which is native to Périgord and the southwest. The meat is first salted, then baked very gently in fat until it so tender, says tradition, that it can be pierced with a straw. Then it is packed in crocks and sealed in fat to keep for several months. Confit can be reheated to eat by itself with potatoes fried in the leftover fat, or it can be used to flavor soups and dishes like the *cassoulet* of Languedoc. Jars of *confit,* together with cans of *pâté de foie gras* and truffles are among the many tempting treasures to take home from Périgord.

Best known dessert is *clafoutis,* a pudding flavored with little black cherries or, out of season, with prunes.

Best known wines are *Monbazillac* and *Cahors* red. *Pécharmant* is an excellent full-bodied red wine. An interesting liqueur is produced locally, *crème de noix,* made from walnuts.

HOTELS AND RESTAURANTS. This is, on the whole, an area for modest inns rather than luxury hotels, in spite of the number of tourists, though many a modest inn harbours an outstanding restaurant. These restaurants can sometimes be chic, not to mention pretentious places, but they are often family-run (often for several generations), and with rustic decor. The food, on the other hand, is generally superb, based on local produce and served in generous portions. Rooms are clean and often attractive, perhaps with antique or typically regional furniture, but don't expect the modern amenities of Ameri-can-style chains. The region also has a large number of *gîtes* and other holiday rentals, as well as an increasing number of farm inns.

For general notes on hotels and restaurants, see "Hotels" and "Restaurants" in *Facts at Your Fingertips.*

BRANTÔME. *Moulin de l'Abbaye* (E), tel. 53-05-80-22. 12 rooms. Closed Nov. through Apr; restaurant closed Mon. Restored and converted watermill with lots of charm and good *nouvelle cuisine.* AE, DC, MC, V. *Chabrol* (M), 59 rue Gambetta (tel. 53-05-70-15). 20 rooms. Closed part of Feb., mid-Nov. to mid-Dec.; restaurant closed Sun. dinner, Mon. (Oct. through June). Small and charming, with excellent restaurant, *Frères Charbonnel,* serving some local dishes. AE, DC, V.

Restaurant. At **Champagnac-de-Belair,** 6 km. (3½ miles) northeast, *Moulin du Roc* (M), tel. 53-54-80-36. Closed mid-Jan. to mid-Feb., mid-Nov. to mid-Dec.; restaurant closed Tues, Wed. lunch. Converted 17th-century walnut-oil mill on the river Dronne, creeper-covered and altogether delightful; melt-in-the-mouth *nouvelle cuisine* cooked by inspired and rightly-famed woman chef. Taste the *foie gras au miel* or the *truite aux cèpes.* Also has 8 very pretty rooms (E). AE, DC, MC, V.

BRIVE LA GAILLARDE. *Truffe Noire* (M), 22 blvd. Anatole France (tel. 55-74-35-32). 35 rooms. Picturesque old building, well-modernized, with garden and well-known restaurant. AE, DC, V.

At **Varetz,** 10 km. (6 miles) northwest, *Château de Castel-Novel* (E), tel. 55-85-00-01. 23 rooms. Closed mid-Oct. through Apr.; restaurant closed Mon.

lunch. 13th-century fortified château, a favorite of Colette's and perfectly situated for sightseeing; pool, tennis, large grounds, and good regional cuisine. AE, DC, V.

Restaurants. *Crémaillère* (M), 53 av. Paris (tel. 55-74-32-47). Closed second half Feb., second half July, Mon., and Sun. dinner. Delicious *nouvelle cuisine* using excellent local produce; also has 12 rooms. AE, V.

At **Meyssac,** 20 km. (12½ miles) away, *Relais du Quercy* (I), tel. 55-25-40-31. Closed Fri. for dinner except school hols. Particularly pleasant little family hotel right by medieval village of Collonges-le-Rouge; local specialties (especially wild mushrooms) at very reasonable prices. Also has 12 modest rooms. AE, MC, V.

CAHORS. *Wilson* (E), 72 rue Wilson (tel. 65-35-41-80). 36 rooms. Central, well-modernized; sauna, but no restaurant. MC, V. *Terminus* (M), 5 av. Freycinet (tel. 65-35-24-50). 31 rooms. Restaurant closed Wed. and throughout Feb. Good, old-fashioned service plus modern comforts; the good restaurant has a different telephone number (65-30-01-97). V. *France* (I), 252 av. Jean-Jaurès (tel. 65-35-16-76). 79 rooms. Closed Christmas and New Year. Comfortable and well-placed, close to the rail station and famous old bridge; no restaurant. AE, DC, MC, V.

At **Lalbenque,** 9 km. (6 miles) south by RN20, *Aquitaine* (M), (tel. 65-21-00-51). 44 rooms. Modern rooms with country views; pool; restaurant.

At **Mercuès,** 8 km. (5 miles) north, *Château de Mercuès* (E), tel. 65-20-00-01. 46 rooms. Closed Nov. to Easter. Comfortable rooms in splendid château overlooking Lot Valley; pool, grounds, tennis, plus stylish restaurant serving a mixture of regional and *nouvelle* cuisine. DC, MC, V.

Restaurant. *Taverne* (M), 41 rue J.B.-Delpech (tel. 65-35-28-66). Closed mid-Nov. to mid-Dec., Sun. dinner and Mon., except May through Sept. An old favorite; delightful inn, newish cuisine. AE, DC, MC, V.

CONQUES. *Ste.-Foy* (M), tel. 65-69-84-03. 20 rooms. Closed mid-Oct. through Mar.; restaurant closed Sun. in July and Aug. (serves dinner only). Delightful spot, facing basilica; nicely furnished, with pleasant restaurant. V.

DOMME. Restaurant. *Esplanade* (M), tel. 53-28-31-41. Closed Feb., Nov., and Mon. Good place for lunch after admiring the views over the Dordogne valley; rich regional cuisine. Also has 19 attractive and peaceful rooms. AE.

ESPALION. *Moderne* (M), 27 blvd. Guizard (tel. 65-44-05-11). 32 rooms. Closed Oct. through Feb., Mon., Sun. dinner. Comfortable and friendly hotel in attractive village with tasty *nouvelle cuisine* using local produce. V.

LES EYZIES. *Cro-Magnon* (M), tel. 53-06-97-06. 24 rooms. Closed mid-Oct. through April. Surrounded by gardens; excellent restaurant, family-run and specializing in "new" versions of regional dishes. Pool. AE, DC, MC, V. *Glycines* (M), rte. Périgueux (tel. 53-06-97-07). 25 rooms. Closed Nov. through Mar. Large garden and good regional cuisine are among the many delights of this pleasant hostelry on the Périgueux road. AE, V.

Restaurant. *Centenaire* (E), tel. 53-06-97-18. Closed Nov. through Mar.; restaurant closed Tues. lunch. Superb regional cuisine cooked "new"-style; also has 27 (M) rooms and 4 luxurious apartments. AE, DC, MC, V.

LIMOGES. *Royal Limousin* (E), pl. République (tel. 55-34-65-30). 75 rooms. Central and well run; no restaurant. AE, DC, MC, V. *Jeanne d'Arc* (M), 17 av. Gal de Gaulle (tel. 55-77-67-77). 55 rooms. Excellent for short stay; well equipped rooms. MC, V. *Mapotel Luk* (M), 29 pl. Jourdan (tel. 55-33-44-00). 53 rooms. Closed mid-Dec. through the New Year; restaurant closed Sun. for dinner. Comfortable and well-modernized; restaurant is called *Taverne Alsacienne.* AE, DC, V. *Richelieu* (I), 40 av. Baudin (tel. 55-34-22-82). 27 rooms. No restaurant. V.

Restaurants. *Pré St.-Germain* (I), 26 rue Loi (tel. 55-34-15-17). Closed Sat. for lunch, Sun., public hols., most of Aug., 2 weeks in Jan. Good cooking with fresh produce; a new find. v. *Versailles* (I), 20 pl. Aine (tel. 55-34-13-39). Closed part of Feb., most of Aug., Mon., Sun. dinner. Family-type meals and good local wines. v.

MONTIGNAC-SUR-VÉZÈRE. *Relais du Soleil d'Or* (E), rue 4-Septembre (tel. 53-51-80-22). 40 rooms. Closed Dec. through March. Beautifully-modernized to provide very comfortable, well-planned rooms; pool, big garden, good restaurant, and excellent service. v. *Lascaux* (I), av. Jean-Jaurès (tel. 53-51-82-81). 16 rooms. Closed Nov. through Mar.; restaurant closed Mon. (Apr. through June only), Sun. evening. Small and modest, with a family-type restaurant. v.

PÉRIGUEUX. *Bristol* (M), 37 rue Gadaud (tel. 53-08-75-90). 29 rooms. Fairly central, with soundproofed rooms, though no restaurant. v. *Domino* (M), 21 pl. Francheville (tel. 53-08-25-80). 37 rooms. Lovely, creeper-covered, traditional hotel; good regional cuisine and delightful courtyard garden. AE, DC, MC, v. *Régina* (I), 14 rue Papin (tel. 53-08-40-44). 46 rooms. Right by the station; no restaurant. AE, MC, v.

At **Antonne**, 6 km. (4 miles) north via route de Limoges, *Ecluse* (I), (tel. 53-06-00-04). 53 rooms. Closed Sat. except in summer. Modern hotel with good facilities. AE, DC, MC, v.

Restaurants. *Léon* (M), 18 cours Tourny (tel. 53-53-41-93). Closed second half of May, Christmas and New Year, Mon. (except July through Sept.). Old-established and popular with locals; mostly regional cuisine. AE, DC, v.*Oison* (M), 31 rue St.-Front (tel. 53-09-84-02). Closed Sun. for dinner, Mon., and mid-Feb. to mid-Mar. *Nouvelle cuisine,* light and well prepared. Good-value *menus.* AE, DC, v.

ROCAMADOUR. *Beau Site et Notre Dame* (M), rue Roland-le-Preux (tel. 65-33-63-08). 53 rooms. Closed mid-Nov. through Mar. Tasty regional cuisine; delightfully located. AE, DC, MC, v. *Château et Relais Amadourien* (M), rte. Château (tel. 65-33-62-22). 58 rooms. Closed Nov. through Mar. Peaceful setting, with separate annexe; good regional cuisine and attractive rooms. AE, DC. *Panoramic* (I), in the Hospitalet district (tel. 65-33-63-06). 13 rooms. Closed mid-Nov. through Jan. Modest, with good-value meals. DC, v. *Ste.-Marie* (I), tel. 65-33-63-07. 22 rooms. Closed Nov. through Mar. Terrace, lovely views, and good cuisine, too. v.

Restaurants. *Augerge de la Garenne* (M), just outside town on the D247 (tel. 65-33-65-88). Pretty garden, with pool; also has 25 rooms.

At **Rignac**, 4½ km. (2½ miles) away, *Château de Roumegouse* (M), tel. 65-33-63-81. Closed mid-Nov. through Mar., Tues. Picturesque château makes fine setting for light and tasty regional dishes as created by a *nouvelle cuisine* chef; also has 12 elegant (E) rooms. AE, DC, v.

RODEZ. *Mapotel Broussy* (M), 1 av. Victor-Hugo (tel. 65-68-18-71). 76 rooms. Pleasant family-run hotel; straightforward cuisine. *Tour Maje* (M), blvd. Gally (tel. 65-68-34-68). 42 rooms. Modern rooms in a building attached to the 14th-century tower that gives it its name; no restaurant. AE, DC, MC, v. *Moderne* (I), 9 rue Abbé-Bessou (tel. 65-68-03-10). 27 rooms. Closed first half of Jan. Central and modernized; good (M) restaurant serves rich and tasty regional dishes. v.

At **Onet**, 3½ km. (2 miles) away, *Hostellerie de Fontanges* (E), tel. 65-42-20-28. 42 rooms. 16th-century building, beautifully furnished, with gardens, pepperpot turrets, pool, tennis and excellent restaurant (M) serving mostly rich regional specialties. AE, DC, MC, v.

Restaurants. *Régent* (M), 11 av. Durand-de-Gros (tel. 65-67-03-30). Closed first half of July, Sun., for lunch (except public hols.). Chic décor, and cuisine to match; must reserve. AE, DC, MC, v. *St.-Amans* (M), 12 rue Madeleine (tel. 65-68-03-18). Closed Sun. for dinner, Mon. and Feb. Good classical cuisine.

ST.-CÉRÉ. *Coq Arlequin* (I), blvd. Dr.-Roux (tel. 65-38-02-13). 30 rooms. Closed Jan. and Feb. and Mon. in Nov. and Dec. Old-established place, still run by same family and still serving tempting regional dishes, though with some *nouvelle cuisine* touches these days; shop next door sells the restaurant's specialties in to-go versions. V.

Restaurants. *France* (M), av. Maynard (tel. 65-38-02-16). Closed Oct. through May. A good place to try Quercy specialties (out of doors in summer), including wines; also has 27 pleasant rooms. V.

At **Sousceyrac**, 16 km. (10 miles) away, *Déjeuner de Sousceyrac* (M), tel. 65-33-00-56. Closed Oct. through Mar., Sat. except July and Aug. Superb, good-value regional cuisine; also has 15 (I) rooms. AE, DC, V.

At **Gramat**, 20 km. (12½ miles) away, *Lion d'Or* (M), tel. 65-38-73-18. Closed mid-Dec. to mid-Jan., and Mon. Nov. through Feb. Excellent-value *menus*, mostly regional cuisine; also a hotel with 15 rooms. V.

SARLAT. *Hoirie* (M), 2 km. (1¼ mile) south (tel. 53-59-05-62). 13 rooms. Closed mid-Dec. through mid-Mar.; no dinners for non-residents. Delightful Relais du Silence converted from an old hunting lodge; now has a restaurant, for which you must reserve ahead. AE, DC, MC, V. *Hostellerie Meysset* (M), 3 km. (2 miles) north (tel. 53-59-08-29). 21 rooms. Closed Oct. through April. Very attractive creeper-covered manorhouse; nicely furnished rooms, friendly service, and mouth-watering regional meals. AE, DC, V. *Madeleine* (M), 1 pl. Petite-Rigaudie (tel. 53-59-12-40). 19 rooms. Closed mid-Nov. through mid-Mar. Nice family-run place with large, comfortable rooms and good, rich regional cuisine. MC, V. *St.-Albert* (M), 10 pl. Pasteur (tel. 53-59-01-09). 57 rooms. Closed Sun. for dinner and Mon. Nov. to mid-March. Another pleasant, family-run spot; restaurant does filling, regional cooking. AE, DC, MC, V. *Salamandre* (M), rue Abbé-Surguier (tel. 53-59-35-98). 23 rooms. Closed Nov. to mid-Apr. Comfortable, simple.

At **La Roque-Gageac**, 13 km. (7½ miles) away, *Belle Etoile* (I), tel. 53-29-51-44. Closed mid-Oct. to mid-Apr. Pretty village setting, good views of Dordogne river, good-value meals. V. *Gardette* (I), tel. 53-29-51-58. 15 rooms. Closed mid-Oct. through Mar. Small and modest, with garden and restaurant.

Restaurants. *Rossignol* (M), blvd. Arlet (tel. 53-59-03-20). Closed second half of both March and Nov., Mon. Family-run and pleasant; traditional regional dishes plus some *nouvelle cuisine* recipes; *menus* are superb value. Terrace.

SORGES-EN-PÉRIGORD. Restaurant. *Hôtel de la Mairie* (I), pl. Mairie (tel. 53-05-02-11). Closed second half of Oct., Wed. Good spot for lunch if you're visiting the Truffle Museum; nice little family-run place specializing in Périgord cuisine. Has 12 modest rooms, too. AE, MC, V.

SOUILLAC. *Ambassadeurs* (I), 12 av. de Gaulle (tel. 65-32-78-36). 28 rooms. Closed Oct., New Year period, Fri. dinner, Sat. (Nov. through June). Quercy cuisine at its best, and at very fair prices, too; well-decorated rooms. V. *Grand* (I), 1 allée Verninac (tel. 65-32-78-30). 27 rooms. Closed Nov. through Mar., Wed. except summer months. Comfortable rooms; light meals available in terrace restaurant. AE, V.

Restaurant. *Vieille Auberge* (M), pl. Minoterie (tel. 65-32-79-43). Closed mid-Nov. to mid-March. Regional cuisine in a charming old inn; must reserve in summer. Also has 20 comfortable rooms in a modern annexe with pool. MC, V. *Renaissance* (I), 2 av. Jean-Jaurès (tel. 65-32-78-04). Regional cooking and delicious wines. Also 24 rooms; half-board compulsory in season. MC, V.

TRÉMOLAT. *Vieux Logis* (E), tel. 53-22-80-06. 14 rooms. Lovely Relais et Châteaux member in typical Dordogne village; country atmosphere and excellent regional cuisine. AE, DC, MC, V. *Panoramic* (I), 2½ km. (1½ miles) northwest (tel. 53-22-80-42). 23 rooms. Closed Jan. and Feb. Modern and well-located for gorgeous views of Dordogne river; no restaurant. MC.

TULLE. *Limouzi* (I), 16 quai République (tel. 55-26-42-00). 50 rooms. Restaurant closed Sun., Jan., and first half of July. Central and well-run; good-value rooms and meals. AE, DC, V.

Restaurants. *Central* (M), 32 rue Jean-Jaurès (tel. 55-26-24-46). Closed most of Aug., Sat., Sun. dinner. Family-run restaurant specializing in regional cuisine. V. *Toque Blanche* (M), 29 rue Jean-Jaurès (tel. 55-26-75-41). Closed most of Jan., Sun. (except public hols. and during July and Aug.). Good-value regional dishes cooked "new" style by young chef; lots of charm. Also has 10 nice rooms. AE, V.

TOURS AND EXCURSIONS. By Car. If you're traveling by car, you can follow a number of well-signposted itineraries referred to as *circuits touristiques*. For instance, in the Lot region you will soon spot the following: *Itineraire touristique Cahors par Gourdon* (70 km./44 miles) from Cahors via Souillac and the Lot and Dordogne valleys; *Circuit du Vin de Cahors* (120 km./75 miles) in the Lot Valley vineyards and visiting Bonaguil château; *Circuit des Vallées du Lot et du Cèle* (155 km./97 miles) from Cahors, including St.-Cinq-la-Popie and Figeac; *Circuit des Merveilles* (75 km./47 miles) from Gramat through the high spots of the Quercy region. Details of these and other circuits, mainly from Cahors, Rocamadour, and Souillac may be obtained from tourist offices, who will supply leaflets and maps.

By Bus. SNCF organize bus excursions from the following towns: Bergerac ("Provencale en Périgord"); Brive-La-Gaillande ("La Préhistoire," "Les Grottes"); Cahors ("Grottes de Cabrerets," "St.-Cinq-la-Popie"); Figeac ("La Vallée du Cèle et du Lot"); Périgueux ("Circuit des Bastides," "Vallée de la Dordogne"); Rocamadour ("Padirac"); Rodez ("Discovering the Aveyron"); Sarlat ("La Préhistoire," "Lascaux II"); Souillac ("Les Eyzies," "Collonges-la-Rouge"); Tulle ("Barrage du Chastany," "Bort-les-Orgues").

Excursions also set out from Périgueux, arranged by the Dordogne tourist office, June to Sept. only: "Val de Bronne" (half-day) and "Sarlat et la Préhistoire," "Circuit des Bastides," and "Journée Préhistoire" (all full-day). Other bus excursions leave from St.-Céré (June through Sept.) and from Bergerac.

By Boat. Boat trips may be made along the Lot and Dordogne rivers. Details available from tourist offices.

SIGHTSEEING DATA. Exploring the villages and little towns of this still largely unspoilt region, and the extraordinary grottos and caves of its landscapes, are perhaps the major attractions here. But, though museums and châteaux may be thinner on the ground here than elsewhere in France, there are nonetheless a number of interesting places to visit. We give details below.

For general notes on visiting museums and historic buildings in France, see "Sightseeing" in *Facts at Your Fingertips*.

BERGERAC. Musée du Tabac (Tobacco Museum). Open Tues. to Sat. 9–12, 2–6; Sun. and public hols. 2–6; closed Mon.

BEYNAC. Château, tel. 53-29-50-40. Open Mar. to mid-Nov., daily 10–12, 2.30–7, 6 in winter.

BIRON. Château, tel. 53-22-62-01. Open daily, Feb. to mid-Dec., 9–11.30, 2–6; closed Tues. (except July and Aug.).

BOURDEILLES. Château, tel. 53-05-73-36. Open daily, Feb. through Sept., 9–11.30, 2–6; closed Tues. (except mid-June to mid-Sept.).

CADOUIN. Abbaye. Open daily, Feb. through June, Sept. to mid-Dec, 9–11.30, 2–6; closed Tues. mid-Oct. through Feb.; July and Aug. daily 9–6.

CASTELNAU-BRETENOUX. Château, tel. 65-38-52-04. Open daily, Apr. through Sept., 9–12, 2–6; closed Tues.; Oct. through Mar., 10–12, 2–5; closed Tues. and public hols.

CASTELNAUD. Château, tel. 53-29-50-12. Open daily, July to mid-Sept., 9.30–12, 2.30–6.30.

LA COUVERTOIRADE. Ramparts, tel. 65-62-25-81. Open daily, Mar. through Dec., 8–6.

CONQUES. Abbatiale Ste.-Foy (Abbey Church). Open daily 9–12, 2–6; stays open until 7 in July and Aug. Closed Feb. and Tues. in winter.

LES EYZIES-DE-TAYAC. Château, housing **Musée National de la Préhistoire,** tel. 53-06-97-03. Open daily, Mar. through Nov., 9.30–12, 2–6; closed Tues.; Dec. through Feb. closes at 5.
   Grotte de Font-de-Gaume, tel. 53-08-00-94. Open daily, Apr. through Sept., 9–12, 2–6; closed Tues.; Oct. through Mar., 10–12, 2–4; closed Tues. Number of visitors daily limited to 700.
   Grottes des Combarelles, tel. 53-08-00-94. Open daily, except Dec., public hols. and Tues.
   Grotte du Grand Roc, tel. 53-06-96-76. Open daily, July to mid-Sept., 9–6.30; Apr. through June and mid-Sept. through Oct., daily 9–12, 2–6.
   Gorges d'Enfer, tel. 53-06-94-71. Open daily, mid-Mar. to mid-Nov., 9.30–6; Nov. through mid-Mar., 10–12, 1–5.
   Laugerie-Basse, tel. 53-06-97-12. Open daily, Apr. through Sept., 9.30–6.30.
   Laugerie-Haute, tel. 53-08-00-94. Open daily, Apr. through Sept., 9–12, 2–6; closed Tues.; Oct. through Mar., 10–12, 2–4; closed Tues. and public hols.

HAUTEFORT. Château, tel. 53-50-40-04. Open daily, Easter to mid-Sept., 9–12, 2–7; mid-Sept. through Oct, 9–12, 2–6; Nov. to Easter, Sun. and public holidays, 2–5.

HERM. Château, tel. 53-05-41-71. Open daily, mid-June through Aug., 10–12, 2–6. Closed Wed.

LACAVE. Grottes de Lacave. Open daily, Apr. through Oct., 9–12, 2–6.30.

LIMOGES. Musée de l'Ancien Évêché, pl. Cathédrale (tel. 55-33-70-10). Open daily, Oct. through Mar., 10–11.45, 2–5; closed Tues.; June through Sept., 10–11.45, 2–6; closed Tues. and public hols.
   Musée National Adrien-Dubouché (Ceramics Museum). Open daily, 10–12, 1.30–5 (or 6); closed Tues. and public hols.
   St.-Martial (Crypt). Open daily, July through Sept., 9.30–12, 2.30–7.

LOSSE. Château, tel. 53-50-70-38. Open daily, July to mid-Sept., 10–12.30, 2–6.30.

MONBAZILLAC. Château, tel. 53-58-30-27. Open daily, May through Oct., 9–12, 2–6.30; Nov. through Apr., 9.30–12, 2–5.30.

MONTIGNAC-SUR-VÉZÈRE. Lascaux II, tel. 53-53-44-35. Open daily, except Mon., mid-June to mid-Sept., 9.30–7; Feb. to mid-June, and mid-Sept. to mid-Dec., 10–12, 2–5.
   Le Regourdou. Open daily, Apr. to Sept., 9–11.30, 2.30–5.30.

PÉRIGUEUX. Guided city tours. July and Aug., Tues. and Fri., 2.30 (Medieval and Renaissance circuit); 5 (Gallo-Roman circuit).

Musée du Périgord, tel. 53-53-16-42. Open daily, 10–12, 2–7; closed Tues. and public hols.

PUYGUILHEM. Château, tel. 53-54-82-18. Open daily, Feb. to mid-Dec., 9–11.30, 2–6; closed Tues. (no Tues. closure in July and Aug.).

ROUFFIGNAC. Grotte aux Cent Mammouths, tel. 53-05-41-71. Open daily, Easter through June and mid-Sept. through Oct., 10–11.30, 2–5; July and Aug., 9–11.30, 2–6; Nov. to Easter, Sun. and Nov. 1 only, visits at 11 A.M. and 3 P.M.

ST.-CÉRÉ. Chatêau de Montal, 1½ km. (1 mile) west. Open daily, Easter to Oct., 9.30–11.30, 2.30–5.30; closed Sat. (no Sat. closure in July and Aug.).

Grottes de Presque, tel. 65-38-07-44. Open daily, Apr. to mid-June and mid-Sept. to mid-Oct., 9–12, 2–6; mid-June to mid-Sept., 8.30–12, 2–7.

SORGES-EN-DORDOGNE. Ecomusée de la Truffe (Truffle Museum). Open daily, 2–5 (until 6 mid-June to mid-Sept.); closed Tues.

TURENNE. Château. Open mid-Mar. through Oct., Mon. to Sat. 9–12, 2–7, Sun. 10–12, 2–5.

SHOPPING. The most popular purchases in this region are undoubtedly food-oriented. Jars or cans of preserved goose and duck, expensive *foie gras,* and even more expensive truffles make good presents to take home to gourmet friends. Look out, too, for glass preserving jars containing tasty local mushrooms, such as *cèpes* (boletus) or *girolles.* Porcelain and enamels are world-famous specialties in Limoges, and many stores in the town center will be happy to supply you. Other worthwhile buys include reproductions of the region's prehistoric cave paintings and a variety of craft items; most of the picturesque villages now have at least one little shop selling the work of local craftsmen, and craft fairs are common occurrences.

THE ARDÈCHE AND THE CÉVENNES

Sapphire-Blue Hills

To the north of the Languedoc coast, sandwiched between the Rhône Valley and the rounded hills of the Auvergne, lie what Robert Louis Stevenson tellingly referred to as "the French Highlands." Indeed, the wild upland reaches of the Cévennes Mountains and the remote Ardèche are in many ways reminiscent of the Scottish Highlands. Away from well-worn tourist routes, they have much to offer those who like exploring regions rich in history, where centuries-old traditions have remained intact. Don't come here if you're looking for the razzmatazz of mass tourism, luxury hotels or big-city entertainment. Do come if you feel you can identify with a proud and fiercely independent people who have managed to preserve their remote territory as a land apart, which draws visitors to return again and again to sample its unique delights.

Not least of these are landscapes of amazing variety, ranging from the chestnut forests and cool mountains of the northern Ardèche—known locally simply as "The Mountain"—to the hot, dry region of Bas-Vivarais in the south, pure Provençal with its olive trees and scrub-filled rocky landscapes bordering on the *garrigue* around Nîmes; from the heather-covered wilderness of the Cévennes to the strange windswept plateaux known as the Causses. This is a land for hiking and for action-packed holidays canoeing down the Ardèche gorges or spelunking in extraordinary grottoes and caves, seeking out prehistoric remains, bathing in brilliantly blue pools overhung by rocky ledges, or even skiing from the newly-equipped little resorts specializing in cross-country skiing.

There is plenty for the less energetic: notably the pleasures of the local cooking, for this is a region where you'll find genuine local cuisine, uncorrupted by convenience foods or the latest fads and fashions that so quickly sweep through less remote areas. And although there are few major historic buildings to be visited, there are many delightful little museums devoted to local arts and crafts and history and culture, often housed in farmhouses or cottages rather than in grand museums of the traditional type. History lovers can trace the stirring events of the 16th and 17th-century Wars of Religion that left such a mark on the region. Those interested in traditional crafts will have a field day: this region is famous for producing beautiful objects that bear little resemblance to the mass-produced articles found elsewhere, and the local authorities are making a conscious effort to revive traditional crafts and thus bring back life and vigor to an area that has suffered badly from depopulation.

Another key attraction of the region is undoubtedly its low prices. This is the area for cosy little family hotels—at least two-thirds of the Ardèche's hotels are members of the good-value Logis de France association—and modest restaurants serving excellent meals at prices totally unrelated to those of the tourist-haunted Mediterranean coast or the consciously gastronomic Rhône Valley area. Self-caterers are well provided for: the Ardèche has the second-largest pool of *gîtes* of any French *département*, over 1,000 of them, and farm camping is common. The Cévennes are full of modest little farm-inns and hikers' shelters. Transport, too, is easier than in many areas: with few of the two-car families found in more affluent regions, the regular bus network is comprehensive and services reasonably frequent.

Exploring the Cévennes

A convenient starting-point for visiting the rugged Cévennes Mountains is Alès, a lively little town not far from Nîmes offering good bus and train services. The perfect literary companion is Robert Louis Stevenson's *Travels with a Donkey in the Cévennes.* No need to go to extremes and take a donkey, but you might like to try following in R.L.S.'s footsteps, as increasing numbers of tourists, many of them from Britain, have been doing since the centenary of his journey in 1978 revived interest in his exploits. Things have changed surprisingly little in those hundred-odd years. You'll still be able to revel in the "high rocky hills, as blue as sapphire . . . ridge upon ridge, heathery, craggy, the sun glittering on veins of rock, the underwood clambering in the hollows, as rude as God made them at the first . . . " that so enthralled R.L.S. The sight of nature in the raw, untouched by man, is what many visitors to the Cévennes find exhilarating.

The rugged nature of the terrain makes it ideal country for guerrilla warfare. During World War II the Cévennes were one of the major centers of the French Resistance against the German occupying powers. Guerrilla skirmishes have been a feature of this region for centuries, for this is where French Protestants held out longest against official attempts to drive the "heretics" into recanting their faith. When

Louis XIV revoked the Edict of Nantes in 1685, thus putting an end to the religious toleration granted to those of the Protestant faith by Henri IV nearly a century earlier, the Protestants in the Cévennes resisted the royal decree. They read the banned Bible in their homes and organized clandestine assemblies in the "Desert" or "Wilderness" of their remote mountain fastnesses, addressed by wandering preachers. Unending persecution finally drove them into open rebellion and the War of the Camisards (the name is said to come from a dialect word for *chemise* or "shirt," for the Cévenol rebels were poor peasants without armor or uniforms) raged from 1702–5, the "guerrillas" keeping thousands of royal troops at bay before their inevitable defeat.

A good place to delve into the turbulent history of the region is the fascinating Musée du Désert (or Wilderness Museum) at the Mas Soubeyran near Alès. This modest hamlet overlooking the Gardon was the home of one of the bravest of the Camisard leaders, Pierre Laporte, always known as Rolland, and Rolland's house (the Maison de Rolland) now forms part of the museum. You can even see the hiding hole in the kitchen where he could escape the king's dragoons when they swooped on the hamlet in their attempt to wipe out the movement. The museum has enthralling exhibits illustrating the life of the persecuted Protestants, including folding lecterns carried by itinerant preachers to their openair services: if the lookout warned that royal troops were in the vicinity the congregation melted into the caves and hollows of the terrain they knew so well, the lectern was folded and hidden, the communion cups thrust into nooks and crannies in the rocks. Every year tens of thousands of Protestants from all over Europe and the U.S. gather at the Mas Soubeyran to commemorate the sufferings of their co-religionists.

Anduze and St.-Jean-du-Gard

Close to the Mas Soubeyran is the first of the many extraordinary underground grottoes and caves you can visit in this part of France, which seems to be pitted with natural "wells" or wide crevasses known locally as *avens* and caused by rain water penetrating the limestone plateaux to the west of the Cévennes. As the wells are gradually widened they form caves and grottoes through which underground rivers then run.

The Grotte de Trabuc is the largest in the Cévennes and is famous for the curious formation of stalagmites known as *Les Cent Mille Soldats* (The Hundred Thousand Soldiers) from their resemblance to an army on the march. Like most of the region's grottoes, it shows signs of human habitation dating back to the Neolithic period and has been used as a hiding place in times of danger, such as the Wars of Religion and World War II. The grotto can be visited, but do make sure—as when visiting any other subterranean caves in the area—that you are suitably equipped with warm clothes and stout, non-slip shoes.

Close by is another extraordinary natural sight: the Bambuseraie de Prafrance, a bamboo and sequoia forest said to be the only one of its kind in Europe and including no fewer than 60 varieties of bamboo. Try to visit in the morning, when the light is best, as you're bound to want to take photos.

The small town of Anduze, picturesquely set beside the Gardon river, is famous for its pottery and makes a pleasant place to stay with its narrow old streets and its 14th-century Tour de l'Horloge, or clock tower. An attractive road leads from here beside the Gardon de Mialet, flowing through a narrow gorge, via the village of Générargues to St.-Jean-du-Gard, a delightful little town that has become an important center for hikers and others exploring the Cévennes. It stages a number of cultural events in the summer and has a charming museum devoted to the life of the Cévenol people down the ages.

From St.-Jean you can take the twisting road known as the Corniche des Cévennes, which offers fabulous views all the way and winds through a number of tempting villages before reaching Florac. Florac is the main town of the Cévennes National Park: designated an official nature reserve in the early '70s, it covers around 85,000 hectares, and is France's second largest. Here you can ramble or enjoy cross-country skiing, study protected species and hunt for rare wild flowers, staying in friendly little hikers' shelters or for bed and breakfast in modest farmhouses. There are breathtaking views for Mont Aigoual, south of Florac, best visited during the cool hours of a summer day, on a clear winter's day, or even at sunrise.

The Causses

Florac is one of several centers for excursions into the strange region known as the Causses, the term given to the windy limestone plateaux that are unique in France. This is wild and harsh country with hot dry summers, torrential rains in fall and bitterly cold winters. But it is also endlessly fascinating and beautiful, and still relatively unexplored. Its isolation is dramatically interrupted each year when hundreds of thousands of sheep are driven up from the Camargue and the Languedoc coastal areas to graze on the high summer pastures. This *transhumance,* as it is known, is often carried out by trucks nowadays, rather than as formerly when shepherds would drive the flocks on day after day; but the arrival of the sheep is still an awesome sight.

The major natural phenomenon in the Causses is the Gorges du Tarn. The river Tarn, which rises on Mont Lozère, sweeps down the Cévennes, becoming a raging torrent which has gouged a canyon separating the Causse Méjean from the Causse Sauveterre and formed a spectacular series of gorges stretching for nearly 50 km. (over 30 miles). You can walk along them, which is rewarding though tiring, or go by boat or canoe, a thrilling experience. Weirdly shaped groups of rocks— graphically referred to in French as *chaos*—seem to fling themselves headlong into the river; russet and ochre cliffs tower over the narrow gorge. This is nature in the raw, and not to be missed.

Millau is another good center for excursions and is itself worth visiting to see its medieval streets, picturesque old wash-house and 12th-century belfry topped by a 17th-century tower. Nearby is a place of pilgrimage for cheese-lovers: Roquefort-sur-Soulzon, where the world-famous ewe's milk cheese has been made since the days of the Romans. A number of the cheese cellars, as well as a small museum, can be visited. The ancient fortified village of La Couvertoirade, once a stronghold of the Knights Templar, is also worth a visit. And no one visiting the Causses should miss the Aven Armand near Meyrueis, one of the world's most famous subterranean sights. It was discovered in 1897 by Louis Armand, a local locksmith who assisted the pioneering French spelunker Edouard-Alfred Martel on many of his explorations. Its chief glory is a soaring cathedral-like cave with a petrified forest of hundreds of huge stalagmites creating a fairyland of magical shapes.

The Grotte de Dargilan, also near Meyrueis, is very nearly as splendid, with its huge "Belltower," over 20 meters (65 feet) high, and its towering "Mosque" made up of glistening stalagmites.

Mende, a bustling little town, and another possible excursion center, has a fine cathedral and graceful 14th-century bridge, the Pont Notre-Dame; its museum is full of artefacts from prehistoric times onwards and also includes a small folk art exhibit. This is the chief town of the Gévaudan region, whose main claim to fame is the Beast of Gévaudan which sowed terror among the populace in the 1760s by attacking women and children watching over the local flocks and allegedly sucking them dry of blood. The creature—which turned out to be a wolf—caught the imagination of the court and Louis XV sent his chief archer to put an end to its depredations, though it was eventually killed by a local peasant. The legend lives on and French mothers still frighten their errant offspring with threats that the Beast will come for them.

The Route des Cévennes

The eastern face of the Cévennes, bordering on the Ardèche, is less wild but nevertheless offers some grandiose scenery. The road and the rail line (this is the route followed by the *Cévenol* tourist train) climb up from Alès to La Bastide, a peaceful little resort popular with hikers and skiers and boasting a Trappist monastery, Notre-Dame-des-Neiges (Our Lady of the Snows), that features in *Travels with a Donkey*. One of the most spectacular views on the way north is the beautiful artificial lake of Villefort fringed by heather-covered hills. Villefort is another popular holiday resort. Génolhac, too, is attractive, while beyond La Bastide, Langogne has an interesting church and some fine Gothic houses.

Exploring the Western Ardèche

From La Bastide an impressive mountain road leads via the tiny spa town of St.-Laurent-les-Bains (which is currently being extensively renovated for a new lease of life after a period of neglect) into the leafy northwestern corner of the Ardèche, famous for its chestnut forests. The mountain village of Valgorge makes a good center for exploring these upland reaches, where many delightful excursions can be made into the Massif du Tanargue, the southernmost tip of the volcanic mountains of the Auvergne. This region has some lovely mountain cols, or passes, such as the Col de la Croix de Bauzon or the Col de Meyrand, both offering superb panoramic views. The little town of Jaujac is a popular holiday center.

To the south you should try to visit the beautiful Romanesque church of Thines, in a wild and lonely area not far from the town of Les Vans. This is the heart of the Bas-Vivarais region that has a strongly Mediterranean feel about it after the mountainous terrain of the rest of the Cévennes. Both Les Vans and Thines are centers for the revival of local crafts, and here you will find showrooms set up by the Compagnons de Gerboul, an association of craftsmen dedicated to repopulating this poverty-stricken part of France by encouraging local youngsters to train as craftsmen rather than seek work elsewhere. Craft workshops are also attracting holidaymakers from Paris and abroad who want to try their hand at a new skill and stay in a local farm or village.

From Les Vans you can visit a number of picturesque villages and make an unusual excursion into the Bois de Païolive, a wilderness of limestone rocks fashioned into strange ruin-like shapes by wind and water erosion. South of here is another interesting grotto, the Grotte de la Cocalière, which you can visit in a little train.

A pleasant spot in easy reach of Les Vans is Joyeuse, a tiny walled town with an imposing castle and a history dominated in the 16th and 17th centuries by the exploits of the lively and versatile Joyeuse brothers, who included a marshal of France, a cardinal and a Capuchin friar. With its busy market this is a popular center for excursions into the wild Beaume valley, where a series of miniature gorges offer many opportunities for bathing and fishing.

The best-known gorges in the Ardèches are of course the Gorges de l'Ardèche. The broad and beautiful river Ardèche is the loveliest natural feature in the region, and shooting the rapids in a canoe is so popular these days that the river banks are becoming unpleasantly crowded with campers in high summer. Swimming and picnicking along the narrow beaches are still delightful, though, and the whole length of the gorges—from Vallon-Pont-d'Arc, with its natural rock bridge, to Pont-St.-Esprit—is a joy for lovers of natural grandeur. Two more subterranean experiences can be enjoyed in this region. The Grotte de la Madeleine, close to the gorges, has a superb gallery with stalagtites and stalagmites seeming to form organ pipes and waterfalls, while the Aven d'Orgnac, discovered as late as 1935, is famous for the strange shapes apparently caused by an earthquake at the end of the Tertiary geological era.

Aubenas and Privas

Just north of the Vallon-Pont-d'Arc lies Ruoms, a pretty little town with several good pottery shops. Close to the Mas de la Vignasse on the edge of Auriolles, is a silk farm which once belonged to the family of the writer Alphonse Daudet, author of *Letters from my Windmill*. It has been turned into a delightful museum with exhibits to do with silkworm breeding and silk making, as well as with the writer and his work.

The silk-weaving industry was once the major source of wealth in the Ardèche, and many of the mulberry trees on which the silkworms fed survive. Aubenas is a busy market town perched high on a hill, with an interesting castle and some attractive old houses. It was once the silk capital of the region and you'll often spot houses here with arched balconies used for drying the silk. Aubenas is now famous for its *marrons glacés,* the chestnut industry bringing a degree of prosperity to the region. A bus or car ride from here will bring you to Largentière, formerly, as its name suggests, a silver-mining town; surprisingly, it is endowed with law courts looking like a Greek temple, though its days of prosperity are long since over. But it has a lively market, a picturesque series of old streets spanning the river, and it offers many interesting excursions into the area heading towards Valgorge and "The Mountain."

Another bus ride from Aubenas takes you to Vals-les-Bains, a mildly fashionable spa town producing millions of bottles of mineral water every year, and a mecca for those suffering from liver and stomach complaints. A picturesque road winds through peaceful villages to Antraigues, a typical hill village with narrow streets and carefully restored houses; several craft and antique shops are an added attraction here. The road continues to a more mountainous area where you will see Mont Gerbier de Jonc, a peculiar cone-shaped peak of blackish volcanic rock. If you're feeling energetic, you could climb it and be rewarded by magnificent views, though a bowl of wild loganberries and cream on one of the café terraces may be equally enticing. For this is a tourist-ridden spot, known to schoolchildren all over France as the place where the mighty Loire, the country's longest river, rises at the foot of the Gerbier de Jonc. The spring, marked by a stone monument, is usually a disappointing trickle, or may even be quite dry, but this is a pleasant place to visit, especially if you combine it with the Mont Mézenc, another volcanic peak, and with Ste.-Eulalie, a village famous for its Violet Fair in July, where dried herbs and flowers are sold alongside the more prosaic items typical of country fairs.

Also easily visited from Aubenas, though right in the other direction, is the village of Voguë, perched above the river Ardèche and the seat of a well-known family whose feudal castle was substantially rebuilt in the 16th century.

The road from Aubenas to Privas climbs spectacularly over the Col de l'Escrinet. From here the whole of the Ardèche is spread out at your feet, its gray and golden mountains stretching to the distant horizon. Privas, the capital of the Ardèche *département*, is a charming market town with an eventful past, particularly during the Wars of Religion, for it was a major bastion of the Protestant Huguenots. The most dramatic incident came in 1629, when the town was razed to the ground by the king's men. A couple of interesting little museums can be visited near Privas. The Musée Agricole du Verdus is housed in a country inn and is full of fascinating exhibits connected with the local way of life. A little further away is the Musée du Vivarais Protestant, at Pranles, this time in a typical local farmhouse. A favorite excursion from Privas is to the Grottes de la Jaubernie, where some of the banned Protestants took refuge from the royal troops, and the pretty old village of Coux.

The Haut-Vivarais

The northernmost region of the Ardèche, the Haut-Vivarais, consists of plateaux and valleys enjoying a temperate climate without the extremes of heat and cold found further south and west, and is mainly farm land. Its major center is Annonay, a busy industrial town with the largest population in the *département*. Annonay's heroes are the Montgolfier brothers, who invented the hot-air balloon (known in French as a *montgolfière*). The city's museum, the Musée Vivarois César Filhol, includes exhibits about their exploits and in 1983 the 200th anniversary of their first public demonstration of their new invention, in the place des Cordeliers, was celebrated with appropriate ceremony. Just outside town is the Haut-Vivarais Safari Park. Right in the north of the Ardèche, on the banks of the Rhône close to Annonay, is Serrières, which has an interesting Boatmen's Museum housed in a Gothic chapel.

The region also boasts its own steam train, "Le Mastrou", which runs on a narrow-gauge track from Lamastre to Tournon, following the Doux gorges. Tournon, an attractive town overlooking the Rhône opposite its twin, Tain-l'Hermitage, is a fitting place to end our journey to the Ardèche and Cévennes. Although technically in the Ardèche, with its castle perched on granite rocks, its lovely terraced gardens suspended above the river and its waterfront promenade, it seems to belong far more to the broad river valley than to the wilder regions to which it provides a gateway.

PRACTICAL INFORMATION FOR THE ARDÈCHE
AND THE CÉVENNES

TOURIST OFFICES. The three *départements* of the Ardèche and the Cévennes have their own regional tourist offices (written enquiries only). These are: **Ardèche,** 8 cours du Palais, 07002, Privas Cedex (tel. 75-64-04-66); **Gard,** 3 pl. des Arènes, BP 122, 30011 Nîmes Cedex (tel. 66-21-02-51); **Lozère,** pl. Urbain-V, BP 4, 48002 Mende Cedex (tel. 66-65-34-55).

There are local tourist offices in the following towns: **Alès,** 3 rue Michelet (tel. 66-52-21-15); **Anduze,** plan de Brie (tel. 66-61-98-17), (mid-June to mid-Sept. only); **Annonay,** pl. Cordeliers (tel. 75-33-24-51); **Aubenas,** pl. Airette (tel. 75-35-24-87); **Lamastre,** rue Hérold (tel. 75-06-48-99), (Easter through Sept. only); **Mende,** blvd. Soubeyran (tel. 66-65-02-69); **Privas,** 1 av. Chomérac (tel. 75-64-33-35); **Vals-les-Bains,** 12 av. Farincourt (tel. 75-37-42-34); **Les Vans,** pl. Ollier (tel. 75-37-24-48), (July and Aug. only); **Villefort,** rue Eglise (tel. 66-46-80-26).

REGIONAL FOOD AND DRINK. The Ardèche's main specialty is chestnuts, and they are to be found in every imaginable form: as *marrons glacés* (this is the major French producing area) or sweet purées and creams, preserved in sugar syrup *(au sirop)* or in brandy *(au cognac),* or in main dishes as savory purée or whole. Chestnuts are particularly good with goose and game birds. Traditional country dishes are braised slowly rather roasted, and are often flavored with wild mushrooms such as the tasty *mousserons* and herbs from the wild upland areas. The best local *charcuterie* is a type of sausage or salami called a *Jésus* (it looks rather like a swaddled baby), but you'll find many other varieties too. Fish are plentiful in the local rivers, with trout pre-eminent; stewed crayfish *(écrevisses)* in a tomato, onion and herb sauce can still sometimes be found. *Crique* is a delicious vegetable dish made from thinly sliced potatoes interleaved with slivers of garlic and baked to form a smooth cake. Salads are often dressed with walnut oil, which gives them a distinctive flavor. Ardèche cheeses are mostly made with goat's milk and are often flavored with local herbs. One of the region's few cow's milk cheeses is *Coucouron,* a fairly soft blue cheese from the plateau of the same name.

Desserts are often based on the superb local fruit, with fat juicy cherries a specialty, and wild raspberries and loganberries a treat not to be missed. Rich dark honey flavored with chestnuts makes desserts and pastries delicious. *Côtes du Vivarais* is a light local wine worth trying, and another local specialty is peach wine, flavored with its kernels, making a slightly bitter, almondy taste.

In the Cévennes the best-known peasant dish (enjoyed by R.L. Stevenson, incidentally) is *bajana,* a thick soup made from chestnuts steeped in milk, though you may have trouble finding it nowadays. In this traditionally poor region food is plain and simple. Local fish and game are flavored with *cèpes* and other delicious local mushrooms. Juicy lamb from animals grazed on the Causses plateaux is renowned, generally served plainly roasted. Small roast thrush and thrush pâté are found in and around Mende and Florac, while *Pélardon,* a flavorsome round goat's cheese is still made in farms and cottages throughout the Cévennes valleys. And you should certainly make sure to taste some *Roquefort* produced in the village that gives it its name, and the *Bleu des Causses,* also aged in natural caves.

HOTELS AND RESTAURANTS. The accent here is very much on small, traditional family hotels and modest restaurants. Long a neglected and poor area of France, there are very few large or expensive hotels or restaurants. Similarly, there are large numbers of *gîtes*—self-catering holiday homes—and camp sites.

For general notes on hotels and restaurants, see "Hotels" and "Restaurants" in *Facts at Your Fingertips*.

ALÈS. *Grand* (M), 17 pl. Gabriel-Péri (tel. 66-52-19-01). 42 rooms. Restaurant closed Dec. and Jan., Sat. for dinner and Sun. (except in July and Aug.). Old-fashioned but adequate; central, with restaurant. MC.
At **La Favède,** 14 km. (8½ miles) northwest, *Auberge Cévénole* (M), (tel. 66-34-12-13). 16 rooms. Closed Nov. through Mar. Delightfully peaceful Relais du Silence, good base for visiting Cévennes; pool, garden; restaurant serving local specialties. MC.
Restaurants. *Clou de Girofle* (M), 58 rte. St.-Martin (tel. 66-86-22-46). Closed Jan. and Sun. Good-value newish cuisine. *Riche* (M), 42 pl. Sémard (tel. 66-86-00-33). Closed July. Near rail and bus stations; popular with locals. AE, MC, V.

ANDUZE. At **Générargues,** 5½ km. (3½ miles) northwest, *Trois Barbus* (M), (tel. 66-61-72-12). Closed Nov. to mid-Mar.; restaurant closed Mon. (except in July and Aug.). AE, DC, MC, V.
Restaurant. At **Mialet,** 10 km. (6 miles) away, *Auberge du Fer-à-Cheval* (M), (tel. 66-85-02-80). Closed Oct. through March, Sun. for dinner and Mon. Right on village square and ideal for lunch combined with a visit to Le Mas Soubeyran museum; marvelous value with some *nouvelle cuisine* touches. V.

ANNONAY. *Midi* (I), 17 pl. Cordeliers (tel. 75-33-23-77). 40 rooms. Closed Christmas through Jan. and Sun. in winter. Comfortable Logis de France in town center; no restaurant. AE, MC, DC, V.
Restaurants. *Château* (M), 2 montée Château (tel. 75-32-19-78). Closed most of Jan., Sun. for dinner and Mon. Interesting cooking by one of the region's few women chefs; newish cuisine; in heart of old town. AE, DC, V. *Célérien* (I), opposite station (tel. 75-33-56-97). Closed Sat. and for dinner on Sun. Popular with locals.

ANTRAIGUES. Restaurant. *Lo Podello* (M), (tel. 75-38-71-48). Closed June, Oct. and Thurs. (except July and Aug.). Delightful spot on central square, crammed with antique furniture and knick-knacks; tasty Ardèche specialties, especially *charcuterie;* must reserve.

AUBENAS. *Pinède* (M), rte. Camping (D235), (tel. 75-35-25-88). Closed mid-Dec. to mid-Jan., and Mon. Just outside town; huge garden, sunny terrace, beautiful views; good restaurant. V.
At **Thueyts,** 20 km. (12 miles) away, *Nord* (I), 102 pl. Champ-de-Mars (tel. 75-36-40-38). Closed Oct. through Mar., Tues. (except mid-June through Sept.). Good modest spot for visiting Cévennes; garden and good-value restaurant.
Restaurant. *Fournil* (I), 34 rue 4 Septembre (tel. 75-93-58-68). Closed Sun. for dinner, Mon., Feb. and June. Excellent *menus,* though limited choice. 15th century house. V.

LA BASTIDE-PUYLAURENT. *Gevaudan* (I), (tel. 66-46-02-52). 33 rooms. Closed Nov. through Apr., Mon. (except June through Aug.). Well-modernized building opposite station run by friendly Franco-Canadian couple; good local specialties in attractive restaurant. AE, DC, MC, V.
Restaurant. *Genets* (I), (tel. 66–46–00–13). Closed mid-Oct. to mid-May. Excellent value, though only 3 *menus.* Also has 10 rooms; half board compulsory in season. V.

FLORAC. *Parc* (M), 47 av. Jean-Monestier (tel. 66-45-03-05). 58 rooms. Closed Dec. to mid-Mar., Sun. for dinner, and Mon. (except in July and Aug.). Old-established friendly hotel with lovely mountain views; adequate restaurant. AE, DC, MC, V. *Gorges du Tarn* (I), (tel. 66-45-00-63). 31 rooms. Closed Oct. through Apr. Welcoming; no restaurant.

GÉNOLHAC. *Mont Lozère* (I), 13 av. Libération (tel. 66-61-10-72). 15 rooms. Closed Nov. through Jan., Tues. (except July to mid-Sept.). Small family hotel with restaurant. MC.
    Restaurant. At Vialas, 8 km. (5 miles) west, *Chantoiseau* (M), (tel. 66-61-00-02). Closed Jan., and Wed. Delightful; a 17th-century building, with tempting regional cuisine (you can even take lessons from the friendly chef!); also has 15 rooms. AE, MC.

GOUDET. *Loire* (I), (tel. 71-57-16-83). 22 rooms. Closed Oct. to mid-April. Owned by a descendant of the innkeeper who welcomed R.L. Stevenson; good base for walkers; good-value restaurant.

JOYEUSE. *Cèdres* (M), (tel. 75-39-40-60). 40 rooms. Closed mid-Oct. to mid-April. Large garden and comfortable rooms; trout fishing available; restaurant is (I), with good choice of *menus.* DC, MC.
    Restaurant. At Maison-Neuve, 13 km. (8 miles) away, *Relais de la Vignasse* (I), (tel. 75-39-31-91). 15 rooms. Closed Nov. through Mar. Attractive Logis de France perched high up on hill with lovely views; family-type restaurant. AE, MC.

LAMASTRE. *Château d'Urbilhac,* 2 km. (1¼ miles) south (tel. 75-06-42-11). 14 rooms. Closed Oct. through Apr. Peaceful 16th-century château attractively converted into delightful hotel; lovely grounds and views, pool and elegant restaurant. AE, DC, V. *Commerce* (I), pl. Rampon (tel. 75-06-41-53). 23 rooms. Closed Nov. through Feb. Close to station; good-value meals.
    Restaurant. *Barattero* (M), pl. Seignobos (tel. 75-06-41-50). Closed mid-Dec. through Feb., Sun. for dinner, Mon. Old favorite run by a delightful family; reliable cuisine is becoming increasingly *nouvelle;* also has a few well-modernized rooms (M). AE, DC, V.

LA MALÈNE. *Château de la Caze* (E), 5 km. (3 miles) northeast (tel. 66-48-51-01). 20 rooms. Closed mid-Oct. through Mar., Tues. 15th-century château, ideal when visiting the Gorges du Tarn as it's actually on the banks of the river; some rooms are in annexe called "The Farm"; restaurant. AE, DC, V. *Manoir de Montesquiou* (M), on D907 bis road (tel. 66-48-51-12). 12 rooms. Closed mid-Oct. through Mar. 15th-century manor-house which once belonged to the famous Montesquiou family; right on the Gorges du Tarn; restaurant and garden. DC.

MENDE. *Lion d'Or* (M), 12 blvd. Britexte (tel. 66-49-16-46). 40 rooms. Closed mid-Nov. to mid-Mar., Sun. and for lunch on Mon. (except July and Aug.). Well modernized hotel with best rooms overlooking garden and pool; excellent regional cuisine cooked "new"-style. AE, DC, MC, V. *France* (I), 9 blvd. Arnault (tel. 66-65-00-04). 28 rooms. Closed mid-Dec. through Jan., Sun. for dinner, Mon. (except in July and Aug.). Typical French provincial hotel; good views from terrace and good-value restaurant. V.

MEYRUEIS. *Château d'Ayres* (E), 1½ km. (1 mile) east on D57 road (tel. 66-45-60-10). 21 rooms. Closed Nov. through Mar. Medieval château in stunning position among lovely old trees; lots of atmosphere and goodish restaurant (M). AE, DC, V. *Renaissance* (M), (tel. 66-45-60-19). 20 rooms. Closed mid-Jan. and Feb. 16th-century Cévenol architecture with antique furniture (also modern rooms in annexe); delicious regional cuisine, good place for lunch if you're visiting the Aven Armand or the Grotte de Dargilan. AE, DC, V. *Europe et Mont-*

Aigoual (I), quai Orléans (tel. 66-45-60-05). 50 rooms. Closed Oct. through Mar. Very good value; pool and garden; good restaurant.

LE MONASTIER. *Ajustons* (I), 2½ km. (1½ miles) south of village (tel. 66-32-70-35). 23 rooms. Closed weekends (Nov. through Feb. only). Good base for walkers (R.L. Stevenson started his journey from Le Monastier); simple, friendly. v.

PRIVAS. *Chaumette* (I), av. Vanel (tel. 75-64-30-66). 35 rooms. Restaurant closed Sat. (mid-Sept. to mid-June). Central but in leafy setting; restaurant *(Les Marronniers)* has tasty classical cuisine. DC, MC, V.
At **Col de l'Escrinet,** 13 km. (8 miles) away, *Escrinet* (M), (tel. 75-87-10-11). 17 rooms. Closed mid-Nov. to mid-Mar., Sun. for dinner, Mon. for lunch (except mid-June to mid-Sept.). Modern, with spectacular views, pool, and a balcony to every room; good restaurant with some regional specialties; friendly atmosphere. AE.
Restaurant. At **Les-Fonts-du-Pouzin,** 10 km. (6 miles) east, *Marcanterie* (M), (tel. 75-63-88-84). Closed Mon. Lovely old building with vaulted ceilings; delicious regional cuisine and wines. v.

ST.-JEAN-DU-GARD. *Oronge* (M), 103 Grand-Rue (tel. 66-85-30-34). 30 rooms. Closed Jan. through Mar., Sun. for dinner and Mon. (except in July and Aug.). 17th-century coaching inn with carefully modernized rooms and tasty regional cuisine. AE, DC, MC, V. *Auberge du Péras* (I), rte. de Nîmes (tel. 66-85-35-94). 10 rooms. Closed Jan. through Feb., Tues. for dinner and Wed. for dinner (except in July and Aug.). Good spot from which to walk or drive along Corniche des Cévennes; typical Cévenol architecture and cuisine; light grills served in summer. DC.

TOURNON. *Château* (M), 12 quai Marc-Seguin (tel. 75-08-60-22). 35 rooms. Closed first halves of both Feb. and Nov., Sat. (except for dinner in summer), also Sun. in winter. Comfortable, with attentive service and dining rooms overlooking river; good traditional cuisine (M). AE, DC, MC, V.
Restaurants. *Chaumière* (M), 76 quai Farconnet (tel. 75-08-07-78). Closed Nov. to mid-Mar., Mon. for dinner; also Tues. (except June to mid-Sept.). Close to river; some local specialties. AE, DC, V.
At **St.-Péray,** 14 km. (9 miles) away, *Château de Châteaubourg* (M), (tel. 75-40-33-28). Closed mid-Jan. to mid-Feb. and second half Aug., Sun. for dinner, and Mon. Lovely site overlooking Rhône; delicious *nouvelle cuisine* and wines. DC, V.

VALGORGE. *Tanargue (Chez Coste),* (M), (tel. 75-93-68-88). 27 rooms. Closed Jan. and Feb. Chalet-type family hotel with garden and mountain views; good local dishes in busy restaurant (I) (especially wild mushrooms).

VALLON-PONT D'ARC. *Parc* (I), (tel. 75-88-02-17). 20 rooms. Closed Jan. and Fri. (except June through Sept.). Modest family hotel, good base for exploring the Ardèches Gorges; good-value meals.
Restaurant. *Manoir de Raveyron* (I), rue Henri-Barbusse (tel. 75-88-03-59). Closed Oct. to mid-Mar., Wed. (except in July and Aug.). 15th-century manor-house; marvelous choice of *menus;* also has 11 (I) rooms. v.

VALS-LES-BAINS. *Grand Hôtel des Bains* (M), (tel. 75-94-65-55). 54 rooms. Closed Oct. to mid-May. Traditional spa-town hotel with delightful flower-filled terrace and garden; pleasant restaurant. AE, DC, V. *Europe* (I), 86 rue Jean-Jaurès (tel. 75-37-43-94). 36 rooms. Closed mid-Oct. to mid-Apr. Fine local architecture, well restored; restaurant (I). AE, DC, MC, V.
Restaurant. *Runel* (M), 43 rue Jean-Jaurès (tel. 75-37-48-57). Closed Sun. for dinner and Mon. New place with classical cuisine; terrace. v.

LES VANS. *Château le Scipionnet* (E), 3 km. (2 miles) northeast on D104A (tel. 75-37-23-84). 26 rooms. Closed Oct. to mid-Mar. Peaceful and well-run converted château on road to Joyeuse in lovely wooded setting; pool, tennis; elegant restaurant (M). MC.

Restaurant. *Cévennes* (I), (tel. 75-37-23-09). Closed mid-Jan. to mid-Feb., second half Oct., Mon. Good-value meals with regional specialties in friendly restaurant; also has 15 modest rooms. AE.

VILLEFORT. *Balme* (I), pl. Portalet (tel. 66-46-80-14). 23 rooms. Closed mid-Nov. through Jan., Sun. for dinner and Mon. (except in July and Aug.). Old-established family hotel with fine restaurant (I). AE, DC, MC. *Nord* (I), (tel. 66-46-80-12). 24 rooms. Simple but adequate; with restaurant.

 TOURS AND EXCURSIONS. By Train. Two steam trains operate in this region. The long-established "Petit Train du Vivarais" runs between Lamastre and Tournon (tel. 78-28-83-34 for reservations); the S.N.C.F. include it in their excursion program (starting from Tournon). More recent is the "Mont-Aigoual Express", with Western coaches and panoramic platforms, running between Ganges and St.-Hippolyte du Fort in the heart of the Cévennes; (weekends and public hols., July through Oct., tel. 67-73-80-33 for reservations).

By Bus. The S.N.C.F. (French railways) runs bus tours into the Ardèche from the Rhône Valley area as well as within the region. You can take an *Ardèche Verte* ("Verdant Ardèche") tour from Valence or visit the famous Gorges de l'Ardèche and Vallon-Pont d'Arc from Montélimar on two separate excursions. Other tours set out from Aubenas (Gorges de l'Ardèche and Vallon-Pont d'Arc); from Joyeuse and Largentière to the Trappist monastery of Notre-Dame des Neiges or to the Haut-Vivarais regional park; and from Vals-les-Bains to the Aven d'Orgnac. The local tourist offices will supply details of privately-run bus tours to these and other sights from main centers in the Ardèche. From Alès various tours go into the Cévennes and a few into the Ardèche. In summer, excursions from Nîmes include the Corniche des Cévennes. Tours to the Gorges du Tarn set out from both Mende and Millau.

On Foot. This is great walking country and you can easily join walking parties led by experienced guides. Walking tours lasting a day, a weekend or several days set out from Largentière into the Tanargue and the Cévennes (information from tourist office). La Bastide is a good center for walking in summer and cross-country skiing in winter, with booklets of maps available and guides too on advance reservation. The information centers in the Cévennes National Park, at Florac (year-round) and at Génolhac, St.-Jean-du-Gard and Villefort (summer months) will help with planning hikes and providing local guides. In summer remember to start early as the days get hot fast.

The British tour operator *Waymark* organizes walking holidays for small groups in the Cévennes, including one ("Travels Without a Donkey") following in the footsteps of Robert Louis Stevenson. If you want to plan your own trip, you should know that he started out from Le Monastier-sur-Gazeille and took 12 days to reach Alès via Goudet, Pradelles, Langogne, La Bastide, Pont-de-Montvert, Florac and St.-Jean-du-Gard.

Walking through the Gorges du Tarn is another classic excursion, wearing but rewarding; there is a marked path from the bridge in La Malène.

By Boat. Excursions in small boats can be made down the Ardèche Gorges. Inquire at local tourist offices in any center about this and about the classic excursion down the Gorges du Tarn, for which reservations are essential: you start out from La Malène in a punt (with boatman), covering around 8–9 km. (5 miles) taking about an hour; most visitors travel back by taxi.

SPORTS. Canoeing. Canoeing down the Ardèche Gorges is easily arranged, either locally or through a British tour operator. You can also canoe down the Gorges du Tarn; the least dangerous section is Ste.-Enimie to Le Pas du Souci.

Riding. Day excursions and longer riding holidays are popular in the Ardèche. One good place among many organizing them is the *Mas de Saflambert* at Blaunac between Largentière and Valgorge (tel. 75-39-16-47). Riding can easily be arranged in the Cévennes National Park (leaflets available from all local tourist offices), with modest accommodations in restored cottages and farmhouses.

Spelunking. Experienced spelunkers may be able to join expeditions organized by local groups. "Subterranean safaris" are organized in the Grotte de Trabuc; inquire at local tourist offices.

SIGHTSEEING DATA. For general notes on visiting museums and historic buildings in France—and an important wanrning—see "Sightseeing" in *Facts at Your Fingertips.*

ALÈS. Musée du Colombier, parc du Colombier (tel. 66-86-30-40). Open daily except Tues. and public hols., 9–12, 2–5.

ANDUZE. Bambuseraie de Prafrance (bamboo and sequoia plantation), 2½ km. (1¼ miles) outside town via D129 road (tel. 66-61-70-47). Open daily 9–12, 2–7; no lunchtime closure in July and Aug. Closed Nov. through Feb.

AURIOLLES. Mas de la Vignasse, housing **Musée Alphonse Daudet** (Daudet Museum) and **Musée de la Soie** (Silk Museum), (tel. 75-39-65-07). Open May through Sept., daily 9.30–12, 2–6.30.

AVEN ARMAND, 11 km. (7 miles) north of Meyrueis. Open Easter through Sept. only, 8–12, 1.30–7. The funicular is included in the admission charge.

AVEN DE LA FORESTIÈRE, on D217 road (tel. 75-38-63-08). Open Apr. and May, weekends only; June through Sept., daily 9–12, 2–6.

AVEN MARZAL, Bidon (tel. 75-04-53-51). Open May through Nov. Opening times depend on weather: check locally. Includes **Musée du Monde Souterrain et de l'Histoire de la Spéléologie** (Underground and Spelunking Museum).

AVEN D'ORGNAC, Orgnac (tel. 75-38-62-51). Open Mar. through Nov. Opening times depend on weather: check locally.

LA BASTIDE-PUYLAURENT. Notre-Dame des Neiges (Trappist monastery). Open daily 9–12, 3–6. Wine made by monks may be bought here.

FLORAC. Château, with exhibit on Cévennes National Park. Open daily 8–12.30, 2–8.

GROTTE DE LA COCALIÈRE, 10 km. (6½ miles) from St.-Ambroix (tel. 66-24-01-57). Open Apr. through Oct., 9–12, 2–6.30; tour through subterranean galleries in a little train.

GROTTE DE DARGILAN, 8 km. (5 miles) northwest of Meyrueis. Open Easter through Sept., 9–7; first half Oct., 1–7; closed rest of year.

GROTTES DE LA MADELEINE, St. Remèze (tel. 75-04-12-24). Open Mar. through Nov. Opening times depend on weather: check locally.

GROTTE DE TRABUC, 11 km. (7 miles) north of Anduze. Open mid-Mar. to mid-Oct., 9.30–12, 2–6; no lunchtime closure June to mid-Sept.; winter, Sun. only, 2–4. Get there early if possible as only a limited number of people allowed in at one time.

LE MAS SOUBEYRAN. Musée du Désert (Wilderness Museum), 8 km. (5 miles) north of Anduze (tel. 66-85-32-72). Open Mar. through Nov. only, 9.30–12, 2.30–6; July and Aug. 9.30–6.30. Guided tours available except Sun. A.M.

MENDE. Musée Fabre. Open daily except Tues., Sun. and public hols., June through Sept., 10–12, 3–7; Oct. through May, 3–6 only.

MILLAU. Musée. Open summer, daily except Sun. and public hols., 10–12, 3–7; winter, Wed. and Sun. 3–6.

PRANLES. Musée du Vivarais Protestant. Open mid-June to mid-Sept., daily 10–12, 2.30–6.30; Palm Sun. to mid-June and mid-Sept. through Oct., weekends only, 10–12, 2.30–6.30.

PRIVAS. Musée Agricole du Verdus (agricultural museum), 6 km. (3½ miles) outside town on road to Villeneuve-de-Berg (tel. 75-64-27-40). Check opening times locally.

ROQUEFORT-SUR-SOULZON. The *Société des Caves* enables you to visit various cheese cellars and two small museums with exhibits tracing the history of the region and cheese making since the Neolithic period. Open daily 9–12, 2–5 (2–7 in July and Aug.). Wear a warm sweater or jacket.

ST.-JEAN-DU-GARD. Musée des Vallées Cévenoles (local history museum), 95 Grand'Rue (tel. 66-85-10-48). Open mid-June to mid-Sept., daily except Sun. A.M. and Mon., 9.30–12.30, 3–7; rest of year, Sun. only, 2.30–6.30.

SERRIÈRES. Musée des Mariniers du Rhône (Rhône Boatmen's Museum). Open Easter through Sept., weekends only, 3–7.

LE VIGAN. Musée Cévenol (Local History Museum). Open Apr. through Oct., daily except Tues. 10–11.30, 2–6.30 (open every day in July and Aug.); winter, Wed. only, same times.

 SHOPPING. The Ardèche is an excellent area for unusual craft items. Local craftsmen display their work in Les Vans and Thines and at craft fairs held throughout the Ardèche in summer. Special to the region are articles in chestnut wood, ranging from tiny objects to beautifully made furniture, carved to traditional designs. In the food line, chestnuts are again preeminent, with *marrons glacés* packed in pretty boxes making good gifts to take home. Local goat's cheeses (the drier, harder sort travel well) and *charcuterie* make welcome presents too.

In the Cévennes, pottery is a specialty of Anduze, and everywhere you will find little packs of wonderfully aromatic local herbs (try the tasty *sariette* or savory); the freshest come from the colorful openair markets, both here and in the Ardèche.

EASTERN FRANCE

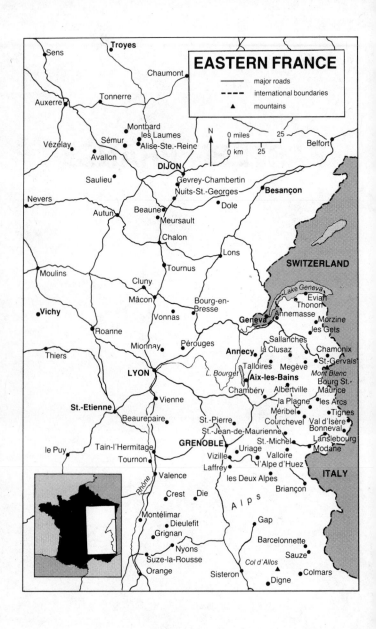

EASTERN FRANCE

— major roads
- - - international boundaries
▲ mountains

N

0 miles 25

0 km 25

Sens

Troyes

Chaumont

Tonnerre

Auxerre

Montbard
les Laumes
Sémur
Alise-Ste.-Reine

Vézelay

Avallon

DIJON

Belfort

Saulieu

Gevrey-Chambertin

Nuits-St.-Georges

Besançon

Nevers

Beaune

Dole

Autun

Meursault

Chalon

Moulins

Lons

SWITZERLAND

Tournus

Cluny

Lake Geneva

Evian

Mâcon

Bourg-en-
Bresse

Thonon

Vichy

Vonnas

Geneva

Annemasse

Morzine
les Gets

Roanne

Mionnay

Pérouges

Annecy

Sallanches
la Clusaz

Chamonix
St-Gervais

Thiers

Talloires

Megève

Mont Blanc

LYON

L. Bourget

Aix-les-Bains

Bourg St.-
Maurice

Vienne

Chambéry

Albertville

la Plagne

les Arcs

Méribel

Tignes

Beaurepaire

St.-Pierre

Courchevel

Val d'Isère

St.-Jean-de-Maurienne

Bonneval

St-Etienne

St.-Michel

Lanslebourg

Tain-l'Hermitage

GRENOBLE

Uriage

Modane

le Puy

Tournon

Vizille

Valloire

Laffrey

l'Alpe d'Huez

ITALY

Valence

les Deux Alpes

Rhône

Crest

Die

A l p s

Briançon

Montélimar

Gap

Dieulefit

Grignan

Barcelonnette

Nyons

Sauze

Suze-la-Rousse

Col d'Allos ▲

Colmars

Orange

Sisteron

Digne

BURGUNDY

Treasure House of History

Famous vineyards drenched with sunshine; undulating countryside with billowing wooded hills; hospitable people who have perfected all that is best in eating and drinking; old towns and villages, rich in history and artistic treasures; and all along the roads from Dijon, the names of world-famous wines greet you as you travel through Burgundy.

Evidence that man has lived in this region since prehistoric times has been found near Beaune, at Solutré, which has given its name to an archeological period, and in the grottos of Arcy-sur-Cure near Auxerre. Just off the A6 motorway south of Beaune, the Archéodrome is an imaginative reconstruction illustrating a thousand centuries of life in Burgundy, with reproductions of huts, temples and fortifications built when Caesar ruled Alesia. The remarkable Treasure of Vix, in the museum of Châtillon-sur-Seine, includes objects that decorated the tomb of a Celtic princess buried more than 2,500 years ago in a nearby village.

Sens and its Cathedral

Sens, about 112 km. (70 miles) south of Paris, was for centuries the ecclesiastical center of France. The cathedral of St.-Etienne, one of the models for England's Canterbury Cathedral, was the first major Gothic cathedral in France. Its treasury, one of the richest in France, is of particular interest, for here can be found the robes of Thomas à Becket, who fled from England to escape the wrath of Henry II. He returned to England only to find himself again differing with the king, this time regarding the legal rights of priests, and was murdered in his own cathedral of Canterbury in 1170. Also in the treasury are the richly woven gold and silver robes of the archbishops of Sens and the 15th-century tapestry presented to the cathedral by Louis de Bourbon.

If you visit the 15th-century château of St.-Fargeau, where la Grande Demoiselle, Louis XIV's cousin, was exiled as a result of her activities during the Fronde rebellion, you'll have, on top of the interest presented by the château itself with its six huge towers, its horse museum and its beautiful furniture, the extra pleasure of knowing that you're helping to save it from ruin. It was bought in 1979 by two energetic young brothers and they are gradually restoring it, doing most of the work themselves. To raise the money needed to complete the restoration they run a summer festival of dance and drama that attracts some big names. There's a *son-et-lumière* here too.

The Abbey of Fontenay

About six km. (four miles) from Montbard is the abbey of Fontenay. Founded in 1118 by Bernard, Abbot of Clairvaux, it was built by a group of Cistercian monks in a remote spot, for it had been decreed that their monasteries could not be established anywhere near "cities, feudal manors, or villages."

By the end of the 12th century, the church and other buildings comprising the monastery were finished. Membership in the order at Fontenay grew steadily until, at the beginning of the 14th century, the abbey had some 300 monks or converts. Under powerful protection the monastery prospered mightily.

The 16th century marked the beginning of the fall of Fontenay. The religious wars were partly responsible for the deterioration, but a more important cause was in the administration of the abbey itself. During this period, abbots were selected by the king with little regard for ecclesiastical capabilities. Exercising their rights as abbots, they dissipated the wealth that had made Fontenay powerful.

The French Revolution spelled the end of Fontenay as a monastery. It was sold for 78,000 francs to a buyer who transformed the monastery buildings into a paper factory. Fontenay served in this industrial capacity until 1906. During this time great care was taken not to damage the historic buildings. After the paper concern relinquished control, restoration of the abbey was undertaken by its new owner, Edouard Aynard. Using ancient plans, he accomplished the remarkable task of returning the church and all of the buildings to their original 12th-century state.

Along the Road to Dijon

The château of Bussy-Rabutin, south of Montbard, was built in the middle of the 17th century by Roger de Bussy-Rabutin, satirist and wit at the court of Louis XIV. The king enjoyed the young man's clever sallies directed at various members of the court, for Bussy-Rabutin made a point of studying minutely the private and public lives of all the noblemen and court hangers-on. But he wrote a book entitled *L'Histoire Amoureuse des Gaules,* a thinly disguised account of the love-life of Louis XIV. The enraged king had the impudent Bussy-Rabutin exiled from Paris. Selecting land near Les Laumes, he built a château. As a further insult to Louis, he personally designed the gardens of his château, taking meticulous care to copy the gardens of Versailles. Bussy-Rabutin's ribald personality persists to this day within the confines of the château, particularly in the Mistress Hall, which contains portraits of all of his mistresses.

Alise-Ste.-Reine, known as Alesia a century before the birth of Christ, was in its day one of the most important towns in Gaul. Well-fortified, and perched on the summit of a hill, it was considered impregnable. Yet it was in this city, in 52 B.C., that Julius Caesar completed the conquest of Gaul, defeating the youthful Vercingetorix.

Although the fortifications built by Caesar at Les Laumes have now been covered over, Alesia is in an excellent state of preservation. Roman occupation forces took over the city, engineers and builders were brought in and the city took on a Roman aspect. A theater, forum and Roman district were built, and a central heating system was installed to heat the houses. Although the Romans destroyed part of the Celts' homes to build their own, a sizable Celtic or Gallic district remains. In it is a dolmen, or Celtic stone altar. A visit to Alesia illustrates how the Celts lived before, and just after, the Roman conquest of Gaul that marked the beginning of the cultural birth of France. Nearby is the Merovingian church of Ste.-Reine.

The two little medieval towns of Avallon and Vézelay, lying on the northern tip of the great Burgundian vineyards, are not only charming but are also excellent centers from which to explore the northern part of the nearby Morvan forest. Avallon, perched on a high rocky promontory and surrounded by ancient ramparts, looks out over the striking valley of the Cousin.

Vézelay's location is if anything even more beautiful. It sits commandingly on a rocky crag, visible for miles around, the little town nestling at its feet, with magnificent views to the south and east. The church itself, the basilica of La Madeleine, founded originally in 860 and rebuilt in the 11th century, attained fame in the 11th century as the resting place of the relics of St. Mary Magdelene. As such, it rapidly became one of northern Europe's major pilgrimage centers, and one of the four departure points for pilgrimages to Compostella in northern Spain. As the monastery grew in wealth, so the little church was further embellished, becoming in the process one of the most beautiful Romanesque, or pre-Gothic, churches in France.

But by the mid-13th century the monastery was in decline as doubt was cast on the authenticity of the relics, a decline that continued until the French Revolution in the late-18th century when the monastery was sold by the Government. The extensive buildings were demolished and only the church, itself rapidly falling into ruin, remained. However, the crumbling buildings were saved and beautifully restored in the mid-19th century by Viollet-le-Duc, high priest of the Gothic revival in France.

Vézelay today, despite the inevitable crowds it draws, survives as an extraordinary memorial to the power and grace of the French Romanesque. Nowhere is this more evident than in the elegant nave of the church, made all the more appealing by the contrast it presents with the later, more elaborate Gothic apse. But the church is similarly and justly famed for the remarkable sculptures of both the nave and the tympanum, the great carved interior entrance to the church. The ingenuity of the builders and the complex religious symbolism that motivated them are enthrallingly explained in the very much better-than-average English guide book available in the church.

A favorite excursion in the Morvan is to an abbey with the strange name Abbaye de la Pierre-qui-Vire, after a huge flat stone balanced on a rock. You can visit parts of the abbey and the monks' famous publishing center, producing superbly illustrated books on religious art under the Zodiaque imprint.

Burgundy's Capital

Dijon, the capital of the province and long the historical center of all Burgundy, is also one of the renowned gourmet cities in France. Its streets are literally crammed with restaurants, delicatessens, markets and pastry-shops, each vying with the others to offer you the best of Burgundian fare.

There is plenty to see in Dijon. The 13th-century cathedral of St.-Bénigne, and the Gothic church of Notre-Dame with its stained-glass windows; the 16th-century church of St.-Michel with its famous Renaissance façade; the 15th-century Hôtel Chambellan, in the picturesque rue des Forges, which contains the beautiful 16th-century Hôtel Maillard; the Chartreuse de Champmol, founded in the 14th century by Philippe le Hardi: its magnificent doorway and the Well of Moses are the work of the 14th-century sculptor Claus Sluter.

The Museum of Fine Arts, which is housed in the old palace of the dukes of Burgundy, is famous throughout France for the wealth and variety of its collections. The tombs of Philippe le Hardi (Claus Sluter's masterpiece) and of Jean sans Peur are celebrated examples of Burgundian art at its finest, while the picture galleries and the section devoted to Renaissance furniture and medieval *objets d'art* have few rivals elsewhere in the country. The magnificent Granville Donation, the modern art section, is housed and excitingly arranged in what used to be the attics.

Passing southwards through strips of well-tended vineyards, you come to places whose names have made Burgundy world-famous. Stop for a moment at the little village of Chenôve, for here is one of the oldest wine-making buildings in France. Built by Alix de Vergy in 1238, it still has two large winepresses dating from the 13th century that can be visited.

The Wine District

At Gevrey-Chambertin you may visit the château and taste the famous Chambertin wine, renowned among connoisseurs and prized by Napoleon above all wines. Clos-Vougeot, with its 16th-century Renaissance château dominating the enormous vineyards that were planted by the monks of the Abbey of Cîteaux, is the place where the members of the Confrérie des Chevaliers du Tastevin (brotherhood of the knights of winetasting) meet some 12 times a year with their guests to dine in Rabelaisian sumptuousness. Nuits-St.-Georges, where wine was made in Roman times, produces a wine that Fagon, the royal physician, prescribed in much later days for Louis XIV on account of its "dry, tonic, and generous qualities." And again journeying southward you pass vineyard after vineyard, until at last you come to Beaune, the capital of the great region known as the Côte de Beaune, which includes such famous vineyards as Pommard, Volnay and Aloxe-Corton.

Beaune itself, despite the crowds it draws and a rather bogus touristic gloss, remains one of the most charming and attractive of French provincial towns. Its raison d'être is wine of course, and there are few more delightful experiences than a visit to one of the many wine-tasting cellars here, where some of the most famous wines in France can be sampled for next to nothing. The Marché aux Vins, located by the tourist office opposite the Hôtel de Dieu, is perhaps the most atmospheric and famous of these. But watch out if you're driving!

The Hôtel-Dieu, or Hospital of Beaune, was built in 1450 by Nicolas Rolin, chancellor of Burgundy. It carried on its activities without interruption until 1971, the nurses still wearing the curious medieval dress they wore when the hospital admitted its first patient in the 15th century; you may still see, in the Hospital Museum, some of the strange instruments used by doctors in those early days. The museum also possesses the polyptych of the *Last Judgement* by Rogier van der Weyden, together with a fine collection of tapestries. Nor should art lovers miss Beaune's beautiful 12th-century basilica.

But the Hospital of Beaune has another claim to distinction. It is so wealthy that it has no need to ask for aid either from the state or from individuals. Under the name of Hospices de Beaune, it is the proud owner of some of the finest vineyards in the region—particularly Pommard and Volnay. These are farmed out on a profit-sharing basis, and each year, on the third Sunday in November, there is an auction sale attended by international connoisseurs and wine dealers.

In the Hôtel des Ducs de Bourgogne is the Wine Museum, where the entire history of winemaking is traced. The mansion housing the museum is itself of great interest. Built in the 15th and 16th centuries, it has been well restored, and is now much as it must have been in the days when it was the country seat of the dukes of Burgundy.

Autun is one of the most interesting old towns in Burgundy. Caesar called it "the sister and rival of Rome itself," and you may still see traces of the Roman occupation in the Temple of Janus and the fine gates of St.-André and Arrouz. Parts of the Roman wall surrounding the town are still standing and give a fair indication of its size in those days. Near Autun, the curious Pierre de Couhard, a pyramid-like Roman construction, has so far baffled archeologists, who are undecided as to its significance. But the 12th-century cathedral of St.-Lazare, with its tympanum of the Last Judgement and its capitals carved by the famous sculptor Gislebertus around 1130, is one of the finest examples of medieval art in France. The Rolin Museum, with its collection of Burgundian sculpture (including Gislebertus's masterpiece, *Eve*, formerly in the cathedral) and its painting of the *Nativity* by the Maître de Moulins, make Autun one of the most richly endowned art cities in Burgundy.

The abbey of Cluny, founded near the beginning of the 10th century and set in lovely rolling countryside was, in its day, famous throughout the Christian world; though little of the original buildings survives, the remains of the church, and the sculpture exhibit, are well worth a visit. The little town of Cluny itself has a wealth of medieval and Renaissance buildings, as well as a number of interesting Romanesque houses.

South of Beaune lies the district of Meursault, where two of the great white wines of Burgundy, Meursault and Montrachet, are produced. If you are lucky enough to be there at the time of the grape harvest, when the *Paulée de Meursault* takes place, you will need a strong constitution to digest all the rich Burgundian fare that is provided at this annual feast.

Tournus and its Romanesque Abbey

At the beginning of the 11th century, after years of invasions and internal dissension, peace and order were established for a while in Burgundy. The countryside flowered with great churches and abbeys built in a new style, known as Romanesque. The most spectacular and best preserved of these is the abbey of St.-Philibert at Tournus. Although massively built, the interior is spacious and light. Unadorned cylindrical pillars, over one meter (four ft.) thick, support the curved arches of the nave. As it was designed purely as a place of prayer, no attempt was made to decorate or embellish it. The sole touch of frivolity is the use of red and white stones arranged alternately in the round arches of the nave.

The town itself retains much of the charm of the Middle Ages and the Renaissance, for most of the houses were built during these periods: all historic buildings are well marked with signs. The antique collector will be delighted with Tournus, for the narrow, winding cobblestone streets abound with antique shops. Tournus is also a good base for visiting Brancion, Cluny and Mâcon.

As far as Mâcon, on the southward journey, the vines grow on limestone soil typical of the great Burgundian vineyards, but from Mâcon almost to the gates of Lyon the land changes and covers a hard granite base that nevertheless produces a number of high-quality wines such as Juliénas, Fleurie, Morgon, Brouilly, Moulin-à-Vent and Pouilly-Fuissé.

Mâcon, an old, sleepy town with wide quays along the banks of the Saône, is dominated by the two octagonal towers of the ruins of its medieval cathedral of St.-Vincent. It was the birthplace of the great poet Lamartine. In the place aux Herbes is a wooden house of the 16th century still in an excellent state of preservation. The Hôtel-Dieu has a superb collection of apothecary jars dating from the 18th century.

PRACTICAL INFORMATION FOR BURGUNDY

TOURIST OFFICES. The regional tourist office for the whole of Burgundy—written enquiries only—is the *Comité Régional de Tourisme,* 55 rue de la Prefecture, 21041 Dijon (tel. 80-55-24-10). In addition, the four *départements* of Burgundy also have their own tourist offices (again, written enquiries only): **Côte d'Or,** 55 rue de la Prefecture 21041 Dijon (tel. 80-73-81-81); **Nièvre,** Prefecture, 58019 Nevers (tel. 86-57-80-25); **Saône-et-Loire,** Conseil General, 71025 Mâcon (tel. 85-38-21-00); **Yonne,** Maison Départementale de Tourisme, 1 quai de la République, 89000 Auxerre (tel. 86-52-26-27).

There are local tourist offices in the following towns: **Beaune,** rue Hôtel-Dieu (tel. 80-22-24-51); **Dijon,** pl. Darcy (tel. 80-43-42-12); **Mâcon,** 187 rue Carnot (tel. 85-38-06-00); **Sens,** pl. Jean-Jaurès (tel. 86-65-19-49); **Tournus,** pl. Carnot (tel. 85-51-13-10).

REGIONAL FOOD AND DRINK. Blessed with a temperate climate, rolling hills and fertile river valleys, Burgundians start with fine ingredients and put them to good use. Famous regional dishes are *boeuf bourguignon* (beef cooked slowly in wine with baby onions, mushrooms and bacon), *oeufs en meurette* (eggs poached and served in a rich red wine sauce), *pochouse* (a freshwater fish stew with herbs, onions and wine), *jambon persillé* (molded ham aspic with white wine and parsley), *boeuf à la mode* (braised beef with vegetables that is served hot or cold) and *saupiquet* (ham in piquant cream sauce). Burgundy's large white snails are famous and for many people Dijon is synonymous with mustard, used in dishes like veal chops or kidneys *dijonnaise*.

For a snack try *gougères* (cheese choux puffs) with a glass of wine, *pain d'épices* gingerbread, or fruit candies, particularly those flavored with *cassis* (black currant). *Cassis* liqueur is another local specialty, a teaspoon or two acting as base for *kir*, the local aperitif made with tart white *aligoté* wine. A *kir royale* is made with champagne or, less expensively, any sparkling white wine. Regional cheeses include the rich, mild *Chaource, St.-Florentin, Soumaintrain*, and the highly prized *Epoisses*, which is slightly stronger. Little goat cheeses, varying from fresh to piquant and hard, abound, the most famous being *Crottin de chavignol*.

Crottin comes from the wine country of Sancerre, strictly speaking part of the Loire. Sancerre is just over the river from Pouilly, home of the smoky white *Pouilly-fumé*. The other Pouilly wine, *Pouilly-fuissé* is an excellent white wine from the Mâcon region.

The wines of Burgundy are of course world-famous—burgundies and bordeaux (clarets) are the two great groups of French wines. Each separate region produces its own distinctive wines: dry, light wines *(Chablis)*, rich, full-bodied reds from the Côte du Nuits, the best-known of which are *Nuits-Saint-Georges, Gevrey-Chambertin* (which was apparently Napoleon's favorite wine!), *Chambolle-Musigny* and *Vosne-Romanée*. The Côte de Beaune also produces some of France's finest red wines, such as *Pommard, Volnay* and *Savigny-les-Beaune*, as well as magnificent white wines *(Meursault, Puligny-Montrachet)*.

HOTELS AND RESTAURANTS. Burgundy has many comfortable and attractive hotels and inns, usually offering excellent food served in generous portions (the Burgundians have a reputation for large appetites). Most hotels, even in city centers, have restaurants and many insist on your eating at least one meal in during the summer months; but this is not a problem as the food is normally excellent. Small country restaurants usually provide splendid meals, and meals can be found all over the region for reasonable prices on the whole, except in the really top-class gourmet restaurants, of which Burgundy has a good number. In country districts you usually have a choice of two or three fixed-price meals (often there is no *carte* at all), but even the cheaper ones may easily consist of a starter, an *entrée*, a main course, cheese and fruit or a dessert. Eating is an important part of life in Burgundy, so don't try to persuade restaurateurs to prepare you a quick snack—meals generally last some time, so that you have plenty of opportunity to savor the splendid wines. Virtually all hotels and restaurants in this tourist-frequented region take credit cards.

For general notes on hotels and restaurants, see "Hotels" and "Restaurants" in *Facts at Your Fingertips*.

AUTUN. *St. Louis* (M), 6 rue Arbalète (tel. 85-52-21-03). 52 rooms. Mostly very comfortable rooms (Napoleon slept in one of them!); plus restaurant and garden. AE, DC, MC, V. *Ursulines* (M), 14 rue Rivault (tel. 85-52-68-00). 29 rooms. Former monastery; comfortable and quiet. Restaurant open daily; terrace. *Moderne et Tête Noire* (I), 1 rue Arquebuse (tel. 85-52-25-39). 20 rooms. Closed Mar., second half Oct. Restaurant closed Sat. Plain but pleasant rooms and good Burgundian cuisine. MC, V.

Restaurants. *Chalet Bleu* (I), 1 rue Bourg-St.-Pantaléon (tel. 85-52-25-16). Closed June; Sun. P.M., Tues. In St. Pantaléon suburb; excellent value, newish cuisine and friendly service. AE, DC, MC, V.

At **airport**, 3 km. (2 miles) north west, *Clef des Champs* (M), (tel. 85-52-12-30). Closed mid-Jan. to Mid-Feb.; Sun. P.M. and Mon. Worth the trip out of town for good *nouvelle cuisine* and interesting wine list. MC.

AUXERRE. *Maxime* (M), 2 quai Marine (tel. 86-52-14-19). 25 rooms. Very comfortable, with restaurant and garden. AE, DC, MC, V. *Parc des Maréchaux* (M), 6 av. Foch (tel. 86-51-43-77). 22 rooms. 19th-century mansion set in own grounds; no restaurant. AE, DC, MC, V. *Clairions* (I), av. Worms (tel. 86-46-85-64). 62 rooms. New, away from main road. Restaurant. AE, MC, V.

Restaurants. *Jardin Gourmand* (M), 56 blvd. Vauban (tel. 86-51-53-52). Closed mid-Aug. to mid-Sept., second half Dec.; Sun. for dinner (except summer) and Mar. Attractive; wonderfully light *nouvelle cuisine.* AE, DC, V. *Salamandre* (M), 86 rue Paris (tel. 86-52-87-87). Closed Sun. for dinner, Mon. Chef specializes in fish. Good-value *menus.* Modern décor. AE, DC, V.

AVALLON. *Hostellerie de la Poste* (E), pl. Vauban (tel. 86-34-06-12). 29 rooms. Closed mid-Nov. to mid-Mar. Old-established and family-run hotel with lots of Burgundian charm and historical associations. Good, expensive restaurant and famous wine cellar; half-board terms only in July and August. AE, DC, V.

At **La Cerce** (exit Autoroute Avallon), *Relais Fleuri* (I), (tel. 86-34-02-85). 48 rooms. Old inn with nice décor. Restaurant with good regional cooking. Terrace, bar, pool. AE, DC, MC, V.

Restaurant. *Morvan* (M), 7 rte Paris (tel. 86-34-18-20). Closed most of Jan., second half Nov.; Sun. P.M., Mon. (except hols.), also closed evening in winter. Interesting and often inventive cuisine. AE, DC, MC, V.

In **Cousin Valley,** 3½ km. (2 miles) away, *Moulin des Ruats* (M), (tel. 86-34-07-14). 21 rooms. Closed Nov. through Feb., restaurant Mon. Delightful converted watermill with garden; restaurant with some regional specialties. AE, DC, MC, V.

BEAUNE. *Le Cep* (E), 27 rue Maufoux (tel. 80-22-35-48). 21 rooms. Closed Dec. through Mar. In charming old building; wine cellar but no restaurant. AE, DC, MC, V. *Poste* (E), 1 blvd. Clemenceau (tel. 80-22-08-11). 25 rooms. Closed mid-Nov. through Mar. An old favorite and very pleasant; rooms renovated; rich cuisine and superb service; half-board terms compulsory in July and Aug. AE, DC, MC, V. *Central* (M), 2 rue Victor-Millot (tel. 80-24-77-24). 22 rooms. Closed mid-Nov. to mid-Mar.; restaurant closed Wed., except in July and Aug. Pleasant city center hotel with good restaurant and charming service. V.

Restaurants. *Auberge St.-Vincent* (M), pl. Halle (tel. 80-22-42-34). Closed Dec., Sun. P.M. except July and Aug. Close to Hospices de Beaune and most attractive; regional dishes plus some *nouvelle cuisine.* AE, DC, MC, V. *Jacques Laine* (M), 10 blvd. Foch (tel. 80-24-76-10). Closed Feb. Very good classical cuisine—a discovery. Terrace. AE, DC, MC, V. *Rôtisserie de la Paix* (M), 47 fbg. Madeleine (tel. 80-22-33-33). Closed first half Mar., Sun. P.M. and Mon. Delicious *nouvelle cuisine;* outdoor meals in fine weather. AE, DC, MC, V. *Ecusson* (I), pl. Malmédy (tel. 80-22-83-08). Closed mid-Feb. to mid-Mar., Wed. Good value and friendly welcome; garden for summer meals. AE, DC, V.

At **Bouilland,** 16 km. (10 miles) out of town, *Vieux Moulin* (M), (tel. 80-21-51-16). Closed Christmas through Jan., Wed. and Thurs. for lunch. Well-known for delicious cuisine (mostly "new") and charming river setting; also has 8 delightful (M) rooms. AE, DC, V.

At **Chagny,** 16 km. (10 miles) away, *Lameloise* (E), 36 pl. Armes (tel. 85-87-08-85). Closed Dec. to mid-Jan.; all day Wed. and lunch on Thurs. One of the best restaurants in France with an excellent mixture of traditional Burgundian cuisine and "new" dishes; also has 25 pleasant rooms. V.

CHALON-SUR-SAÔNE. Restaurant. 2 km. (1 mile) south at St.-Rémy, *Moulin de Martorey* (I), (tel. 85-48-12-98). Closed Sun. for dinner, Mon., 2 weeks in Feb. and 2 weeks after Aug. 25. Good new restaurant with good-value *menus. Nouvelle cuisine.* Charming décor. MC, V.

CLUNY. *Bourgogne* (M), pl. Abbaye (tel. 85-59-00-58). 18 rooms. Closed mid-Nov. to mid-Mar., restaurant closed Tues. and for lunch on Wed. except mid-July through Sept. Right beside abbey and very pleasant; garden and good (M) restaurant; half-board terms compulsory in July and Aug. AE, DC, V.

Restaurant. *Moderne* (M), pont-de-l'Etang (tel. 85-59-05-65). Closed Nov, first half of Feb., Sun. P.M., Mon. (except mid-June to mid-Sept.). Charming traditional restaurant now has *nouvelle cuisine* as well as rich Burgundian specialties; also a hotel with 16 (I) rooms. AE, DC, V.

DIJON. *Chapeau Rouge* (E), 5 rue Michelet (tel. 80-30-28-10). 33 rooms. Closed mid-Dec. to mid-Jan. Lovely old building in town center close to cathedral with excellent restaurant (M); belongs to Mapotel group. AE, MC, V. *Cloche* (E), 14 pl. Darcy (tel. 80-30-12-32). 80 rooms. Closed Feb. Marvelous old "grand hotel" in town center; was given a facelift in the early '80s and is now equipped with all modern amenities; best restaurant in Dijon, with terrace and garden. AE, MC, V.

Central Ibis (M), 3 pl. Grangier (tel. 80-30-44-00). 90 rooms. Restaurant closed Sun. Old-established, now belongs to Ibis chain; central, but soundproofed and airconditioned with modernized rooms; very popular grillroom. AE, V. *Morot et Genève* (I), 15 av. Foch (tel. 80-43-40-01). 90 rooms. Modest but convenient for rail and bus stations and town center; brasserie open all day and most of the night. V. *Villages* (I), 15 av. Albert ler (tel. 80-43-01-12). 128 rooms. Plain, comfortable, welcoming; near station; restaurant. V.

Restaurants. *Château Bourgogne* (M), 22 blvd. Marne (tel. 80-72-31-13). In hotel *Pullmann* (E). Good classical cooking with good-value *menus*. AE, DC, MC, V. *Rallye* (M), 39 rue Chabot-Charny (tel. 80-67-11-55). Closed second half Feb., second half July, Sun., Mon. and public hols. Good-value *nouvelle cuisine* and particularly pleasant atmosphere. AE, DC, V. *Thibert* (M), 10 pl. Wilson (tel 80-67-74-64). Closed first half of Aug., Sun. and Mon. for lunch. Inventive *nouvelle cuisine* variants on traditional Burgundian recipes. AE, V.

Toison d'Or (M), 18 rue Ste.-Anne (tel. 80-30-73-52). Closed part of Feb., most of Aug., Sat. for lunch, Sun. and public hols. A miniature wine museum belonging to the Burgundian Company of Wine Tasters, in superb 17th-century setting; excellent classical Burgundian cuisine and reasonably-priced wines. AE, DC, MC, V. *Vinarium* (M), 23 pl. Bossuet (tel. 80-30-36-23). Closed Feb., Sun. 13th-century crypt makes perfect setting for sturdy Burgundian cuisine and wines. AE, DC, V.

At **Fixin**, 10 km. (6 miles) away, *Chez Jeannette* (M), (tel. 80-52-45-49). Closed mid-Dec. to mid-Jan., Thurs. Well-known for rich Burgundian cuisine in unpretentious setting. AE, DC, MC, V.

At **Marsannay**, 7 km. (4½ miles) southwest of town, *Gourmets* (M), (tel. 80-52-16-32). Closed Jan., Mon. P.M., Tues. Attractive old building with pretty garden; well worth the trip out of town. AE, DC, V.

GEVREY-CHAMBERTIN. Restaurants. *Rôtisserie du Chambertin* (E), rue Chambertin (tel. 80-34-33-20). Closed Feb., first half of Aug., Sun. P.M. and Mon. A famous name and it lives up to it; remarkably reasonable prices for the quality of the cuisine and the wine. *Millésimes* (M), 25 rue Eglise (tel. 80-51-84-24). Closed mid-Jan. to mid-Feb., Tues. and for lunch on Wed. Delightful restaurant in 17th-century wine cellar with lots of regional touches, including a whole wine press; good, mostly classical cuisine; friendly service and fine wines. AE, DC, MC, V.

MÂCON. *Frantel* (M), 26 rue Coubertin (tel. 85-38-28-06). 63 rooms. Restaurant closed Sat. and Sun. lunch-times. Modern and comfortable, overlooking river, with pleasant restaurant; closed both Sat. for lunch, and Sun. Very welcoming. AE, DC, MC, V.

Restaurants. *Auberge Bressane* (M), 114 rue 28-Juin-1944 (tel. 85-38-07-42). Closed Wed. Good for regional dishes. AE, DC, MC, V. *Rocher de Cancale* (M), 393 quai Jean-Jaurès (tel. 85-38-07-50). Closed first half Jan., first half July; Sat. lunchtime, Sun. P.M., all day Mon. Good fish dishes go well with river views, and the meat's good too. AE, DC, MC, V.

NUITS-ST.-GEORGES. 1 km. (½ mile) northwest, *Gentilhommière* (I), route Serrée (tel. 80-61-12-06). 20 rooms. Closed first 3 weeks of Jan. Modern, plain, for quiet nights. Restaurant in 16th-century hunting pavilion. AE, MC.
Restaurant. *Côte d'Or* (M), 1 rue Thurot (tel. 80-61-06-10). Closed most of July and Jan., Sun. P.M. and Wed. Delicious classical cuisine accompanies marvelous wines; also has 7 attractive (M) rooms.

SAULIEU. *Poste* (M), 1 rue Grillot (tel. 80-64-05-67). 48 rooms. Beautifully modernized 17th-century coaching inn; restaurant. AE, MC, V. *Tour d'Auxois* (I), pl. L'Abreuvoir (tel. 80-64-13-30). 30 rooms. Closed Dec.; restaurant closed Sun. for dinner and Mon. Very simple; near basilica.
Restaurants. *Côte d'Or* (E), 2 rue Argentine (tel. 80-64-07-66). Closed mid-Nov. to mid-Dec., first half of Mar., Tues. in winter. One of the finest restaurants in the whole of France for *nouvelle cuisine;* now has some stylish apartments to match; the whole building has been beautifully redecorated and modernized. Relais et Châteaux member. AE, DC, MC, V. *Borne Impériale* (M), 14 rue Argentine (tel. 80-64-19-76). Closed mid.-Nov. to mid-Dec., Mon. P.M., Tues. (except in July and Aug.). Classical cuisine and smiling service. AE, MC, V.

SÉMUR-EN-AUXOIS. Restaurants. *Carillon* (M), 13 rue Buffon (tel. 80-97-07-87). Closed Mon. for dinner, Tues. and Oct. Cooking classical and generous; terrace. MC, V. *Côte-d'Or* (M), pl. Gaveau (tel. 80-97-03-43). Closed Jan. to mid-Mar., Wed. Good home-style food; also has some (I) rooms. AE, DC, V.

SENS. *Paris et Poste* (M), 97 rue République (tel. 86-65-17-43). 32 rooms. Pleasant; near cathedral; with good classical restaurant. AE, DC, MC, V.
Restaurants. *Clos Jacobins* (M), 49 Grande-Rue (tel. 86-95-29-70). Closed Sun. for dinner (except in summer), Tues. for dinner, Wed., second half of Aug., beginning of Jan., first 2 weeks of March. New place with good, plain cuisine. V. *Palais* (I), 18 pl. République (tel. 86-65-13-69). Closed first half Jan., Sun. P.M., all day Mon. Right by cathedral; modest but lively and good value. MC, V.

TONNERRE. *Abbaye St.-Michel* (E), Montée St.-Michel (tel. 86-55-05-99). 11 rooms. Closed Jan. to mid-Feb. Restaurant closed Sun. P.M. and Mon. Benedictine abbey converted into delightful hotel-restaurant in vineyard setting (half-board terms compulsory in July and Aug.); Relais et Châteaux member. AE, DC, V.

TOURNUS. *Rempart* (M), 2 av. Gambetta (tel. 85-51-10-56). 32 rooms. Close to St. Philibert, rather grand, with good restaurant. AE, DC, MC, V. *Paix* (I), 9 rue Jean-Jaurès (tel. 85-51-01-85). 19 rooms. Closed second half Jan., first half May, second half Oct., Wed. for lunch and Tues. (except mid-June to mid-Sept.). Close to river; modest but adequate, with (I) restaurant. AE, DC, V. *Terrasses* (I), 18 av. 23-Janvier (tel. 85-51-01-74). 12 rooms. Closed in Jan. Restaurant closed Sun. for dinner and Mon. Family-type hotel with good, generous meals; excellent new find. V.
Restaurants. *Greuze* (M), 1 rue Albert-Thibaudet (tel. 85-51-13-52). Closed mid-Nov. to mid-Dec.; Thurs. for dinner, except hols. One of the best restaurants in France for classical cuisine; an institution. AE, V. *Sauvage* (M), pl. Champ-de-Mars (tel. 85-51-14-45). Closed mid-Nov. to mid-Dec. Rich Burgundian cuisine; also has 31 pleasant and airconditioned rooms. AE, DC, MC, V.

VÉZELAY. *Poste et Lion d'Or* (E), pl. Champ-de-Foire (tel. 86-33-21-23). 49 rooms. Closed Nov. through Mar.; Weds. and Thurs. for lunch. Good place for lunch or a peaceful stay while visiting marvelous basilica; reserve well ahead; classical cuisine. V.
Restaurant. At **St.-Père-sous-Vézelay**, 3 km. (two miles) southeast, *Espérance* (E), (tel. 86-33-20-45). Closed Jan., Tues. and for lunch on Wed. One of half-dozen top restaurants in France; absolutely superb *nouvelle cuisine.* Also has 19 charming rooms. AE, V.

TOURS AND EXCURSIONS. By Bus. The Dijon tourist office organizes two whole-day tours with wine tastings from July through Sept., with optional gourmet lunch: *Côte de Nuits* tour leaves from Dijon, *Côte de Beaune* from Beaune. Many other excursions are run by local operators and travel agents to places of interest, usually including wine tasting; departures from Beaune and Dijon. Details from tourist offices.

By Boat. Various excursions are available on Burgundy's inland waterways; over 30 local companies organize trips on portions of the region's 3,500 km. (2,175 miles) of navigable waterways, some including gourmet meals and/or musical accompaniment, with flute and piano recitals on board. Many trips last a weekend or longer, but occasional day cruises too, often from Joigny on the river Yonne. *Tourisme Fluvial* brochures, available from tourist offices and travel agents, give details.

By Balloon. Hot air balloons are the latest craze, and tours of vineyards in Burgundy, combined with luxury bus travel, gourmet meals and deluxe accommodations certainly make for a vacation-to-remember. Check with your travel agent for the latest possibilities; most tours are organized by American operators.

City Tours. Walking tours of Beaune and Dijon, accompanied by official approved guide-lecturers, are available in July and Aug. and sometimes at other seasonal highpoints such as Easter if the weather is suitable. Most guides speak English. Tours last around 1½ hrs. Private tours within and outside these cities, accompanied by English-speaking guides, can be arranged for reasonable fees; ask at tourist offices.

By Train. Burgundy now has its own "tourist steam train" operating in the Ouche Valley some 15 km. (10 miles) from Beaune. Apr. through Sept., Sun. and public holidays only, but a diesel train runs on the same track on Tues., Thurs. and Sat. Another must for train enthusiasts is the *Petit Train touristique de la Côte d'Or,* setting out from Velars-sur-Ouche, mid-Mar. through Sept.; this is the delightful little train once used by anglers to travel between the river and the Burgundy Canal.

 SIGHTSEEING DATA. For general notes on visiting French museums and historic buildings—and an important warning—see "Sightseeing" in *Facts at Your Fingertips.*

ALISE STE.-REINE. Musee Alésia, (tel. 80-96-20-95). Open daily, Easter through June and mid-Sept. through Oct. 10–6; July to mid-Sept. 9–7.

ANCY-LE-FRANC. Château. Open daily, Easter through Oct., 10–12, 2–6. Guided tours.

ARCHÉODROME. Off A6 motorway near Beaune (tel. 80-21-48-25). Open daily Oct. through Apr. 10–6; May through Sept. 10–8. No admission charge for children under 12.

ARCY-SUR-CURE. Prehistoric grottoes. Open daily, Mar. through Nov., 9–12, 2–6.

ARNAY-LE-DUC. Maison régionale des Arts de la Table, 15 rue St.-Jacques (tel. 80-90-11-59). Open daily, except Mon., mid-Mar. through Oct. 10–12, 2–6.

AUTUN. Musée Ronis, 5 rue Bancs (tel. 85-52-09-76). Open daily, except Tues., Feb. and public hols., 10–12, 2–6; mid-Mar. through Sept., 9.30–12, 2–6; Oct. to mid-Nov., 10–12, 2–5; mid-Nov. through Dec. 10–12, 2–4.

AUXERRE. Cathédrale St.-Etienne: Trésor, Crypte, Tour (cathedral treasury, crypt and tower). Open Mon. to Sat. 9–12, 2–6; Sun. and public hols. 10.30–11.30.

BEAUNE. Hôtel-Dieu and **Musée de l'Hôtel-Dieu,** (tel. 80-22-14-14). Open daily, 9–11, 2–5; July and Aug., 9–6.40. No admission charge for children under 12.
Musée du Vin de Bourgogne (Wine Museum), rue d'Enfer (tel. 80-22-08–19). Open daily, May through Sept., 10–12.30, 2–6.15; Oct. through Apr., 9–12, 2–5.45.
Son-et-Lumière at Hôtel des Ducs de Bourgogne. Nightly from Easter to the famous fall sales of the Hospice wines.

BUSSY-RABUTIN. Château, (tel. 80-96-00-03). Open daily, except Tues., and public hols. Apr. through Sept., 9–11, 2–5. Oct. through Mar., 10–11, 2–3.

CHÂTILLON-SUR-SEINE. Musée Archéologique, housing *Trésor de Vix,* (tel. 80-91-24-67). Open daily 9–12, 2–6 (7 in summer, 5 in winter); afternoons only mid-Nov. to mid-March.

CHÊNOVE. Duke of Burgundy's 13th-cent. **wine presses,** (tel. 80-52-39-80). Open daily, at any time.

CÎTEAUX. Abbaye, (tel. 80-61-11-53). Open 9–12, 2–7; closed Sun. A.M. No admission charge.

CLUNY. Abbaye, (tel. 85-59-12-79). Open Apr. through Sept. 9–11.30, 2–6; Oct. through Mar. 10–11.30, 2–4. Closed public hols.

DIJON. Chartreuse de Champmol, 7 blvd. Chanoine-Kir, (tel. 80-43-23-23). Open daily, 8–6. No admission charge.
Musée des Beaux Arts, (tel. 80-30-31-11). Open daily, except Tues. and public hols. 10–6. Guided tours in French, Nov. through Apr. on Fri. 6.30–7.30 and Sat. 2.30–3.30; in English on request.
Tour Philippe-le-Bon. Open daily except Tues., mid-Apr. to mid-Sept., 9.30–11.30, 2.30–5.30. Rest of year open Wed. and Sun. only, same times.

FONTENAY. Abbaye, (tel. 80-92-15-00). Open daily, July through Sept., 9–12, 2 or 2.30–6.30. Guided tours every hour on the hour, excluding 1.00 P.M.

GEVREY-CHAMBERTIN. Château, (tel. 80-34-36-13). Open daily, 10–12, 2.15–6.15. Closed Sun. A.M. and some public hols.

ST.-FARGEAU. Château (tel. 86-74-05-67). Open daily, Apr. through Oct., 10–12 and 2–7; *son-et-lumière* with costumed actors some summer evenings (check dates locally).

SENS. Palais Synodal, 133 rue des Déportés de la Résistance, (tel. 86-65-05-30). Open daily, except Tues. and public hols. Apr. through Sept. 9–12, 2–6; Oct. through Mar. 10–12, 2–4.

WINE TASTING. There are innumerable opportunities here for tastings in wine cellars as well as visits to the great wine châteaux such as Clos Vougeot. Tourist offices in Beaune and Dijon have full details. The following places can be visited: Aloxe-Corton (Château Corton-André); Beaune (a large number of wine cellars, including the Halle aux Vins in a 9th-century church crypt and the well-known Patriarche cellars; many have small museums on the premises); Chorey-les-Beaune (two well-known estates); Dijon (Caveau Darce, in town center); Gevrey-Chambertin (vaulted Burgundian cellar used solely for tastings); Marsannay-la-Côte (local wine cooperative's cellar); Meursault (Château's 14th-century cellars plus another estate); Nuits-St.-Georges (18th-century cellars); Santenay (three different cellars); Savigny-les-Beaune (wine cellars plus motorbike museum); Vougeot (two different cellars).

Most of the region's excursions, whether by boat, coach, balloon or train, include at least one wine-tasting (see "Excursions" above).

COOKERY CLASSES. Next to drink in Burgundy comes food. This is one of France's best-known gastronomic regions and you may well want to combine sightseeing with instruction in the rich Burgundian cuisine.

In late spring and early fall, *École de Cuisine la Varenne* of Paris offers special one-week gastronomic courses at the historic Château du Fey near Joigny in northern Burgundy. In addition to cooking lessons, participants sample the best Burgundy has to offer during wine tastings, excursions to vineyards, and visits to Michelin-starred restaurants. For information contact: *La Varenne,* P.O. Box 27320, Seattle, WA 98125.

One-day instruction, including lunch, is available at the *Chez Camille* hotel in Arnay-le-Duc, year-round except July and Aug. Cookery demonstrations are occasionally held at the *Chapeau Rouge* hotel in Dijon, but not for fewer than 15 people.

SHOPPING. The most obvious present or souvenir hereabouts is some of the region's splendid wine. If that proves too heavy or fragile you can always buy wine implements: many local shops specialize in attractive corkscrews, bottle stands, coasters and the like. Dijon has three other famous food specialties: mustard, blackcurrants and *crème de cassis.* China jars of mustard are particularly attractive, as are prettily packed boxes of blackcurrant-flavored candy. *Cassis,* the strong liqueur distilled from blackcurrants, is a good buy: use it as a *digestif* after meals or for making the delicious *kir apéritif* before meals.

THE RHÔNE VALLEY

Silk, Lavender and Nougat

Even though Lyon is France's second-largest city, this part of the country is surprisingly little known to foreign tourists, who tend to hurtle through it on their way down south to the Côte d'Azur or to Italy, maybe stopping off for a gastronomic meal, but rarely exploring the region beside the mighty river.

Yet the Rhône valley certainly doesn't deserve this neglect. It is full of interest, with a long history stretching back to the Romans, hundreds of churches, châteaux and abbeys, magnificent scenery, fine wines, unspoilt villages—and many small restaurants serving excellent local dishes at only a fraction of the prices charged in the better-known centers. To the east, between the Rhône and the Alps, is the lavender-scented Drôme, full of delightful little towns offering a foretaste of sunny Provence. To the north is the Beaujolais wine-producing district, which is in a way a continuation of the great Burgundy vineyards.

And right in the center of course is busy, bustling Lyon, which makes a good starting-point for your journey.

Lyon—Silk and Industry

Lyon, center of the French mechanical industry, with its many bridges spanning the mighty Rhône and Saône rivers, its massive stone houses, its prosperous, perpetually hurrying inhabitants, is very different from the Old Burgundian towns you may have passed through before reaching this great metropolis, second only to Paris in size and population. Although it can trace its history back to Roman Lugdunum, it is essentially a modern city, surrounded by motorways. Its traditional silk industry is today somewhat in decline, but it has numerous large mechanical and chemical firms and is also recovering something of its former role as a capital of banking and international commerce. It has a new civic and commercial complex (La Part-Dieu) and a handsome new university campus in the suburbs. It also has its own Métro (subway) and its main street has been banned to traffic, in keeping with the current "quality of life" vogue. Thousands of people attend its annual International Fair, held in early April in special buildings along the Rhône, and throng to the great summer festival of Lyon-Charbonnières. Lyon also has the country's leading provincial theater: Roger Planchon's remarkable Théâtre National Populaire, in the suburb of Villeurbanne, specializing in radical and experimental plays.

Many people have drawn parallels between Lyon and the industrial towns of northern England, mainly because the Lyonnais is traditionally taciturn and difficult to get to know. His life still revolves largely around his family, and strangers are rarely invited into his home. But though you may be disappointed at not being invited for dinner to sample the region's magnificent cuisine as cooked for an ordinary family, Lyon is so full of restaurants that you won't have any difficulty finding somewhere to eat.

The 18th-century place Bellecour is the lively heart of this bustling city, and here you'll find a whole host of restaurants and cafés (the Lyonnais are fond of café life). Leading off it, the pedestrians-only rue Victor Hugo has some good shops. Not far from here are the city's major museums. The interesting Musée Historique des Tissus (the Textile Museum), in an 18th-century mansion, reflects Lyon's former importance as the center of the silk trade, but also on display are magnificent tapestries going back almost 2,000 years, as well as a fine collection of Persian and Turkish fabrics. Close by is the Musée des Arts Décoratifs, a must for lovers of 18th-century furniture and porcelain, and a little further away the Musée des Beaux-Arts, with a varied collection including some fine modern paintings.

On the other side of the Saône from the place Bellecour is the old town, known as the Vieux Lyon, with many fine Renaissance mansions, plus a sprinkling of late Gothic houses. This area is well worth exploration, with its covered passages *(traboules)*, inner courtyards and decorative wrought ironwork, and the fine Gothic cathedral of St.-Jean, with beautiful stained glass and an astronomical clock. Close to the cathedral is the base of the funicular taking you up to the late 19th-century basilica of Notre-Dame-de-Fouvière, the scene of special pilgrimages and celebrations on September 8 and December 8, and commanding a magnificent view. Not far from here are the ruins of two Roman theaters and the excellent modern Gallo-Roman Museum.

Don't leave Lyon without strolling along by the Rhône—a favorite pastime for the Lyonnais, as is the traditional Sunday outing to the little spa of Charbonnières-les-Bains, with its racecourse and casino and, in March, a famous motor rally.

A classic excursion from Lyon is to medieval Pérouges, a picturesque walled village originally dating from before the Roman occupation. Allow time to wander through the old streets and sample some medieval food-and-drink specialties. If you're interested in birds, continue from here to the huge Dombes Ornithological Reserve, which has about 400 different species of birds, some of them extremely rare. A minor road from Pérouges leads to Villefranche-sur-Saône, a busy industrial town best known to foreign visitors as the capital of the Beaujolais wine-producing area. It has an interesting church where a miracle is said to have taken place, but otherwise has little to attract the holidaymaker.

South to the Drôme

If you continue south down the Rhône valley from Lyon you come first to ancient Vienne, famous for its superb restaurants, but also for its temples and a theater dating from the Roman period, plus a Gothic cathedral and Romanesque cloisters. To the west lies St.-Etienne, an important industrial and mining center that has been the scene of serious industrial unrest in recent years. Although a lively city culturally, it has little to interest the foreign visitor. A favorite excursion from Vienne is to the Ideal Palace, an extraordinary folly built by a local postman in Hauterives, but check that it is still open to the public as it has been suffering from too many sightseers.

South of Vienne lie Tain-l'Hermitage and Tournon, where the celebrated L'Hermitage wine is made, and then Valence, the capital of the Drôme, a busy industrial and market town with a university once attended by François Rabelais. Its 16th-century Maison des Têtes, in the Grande-Rue, is known for its richly carved façade. Further south still is Montélimar, famous throughout France as the center of nougat production (you can even visit a nougat factory if you feel like it, but anyway you're sure to want to take home a prettily packed box of this great delicacy). But the chief interest of Montélimar is as a center for excursions into the unspoilt Drôme, a region of lavender-scented hills and peaceful little towns unknown, fortunately, to the developers. One attractive road from here leads to the busy little town of Crest, with delightful gardens and a 12th-century keep; another to tiny Grignan, where the great marquise de Sévigné is buried (she used to stay with her daughter, the countless of Grignan, in the 16th-century château, which can be visited, and wrote many of her celebrated letters in the countryside around here).

From here you can continue to Nyons, an ancient town with medieval houses and ramparts, popular with summer visitors, passing on the way through Valréas and the "Enclave of the Popes," which was part of the papal dominions from the 14th to the 16th centuries. A different road takes you to Dieulefit, a center of craftsmanship where many of the traditional crafts (especially glass-blowing) are being revived, and to Le Poët-Laval, with the ruins of a fortress built by the Knights of Malta, and a Protestant Museum. The whole of this unspoilt area is an ideal hunting ground for those who like exploring off the beaten tourist track.

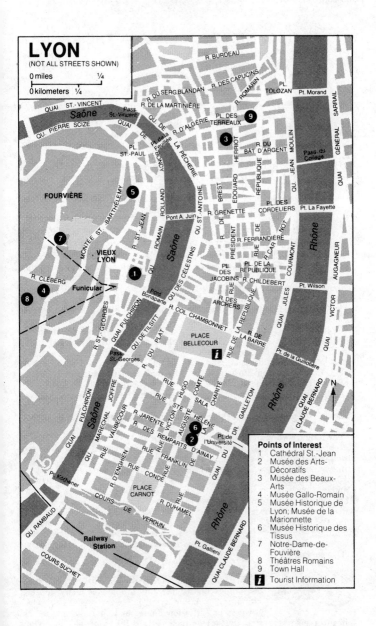

LYON
(NOT ALL STREETS SHOWN)

0 miles ¼
0 kilometers ¼

QUAI ST.-VINCENT
Saône
QU. PIERRE SCIZE
Pass. St-Vincent
R. DE LA MARTINIÈRE
R. DU SERG. BLANDAN
R. DES CAPUCINS
R. BURDEAU
PL. TOLOZAN
Pt. Morand
SARRAIL
R. ROMARIN
R. D'ALGÉRIE
PL. DES TERREAUX
9
GÉNÉRAL
QUAI
PL. ST-PAUL
QU. DE LA FEUILLÉE
R. DES DE BONDY
LA PÊCHERIE
3
R. DU BÂT D'ARGENT
HERRIOT
ÉDOUARD
RÉPUBLIQUE
R. JEAN MOULIN
Pass. du Collège
FOURVIÈRE
MONTÉE ST-BARTHÉLEMY
R. ST. JEAN
R. ROMAIN ROLLAND
Pont A. Juin
QU. ST.-ANTOINE
Saône
PL. DES CORDELIERS
Pt. La Fayette
Rhône
AUGAGNEUR
5
R. DE BREST
PRÉSIDENT
R. GRENETTE
R. FERRANDIÈRE
RUE DE LA CARNOT
R. DE LA RÉPUBLIQUE
7
VIEUX LYON
1
QU. DES CÉLESTINS
Pont Bonaparte
PL. DE LA RÉPUBLIQUE
R. CHILDEBERT
PL. DES JACOBINS
Pt. Wilson
R. CLÉBERG
4
Funicular
8
R. COL. CHAMBONNET
R. DES ARCHERS
RUE DE LA BARRE
QUAI JULES
VICTOR
QUAI
R. ST-GEORGES
QUAI FULCHIRON
QU. DE TILSITT
QU. DU PLAT
PLACE BELLECOUR
i
R. DE
Pt. de la Guillotière
Pass. St-Georges
Rhône
QUAI CLAUDE BERNARD
N
RUE VICTOR HUGO
RUE STE HÉLÈNE
RUE AUGUSTE COMTE
SALA
CHARITÉ
RUE DE GAILLETON
FULCHIRON
MARÉCHAL JOFFRE
VAUBECOUR
R. JARENTE
R. DES REMPARTS D'AINAY
6
2
Pt. de l'Université
Saône
QUAI
R. D'ENGHIEN
RUE FRANKLIN
RUE CONDÉ
R. DU DR
PLACE CARNOT
R. DUHAMEL
QU. RAMBAUD
COURS DE VERDUN
Pt. Kitchener
Railway Station
Pt. Gallieni
COURS SUCHET
QUAI CLAUDE BERNARD

Points of Interest
1 Cathédral St.-Jean
2 Musée des Arts-Décoratifs
3 Musée des Beaux-Arts
4 Musée Gallo-Romain
5 Musée Historique de Lyon; Musée de la Marionnette
6 Musée Historique des Tissus
7 Notre-Dame-de-Fourvière
8 Théâtres Romains
9 Town Hall
i Tourist Information

PRACTICAL INFORMATION FOR THE RHÔNE VALLEY

TOURIST OFFICES. There are regional tourist offices —written enquiries only—in the following *départements: Lyonnais-Bresse*—**Ain,** 2 rue Guichenon, BP 78 01002 Bourg-en-Bresse (tel. 74-23-66-66); **Loire,** 5 pl. Jean-Jaurès, 42021 St.-Etienne (tel. 77-33-15-39); **Rhône,** 69223 Lyon (tel. 78-42-25-75). *Dauphiné*—**Drôme,** 1 av. de Romans, 26000 Valence (tel. 75-43-27-12).

There are local tourist offices in the following towns: **Lyon,** pl. Bellecour (tel. 78-42-25-75) and Centre d'Echange de Perrache (beside Perrache rail station), (tel. 78-42-22-07); **Montélimar,** allée Champ-de-Mars (tel. 75-01-00-20); **St.-Etienne,** 12 rue Gérentet (tel. 77-25-12-14); **Tain-l'Hermitage,** 70 av. Jean-Jaurès (tel. 75-08-06-81); **Vienne,** 3 cours Brillier (tel. 74-85-12-62); **Valence,** 33 bis av. Félix-Faure (tel. 75-43-04-88).

REGIONAL FOOD AND DRINK. Lyon claims to be the heartland of French regional cuisine, and there must be more good restaurants to the square mile here than anywhere outside Paris. The great strength of Lyonnais cooking is its simplicity, with excellent ingredients carefully cooked. Typical are *quenelles de brochet* (dumplings of pounded pike, usually served in a rich crayfish sauce), *poularde demi-deuil* (poached chicken with truffle slices beneath the skin), or the less expensive *poularde à la crème.* (The finest French chickens come from Bresse, just 60 km. (35 miles) north of Lyon). Equally renowned is *gâteau de foies de volaille,* a hot pâté of chicken livers, usually served with a tomato sauce. Simpler fare includes the famous *saucisson de Lyon,* often served hot with a warm potato salad, and *gras double à la lyonnaise,* a feast for tripe lovers. Lyon draws on Burgundy, the Alps and the Auvergne for its cheeses while, to complete the feast you are likely to find the richest of chocolate cakes.

In the Rhône valley due south of Lyon, the cuisine resembles that of Provence with an Alpine influence obvious from the number of potato dishes. Montélimar is famous for nougat, made there since the late 16th century. Packed in pretty boxes, it travels well.

The long tradition of gastronomy in this part of France is, not surprisingly, accompanied by an equally long tradition of wine production. Beaujolais, produced in the north of the region, is a light wine tasting of the grape and is often drunk as a refreshing drink outside ordinary mealtimes. The famous *Beaujolais nouveau,* drunk in Nov. almost as soon as it has been bottled, is particularly popular. Lower down the Rhône valley you will come across the Côtes-du-Rhône wines, made from wines grown in the vineyards on both sides of the river. Particularly well known are the excellent *Condrieu* and *Château-Grillet,* both white and drunk very cold, and the slightly sparkling *Clairette de Die,* while the Hermitage wines, from the area round Tain and Tournon, are unusually fruity. Also try the *St.-Joseph* or the *Cornas,* which was appreciated by Charlemagne 1,200 years ago.

HOTELS AND RESTAURANTS. This part of France is famous for its fine cuisine and has many gourmet restaurants. A new trend is for the region's top chef-owners to add a few deluxe and charming rooms and suites to their restaurants, thus giving their patrons the bonus of a marvelous overnight stop or weekend. Reserve well ahead for these delights as they are much sought after. For incorrigible gourmets the first place to head for must be Lyon. We can offer only a small selection in our lists each year. Lyon also has the usual big-city range of hotels, while elsewhere in the region you'll find pleasant country inns and modest hotels, often with excellent restaurants.

For general notes on hotels and restaurants, see "Hotels" and "Restaurants" in *Facts at Your Fingertips*.

BEAUREPAIRE. Restaurant. *Fiard* (M), 23 rue République (tel. 74-84-62-02). Closed Jan. and Feb., Sun. for dinner (except in July and Aug.). Deserves its high reputation with locals; excellent classical cuisine at reasonable prices; also has 15 rooms with bath or shower (I). AE, DC, MC, V.

BOURG-EN-BRESSE. *Prieuré* (E), 49 blvd. Brou (tel. 74-22-44-60). 15 rooms. New, modern; some rooms have terrace overlooking garden or church; some (M) rooms. No restaurant. AE, DC. *Logis de Brou* (M), 132 blvd. Brou (tel. 74-22-11-55). 30 rooms. Beside famous church; modern and comfortable; no restaurant. AE, DC, V.
Restaurant. *Auberge Bressane* (M), 166 blvd. Brou (tel. 74-22-22-68). Closed mid-Nov. to mid-Dec., Mon. for dinner, Tues. Right by church; serves genuine regional cuisine at moderate prices. AE, DC, V.

DIE. *Petite Auberge* (I), av. Sadi-Carnot (tel. 75-22-05-91). 13 rooms. Closed mid-Dec. through Jan., Sun. for dinner and Mon. (except in July and Aug.). Facing station; good food. V.

DIEULEFIT. At Poët-Laval, 4 km. (2½ miles) west, *Hospitaliers* (E), (tel. 75-46-22-32). 20 rooms. Closed mid-Nov. through Feb. Medieval building in heart of lovely old village; glorious views from terrace; pool; good restaurant (M) with newish cuisine. AE, DC, MC, V.
Restaurant. *Brises* (I), route de Nyons (tel. 75-46-41-49). Closed Mon. for dinner, Tues. and Jan. Charming, with lovely terrace for warm days; good-value *menus*. Also 9 rooms (I) with half-board terms compulsory in season (a real bargain).

GRIGNAN. *Sévigné* (I), (tel. 75-46-50-97). 20 rooms. Closed Dec. to mid-Jan, and Mon. (except in July and Aug.). Modest but convenient base for exploring the Drôme and visiting Mme. de Sévigné's château; no restaurant. MC.

LYON. *Concorde* (E), 11 rue Grôlée (tel. 78-42-56-21). 140 rooms. Large comfortable rooms in this airconditioned traditional hotel in town center; restaurant. AE, DC, MC, V. *Pullman Prestige* (E), 129 rue Servient (tel. 78-62-94-12). 245 rooms. Restaurant closed mid-July to mid-Aug., Sun. and for lunch on Mon. In eastern sector of city near Part-Dieu rail station; modern airconditioned rooms; very good restaurant *(Arc-en-Ciel)* on 32nd floor (worth it for the views alone!). AE, DC, MC, V. *Royal* (E), 20 pl. Bellecour (tel. 78-37-57-31). 90 rooms. Restaurant closed Sun. Right in town center; huge price range, (I) to (E)!, well-equipped rooms in traditional building, plus restaurant for straightforward grills. AE, DC, MC, V. *Sofitel* (E), 20 quai Gailleton (tel. 78-42-72-50). 196 rooms. Well-planned modern rooms; 8th-floor restaurant *(Trois Dômes)* offering some interesting regional dishes; boutiques, hairdresser. AE, DC, MC, V.

Carlton (M), pl République (tel. 78-42-56-51). 87 rooms. Welcoming; all rooms refurbished. No restaurant. AE, DC, MC, V. *Grand Hotel des Beaux Arts* (M), 73 rue Pdt.-Herriot (tel. 78-38-09-50). 79 rooms. Good central location; completely refurbished; most rooms airconditioned. No restaurant. AE, DC, MC, V. *Tourinter* (M), 23 cours Charlemagne (tel. 78-92-81-61). 120 rooms. Impersonal but well-run modern hotel near Perrache station; the best (and most expensive) rooms have own balcony. AE, DC, V.

Bristol (I), 28 cours Verdun (tel. 78-37-56-55). 131 rooms. Old-established, well run hotel by Perrache rail station. No restaurant. AE, DC, V. *Ibis* (I), pl. Renaudel (tel. 78-95-42-11). 144 rooms. Modest but efficiently run, near Part-Dieu rail station; restaurant. MC, V. *Laennec* (I), 36 rue Seignemartin (tel. 78-74-55-22). 14 rooms. Good little modern hotel. No restaurant. V. *Phenix* (I), 7 quai Bondy (tel. 78-28-30-40). 36 rooms. Rooms charming and comfortable. A good place to stay in Lyon. No restaurant. AE, DC.

Restaurants. *Léon de Lyon* (E), 1 rue Pléney (tel. 78-28-11-33). Closed Christmas and New Year period, Sun., Mon. for lunch and public hols. Mixture of Lyon specialties and interesting *nouvelle cuisine* makes this one-time bistrot one of best in town. V. *Mère Brazier* (E), 12 rue Royale (tel. 78-28-15-49). Closed Aug., Sat. for lunch, Sun. Here you can understand why Lyon has such a reputation. Try the *Côte-de-Brouilly, réserve maison.* AE, DC, V. *Nandron* (E), 26 quai Jean-Moulin (tel. 78-42-10-26). Closed Aug., Fri. for dinner, Sat. Deservedly renowned for its outstanding regional cuisine, often "new"-style. AE, DC, MC, V. *Orsi* (E), pl. Kléber (tel. 78-89-57-68). Closed Aug., Sat. May through July, Sun. and public hols. Very pretty restaurant serving superb *nouvelle cuisine;* good-value (M) *menu.* AE, V. *Vettard* (E), 7 pl. Bellecour (tel. 78-42-07-59). Closed mid-July to mid-Aug., Sat. for dinner June and July and Sun. One of best in town for *nouvelle cuisine* versions of rich regional dishes; central (on main square). AE, DC. V.

Ty-Coz (M), 15 rue Royale (tel. 78-27-36-29). Closed Sun. and Mon. Opened 1985 by owner of famous Breton restaurant of same name in Paris, and quickly made a name for itself. AE, DC, V.

Café des Fédérations (I), 8 rue Major-Martin (tel. 78-28-26-00). Closed Aug. and weekends. Typical Lyon restaurant with the accent on charcuterie. AE, DC. *Café Jura* (I), 25 rue Turpin (tel. 78-42-20-57). Closed Sat., Sun., Aug. and one week in winter. One of the best simple restaurants in Lyon, typical of its kind; good, plain cooking. V. *Chez Mounier* (I), 3 rue Marronniers (tel. 78-37-79-26). Closed Wed. for dinner and Mon. Just behind pl. Bellecourt, and worth discovering for its atmosphere and typical, good cooking. *Fourvière* (I), closed Mon. High up by the pilgrimage church of Notre-Dame-de-Fourvière, with stunning views over Lyon and good-value food. *Pied de Cochon* (I), 9 rue St.-Polycarpe (tel. 78-28-15-31). Closed Aug. and weekends. Genuine Lyonnais pork dishes washed down with marvelous wines. AE, DC. *Tante Alice* (I), 33 rue Remparts-d'Ainay (tel. 78-37-49-83). Closed mid-July through Aug., Christmas and New Year period, Fri. for dinner, Sat. Good home cooking, pleasantly served in traditional bistrot-style restaurant. AE. *Voûte* (I), 11 pl. Antonin-Gourju (tel. 78-42-01-33). Closed Aug., and Sun. Old favorite, though the long-time woman chef-owner has now handed on to a young man; tasty tripe and other Lyon specialties. AE, DC.

At **Charbonnières-les-Bains,** 8 km. (5 miles) west, *Gigandon* (M), (tel. 78-87-15-51). Closed Aug., Sun. for dinner, Mon., Christmas and New Year period. Delightful spot for lunch, very popular with the people of Lyon on outings; mixture of traditional and more inventive cuisine. AE, V.

At **Collonges-au-Mont-d'Or,** 9 km. (5½ miles) north, *Paul Bocuse* (E), (tel. 78-22-01-40). Run by probably France's best-known chef-restaurateur and vocal champion of ultra-fresh ingredients (not only for *nouvelle cuisine*); delicious and sophisticated; reserve well ahead. AE, DC, V.

At **Crépieux-la-Pape,** 9 km. (5½ miles) north, *Larivoire* (M), (tel. 78-88-50-92). Closed part of Feb., part of Sept., Tues. and Mon. for dinner. Old favorite overlooking Rhône; newish cuisine. Good-value *menus.* AE, DC, V.

MIONNAY. **Restaurant.** *Alain Chapel* (E), on N83 road (tel. 78-91-82-02). Closed Jan., Mon. (except if public hol.) and for lunch on Tues. Belongs to one of France's most brilliant chefs; marvelously light and inventive cuisine, plus 14 beautifully renovated rooms (E)—great breakfast!, but reserve months ahead. AE, DC, V.

MONTÉLIMAR. *Parc Chabaud* (E), 16 av. Aygu (tel. 75-01-65-66). 22 rooms. Closed Christmas through Jan.; restaurant closed weekends. Central, yet with big garden; very comfortable, with restaurant. AE, DC, V. *Relais de l'Empereur* (E), 1 pl. Marx-Dormoy (tel. 75-01-29-00). 40 rooms. Closed mid-Nov. to mid-Dec. Converted coaching inn, old-fashioned but charming; restaurant usually good, though some readers have been disappointed. AE, DC, MC, V.

Restaurant. At **Malataverne,** 9 km. (6 miles) south by D144a, *Domaine Colombier* (M), (tel. 75-51-65-86). Typical old house with home-style cooking. Also has 13 rooms; very quiet; park, pool. AE, DC, V.

PÉROUGES. Restaurant. *Hostellerie Vieux Pérouges* (E), (tel. 74-61-00-88). 23 rooms. Closed Wed. (except in July and Aug.), Thurs. for lunch. Picturesque atmosphere in half-timbered 13th-cent. building in medieval village; a few (M) rooms in annex; good restaurant. V.

ROANNE. *Troisgros* (E), pl. Gare (tel. 77-71-66-97). Closed Jan. and most of Aug., Tues. and Wed. for lunch. One of finest in France. Michel Troisgros has now joined his father Pierre to prepare the most imaginative *nouvelle cuisine*. Reserve well in advance. Also garden and 24 comfortable (E) rooms. AE, DC, V.

ST.-ETIENNE. *Altea* (M), rue Wuppertal (tel. 77-25-22-75). 120 rooms. Restaurant closed Sat. for lunch and Sun. On outskirts beside Parc de l'Europe; modern, with good restaurant, *Ribandière.* AE, MC, V. *Arts* (I), 11 rue Gambetta (tel. 77-32-42-11). 63 rooms. Central, renovated and well-equipped. Good value. No restaurant. V. *Astoria* (I), 60 rue Déchaud (tel. 77-25-09-56). 33 rooms. Central, pleasant; no restaurant. AE, DC, MC, V.

Restaurants. *Pierre Gagnaire* (E), rue Georges-Teissier (tel. 77-27-57-93). Closed part of Feb., Aug., Sun. and Mon. Brilliantly inventive cuisine. One of the best in the region; very good value. AE, DC, V.

At **St.-Priest-en-Jarez,** 4 km. (2⅜ miles) out, *Clos Fleuri* (M), (tel. 77-74-63-24). Closed part of Feb., Sun. for dinner, Mon. Pleasant garden setting; popular with local businessmen. AE, DC, V.

SUZE-LA-ROUSSE. *Relais du Château* (I), (tel. 75-04-87-07). 20 rooms. Closed mid-Dec. to mid-Jan. Right opposite the château; modern, with pool, tennis court and restaurant; good half-board rates. AE, MC, V.

At **La Beaume de Transit,** 5 km. (3 miles) away, *Domaine de St.-Luc* (I), (tel. 75-98-11-51). 5 rooms. No lunches. Delightful farm-inn, very friendly welcome; attractive rooms and regional home cooking (meals served to inn guests only).

TAIN L'HERMITAGE. *Commerce* (M), 69 av. Jean-Jaurès (tel. 75-08-65-00). 28 rooms. Closed mid-Nov. to mid-Dec. Nice little family hotel with pleasant restaurant (some local specialties). AE, DC, MC, V.

Restaurant. *Reynaud* (M), 82 av. Pdt. Roosevelt (tel. 75-07-22-10). Closed Sun. for dinner, Mon. and Jan. Terrace overlooking Rhône. Good regional cooking with touch of *nouvelle.* Also (I) meals and nice *menus.* Pool. AE, DC, V.

VIENNE. At **Chasse sur Rhône,** 8 km. (5 miles) north, *Mercure* (M), CD4 "les Roues" (tel. 78-73-13-94). 108 rooms. Rooms well equipped and aircondi-tioned. AE, DC, MC, V.

At **Pont-Evêque,** 3 km. (2 miles) east, *Midi* (I), (tel. 74-85-90-11). 16 rooms. Closed Jan. Set in lovely garden, friendly service; no restaurant. AE, DC, V.

At **Chonas l'Amballan,** 9 km. (5 miles) south, *Hostellerie Marais St.-Jean* (E), (tel. 74-58-83-28). 10 rooms. Closed Feb., Tues. for dinner, Wed. Delightful restored farmhouse in peaceful countryside; lovely garden; traditional cuisine. AE, DC, V.

Restaurants. *Pyramide* (E), 14 blvd. Fernand-Point (tel. 74-53-01-96). Closed Feb., Mon. for dinner, Tues. One of the high spots in France for classical cuisine. AE, DC. *Bec Fin* (M), 7 pl. St.-Maurice (tel. 74-85-76-72). Closed Sun. for dinner, Mon. Close to cathedral; Lyonnais cuisine; good-value *menus.* AE, DC, MC, V. *Magnard* (M), 45 cours Brillier (tel. 74-85-10-43). Closed part of Feb., most of Aug., Tues. and Wed. Good for regional dishes cooked in classical style; must reserve. AE, DC, MC, V. *Molière* (M), 11 rue Molière (tel. 74-53-08-41). Closed Sat. for lunch and Sun. Classical cooking and good wines.

At **Les Roches de Condrieu,** 12 km. (7½ miles) away, *Bellevue* (M), 1 quai Rhone (tel. 74-56-41-42). Closed mid-Feb. to mid-Mar., first half Aug., Mon., for lunch on Tues. (Apr. through Sept.), Sun. for dinner (Oct. through Mar.). Excellent classical cuisine and interesting wine list; also has 20 rooms. AE, DC, MC, V.

VONNAS. *Georges Blanc* (E), (tel. 74-50-00-10). Closed Jan. to mid-Feb., Wed., Thurs. (but open Thurs. for dinner mid-June to mid-Sept.). Run by the same family for generations and now one of the most famous in all France; superb *nouvelle cuisine;* also has 26 deluxe rooms and 6 suites, plus pool, tennis court—even a heliport! Must reserve well ahead. AE, DC, V.

TOURS AND EXCURSIONS. By Bus. The S.N.C.F. (French Railways) has tours of the Beaujolais wine region from Lyon. There are various bus tours from Ardèche centers such as Aubenas and Privas into the Drôme, visiting Nyons, Tain-l'Hermitage, Dieulefit, among other places. Excursions into the Drôme and its lavender hills start from Montélimar.

Various tours of Lyon accompanied by official guide-lecturers are available: Old Lyon, Modern Lyon, Technical Lyon, etc. Inquire at tourist offices.

By Boat. Excursions by boat or canoe can be made in the Loire-Forez area in the northwest of the region, based on the Pilat nature reserve. Occasional trips are organized down the Rhône from Lyon, mostly into Provence (Arles and the Camargue). For details inquire at tourist offices.

On Foot. For walking tours of Lyon, cassette players (cassettes available in English) can be hired, together with an illustrated leaflet.

There is a marked itinerary for hikers from Tain-l'Hermitage called *Le Circuit des Crêtes* (the Mountain Ridge Circuit), starting in the south at La Roche-de-Glun and ending at Serves in the north (look out for green arrows and *route panoramique* signs). Leaflets are available from the tourist office in Tain. Walking tours in the *Parc naturel régional du Pilat* (Pilat nature reserve) set from St.-Etienne.

SIGHTSEEING DATA. For general notes on visiting historic buildings and museums in France—and an important warning—see "Sightseeing" in *Facts at Your Fingertips.*

BOURG-EN-BRESSE. Abbaye de Brou (Brou Abbey). Open Apr. through Sept., daily 8.30–12, 2–6.30; rest of the year, daily 10–12, 2–4. Closed public hols. *Son-et-Lumière* takes place at Easter and from the last Sat. in May to last in Sept., on Thurs., weekends and public hols., at around 9.30 P.M.

CORCELLES. Château. In the Beaujolais hills. Open daily, except Sun. and public hols., 10–12, 2.30–6.30.

CREST. Tour Vieille and **Tour Neuve** (Old and New Towers), (tel. 75-75-00-22). Open daily 9–12, 2–6. Closed weekdays in winter.

GRIGNAN. Château (tel. 75-46-51-56). Open Wed. P.M. to Mon., 9.30–11.30, 2.30–5.30; closed Nov.

LYON. Hôtel Gadagne, housing **Musée Historique de Lyon** and **Musée de la Marionnette** (Puppet Museum), 10–14 rue Gadagne (tel. 78-42-03-61). Open daily except Tues. and public hols., 10.45–6.

Musée des Beaux-Arts (Fine Arts Museum), pl. Terreaux. Open daily except Tues. and public hols., 10.45–6.

Musée Gallo-Romain, 17 rue Cléberg. Open Wed. to Sun., except public hols., 9.30–12, 2–6.

Musée Historique des Tissus (Textile Museum), Hôtel de Villeroy, rue Charité. Open daily except Mon. and public hols., 10–12, 2–5.30.

Musée de l'Imprimerie et de la Banque (Printing and Banking Museum), 13 rue Poulaillerie. Open Wed. to Sun., except public hols.

Musée Lyonnais des Arts-Décoratifs (Applied Arts Museum), 30 rue Charité. Open daily except Mon. and public hols., 10–12, 2–5.30. Same ticket as Textile Museum.

MONTÉLIMAR. Château des Adhémar (tel. 75-01-07-85). Open Wed. P.M. to Mon., 10–12, 2–5; guided tours Wed., Sat. and Sun. at 3 P.M. Closed Dec.

LE POËT-LAVAL. Musée du Protestantisme Dauphinois (Protestant Museum). Open summer months 3–6.30 (dates vary, so check locally).

ST.-BONNET-LE-CHÂTEAU. Crypte, Caveau des Momies, Bibliothèque (crypt, burial vault of mummies, and library, the latter in the Collégiale). Between Montbrison and St.-Etienne. Open daily 8–12, 2–7 (to 6 in winter); closed Tues. and Thurs. in winter.

SUZE-LA-ROUSSE. Château (tel. 75-46-51-56). Open July through Sept., daily, guided tours only, at 3, 3.45, 4.30 and 5.15; rest of year, Sun. only, same times. Closed Nov.

TOURNON. Château, housing **Musée du Rhône,** pl. Auguste-Faure (tel. 75-08-10-30). Open Apr. through Oct., daily 2.15–6; June through Aug., also 10–12. Closed Wed.

VIENNE. Cloître St.-André-le-Bas (monastery), (tel. 74-85-18-49). Open Apr. to mid-Oct., daily except Mon. and Tues., 9–12, 2–6.30; winter, Wed. to Sat., 10–12, 2–5; Sun. 2–6. Also closed on public hols.

Musée Lapidaire (Roman sculpture and mosaics), Eglise St.-Pierre. Open Apr. to mid-Oct., daily except Tues., 9–12, 2–6.30; winter, daily except Tues., 10–12, 2–5.

Théâtre Romain (Roman amphitheater). Opening times as *Musée Lapidaire.*

SHOPPING. Montélimar's famous nougat is packed into pretty boxes and sold in various shapes and sizes. Nyons is known all over France for its olives; packed in pottery jars, they make good presents to take home, or you might like to take a traditional wooden olive spoon with drainage holes, used to scoop olives out of barrels. A special type of rug, called a *scourtine,* is made in Nyons, and nearby Dieulefit is an important craft center, specializing in pottery and glass-blowing.

THE FRENCH ALPS

One Area, Two Countries

Along the southeastern border of France rises a mighty barrier of mountains that provides some of the most spectacular scenery in Europe—The French Alps, soaring 4,805 meters (15,775 ft.) to their climax in Europe's highest peak, Mont Blanc. Its chief divisions, north to south, are—the Mont Blanc country; Savoie, lying along the Italian border; the Dauphiné, of which Grenoble is the capital; the Hautes-Alpes, centered about Briançon; and the Alpes-de-Haute-Provence and Alpes Maritimes, which extend down to the lemon and the orange trees, the palms and the bougainvillaea, and the warm blue waters of the Mediterranean.

The northern part of the French Alps, the Mont Blanc area and the Savoie, is double-treat playground country—lakes for summer vacationists, mountains for both summer and winter. The lakes, north to south, are those of Geneva, Annecy and Bourget; the great mountain is Mont Blanc, which dominates the scenery for miles around.

Of the lake resorts, the best known is undoubtedly Aix-les-Bains. On Lac du Bourget, this resort has all the amenities of a typical European spa. This might sound expensive, and it can be, but Aix-les-Bains is large enough for hotels to exist at all levels. The lake becomes rather polluted in high summer, and bathing is inadvisable (a new purification plant is easing this problem), but you can sail, fish, and, around the shores, play golf and tennis. The city has some interesting Roman remains, and you can make an excursion, preferably by boat, to Hautecombe Abbey, where you can visit the tombs of the princes of the House of Savoy and listen to Gregorian plainsong.

Annecy, on the lake of the same name, is dominated by the four towers of its 12th-century castle. Arcaded lanes alternate with quiet canals in the old quarter round the lovely 16th-century Palais de l'Isle, and the relics of the monastery of the Visitation are widely venerated. The lake is marvelously clean, and is a paradise for all water sports.

Evian, on Lake Geneva, is smaller, but no less pleasant, and it has the resources of Europe's largest lake to draw upon. A noted spa, its still mineral water is bottled and may be bought anywhere in the country. It shares its lakeside position with Thonon, also a spa, and a comparatively inexpensive one. The nearby Château de Repaille is an impressive, castle-cum-monastery surrounded by vineyards.

Chambéry, which lies only a few miles south of Aix-les-Bains, is a delightful old city, with the château of the dukes of Savoy rising above the arcades of its picturesque old streets, and an interesting cathedral.

Mont Blanc Region

On one side of Mont Blanc lies Chamonix, the oldest and biggest of French winter sports resorts. Site of the first Winter Olympic Games in 1924, it still challenges experts to get down the Brévent run used on that occasion.

In summer, Chamonix is a center for mountain climbers interested in scaling Mont Blanc—and for the less experienced and adventurous, there are some relatively easy routes, requiring no ropes or special equipment. Chamonix is also the starting point for spectacular cablecar rides across the glaciers to Courmayeur, in Italy. For truly energetic skiers, there is the famous six-day Chamonix-Zermatt trip: for this you need to be a good skier *and* very fit.

Avoriaz, reached by cablecar from the old resort of Morzine, has most attractive architecture, and a chic clientele. The absence of automobiles makes the atmosphere particularly restful. Flaine, designed by Marcel Breuer, seems rather stark and chilly for many. Deliberately designed to be the intellectual's ski resort, it provides avantgarde art galleries, double-dome seminars, far-out films as well as particularly well-organized skiing.

In the next valley is the smartest of the Mont Blanc region resorts, Megève, which is inevitably one of the most expensive. It has a lively non-skiing life, like Chamonix. Indeed, perhaps the after-ski amusements tend to submerge the skiing, for in general the slopes here are comparatively easy, and skiers of only modest ability will find Megève more to their liking than Chamonix. It also has attendant resorts, which can be reached easily—St.-Gervais, and the smaller Praz-sur-Arly, Combloux and Col de Voza-Prarion. St.-Gervais is a winter sports resort that is also popular in the summer, and is famous for its sulfuric thermal springs, used with success to treat very bad burn cases.

Lesser resorts are Les Contamines tucked away in the mountains between Chamonix and Megève; La Clusaz (conveniently reached from Annecy by bus); Samoëns and Les Gets, near Morzine.

Resorts in Savoie

In Savoie, the leading winter resorts are the high-altitude Val d'Isère and its twin, Lac de Tignes, just over the mountain tops. Courchevel, with its twin Méribel just over the ridge, is connected by ski lift with St.-Martin-de-Belleville, Les Menuires and Val Thorens, all of which make for a vast skiing area. Tignes is one of the largest resorts in the area, with an enormous complex of lifts which connect it not only with Val d'Isère, but with the smaller resorts of La Daille, Les Boisses and Les Brevières. Tignes and Val are very sporty, and there is little nightlife, since everyone skis all day long, every day. Courchevel is the smartest of the Savoie resorts, with lots of nightlife. Méribel, just over the mountain, is a rather strung-out place, where the smart set go in for villas.

La Plagne, nor far from Tignes, is attractive and well-organized. Les Arcs, a budding resort reached by cable car (or road) from Bourg St.-Maurice, is for those who like a quiet, early-to-bed life after a day on the slopes. Tignes offers a nine-hole golf course, sailing on its lake, swimming, and excursions to the Vannoise National Park during the summer months; Les Arcs also has a golf course and special crash courses for beginners.

This is lovely summer vacation country, too; you can stay at Courchevel itself, or seek a vacation spot more associated with summer holidays than winter ones—say Bourg St.-Maurice, to the northeast, set in a basin of meadows and orchards. Bourg St.-Maurice is a junction of valleys and roads, and also a rail terminus, and from here you can make a magnificent trip which is possible only in summer: through Val d'Isère and beyond it over the summer road through the Alps.

This trip will offer you some unparalleled high-altitude mountain scenery. You pass along the highest mountain highway in Europe and approach its culminating point—the Iseran Pass, 2,767 meters (9,084 ft.) up; and if the air is clear, you might stop at the inn right on the pass and drink in, among other things, the unbeatable view over the Tarentaise mountain range and the glacier-streaked peaks of Albaron and de Charbonel. The latest date at which you can expect to make this trip is the end of September. By October the pass is usually choked with snow, and it stays that way until the end of June.

Places to visit hereabouts include Albertville and the old walled part of town, Conflans, perched on a rocky spur and full of picturesque streets and buildings. St.-Jean-de-Maurienne has a fine cathedral with a separate bell tower and lovely carved choirstalls.

Dauphiné and Grenoble

Grenoble, capital of the Dauphiné, has grown faster since World War II than any other French city. "France's little Chicago in the Alps," this boom city has been called, for its rows of new skyscrapers fill a narrow plain with mountains on all sides. In this striking setting, ultra-modern industries specialize in electronics and engineering, while nuclear research flourishes, and the large universities attract thousands of foreign students. Grenoble, the venue for the 1968 Winter Olympics, prides itself on being a pace-setter in France for all kinds of new developments, social and cultural as well as industrial.

Modernistic and cosmopolitan, Grenoble has an air of self-assertiveness that some may find more American than European. Yet it is also well rooted in French culture and tradition. Its art museum is a fine one, with works by Rubens, Cranach, Watteau and other old masters, and a fine modern collection including Gauguin, Matisse, Rouault, Utrillo and Picasso. It has notable architecture as well—the church of

St.-Laurent, with a 6th-century crypt; the early Renaissance Palace of Justice; and the 12th-century cathedral, in the district where Stendhal, author of *Le Rouge et le Noir* and *La Chartreuse de Parme,* was born. Canalized between stone banks, the river Isère rushes swiftly through the city, and over it swings the *téléférique,* which takes you up to the Fort de la Bastille, with gardens, restaurants and cafés on the hill beyond the river, for a remarkable view over the city and the surrounding countryside.

An interesting excursion from Grenoble is to the Grottes de la Balme caves. A bit farther afield is the famous monastery of the Grande Chartreuse in a setting that is both austere and serene, enclosed by wooded heights and limestone crags. Situated about a mile from the main road, the vast complex of buildings covers almost five hectares (12 acres). Here originated the distinctive style of hermitages and communal institutions followed by 24 charterhouses throughout the world. Founded by St.-Bruno in 1084, the monastery was destroyed many times by fire, and rebuilt. During the Revolution, it was stripped of its possessions and the monks were expelled. When they were allowed to return a few years later, they began to make the Chartreuse liqueurs that provided their main source of income. Expelled again in 1903, they finally returned in 1940. The Grande Chartreuse itself cannot be visited, but the liqueur cellars can be, and the Correrie, about three km. (two miles) from the main road, presents an excellent picture of the contemplative life.

To the south is the pleasant little spa of Uriage-les-Bains, and then Vizille, where the first rebellion against royalty occurred in 1788 when the deputies of Dauphiné demanded the convocation of the States General. They had last met in 1614, and their return to activity set in action the chain of events that led to the French Revolution. A museum was opened in the castle in 1984. Also near Grenoble are two gorges and two châteaux, Béranger and Crownes, as well as the Château de Sérivantin, although unfortunately this is only open to the public in high summer. A little farther south is the lake of Laffrey, where the royal troops sent to arrest Napoleon caught up with their man—and promptly joined his army. A splendid statue, isolated in lonely grandeur on a wind-swept plateau, commemorates this *volte-face.* Be very careful driving around here, the roads are very steep and full of sharp turns.

Hautes-Alpes and Briançon

The eastern part of what was once the old province of Dauphiné is now the modern Hautes-Alpes, and its heart is Briançon, a city of much more than passing interest. If you visit it in the summer, you would do well to take the high-altitude Route des Grandes Alpes, for its scenery is magnificent. From the north you would come from Val d'Isère over the Iseran Pass, and then through Bonneval and Lanslebourg where the road joins the N6 west through Modane, the frontier point for train travel into Italy. In July, the famous Tour de France bicycle race passes over this gruelling route. At St.-Michel it turns south, again over a road that demands a little effort from the driver but repays him by the scenery of the Col du Télégraphe and the Galibier Pass, 2,642 meters (8,675 ft.) up, before reaching Briançon.

Briançon is old and intriguing, and prides itself on being the highest city (as distinguished from towns or villages) in Europe—its altitude is 1,325 meters (4,350 ft.). Fortified by Vauban, the military architect of Louis XIV, it still has its old ramparts into which the cathedral snugly fits. The citadel is crowned by Bourdelle's statue of France, presiding over a superb alpine panorama. Outside the walls, spread out along slopes that descend towards the resort, is the new town, called Briançon-Ste.-Catherine. Briançon is a wonderful center from which to set out on hikes into the mountains, and it is also a starting point for bus excursions in all directions—for instance into the charming rustic beauty of the Var and Queyras valleys.

If you visit Briançon for winter sports, you will not be able to take the routes suggested above. Whether you come from north or south, you will have to travel by way of Gap, the only road left open after the snow begins to pile up in the passes. Close by are two leading winter sports resorts, Serre-Chevalier and Montgenèvre, the latter with one of the most famous ski jumps in France.

A few minutes' drive from Chorges, the old capital of the Cartigues, the vast 3,040-hectare (7,500-acre) lake formed by the Serre-Ponçon dam provides a whole new pleasure-ground for water sports. A little farther down the valley, the small lake at Le Lauzet does the same on a miniature scale.

The National Park of Les Ecrins, east of Briançon, is France's largest, the purpose of its creation in 1973 being the conservation of nature. Not to be missed are the Meije and the majestic Barre des Ecrins, 4,102 meters (13,470 ft.) high.

Alpes-de-Haute-Provence

South of Briançon and Gap (which is becoming rather built-up and terribly noisy) are the Alpes-de-Haute-Provence. The mountains are less majestic, and the tall pines give way to a drier, stubbier kind of vegetation. The scent of lavender and thyme wafts from the fields, the skies are bluer (we are approaching the Mediterranean) and the atmosphere is less austere. There are a number of small, picturesque towns to visit; Seyne-les-Alpes is a good center for exploration.

Among the hill towns worth visiting are Sisteron, with its fortress rising sheer from the great cliff that springs from the river bed; Allos, the starting point for an excursion to the glistening emerald Lac d'Allos in a wild mountainous setting; and Digne, with its old cathedral and basilica, Notre-Dame-du-Bourg, one of the finest Romanesque churches in France.

On the Route des Grandes Alpes, the chief town is pleasant, rather sleepy Barcelonnette, which in winter is a minor sports center and is well-known for the luxury villas and marinas surrounded by large gardens. The gardens were built by locals who, in the 19th century, emigrated to Mexico, made their fortune, then returned to enjoy their wealth in their native valley. The two modern resorts nearby, Sauze and Super-Sauze, are fairly lively. If you have a good head for heights and steady nerves on the hairpin bends, a spectacular day's tour from Barcelonnette twists up through the mountains to the 2,250-meter (7,385-ft.) Col d'Allos, then down through the fortified town of Colmars and across a luxuriant valley to Digne. Between Barcelonnette and the coast, there are a few ski resorts reached from the Riviera: Auron, Valberg or Beuil. Surprisingly, sometimes there is more snow and it is colder at Auron or Valberg than in the northern Alpine resorts. The new ski resort of Isola 2000—the odd name comes from its height in meters—close to the Italian border, is becoming increasingly popular.

PRACTICAL INFORMATION FOR THE FRENCH ALPS

TOURIST OFFICES. The *départements* of the Alps have their own regional tourist offices (written enquiries only). These are: *Dauphiné*—**Hautes Alpes**, 16 rue Carnot, 05000 Gap (tel. 92-51-39-49); **Isère**, 14 rue de la République, BP 227, 38019 Grenoble (tel. 76-54-34-36). *Savoie*—**Haute-Savoie**, 45 rue Sommeiller, BP 348, 74102 Annecy; **Savoie**, 4 rue du Château, 73000 Chambery (tel. 79-85-12-45).

There are local tourist offices in the following towns: **Aix-les-Bains**, pl. Mollard (tel. 79-35-05-92); **Albertville**, pl. Gare (tel. 79-32-04-22); **Alpe d'Huez**, pl. Paganon (tel. 76-80-35-41); **Annecy**, Clos Bonlieu, 1 rue Jean-Jaurès (tel. 50-45-00-33); **Annemasse**, rue Gare (tel. 50-92-53-03); **Autrans**, pl. Mairie (tel. 76-95-30-70); **Barcelonnette**, pl. Manuel (tel. 92-81-04-71); **Chamonix**, pl. Eglise (tel. 50-53-00-24); **Chamrousse**, Le Recoin (tel. 76-97-02-65); **Courchevel**, La Croisette (tel. 79-08-00-29); **Les Deux Alpes** (tel. 76-79-22-00); **Evian**, pl. Allinges (tel. 50-75-04-26); **Flaine** (tel. 50-90-80-01); **Les Gets** (tel. 50-79-75-55); **Grenoble**, 14 rue de la République (tel. 76-54-34-36); **Megève**, rue Poste (tel. 50-21-27-28); **Les Ménuires** (tel. 79-08-20-12); **Meribel** (tel. 79-08-60-01); **Montgenèvre** (tel. 92-21-90-22); **Morzine**, pl. Crusaz (tel. 50-79-03-45); **La Plagne**, Le Chalet (tel. 79-09-79-79); **Pralognan-la-Vanoise** (tel. 79-08-71-68); **Pra Loup** (tel. 92-84-10-04); **St.-Jean-de-Maurienne**, Ancienne Evêché (tel. 79-64-03-12); **St.-Gervais-les-Bains**, av. Paccard (tel. 50-78-22-43); **Sallanches**, quai Hôtel-de-Ville (tel. 50-58-04-25); **Samoëns** (tel. 50-34-40-28).

REGIONAL FOOD AND DRINK. Cooking in the Alps focuses on the cow, with fine cream, butter, veal and above all, cheese. Specialties include *poulet au comté* (chicken with a wine cheese sauce), *escalope de veau belle comtoise* (veal escalope topped with ham and cheese), *noix de veau aixoise* (braised veal with vegetables and chestnuts), and gratins like the famous potato *gratin dauphinois* baked with cream and topped with cheese, and *gratin savoyard*, potatoes baked with onions, stock and cheese. Delicious fish dishes are made with mountain trout and the rare *omble chevalier*, or char, found in lake Annecy. In season look for game and wild mushrooms, with raspberries and wild strawberries in summer, and soups and chesse fondue in winter.

The famous Alpine *Gruyère* cheese is in fact a generic term which covers *Beaufort*, *Comté* (both excellent table cheeses), and the less refined *Emmenthal*, recognisable by its large holes and usually reserved for cooking. Other varieties include blue cheeses like *Sassenage* and *Morbier*, a dozen different varieties of *Tomme* (a term meaning simply "round"), creamy *Vacherin* which can be mild or quite strong, and *Reblochon*, a small soft cheese distributed throughout France. As if these cow's cheeses were not enough, *St.-Marcellin* is a reliable little goat cheese.

So close to Switzerland, pastries are good, especially with chocolate or local fruits. Look, too, for *biscuit de Savoie* (a light sponge cake), for the delectable *roseaux d'Annecy* liqueur chocolates, and for *mont blanc*, a tall confection of meringue, chestnut purée and whipped cream sprinkled with grated chocolate.

This is not a region of great wines, but the slopes do produce a few wines of superior quality, notably *Crépy, Ayse, Chignin, Montmélian*, and the *Roussettes* of Frangy and Seyssel. And sample the justly famed liqueur of the Grande Chartreuse and the potent *framboise* made from an aromatic local raspberries. *Génépi* is an unusual liqueur made from an aromatic local plant which grows only high up in the mountains (above 8,000 ft.).

HOTELS AND RESTAURANTS. Accommodations range from the luxurious in larger cities and resort centers to modest ones for the budget-minded. Most hotels are only open seasonally (Easter, summer and the winter-sports season for the most part) so always check in advance. Many insist on at least half-board terms.

For general notes on hotels and restaurants, see "Hotels" and "Restaurants" in *Facts at Your Fingertips*.

AIX-LES-BAINS. *Adélaïde* (E), av. Marlioz (tel. 79-88-08-00). 60 rooms. Comfortable rooms, some (M), some with terraces overlooking park; pool. Restaurant with terrace. *Manoir* (M), 37 rue Georges-ler (tel. 79-61-44-00). 72 rooms. Closed 24 Dec. through Jan. Fine old mansion in big garden behind baths; restaurant serves wonderful classical food. DC, MC, V. *Central* (I), 6 rue Murger (tel. 79-35-21-19). 20 rooms. Closed mid-Nov. through Feb. In town center; restaurant with good-value meals.

At **Ruffieux,** 21 km. (13 miles) north, *Château de Collonges* (E), (tel. 79-54-27-38). 12 rooms. Closed Jan. Historic castle furnished with antiques; lovely grounds; good restaurant; closed for lunch on Tues. and Mon. (except summer). (E). AE, DC.

Restaurants. *Lille* (M), at **Grand Port** (tel. 79-35-04-22). Closed Jan., Feb., and Wed. Pleasant location near lake, calm and luxurious atmosphere; great classical cuisine. Also has 12 comfortable rooms (M). AE, DC. *Platanes* (M), at **Petit Port** (tel. 79-61-40-54). Closed Nov. through Mar., and Tues. Peaceful, with garden. AE, DC, MC, V.

ALBERTVILLE. *Million* (M), 8 pl. Liberté (tel. 79-32-25-15). Closed mid-April to mid-May, mid-Sept. to mid-Oct.; restaurant also closed Sun. for dinner, Mon. for dinner, also Mon. for lunch mid-July through Aug. Old-established, elegant, with comfortable rooms; restaurant's (E) classical cuisine, is not to be missed! AE, DC, V.

Restaurant. *Ligismond* (M), Cité Médiéval de Conflans (tel. 79-32-53-50). Closed Mon. and first half of Oct. On the beautiful medieval square. Good *nouvelle cuisine* and good-value *menus.* AE, DC, V.

ALPE D'HUEZ. *Christina* (E), pl. Cognet (tel. 76-80-33-32). 27 rooms. Closed May, June, and Sept. through Nov. Chalet with fine views of massif de l'Oisans. V. *Chamois d'Or* (M), near Grandes Housses télécabine (tel. 76-80-31-32). 42 rooms. Closed May to mid-Dec. Conveniently placed for skiing facilities; restaurant has good classical cuisine.

Restaurant. *Outa* (I), rue Poutat (tel. 76-80-34-56). Open July, Aug., and Christmas through Apr. In lovely garden; popular with locals. Also has 11 rooms. DC, MC, V.

ANNECY. *Trésoms et Forêt* (E), 3 blvd. Corniche (tel. 50-51-43-84). 33 rooms. Closed Nov. through Feb. Forest location; luxurious. AE, DC. V. *Carlton* (M), 5 rue Glières (tel. 50-45-47-75). 44 rooms. Comfortable, in town center, facing station; no restaurant. AE, DC, V. *Belvédère* (I), 2 km. (1 mile) by route de Semnoz, 7 chemin Belvédère (tel. 50-45-04-90). 10 rooms. Closed Oct. through Apr. Very quiet rooms and lake views. Restaurant (M), one of the best in town, closed Sun. for dinner, Mon., Nov. V.

At **Chavoires,** 4½ km. (3 miles) away, *Pavillon de l'Ermitage* (E), 79 rte. Annecy (tel. 50-60-11-09). 11 rooms. Closed Nov. through Feb. Traditional; has 2 family apartments; garden. Worth the trip for its excellent (M) restaurant. AE, DC. V.

Restaurants. *Auberge de l'Eridan* (E), 7 av. Chavoires, Petit Port (tel. 50-66-22-04). Closed Christmas, Feb., mid-Aug. to mid-Sept., Wed., and Sun. for dinner. Elegant décor; deliciously inventive cuisine. AE, DC, MC, V. *Salino* (M), 13 rue Jean-Mermoz (tel. 50-23-07-90). Closed part of Feb., mid-June to mid-July, Sun. for dinner, and Wed. In old town, near church; classical cuisine; eat outside to enjoy view of lake. AE, V. *Pré de la Danse* (I), 16 rue Jean-Mermoz (tel.

50-23-70-41). Closed June, Sat. for lunch, and Mon. In old town, good value.
DC, MC, V.

ANNEMASSE. *Genève* (M), 38 route de Genève (tel. 50-38-70-66). 100
rooms. Ask for rooms at the rear (*sur l'arrière*). Modern, practical; close to
Geneva. AE, DC, MC, V.
Restaurant. At **Gaillard**, 2 km. (1¼ miles) southwest, *Château* (M), 47 rue
Vignes (tel. 50-38-65-38). Closed Sun. for dinner and Mon. Very light food,
served in elegant dining room or outside in park. MC, DC, V.

LES ARCS. *Golf* (E), arc Chantel (tel. 79-07-25-17). 280 rooms. Closed
mid-Apr. to mid-June, and mid-Sept. to mid-Dec. Huge modern hotel in beautiful scenery; pool, tennis. AE, V.
Restaurant. *Logis du Guetteur* (M), northeast via D57 (tel. 94-73-30-82).
Closed mid-Nov. to mid-Dec. Picturesque and peaceful location in old fortress;
also has 10 rooms. AE, DC, MC, V.

ARGENTIÈRE. *Grands Montets* (M), (tel. 50-54-06-66). 40 rooms. Closed
May and Oct. to mid-Dec. Near Lognan téléférique. MC, V.
At **Montroc-le-Planet**, 2 km. (1 mile) northeast by RN 506 and VO7, *Becs
Rouges* (M), (tel. 50-54-01-00). 24 rooms. Closed mid-Apr. to mid-June and
mid-Sept. to mid-Dec. Very well maintained; good, practical take-away meals
with half-board terms. AE, DC, V.
Restaurant. *Dahu* (I), (tel. 50-54-01-55). Closed mid-June through Oct., and
mid-Dec. to mid-May, Wed. in Sept. Good value; also has 22 rooms. AE, DC, V.

AURON. *Pilon* (E), (tel. 93-23-00-15). 26 rooms. Open July and Aug., Christmas to mid–Apr. Peaceful; ice rink and pool (in summer). AE, DC, MC, V.

AUTRANS. *Buffe* (E), la Côte (tel. 76-95-33-26). 18 rooms. Closed mid-Apr.
through May, and Sept. Comfortable chalet; good food (M). MC, V. *Poste* (M),
(tel. 76-95-31-03). 30 rooms. Closed mid-Apr. to mid-May, mid-Oct. to mid-
Dec. With garden and pool; pleasant restaurant is (I). DC, MC. V.

AVORIAZ. *Dromonts* (E), by cable car (tel. 50-74-08-11). 40 rooms. Closed
mid-Apr. to mid-Dec. Comfortable; sauna, massage; inventive cuisine; warm
welcome. AE, DC, MC, V.

BARCELONNETTE. *Grande Epervière* (I), rte. Gap (tel. 92-81-00-70). 10
rooms. Closed part of Apr., mid-Nov. to mid-Dec., first half Jan., Mon. for
lunch (except in winter), and Sun. for dinner. Small, with garden and (I)
restaurant.
At **Sauze-sur-Barcelonnette**, 4 km. (2½ miles) southeast, *Alp* (E), (tel. 92-
81-05-04). 36 rooms. Closed May to mid-June and Nov. to mid-Dec. Great
hotel; quiet, with view and garden. Restaurant (I) is very good value. AE, DC, V.
At **Pra Loup**, 8½ km. (5¼ miles) southwest, *Auberge Clos Sorel* (E), Village
Clos Sorel (tel. 92-84-10-74). 11 rooms. Closed first half June, Nov. to mid-Dec.
Renovated old farm with very comfortable rooms. Pool, tennis. Restaurant. AE,
DC, V.
Restaurant. *Mangeoire* (M), pl. 4-Vents (tel. 92-81-01-61). Closed Jan., first
half June, Sun. (except July and Aug.) and Mon.; no lunches Feb. and Mar.
Near church, pleasant. V.

BONNEVAL-SUR-ARC. *Marmotte* (M), (tel. 79-05-94-82). 28 rooms.
Closed May to mid-June, mid-Sept. to mid-Dec. Peaceful chalet near ski slopes.
Bergerie (I), (tel. 79-05-94-97). 22 rooms. Open mid-June to mid-Sept., mid-
Dec. through Apr. Tranquil, lovely views; restaurant. MC, V.

LE BOURGET-DU-LAC. *Ombremont* (E), rte. Tunnel du Chat, 2 km. (1¼ miles) north via N504 (tel. 79-25-00-23). 20 rooms. Closed Dec., Jan., Sat. for lunch (except July and Aug.) and Mon. for lunch. Very comfortable. Mansion in attractive setting; private harbor with little boat; excellent cuisine. AE, DC, MC, v. *Port* (M), (tel. 79-25-00-21). 30 rooms. Closed Christmas through Jan. and on Thurs. Lovely views and (I) restaurant. MC, V.
  Restaurant. *Auberge Lamartine* (M), route du Tunnel du Chat (tel. 79-25-01-03). Closed Sun. for dinner, Mon., Dec. through Jan. Good classical cuisine; lovely views of lake; terrace. MC, V.

BOURG ST.-MAURICE. *Concorde* (M), av. Maréchal-Leclerc (tel. 79-07-08-90). 32 rooms. Closed mid-April through May, Oct. and Nov. Near station and téléférique; with restaurant. *Petite Auberge* (I), by bridge, rte. Moutiers (tel. 79-07-05-86). 15 rooms. Closed May to Oct. Good-value restaurant; tennis.

BRIANÇON. *Auberge Le Mont Prorel* (M), 5 rue René-Froger (tel. 92-20-22-88). 18 rooms. Closed second half of April and two weeks before Christmas. Chalet near town center, in own grounds. AE, DC, MC, V. *Vauban* (M), 13 av. Général-de-Gaulle (tel. 92-21-12-11). 44 rooms. Closed mid-Dec. Comfortable rooms, friendly service; garden. *Mont-Brison* (I), 3 av. Général-de-Gaulle (tel. 92-21-14-55). 44 rooms. Closed Nov. to mid-Dec. Good traditional hotel; no restaurant.
  Restaurant. *Paris* (I), 41 av. Général-de-Gaulle (tel. 92-20-15-30). Closed Oct., Fri. (except summer), Sat. for lunch. Good value and lovely views; also has 24 (M) rooms. AE, DC, V.

CHAMBÉRY. *Grand* (E), 6 pl. Gare (tel. 79-69-54-54). 50 rooms. Traditional hotel with all modern comforts; facing station. AE, DC, V. *Princes* (M), 4 rue Boigne (tel. 79-33-45-36). 45 rooms. Newly renovated, good facilities; central. Good classical cooking. AE, DC, MC, V.
  At **Challes-les Eaux,** 6 km. (3¾ miles) southeast. *Château* (M), 247 rue Château (tel. 79-85-21-45). 80 rooms. Closed Nov. through Jan. Magnificent 15th-century castle set in huge grounds; pool, tennis court; restaurant. AE, DC, MC, V. *Château de Trivier* (M), (tel. 79-85-07-27). 30 rooms. Successful blend of traditional elegance and modern comfort; set in large garden; restaurant (I). AE, DC, MC, V.
  Restaurants. *Roubatcheff* (E), 6 rue Théâtre (tel. 79-33-24-91). Closed mid-June to mid-July, Sun. for dinner, and Mon. A few Russian dishes plus fine *nouvelle cuisine,* elegant décor. AE, DC, MC, V. *Ducs de Savoie* (M), 6 pl. Gare (tel. 79-69-54-54). Closed Sun. Classical yet inventive cuisine; plenty of fish. *Vanoise* (M), 6 pl. Gare (tel. 79-69-02-78). Closed Sun. Excellent food in attractive small dining room. AE, DC, MC, V. *Trois Voûtes* (I), 110 rue Croix d'Or (tel. 79-33-38-56). Closed Nov. and Sun. (except July and Aug.). Unpretentious; good food and warm atmosphere.

CHAMONIX-MONT-BLANC. *Mont Blanc* (E), pl. Eglise (tel. 50-53-05-64). 50 rooms. Closed mid-Oct. to mid-Dec. Luxurious traditional hotel, with big garden in heart of resort. AE, DC, MC, V. *Alpes* (M), 89 rue Docteur-Paccard (tel. 50-53-07-27). 35 rooms. Closed mid-Nov. to mid-Dec., first half May. Central, newly modernized, surrounded by gardens. AE, DC. V. *Sapinière-Montana* (M), 102 rue Mummery (tel. 50-53-07-63). 30 rooms. Closed May and Oct. to mid-Dec. Beautiful views of Mont Blanc. Surrounded by forest and very quiet. AE, DC, MC, V.
  At **Le Lavancher,** 5 km. (3 miles) northeast via N506, *Beausoleil* (M), 60 allée Peupliers (tel. 50-54-00-78). 17 rooms. Closed mid-Sept. to mid-Dec. Tranquil setting in village; big garden; tennis. Half-board terms compulsory; restaurant is (I).
  Restaurants. *Albert Ier et Milan* (M), 119 impasse Montenvers (tel. 50-53-05-09). Closed May, Oct. and Nov. Welcoming dining room, with good cuisine. AE, DC, V. *Matafan* (M), in *Mont Blanc* hotel (tel. 50-53-05-64). Closed mid-Oct. to mid-Dec. Classical yet light food. AE, DC, MC, V. *Tartiffle* (M), 87 rue Moulins

(tel. 50-53-20-02). Closed Oct. to Christmas, most of Apr. through Mar., and Tues. Local dishes, warm welcome. AE, DC, V. *Bartavel* (I) at lunch, (M) at dinner, 26 cour Bartavel (tel. 50-53-26-51). Closed May, Oct. to mid-Dec., and Tues. except in Aug. Small chalet with friendly atmosphere, local dishes and good wine. AE, DC, V.

CHATEL. *Fleur de Neige* (E), rte. Morgins (tel. 50-73-20-10). 45 rooms. Closed mid-April to mid-June and mid-Sept. to mid-Dec. You can choose the chalet rooms or the regular ones. Chalet-type restaurant (M), with inventive classical cuisine; lovely views. MC. *Panoramic* (M), rte. Linga (tel. 50-73-22-15). 28 rooms. Closed Easter to mid-July and mid-Aug. to mid-Dec. Comfortable and quiet.

LA CLUSAZ. *Aravis* (M), (tel. 50-02-60-31). 41 rooms. Closed Easter through June and mid-Sept. to mid-Dec. In center of village, with big garden; tennis; restaurant.
Restaurant. *Vieux Chalet* (M), rte. de Crêt du Merle (1 km. northeast), (tel. 50-02-41-53). Closed second half June, and mid-Oct. to mid-Nov.; Tues, also Wed. and Thurs. (except July and Aug.). Excellent cuisine; also has 7 rooms.

COURCHEVEL. *Annapurna* (E), at **Super Pralong 2000,** rte. Altiport (tel. 79-08-04-60). 68 rooms. Closed Easter to mid-Dec. One of the best hotels in the French Alps, extremely comfortable with luxurious amenities; restaurant. AE, DC, MC, V. *Carlina* (E), at **Courchevel 1850** (tel. 79-08-00-30). 58 rooms. Closed Easter to Christmas. Conveniently near the slopes, yet peaceful. AE, DC, MC, V. *Crystal 2000* (E), route de l'Altiport (tel. 79-08-28-22). 51 rooms. Closed May to mid-Dec. Excellent hotel with huge terrace. Restaurant. Half-board terms only. DC, V. *Potinière* (M), at **Courchevel 1850** (tel. 79-08-00-16). 30 rooms. Closed May and June, mid-Sept. to mid-Nov. In heart of town, small and cozy. AE, V.
At **Praz St.-Bon,** 8 km. (5 miles) away, *Peupliers* (I), (tel. 79-08-11-61). 33 rooms. Closed Oct. and Nov. Lovely views and good-value restaurant. AE, V.
Restaurants. At **Courchevel 1850.** *Bateau Ivre* (E), (tel. 79-08-02-46). Closed Easter to Christmas. Particularly fine fish and good choice of wines. AE, DC, V. *Byblos des Neiges* (E), Jardin Alpin (tel. 79-08-12-12). 69 rooms. Closed May to mid-Dec. Pool, terraces, fireplaces. Restaurant with spectacular mountain views. AE, DC, V. *Chabichou* (E), (tel. 79-08-00-55). Closed mid-Apr. to mid-Dec. Elegant, one of best in region, with lots of fish.

LES DEUX ALPES. *Farandole* (E), rte. Farandole (tel. 76-80-50-45). 46 rooms. Closed May through June, Sept. through Nov. Modern chalet with comfortable rooms and apartments; pool. AE, DC, MC, V. *Belle Epoque* (M), (tel. 76-80-51-19). 29 rooms. Closed mid-Sept. through Nov., May through June. Traditional chalet with lovely views of the Muzelle; pool; restaurant. V. *Mariande* (M), (tel. 76-80-50-60). 25 rooms. Closed May through June, Sept. to mid-Dec. Quiet hotel near chapel, with comfortable rooms; garden with pool.
Restaurant. *Bérangère* (M), (tel. 76-79-24-11). Closed May through June and Sept. to mid-Dec. Original *nouvelle cuisine* and good-value *menus.* 59 (E) rooms. V.

EVIAN. *Prés Fleuris* (E), rte. Thollon, 7 km. (4½ miles) southeast (tel. 50-75-29-14). 12 rooms. Closed mid-Oct. to Palm Sun. Large luxurious mansion surrounded by fields. Marvellous classical cuisine in (E) restaurant. AE, DC, MC, V. *Royal* (E), on south bank of lake (tel. 50-75-14-00). 200 rooms. Closed mid-Dec. to mid-Feb. Old style "grand hotel," luxurious and comfortable; 3 restaurants, 2 of them famous. AE, DC, MC, V. *Bourgogne* (M), 73 rue Nationale (tel. 50-75-01-05). 8 rooms. Closed Nov. to Christmas. Modern, comfortable. AE, DC, MC, V.
Restaurants. *Café Royal* (E), in Royal Hotel (tel. 50-75-14-00). Closed mid-Dec. through Jan. Inventive cuisine, luxurious décor and excellent service. AE,

DC, V. *Verniaz* (M), Neuvecelle (tel. 50-75-04-90). Classical cooking. Lake views. 41 (E) rooms; pool, tennis. AE, DC, MC, V.

MÉGÈVE. *Chalet du Mont d'Arbois* (E), 3 km. (2 miles) via rte. Mont-d'Arbois (tel. 50-21-25-03). 12 rooms. Closed end Apr. to mid-June. Luxurious chalet in exceptional scenery; garden. AE, DC, MC, V. *Mont Blanc* (E), pl. Eglise (tel. 50-21-20-02). 55 rooms. Closed end Apr. to mid-June, Oct. Best in the resort; elegant atmosphere. AE, DC, MC, V. *Résidence* (E), at Rochebrune (tel. 50-21-43-69). 56 rooms. Closed mid-April to mid-May, Oct. Smart old hotel with pool, ice rink and (M) restaurant. AE, DC, MC, V. *Coin du Feu* (M), rte. Rochebrune (tel. 50-21-04-94). 25 rooms. Closed Easter through June, mid-Sept. to mid-Dec. Modern, comfortable, central, near slopes. V. *St.-Jean* (I), (tel. 50-21-24-45). 15 rooms. Closed mid-Apr. through May and mid-Sept. to mid-Dec. All rooms have good views. Convenient for skiing. Restaurant.

Restaurants. *Chez Nano's* (E), rue Arly (tel. 50-21-02-18). Closed Oct. to mid-Dec., May and June. Excellent, with modern cuisine, warm welcome and good atmosphere. AE, DC, V. *Enfants Terribles* (E), pl. Eglise (tel. 50-21-20-02). Closed end Apr. to mid-June, Oct. In *Mont Blanc* hotel; chic with inventive cuisine, good wine list and perfect service. AE, DC, V. *Au Capucin Gourmand* (M), rue du Crêt du Midi (tel. 50-21-01-98). Closed Mon. except summer, Oct. to Christmas, May and June. Good food and well-priced *menus*. AE, DC, MC, V. *Prieuré* (M), pl. Eglise (tel. 50-21-01-79). Closed Sept. to mid-Dec. and mid-Apr. through June. Nice, typical décor; generous cooking, also (I) and good-value *menus*. AE, DC, V.

MÉRIBEL-LES-ALLUES. *Grand Coeur* (E), (tel. 79-08-60-03). 24 rooms and 12 apartments. Closed mid-Apr. through June, and Sept. to mid-Dec. Chalet with comfortable rooms and good (E) restaurant. Half-board terms only. AE, DC, V. *Belvedère* (M), (tel. 79-08-65-53). Closed mid-Apr. to mid-Dec. 21 rooms. Peaceful hotel on the slopes; half-board only.

Restaurant. At **Mottaret**, 6 km. (4 miles) south, *L'Estaminet* (M), (tel. 79-08-64-25). Closed end Apr. to mid-Dec. Small, with traditional cuisine.

MONTGENÈVRE. *Montgenèvre* (M), Grand rue (tel. 92-21-92-64). 42 rooms. Closed May, June, and Sept. through Nov. Comfortable; restaurant has terrace. AE, DC, V. *Alpet* (I), (tel. 92-21-90-06). 10 rooms. Closed mid-Apr. through June, Sept. to mid-Dec. Small and peaceful, with lovely views and good-value meals. Restaurant closed for lunch in July and Aug.

MORZINE. *Dahu* (M), le Mas Metoud (tel. 50-79-11-12). 26 rooms. Closed mid-Apr. through June, Sept. to mid-Dec. Modern; pleasant service and ambiance; restaurant. V. *Musardière* (I), (tel. 50-79-13-48). 10 rooms. Open mid-June to mid-Sept., mid-Dec. to mid-Apr. Quiet, with small garden; no restaurant.

At **Avoriaz**, 7 km. (4½ miles) east or by cable car, *Dromonts* (E), (tel. 50-74-08-11). 40 rooms. Closed mid-April to mid-Dec. Modern and comfortable; restaurant with terrace. AE, DC, MC, V.

LA PLAGNE. *Christina* (E), (tel. 79-09-28-20). 55 rooms. Closed mid-Apr. to mid-Dec. Near slopes; peaceful with good restaurant *Edelweiss,* closed Thurs. for lunch; half-board. AE, DC, MC, V. *Graciosa* (M), (tel. 79-09-00-18). 10 rooms. Closed May through Nov. Large rooms, great views; restaurant (M), *Etoile d'Or,* is good but a bit overpriced à la carte. AE, DC, MC, V.

PRALOGNAN-LA-VANOISE. *Airelles* (M), Les Darbelays, ½ mile north on rte. des Granges (tel. 79-08-70-32). 16 rooms. Closed Easter through May, mid-Sept. to mid-Dec. Chalet-type hotel with comfortable rooms and lovely view; restaurant. *Grand Bec* (I), (tel. 79-08-71-10). 39 rooms. Closed mid-Sept. to mid-Dec., mid-Apr. to mid-June. With small garden and good-value restaurant.

ST.-GERVAIS-LES-BAINS. *Carlina* (E), Le Rosay (tel. 50-93-41-10). 34 rooms. Closed Nov. to mid-Dec., mid-Apr. to mid-June. Comfortable chalet with fine dining room and view of Mont Blanc. Pool. AE, DC, MC, V. *Couttet* (M), 23 av. du Mont-d'Arbois (near pl. Eglise), (tel. 50-78-26-65). 20 rooms. Closed mid-Nov. to mid-Dec., and third week of Apr. Old hotel, central, well-modernized; restaurant (I). AE, DC. V.

At **Bettex,** 8½ km. (5 miles) southwest, *Arbois-Bettex* (M), (tel. 50-93-12-22). 27 rooms. Closed mid-Apr. through June and Sept. to mid-Dec. Well equipped rooms; pool in summer; good simple restaurant. Well situated for skiing and hiking. DC, V.

ST.-JEAN-DE-MAURIENNE. *St.-George* (M), 334 rue République (tel. 79-64-01-06). 23 rooms. Quiet; no restaurant. *Bernard* (I), 18 rue Libération (tel. 79-64-01-53). 15 rooms. Closed Nov. and Mon. Near cathedral, with good-value restaurant. AE.

ST.-JULIEN EN GENEVOIS. Restaurants. *Abbaye de Pomier* (E), at Présilly (tel. 50-04-40-64). Closed Jan. to early March., Tues. and Wed. for lunch. 18th-cent. abbey serving excellent, inventive cuisine. DC, MC, V. *Diligence* (E), av. de Genève (tel. 50-49-07-55). Closed second half Jan., Sun. for dinner and Mon. Near church; perfectly-prepared classical cuisine served in elegant ambiance. AE, DC, V.

SALLANCHES. *Sorbiers* (M), 17 rue Paix (tel. 50-58-01-22). 40 rooms. Restaurant closed Sun. except school hols. Traditional, in peaceful grounds, with superb view; restaurant (I). AE, DC, MC, V. *Beauséjour* (I), pl. Gare (tel. 50-58-00-06). 35 rooms. Closed first half May and first half Nov. Central, modernized, with view of Mont Blanc and (M) restaurant.

SAMOËNS. *Sept Monts* (M), (tel. 50-34-40-58). 36 rooms. Closed mid-Sept. to mid-Dec., mid-Apr. through May. Pleasant, with pool and garden; restaurant is (I). MC, V.

At **Vercland,** 3 km. (2 miles) southwest, *Eteski* (I), (tel. 50-34-44-60). 22 rooms. Closed mid-Sept. to mid-Dec. Tranquil with garden; mountain views; restaurant, must book for dinner.

SERRE-CHEVALIER. *Plein Sud* (E), (tel. 92-24-17-01). 42 rooms. Closed mid-Sept. to mid-Dec., mid-Apr. through June. Comfortable and modern; pool; no restaurant. AE, V. *Boule de Neige* (I), (tel. 92-24-00-16). 10 rooms. Closed Easter to mid-Dec. Simple, comfortable hotel; half-board terms only in high season. V.

TALLOIRES. *Auberge du Père Bise* (E), rte. du Port (tel. 50-60-72-01). 24 rooms. Closed mid-Apr. to mid-May, Dec. and Jan. 18th-cent. mansion in wide grounds with own harbor; beautiful rooms; restaurant is famous for its classical cuisine and excellent service. Closed Tues. and Wed. for lunch. AE, DC, V. *Cottage* (E), (tel. 50-60-71-10). 33 rooms. Closed mid-Oct. to mid-Mar. Chic and comfortable; half-board terms compulsory in season. Restaurant uses local produce for classical dishes; excellent wine list. Private harbor, fine view of Lake d'Annecy. AE, DC, V.

THONON-LES-BAINS. *Clos Savoyard* (M), 50 av. Génève (tel. 50-71-03-91). 17 rooms. Beautiful setting; some quiet rooms in bungalows in garden. Good restaurant. AE, DC, V. *Corniche* (M), 24 blvd. Corniche (tel. 50-71-10-73). 23 rooms. Closed mid-Sept. to mid-May. Pleasant and welcoming; garden and pool; good (I) restaurant.

At **Bonnatrait,** 7 km. (4½ miles) southwest, *Château de Coudrée* (E), (tel. 50-72-62-33). 20 rooms. Closed Nov. through Apr. Wonderful partly-medieval castle beside lake, beautifully furnished; garden and private beach; good restaurant. AE, DC.

TIGNES. *Gentiana* (M), (tel. 79-06-52-46). 18 rooms. Closed Sept. to mid-Nov., May through June. Tranquil; lovely view; restaurant is (I).

At **Val Claret,** 2 km. (1¼ miles) southwest, *Ski d'Or* (E), (tel. 79-06-51-60). 22 rooms. Closed May to mid-Dec. Excellent, quiet hotel, facing slopes; good restaurant.

VAL D'ISÈRE. *Grand Paradis* (E), (tel. 79-06-11-73). 42 rooms. Closed May through June and Sept. through Nov. Rooms have terraces. Restaurant; nightclub; tennis. AE, DC, MC, V. *Galise* (M), (tel. 79-06-05-04). 32 rooms. Closed mid-Apr. to mid-Dec. Near post office; pleasant rooms and good-value restaurant (I).

VALLOIRE. *Setaz* (I), (tel. 79-59-01-03). 22 rooms. Closed mid-Apr. through May and mid-Sept. to mid-Dec. Rooms recently renovated; pool; fine mountain views; generous, good cooking. Excellent value.

TOURS AND EXCURSIONS. By Train. A scenic route along lakesides and through gorges in the 30 km. (18½ miles) *Chemin de Fer de la Mure,* from St.-Georges-de-Commiers to La Mure. The fare is around 75 fr. (reductions for children under 14 and students); for further details call 76-54-10-55.

By Car. A new marked route has been organized across the Dauphiné: *La Route des Dauphins,* visiting 11 historical mansions and museums: Ask for a map of this and other routes at any tourist office.

On Foot. Guided tours of the Old Town in Grenoble take place from July to Sept., daily except Thurs., at 10, 2.30 and 4.30, starting in front of the St.-Laurent church. The rest of the year, call 76-44-78-68 for an appointment.

By Boat. A boat trip on an Alpine lake is a delightful experience. From Evian you can take a round trip on Lac Léman (Lake Geneva), from June to Sept., about 9 hours, or simply cross the lake; there are evening cruises on Sat. in July and Aug. At Annecy round trips on the lake are available from Mar. to Oct., 8.30 A.M. to 8 P.M. from the Quai du Thiou. You can visit the Abbaye de Hautecombe across Lake Bourget, departing from the Grand Port at Aix-les-Bains at 10, 2.45 and 3.45. For further details of these and other trips, inquire at local tourist offices.

SIGHTSEEING DATA. For general notes on visiting historic buildings and museums in France—and an important warning—see "Sightseeing" in *Facts at Your Fingertips.*

ABONDANCE. **Cloître** (monastery with 14th-century frescoes). Open 10–12, 2–6 (to 4 or 5 in winter). Ask at Tourist Office.

AIME. **Basilique St.-Martin** (St. Martin's Basilica), La Plagne village. Open July to first week in Sept., daily except Tues., 9–12, 2–6. Other months, ask for the keys at the Tourist Office.

AIX-LES-BAINS. **Abbaye de Hautecombe** (Abbey, accessible by boat across Lake Bourget). Guided tours daily every 6 min., 10.20–11.25, 2.30–5.40 (4.25 in winter). Open Sun., public hols. (also Thurs. in July and Aug.) at 8.30 A.M. for Gregorian plainsong.

Roman remains. Spa and caves: guided tour only, daily except Sun. and hols., at 3, meet in front of the Nouveaux Thermes. Nearby are the **Arc de Campanus** and **Temple of Diana.** Closed Sun., public hols. and Nov. through Mar.

ANNECY. Château, rue Ste.-Claire. Housing **Musée Regional** (Local Museum). Open daily except Tues. and public hols., 10–12, 2–6.

BARRAUX. Château Le Fayet, (tel. 76-97-37-43). Open July and Aug. on Sat., Sun. and Mon.

BAYARD. Château housing **Bayard Museum** (tel. 76-97-63-60). Open June to mid-Sept., daily except Tues., 2–6.

BRIANÇON. Citadelle de Vauban. Guided tours July through Aug., daily at 10 and 3 (Tues. at 9.30).

CHAMBÉRY. Château des Ducs de Savoie, rue Basse du Château. Guided tours mid-June to mid-Sept., daily at 10.30 and 2.15–4.45; rest of year Sat. only at 2.30.
Musée Savoisien (Savoy Museum, prehistory and local history). Open daily except Tues., 10–12, 2–6.

CHAMONIX. Musée Alpin (Alpine Museum). Open June to Sept., and in school hols., daily 2–7.

CLUSES. Ecole Nationale d'Horlogerie (Clockmaking College). Open to visitors in summer, Mon., Wed. and Sat.

DIE. Musée Municipale (Local Museum with Roman collection), rue Buffarde. Open mid-June to mid-Sept., Mon., Tues., Thurs. and Sat., 3.30–6.30.

GRENOBLE. Eglise St.-Laurent, near quai Jouvin. Guided tours July through Sept., daily except Tues., 10–12, 2–6.
Grottes de la Balme (caves), 5 km. (3 miles) away. Open Apr. through Sept., daily 9–7; some weekends and public hols. in winter.
Musée des Automobiles Anciennes (Veteran Car Museum), (tel. 76-54-50-69).
Musée Dauphinois (Local History Museum), 30 rue Maurice Gignoux. Open daily except Tues. and public hols. 9–12, 2–6.
Musée de Peinture et de Sculpture (Painting and Sculpture Museum), pl. Verdun (tel. 76-54-09-82). Open daily except Tues. and public hols., 12.30–7.
Musée de la Résistance et de la Déportation (Resistance Museum), 14 rue Rousseau (in Stendhal's home), (tel. 76-44-51-81). Open Wed. to Sat., 3–6.
Musée Stendhal, 20 Grand Rue (tel. 76-42-02-62). Open daily except Mon., 10–12, 2–6.
Palais de Justice (Law Courts, early Renaissance building), pl. St.-André. Open daily except Sat., Sun. and public hols., 9–11.30, 2.30–5.

LONGPRA. Château (tel. 76-07-50-21). Open mid-June to mid-Sept., Tues., Thurs., Sat., 2.30–6.

MOIDIÈRE. Château, housing **Natural History Museum** (tel. 74-96-44-63). Open daily except Tues., 2–6; closed part of Sept.

ST.-MARCELLIN. Abbaye de St.-Antoine (13th-15th cent. abbey, former place of pilgrimage). Open June through Aug., daily tours at 3; rest of year, Sat. and Sun., 2.30–5. Venue of many fairs and festivals.

ST.-PIERRE D'ALBIGNY. Château de Miolans, 3 km. (2 miles) northeast. Open Apr. to Sept., daily 10–11.30, 2.30–6.

SAMOËNS. Jaysinia Alpine Garden. Open daily, 8–12, 1.30–5 (to 8 in July and Aug.). Access to the west of the church.

SASSENAGE (6 km., 4 miles, from Grenoble). **Château de Bérenger,** (tel. 76-27-54-44). Open July and Aug., 10–12, 2–6.
Château de Crolles, (tel. 76-08-01-01). Open July to Sept., by arrangement.
Grottes, (tel. 76-27-55-37). Open May to Oct., daily except Tues., 9–11, 2–6.

SERVIANTIN. Château (16th-cent. castle), (tel. 76-52-27-65 or 76-52-25-30). Open mid-July through Aug., 9–12, 2–5.

THONON-LES-BAINS. Château de Ripaille. Open Apr. to Oct., daily except Mon. in winter, 10–12, 2–6. Guided tours.
Musée du Chablais (Regional Museum), in Château de Sonnaz. Open daily except Sun. and public hols., July to mid-Sept., 10–12, 3–6.

THORENS GLIÈRES. Château de Thorens. Guided tours Easter to Oct., daily 10–12, 2–6 (Sun. and public hols., 2–6 only).

LE TOUVET Château (15th-17th cent. castle with 18th-cent. gardens), (tel. 76-08-42-27). Open May through Oct., Sat. Sun. and public hols., 2–6.

VERCORS. Grotte de Coufin (Choranche). Guided tours every hour, 10–4.

VIZILLE. Château, housing **Musée de la Révolution** and *Son et Lumière* (Sound and Light) shows in summer (tel. 76-68-00-19). Open Apr. through Sept., daily except Tues., 9–12, 2–5.30; in winter, 2–5.30 on Wed., Thurs. and Fri., 9–12 on Sat. and Sun. Guided tours.

VOIRON. Caves de la Chartreuse (liqueur cellars), 10 blvd. Edgar Kofler (tel. 76-05-81-77). Open daily except Sat., Sun. and public hols., 8.30–11.30, 2–6.30 (5.30 in winter).

SKI RESORTS. Alpe d'Huez. 1,858 meters (6,100 ft.). Large and fashionable with very lively night life; one of Dauphiné's most famous resorts. Good for all types of skiers. Be sure to take the *téléférique* (cable car) to Lac Blanc.
Les Arcs. 1,584 meters (5,200 ft.). Recent resort made up of three separate places: **Arc 1600,** small and brand new, with a lot of chalet accommodations; **Arc 1800,** with exceptional scenery; and **Arc 2000,** at over 3,226 meters (10,580 ft.). Quite a sporty resort, with a golf course and very little night life.
Argentière. 1,252 meters (4,110 ft.). The highest resort in the Chamonix valley. Suitable for all skiers. Non-skiers can always hike or take the *téléférique* to the Aiguille des Grands Monts (over 60 fr.).
Auris. 1,600, 2,200 and 3,350 meters (5,250, 7,220 and 10,990 ft.). New resort near Alpe d'Huez. A lot of activities for children as well as a large variety of summer sports. Mostly chalet accommodations.
Auron. 1,607 meters (5,275 ft.). Lots of winter sun thanks to the Mediterranean climate. Slopes face north, which means powdery snow stays on them, excellent for skiing. Chic atmosphere, with slopes for every kind of skier.
Autrans. 1,000–1,710 meters (3,283–5,613 ft.). 35 km. (21 miles) from Grenoble. The capital of cross-country skiing.
Bónneval-Sur-Árc. 1,005 meters (3,301 ft.). Near Modane. Nice little resort, very peaceful but rather remote.
Chamonix. 1,847 meters (6,063 ft.). Famous skiing resort, also the oldest and biggest, and extremely popular. Most of the slopes are for experienced skiers, but if you are not a good skier there are still plenty of things to do: hiking, visiting the casino or the restaurants, or simply admiring the wonderful scenery.

You should not miss the cable car trip to the Aiguille du Midi. Chamonix is also an important summer sports center.

Chamrousse 1,614 meters (5,300 ft.). Near Grenoble. Very sporty resort with a lot of facilities. Take the cable car to the Crois de Chamrousse for the view, but also because it offers late spring skiing, with the fantastic feeling of skiing towards the clouds.

Châtel. 1,188 meters (3,900 ft.). Near Evian. Family resort for all types of skiers. Super Châtel, at 1,647 meters (5,400 ft.) offers chalet accommodations and lovely views.

La Clusaz. 1,039 meters (3,411 ft.). Well-equipped winter sports resort near Annecy; small and peaceful; late spring skiing is possible here.

Collet d'Allevard. 1,450 meters (4,760 ft.). Near Montmélian, in the Chaîne de Belledonne. Quiet family resort, one of France's least expensive ski resorts.

Courchevel. 1,848 meters (6,068 ft.). Very chic resort made up of several resorts, including: **Le Praz,** at 1,300 meters (4,260 ft.) the lowest; **Courchevel 1650,** a family-type resort; and **Courchevel 1850,** the biggest and busiest from March onwards. On the whole, a very lively resort, wonderfully equipped, both for skiing and après-ski.

Les Deux Alpes. 1,797 meters (5,900 ft.). Not far from Grenoble. A peaceful resort, popular in winter for its cross-country skiing, but also in summer, where you can practice at above 2,600 meters (8,530 ft.). Has a brand new 600-meter (1,970 ft.) luge run.

Flaine. 1,828–2,437 meters (6–8,000 ft.). Near Cluses. Rather an intellectual resort, with shows or concerts throughout the year: well organized skiing.

Les Gets. 1,850 meters (6,075 ft.). This resort near Cluses has been developed to complement the skiing terrain near Morzine; good for both beginners and experienced skiers.

Gresse-en-Vercors. 1,205 meters (3,960 ft.). Very picturesque resort, still looking a bit like a village, 45 km. (28 miles) from Grenoble, with peaceful homely atmosphere, yet very sporty.

Les Houches. 1,009 meters (3,313 ft.). A family resort with slopes best suited to expert skiers, but can be used by beginners. Run from Bellevue *téléférique* is used in international competitions.

Isola 2000. 2,437 meters (8,000 ft.). A recent resort with lovely sunny climate, good slopes for beginners, and very well equipped.

Lans-en-Vercors. 1,000–2,000 meters (3,283–6,565 ft.). Not far from Grenoble, in the Parc Naturel Régional du Vercors, with three international slopes and over 50 km. (30 miles) for cross-country skiing; also a registered health resort.

Meaudre. 1,000–1,580 meters (3,283–5,187 ft.). Another resort in the Parc du Vercors; traditional village with friendly family atmosphere.

Mégève. 1,113 meters (3,650 ft.). A very chic and expensive resort with lively night life in the casino, nightclubs or restaurants. Impressive network of *téléfériques*; also a lot of sports facilities.

Meribel-Les-Allues. 1,653 meters (5,428 ft.). Courchevel is located on the other side of the mountain. Very chic too, but more for real skiers, with some difficult slopes; late spring skiing possible.

Montgenèvre. 1,854 meters (6,086 ft.). Near Briançon, close to the Italian border; this resort's climate is favorable for skiing right through to late spring; also famous for its ski jump.

Morzine. 1,000 meters (3,280 ft.). Very popular small resort, whose varied slopes join up with those of Avoriaz—particularly for beginners; family ambiance.

La Plagne. 2,010 meters (6,600 ft.). A very modern resort built from nothing into a sophisticated village curiously interconnected by underground galleries. Late spring skiing is possible.

Pralognan-la-Vanoise. 1,377 meters (4,520 ft.). A little resort near Moutiers, popular for easy skiing (fine for beginners), and its season lasts through to May.

Pra-Loup. 1,630 meters (5,350 ft.). Near Embrun, with a great variety of slopes and lovely scenery.

St.-Gervais-les-Bains. 907 meters (2,987 ft.). Family resort, where you'll find more locals than tourists. Good slopes for beginners; also a popular climbing spot.

St.-Martin-de-Belleville-les-Menuires. 1,700 meters (5,580 ft.). Twin resorts offering a vast amount of skiing terrain (100 km., 62 miles of slopes). Very popular.

St.-Pierre-de-Chartreuse. 900–1,800 meters (2,954–5,909 ft.). Near Grenoble, it offers the advantages of being in a village, and having beautiful scenery and 15 slopes ranging from Olympic to beginners'.

Samoëns. 822 meters (2,700 ft.). A bit remote, but very peaceful, with very good slopes. Also specializes in skydiving.

La Sauze-sur-Barcelonnette. 1,370 meters (4,500 ft.). Near Embrun, with dry and sunny climate; very popular with French families. Higher up, at 1,700 meters (5,580 ft.), is the newer **Super-Sauze.**

Serre-Chevalier. 1,349 meters (4,428 ft.). A major ski center, made up of several villages near Briançon, offering 160 km. (100 miles) of slopes for both experts and beginners. Also an important summer resort (Villeneuve la Salle), and a favorite with many Americans.

Tignes. 2,111 meters (6,930 ft.). Highest of the Savoie resorts, with a wide range of slopes and excellent spring and summer snow; also the starting-pont for hiking trips into the nearby Parc National de la Vanoise.

Val d'Isère. 1,848 meters (6,068 ft.). One of Europe's best-known resorts, mainly for good skiers, with a lot of cross-country skiing as well as summer skiing. Very sporty atmosphere.

Valloire. 1,428 meters (4,690 ft.). A very well equipped resort near St.-Jean-de-Maurienne, with excellent slopes for skiers with all types of skills. Family atmosphere.

Val-Thorens. 2,300 meters (7,550 ft.). One of the highest resorts in Europe, known for its cross-country skiing and also its summer skiing.

Valleys of Vars and Queyras. 1,600–2,130 meters (5,000–7,000 ft.). A group of villages and little resorts offering good skiing conditions and a lot of marked trails.

Villard de Lans. 1,050 meters (3,445 ft.) Not far from Grenoble, this now forms a much bigger resort since its recent link-up with Corrençn. Very well equipped; artificial snow can be spread all over the terrain if the weather is poor.

SOUTHEAST FRANCE

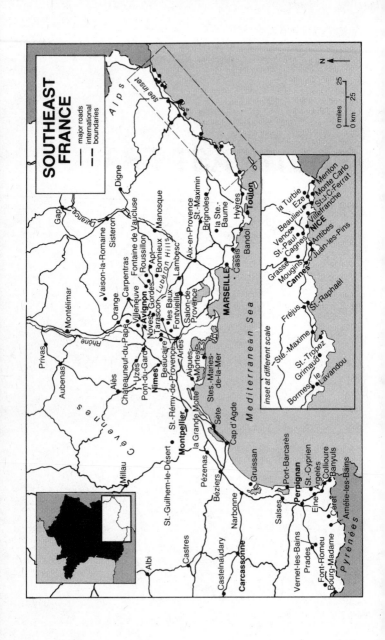

SOUTHEAST FRANCE

— major roads
--- international boundaries

N

0 miles   25
0 km   25

inset at different scale

see inset

Alps

Cévennes

Rhône

Durance

Luberon Hills

Mediterranean Sea

Pyrénées

Digne
Gap
Sisteron
Vaison-la-Romaine
Montélimar
Privas
Aubenas
Alès
Orange
Carpentras
Fontaine de Vaucluse
Apt
Roussillon
Bonnieux
Gordes
Manosque
Lambesc
Aix-en-Provence
St.-Maximin
Brignoles
la Ste.-Baume
Villeneuve
Avignon
Noves
les Baux
Fontvieille
Salon-de-Provence
Cassis
Bandol
Hyères
Toulon
Châteauneuf-du-Pape
Uzès
Pont-du-Gard
Beaucaire
Tarascon
St.-Rémy-de-Provence
Arles
Nîmes
Aigues-Mortes
Stes.-Maries-de-la-Mer
la Grande Motte
Sète
Montpellier
Cap d'Agde
Pézenas
St.-Guilhem-le-Désert
Millau
Béziers
Gruissan
Narbonne
Castres
Castelnaudary
Albi
Carcassonne
Salses
Port-Barcarès
St.-Cyprien
Argelès
Collioure
Banyuls
Elne
Perpignan
Céret
Amélie-les-Bains
Vernet-les-Bains
Prades
Font-Romeu
Bourg-Madame
MARSEILLE

Inset:

Menton
Monte Carlo
St.-J.-C.-Ferrat
la Turbie
Èze
Beaulieu
Villefranche
Vence
St.-Paul
Cagnes
NICE
Grasse
Mougins
Antibes
Juan-les-Pins
Cannes
St.-Raphael
Fréjus
Ste.-Maxime
St.-Tropez
Grimaud
le Lavandou
Bormes

MONACO

The Sybarites' Haven

Monaco is one of the tiniest countries in the world—a horseshoe-shaped strip of Mediterranean coast about two miles long, its 473 acres washed by the sea on one side and shielded by the first peaks of the Maritime Alps on the other. It has a proportion of five immigrant residents (around 27,000) to every citizen—who call themselves Monégasques. But, since Monaco is such a sought-after place, the number of bodies packed into its constricted boundaries can easily top a million over the year.

With territory so limited, expansion in the past was mostly vertical—even the tombs and headstones in the cemetery were stacked one on top of another. But, more recently, Monaco has beaten all world records for peaceful expansion, increasing its area by something like 20 per cent by reclaiming land from the sea, the infill providing valuable space for development and beaches for visitors.

The principality consists of four main neighborhoods: the ancient community of Monaco, built on its rock; La Condamine, where business thrives and most Monégasques live; Monte Carlo, casino-land, where Belle-Epoque stuccoed villas have reluctantly given way to high-rise hotels and apartment blocks; and, secure on some of the reclaimed land, Fontveille, now a flourishing industrial district.

One of the most firmly entrenched myths about Monaco is that people pay no personal income taxes because all government expenses are financed through the proceeds of the world's most famous Casino.

While it is true that the citizens of Monaco are less burdened by taxes than most of us, the casino now provides only about four per cent of the annual State income. And if you dream of becoming a Monégasque to save on income tax, you'd better think again. Citizenship here is one of the hardest in the world to obtain, and is not given automatically even to everyone born and raised in the principality. Mark you, it is a society that guards its wealth jealously. It's reported that there is around one cop or security man for every dozen residents. Given the sheer volume of solid wealth tucked away in the strong boxes and jewel cases here, the *flics* have plenty to keep an eye on. It's no wonder that the place has the lowest crime rate in Europe!

Grimaldi's "Golden Ghetto"

His serene Highness Rainier III (Louis-Henri-Maxence Bertrand), the Sovereign Prince, 30th descendant of the Grimaldi dynasty, has no less than 24 official titles, giving him the distinction of being one of the world's most titled monarchs. Mind you, as the Grimaldi have ruled Monaco since the Middle Ages—and are in fact Europe's oldest reigning dynasty—this is hardly a surprise. The family first came to Monaco at the end of the 13th century, with the expulsion from Genoa of Francesco Grimaldi, popularly known as Frank the Rogue, whose story reads like a plot from a wilder-than-usual Romantic opera. With the aid of followers disguised as monks he managed to seize the Monaco fortress, a feat commemorated in the Grimaldi coat of arms by two monks with swords.

Thereafter, Monaco was subsequently—and prudently—allied to France. For a brief period, from 1793, the Grimaldi were dispossessed by Revolutionary France but, by 1814, with Napoleon's downfall, the family were back in power. The Franco-Monégasque Treaty of February 2, 1861, restored independent sovereignty to the principality.

Among the Grimaldi of note was Prince Albert I, who died in 1925. World-famous for oceanographic researches, he also found time to endow his country, in 1911, with a democratic constitution and, at the same time, to increase its prosperity in a spectacular fashion.

Rainier III succeeded his grandfather in 1949 and, in one of this century's most unexpected and glamorous weddings, married the beautiful American film star, Grace Kelly. Together they created a vibrant social and cultural life for the principality and brought up a family of three children—two girls, the Princesses Caroline and Stephanie, and the heir to the throne, Prince Albert. In 1962 Prince Rainier promulgated a new constitution which managed to combine the hereditary monarchy with modern social rights—especially giving guarantees to trade unions. In 1982 the tiny nation was the sad focus of world attention when Princess Grace died in a tragic auto accident.

Despite a deceptive fairytale aspect, with its miniscule army renowned for tall shakos and fancy dress, Monaco is a serious State, maintaining firm representation abroad with 95 chancelleries and consulates. At home, Prince Rainier has been an extremely adept manager of his principality's resources, guiding Monaco through the turbulent waters of modern finance and ensuring that it hasn't become a feeding ground for predatory international sharks. Which doesn't mean to say that money does not flow into Monaco. The place simply breathes wealth—its cars, its apartments, its beautiful jetsetters, its chic fashions and its opulent yachts all ensure that it maintains its reputation as a "golden ghetto," one of the last enclaves left in the world where the rich, the noble and the famous can feel both at home and protected.

Exploring Monaco

The Place d'Armes, where there is a daily market from six to noon, is a good spot from which to start exploring the town. To the right of the square you'll find the Rampe Major—a steep carriageway and footpath laid out in 1714 by Prince Antoine I. Pass the 16th-century fortified gateways and you'll come to the Oreillon Tower, its high sides smooth to repel beseigers. Above, a battery of cannon was intended to command the port below. At the top of the Rampe is the Palace Square, with its neat piles of cannon balls, trees, and the soldiers who change guard just before midday. The State Rooms of the palace, with their painted ceilings, glistening chandeliers, and immaculate antiques, are open for guided tours in July, August and September, and are well worth visiting. The royal family lives in the southern wing, rebuilt with modern plate-glass windows and shielded from public view by a rapidly growing screen of pine trees.

The palace also houses the Musée Napoléonien et des Archives Monégasques, begun in 1919 by Prince Louis. It contains many personal mementoes of Napoleon—a hat, sashes, his field-glasses, a scrap of his coronation robe—plus busts of him by Canova and Houdon, and of Joséphine, his wife, the Empress of Bosio, a Monégasque sculptor. One whole floor is devoted to the history of Monaco.

Looking down from the promenades you'll see, beyond the Rock on the Nice side, the new area of Fontveille, bristling with the hard lines of apartment blocks and factories. Much more attractive to the eye is the medieval town with its ancient buildings which nestles round the base of the Rock. This is an area that will amply repay a quiet wander, particularly in the evening when the narrow alleys are at their most atmospheric. One of the more modern buildings, the neo-Classical Cathedral, dating from 1884, shelters the tombs of the Princes of Monaco. It is here that Princess Grace rests. You will also be able to see several paintings by local (Nice) 16th-century artists in the cathedral, especially a fine altarpiece.

At the base of the Rock, by the sea, is the Musée Océanographique, founded in 1911 by Prince Albert I, Rainier's great-grandfather, as a permanent memorial to his interest in the study of the seas and their life. It has the cabin of his ship, with the scientific instruments invented by him, and what is reputed to be the world's largest aquarium.

Near to the museum are the St.-Martin Gardens on the site of some ancient fortifications, the broad walks along the almost vertical seawall edged with a romantic profusion of plants. The paths descend past the Théâtre St.-Antoine, where openair summer concerts are held, to steps that will finally lead you out to the port near the Yacht Club.

A walk round the waterfront will take you past Loews Hotel to the Casino. It was in the middle of the last century that Princess Caroline— who, like Princess Grace a hundred years later, had been an actress before her marriage—with memories of the casino at Bad-Homburg, decided to try to replace the lost income from the Principality's vast lemon groves at Menton by opening a public gambling house. After teething pains a company was formed, the Societé des Bains de Mer, to run the project and the Casino was built in Spélugues, then a wild and rocky area, browsed by goats. The western part was designed by

Charles Garnier, who also created the Paris Opéra. Caroline's son, Prince Charles, was so thrilled by the whole undertaking that, in 1866, he decided to give the surrounding hillside his own name—and it became Monte Carlo. Within four months of the first trains arriving loaded with gamblers (gambling was prohibited in France at the time) the prince was able to announce that taxes would be abolished and his State could be financed by the proceeds of the Casino.

Once the most important element in Monaco's economy, much of the Casino's revenue now comes from the Las-Vegas-style slot machines which fill the American Room in the front of the building, populated by punters in decidedly non-chic clothes. For a glimpse of the old Casino elegance you'll have to pay an extra fee and visit the Salles Privées, but even there things are not what they once were. In some ways more serious gamblers prefer to follow their bent at Loews Hotel gambling room.

Beyond the Casino, on the avenue Princesse Grace, is the Museum of Dolls and Automata located in yet another Garnier-designed building, surrounded by rose-filled gardens. The collection of working 18th- and 19th-century mechanical figures and dolls appeals to all ages.

In a section lying a little inland from the Rock (it may be too far to walk, but local buses go there) are the Jardin Exotique, with thousands of cacti and succulents from countries as far apart as Mexico and tropical Africa; the Grotte Observatoire, a cavern which was discovered when the garden was being constructed, containing prehistoric bones and artefacts; and the Musée d'Anthropologie Préhistorique, which boasts, among many other items fascinating to the student of prehistory, the *Grimaldi Venus*, a small female figure from the Stone Age.

Other places worth visiting in town are the waxworks, setting out the story of the Grimaldis by means of wax figures; and the Casino theater, also designed by Garnier, a Second-Empire masterpiece which still provides as suitable a setting for concerts and ballet performances as it did when it was the home of Diaghilev's Ballets Russes.

There are two automobile events that always serve to remind the world at large of Monaco's continued existence. One is the Grand Prix, held in May, whose thrills count as the fourth stage in the Formula One Championship. The whole city is turned into one giant racecourse, with cars scorching through the elegant streets in what winner Alain Prost has called "a cat-and-mouse game." The second major event is the Monte Carlo Rally, which takes place earlier in the year, in January.

You may go to Monaco for its history, its setting, its sports—golf, tennis and swimming are especially well catered for—or you can enjoy the beach, with its support system of tents and delicious summer food and drinks, and its endless parade of trim tanned torsos. Whichever you go for, you are unlikely to be disappointed. With all its wealth and glamor, Monaco provides just about the only place left which still personifies the popular idea of a sybaritic life in the Mediterranean sun.

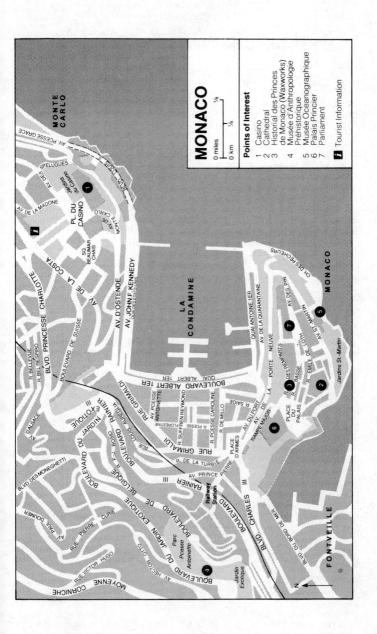

MONACO

0 miles 1/8
0 km 1/8

Points of Interest

1 Casino
2 Cathedral
3 Historial des Princes
  de Monaco (Waxworks)
4 Musée d'Anthropologie
  Préhistorique
5 Musée Oceanographique
6 Palais Princier
7 Parliament

i Tourist Information

PRACTICAL INFORMATION FOR MONACO

 TOURIST OFFICES. The principal tourist office for Monaco is at 2A blvd. Moulins (tel. 93-30-87-01). In addition, the principality also maintains offices in the U.S. (Government Tourist and Covention Bureau, 20 East 49th St., New York, N.Y. 10017) and the U.K. (Monaco Government Tourist Office, 34 Sackville St., London W.1).

 **HOTELS AND RESTAURANTS.** Most hotels and restaurants in Monaco are, needless to say, the last word in luxury. But it is possible to find relatively inexpensive accommodations, and you can also eat well for surprisingly little, especially at lunchtime, when many restaurants have moderately-priced set menus. Most locals seek restaurants with tables outside at lunch, so make sure you get there before 1 P.M. to be sure of a table. The range is wide, from simple family cooking in bistros and cafés to exquisitely served meals under the frescos of the Rococo Hôtel de Paris.

Hotels

Deluxe

Beach Plaza, av. Princesse-Grace (tel. 93-30-98-80). 320 rooms. Modern and deluxe; belongs to Trust House Forte chain; 3 pools; extended in mid-'80s to provide another 120 very comfortable rooms; two restaurants (M). AE, DC, MC, V.

Hermitage, sq. Beaumarchais (tel. 93-50-67-31). 210 rooms. Very grand old-style hotel with all modern amenities; pool and opulently decorated restaurant *(Belle Epoque)*. AE, DC, MC, V.

Hôtel de Paris, pl. Casino (tel. 93-50-80-80). Restaurant closed Oct. through Nov., Jan. 7 to April 15, and Wed. Incomparable, not only the best and most elegant in Monaco, but one of the best in the whole of Europe; very expensive, as are the chic grillroom and the fabulous Salle Empire restaurant, *Louis XV,* now with well-known chef, Alain Ducasse; heated pool; tennis courts. AE, DC, MC, V.

Loews, av. Spélugues (tel. 93-50-65-00). 550 rooms. Perched on stilt-like piers below the old casino, with its own casino, shops, cabaret, pools, Jacuzzi, gaming room. Brash rather than chic, but very comfortable and modern. Three restaurants. AE, DC, MC, V.

Expensive

Mirabeau, 1 av. Princesse Grace (tel. 93-25-45-45). 100 rooms. Extremely comfortable rooms; terrace overlooking sea; pool and direct access to beach; tennis. Casino; good restaurant with terrace. AE, DC, MC, V.

Moderate

Alexandra, 35 blvd. Princesse-Charlotte (tel. 93-50-63-13). 55 rooms. Old building, quite comfortable; restaurant. AE, DC, V.

Balmoral, 12 av. Costa (tel. 93-50-62-37). 67 rooms. Friendly, somewhat old-fashioned hotel overlooking harbor; good value; restaurant. AE, DC, MC, V.

Inexpensive

France, 6 rue Turbie (tel. 93-30-24-64). 26 rooms. Behind station; modest but well-run; no restaurant.

Poste, 5 rue Oliviers (tel. 93-30-70-56). 22 rooms. Modest, in side street below casino, with restaurant.

Restaurants

Expensive

Argentin, in Hôtel Loews (tel. 93-50-65-00). No lunches. South American décor, ambiance and cuisine; stays open till the small hours. AE, DC, MC, V.

Dominique Le Stanc, 18 blvd. Moulins (tel. 93-50-63-37). Closed Sat. for lunch, Sun. (except in July and Aug.), Mon. Opened in the mid-'80s and provided a very welcome breath of fresh air in Monaco's sometimes stuffy gastronomic scene; cuisine is marvelously light and décor delightful, including a collection of toys old and new. AE, DC, V.

Foie Gras, in Hôtel Loews (tel. 93-50-65-00). No lunches. Mostly classical cuisine; marvelously stylish service. AE, DC, MC, V.

Potinière, av. Bord de Mer, St.-Roman, Roquebrune-Cap-Martin (tel. 93-78-21-40). In *Monte Carlo Beach Hotel.* Closed mid-Oct. through Mar. Very elegant room, with terrace by pool. AE, DC, MC, V.

Rampoldi, av. Spélugues (tel. 93-30-70-65). Closed Nov. Very chic, and popular with the yachting fraternity. Mostly Italian cuisine. AE, DC, V.

Moderate

Café de Paris, pl. Casino (tel. 93-50-57-75). Where people go to see and be seen and often eat very little—perhaps just a hamburger and a glass of wine, though there are good brasserie-type dishes too. AE, DC, MC, V.

Chez Gianni, 39 av. Princesse Grace (tel. 93-30-46-33). Closed Tues. and Feb. Italian specialties. AE, DC, V.

Pinocchio, 30 rue Comte-Félix Gastaldi (tel. 93-30-96-20). Closed Wed. for dinner, plus Dec. and Jan. No lunches. Up on the Rock. Openair terrace is very popular. Good for fresh pasta.

Pistou, in Hôtel Loews (tel. 93-50-65-00). Specializes in regional cuisine. AE, DC, MC, V.

Restaurant du Port, quai Albert-ler (tel. 93-50-77-21). Closed Nov. and Mon. Italian cuisine; very popular, with tables outside even in winter. AE, DC, MC, V.

Inexpensive

Polpetta (I), 6 av. Roqueville (tel. 93-50-67-84). Closed Jan., Feb. and Tues. Tasty Italian cuisine; very popular.

TOURS AND EXCURSIONS. By Bus. Excursions organized by local operators to places such as La Turbie and Eze, St.-Jean-Cap-Ferrat, Villefranche and Biot (see *Upper Provence and Riviera* chapter) and also into Italy.

By Helicopter. Organized by *Héli-Air Monaco* (Heliport, tel. 93-30-80-88 for information and reservations).

SIGHTSEEING DATA. Historical des Princes de Monaco (Waxworks), tel. 93-30-39-05. Open daily 9–6; closed Dec. and Jan.

Jardin Exotique and Musée d'Anthropologie Préhistorique (Exotic Gardens and Prehistoric Anthropology Museum). Open daily, Oct. through April, 9–12 and 2–6; May through Sept., 9–7.

Musée National des Automates et Poupées d'Autrefois (Museum of Dolls and Automata) tel. 93-30-91-26. Open daily 10–12.15 and 2.30–6.30.

Musée Océanographique (Oceanography Museum), housing Aquarium (tel. 93-30-15-14). Open daily, Oct. through May, 9.30–7; June and Sept., 9–7; July through August, 9 A.M.–9 P.M.

Palais Princier (Prince's Palace): Grands Appartements open daily July through Sept., 9.30–12.30, 2–6.30; **Musée Napoléonien et des Archives Monégasque** open daily, July through Sept., 9.30–12, 2–6.30; Oct. through June, open daily except Mon., 9–11.30 and 2–5.30.

GAMBLING. The famed Monte-Carlo Casino is operated by the Société des Bains de Mer, which pays the Monaco government for the right to operate its gambling monopoly. In addition to Monégasques, inhabitants of neighboring French districts, minors, soldiers, and certain public officials are forbidden entrance. Admission to the public gaming rooms (open 10 A.M. to 2 A.M.) is about 35 frs. Entrance to the private rooms *(Salles Privées)* costs considerably more. They do not open until 4 P.M. Indicated at each table is the minimum stake *(unité de mise),* which may vary from about 10 frs. up. Stakes or bets are placed with counters or chips of different colors that represent various sums in French frs. These are sold and redeemed in the gaming rooms. Roulette, baccara, chemin-de-fer, trente-et-quarante, boule, craps and blackjack are played. In fact, the main room has been christened the *Salle des Amériques* and has two crap tables, two or three blackjack tables and two American-style roulette tables (American-style roulette is played with fewer people and each person has different-colored chips). Slot machines (made in Chicago) are scattered about here and there. The gaming rooms in Loew's Casino are open Mon. to Fri. from 4 P.M., Sat. and Sun. from 1 P.M. Entrance is free.

 NIGHTLIFE. The place to be seen (if you can afford it) is the elegant *Monte-Carlo Sporting Club,* a restaurant and nightclub complex by the sea which includes a gaming room, the *Maona* restaurant, *Jimmy's, Chez Regine,* nightclub queen Régine's spot (open May-Sept.), pool, and the *Salle des Etoiles* for dancing and big shows. *Jimmy's d'hiver* is the winter version of the disco in the Casino.

During the winter season, the *Sporting d'Hiver* and the *Cabaret du Casino* (open Dec.-June), provide dancing and spectacular shows. The casino theater offers excellent opera, concerts, theater and ballet.

Popular nightspots are: *Parady's; Living Room; Tiffany's* (disco); *Boccaccio* and *Gregory's . . . after dark,* both on av. Princess Grace and open year-round. *Folie Russe,* in Loew's hotel.

Out of town, on av. Winston Churchill (rte. du Littoral), Robert Viale's *Pirate* and *Les Frères de la Côte* attract the young from both Italy and France.

THE RIVIERA AND UPPER PROVENCE

High Life with a Suntan

Few visitors to France come without a vivid mental picture of the fabled Riviera, the southeastern Mediterranean coast between Marseille and Menton, rightly called by the French the Côte d'Azur—the Azure Coast. Here the sea is brilliant blue and sparkles in the endless sunshine, and glamorous creatures parade along the beaches by day and haunt nightclubs and casinos by night. The reality these days isn't quite like the travel agents' posters—unthinking development, snarled-up traffic and pollution have seen to that—but this area of France still has an enormous amount to offer visitors of any age. And those who are prepared to explore off the beaten track will find the idyll remains untarnished.

However, we should start by saying that we strongly recommend you avoid this region in high summer: mid-July through August can be, frankly, a nightmare. The opulence of the plush hotels and restaurants is overshadowed by the dusty and unhygienic roadside campsites. The resorts go decidedly down-market as crowds of holidaymakers pour in, and restaurants, transportation and beaches become packed. But if you visit France at any other time of year, you certainly shouldn't miss the Riviera off your itinerary. Apart from the unspoilable beauty of many of its land- and seascapes, you can choose between family resorts and chic, private beaches; superb, modern art museums and craft work-shops; beautiful coast roads and awe-inspiring mountain scenery; gour-met restaurants and country inns serving tasty regional specialties. Better still, ring the changes between all of these, thus ensuring that your holiday is as varied as it is enjoyable.

Marseille, the Age-old Harbor, and Cassis

Marseille, the third largest city in France after Paris and Lyon, has been a dominant port in the Mediterranean for more than 2,500 years, since the arrival of the first Greek settlers in the splendid natural harbor of what is today called the Vieux Port (Old Harbor). The remains of the original harbor can still be seen nearby. But today, the main ship-ping traffic is from modern and rather depressing docks. In 1943 the Germans blew up the port area, with its narrow streets, its subter-ranean passages, and its houses of ill fame.

Yet, although much of the character of this central part of the city has vanished for ever, the Vieux Port is still a magnet, and one of the most pleasant spots to enjoy the superb local fish—expensive in one of the well-known fish restaurants overlooking the harbor, inexpensive in the cheap-and-cheerful bistrots beside the harbor, vying with one an-other to offer the greatest number of courses for the lowest fixed-price figure. Leading off the harbor is Marseille's best-known street, the famous Canebière, shaded by plane trees, and still a pleasant place to stroll if you can stand the noisy Mediterranean traffic. But it is wise not to wander alone in downtown Marseille at night: the city has a high crime rate and you may feel you are in New York or Chicago at times, mainly because of friction between the Marseillais and the immigrants from North Africa.

To get a taste of another aspect of Marseille, and one that is making the city a more rewarding place to visit or stay in, take the metro to the Cours Julien, or walk up the steep streets behind the Vieux Port. This recently-renovated, traffic-free area is a revelation to those who have known Marseille of old: charming sidewalk cafés and restaurants, good bookshops and boutiques, a truly Mediterranean feel without the somewhat sinister flavor of the town center.

The district extending from the port to the cathedral of La Major, the original church built on the foundations of a Roman temple, is frankly uninspiring; this is even true of Marseille's landmark, Notre-Dame de la Garde, consecrated in 1864 high upon a hill above the opposite side of the port, and topped by a gilded statue of the Virgin. But the view from its terrace is stunning: huge skyscrapers, spreading to Le Corbusier's "Cité Radieuse," an architectural project of the 1930s, rise from the vast conglomeration hemmed in by barren hills and the sea. An ancient monument is the 5th-century St. Nicolas, a base for the Foreign Legion just near the ancient Greek port, where officers in tropical uniform and *képis* still saunter about, while the most modern, the Mediterranean Center of International Commerce, and an attrac-tive theater, the Criée, overlooking the Old Harbor in the old fish auction building, have been there only since the early '80s.

Marseille has a number of interesting museums, one of which, the Musée du Vieux Marseille (Museum of Old Marseille), is housed in one of the few remaining old buildings, the 16th-century Maison Diaman-tée, named for its strange façade, carved into diamond shapes. It has a superb staircase with an intricately carved ceiling, and is crammed with plans, engravings and models illustrating the old city, plus many exhibits connected with local folk art and traditions. The Musée d'Histoire de Marseille (Museum of the History of Marseille) includes objects from the city's Greek and Roman past, while the Roman Docks Museum contains the remains of just that, discovered when the Vieux Port was being rebuilt. The remains are accompanied by amphorae, pottery, parts of boats and so on. If you have time, you can also visit the city's good natural history and fine arts museums. The Navy Museum has some good displays.

The classic excursion by boat is to the Château d'If on an island near the Vieux Port. The guide will solemnly show you the hole through which Dumas' legendary hero, the Count of Monte Cristo, made his escape. Another excursion is to pretty Cassis east of Marseille. The coast road climbs steeply, until, at the Vaufrège Pass, it affords a magnificent view of the bay of Marseille and the islands of Calseraigne and Riou. Cassis is a small sheltered fishing port with three beaches surrounded by rocks and beautiful scenery, beneath Europe's highest cliff, the vertiginous Cap Canaille (365 meters/1,200 ft.). It attracted many artists in search of the unspoiled until it became too fashionable.

The *calanques* of Cassis, the most celebrated in the Mediterranean, are long creeks between steep rocks that often reach a height of 146 to 198 meters (480–650 ft.); the deep clear water, exposed only to the sky, takes on an intense blue, that contrasts dramatically with the whiteness of the rocks. An excursion along these twisting, fiord-like waterways lasts about two hours, and is generally made in boats hired in Cassis. Don't be surprised to see what the French call "total sunbathers." The secluded rocks attract many naturalists. Other *calanques* abound along the coast between Marseille and Toulon, and are best visited by boat, though some can be reached by scrambling down the cliffs.

Nearby, La Ciotat, in ancient times called Citherista, has long been a shipbuilding center. Its bay, with exceptionally deep waters, and its favored situation have contributed largely to the importance it has enjoyed since the 16th century.

Bandol and Toulon

Bandol, pleasant both in winter and summer, has two sandy beaches and a casino. The promenade along the quai du Port is flanked by acacias and palm trees. In summer a carnival atmosphere prevails on the nearby Ile de Bendor with its beaches, zoo, Provençal village, theater and wine museum.

Sanary, a fishing port sheltered by wooded hills that keep the *mistral,* a violent wind, at bay, is a perfect winter resort; in summer, when the little port is crowded with fishing boats and yachts, fresh breezes cool the Mediterranean sun.

Toulon, the capital of the Var *département,* has managed to retain something of its Mediterranean atmosphere in spite of its importance as a naval base and a center for the munitions industry. Yet much has changed, especially in the picturesque district adjoining the Old Harbor, though the modern buildings blend quite well with the older surroundings. The rectangular basin of the Old Harbor, crowded with yachts and fishing boats, is wisely barred to motor traffic. The restaurants overlooking the huge harbor offer quite spectacular views as well as good local fish.

On the Corniche de Tamaris, leading west to La Seyne-sur-Mer, George Sand wrote her most famous novel, *Tamaris,* and though well into her 60s received her lover, who rowed over all the way from Toulon. Nearby is the Naval Museum on the Fort de Balaguer, and from the heights above Captain Napoleon Bonaparte drove an English garrison in 1793. Below are the long gray walls behind which convicts once awaited deportation to Guyana.

Hyères to St.-Tropez

Hyères-les-Palmiers (of the Palm Trees), as it is sometimes called because of the luxuriant palm trees that line its wide roads, is the oldest of the Mediterranean winter resorts with luxurious villas for those who favor quiet and comfort. When bathing became fashionable in the 1920's, it established the beach of Almanarre in the Golfe de Giens, to which a vast municipal camping ground, La Capte, was later added; Port de Hyères provides anchorage for thousands of pleasure craft. This combination resulted in such great pollution that in 1972 bathing had to be prohibited. Thanks to the establishment of a purification plant and of floating buffers to protect the Salt Route along the promontory, all the 22 km. (14 miles) of beach were declared safe again in 1978. Hyères is the horticulture center of the western Côte d'Azur.

The tree-covered Ile d'Hyères makes a charming excursion easily accessible by boat (frequent services), though the actual point of embarkation is difficult to find. Although there are four islands in the group, Porquerolles, Port-Cros, Ile du Levant and Bagau, it is the first two that are usually visited. The crossing is made from Toulon, Hyères, Le Lavandou, or the tiny port of La Tour Fondue at the tip of the promontory of Giens. Although short, at some seasons of the year it can be uncomfortably rough.

Porquerolles, the largest of the islands, has many sandy beaches bordered by pine and briar, luxuriant vegetation, a riot of brilliantly colored wild flowers, and a climate that although cooler in summer and warmer in winter than on the mainland, is occasionally marred by violent storms.

Port-Cros, more rugged and hilly than Porquerolles, is almost entirely wooded. Pine and eucalyptus perfume the air, while in the thick undergrowth myrtle, briar, lavender and a variety of subtropical vegetation make exploration frequently impossible. Although the island may be visited, it is private property and there is a ban on camping, lighting fires—and even smoking. It is officially classified as a national park, so all wild life is under protection (including plants).

The Ile du Levant is known throughout France for its nudist colony, Heliopolis. In recent years, however, the nudists have had to share their Eden with a French naval base.

Traveling eastward along the coastline, beaches are superseded by salt marshes, and it is not until you reach the tiny town of Cabasson that you find good bathing again. Crescent-shaped and dominated by the brooding fortress of Bregançon, its charming beach slopes gently into the sea, reached by a road from the foot of the hill leading to Bormes.

Although now some distance from the beach, the ancient town of Bormes-les-Mimosas was originally by the sea, but Saracen invaders forced the townsfolk to settle on the steep hillside in 730. There is so little level ground that the houses have alleys and streets tunneled through their ground floors. Winding streets abruptly change to stairways as they wander through the town. Often you will be convinced that you have blundered on to someone's private walk as the street emerges into a lovely garden, only to plunge into another tunnel that opens on to yet another cobbled street. Bormes' beautiful gardens, its old houses and the breathtaking view of the sea and the Iles d'Hyères more than outweigh the minor disadvantage of its distance (three kms./ two miles) from the sea. During the season, buses make regular trips to the beach from place Gambetta. The old castle of Fos above the town is now private property. Built between the 11th and 13th centuries, it appears to be a ruin, but the inside has been rebuilt.

Behind the sandy beach of Le Lavandou has arisen a crowded, busy town, full of cheerless concrete buildings, cars and fumes, surrounded by the tent cities erected by campers. The little fishing port, the lovely bay, and the view looking across to the islands remain, however. It is reputed to have derived its name from the wild lavender that grows in profusion on the neighboring hills. The liveliest spot is the place Ernest-Reyer, where locals and visitors alike assemble to watch the fishermen. Its sheltered climate attracts visitors all year.

St.-Tropez to Fréjus

St.-Tropez, or "St. Trop" as the would-be fashionable still like to call it, is a name to conjure with. Once a little fishing village like many others along the coast, it has become a byword for a certain image of the South of France, full of yachts and beautiful people and celebrities.

It came by its name in a curious way, according to legend. In A.D. 68, when Nero was emperor of Rome, a Christian named Torpes refused to give up his religion. Nero had him beheaded and his body set adrift in an open boat. The boat came ashore at what became St. Torpes and, eventually, St.-Tropez.

St.-Tropez first came gently into the limelight when it was discovered by painters like Signac and Segonzac, closely followed by the writers Colette, Kessel, and others. But it was in 1956, when Roger Vadim and Brigitte Bardot shot *And God Created Woman . . .* here, that St. Tropez suddenly acquired the blazing notoriety that has never left it since.

It is difficult to be objective about St.-Tropez. Its problem is that it never built up a solid reputation with the rich and fashionable over decades, as did the chic resorts farther east, and its position, jutting out into the sea, puts it at the mercy of the menacing *mistral* wind. It has never had a winter season—in fact it's quite hard to find a restaurant open here in the winter months—but then it suffers a truly horrendous influx of visitors in high summer. The best times to visit are therefore May, June, Sept. and very early Oct. Yet, in spite of all this, if you sit at a café terrace before lunch or between 5 and 8 P.M., and watch the world go by, or walk along the still lovely port and admire the fabulous yachts, you will understand the attraction it still exerts, and why its habitués remain faithful.

Across the place de l'Hôtel de Ville is a low-arched gateway leading to the Vieux Port. This is the really old part of St.-Tropez. Here are twisting narrow streets designed to break the impact of the *mistral,* tiny squares with fountains, and old houses with curious doorways. If you keep climbing, you will ultimately reach the citadel, a fortress overlooking the vast panorama of the gulf of St.-Tropez. It was built over the remains of a Greek temple—for St.-Tropez was originally settled by the Greeks in about 470 B.C.

There are two *fêtes* in St.-Tropez, called *bravades,* which take place in May and June. The most important is the one in May honoring St.-Tropez, the patron saint. For two days the town is alive with banners and flowers and the air is filled with the music of fife and drum. A bust of St.-Tropez is hoisted to the shoulders of sturdy Tropéziens, traditionally dressed, and paraded to the quayside where sailors fire a salute.

A major attraction in St.-Tropez is the excellent Annonciade Museum of modern art, with paintings by many 20th-century greats.

There are no beaches in St.-Tropez proper, so you really need a car—or at least a bicycle. Outside town, where, incidentally, many of the most pleasant hotels can be found, the beaches are wide and sandy, and expensive, once you have rented umbrella, mattress, etc.—though it is always possible to go on any public beach free. The most popular are Pampelone and Tahiti.

St.-Tropez is an excellent base from which to visit a fascinating group of hilltop villages. Close to Pampelone beach is Ramatuelle, a typical old Provençal town, with several good hotels and restaurants. A climb up to the three abandoned windmills is worth the effort for the rewarding view of the coastline. Nearby is Gassin, where the houses are huddled together high above the Mediterranean. Behind the ramparts of the town, farmers and fishermen retreated to wait out the raids of the Saracen hordes. From the church the view is superb over the gulf of St.-Tropez and, to the south, all the way to the Iles d'Hyères. On a clear day you can even see the snowcapped Alps.

Less attractive than either Gassin or Ramatuelle, Cogolin does offer two visits of great interest. The first is the rug-weavers establishment called Tapis et Tissus de Cogolin. The management is happy to show visitors through every stage of the process. The second industry in Cogolin is that of pipemaking. Several craftsmen in hole-in-the-wall workshops carve pipes in strange and delightful shapes. Grimaud is another attractive hilltop village with lovely views. And back on the coast again, be sure to visit Port Grimaud, a true operetta village, a totally man-made pastiche of an Italian fishing village, very fashionable, though again, horribly crowded in high summer.

The road between Port Grimaud and the next resort of Ste.-Maxime is a mere eight kilometers (five miles) in length, but you'll find it hard to believe if you try to drive (or even walk) along it in high summer. Lined with overcrowded, unhygienic campsites, it seems like a hideous parody of the Riviera, with traffic never speeding up beyond a crawl. Yet Ste.-Maxime itself is as fashionable in its way as St.-Tropez, although it attracts a very different type of holidaymaker. It has long been popular as a family resort, but for wealthy French professional people with elegant villas as second homes. It has a better choice of hotels than St.-Tropez and is a good place to stay, although, since many of its well-heeled visitors have servants and prefer to eat at home, there are not as many restaurants. All seems orderly here, and the noise and bustle of St.-Tropez are viewed with a certain amount of disapproval. Its inhabitants' sense of superiority is enhanced by the town's sheltered position, which means that it has a year-round season.

Fréjus, founded by Julius Caesar in 49 B.C., became the thriving Roman naval base where Octavius built the ships that defeated Antony and Cleopatra at the Battle of Actium and to which he brought back their captured galleys. The town's extensive Roman ruins, including an amphitheater still used for bullfights, have earned it the name of the "Pompeii of Provence." Equally impressive is the cathedral with its beautiful 13th-century cloister and its superb baptistry dating from the 5th century. Among the nearby attractions are an Indo-Chinese pagoda, a Sudanese mosque, a full-scale safari park, the wide beach of Fréjus Plage, and orchards that produce Fréjus peaches, renowned throughout Europe. In recent years a great deal of building has been done on the outskirts of the town, mainly holiday flats and villas, and Fréjus is now a thriving tourist center.

St.-Raphaël and the Esterel Coast

St.-Raphaël is outshone by the attractions of St.-Tropez and Ste.-Maxime, but it is still a favorite resort of many families who swarm over its beaches and in the streets of the little town. Holiday camps abound in the region, offering inexpensive vacations.

St.-Raphaël likes to be known as the town where the "true" Côte d'Azur begins, and with its palm-lined boulevards, sun-splashed port, its life concentrated in the narrow streets and on the beach, it is indeed the prototype that many British and American visitors imagine when they plan their trip to the south of France.

Between St.-Raphaël and Cannes there is a cluster of little resorts, most booked solid by French families in summer, set in the bays and creeks along the Corniche de l'Esterel. The full beauty of this rugged coast can be appreciated whether you travel by train or by car. Agay, with its delightful little bay dominated by the jagged red rock of the Rastel d'Agay, is often used as a place of refuge in the occasional rough weather that can transform this usually placid coast into a sailor's nightmare. Le Trayas possesses innumerable creeks and *calanques* where you may still come across deserted little beaches, protected by the rocks from the wind, though many of these are more accessible by boat than from the coast road. The red rock formation is characteristic of this region and affords a dramatic contrast with the deep blue of the sea. Théoule and La Napoule, with their small pebble beaches and heavy traffic, are not the best places to bathe, but they are good places to eat. The twin marinas in La Rague and La Napoule are filled with yachts, and a little outside Théoule is one of the Riviera's many handsome complexes of small apartment buildings, plus club, hotel, restaurants and pools. Between Le Trayas and Théoule is the Pointe de l'Esquillon, where the Free French landed during the operations of August, 1944.

Cannes and Its Islands

Three names—Cannes, Nice, Monte Carlo—are to be found postered on the walls of every travel agency in the world, conjuring up the sunshine, the blue Mediterranean, and the best-known playgrounds of Europe. Of these three, Cannes is a mixture of the lively and the dignified, with many "grand hotels" now sensitively modernized, and, of course, the world-famous Film Festival.

Cannes is in many ways the infant prodigy of the Côte d'Azur. Although its origins lie deep in the past—it was a center of defense in the 10th century against the Saracens—it was a small fishing port until a chance visit by Lord Brougham, the British Lord Chancellor, nearly 150 years ago. He was on his way to Nice when an outbreak of cholera prevented him from continuing his journey, and he decided to stay in Cannes. He found the place delightful, and built himself a house there. Thenceforth, from 1834, when he first arrived, until his death in 1868, he never failed to spend the winter in Cannes. His example was soon followed by others, and Cannes quickly grew into a winter resort for the aristocracy seeking refuge from the rigors of the English winter. King Edward VII was a devoted visitor.

Today Cannes is fashionable year-round, with a lively winter season when you will find an older age group, and a brasher summer season for Europe's bright young things. It has a strong resort feel still, though the busy rue d'Antibes running parallel to the famous seaside promenade, La Croisette, is the sort of main street or high street you might find in any provincial town except that the prices are higher. Cannes has only one good museum, the Musée de la Castre, with anthropology collections from five continents, and few of the big-city attractions of Nice, but it does have lovely gardens—with lawns grown from turf brought over by the British colony that once was—and palm trees, exclusive jewelers, a dazzling new Palais des Festivals to complement the older model, a winter and summer casino and a luxury yacht marina. Add to that a large number of expensive restaurants (and, fortunately, a few cheaper ones too) and you'll soon see why Cannes continues to attract many visitors.

A funicular runs up to Super-Cannes—climb the observation tower for a magnificent panorama. If you prefer more picturesque surroundings go up to Mougins, an ancient Roman village, now best known for its excellent restaurants. From the top of its monastery tower you will get an unparalleled view of the whole Riviera coastline.

Just off the coast of Cannes two islands are silhouetted against the horizon. They are the Ile Ste.-Marguerite and the Ile St.-Honorat, known collectively as the Iles de Lérins. The fort in the Ile Ste.-Marguerite is famous, for it was here that the 'Man in the Iron Mask' was imprisoned in 1687 and kept in solitary confinement by order of Louis XIV. Crossings, by frequent boat service from Cannes, take 15 minutes to Ste.-Marguerite and half an hour to St.-Honorat. During the summer season thousands of holidaymakers visit the islands to picnic and spend the day in the cool pine woods.

Inland from Cannes you'll enjoy an excursion to the pottery village of Vallauris, made famous by Picasso, who went to work in one of the local workshops in 1947. His stunning *War and Peace* painting on a huge panel is displayed in the tunnel-like, medieval chapel of the local château, referred to as the National Museum of Modern Art or the National Picasso Museum. A vast choice of pottery is on sale in the village most of the year. Farther inland is another "must," Grasse, the center of the world's perfume-making industry. The essence of three-quarters of the world's scents are made here, either from the cultivated flowers, fields of which are everywhere, or the fragrant wild flowers, especially lavender. Visits to the factories are fascinating. The old part of the town is also worth visiting, as is the cathedral, the museum (devoted to Provençal art and history), and the Villa Fragonard, an attractive museum full of work by the famous 18th-century painter Honoré Fragonard, who was born in Grasse.

Grasse is on the Route Napoléon, a highly romantic road following the route of the Emperor when he returned from exile on Elba, landing at Golfe-Juan, farther east along the coast from Cannes. This road makes a fine excursion up into the Lower Alps to the lavender capital of Digne. It continues on through wild scenery to Grenoble (see *The*

Alps). Not far from Grasse perches the hilltop village of Gourdon, which offers fantastic views over the coast and the Esterel chain of mountains. Its château has a good collection of naïve art, and a separate history museum. From here you should try to visit the spectacular Gorges du Loup, with many impressive natural sites and picturesque villages.

A round trip takes you to Vence and nearby St.-Paul-de-Vence, both of which can also be reached from the coast at Cagnes-sur-Mer. Vence has another modern art treat: the Rosary Chapel, designed and decorated by Henri Matisse. It is also an attractive little town, ringed at its heart by a boulevard. The cathedral has lovely Gothic choir stalls, and the Old Town is a delightful place for rambling. St.-Paul is another joy for lovers of the picturesque. In spite of the summer crowds, many of them up for the day from the coast, the village remains most attractive, and you might consider spending a night or two here in one of the fine hotels. St.-Paul's contribution to the Riviera's "Modern Art Road" is one of France's most famous and unusual museums, the partly-openair Maeght Foundation, which has a superb collection of modern paintings and sculpture and outstanding temporary shows.

Two more inland villages are best reached from Cagnes. Villeneuve-Loubet is famous for its grandiosely-named Museum of Culinary Art. It was here that one of France's greatest-ever master-chefs, Auguste Escoffier, inventor of that famous dessert, *pêche melba,* was born in 1847. His home has been turned into a particularly charming museum that includes a collection of thousands of old menus. Biot's specialty is pottery once again, though some fine modern glass is also made here. But you should make sure not to miss the well-displayed modern museum devoted to the painter Fernand Léger. Biot has some good lunch places, so aim to make it a day's excursion if you're staying on the coast.

The Coast between Cannes and Nice

The main coast resorts between Cannes and Cagnes (don't confuse the two) are brash Juan-les-Pins and sedate Antibes. Juan-les-Pins, technically a suburb of Antibes, is one of the flashiest places on the Riviera. The sand is better than the artificial beaches of Cannes, but Juan is better known for the quality—or quantity, if you will—of its nightlife rather than its daylife. It goes in for the big and brassy attitude —lots of noise-making. In spite of its luxury hotels, it is not really elegant, but it is very popular and horribly overcrowded in summer.

About midway between Cannes and Nice lies the picturesque old town of Antibes. Although flower-growing (principally roses) for perfume and Europe's flower markets is the mainstay of Antibes, it has not forgotten the visiting tourist. There are beaches and a casino, and visitors wander through the streets every summer to visit the market place, stacked with fruit and flowers, and to visit the Musée Grimaldi in the ancestral castle of the Grimaldi family, built on a terrace overlooking the sea. It is an excellent small museum of modern painting and ceramics, dominated by Picasso, and worth a visit.

From the bustling market place the street in front of the town hall descends sharply to the old harbor. In spite of the deluxe modern yachts and the uninspiring apartment blocks in the background, it still has a timeless Mediterranean charm, and the fishermen with their weather-beaten faces, lounging beside their tiny craft, might well belong to any other century than the 20th. Antibes also has an archeological museum in the bastion St.-André, part of fortifications built by the military architect Vauban. Make sure you visit the fabulous Cap d'Antibes, a rocky promontory jutting out into the sea beyond Antibes and adorned with the villas of the rich and famous. It has a couple of reasonable family hotels as well as one of the country's most famous luxurious spots. Walking or driving around the peninsula offers an endless series of superb views, several good beaches, a museum almost at the tip full of Napoleana, and the lovely chapel of Notre-Dame-de-la-Garde, resplendent with votive offerings.

Midway between Antibes and Nice is Haut-de-Cagnes, vine-covered and artist-inhabited, made famous by Renoir, who spent the last years of his life nearby (his house has been turned into an attractive small museum). You can also visit a Grimaldi château, also housing a museum. From its tower there is a good view of the old town below and the countryside around. About two kilometers (one mile) away is the not particularly exciting resort of Cros-de-Cagnes, close to the huge Côte d'Azur racecourse (racing runs from December to March, and then again in August and September).

Nice, Queen of the Riviera

And so to Nice, the undisputed capital of the Riviera and for many people almost synonymous with it. Superbly set along the lovely Baie des Anges against a backcloth of hills and mountains, it has attracted visitors for well over 100 years. With their palatial hotels lining the Promenade des Anglais and reflected in the deep-blue waters of the Mediterranean, the Niçois have long been accustomed to receiving foreign visitors—once the English aristocracy and American millionaires, now more often sheiks from the oil-rich Middle East.

If you have known Nice in the past you'll find that it has changed a great deal in recent years. It still has the attractions of sun and sea and flowers, casino and carnival, glittering boutiques and gourmet restaurants, but with changing patterns in holidaymaking the dynamic Niçois have been rethinking their whole approach to tourism, on which much of the town's prosperity is based. Once a mecca for rich foreigners (and the French) seeking refuge from the rigors of the northern winter, this large city—it has nearly 350,000 inhabitants—is now increasingly attracting visitors from a less rarefied income bracket.

To make up for the loss of much of the winter tourist trade a determined effort is being made to attract congresses and conferences and Nice now has a huge and attractive "complex" running from the old place Masséna and stretching eastwards, with a spanking-new congress center, the Acropolis, restaurants, chic boutiques, the whole adorned with paved patios and flower-decked gardens. Traffic has been banned from much of the town center, an enormous bonus for visitors, who can now stroll and window-shop without fear of being mown down by the happy-go-lucky Mediterranean drivers. The picturesque old town with its winding alleyways, Italianate churches and famous flower market in the cours Saleya is now mostly traffic-free too. The busy old harbor to the east, from which the huge car ferries sail to Corsica, is soon to lose the pleasure craft now moored there—by the end of the '80s they will have a new berth to the west, where land has been reclaimed from the sea to build a marina and to extend the busy Nice-Côte d'Azur airport, France's second largest.

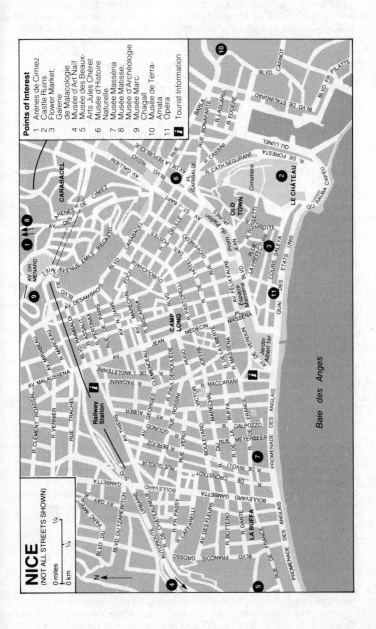

NICE
(NOT ALL STREETS SHOWN)

0 miles   ¼
0 km   ¼

Points of Interest

1 Arènes de Cimiez
2 Castle Ruins
3 Flower Market;
   Galerie
   de Malacologie
4 Musée d'Art Naïf
5 Musée des Beaux-
   Arts Jules Chéret
6 Musée d'Histoire
   Naturelle
7 Musée Masséna
8 Musée Matisse;
   Musée d'Archéologie
9 Musée Marc
   Chagall
10 Musée de Terra-
   Amata
11 Opéra
i Tourist Information

Nice's best-known event is its Mardi Gras carnival, the only winter one these days to pack the city till it almost bursts at the seams. The place Masséna and the surrounding streets and squares are lavishly decorated and lit and His Majesty King Carnival makes his ceremonial entry while processions of flower-decked floats parade along the Promenade des Anglais. But if you come at other times of year you won't be disappointed—sports of all kinds are catered for (including winter sports in the ski resorts up in the nearby mountains), while nightclubs and concerts take care of your evenings.

In the daytime we recommend a guided tour of the Old Town (inquire at the Palais Lascaris or the tourist office) with its interesting churches, and Nice's excellent museums. Perhaps the least known is the Terra Amata paleontological museum, which recently won one of the coveted European Museum of the Year awards. Close to the old harbor, this well-displayed museum is on the spot where the remains of an elephant hunters' camp no less than 400,000 years old were discovered during site preparation for an apartment block. Also on the eastern side of the city is the ruined castle, with a peaceful garden perched on a high mound offering breathtaking views.

As for the city's art museums, you're spoiled for choice. Many of them are in the resort area of Cimiez, up behind the town center, once a Roman settlement. Here you'll find the excellent Matisse Museum, which has a fine collection including a recent donation by the painter's family of some interesting sculptures. Also in Cimiez is a museum built specially to display a series of mystical biblical paintings by the Russian-born Marc Chagall, who lived on the Riviera for much of his long life. There are also nearly 200 preparatory sketches for these charming paintings, as well as lithographs, stained-glass, sculpture, mosaics, tapestries and engravings. You can see the remains of the Romans' arena in Cimiez too, and an archeological museum.

In the town center is the old-established Musée Masséna, a magnificent 19th-century building with many exhibits of the Napoleonic era, and some lovely examples of the work of the Nice School 16th- and 17th-century painters, of whom the best-known belonged to the Bréa family. The Jules Chéret fine arts museum is also housed in a splendid 19th-century building. It has a good range of paintings from the 17th to 19th centuries, including some by locally-born artists such as Carle Vanloo and Fragonard, and some interesting 20th-century work by Picasso and Van Dongen among others. Farther away, quite near the airport, is the Naïve Art Museum, an absorbing collection opened to the public in the early '80s.

As if this weren't enough, Nice also has a good natural history museum and an enthralling Shell Gallery in the Old Town, now thoroughly modernized and displaying a vast collection of shells and some ultra-modern aquaria.

The Hinterland

Nice's *Arrière-Pays,* or Hinterland, offers many delights to those who find the coast over-sophisticated, or overcrowded. Various roads lead up into the Maritime Alps, as they are called, from both Nice itself and from the far end of the French coast at Menton. Not far from the coast are the picturesque perched villages of Peille and Peillon, Gorbio, Ste.-Agnès, and Roquebrune. But all of these, though charming, are full of tourists for much of the year. Farther inland is peaceful Lovens at the entrance is the lovely Vallée de la Vésubie, which offers wonderfully varied scenery from the narrow rocky gorges farther south to the verdant upper valley around the little ski and hiking resort of St.-Martin-Vésubie, where you really feel you've reached the Alps proper. A favorite excursion is to the Madonna of Utelle, a pilgrimage sanctuary. The Tinée Valley leads up to ski resorts such as Valberg, Auron and Isola 2000 (see *The Alps*), while perhaps the loveliest valley of all is the Roya valley, close to the Italian border. Sights include the strange village of Saorge, seemingly hanging over the road, and the remote church of Notre-Dame-des-Fontaines, whose interior is covered with weird 15th-century frescos. Many of these little villages have altarpieces or other paintings by members of the "School of Nice," but you may have trouble finding someone to unlock them. In between the Roya and Vésubie valleys lies the extraordinary Vallée des Merveilles, or Valley of Wonders. The main wonder, apart from the spectacular mountain scenery, is a huge number of Bronze Age rock carvings. Best organize a guide (inquire at the tourist office in Nice or Menton before you set off, or at local-hotels once you get there) as the rock carvings are hard to spot and very scattered; and don't attempt this excursion if you're not an experienced walker (though jeeps are sometimes available).

Along the Corniches to Menton

Back on the coast, going eastward from Nice, you encounter one delightful spot after another. Villefranche, whose bay, squeezed between Mount Boron on one side and Cap Ferrat on the other, is deep enough for large ships to anchor, sometimes plays host to ships from the U.S. Mediterranean fleet and they dwarf the local fishing boats. Villefranche has played host to the sailors of the world since the Saracens first came here. Their influence can still be seen in the rue Obscure in the old town, a tunnel recalling the covered streets of North African *souks*. A 16th-century fortress dominates the waterfront. One of the greatest attractions of Villefranche, apart from its lively fish restaurants along the quayside, is the little fishermen's chapel of St.-Pierre, decorated with biblical scenes by Jean Cocteau.

Cap Ferrat is a world-famous resort but is still relatively peaceful because it forms a peninsula and is thus off the busy main road between Nice and the Italian border. It is a delightful place for long walks, with magnificent views over the Mediterranean and as far as the Italian Riviera in clear weather. The finest walk is along the footpath starting at Paloma Beach, which winds right round the beautiful Pointe St. Hospice. St.-Jean, at the tip, is an old fishing port, now equipped with a large marina to house the many luxury yachts moored here. Up above it is a cemetery containing a curious gigantic statue known locally as the Black Virgin, and also a zoo displaying small animals (many of them from South Africa, which has a similar climate), lizards, insects, and a butterfly farm. There are many beautiful private homes and gardens on Cap Ferrat, many of them owned by movie stars, but they can barely be glimpsed through high hedges. The Ephrussi de Rothschild Foundation and Musée de l'Ile-de-France, set in beautiful grounds, is well worth a visit. It has fine porcelain and furniture collections, and is the setting for concerts in the summer.

The next resort, Beaulieu-sur-Mer, has a big casino and several attractive hotels. An interesting visit can be made to the Villa Kérylos, a reconstruction of an ancient Greek patrician home designed by a well-known French archeologist. Beyond Beaulieu is the seaside resort of Eze-sur-Mer, but you should leave the coast road and go up to the Moyenne Corniche to visit Eze-Village, perched like an eagle's nest on its crag. Seen from afar, the village looks much as it did in the Middle Ages except that its former château is now a ruin surrounded by a garden of exotic plants and flowers. Eze has both good hotels and restaurants, and superb views.

For this same easterly trip from Nice you can also take the Grande Corniche, the high road along the crests of the mountains, with a plunging view down towards the sea. Don't gaze fascinated seaward during the whole trip, or you'll miss a point where there's a break in the mountains, through which in clear weather with no heat haze you can look northward into a region of ever higher peaks until those in the distance glitter with snow in the Mediterranean sun.

On this route you will pass through La Turbie, where a few columns perched curiously on a rock above the town are all that remain of the Trophy of the Alps, built by the Emperor Augustus in 5 B.C. to commemorate Rome's subjection of the Ligurians. Another attraction of La Turbie is the view from its terrace—the panorama of Monaco lying far below, spread out like a map against the sea, below the massive gray mountain known as the Tête de Chien—the Dog's Head.

On the way down from La Turbie to Monte Carlo (see previous chapter), you pass Roquebrune, another hill town and one well worth visiting with its feudal château hewn directly out of the rock. The curious religious procession held there on August 5 commemorates a happy deliverance that took place in the town during the Middle Ages, when an epidemic of cholera was miraculously stopped.

Menton

At the extreme tip of the Riviera, with the Italian border only a few hundred yards away, stands Menton, which was once two separate towns. The eastern side is still inhabited by fishermen living in tall, typically Mediterranean old buildings in narrow little streets, while the much larger western side, devoted mostly to wealthy retired people and tourists, has spacious avenues, first-class hotels, a casino and a beach that is thronged in summer by countless devotees of sea and sunshine. But there is now a yacht marina and a wide sandy beach (Les Sablettes) to the east, both of which have added a youthful attraction to this resort which has the mildest climate on the whole coast.

Menton has a picturesque Lemon Fair in February (lemon trees flourish all year here) and an internationally known chamber music festival in August, with some of the concerts held in the attractive Italianate churches in the old town. They are well worth a visit, as is the Cocteau Museum down by the harbor. Cocteau also painted the famous frescoes in the Salle des Mariages in Menton's town hall. Menton is also one of the best centers on the Riviera from which to make excursions. A few minutes' walk and you are across the frontier into Italy, where you can take a bus to San Remo or (a favorite with tourists) to the Friday flower market in Ventimiglia (called Vintimille in French). Don't forget your passport. Or you can leave the hot sunshine of the beach and go up into the hills to visit the picturesque inland areas that we have already described.

PRACTICAL INFORMATION FOR THE RIVIERA
AND UPPER PROVENCE

TOURIST OFFICES. The regional tourist office for Provence and the Riviera—written enquiries only—is the *Comité Régional du Tourisme* (Riviera/Côte d'Azur), 55 promenade des Anglais, 06000 Nice (tel. 93-44-50-59). In addition, the *départements* of the Riviera also have their own tourist offices (again, written enquiries only): **Alpes-de-Haute-Provence,** rond-point du ll-Novembre, Maison du Tourisme, 04000 Digne (tel. 92-31-29-26); **Alpes-Maritimes,** 55 promenade des Anglais, 06000 Nice (tel. 93-44-50-59); **Var,** 1 blvd. Foch, 83300 Draguignan (tel. 94-68-58-33).

There are local tourist offices in the following towns: **Antibes,** 11 pl. Général-de-Gaulle (tel. 93-33-95-64); **Bandol,** allées Vivien (tel. 94-29-41-35); **Beaulieu-sur-Mer,** pl. Gare (tel. 93-01-02-21); **Cagnes-sur-Mer,** 26 av. Renoir (tel. 93-20-61-64); **Cannes,** Palais des Festivals et des Congrès, blvd. Croisette (tel. 93-39-24-53); also at rail station (tel. 93-99-19-77); **Cassis,** pl. Baragnon (tel. 42-01-71-17); **Grasse,** pl. Foux (tel. 93-36-03-56); **Hyères,** av. Belgique (tel. 94-65-18-55); **Juan-les-Pins,** blvd. Guillaumont (tel. 93-61-04-98); **Le Lavandou,** quai Gabri-el-Péri (tel. 94-71-00-61); **Marseille,** 4 La Canebière, (tel. 91-54-91-11); **Menton,** Palais de l'Europe (tel. 93-57-57-00); **Nice,** av. Thiers (tel. 93-87-07-07); also at 5 av. Gustave-V (tel. 93-87-60-60) and 10 rue G.-Fauré (tel. 93-62-12-12); **St.-Jean-Cap-Ferrat,** 59 av. Denis-Semeria (tel. 93-01-36-86); **St.-Paul-de-Vence,** rue Grande (tel. 93-32-86-95); **St.-Raphaël,** rue Waldeck-Rousseau (tel. 94-95-16-87); **St.-Tropez,** 23 av. Général-Leclerc (tel. 94-97-41-21); **Ste.-Max-ime,** prom. Simon-Lorrière (tel. 94-96-19-24); **Toulon,** 8 av. Colbert (tel. 94-22-08-22); **Venice,** pl. Grand-Jardin (tel. 93-58-06-38); **Villefranche,** sq. Binon (tel. 93-01-73-68).

REGIONAL FOOD AND DRINK. The Riviera shares its cuisine with Provence, enjoying the same vegetable and fish dishes with vivid seasonings. Most famous is *bouillabaisse,* a fish stew from around Marseille. Genu-ine *bouillabaisse* contains *rascasse* (scorpion fish) and half a dozen others, including eel. Optional extras are *langoustines* (scampi), crabs and lobster. All are cooked with olive oil, tomato, garlic, saffron, fennel and a touch of anise liqueur to a wonderfully aromatic brew, half-soup, half-stew. Important accom-paniments are garlic toasts and *rouille,* a rust-colored mayonnaise flavored with garlic and red chili pepper.

Bouillabaisse is just one of fish stews like *bourride,* with herbs, fennel and garlic, and modest *soupes de poissons* (fish soups) puréed from the less presti-gious part of the day's catch. Unfortunately local fish is scarce, so dishes like *loup flambé* (sea bass flamed with fennel and anise liqueur), braised fresh tuna, even fresh sardines, are expensive.

With Italy so close, it's no surprise to find ravioli and potato gnocchi. Vegeta-ble *soupe au pistou* comes with a basil, garlic, olive oil, and Parmesan cheese sauce, as in Italy; *pissaladière* is a pastry or bread-based version of pizza, topped with tomato, olives, anchovy and lots of onion. Nice claims its own specialties, often containing the tiny piquant black Niçois olives—dishes like *salade niçoise* with green beans, potato, tuna, olives and hard cooked eggs, *pan bagna* (a kind of salad in a bun), and *poulpe à la niçoise* (octopus with tomato sauce).

Almond trees grow all along the Riviera and in the sheltered corner near Italy are citrus orchards, both contributing to the delicious *tarte au citron.*

Except for the white wines of Cassis, the region's wines are not great, but they are pleasant. Most of them are *rosés,* pinkish in tint, pleasant in hot weather, light to the palate, but don't be deceived—they can be heady. The traditional drink in this part of France is the aniseed-flavored *pastis,* drunk as an apéritif— or at any other time for that matter.

 HOTELS AND RESTAURANTS. The Riviera, or Côte d'Azur, is the most expensive region in France. Generally speaking, the eastern end (starting at the Italian border) has the deluxe resorts and the highest prices, while the western end has a number of little family resorts where prices are lower. However, these resorts are booked out by French families from one year to the next; they also lack the glamor you may have come here for. Budgeteers need not despair totally because Nice, large and cosmopolitan, with its broad range of hotels (some 20,000 beds in all) offers modest spots in side-streets well away from the seafront. But it is essential to reserve well ahead in all categories.

On the restaurant front, you will soon notice that we list fewer (I) places than in most other regions. This is not only because this is deluxe territory but because we find that while (I) places do exist—after all the locals have to eat somewhere!—they tend to be less reliable and shorter-lived. Fashion is all-important on the Riviera, so restaurants come and go accordingly. Rather than disappoint you by recommending places that may go downhill, raise their prices (or both), or even close altogether, we prefer to suggest (E) and (M) places that are truly reliable and advise you to scout around for (I) spots offering value for money during your visit—you can soon tell by the crowds eating there. You may also like to economize some days by buying delicious picnic-makings from the many Provençal markets and then enjoy an (M) or (E) restaurant on other days.

For general notes on hotels and restaurants, see "Hotels" and "Restaurants" in *Facts at Your Fingertips.*

ANTIBES. *Bleu Marine* (M), 3 km. (2 miles) from town center on rte. Quatre-Chemins (tel. 93-74-84-84). 18 rooms. Closed Dec. and first half of Jan. Modern; good views; no restaurant. AE, MC, V. *Mas Djoliba* (M), 29 av. Provence (tel. 93-34-02-48). 14 rooms. Restaurant closed Oct. through Mar. Typical Provençal farmhouse style; between beach and town; pool, garden. AE, DC, V. *Tananarive* (M), 763 rte. Nice, 4 km. (2½ miles) away on N7 (tel. 93-33-30-00). 50 rooms. Modern, well-run, with airconditioning, pool, tennis, hairdresser, boutiques, bank, the lot—but no restaurant. AE, DC, MC, V.

At **Cap d'Antibes,** 10 km. (6 miles) away. *Gardiole* (E), chemine Garoupe (tel. 93-61-35-03). 21 rooms. Closed Dec. through Feb. Near beach, quiet; nice terrace and restaurant. AE, DC, MC, V.

Restaurants. *Auberge Provençale* (M), 61 pl. Nationale (tel. 93-34-13-24). Closed mid-Nov. to mid-Dec. and two weeks Apr.–May, Mon. In old town near harbor; lots of atmosphere; newish cuisine; also has 6 rooms. AE, DC, MC, V. *Marguerite* (M), 11 rue Sadi-Carnot (tel. 93-34-08-27). Closed Sun. for dinner (except in season), Tues. for lunch, Mon. Welcoming, very good-value *menu;* away from tourists. *Caméo* (I), pl. Nationale (tel. 93-34-24-17). Closed Jan., Tues. (except mid-June through Sept.). Central, very popular; tables outside on typically Provençal square; also has 10 rooms. *Oursin* (I), 16 pl. République (tel. 93-34-13-46). Closed Aug., Tues. for dinner, Wed. Good-value fish and shellfish; on edge of old town.

At **Cap d'Antibes,** 10 km. (6 miles) away. *Bacon* (E), blvd. Bacon (tel. 93-61-50-02). Closed mid-Nov. through Jan., Sun. for dinner, Mon. Excellent seafood and lovely views over bay. AE, DC. *Pavillon Eden Roc* (E), in *Grand Hotel du Cap* (tel. 93-61-39-01). Closed mid-Oct. to Easter. Supremely elegant, with lovely terrace; good *nouvelle cuisine.*

At **La Brague,** 5 km. (3 miles) north, *La Bonne Auberge* (E) (tel. 93-33-36-65). Closed mid-Nov. to mid-Dec., first week in Mar., Mon. Still one of the best on Riviera; Provençal dining room, pricey *nouvelle cuisine.* AE, V.

BANDOL. *PLM Ile Rousse* (E), blvd. Louis-Lumière (tel. 94-29-46-86). 53 rooms. Right on private beach, airconditioned and well run, with good service, pool and restaurant, *Oliviers.* AE, DC, MC, V. *Ker Mocotte* (M), rue Raimu (tel.

94-29-46-53). 19 rooms. Closed mid-Oct. through Feb. Converted seaside villa with lots of charm, in attractive garden; private beach; restaurant.

On **Bendor island,** *Le Delos* (E), (tel. 94-29-42-33). 55 rooms. Closed mid-Dec. to mid-Feb. Comfortable and secluded; pool, tennis, sailing; restaurant. AE, DC, MC, V.

At **Cadière-d'Azur,** 10 km. (6 miles) away, *Hostellerie Bérard* (M), rue Gabriel-Péri (tel. 94-29-31-43). Closed Nov. Attractive building in Provençal village overlooking Bandol vineyards; pool; terrace restaurant. AE, V.

Restaurants. *Auberge du Port* (E), 9 allées Jean-Moulin (tel. 94-29-42-63). Closed Jan., Sun. for dinner and Mon. (except school hols.). Good *bouillabaise* and other fish dishes. AE, DC, MC, V. *Réserve* (M), rte. Sanary (tel. 94-29-42-71). Closed approx. last week in May and first week in June, Dec. to mid-Jan., Sun. for dinner (except in July and Aug.) and Mon. Terrace with sea views; also has 16 comfortable rooms. DC, V.

BEAULIEU. *Métropole* (L), 15 blvd. Leclerc (tel. 93-01-00-08). 50 rooms. Closed Nov. to Christmas. Elegant Relais et Châteaux member overlooking sea; lovely gardens, private beach, pool; airconditioning; good *nouvelle cuisine*. *Réserve* (L), 5 blvd. Leclerc (tel. 93-07-00-01). 50 rooms. Closed Dec. to mid-Jan. Deluxe airconditioned rooms and apartments in charming turn-of-the century building; flower-filled gardens, private beach, pool, sauna; excellent cuisine, in the grand manner. *Residence* (E), 9bis av. Albert Ier (tel. 93-01-06-02). 21 rooms. Closed Oct. through Jan. Close to beach, welcoming, modern; garden. No restaurant. AE, V. *Comté de Nice* (I), 25 blvd. Marinoni (tel. 93-01-19-70). 33 rooms. Closed Nov. to mid-Dec. A bit away from beach but reasonable prices for this expensive resort; no restaurant. AE, DC, V.

Restaurants. *African Queen* (M), Port de Plaisance (tel. 93-01-10-85). Very popular and crowded in July and Aug. Terrace. Good *menus*. AE, DC, V. *Pignatelle* (I), 10 rue Quincenet (tel. 93-01-03-37). Closed Wed. Friendly welcome and home-style cooking with regional flavor. AE, V.

BIOT. Restaurants. *Auberge Jarrier* (M), 30 passage Bourgade (tel. 93-65-11-68). Closed mid-Nov. to mid-Dec., Mon. for dinner, Wed. for lunch from June to Aug. and Tues. Regional dishes cooked "new"-style; good value. AE, DC, MC, V. *Arcades* (M), pl. Arcades (tel. 93-65-01-04). Closed Nov., Sun. for dinner, Mon. Attractive 14th-century building full of paintings; good regional dishes; also has 10 rooms.

CAGNES. At Hauts-de-Cagnes. *Cagnard* (E), rue Pontis-Long (tel. 93-20-73-21). 19 rooms. Closed Nov. to mid-Dec.; restaurant also closed for lunch on Thurs. Attractive old Provençal building once part of Grimaldi château; good *nouvelle cuisine*. AE, DC, MC, V.

Restaurants. At Cros-de-Cagnes, 2 km. (1¼ miles) southeast. *Auberge du Port* (M), 93 blvd. Plage (tel. 93-07-25-28). Closed Nov. and Dec., Wed. (except in July and Aug.). Old favorite for fish caught by the chef-owners in person. AE, DC, MC, V. *Réserve* (M), 91 blvd. Plage (tel. 93-31-00-17). Closed July and Aug., Sat., Sun. Superbly fresh fish for those who wisely avoid the high-summer crowds. MC, V.

At **Hauts-de-Cagnes.** *Josy-Jo* (M), 2 pl. Planastel (tel. 93-20-68-76). Closed mid-Dec. to mid-Jan., Sun. Lots of atmosphere, with good, mainly regional, cuisine. *Cassolette* (I), 92 montée Bourgade (tel. 93-73-71-16). Closed 2 weeks in Nov. Simple cooking; recommended for *menus*. Serves to 1 A.M. AE, MC, V.

CANNES. *Carlton* (L), 58 blvd. Croisette (tel. 93-68-91-68). 335 rooms. The grand old lady of Cannes's deluxe hotels and still excellent after extensive modernization; private beach, hairdresser's, boutiques, grillroom, airconditioning. AE, DC, MC, V. *Gray d'Albion* (L), 6 rue Etats-Unis (tel. 93-68-54-54). 187 rooms. The last word in luxury (dating from 1981); private beach, disco, airconditioning, and the best restaurant in town (see below). AE, DC, MC, V. *Majestic* (L), 6 blvd. Croisette (tel. 93-68-91-00). 262 rooms. Closed Nov. to mid-Dec. Luxurious in the old "grand hotel" style; private beach, pool, airconditioning;

elegant restaurant. AE, DC, MC, V. *Martinez* (L), 73 blvd. Croisette (tel. 93-68-91-91). 400 rooms. Closed mid-Nov. to mid-Jan. Twenties "grand hotel" superbly modernized and renovated; stunning octagonal pool beside dining room and terrace for outdoor meals; chic private beach with good light meals available to non-residents; airconditioning. AE, DC, MC, V. *Pullman Beach* (L), 13 rue Canada (tel. 93-38-22-32). 94 rooms. Closed Nov. to mid-Mar. Well equipped rooms; sauna, pool; tours, car rental. No restaurant. AE, DC, MC, V.

Canberra (E), 120 rue Antibes (tel. 93-38-20-70). 37 rooms. Closed Dec. (but open for Christmas period). In town center, with garden and pool; airconditioning; no restaurant. AE, DC, V. *Fouquet's* (E), 2 rond-point Duboys-d'Angers (tel. 93-38-75-81). Closed mid-Oct. to mid-Dec. Attractive, close to blvd. Croisette; airconditioned and sound-proofed rooms; no restaurant. AE, DC, MC, V. *Paris* (E), 34 blvd. Alsace (tel. 93-38-30-89). 48 rooms. Closed Nov. through Jan. Airconditioned and sound-proofed rooms; pool and garden; no restaurant. DC, V.

Century (M), 133 rue Antibes (tel. 93-99-37-64). 35 rooms. Closed mid-Nov. to mid-Jan. Very central, own garage; well run, no restaurant. AE, DC, V. *Palma* (M), 77 blvd. Croisette (tel. 93-94-22-16). 52 rooms. Attractive, and well-placed on the famous seafront promenade; a few rooms in (E) category; no restaurant. AE, DC, MC, V. *Ruc* (M), 15 blvd. Strasbourg (tel. 93-38-64-32). 30 rooms. Closed Nov. to Christmas. Modern but built in 18th-century style; terrace and small garden; no restaurant. AE, V.

Molière (I), 5 rue Molière (tel. 93-38-16-16). 34 rooms. Closed mid-Nov. to mid-Dec. Most rooms with terraces; central, quiet, lovely garden. No restaurant. DC, V. *Cheval Blanc* (I), 3 rue Maupassant (tel. 93-39-88-60). 16 rooms. Away from center but good value; no restaurant. *St.-Ives* (I), 49 blvd. d'Alsace (tel. 93-38-65-29). 8 rooms. Recently renovated; lovely garden. No restaurant. V.

At **La Napoule,** 8 km. (5 miles) west, *Ermitage du Riou* (E), 3 blvd. Bord de Mer (tel. 93-49-95-56). 42 rooms. Some rooms have balcony or terrace. Pool, garden. Restaurant. AE, DC, MC, V.

Restaurants. *Palme d'Or* (E), 73 La Croisette, in Martinez. Closed mid-Nov. to mid-Jan. Chef (Chavance) prepares excellent *nouvelle cuisine.* A new discovery. AE, DC, MC, V. *Royal Gray* (E), in *Gray d'Albion* hotel (tel. 93-48-54-54). Closed Feb. to mid-Mar., Sun. for dinner, also Mon. (except in July and Aug.). Excellent *nouvelle cuisine* at good prices if you keep to the *menus.* AE, DC, MC, V.

Bistingo (M), Jetée Albert-Edouard (tel. 93-38-12-11). In new Palais des Festivals with lovely terrace overlooking harbor; *nouvelle cuisine.* AE, DC, V. *Félix* (M), 63 blvd. Croisette (tel. 93-94-00-61). Closed Nov. to Christmas, Wed., and Thurs. for lunch. Still attracts the "in" crowd; straightforward meals. AE. *Festival* (M), 52 blvd. Croisette (tel. 93-38-04-81). Closed Dec. Chic and lively, especially at movie festival time; good-value *menu.* AE, DC. *Mal Assis* (M), 15 quai St.-Pierre (tel. 93-39-13-38). Closed mid-Oct. to mid-Dec. Harbor views; good value if you stick to the *menus;* mostly fish. AE, DC, MC, V.

Bec Fin (I), 12 rue 24-Août (tel. 93-38-35-86). Closed Sun. Crowded and fun; good plain cooking. AE, DC, V. *Caveau Provençal* (I), 45 rue Félix-Faure (tel. 93-39-06-33). Closed second half Mar. Beside harbor, with good ambiance and fish in generous portions. AE, DC, V. *Coquille* (I), 65 rue Félix-Faure (tel. 93-39-26-33). Closed first half Dec. Excellent value fish; by old harbor. AE, DC, MC, V. *Gilbert l'Ecailler* (I), 67 rue Félix-Faure (tel. 93-39-41-01). Closed Oct., Tues. Next door to old-established *Coquille* and just as good; mostly shellfish. *Pompon Rouge* (I), 4 rue Emile-Négrin. Closed second half of June, Sun. and Mon. Old favorite for home-style cooking.

At **La Napoule,** 8 km. (5 miles) west, *L' Oasis* (E), rue Carle (tel. 93-49-95-52). Closed Nov. to Christmas, Mon. for dinner, Tues. and Nov. One of finest in whole of France; particularly delicious *nouvelle cuisine* thanks to interesting use of spices. AE, V.

At **Théoule-sur-Mer,** 10 km. (6½ miles) away on the Golden Corniche, *Chez Aristide* (M), 46 av. Lérins (tel. 93-49-96-13). Closed Jan. and Mon. (except in July and Aug.). Well-run spot facing harbor, presided over by young couple specializing in *bouillabaise,* lobsters and fresh-caught fish. AE, DC, V.

CASSIS. *Jardins du Campanile* (M), rue Auguste-Favier (tel. 42-01-84-85). 30 rooms. Closed mid-Oct. through Mar. Attractive Provençal building in orange-and-lemon grove; rooms overlook patio and pool; tennis; no restaurant. AE, DC, V. *Grand Jardin* (I), 2 rue Eydin (tel. 42-01-70-10). 26 rooms. Closed Jan. to mid-Feb. Attractive and peaceful, surrounded by gardens, near casino and only a short walk from harbor; no restaurant. AE, DC, MC, V. *Rade* (I), 1 av. Dardanelles (tel. 42-01-02-97). 27 rooms. Closed mid-Nov. through Feb. Modern and well equipped, with nice views, pool and restaurant serving simple food. AE, DC, V.

Restaurants. *Presqu'ile* (E), 2 km. (1¼ miles) southwest (tel. 42-01-03-77). Closed Jan. to early March. (except in July and Aug.). Lovely views over harbor and Calanques; good regional cuisine (particularly fish). AE, DC, V. *Chez Gilbert* (M), 19 quai Baux (tel. 42-01-71-36). Closed mid-Dec. to mid-Feb., Sun. for dinner (except in July and Aug.), and Tues. (but open for dinner in July and Aug.). Overlooking harbor and always busy; good for fish. AE, DC, V. *Oustau de la Mar* (I), 20 quai Baux (tel. 42-01-78-22). Closed Thurs. and mid-Nov. to mid-Dec. Close to harbor; terrace; excellent *menus;* good value. V.

CHÂTEAU-ARNOUX. Restaurant. *La Bonne Etape* (E), Chemin du Lac (tel. 92-64-00-09). Closed Jan. to mid-Feb., Sun. for dinner, and Mon. (except in June, July and Aug.). Stylish Relais et Châteaux member converted from a 17th-century coaching inn; family-run and welcoming; delicious regional "new" cuisine. Also has 18 attractive rooms and pool. AE, DC, MC, V.

EZE. At **Eze-Bord-de-Mer.** *Cap Estel* (E), (tel. 93-01-50-44). 37 rooms. Closed Nov. through Jan. Beautifully situated on rocky promontory jutting out to sea; luxury rooms and apartments, pools, private beach; restaurant. MC, V.

In **Eze-Village.** *Château Eza* (L), (tel. 93-41-12-24). 7 rooms. Closed Nov. through Mar. Fantastic views from what was once a private residence of the king of Sweden; good (E) restaurant. AE, DC, V. *Château de la Chèvre d'Or* (L), rue Barri (tel. 93-41-12-12). 6 rooms. Closed Dec. through Feb., Wed. (Oct. to Easter only). Well-known Relais et Châteaux member with superb views, comfortable rooms, pool and excellent restaurant; reserve well ahead. AE, DC, V.

Restaurants. At **Eze-Bord-de-Mer,** *Soleil* (I), on Basse Corniche (tel. 93-01-51-46). Closed mid-Nov. to mid-Dec. Good-value meals and friendly welcome; close to beach; also has 11 (I) rooms. V.

In **Eze-Village.** *Bergerie* (M), on Grande Corniche (tel. 93-41-03-67). Closed mid-Oct. to mid-Jan., and Wed. Good-value charcoal-grilled meat plus some local specialties. V. *Taverne* (I), rue Barri (tel. 93-41-00-17). Closed Mon. In old village; excellent classical cooking served on terrace. V.

GRASSE. *Panorama* (M), 2 pl. Cours (tel. 93-36-80-80). 36 rooms. Welcome new arrival, well-run and friendly; nicest rooms overlook garden. MC, V.

Restaurants. *Amphitryon* (M), 16 blvd. Victor-Hugo (tel. 93-36-58-73). Closed part of April, Aug., Dec. and Sun. Good classical cuisine with a lot of fish. AE, DC, V. *Maître Boscq* (I), 13 rue Fontette (tel. 93-36-45-76). Closed first week in July, Mon. (except July and Aug.), Sun. In old part of town; some good regional dishes.

At **Spéracèdes,** 6 km. (4 miles) west, *Soleillade* (I). Closed Wed. (except in summer) and Nov. Excellent menu; very good value; terrace. Also has 8 rooms, half-board only at very good prices.

HYÈRES. At **Giens,** 12 km. (7½ miles) away, *Provençal* (M), pl. Eglise (tel. 94-58-20-09). 50 rooms. Closed mid-Oct. to mid-March. Views over bay; pool, tennis, garden; restaurant (M). DC, MC, V.

At **Hyères-Plage,** 5 km. (3 miles) southeast, *Pins d'Argent* (M), (tel. 94-57-63-60). 20 rooms. Peaceful setting beside beach, with pool and restaurant. AE, V.

Restaurants. *Roy Gourmet* (M), 11 rue Ribier (tel. 94-65-02-11). Closed Mon. for dinner, Tues. (except July, Aug. and hols.). Small and elegant (waiters dressed as court lackeys!); short but interesting menu. AE, DC, MC, V. *Le Delfin's*

(I), 7 R. R. Seigneuret (tel. 94-65-04-27). Closed mid-Jan. to mid-Feb., Sun. for dinner, Wed. (except in July and Aug.). Good fresh fish and homely décor. AE, DC, MC, V.

JUAN-LES-PINS. *Belles Rives* (L), blvd. Littoral (tel. 93-61-02-79). 48 rooms. Closed mid-Oct. through Mar. Right by the sea with lovely views from terrace; good classical cuisine in restaurant. AE. *Juana* (L), av. G. Gallice (tel. 93-61-08-70). 47 rooms. Closed Nov. through Mar. Old-established, chic and expensive; airconditioned rooms and suites, pool, private beach. Restaurant. *Hélios* (E), av. Dautheville (tel. 93-61-55-25). 70 rooms. Closed mid-Oct. to Easter. Modern and airconditioned; private beach where you can lunch pleasantly. AE, DC, V. *Parc* (E), av. Maupassant (tel. 93-61-61-00). 20 rooms. Closed mid-Oct. to mid-Dec.; restaurant closed Wed. Central yet quiet; sea views from most rooms; restaurant is (M). AE, DC, MC, V. *Admiral* (M), 136 blvd. Wilson (tel. 93-67-08-08). 21 rooms. Good value for budget hols. No restaurant. AE, DC, MC, V. *Mimosas* (M), rue Pauline (tel. 93-61-04-16). 37 rooms. Closed Oct. through Mar. Modern, with garden and pool; no restaurant. *Welcome* (M), 7 av. Dr.-Hochet (tel. 93-61-26-12). 29 rooms. Closed mid-Oct. to mid-Mar. Palm trees surround you in this quiet little spot near beach; no restaurant. AE, DC, MC, V.

Restaurants. *Auberge de l'Esterel* (M), 21 rue Iles (tel. 93-61-86-55). Good *nouvelle cuisine;* good-value *menus,* especially the less expensive. Terrace, lovely garden. Also has 16 rooms. *Bijou-Plage* (M), (tel. 93-61-38-55). Open in summer, dates depending on weather. Popular beach restaurant, also serves good light salads and grills right on beach. *Perroquet* (M), av. Gallice (tel. 93-61-02-20). Closed Dec. to Jan., Wed. Close to casino and pine woods; good choice of *menus.* AE, DC, V. *Girasole* (I), 17 av. Maupassant (tel. 93-61-22-39). Closed mid-Dec. through Jan., Wed. (in Feb. and Mar. only). Good-value *menus;* good regional fish specialties. AE, DC, V. *Potager* (I), 24 av. Esterel (tel. 93-61-13-69). Sea views from dining room; generous portions.

LE LAVANDOU. *Calanque* (M), 62 av. de Gaulle (tel. 94-71-01-95). 39 rooms. Closed Nov. through Jan., restaurant closed Mon. (except in July and Aug.). Overlooking harbor; garden and good classical cooking. AE, DC, MC, V.

At **Aiguebelle,** 5½ km. (3½ miles) northeast, *Roches Fleuris* (E), 1 av. Trois Dauphins (tel. 94-71-05-07). 48 rooms. Good location overlooking sea. Half-board terms compulsory. Pool. Restaurant. AE, DC, MC, V.

On **Ile de Port-Cros,** *Le Manoir* (M), (tel. 94-05-90-52). 22 rooms. Closed Oct. to Easter. Attractive, with lovely garden and fine views; reliable restaurant; full-board only.

On **Ile de Porquerolles,** *Mas du Langoustier* (E), (tel. 94-58-30-09). 48 rooms. Closed Oct. through April. Charming hotel in lovely grounds with tennis, sailing and restaurant; full-board only. v.

Restaurants. *Algue Bleue* (M), in *Calanque* hotel (see above). Closed Nov. through Apr. Excellent *nouvelle cuisine;* taste the *Bourride.* Terrace. AE, DC, MC, V. *Vieux Port* (M), quai Gabriel-Péri (tel. 94-71-00-21). Closed Jan. to first week in March. Elegant; imaginative cuisine. AE, DC, V. *Denise et Michel* (I), 6 rue Patron-Ravello (tel. 94-71-12-81). Closed Nov. through Mar., Mon. (except in July and Aug.), Thurs. for lunch. Straightforward regional dishes; popular.

At **Aiguebelle,** 5½ km. (3½ miles) northeast, *Hervé Vinrich* (M), 22 rue Patron-Ravello (tel. 94-71-06-43). Dinner only except Sun. and public hols. Good *nouvelle cuisine;* delightful little terrace. AE, DC, MC, V.

On **Ile de Porquerolles,** *Arche de Noé* (I), (tel. 94-58-30-74). Closed Nov. through Mar. Good value; also has 11 rooms (full-board only).

At **Bormes-les-Mimosas,** 5 km. (3 miles) away, *Tonnelle des Délices* (I), (tel. 94-71-34-84). Closed Oct. through Mar.; no lunches weekdays. Creeper-covered spot in village setting serving tasty Provençal cuisine.

MARSEILLE. *Petit Nice* (L), Anse Maldormé (tel. 91-52-14-39). 20 rooms. Closed Jan.; restaurant closed Mon. Perched just off Corniche road above sea, so you need a car; comfortable and pleasant, with pool, airconditioning, and excellent "new" regional cuisine. AE, V. *Sofitel Vieux-Port* (L), 36 blvd. Charles-

Livon (tel. 91-52-90-19). By Vieux Port, as name suggests; modern, air-conditioned, sound-proofed rooms; pool, two restaurants (one, *Trois Forts,* is among best in town). AE, DC, MC, V.

Concorde Palm Beach (E); prom. Plage (tel. 91-76-20-00). 145 rooms. Modern and right by sea; airconditioning, pool, private beach, hairdresser, disco and good classical (M) restaurant. AE, DC, MC, V. *P.L.M. Beauvau* (E), 4 rue Beauvau (tel. 91-54-91-00). 72 rooms. Ideally located where Canebière meets Vieux Port; modern and comfortable; airconditioned; no restaurant. AE, DC, MC, V.

Astoria (M), 10 blvd. Garibaldi (tel. 91-33-33-50). 58 rooms. Recently renovated; near the Canebière and Vieux Port. No restaurant. AE, DC, V. *Grand Hotel de Genève* (M), 3bis rue Reine-Elisabeth (tel. 91-90-51-42). 49 rooms. Modernized, quiet, in pedestrian zone. No restaurant. DC, V.

Esterel (I), 124 rue Paradis (tel. 91-37-13-90). 27 rooms. A bit away from center, but just by metro stop. Soundproofed rooms, good service. No restaurant. DC, MC, V. *Européen* (I), 115 rue Paradis (tel. 91-37-77-20). 43 rooms. Closed Aug. A bit out of center, but not far from metro stop; modest but welcoming; airconditioned; no restaurant.

Restaurants. *Maurice Brun* (E), 18 quai Rive-Neuve (tel. 91-33-35-38). Closed Sun. and Mon. One of the best in town; reliable regional cuisine served on second floor overlooking Vieux Port; must reserve. DC. *Calypso* (E), 3 rue Catalans (tel. 91-52-64-00). Closed Aug., Sun. and Mon. Fresh-caught fish; views of harbor too. Try *Michel* across the street (same ownership). V. *Mavro* (E), 2 La Canebière (tel. 91-33-00-94). Closed Sun. and for lunch on Mon., also closed Sat. in July and Aug. Right by Vieux Port; marvelous fish. AE, DC.

Chaudron Provençal (M), 48 rue Caisserie (tel. 91-91-02-37). Closed first half July, Christmas and New Year period, and Sun. Not far from Vieux Port and Canebière, deservedly popular for regional fish dishes and friendly service. AE, V. *Cousin-Cousine* (M), 102 cours Julien (tel. 91-48-14-50). Closed second half Feb., first half Oct., Sun. and Mon. One of many in the attractive, traffic-free cours Julien; newish cuisine; good-value *menu.* AE, DC, V. *La Ferme* (M), 23 rue Sainte (tel. 91-33-21-12). Closed Aug., Sat. for lunch and Sun. Just by opera house; good *nouvelle cuisine.* AE, V. *Oursinade* (M), rue Neuve-St.-Martin (tel. 91-91-91-29). Closed Aug., New Year period, Sat. lunch, Sun. Delicious Provençal specialties cooked "new"-style at reasonable prices. AE, DC, V. *Tire-Bouchon* (M), 11 cours Julien (tel. 91-42-49-03). Closed July and Aug., Sun. and Mon. Charming bistrot in lively pedestrian area; family-style cooking; very good wines. AE, DC, MC, V.

Arcenaulx (I), 25 cours Estienne-d'Orves (tel. 91-54-39-37). Closed Sun. and Mon. Attached to delightful bookshop in old arms factory behind the Vieux Port; light meals and good teas. AE, V. *Jardin Gourmand* (I), 70 cours Julien (tel. 91-48-49-24). Closed Sun. Attractive green-and-white décor with tables outside on pedestrian promenade; good spot for a refreshing lunch. *Julien* (I), 45 cours Julien (tel. 91-48-11-25). Closed Sat. and Sun. Traditional bistrot with lacy café curtains and pictures on the walls; good-value home-style cooking. V.

MENTON. *Napoléon* (E), 29 Porte de France (tel. 93-35-89-50). 40 rooms. Closed Nov. to mid-Dec. Lovely views; pool and pleasant restaurant (M), AE, DC, MC, V. *Aiglon* (M), 7 av. Madone (tel. 93-57-55-55). 30 rooms. Closed Nov. to mid-Dec. Good-value, old-established spot with pool and garden; no restaurant but light suppers available to guests. AE, MC, V. *Méditerranée* (M), 5 rue République (tel. 93-28-25-25). 90 rooms. Modern (opened 1982) and central; roof terrace for sunbathing with marvelous views over the bay; no restaurant. AE, DC, MC, V. *Europ* (M), 35 av. Verdun (tel. 93-35-59-92). 33 rooms. Modern hotel near old town and sea. No restaurant. AE, DC, MC, V. *Céline-Rose* (I), 57 av. de Sospel (tel. 93-28-28-38). 14 rooms. Closed Dec. Family-style hotel with garden; good full-board rates. *Londres* (I), 15 av. Carnot (tel. 93-35-74-62). 26 rooms. Closed mid-Oct. to mid-Dec.; restaurant closed Wed. Close to beach; family-style restaurant. V.

Restaurants. *Arcimboldo* (M), 6 pl. Cap (tel. 93-35-24-24). Closed second half Nov. and Tues. Pretty place in pedestrian area; good local specialties. AE, DC, V. *Chez Mireille-l'Ermitage* (M), 2080 prom. Soleil (tel. 93-35-77-23). Elegant yet cozy ambience; good for local dishes; also has 21 (M) rooms. AE, V. *Table du*

Roy (M), 31 av. Cernuschi (tel. 93-57-38-38). Closed first half of Dec., Sun. for dinner, Mon. Classical cuisine; good-value *menus.* AE, MC, V. *Nautic* (I), (tel. 93-35-78-74). Closed Jan. and Mon. Modest spot by harbor; good-value family-type meals. AE, MC, V.

Out of town. *Hacienda* (M), 3½ km. (2½ miles) along road to Gorbio (tel. 93-35-84-44). Attractive setting; farmhouse cooking. V. *Auberge des Santons* (M), 2½ km. (1½ miles) up on Annonciade hill (tel. 93-35-94-10). Closed mid-Nov. to mid-Dec., Sun. for dinner and Mon. Charming inn just below monastery; an old favorite with newish cuisine; also has 10 (I) rooms. AE, V.

MOUGINS. *Mas Candille* (E), blvd. Rebuffel (tel. 93-90-00-85). 24 rooms. Closed Nov. to Christmas; restaurant closed Tues. (except dinner in July and Aug.), Wed. Lovely old olive-tree-surrounded building with comfortable rooms and good "new" regional cuisine; pool. AE, DC, V. *Acanthe* (I), Val de Mougins, 95 av. Maréchal Juin (tel. 93-75-35-37). 26 rooms. Newly opened and well equipped; sea views; restaurant.

Restaurants. *Relais à Mougins* (E), pl. Mairie (tel. 93-90-03-47). Closed Sun. for dinner and Mon. (except in July and Aug.). Excellent *nouvelle cuisine;* elegant; good-value lunchtime *menus.* V. *Amandier* (M), pl. Lamy (tel. 93-90-00-91). Closed Jan. to mid-Feb., Wed., Sat. for lunch. Delightful Provençal architecture and décor; good-value *nouvelle cuisine.* AE, DC, V. *Estaminet des Remparts* (I), 24 rue Honoré-Henri (tel. 93-90-05-36). Closed Tues. Modest bistrot with open kitchens so you can see how fresh the food is; good value. *Feu Follet* (I), pl. Mairie (tel. 93-90-15-78). Closed Sun. for dinner, Mon., Nov. and first 2 weeks of Mar. Serves three *menus,* all very good value; good wines; terrace.

At **Notre-Dame-de-Vie,** 2½ km. (1½ miles) southeast, *Moulin de Mougins* (E), (tel. 93-75-78-24). Closed mid-Feb. through Mar., mid-Nov. to Christmas, Mon. and for lunch on Thurs. One of best-known restaurants in France; light and inventive *nouvelle cuisine,* worth the very high prices; a converted mill which also has 5 beautiful rooms which you must reserve months ahead. AE, DC, V.

NICE. *Méridien* (L), 1 prom. des Anglais (tel. 93-82-25-25). 315 rooms. Modern and well-run, very welcoming; central, on the fabled promenade; pool on roof; restaurant (M). AE, DC, MC, V. *Negresco* (L), 37 prom. des Anglais (tel. 93-88-39-51). 130 rooms. A byword for old-world elegance, an official "historical monument," airconditioning; one of the best restaurants in France (see below). AE, DC, MC, V.

Aston (E), 12 av. Félix-Faure (tel. 93-80-62-52). 157 rooms. Well-known for lovely roof garden; central (right by new Masséna area in old town); restaurant is (I). AE, DC, MC, V. *La Pérouse* (E), 11 quai Rauba-Capeu (tel. 93-62-34-63). 66 rooms. Well-located at eastern end of Baie des Anges with marvelous views; lovely gardens, pool, airconditioning, delightful ambience, but no restaurant. AE, DC, MC, V. *Plaza-Concorde* (E), 12 av. Verdun (tel. 93-87-80-41). 200 rooms. "Grand hotel," well-renovated, overlooking gardens and sea; wonderful sunroof terrace with gorgeous views; airconditioning and sound-proofing; restaurant. AE, DC, MC, V. *Sofitel-Splendid* (E), 50 blvd. Victor-Hugo (tel. 93-88-69-54). 130 rooms. Modern amenities in long-standing family-run hotel with personal service; pool, sun terrace, airconditioning and restaurant. AE, DC, MC, V.

Marina (M), 11 rue St.-Philippe (tel. 93-44-54-04). 40 rooms. Closed Nov. One of few central hotels with garden; gradually being modernized; no restaurant. AE, DC, V. *Vendôme* (M), 26 rue Pastorelli (tel. 93-62-00-77). 58 rooms. Well-furnished and nice garden; no restaurant. *Victoria* (M), 33 blvd. Victor Hugo (tel. 93-88-39-60). 39 rooms. Quiet, comfortable hotel near the sea. AE, DC, MC, V. *Windsor* (M), 11 rue Dal Pozzo (tel. 93-88-59-35). 60 rooms. Traditional hotel with garden, pool, sauna; light meals. AE, DC, MC, V.

Georges (I), 3 rue Henri-Cordier (tel. 93-86-23-41). 18 rooms. Family atmosphere; third-floor terrace for sunbathing and breakfast. No restaurant. Near sea. AE, V. *Pavillon de Rivoli* (I), 10 rue Rivoli (tel. 93-88-80-25). 20 rooms. Member of small group of family-style hotels; converted villa not far from prom. des Anglais; no restaurant. *Radio* (I), 6 rue Miron (tel. 93-62-10-65). 40 rooms. Modest but friendly city-center hotel near station; no restaurant. *Régence* (I),

21 rue Masséna (tel. 93-87-75-08). In pedestrian area so reasonably quiet; no restaurant. AE, DC, MC, V.

Restaurants. *Ane Rouge* (E), 7 quai des Deux-Emmanuel (tel. 93-89-49-63). Closed mid-July through Aug., Sat., Sun. Famous for generations for its superb fish, cooked in the classical manner. AE, DC, V. *Chantecler* (E), in *Negresco* hotel (tel. 93-88-39-51). Closed Nov. One of the very top places in France for *nouvelle cuisine;* delicious regional *menu,* marvelous wine list. AE, DC, MC, V. *Coco Beach* (E), 2 av. Jean-Lorrain (tel. 93-89-39-26). Closed Nov. and Dec., Sun. Good fresh fish and marvelous views of the Baie des Anges, so worth the high prices; away from town center, east of harbor. AE, DC, MC, V.

Barale (M), 39 rue Beaumont (tel. 93-89-17-94). Closed Sat., dinners only. In old town and very popular (must reserve); genuine Niçois dishes, fun atmosphere and knick-knacks everywhere. *Los Caracoles* (M), 5 rue St.-François-de-Paule (tel. 93-80-98-23). Closed first half Feb., July, Sun. for dinner, and Wed. By the flower market and opera house; well-known for fish. AE, MC, V. *La Poularde Chez Lucullus* (M), 9 rue Gustave-Deloye (tel. 93-85-22-90). Closed mid-July to mid-Aug., Wed. Elegant old favorite for classical cuisine. AE, DC, MC, V. *Rendezvous des Sportifs* (M), 120 blvd. Madeleine (tel. 93-86-21-39). Closed Sun. Lots of atmosphere with good regional cooking and wines. V.

La Merenda (I), 4 rue Terrasse. Closed Feb. and Aug., Sat. for dinner, Sun. and Mon. No telephone reservations, so get there early for a table in this genuine Niçois old-town bistrot. *Nissa-Solla* (I), 5 rue Ste.-Réparate (tel. 93-80-18-35). Closed Sun. for dinner, Mon. In heart of old town, friendly; excellent regional dishes at low prices. *Le Safari* (I), 1 cours Saleya (tel. 93-80-18-44). Closed Mon. Just by flower market; very crowded and lively, with tasty Niçois specialties. Terrace. AE, DC, MC, V. *Tramway* (I), 11 rue Lamartine (tel. 93-62-16-74). Closed Sat. for lunch, Sun. and Aug. Old, well-known restaurant with new decor; one *menu;* extremely good value.

PORT GRIMAUD. *Giraglia* (E), Grand-Rue (tel. 94-56-31-33). 48 rooms. Closed mid-Oct. to Christmas Eve. Provençal-style complex with private beach and yacht harbor; good restaurant (see below). AE, DC, V. *Port* (M), pl. Marché (tel. 94-56-36-18). 20 rooms, all with balconies. Some rooms can be grouped in suites for families; restaurant. DC, MC, V.

Restaurants. *L'Amphitrite* (E), in hotel *Giraglia* (tel. 94-56-31-33). Closed mid-Oct. to March. Good *nouvelle cuisine;* terrace for outdoor meals. AE, DC, V. *Marine* (M), pl. 14-Juin (tel. 94-56-25-50). Open daily; pleasant terrace by harbor; meals in garden.

At **Grimaud,** 3 km. (2 miles) inland. *Boulangerie* (E), (tel. 94-43-23-16). 10 rooms. Closed Oct. through Mar. Quiet and delightful, yet only 10 km. (6 miles) from busy St.-Tropez; pool, tennis court, restaurant (half-board terms only in July and Aug.). *Bretonnière* (M), (tel. 94-43-25-28). Closed Mon.; open for dinner only. Attractive vaulted dining room; good-value *menu.* AE, V. *Le Gacharel* (M), (tel. 94-43-24-40). Closed mid-Oct. to Palm Sun. weekend., Wed., dinners only in July and Aug. Old favorite now run by dynamic young chefs; good local recipes.

ST.-JEAN-CAP-FERRAT. *Grand Hôtel du Cap Ferrat* (L), blvd. Général-de-Gaulle (tel. 93-01-04-54). 66 rooms. Closed Oct. to Easter. Right on tip of peninsula; old established but well modernized, with lovely gardens, private beach, pool, tennis; grand classical restaurant. AE, DC, MC, V. *Voile d'Or* (L), (tel. 93-01-13-13). Closed Nov. through Feb. One of best-known hotels on Riviera, overlooking harbor and sea; 2 pools, airconditioning and very good restaurant. *Belle Aurore* (E), 49 av. Denis Séméria (tel. 93-01-31-03). 20 rooms. Closed Nov. through Mar. Away from beach, but well located for village and exploring the Cap; friendly ambience, pool; restaurant. AE, MC, V. *Brise Marine* (M), av. Jean-Mermoz (tel. 93-76-04-36). 15 rooms. Closed Nov. through Jan. Converted Provençal villa close to beach, with sea views; restaurant (I) open evenings only. *Panoramic* (M), av. Albert-ler (tel. 93-01-06-62). 20 rooms. Closed Nov. through Jan. A bit away from village and harbor but lovely views; modern rooms; no restaurant. AE, DC, MC, V.

Restaurants. *Hirondelles* (E), 36 av. Jean-Mermoz (tel. 93-76-04-04). Closed mid-Nov. through Jan., Sun. and Mon. Long famous for beautifully fresh fish and lovely vine-covered terrace overlooking harbor. v. *Petit Trianon* (M), blvd. Général-de-Gaulle (tel. 93-01-31-68). Closed mid-Oct. to mid-Mar., Wed. for dinner and Thurs. Elegant; good classical cuisine and excellent service. AE, DC, MC, v. *Sloop* (M), (tel. 93-01-48-63). Dinner only Mon. to Fri. Closed Sun. for dinner and Wed. except July and Aug. Terrace and meals in garden. Beside marina; cheerful atmosphere and varied menu. AE, DC, V.

ST.-RAPHAËL. Out of town. *Mapotel Golf de Valescure* (M), 5 km. (3 miles) north, av. Paul-Lermite (tel. 94-52-01-57). 40 rooms. Closed Oct. 15 to Dec. 15. Comfortable rooms by golf course; tennis, pool; good (M) restaurant. AE, DC, MC, v.

At **Boulouris**, 5 km. (3 miles) away, *La Potinière* (M), (tel. 94-95-21-43). Closed Nov. to Christmas, Thurs. for lunch (in winter). Peacefully set in garden; tennis, pool; good restaurant. AE, DC.

Restaurants. *Cheneraie* (M), blvd. Gondins (tel. 94-52-08-02). Near *Golf de Valescure*, views of golf course and mountains. Closed Mon. for lunch, mid-Feb. to mid-Mar. Excellent produce, good cooking; garden; also has 10 modern, quiet rooms. v. *La Voile d'Or* (M), 1 blvd. Général-de-Gaulle (tel. 94-95-17-04). Closed mid-Nov. to Christmas, Tues. for dinner and Wed. Good regional cuisine (mainly fish); good views over bay. AE, DC, V.

ST.-TROPEZ. *Byblos* (L), av. Paul-Signac (tel. 94-97-00-04). 108 rooms. Closed Nov. through Mar. Legendary hotel arranged to feel like a miniature Provençal village centered round a pool; expanded in 1985 with deluxe bungalows and apartments in an olive grove; sauna, 2 discos, boutiques, hairdresser; gourmet restaurant. AE, DC, V. *Levant* (E), rte. Salins (tel. 94-97-33-33). 28 rooms. Closed mid-Oct. through Mar. Just outside town, with comfortable bungalows spaced in pleasant grounds; pool; grillroom. AE, DC, V. *Yaca* (E), blvd. Aumale (tel. 94-97-11-79). 22 rooms. Closed Oct. through Mar. In old town; attractive, with pool and garden; restaurant. AE, DC, MC, V. *Dei Marres* (M), route Plages, Ramatuelle (tel. 94-97-26-68). Closed mid-Oct. to mid-Mar. 24 rooms. Pleasant rooms; at feet of hills; great for tennis and other sports. AE, DC. *Lou Troupelen* (M), chemin des Vendanges (tel. 94-97-44-88). 43 rooms. Closed mid-Oct. through April. Modernized Provençal farmhouse surrounded by vines and gardens, not far from beach; no restaurant. DC, v. *Coste* (I), port Pilon (tel. 94-97-00-64). 30 rooms. Closed Nov. through Jan. One of very few (I) hotels in expensive St.-Tropez; no restaurant. AE, DC.

Restaurants. *Chez Fuchs* (E), 7 rue des Commercants (tel. 94-97-01-25). Closed Oct. and Nov., Mon. (except in July and Aug.); no lunches in July and Aug. Old-established and still popular. *La Ponche* (E), rue Remparts (tel. 94-97-02-53). Closed Oct. through Mar. Antique furniture and paintings, lots of chic atmosphere; excellent fish; also a small hotel (23 rooms). *Echalote* (I), 35 rue Général Allard (tel. 94-54-83-26). Closed mid-Nov. to early Dec. Good place to eat in garden; *menu* recommended.

Just outside **Cogolin**, 13 km. (8 miles) away on N98, *Ferme du Magnan* (M), (tel. 94-49-57-54). Closed Tues. True farmhouse setting, worth the trip for a change from the hectic coast; country-style chicken and rabbit or grilled meat on a bed of vine leaves.

At **Gassin**, 8 km. (5 miles) away, *Auberge La Verdoyante* (M), (tel. 94-56-16-23). Closed Dec. to mid-Mar., and Wed., except July and Aug. Surprisingly rural, with good regional specialties. v.

At **Ramatuelle**, 12 km. (7½ miles) south, *Chez Camille* (M), (tel. 94-79-80-38). Closed Oct. through March, Tues. (except July and Aug.). Beside Bonne-Terrasse beach; well-known for *bouillabaisse*. Good-value *petit menu*.

STE.-MAXIME. *Belle Aurore* (E), 4 blvd. Jean-Moulin (tel. 94-96-02-45). 18 rooms. Closed mid-Oct. to mid-Mar. Gorgeous sea views and pleasant restaurant serving good *nouvelle cuisine;* full board only in July and Aug. *Croisette* (M), 2 blvd. des Romarins (tel. 94-96-17-75). 20 rooms. Closed mid-Oct. to mid-Mar. Surrounded by pine trees and terraced garden, convenient for beach; no restaurant. MC, V. *Poste* (M), 7 blvd. Frédéric-Mistral (tel. 94-96-18-33). 24 rooms. Closed Nov. through Mar. Exceptionally pleasant and attractive, near beach, with pool and 4 restaurants. AE, DC.

At **Beauvallon**, 4½ km. (3 miles) south, *Hostellerie Beauvallon* (M), (tel. 94-43-81-11). 27 rooms. Closed Nov. to Easter. Modern and well equipped, around large pool and close to beach. Restaurant.

At **Plan-de-la-Tour**, 10 km. (6 miles) away, up in the hills, *Ponte-Romano* (E), rte. Grimaud (tel. 94-43-70-56). 10 rooms. Closed Oct. through Mar. Delightful hideaway from the crowded coast; elegant gardens, pool, friendly service and good cuisine. AE, MC, V.

Restaurants. *Gruppi* (E), av. Charles-de-Gaulle (tel. 94-96-03-81). Closed Mon. (except in July and Aug.). Good views to St.-Tropez from second floor; best in town for fish. *Esquinade* (M), (tel. 94-96-01-65). Closed Nov. to mid-Dec., Wed. (except in July and Aug.). Overlooks harbor; good fish. DC. *Citronnière* (I), La Petite Toscane, av. Clemenceau (tel. 94-96-75-94). Closed Nov. and first half Jan. Excellent, simple cooking; good-value *menus;* terrace. DC, V.

TOULON. *Frantel* (E), blvd. Vence (tel. 94-24-41-57). 93 rooms. Closed Sat. for lunch and Sun. (except July and Aug.). Well situated with fabulous views over huge harbor; modern, comfortable rooms and good *nouvelle cuisine* with regional flavor in restaurant—*La Tour Blanche* (M). AE, DC, MC, V. *Corniche* (M), 1 littoral Frédéric-Mistral (tel. 94-41-39-53). 18 rooms. Restaurant closed mid-Jan. through Feb., Sun. for dinner and Mon. In Mourillon district, with stunning sea views and quite good restaurant. AE, DC, MC, V.

Restaurants. *Le Lutrin* (E), 8 littoral Frédéric-Mistral (tel. 94-42-43-43). Closed Sat. Attractive 19th-cent. building overlooking harbor; very elegant; expensive, though *menus* are good value. AE, DC, MC, V. *Le Dauphin* (M), 21 rue Jean-Jaurès (tel. 94-93-12-07). Closed July, weekends and two weeks in Feb. Good value fish restaurant with friendly welcome. V. *Madeleine* (M), 7 rue Tombades (tel. 94-92-67-85). Closed Tues. for dinner, Wed. and Jan. Particularly friendly service and good food too, with some dishes from the *patron's* native southwest; excellent *menu.* DC, V. *Chantilly* (I), pl. Puget (tel. 94-92-24-37). Closed Sun. Cheerful spot for light meals on the edge of old town.

VENCE. *Château St.-Martin* (L), rte. Coursegoules (tel. 93-58-02-02). 25 rooms. Closed Dec. through Feb.; restaurant closed Wed. Deluxe Relais et Châteaux member with apartments in large château plus rooms in converted outbuildings and bungalows dotted around grounds; pool, tennis; exquisite service; good restaurant. AE, DC, MC, V. *Floréal* (M), 440 av. Rhin-et-Danube (tel. 93-58-64-40). Closed Jan. and Feb. Modern, well-run hotel on road to Grasse; most rooms have balconies overlooking pool and garden; no restaurant. V. *Miramar* (M), Plateau St.-Michel (tel. 93-58-01-32). 17 rooms. Closed Nov. through Feb. Well equipped rooms with views of sea and Alps; bar but no restaurant. AE, V.

At **St.-Paul-de-Vence**, 4½ km. (3 miles) away. *Mas d'Artigny* (L), chemin Salettes (tel. 93-32-84-54). 81 rooms. Relais et Châteaux member offering superb views; many suites with private pool and garden; mixture of classical and *nouvelle* cuisine in elegant restaurant. V. *Colombe d'Or* (E), pl. de Gaulle (tel. 93-32-80-02). 17 rooms. Closed Nov. and Dec. Known for its collection of paintings by Picasso et al.; beautiful rooms; pool; reliable classical cuisine in generous portions. AE, DC, MC, V. *Orangers* (M), rte. Colle (tel. 93-32-80-95). 9 rooms. Charming old Provençal building in olive-and-orange grove; no restaurant.

Restaurants. *Portiques* (M), 6 rue St.-Véran (tel. 93-58-36-31). Closed Sun; no lunches. Excellent service and good cooking; generous *menu* and *nouvelle cuisine*. Must reserve. V. *Farigoule* (I), 15 rue Jean-Isnard (tel. 93-58-01-27). Closed mid-Nov. to mid-Dec., and Fri. Good-value Provençal cuisine; friendly.

At **St.-Paul-de-Vence**, 4½ km. (3 miles) away, *Oliviers* (E), rte. Colle (tel. 93-32-80-13). Closed Dec. through Feb., and Tues. (except in July and Aug.). On edge of village surrounded by olive and orange trees; perfect spot for outdoor meals; very good fish and shellfish. AE, DC, V. *Auberge du Soleil* (I), rte. Colle (tel. 93-32-80-60). Closed Jan. and first of Feb. Tues for dinner and Wed. Attractive inn with pool and regional cuisine; also has 7 (M) rooms. MC, V.

VILLEFRANCHE-SUR-MER. *Versailles* (E), av. Princesse-Grace (tel. 93-01-89-56). 45 rooms. Closed mid-Oct. to mid-Dec. Modern and well-run, with pool and airconditioning; lovely views from restaurant. AE, DC, V. *Welcome* (E), 1 quai Courbet (tel. 93-55-27-27). 32 rooms. Old-established but well modernized; right by harbor; elegant classical restaurant (M) with some light touches. Closed Nov. 15 to Dec 15. AE, DC, MC, V. *La Flore* (I), av. Princesse-Grace (tel. 93-56-80-29). Closed first half Nov. Good views over harbor, pretty gardens; pleasant restaurant.

Restaurants. *La Campanette* (M), 2 rue Baron-de-Brès (tel. 93-01-79-98). Closed first half Nov., and Sun.; no lunches. In picturesque street above harbor; inventive cuisine. AE, V. *Carpaccio* (M), promenade Marinières (tel. 93-01-72-97). Closed Tues. Good for fish, pizzas and, of course, *carpaccio.* Terrace by sea. AE, V.

TOURS AND EXCURSIONS. By Bus. Bus excursions are available from many travel agents in the main centers, and are also offered by the *S.N.C.F.* Some examples are: Cannes to the spectacular Verdon gorges or to St.-Paul-de-Vence; Grasse to the Verdon Gorges; Hyères or Toulon to St.-Tropez, Port-Grimaud and the Levant islands; Nice up into Upper Provence (Beuil and Valberg); and sea-fishing trips from St.-Raphaël or St.-Tropez. Bus (and train) excursions into Italy (San Remo and Ventimiglia) from Nice or Menton are very popular—don't forget your passport.

By Boat. Boat excursions are not to be missed. You might like to avoid the traffic by traveling from Nice to Marseille by boat, but the classic trips are to the various islands: to les Iles d'Hyères (Ile du Levant, Porquerolles and Port-Cros) from Giens (Hyères), Le Lavandou, St.-Tropez or Toulon; to the Iles de Lérins (St.-Honorat and Ste.-Marguerite) from Antibes, Cannes or Juan-les-Pins; and to the Château d'If from Marseille. Boat trips along the lovely Calanques from Cassis and Marseille are also delightful. You can usually find local fishermen organizing trips from smaller resorts, or inquire at tourist offices.

On Foot. The Provençal Alps can be highly rewarding to walkers. Good walkers should consider the stupendous excursion to the Vallée des Merveilles (inland from Menton), with its thousands of Bronze Age rock carvings and wild scenery. Plan to spend a night in the mountain hut open to tourists.

SIGHTSEEING DATA. For general comments on visiting museums and historic buildings in France see "Sightseeing" in *Facts at Your Fingertips.* Sightseeing can be frustrating in this part of France because in summer places of interest are often closed for a long gap at mid-day (frequently 12–3); best plan to combine a morning on the beach with an afternoon's sightseeing or vice versa. The tiny chapels and churches in the Roya Valley are well worth seeking out but are rarely left open: inquire locally which café, hotel or office holds the key.

ANTIBES. Musée Picasso (housed in Château Grimaldi), (tel. 93-33-67-67). Open daily except Tues., Mar. to mid-Sept., 10–12, 3–6 or 7 (closes at 5 in winter). Closed Nov.

Fort Carré, on St.-Roch peninsula. Open July and Aug. only, daily 9–12, 2–7.

Marineland. Shows two or three times daily starting at 2.30; extra show in July and Aug. at around 9.30 P.M.

Musée d'Archéologie Terrestre et Sous-marine (Land and Marine Archeology Museum), Bastion St.-André (tel. 93-34-48-01). Open daily except Tues., 9–12, 2–6. Closed Nov.

Musée Naval et Napoléonien (Naval and Napoleonic Museum), Cap d'Antibes (tel. 93-61-45-32). Open daily except Tues., 10–12, 2–5 (3–7 in July and Aug.). Closed Nov. to mid-Dec.

BANDOL. Musée des Vins et Spiritueux (Wine and Spirits Museum), Ile de Bendor. Open daily except Wed., 10–12, 2–5 or 6.

BEAULIEU. Villa Kérylos, rue Gustave-Eiffel (tel. 93-01-01-44). Open daily except Mon., Sept. through June, 2–6 (July and Aug., 3–6). Closed Nov.

BIOT. Musée Fernand Léger. Open daily except Tues., 10–12, 2–5 (2.30–6.30 July and Aug.).

CAGNES. Château (tel. 93-20-85-57). Open daily except Tues. and public hols., 10–12, 2–5.
Domaine des Collettes (Renoir's Home), (tel. 93-20-61-07). Open daily except Tues., 2–5 (2–6 June through Aug.). Closed mid-Oct. to mid-Nov.

CANNES. Musée de la Castre. Open daily except Mon., 10–12, 2–5 (3–7 in July and Aug.). Closed Nov. and public hols.

FRÉJUS. Musée Archéologique (Archeological Museum), **Baptistère** (Baptistery) and **Cloître** (Cloisters). Open daily except Tues., 9.30–12, 2–4.30 (to 6 in summer).
Musée des Troupes de Marine (Navy Museum), quartier Lecoq, rte. Bagnols-en-Forêt. Open mid-May to mid-Sept., Mon. to Fri., 3–5.50 (2.30–5 in winter), and on Fri. eve., 8 P.M.–10 P.M.; for further times please check locally.

GOURDON. Château (housing **History Museum** and **Naive Painting Museum**), (tel. 93-42-50-13). Open daily July through Sept., 11–1, 2–6, guided tours available; rest of year, daily except Tues., 10–12, 2–6.

GRASSE. Musée d'Art et d'Histoire de Provence (Provençal Art and History Museum), Hôtel de Clapiers-Cabris (tel. 93-36-01-61). Open daily except Mon., public hols. and second and fourth Sun. in month, 10–12, 2–5 (to 6 in summer).
Villa Fragonard, blvd. Fragonard (tel. 93-36-01-61). Opening times as museum above.

HYÈRES. Musée Municipal, pl. Théodore-Lefèvre. Open daily (except Tues. and public hols.), 10–12, 3–6; Sat. and Sun., 3–6 only.

MARSEILLE. Unless otherwise indicated, the museums are closed Tues. all day and Wed. morning.
Château d'If. Open daily 1.30–6.
Musée d'Archéologie (Archeology Museum), Château Borély (tel. 91-73-21-60). Closed Tues., Wed. morning, and some public hols.
Musée des Beaux-Arts (Fine Arts Museum), Palais Longchamp (tel. 91-62-21-17). Open 10–12, 2–6.30. Closed Tues., Wed. morning, some public hols.; free Sun. morning.
Musée Cantini, 19 rue Grignan (tel. 91-54-77-75). Open 10–12, 2–6. Closed Tues., Wed. morning, some public hols.
Musée des Docks Romains, pl. Vivaux. Open 10–12, 2–6. Closed Tues., Wed. morning, some public hols.
Musée d'Histoire de Marseille (History of Marseille Museum), centre Bourse, (tel. 91-90-42-22). Open daily except Sun. and Mon., 10–7.
Musée d'Histoire Naturelle (Natural History Museum), Palais Longchamp (tel. 91-62-30-78). Open 10–12, 2–6. Closed Tues., Wed. morning, some public hols.; free Sun. morning.

Musée de la Marine (Navy Museum), Palais de la Bourse (tel. 91-91-91-51). Open daily except Tues., 10–12, 2–6.30; winter 2.30–7.

Musée du Vieux Marseille (History of Old Marseille Museum), 2 rue Prison (tel. 91-55-10-19). Open 10–12, 2–6.30. Closed Tues., Wed. morning, public hols.

MENTON. Palais Carnoles, 3 av. Madone (tel. 93-35-49-71). Open daily except Mon. and Tues., 10–12, 3–6 (2–5.30 mid-Sept. to mid-June).

Salle des Mariages (decorated by Cocteau), Mairie, rue République (tel. 93-35-78-83). Open daily except Sun. and public hols, 9–12, 2–6 (3–6 in July and Aug.).

Musée Jean-Cocteau, bastion du Port. Open daily except Mon., Tues., public hols. and Nov., 9–12, 2–6 (3–6.15 June through Aug.).

NICE. Many of Nice's museums have no admission charge on Sat.

Arènes de Cimiez. Open June through Aug., 7.30–8; Apr., May and Sept., 7.30–7; 7.30–5.30 in winter. Guided tours of monastery daily except Sat. P.M. and Sun., at 10, 11, 3, 4 and 5.

Musée International d'Art Naïf (Naive Art Museum), Château Ste.-Hélène, av. Fabron. Open daily except Tues., May through Sept., 10–12, 2–6 (to 5 in winter). Closed Nov.

Musée des Beaux-Arts Jules Chéret (Fine Arts Museum), 33 av. Baumettes (tel. 93-88-53-18). Open daily except Mon., public hols., June through Sept., 10–12, 2–7 (to 5 rest of year).

Muséum d'Histoire Naturelle (including aquaria and Galerie de Malacologie or Shell Gallery), 3 cours Saleya (tel. 93-85-18-44). Open daily except Tues. and Aug., 11–7.

Musée Masséna, 65 rue France (tel. 93-88-11-34). Open daily except Mon., 10–12, 2–5.

Musée Matisse, 164 av. Arènes-de-Cimiez (tel. 93-81-59-57). Open daily except Sun. A.M. and Mon., June through Sept., 10–12, 2–7; rest of year, 2–5 only. Closed Nov.

Musée National du Message Biblique Marc Chagall, av. Dr.-Ménard (tel. 93-81-75-75). Open daily except Tues. and public hols., July through Sept., 10–7; rest of year, 10–12.30, 2–5.30.

Palais Lascaris, 15 rue Droite (tel. 93-62-05-54). Open daily except Mon., Jan. through Sept., 9.30–12, 2.30–6 or 6.30; winter, 8.30–12, 2.30–6.

Musée de Terra-Amata (Prehistoric Site), 25 blvd. Carnot (tel. 93-55-59-93). Open daily except Mon., mid-Apr. to mid-Nov., 10–12, 2–7 (to 6 in winter). Closed mid-Nov. to mid-Dec.

ROQUEBRUNE-CAP-MARTIN. Donjon (castle keep). Open daily, except Fri., 9–12, 2–7; winter 10–12, 2–5; closed Nov.

ST.-JEAN-CAP-FERRAT. Fondation Ephrussi de Rothschild, av. Ephrussi-de-Rothschild (tel. 93-01-33-09). Open daily except Mon. and Nov., 2–6 (3–7 in July and Aug.).

ST.-PAUL-DE-VENCE. Fondation Maeght (tel. 93-32-81-63). Open daily 10–12.30, 2.30–6 (3–7 in July and Aug.).

ST.-RAPHAËL. Musée de la Mer (Sea Museum), in front of Templiers church. Open daily except Tues., mid-June to mid-Sept., 10–12, 3–6; rest of year, daily except Sun., 11–12, 2–5. Closed public hols.

ST.-TROPEZ. Musée de l'Annonciade, beside harbor. Open daily except Tues., June through Sept., 10–12, 3–7 (to 6 rest of year). Closed Nov.

Musée de la Marine (Navy Museum), citadelle. Open daily except Thurs., 10–5 (10–6 June through Aug.).

TOULON. Musée d'Art et d'Archéologie (Art and Archeology Museum), 20 blvd. Leclerc. Open daily 10–12, 2–6.

Musée National du Débarquement en Provence (Provence Landings Museum), Mont-Faron. Open daily, except Thurs. and Nov., June through Sept., 9–7; rest of year, 9–11.30, 2–5.30.

Musée du Vieux Toulon (Museum of Old Toulon), 69 cours Lafayette. Open Sat. only, 3–6.

VALLAURIS. Musée Municipal (including modern ceramics collection). Open daily except Tues., 10–12, 2–5 (to 6 in July and Aug.).

Musée National Picasso, pl. Libération. Open daily except Tues., 10–12, 2–5 (to 6 in July and Aug.).

VENCE. Chapelle du Rosaire (Rosary Chapel, decorated by Matisse), 46 av. Henri-Matisse (tel. 93-58-03-26). Open Tues. and Thurs., 10–11.30, 2.30–5; other days by appointment only.

VILLEFRANCHE. Chapelle St.-Pierre (decorated by Cocteau), (tel. 93-80-73-68). Open daily except Fri., Apr. to mid-Nov., 9–12, 2–6 (2.30–9 in July and Aug.); winter, 9–12, 2–4.30. Closed Nov.

Citadelle St.-Elme (tel. 93-55-45-12). Open daily except Sun. A.M. and Tues., May through Sept., 10–12, 3–7 (2–5.30 Oct. through Apr.).

VILLENEUVE-LOUBET. Musée Escoffier de l'Art Culinaire (Escoffier Art of Cooking Museum), (tel. 93-20-80-51). Open daily except Mon. and public hols, 2–6. Closed Nov.

SHOPPING. Pottery and ceramics are a specialty of the region and can be found in the hill villages, notably in Vallauris, where there is a very wide range; in Biot, where potters have worked for centuries; and in Vence, famous for its plain and elegant oven-to-table ware.

The essence for most of the world's perfumes comes from Grasse, so you should buy at least one little bottle. Dried flowers from the wonderful flower fields around Grasse and elsewhere along the coast are temptingly presented in bunches, or balls to hang up, or in little wicker baskets. Also conveniently light to transport are the local dried herbs (the tasty *poivre d'âne,* a form of wild savory, is rarely found elsewhere). Wild herbs enhance the special flavor of the local olives, which you can buy attractively packed in pottery or earthenware jars. Olivewood articles abound: typical are salad bowls and servers, and deep perforated spoons for scooping out olives.

Preserved or candied fruits are a specialty of Nice: don't miss the excellent *Henri Auer* café, 7 rue François de Paule, near the flower market. On the north side of the flower market are families with generations of experience in carefully packing flowers to survive the journey to anywhere in the world.

The chic boutiques in the resorts and the upmarket department stores have beautifully-cut bathing costumes and bikinis that will make you feel as glamorous as any Riviera beach beauty. Evening outfits and accessories are also stunning here, where nightlife plays an important part in many people's vacations.

LOWER PROVENCE

Rome Away From Rome

No other region of France is so steeped in history as Provence, so blessed by nature, so full of beautiful things to see. The Romans called it *provincia*—the province—for it was the first part of Gaul they occupied and it needed no further name. Then, from the 9th to the 15th centuries it was an independent realm, ruled by kings and counts; right up to the Revolution it retained some of this autonomy. Today Provence-Côte d'Azur is just one among the 22 administrative regions of France. But it has kept alive its traditions and folklore and is justly proud of its glorious past, of the Romans and troubadours, popes and princes that forged its history, and of its beautiful old Provençal language.

It is a land on which history lies in thick layers. The Romans have left their finest remains outside Italy here: there is Nîmes and the Pont du Gard, Arles and St.-Rémy, Orange and Vaison. Superb medieval abbeys and churches are everywhere, many of them in the purest Romanesque style. And there are sophisticated modern cities too, for places like Aix and Avignon are anything but dead museum-towns: they possess a vibrant life of their own.

It is a land of clear, dazzling light and pure Mediterranean landscapes, of fertile plains and dry limestone hills. Slender cypresses stand beside red-roofed farmsteads, and the air is heavy with the scent of lavender or alive with the whirr of cicada. These are the harsh, brightly-colored landscapes that inspired Van Gogh and Cézanne and that pulsate through many of their finest paintings.

Nîmes, Uzès and the Pont du Gard

At the western gateway to Provence, on the border of Languedoc, stands the city of Nîmes. It was for long a center of defiance against Paris and played a leading role in the 16th- and 17th-century Protestant revolts. Today, it is an industrial center but shares the typically sleepy feel of the Midi. The locals like to call it "the Rome of France"—an exaggeration, though it does contain two of the finest Roman remains in Europe. One is the majestic Arena, well preserved, which held 21,000 spectators and is still used for operas, concerts and corridas. The other is the graceful Maison Carrée ("square house"), built by Agrippa as a temple in Hellenic style. It has delicate carvings above its fluted Ionic columns, while its interior is a museum of Gallo-Roman art (note the statue of Apollo and the Venus of Nîmes). The area round the Maison Carrée is being pedestrianized and will be enlivened with a magnificent new contemporary arts center and concert hall.

In addition, next to the ornate 18th-century Garden of the Fountain, are the ruins of a temple of Diana, all that remains of the big thermal center the Romans built beside a gushing spring. From here a path leads up to the Tour Magne, a massive tower on a hilltop that the Romans put up probably as a watchtower (fine views from its summit). In town, the old quarter of Nîmes north of the Arena has now been renovated and is a fine place for strolling, with its medieval walkways covered over as protection from the sun (the old street names appear in Provençal as well as French in these days of minority-language revival); there are some attractive Renaissance houses too. (The tourist office will supply a good walking map.) The Musée des Beaux Arts contains a splendid Roman mosaic, and don't miss the classical Jesuit chapel dating from the 17th century; it has now been beautifully restored and provides the perfect setting for art exhibits and chamber-music concerts.

North of Nîmes, a road winds over dry scrub-covered hills, known as *la garrigue,* to the enchanting little medieval town of Uzès, seat of a great ducal family that can be traced back to Charlemagne. They still live in their romantic castle above the town, built in a mixture of styles from early feudal via Renaissance to 19th century. Uzès has many fascinating old streets and buildings: notably, the arcaded Place aux Herbes, and the Tour Fenestrelle, a curious circular six-story bell-tower, of a kind common in north Italy but in France unique to Uzés.

South of here is the famous Pont du Gard, one of the grandest and most elegant of Roman monuments. It was built in 19 B.C. as an aqueduct to carry water to Nîmes. Very much later, Napoleon, the modern Emperor, repaired it. It is 275 meters (902 ft.) long and 49 meters (160 ft.) high and consists of three tiers (you can walk along the top, so long as you're not afraid of heights). The stones weigh up to six tons each, and engineers today still find the whole construction a marvel. An underground museum is being built at the foot of the aqueduct, with the entrance on the Right Bank of the river.

South of Nîmes, the small town of St.-Gilles is worth visiting for its 12th-century abbey church, with marvelously vivid sculptures on its Romanesque façade. In the crypt is the tomb of St.-Gilles, a 7th-century hermit who, according to legend, sailed from Greece to Provence on a raft. Little remains now of the great medieval monastery that flourished here. However, you can still inspect Le Vis, a curious spiral staircase with roofed-over steps, giving a funnel effect.

Amid the lagoons and marshes of the coast southwest of Nîmes is the imposing walled medieval city of Aigues-Mortes, a very busy harbor until the 14th century. Here St.-Louis set sail for the Seventh Crusade in 1248; here today 4,000 people still live within the ramparts. At one corner is the Tower of Constance, once used as a political prison: on some walls you can still read the brave and poignant graffiti of the prisoners.

The Camargue: Horses, Bulls and Flamingoes

These 300-square-miles of lagoons and marshy plains in the Rhône delta are a haunting region like none other in France. Birds and animals in rich variety here lead their special life; herds of half-wild white horses roam the marshes, and at dusk a flock of pink flamingoes may soar up from the reeds. The northern part of the Camargue near Arles, desalinated after World War II, is now France's main rice-growing area. To the south is the large lake of Vaccarès, now the center of a nature reserve with many unusual wild plants and flowers: special permission is needed to enter, but even from outside you can often see flamingoes and other birds by driving along the lake's east side to the Gacholle lighthouse.

The Camargue is divided into 30 private ranches, each with its own herd *(manade)* of bulls and horses, cohabiting happily. The bulls are not bred to die in the local corridas, but for the more harmless sport of *courses à la cocarde,* when young men compete to pluck cockades from the horns of young bulls. The famous white horses are sturdy, hardy animals with short legs, yet nimble and amenable; the herds are allowed to roam freely. This is a great place for a riding holiday—you can gallop alone across the marshes, or go in a group with one of the local *gardians* who look over the herds. Known as "the aristocrats of the Camargue," these tough, gipsy-like men and women live out on the marshes in remote thatched cottages. One of their annual rituals is the *ferade* (branding of yearlings), which takes place amid much drinking and jollity and has become a popular tourist spectacle. There are museums of Camargue history, traditions and wildlife at the Pont de Rousty on N570 and at Les Saintes-Maries-de-la-Mer.

There are still some true gipsies in the Camargue, though today their caravans are all motorized. Every May gipsies from many lands gather at Les Saintes-Maries for their famous and colorful festival. This little town by the sand dunes is partly a family seaside resort, now sporting a chic little yacht harbor, and partly a center of strange legend: Mary Magdalene and two other holy Marys are said to have arrived here in a boat without sails, together with Sarah, their African servant, who today is the gipsies' patron saint. Her shrine is in the crypt of the town's curious, tall fortified church, built in the 11th century as a defense against the Saracens.

Arles, Les Baux and Tarascon

Arles breathes history in its every stone. In Roman days it was a major trade center and key port on the lower Rhône, rivaling Marseille. The Romans made it capital of Provence and then of the "three Gauls"

(France, Spain, Britain). Later it became a powerhouse of early Christianity (St. Augustine was consecrated first Bishop of Canterbury here). In the 10th century it was the capital of a sizeable kingdom, but then fell into decline. Today, a sleepy town of 50,000 people, it contains an astonishing wealth of monuments and museums that tell of Roman and medieval glories.

The Arena (46 B.C.) was one of the largest in the Roman world, holding 25,000 spectators, and is still in good condition. It was used for gladiatorial contests and fights with wild beasts. Today, this gory tradition continues with bullfights in the summer. But the gentler *courses à la cocarde* are also held here.

The Roman Theater, begun under Augustus, is today a ruin, though its two surviving columns are impressive. A drama and music festival is held here in July. On the banks of the Rhône, the vast baths of Constantine are all that remain of the palace built by the emperor. Nearby, the Museum of Pagan Art offers a rich display of Greek and Roman works, found locally, including statues of Venus and Augustus and Greek sarcophagi.

Early-Christian sarcophagi, richly carved, are in the Museum of Christian Art, formerly a Jesuit chapel. From here, steps lead down to the huge basement gallery that the Romans built below their Forum and used as a granary. In the southeast suburbs, yet more sarcophagi are to be seen at Les Alyscamps, a wide tree-lined avenue that was one of the most fashionable cemeteries of early Christendom. Back in town, the ex-cathedral of St.-Trophime is famous for the rich carvings on its 12th-century Romanesque portal, a contrast with the interior's cool simplicity. The adjacent cloister is probably the loveliest in Provence: note the graceful marble pillars, the vivid carvings on the capitals, and the tapestries in a side chapel.

The Réattu Museum, in a former priory of the Knights of Malta, brings a leap forward in time: its eclectic art displays include some Brussels tapestries bizarrely depicting the Wonders of the World; works by Léger and other modern masters, including a set of satirical colored cartoons by Picasso. After this, another abrupt change of mood is needed for a visit to the Muséon Arlaten, a somewhat old-fashioned but charming folklore museum lovingly assembled by the great Provençal poet Frédéric Mistral (1830–1914). Here you'll find a fascinating array of costumes, coiffures, puppets, mascots, tableaux of rural life, and much else. Alas, the famed Arlésienne beauties no longer use the lovely local costumes for daily wear, only for special festivals.

Arles is a lively cultural center these days, staging a major international photography festival, a dance festival and many other exhibits. Future plans include a splendid Archeological Museum overlooking the Rhône, work on which will start in 1986. Northeast of Arles you should visit Montmajor, Les Baux, St.-Rémy and Tarascon. Built on a low hill, the former Benedictine abbey of Montmajor dates from the 10th century and was once a wealthy and powerful religious center. Today it is partly ruined, but still worth seeing for its lofty *donjon* (inner tower), its Romanesque church and crypt and charming cloister. The nearby chapel of Ste.-Croix is another Romanesque gem. Further east, on a hill outside Fontevieille, is the windmill that inspired Alphonse Daudet's stories, *Lettres de Mon Moulin:* the mill can be visited, and contains a small Daudet museum.

A little further on, the mysterious ghost-village of Les Baux perches on a spur of the craggy Alpilles hills. The ruined castle here was the home of one of the great feudal families of medieval France. First it was a center of the "Courts of Love," where troubadours sang. Then it was the stronghold of a cruel despot who kidnapped local people in order that they might amuse him by jumping to their deaths from the clifftop. Les Baux then fell into decay and today is largely deserted. You can walk up past the village's museums and souvenir shops to the gaunt castle above, with its fine view over the valley. A visit by moonlight is a haunting experience.

Just south of St.-Rémy is ancient Glanum, where you can see the remains of Greek houses and of Roman baths and temples; there is also a small, well-preserved Roman triumphal arch and a cenotaph honoring two grandsons of Augustus. Close by, the former priory of St.-Paul-de-Mausole (lovely Romanesque chapel and cloister) is now a mental home: Vincent Van Gogh was a patient here after cutting off his ear in Arles. In St.-Rémy is a museum of Greek and Gallo-Roman finds from Glanum.

Westwards a road leads to Maillane, where Mistral lived: his house is now a museum. Further on is Tarascon, where King René's splendid medieval turreted castle stands above the Rhône. Inside, there is an elegant inner court with a minstrels' gallery, and a spacious banqueting hall. The castle was subsequently used as a prison: on one wall are the pathetic graffiti of English seamen captured in the 18th century. Tarascon is famous also as the setting of Daudet's *Tartarin* novels, and for the weird ancient legend of Ste.-Martha and the Tarasque. The saint, so the tale goes, found the town terrorized by a child-devouring dragon whom no knight could defeat. But Ste.-Martha did so, with the sign of the Cross. She is venerated in the lovely Gothic church that bears her name; and the dragon, the Tarasque, is the subject of a quaint annual pageant.

Across the river lies Beaucaire, with its half-ruined hilltop castle (fine views). From the 13th to 19th centuries the town was the site of Europe's greatest annual trade fair.

Avignon and the Palace of the Popes

Though 14th-century ramparts (much restored 500 years later) ring the noble city of Avignon, the city itself is dominated by the giant fortress-like hulk of the Palace of the Popes, often thought of as Europe's greatest medieval building. Finding Rome too corrupt and disorderly, the Papacy moved here in 1307 and set about building their palace. The popes ruled in it till 1377, then officially moved back to Rome. However, a number of cardinals contested the return. They stayed in Avignon and elected an Antipope, thereby precipitating the Great Schism of the West, which was to last till 1449.

The palace is in two contrasting parts, the result of having been built in two phases by two very different popes. Benedict XII's "old palace" reflects his own austerity (he had been a Cistercian monk); the "new palace," on the other hand, is far more ornate. It was built by Clement VI who loved the arts and high living. In his day, Avignon was a city of luxury, pomp and loose morals—to the fury of some puritans at court such as the poet Petrarch who called it a "sink of vice." The guided tour (not to be missed, despite dense crowds in summer) will enable you to see the very worldly decor in Clement's bedroom and study, clear evidence of his less than entirely spiritual tastes. There is much else to admire too—frescos, tapestries, portraits—in this vast labyrinth of corridors, halls and chapels. The palace is also the focal point of Avignon's famous drama festival in July.

Close by, the 12th-century cathedral contains the Flamboyant-Gothic tomb of Pope John XXII. From here it is a short walk to the hilltop garden of the Rocher des Doms, with a fine view. Below, on the Rhône, is the half-ruined 12th-century bridge of St.-Bénézet, the "pont d'Avignon" of the well-known song. The best museums in town are the Petit Palais (splendid French and Italian paintings of the 13th to 15th centuries) and Calvet (variable French 16th- to 20th-century works). It is also worth strolling in the narrow streets of the old town south of the palace. You will quickly note that Avignon today is an unusually sophisticated and lively town, with an air of youthful *joie de vivre*—a place that even Parisians admit to be fashionable.

Just across the Rhône is Villeneuve-lès-Avignon, formerly a fortress town: hence its two major military buildings, the Tower of Philippe le Bel and the Fort St.-André. Also worth seeing are the enormous Charterhouse and two exquisite works of art: Quarton's *Coronation of the Virgin* (1453) in the Musée de L'Hospice; and the carved ivory statuette of the Virgin and Child in the church of Notre-Dame. Climb, too, to the terrace of the Fort St.-André for a glorious view of the Papal Palace in the setting sun.

From Orange to the Lubéron Hills

Orange was a thriving city in Roman days, with baths and a big stadium. These are now gone. But two of the finest Roman buildings in Europe remain: the Triumphal Arch, built by Julius Caesar to mark his victories over local Gauls; and the Theater, well preserved, vast, with a large statue of Augustus in the central niche of its stage. The theater is best seen from the hill of St.-Eutrope to the south, and preferably by moonlight. At the music and opera festival here in July, the audience sits on the rows of stone seats, just like Roman nobles of old.

The Romans called the town Arausio—hence, "Orange," which has nothing to do with the fruit (that name comes from the Arabic *narandji*). Orange was a tiny principality in the 13th to 17th centuries. It was acquired by the Dutch prince, William of Nassau, who liked it so much that he called his dynasty the House of Orange, a title that his descendants, the Dutch royal family, carry to this day. The Protestant "Orange" movement in Ulster gets its name from the same connection.

South of Orange, the famous vineyards of Châteauneuf-du-Pape once belonged to the Avignon popes (hence the name); the village has a small wine museum. To the east, the old city of Carpentras has much of interest: a 15th-century cathedral rich in works of art; several good museums; a small Roman arch with bas-reliefs of captives; and one of France's earliest synagogues (the town was once a major Jewish center). Venasque, nearby, has a 7th-century Merovingian baptistry.

Memorials of Roman grandeur survive also at Vaison-la-Romaine which the Romans built as a wealthy residential town with patrician villas. Excavations have revealed shops, hanging gardens, salons, baths, even latrines and kitchens—a whole way of life, in fact, as at Pompeii. Do not miss the museum of local Roman art, the Romanesque cathedral, and the medieval quarter across the river. Southward rises the lofty pyramid-shaped Mont Ventoux, "windy mount" (290 meters/

6,260 ft. high), with a good road leading to its summit; also the dramatic limestone crags of the Dentelles de Montmirail.

South of Mont Ventoux is the region of the Plateau de Vaucluse and the Lubéron, with medieval villages and wonderful scenery, including purple lavender fields in June and July. Fontaine de Vaucluse is so called because here the river Sorgue surges out of a cavern to form a dramatic cascade of spray in the wet season or when snows are melting (in dry weather it is much duller). The Italian poet Petrarch spent 16 years here, 1337–53, pining for his Laura, and it inspired some of his work.

Eastward is the lovely hilltop village of Gordes, whose château is now a museum of the works of Vasarély. In this area are scores of strange primitive stone huts, beehive-shaped, known as *bories:* the *village des bories* is a museum of rural life. Just north of Gordes, the beautiful 12th-century Cistercian abbey of Sénanque stands majestically alone in a wild valley. It is well preserved, and among much else it houses, oddly, a museum of the Sahara. Good concerts and exhibitions are held in this lovely setting.

East again is the hill-village of Roussillon, popular with artists. Its houses of local stone are all shades of orange, red and pink, for this is ochre country where quarrying has slashed the cliffs into bizarre shapes. Going southeast you come to Apt, whose cathedral contains remarkable treasures relating to the local cult of Ste.-Anne, mother of the Virgin.

Southwards there rises the long range of the Lubéron hills, part wild and craggy, part lush plateau covered with vines and lavender. Here you should visit Bonnieux, to see the impressive 15th-century German paintings in its basilica; and, high on a rocky spur, the medieval village of Oppède-le-Vieux which, having fallen into ruin, is now being carefully restored by local artists and others. South again, on your way to Aix, do not miss another lovely Cistercian abbey: Silvacane.

Aix-en-Provence

Of all French cities, Aix-en-Provence could most readily be mentioned in the same breath as Florence or Oxford—a proud, patrician place whose modern student life is enacted against an elegant backdrop of classical buildings and historic monuments.

From the 12th to the 18th centuries it was Provence's dazzling capital. Then it became overshadowed by the rise of Marseille. But today it is still a lively town, with a major university and busy cultural activity: its music and drama festival in July is world-famous.

Since Roman days it has been a spa town ("Aix" comes from the Latin *aquae,* "waters"). Its golden age was in the 15th century under "Good King René," count of Provence, a jovial and beneficent ruler, intellectual and patron of the arts, who is still venerated by Aixois today. After his death Provence was united with France, but it retained some autonomy and Aix was the seat of its parliament. Its many graceful 17th- and 18th-century mansions were built by wealthy local dignitaries.

The main avenue is the famous Cours Mirabeau, named after the Revolution's orator, Count Mirabeau, who lived here. It is shaded with plane trees and has four fountains, plus a statue of King René. Nearby, the Musée Granet contains works by Ingres and other French painters, and striking Celto-Ligurian sculptures, excavated locally.

The heart of the "Vieil Aix," the old town, is a fascinating network of narrow, traffic-free streets and picturesque little squares, notably the place Albertas. Here there is much to explore. The cathedral of St.-Sauveur is built in an odd mix of styles, from its 5th-century Gallo-Roman baptistry to the 16th-century late-Gothic facade. The sacristan will unlock for you the ornate wood-carvings on the door-panels and Froment's superb triptych, *The Burning Bush*. The famous Brussels tapestries are no longer on view, alas. But in the adjacent Archbishop's Palace you can see some fine Beauvais tapestries, including a set depicting the life of Don Quixote. The courtyard of this palace is the main venue for Aix's celebrated music and drama festival in summer, rebuilt and expanded in 1985 and now called the Théâtre de l'Archevêché.

Nearby, the Vieil Aix museum of folklore has a large collection of Provençal *santons* (dolls and puppets), while the 17th-century church of Ste.-Marie-Madeleine contains a remarkable 15th-century painting of the *Annunciation*. Out in the suburbs, it is worth visiting the Pavillon Vendôme, former home of a cardinal; and the Fondation Vasarély, a big ultra-modern museum full of the highly-colored murals, mosaics and glass sculptures by that provocative Hungarian-born artist.

Aix was also long the home of one of France's greatest artists, Paul Cézanne, who is buried in the town cemetery. You can visit his rather austere studio on a hillside above the town, near to the spot where in varying lights and hues he would obsessively paint and repaint the Montagne Ste.-Victoire, the high, conical limestone ridge that looms above Aix.

The market town of Salon-de-Provence, northwest of Aix, was the home of the astrologer Nostradamus. His tomb is in the 14th-century church of St.-Laurent. The house where he lived is now a museum devoted to him. Another museum, this one of military history, is in the 10th-century Château de l'Empéri on a rock above the town. Finally, 16 km. (ten miles) west of Aix is the impressive 19th-century aqueduct of Roquefavour, which carries the Durance's water to Marseille. It is much larger than the Pont du Gard: 375 meters (1,230 ft.) long and 83 meters (272 ft.) high.

The Hinterland: Abbeys, Museums, Gorges

The sprawling hinterland of central Provence between Aix and Fréjus, though less well known than the coast or the Rhône valley area, holds much of interest. East of Aix, at St.-Maximin-la-Ste.-Baume, the beautiful 13th- to 16th-century basilica is the noblest building in Provence; it also has sarcophagi dating from the 4th century. Just south of here, the craggy limestone massif of La Ste.-Baume is both very scenic and a place of legend and mystery, for near its summit is a cave where Mary Magdalen is said to have spent her final years, in solitude; it is now a shrine and pilgrimage center.

A spiritual atmosphere also infuses the lovely 12th-century Romanesque abbey of Thoronet, built by Cistercian monks in a secluded valley northeast of Brignoles. With its charming cloister and chapter-house, it forms an ensemble of rare purity and harmony. Try to attend vespers in the chapel on a fine evening, when the stone glows gold in the setting sun. Or go north for a total change of mood to the château at Entrecasteaux, turned into the most bizarre museum in Provence by the late Ian McGarvie-Munn, surrealist painter and Scottish nationalist, and sometime soldier, adventurer and art-fancier.

North again, you come to the Grand Canyon of Verdon, a winding gorge 20 km. (13 miles) long and 580 meters (2,000 ft.) deep, the most spectacular in France. Its bed is impassable, but good roads dizzily follow the clifftop on either side, while for hardy and experienced hikers there are footpaths zigzagging down the cliff towards the rushing river Verdon. Just to the west, the pottery village of Moustiers-Ste.-Marie is worth a visit for its *faience* (decorated earthenware) museum and its setting at the foot of a ravine, while the tiny ancient town of Riez has a 5th-century Christian baptistry *and* the remains of a Roman temple —yet another surprise of the delightful Provençal hinterland.

PRACTICAL INFORMATION FOR LOWER PROVENCE

TOURIST OFFICES. The regional tourist office for the whole of Provence, including those areas covered in our *Riviera and Upper Provence* chapter, is the *Comité Régional du Tourisme,* 22A rue Louis-Maurel, 13006 Marseille (tel. 91-37-91-22); written enquiries only. In addition, the two *départements* of Provence covered in this chapter also have their own tourist offices (again, written enquiries only): **Bouches-du-Rhône,** 6 rue du Jeune-Anacharsis, 13001 Marseille (tel. 91-54-92-66); **Vaucluse,** 2 rue St.-Etienne, quartier de la Balance, BP 147, Avignon Cedex (tel. 90-86-43-42).

There are local tourist offices in the following towns: **Aix-en-Provence,** pl. Général-de-Gaule (tel. 42-26-02-93); **Arles,** esplanade des Lices (tel. 90-96-29-35); **Avignon,** 41 cours Jean-Jaurès (tel. 90-82-65-11); **Nîmes,** 6 rue Auguste (tel. 66-67-29-11); **Les Stes.-Maries-de-la-Mer,** av. Van-Gogh (tel. 90-47-82-55).

REGIONAL FOOD AND DRINK. Of all French regional cuisines, Provençal is probably the most famous. Its colorful mix of fish and vegetables like peppers and tomato with the flavor of garlic, saffron, and wild herbs is extraordinarily evocative of the Mediterranean sun. On the coast, fish dishes echo those of the Riviera, though inland fresh fish tends to be a luxury, so you'll find salt cod in *brandade* (a hot garlicky purée served with potato) and *morue provençale* (salt cod fried with garlic and tomato).

Pride of the local table are vegetable dishes like *ratatouille* (a garlic and herb-laden stew of tomato, bell pepper, onion, eggplant and zucchini), *oignons braisés* (onions braised with wine), *aubergines farcies* (stuffed eggplant) and *tian* of vegetables baked in a shallow earthenware *tian* dish. Classic accompaniment to a *crudité* raw vegetable salad is *aïoli,* an olive oil and garlic mayonnaise.

The famous Provençal *daube* should, correctly speaking, also be cooked in a special earthenware pot. Usually of beef with olives and a variety of vegetables, a *daube* can also be made with lamb or chicken. Lamb is, in fact, the best meat in Provence for cows do badly in the heat except in the Camargue, where *daube* is called *boeuf gardien.* From the Camargue comes the only rice grown in France, leading to dishes like *pigeons valencienne,* made with rice pilaf and sausages.

Olive oil takes the place of butter for cooking and local cheeses are confined to goat's milk, with a few sheep cheeses. As dessert you'll do well with fruit— melons, figs, peaches and apricots are outstanding. For a sweet treat you might try the candied fruit of Apt, the famous honey, *miel de lavande,* or the almond *calissons* of Aix.

Native to the region are the Côte du Rhône wines (Châteauneuf du Pape, Tavel and Gigondas are the best), the red and *rosé* wines of the Costières du Gard; the *rosés* of Var and the Provençal coast.

HOTELS AND RESTAURANTS. Accommodations are very varied in this much-visited part of France, ranging from luxurious *mas* (converted Provençal farmhouses) to modest city-center hotels convenient for sightseeing. Reservations are essential for much of the year, although many hotels are closed in winter. Restaurants tend to offer regional specialties in all price ranges.

For general notes on hotels and restaurants, see "Hotels" and "Restaurants" in *Facts at Your Fingertips*.

AIGUES-MORTES. *Remparts* (E), 6 pl. d'Armes (tel. 66-53-82-77). 20 rooms. Closed Nov. to mid-Dec., first half Jan.; restaurant closed Mon. (except July, Aug., Sept. and public hols.) and Nov. through Jan. Lovely old building right beside Tour de Constance inside ramparts; large, attractive rooms and excellent cuisine in (M) restaurant. AE, DC, MC, V. *St.-Louis* (M), rue Amiral-Courbet (tel. 66-53-72-68). 22 rooms. Closed Jan. and Feb.; restaurant closed Wed., except July and Aug. Friendly, old-style hotel with good service and nice restaurant.

Restaurant. *Camargue* (M), 19 rue République (tel. 66-53-86-88). Open for dinner only (except Sun.); closed Mon. (except mid-June to mid-Sept.). Crowded and fun, with flamenco music to accompany candlelit dinners; generous helpings of regional specialties. Reservations essential AE, DC, MC, V. *Minos* (I), pl. St.-Louis (tel. 66-53-83-24). Good-value *menu* and charming service—a new discovery.

AIX-EN-PROVENCE. *Augustins* (E), 3 rue Masse (tel. 42-27-28-59). 29 rooms. Closed mid-Dec. to early Jan. In former convent, beautiful 12th-century house near town center. Good bathrooms. No restaurant. AE, DC, MC, V. *Cézanne* (E), 40 av. Victor-Hugo (tel. 42-26-34-73). 44 rooms (airconditioned). Very attractive, near station; no restaurant.

Le Nègre-Coste (M), 33 cours Mirabeau (tel. 42-27-74-22). 37 rooms. Lovely 18th-century building on Aix's main (pedestrian) street; good service, no restaurant. AE, DC, MC, V. *Thermes* (M), 2 blvd. J. Jaurès (tel. 42-26-01-18). 64 rooms. Set in large garden and attached to thermal baths; pool, restaurant. AE, DC, MC, V.

Caravelle (I), 29 blvd. Roi-René (tel. 42-62-53-05). 30 rooms. Nicest rooms overlook walled gardens; well run and maintained, no restaurant. MC, V. *Pasteur* (I), 14 av. Pasteur (tel. 42-21-11-76). 19 rooms. Good-value, family-style hotel with tasty food in restaurant.

Outside town: *Prieuré* (I), rte. de Sisteron, 2 km. (1¼ miles) north (tel. 42-21-05-23). 30 rooms. Converted priory once belonging to the local bishopric; attractive, peaceful rooms with garden views; no restaurant.

Restaurants. *Clos Violette* (E), 10 av. Violette (tel. 42-23-30-71). Closed Sun., Mon., and Aug. Regional and *nouvelle cuisine*. Good-value *menu* at lunch only. V.

Abbaye Cordeliers (M), 21 rue Lieutaud (tel. 42-27-29-47). Closed Dec., Oct., Wed. for lunch and Tues. from April through Sept. 14th-century cloister, now deservedly popular restaurant serving newish cuisine. AE, DC, MC, V. *Arbaud* (M), 19 cours Mirabeau (tel. 42-26-66-88). Open 10 A.M. to midnight. Delightful restaurant on first floor of lovely old mansion on Aix's liveliest street. A series of elegant salons adorned with chandeliers and mirrors; for morning coffee, light salad-type lunches, teas, and ices, and more elaborate dinners. AE, MC, V. *Cahuzac* (M), 7ter rue Mignet (tel. 42-20-69-77). Closed Sun. all day and Mon. for lunch. On edge of old town near Palais de Justice; a former Gothic chapel with attractive décor and good southwestern specialties. V.

Bar à Thé (I), 66 pl. Richelieu (tel. 42-23-51-99). Closed Sun. Tiny spot with tables outside overlooking picturesque fish market; good for light lunches of vegetable pies and salads. *Brocherie* (I), 5 rue Fernand-Dol (tel. 42-38-33-21). Closed Sun. and Mon. Simple cooking and good-value *menus.* Terrace and garden. AE, DC, MC, V. *Jardin* (I), 7 av. Victor-Hugo (tel. 42-26-07-04). Closed Mon. Very friendly, family-type restaurant close to Rotonde, tempting, help-yourself hors d'oeuvre as a starter to good-value *menu.* DC.

ARLES. *Jules César* (E), blvd. Lices (tel. 90-93-43-20). 60 rooms. Closed Nov. and most of Dec. Central, converted from Carmelite convent, interior garden, and comfortable with good restaurant (see below). AE, DC, MC, V.

D'Arlatan (M), 26 rue Sauvage (tel. 90-93-56-66). 46 rooms. Very attractive 15th-century building near river, with garden and beautifully-furnished rooms, though not always very welcoming; no restaurant. AE, DC. *Mas Chapelle* (M), route de Tarascaon (tel. 90-93-23-15). 14 rooms. Beautiful hotel near Camargue, quiet and comfortable, with some rooms overlooking park. Restaurant in 16th-century chapel. V.

Calendal (I), pl. Pomme (tel. 90-96-11-89). 27 rooms. Closed mid-Nov. to mid-Feb. Small, family-type hotel with pretty garden, just by Arena and Theater; no restaurant. DC, MC, V. *St.-Trophime* (I), 16 rue Calande (tel. 90-96-88-38). 22 rooms. Closed early Nov. through Feb. Central, good-sized rooms, particularly helpful management; no restaurant.

Restaurants. *Lou Marquès* (E), in *Jules César* hotel (above). Pleasant terrace for summer meals, mixture of regional and *nouvelle cuisine;* good-value *menu. Olivier* (M), lbis rue Réattu (tel. 90-49-64-88). Closed Mon. for lunch, Sun., Apr. and first half Nov. New, near arena and forum; serves *nouvelle cuisine;* especially good-value *menus;* wine by the glass. V. *Paillotte* (M), rue Dr.-Fanton (tel. 90-96-33-15). Closed Wed. and for lunch on Thurs. Close to pl. Forum; quite elegant, with good fish. DC, MC, V. *Vaccarès* (M), rue Favorin (tel. 90-96-06-17). Closed Sun. and Mon. (except public hols.), Christmas to Jan. 20 and second half June. Old favorite for excellent regional cuisine, pleasant served on terrace overlooking picturesque pl. Forum.

Balance (I), rue Tardieu (tel. 90-93-55-76). Friendly, family-run spot just by Roman arena, with good-value regional specialties. *Grillon* (I), rond-point des Arènes. Tiny café with tables outside overlooking Roman arena and close to Roman theater; local specialties and convenient for sightseers. *Agneau sur le Toit* (I), quai Marx-Dormoy (tel. 90-49-67-28). Closed for lunch on Sat. and all day Sun. Adjoining pleasant bookshop close to Rhône, some regional dishes.

AVIGNON. *Europe* (E), 12 pl. Crillon (tel 90-82-66-92). 53 rooms. Restaurant closed most of Jan., part of Aug., part of Nov., Sun. and for lunch on Mon. Delightful 16th-century building, finely furnished with airconditioned rooms; good old-fashioned service and excellent restaurant. AE, DC, MC, V.

Bristol Terminus (M), 44 cours Jean-Jaurès (tel. 90-82-21-21). 91 rooms. Closed mid-Jan. through Feb. Traditional city-center hotel with spacious rooms; only light meals available. AE, DC, MC, V. *Cité des Papes* (M), 1 rue Jean-Vilar (tel. 90-86-22-45). 63 rooms. Closed mid-Dec. through Jan. Conveniently close to Palais des Papes; modern airconditioned rooms, no restaurant. AE, DC, V.

Mignon (I), 12 rue Joseph Vernet (tel. 90-82-17-30). 15 rooms. Close to Palais des Papes; rooms charming and well equipped. Restaurant for groups only.

At **Montfavet**, 5 km. (3 miles) east, *Les Frênes* (E), av. Vertes-Rives (tel. 90-31-17-93). 18 rooms. Closed Nov. through Feb.; restaurant closed Nov. through Mar. Nicely decorated Relais et Châteaux member with pool, lovely garden and good classical cooking in restaurant (E). AE, DC, MC, V.

At **Les Angles**, 4 km. (2½ miles) west on Nîmes road, *Ermitage Meissonnier* (M), av. Verdun (tel. 90-25-41-68). 16 rooms. Closed Jan. and Feb.; restaurant closed Sun. for dinner (Nov. through Mar. only) and Mon. (except July and Aug.). Comfortable rooms, pretty garden, and good *nouvelle cuisine;* choose the good-value *menu.* AE, DC, V.

Restaurants. *Brunel* (E), 46 rue Balance (tel. 90-85-24-83). Closed mid-Feb. to mid-Mar., Sun. and Mon. (except April through Sept.). Close to Palais des Papes, well-known family-run place for *nouvelle cuisine.* MC, V. *Hiély-Lucullus* (E), 5 rue République (tel. 90-86-17-07). Closed mid-June to early-July, Christmas and New Year, Mon. (except July) and Tues. Sober, old-established restaurant serving superb classical Provençal specialties.

St.-Didier (M), 41 rue Saraillerie (tel. 90-86-16-50). Closed Mon., Tues. and May. Popular spot in old part of town; good-value regional cuisine cooked new-style. AE, DC, V. *Vernet* (M), 58 rue Joseph-Vernet (tel. 90-86-64-53). Closed Sun. (but open May through Aug.), Jan. and Feb. 18th-century building opposite Musée Calvet with charming garden; good regional cuisine. AE, DC.

La Férigoulo (I), 30 rue Joseph-Vernet (tel. 90-82-10-28). Closed most of June, first half Nov., Sun. and Mon. for lunch. Oct. through June. Cheerful, good value, mostly "new" cuisine. AE, DC, MC. *La Fourchette* (I), 17 rue Racine (tel. 90-85-20-93). Closed two weeks in June, Oct. and Jan. Stylish, much less expensive sister to *Hiély* (same owner); very crowded, must reserve.

LES BAUX. *La Cabro d'Or* (E), (tel. 90-85-20-93). 22 rooms. Closed mid-Nov. to mid-Dec.; restaurant also closed Mon. and Tues. for lunch. Oct. 15 to Dec. 20. Large garden surrounds this lovely Relais et Châteaux member below old village; good cuisine. AE, DC, MC, V. *Oustau de Baumanière* (E), (tel. 90-54-33-07). 26 rooms. Closed mid-Jan. through Feb.; restaurant also closed Wed. and for lunch on Thurs., Nov. to Mar. 15. Deluxe Relais et Châteaux member (same owner as *Cabro d'Or*) with pool, tennis courts, and one of France's best classical restaurants. AE, DC, MC, V.

Mas d'Aigret (M), (tel. 90-97-33-54). 17 rooms. Closed Jan. through Mar.; restaurant closed lunchtime and Thurs. Large converted farmhouse; good-value restaurant carved into rockface. AE, DC, V.

Hostellerie Reine Jeanne (I), (tel. 90-97-32-06). 12 rooms. Closed mid-Nov. through Jan.; restaurant also closed Tues. (except mid-Mar. to mid-Oct.). The only hotel actually in the old village; very pleasant, with lovely views over valley and terrace for outdoor meals. V.

BEAUCAIRE. *Les Doctrinaires* (M), 32 rue Nationale (tel. 66-59-41-32). 30 rooms. In town center, in the 18th century a meeting-place of political theorists; comfortable rooms, garden, patio, restaurant. MC, V.

BONNIEUX. *Prieuré* (M), rue Aurard (tel. 90-75-80-78). 10 rooms. Closed Nov. to mid-Feb.; restaurant also closed Tues. and lunch on Wed., Sept. through June; and also for lunch on Tues., Wed. and Thurs. July through Sept. Attractive converted priory at foot of ramparts, antique furniture, garden and restaurant. *Aiguebrun* (M), just off D943, 6 km. (4 miles) southeast (tel. 90-74-04-14). 8 rooms. Closed Nov. 15 to Mar. 15. Secluded and idyllic, with huge garden and inventive (E) cuisine.

CARPENTRAS. *Fiacre* (M), 153 rue Vigne (tel. 90-63-03-15). 17 rooms. Attractive 18th-century building, central yet quiet, especially on the patio; no restaurant. Closed first half Nov. DC, MC, V.

FONTAINE DE VAUCLUSE. *Parc* (I), (tel. 90-20-31-57). 12 rooms. Closed Jan. to mid-Feb.; restaurant also closed Wed. Overlooking river, pleasant terrace for outdoor meals, big garden. AE, DC, V.

Restaurant. *Château* (M), (tel. 90-20-31-54). Closed Feb. and Tues. Lovely river views from dining room; mostly classical cuisine, with good-value *menus*. Also has 5 (I) rooms. AE, DC, MC.

FONTVIEILLE. *La Régalido* (E), rue Mistral (tel. 90-97-60-22). 12 rooms. Closed Dec. to mid-Jan.; restaurant also closed Mon. and for lunch on Tues. Luxurious and welcoming Relais et Châteaux member, with attractive garden and delicious food. AE, DC, MC, V. *Valmajour* (M), 22 rte. d'Arles (D17), (tel. 90-97-62-33). 28 rooms and 5 suites. Closed Nov. through Feb. Large Provençal-style building with pool and tennis courts, no restaurant. AE, V.

GORDES. *La Mayanelle* (M), 6 rue Combe (tel. 90-72-00-28). 10 rooms. Closed Jan. and Feb.; restaurant also closed Tues. Gracefully-converted and furnished 17th-century mansion right in village; lovely views and tasty regional cuisine. Relais et Châteaux member. AE, DC, MC, V.

Restaurants. *Bories* (E), 2 km. (1¼ miles) northwest on road to Senanque abbey (tel. 90-72-00-51). Closed Dec. and Wed. Lunches only. Converted from old stone huts *(bories)* typical of region; excellent regional cooking; also has 4 rooms. *Domaine l'Enclos* (M), rte. de Senanques (tel. 90-72-08-22). Closed Nov. through Mar. and Mon. Good *nouvelle cuisine* and some good-value *menus*. Exquisite setting. Also has 10 (E) rooms, pool, tennis, one of the best places to stay in Provence. AE.

LAMBESC. Restaurant. *Moulin Tante Yvonne* (E), rue Raspail (tel. 42-28-02-46). Closed Feb., Aug., Tues., Wed. and Thurs. Picturesque 15th-century oil mill converted into delightful, popular restaurant still presided over by Aunt Yvonne in person; reservations essential.

MANOSQUE. *Hostellerie La Fuste* (E), 6½ km. (4 miles) southeast via D907 and D4 (tel. 92-72-05-95). 10 rooms. Closed Sun. for dinner and Mon. Thoroughly deluxe 17th-century coaching inn; lovely terrace meals, *nouvelle cuisine* versions of regional specialties. AE, DC, MC, V.

MEYRARGUES. *Château Meyrargues* (E), (tel. 42-57-50-32). 14 rooms. Closed Nov. through Jan.; restaurant also closed Sun. for dinner and Mon. Imposing 12th-century château, baronial and romantic, perched on hilltop with sweeping views; quiet. AE, DC.

NÎMES. *Imperator* (E), pl. A. Briand (tel. 66-21-90-30). 61 rooms. Closed Feb. Central, airconditioned, with tiny garden and a good restaurant, *L'Enclos de la Fontaine,* closed Sat. for lunch and Feb. AE, DC, MC, V. *Cheval Blanc et Arènes* (M), 1 pl. Arènes (tel. 66-67-20-03). 50 rooms. Right opposite Roman arena; large rooms (some airconditioned). Restaurant. AE, DC, MC, V. *Louvre* (M), 2 sq. Couronne (tel. 66-67-22-75). 35 rooms. 17th-century mansion in town center, comfortable, with good-value restaurant. AE, DC, MC, V. *Michel* (I), 14 blvd. Amiral-Courbet (tel. 66-67-26-23). 28 rooms. Close to major sights; modest but well modernized; no restaurant. AE, DC, MC, V. *Milan* (I), 17 av. Feuchères (tel. 66-29-29-90). 32 rooms. Right by station; no restaurant. AE, MC, V.

Restaurants. *Lisita* (M), 2 blvd. Arènes (tel. 66-67-29-15). Closed Aug. and Sat. By Roman arena; regional specialties. AE, DC, V. *Magister* (M), 5 rue Nationale (tel. 66-76-11-00). Closed Sun. (except public hols.). Original *nouvelle cuisine;* good-value *menus,* also (I); nice modern decor. AE, DC, V.

NOVES. *Auberge Noves* (E), rte. Châteaurenard (tel. 90-94-19-21). 22 rooms. Closed Jan. and Feb.; restaurant also closed Wed. for lunch. Luxurious converted manor-house with large garden and pool in lovely open country; superb, imaginative cuisine, mostly "new." AE, DC, MC, V.

ORANGE. *Louvre et Terminus* (M), 89 av. Mistral (tel. 90-34-10-08). Closed mid-Dec. to mid-Jan. Just by station; most rooms airconditioned; restaurant; half-board terms compulsory in season. V *Arène* (I), pl. Langes (tel. 90-34-10-95). Closed Nov. to mid-Dec. 30 rooms. Central (close to Roman theater) but quiet; no restaurant. AE, MC, V.

At **Rochegude,** 14 km. (9 miles) north, *Château Rochegude* (E), (tel. 75-04-81-88). 29 rooms. Closed Nov. to mid-Mar.; restaurant also closed Mon. for lunch. Splendid Relais et Châteaux member with 12th-century keep (the rest dates from 17th and 18th centuries), lovely grounds, pool, tennis and elegant restaurant. AE, DC, MC, V.

Restaurants. *Pigraillet* (M), chemin Colline St.-Eutrope (tel. 90-34-44-25). Closed Mon., Sun. for dinner and Jan. to mid-Feb. Attractive building on hill above town, good-value newish cuisine. AE, DC. *Côté Cour* (I), 5 impasse Parliament (tel. 90-34-55-57). Closed Sun. and Mon. Convenient to Roman theater; some tables outside. AE, DC, V.

PONT-DU-GARD. At **Castillon-du-Gard,** 4 km. (2½ miles) away, *Le Vieux Castillon* (E), (tel. 66-37-00-77). 35 rooms. Closed Jan. to mid-Mar. Elegant Relais et Châteaux member in medieval village; pool, tennis and restaurant.

ROUSSILLON. *Mas Garrigon* (E), rte. St.-Saturnin (tel. 90-05-63-22). 8 rooms. Restaurant closed mid-Nov. through Dec., Sun. for dinner and Mon. Provençal-style building just outside town in country setting; pool, good cuisine. AE, DC, MC, V. *Résidence des Ocres* (I), (tel. 90-75-60-50). 15 rooms. Closed Feb. and last half Nov. Neat and modern, with airconditioned rooms, garden, but no restaurant. MC, V.

Restaurants. *David* (M), pl. Poste (tel. 90-05-60-13). Closed Jan. through Mar., Mon. and Tues. (except mid-June to mid-Sept.). Well-known for classical cuisine; fine views. DC, V. *Tarasque* (M), rue Casteau (tel. 90-75-63-86). Closed Feb. to mid-Mar. and Wed. Delicious regional cuisine; reservations essential. AE, DC, MC, V. *Val Fées* (M), rue Casteau (tel. 90-75-64-99). Closed Wed. for dinner and Thurs. except in summer. Pleasant ambience, good-value newish cuisine, particularly good desserts. AE, DC, MC.

ST.-RÉMY-DE-PROVENCE. *Château Alpilles* (E), on D13 (tel. 90-92-03-33). 18 rooms. Closed mid-Nov. to mid-Mar. Grand 19th-century building set in delightful grounds, once frequented by France's literary lions; very comfortable; grilled food and snacks served by pool in summer. AE, DC, MC, V. *Château Roussan* (E), 2 km. (1¼ miles) outside town on Tarascon road (tel. 90-92-11-63). 12 rooms. Closed mid-Oct. to around Easter. 18th-century manor-house run by charming owners, with rambling, romantic garden; no restaurant. V.

Le Castelet Alpilles (M), pl. Mireille (tel. 90-92-07-21). 19 rooms. Closed mid-Nov. to mid-Mar. Provençal architecture, attractive gardens and restaurant. AE, DC, V. *Arts* (I), 30 blvd. Victor-Hugo (tel. 90-92-08-50). 17 rooms. Closed Jan. through Mar.; restaurant also closed Wed. Lively and bohemian, crammed with colorful paintings; good regional cooking; very good-value *menus.* AE.

Restaurant. *Jardin de Frederic* (M), 8 blvd. Gambetta (tel. 90-92-27-76). Closed Nov. through Jan. and Tues. Friendly and popular bistrot with good *menus.* V.

STES.-MARIES-DE-LA-MER. *Galoubet* (M), rte. Cacharel (tel. 90-97-82-17). 20 rooms. Closed last week in Dec. and mid-Jan. to mid-Mar. In town, with pool but no restaurant.

Ranch-hotels outside town: *Mas de la Fouque* (E), 4 km. (2½ miles) northwest on road to Aigues-Mortes (tel. 90-47-81-02). 13 rooms. Closed Nov. through Mar.; restaurant also closed Tues. Chic yet friendly, with great views over Camargue, pool; good regional meals in restaurant (M). AE, DC, V. *Pont des Bannes* (E), north on D570 (Arles road), (tel. 90-47-81-09). 20 rooms. Closed mid-Oct. through Mar. Genuine *gardians'* huts now the last word in deluxe comfort; pool, good restaurant, gipsy music some nights.

Le Boumian (M), 1½ km. (1 mile) north on D570 (Arles road), (tel. 90-47-81-15). 28 rooms. Closed Jan. to mid-Feb. Pleasant rooms overlooking pool; garden and restaurant. AE, DC, V. *Etrier Camarguais* (M), chemin Bas des Launes (just off D570), (tel. 90-47-81-14). 33 rooms. Closed mid-Nov. through Mar.; restaurant also closed Mon. (except in July and Aug.). Attractive views; pool, disco, restaurant. AE, DC, MC, V.

Restaurants. *Brûleur Loups* (M), av. Leroy (tel. 90-97-83-31). Closed mid-Nov. to mid-Mar., Tues. for dinner and Wed. (except in Aug. and Sept.). Good-value regional cuisine served on flower-covered terrace on fine days. AE. *Hippocampe* (I), rue Pelletan (tel. 90-97-80-91). Closed mid-Nov. to mid-Mar. and Tues. (except July through Sept.). Quite near beach, friendly; also has 4 rooms.

SALON-DE-PROVENCE. 5 km. (3 miles) northeast via D16, *Abbaye Ste.-Croix* (E), (tel. 90-56-24-55). 24 rooms. Closed Nov. through Feb. Restaurant closed Mon. for lunch. Elegantly converted 12th-century abbey (Relais et Châteaux member) with pool and excellent restaurant. AE, DC, MC, V.

Restaurant. *Robin* (E), 1 blvd. Clemenceau (tel. 90-56-06-53). Closed Sun. for dinner, Mon., and two weeks in Feb. Tasty *nouvelle* regional specialties; reservations essential. AE, DC, MC.

TARASCON. *Provence* (M), 7 blvd. Victor-Hugo (tel. 90-91-06-43). 11 rooms. Closed mid-Dec. to mid-Jan. Central and good-value, with well-planned, airconditioned rooms; no restaurant. DC, MC, V. *St.-Jean* (I), 24 blvd. Victor-Hugo (tel. 90-91-13-87). 12 rooms. Closed mid-Dec. to mid-Jan.; restaurant also closed Wed. (except July and Aug.). Modest but nicely decorated rooms; restaurant has reputation for good value. AE, DC, MC, V.

UZÈS. *Entraigues* (M), pl. Evêché (tel. 66-22-32-68). 18 rooms. Closed Jan. Restaurant also closed Tues. and Wed. for lunch. Tastefully converted 15th-century mansion; grillroom (I) for light meals. DC, MC, V.

At **Arpaillargues**, 4 km. (2½ miles) west via D982, *Château d'Arpaillargues Hotel d'Agoult* (E), (tel. 66-22-14-48). 26 rooms. Closed Nov. to mid-Mar., restaurant also closed Wed. (except in July and Aug.). Elegantly furnished 18th-century manor-house in large grounds; sophisticated ambience, pool, tennis; restaurant with open fireplace, mostly *nouvelle cuisine.* AE, DC, MC, V.

VAISON-LA-ROMAINE. *Beffroi* (M), rue Evêché (tel. 90-36-04-71). 21 rooms. Closed mid-Nov. to mid-Mar. (except second half Dec.); restaurant also closed Mon. and for lunch on Tues. Quaint 16th-century mansion in old town, furnished with antiques; good-value restaurant serves true classical cuisine. AE, DC, MC, V.

Restaurants. At **Séguret**, 9½ km. (6 miles) west, *La Table du Comtat* (M), (tel. 90-46-91-49). Closed mid-Jan. through Feb.; restaurant also closed Tues. for dinner and Wed. 15th-century building with sweeping views, pool and very good food; reservations essential. Also has 8 peaceful, well-furnished rooms. AE, DC, MC. *Domaine de Cabasse* (M), (tel. 90-46-91-12). Closed mid-Sept. to mid-Mar. Set among vineyards, a friendly inn with mouthwatering cooking; also has 8 comfortable (I) rooms and pool. V.

VILLENEUVE-LÈS-AVIGNON. *Le Prieuré* (E), 7 pl. Chapitre (tel. 90-25-18-20). 35 rooms. Closed mid-Nov. to mid-Mar.; restaurant also closed Sun. for dinner. Gracious and sophisticated converted priory, with lovely garden, tennis, and pool; elegantly served classical cuisine, but prices are steep. AE, DC, MC, V. *Magnaneraie* (M), 37 rue Camp-de-Bataille (tel. 90-25-11-11). 21 rooms. Lovely 15th-century house on a hill; elegant décor, pool, tennis; excellent restaturant (M) with outdoor meals in fine weather. AE, DC, MC, V. *Hostellerie Vieux Moulin* (I), rue Vieux Moulin (tel. 90-25-00-26). 14 rooms. Closed Nov. and Dec. Very pleasant hotel in former windmill overlooking the Rhône; boat trips. Restaurant.

 TOURS AND EXCURSIONS. By Bus. From Aix-en-Provence, the tourist office arranges excursions with English-speaking guides, daily, Easter through Oct. Half-day itineraries include: Silvacane Abbey and Lubéron châteaux; St.-Rémy, Glanum and Les Baux; Cassis (no guide). Full-day trips: the Camargue; Fontaine de Vaucluse and Avignon; the Pont du Gard, Beaucaire, Tarascon and Arles.

At Arles, the tourist office has a program of visits (mid-June to mid-Sept.) with excellent guides, organized under the auspices of the *Caisse Nationale des Monuments Historiques*, as well as various city tours, including "In the Footsteps of Van Gogh." Excursions to Aigues-Mortes, Avignon, the Camargue, Nîmes and Les Stes.-Maries-de-la-Mer are run by *Arles Voyages* (tel. 90-96-88-73) and *Camargue Voyages* (tel. 90-96-13-25).

From Avignon, a variety of excursions to major sights and towns in Provence are run by the tourist office (but not in July and Aug.) and by private companies: details from the tourist office.

From Marseille, day trips once a week, called "Camargue and its Wildlife Reserve," will take you to Arles and Albaron, then on a 1½-hr. paddlesteamer trip through the Camargue, and to Les Stes.-Maries-de-la-Mer and various other Camargue sights.

From Nîmes, there are city tours and a full program of excursions to local sights (mainly mid-July to mid-Sept.), some with guides from the *Caisse Nationale des Monuments Historiques.*

By Jeep. An excellent way of seeing the Camargue and photographing its fauna and flora is to go on a "photo safari" in a jeep (suitable for elderly or disabled people, too). Trips, from 1½ hrs. to around 9 hrs., depart from Les Stes.-Maries-de-la-Mer frequently, Apr. to Sept. Contact *M. Gallon,* 14 av. Van-Gogh (tel. 90-97-86-93 or 90-47-84-12); or call 90-98-60-31 in Arles.

Trips into the wine region around Aix-en-Provence, visiting cellars and tasting wine, also visiting a wild boar breeding farm and several little known châteaux and museums, are offered by *La Piste des Vins,* 16 rue Barthélemy-Niollon, 13710 Fuveau (tel. 91-62-65-63). The tourist office in Aix-en Provence can supply you with full details.

By Boat. Various short canal trips can be made from Aigues-Mortes into the heart of the Camargue in cabin cruisers or more modest craft, or northwards to Arles or Beaucaire and Tarascon. Contact *Cap au Sud,* 1 av. Pasteur, 13100 Aix-en-Provence (tel. 42-21-52-85) or ask at tourist offices. There are other departures from Les Stes.-Maries-de-la-Mer in the *Tiki III* or *Le Camargue* (ask at tourist office); and weekly boat trips, also into the Camargue, setting out by bus from the tourist office at Nîmes.

On Foot. The Arles tourist office organizes nature rambles in the interesting countryside around the town, and to Montmajour Abbey. The Avignon tourist office organizes city walking tours daily at 10–11.30 A.M.

 SIGHTSEEING DATA. For general hints on museums and historic buildings, and an important warning, see "Sightseeing" in *Facts at Your Fingertips.* Admission to many museums and monuments is reduced for children, students and senior citizens, and there is reduced or free admission for all on certain days; enquire locally.

AIGUES-MORTES. Tour de Constance and **Remparts** (Ramparts), (tel. 68-51-01-55). Open daily, Apr. through Sept., 9–12, 2–6; Oct. through Mar., 10–12, 2–5. Guided tours available. Closed certain public hols. Half price on Sun. and public hols.

AIX-EN-PROVENCE. Atelier de Cézanne (Cézanne's Studio), 9. av. Paul-Cézanne. Open daily except Tues. and public hols., 10–12, 2–5 (to 6 in June to Sept.). Audiovisual presentation available.

Fondation Vasarély, av. Marcel-Pagnol, Jas-de-Bouffan. Open daily except Tues., 9.30–12.30, 2–6.

Musée Arbaud (Ceramic Museum), 2 a rue Quatre-Septembre. Open daily except Sun., public hols. and Oct. 2–5.

Musée Granet (Art Museum), pl. St.-Jean-de-Malte. Open daily except Tues. and public hols., 10–12, 2–6; temporary exhibits open to 8 on weekdays.

Musée d'Histoire Naturelle (Natural History Museum), 6 rue Esperiat. Open daily except Sun. and public hols., 10–12, 2–6.

Musée du Vieil Aix (Local History Museum), 17 rue Gaston-de-Saporta. Open daily except Mon., 10–12, 2–5 (to 6, Apr. to Sept.); also closed public hols.

Musée des Tapisseries (Tapestry Museum), Ancien Archevêché. Open Feb. through Dec., 10–12, 2–5 (to 6, June to Sept.). Closed on Tues. Appointments only (tel. 42-21-05-78).

Pavillon Vendôme, 32 rue Célony. Open daily except Tues., 10–12, 2–5 (to 6.30, June to Sept.).

ANSOUIS. Château. Open daily, except Tues., 2.30–6.30. Closed Christmas and New Year's Day.

APT. Cathédrale Ste.-Anne. *Trésor* (treasury) can be visited July and Aug. only, at 11 A.M. and 5 P.M., daily except Sun., Mon. and public hols.

ARLES. The sights of Arles have the same opening hours: daily, June to mid-Sept., 8.30–12.30, 2–7; shorter hours for the rest of the year—inquire locally. Special tickets *(billets globaux)*, costing around 20 fr. (15 fr. for students and children) cover all the city's museums and monuments; they need not be used on a single day.

Alyscamps, av. Alyscamps (tel. 90-96-83-17).

Arènes (Roman arena), (tel. 90-96-93-37).

Cloître St.-Trophime (cloisters), entrance in pl. République beside church.

Crèche (giant Christmas crib), Chapelle de la Charité (entrance beside Hotel Jules César). Open daily, 9–12, 2–7.

Musée d'Art Païen (Museum of Pagan Art), pl. République.

Musée d'Art Chrétien (Museum of Christian Art), pl. République.

Musée Réattu, 10 rue Grand-Prieuré (tel. 90-96-37-68).

Muséon Arlaten, rue République (tel. 90-96-08-23).

Palais Constantin (Baths of Emperor Constantine), entrance in rue D-Maïsto; key available from Musée Réattu (see above) if there is no attendant to let you in.

Théâtre Antique (Roman Theater), entrance in rue Calade (tel. 90-96-93-30).

AVIGNON. Musée Calvet, Hôtel de Villeneuve-Martignan, 65 rue Jospeh-Vernet (tel. 90-86-33-84). Open daily except Tues., 10–12, 2–6. Closed public hols.

Palais des Papes (Palace of the Popes), (tel. 90-86-03-32). Open daily, Oct. through Mar., 9–11.15, 2–4.15; Apr. through June, 9–11.30, 2–5.30; July through Sept., 9–6. Guided tours only (except July through Sept.).

Petit Palace (Small Palace), pl. Palais des Papes (tel. 90-86-44-58). Open daily except Tues. and public hols., 9.15–12, 2–6. Free Sun. in winter.

LES BAUX. Ville Morte (ruined town), including *Château, Musée d'Art Moderne* (Museum of Modern Art) and *Musée Lapidaire* (Sculpture Museum). Open daily, May through Sept., 8.30–8; Oct. through Apr., 9–7; tickets from Musée Lapidaire. After 7 or 8 P.M. you can visit the *Ville Morte* free of charge, but all the buildings are closed.

BEAUCAIRE. Château, (tel. 66-59-25-20). Open daily except Tues., Apr. through Sept., 10–12, 2.15–6.30; Oct. through Mar., 10–12, 1.30–5.30.

CAMARGUE. Musée Camarguais, Mas du Pont-de-Rousty, Albaron (tel. 90-97-10-82). Open daily 9–12, 2–6.

Parc Ornithologique (Bird Sanctuary). Open daily, 8–8.

Réserve Zoologique (Nature Reserve). Open only to bonafide naturalists and scientists requesting permission in advance. Write: Directeur, *Réserve Zoologique de Camargue,* 1 rue Stendhal, 13200 Arles.

CARPENTRAS. The four museums listed below have the same opening hours: Apr. through Sept., 10–12, 2–6 (to 4 in winter). A single ticket covers all four and the cathedral treasury.

Ancienne Cathédrale St.-Siffrein. To visit the *Trésor* (treasury) apply to the nearby Bibliothèque Inguimbertine, which is open 9.30–12, 2–7 (except Mon. A.M., Sat. P.M., Sun. and public hols.).

Musée Comtadin, Hôtel d'Allemand, rue Fornery (ground floor).

Musée Duplessis, Hôtel d'Allemand, rue Fornery (first floor).

Musée Sobirats, rue Collège.

Musée d'Archéologie (Archeological Museum), rue Carmel Stes.-Maries.

Synagogue, rue Sous-Préfecture. If ticket office closed, ask at the cafe opposite. Open daily 10–12, 3–5, closed weekends.

CHÂTEAUNEUF-DU-PAPE. Musée Vigneron (Wine Museum), Caves du Père Anselme. Open daily, 8–12, 2–6.

ENTRECASTEAUX. Château, (tel. 94-04-43-95). Open daily, Apr. through Sept., 10–8; winter, 10–6.

FONTAINE DE VAUCLUSE. Musée. Open daily 9–12, 2–7.

FONTVIEILLE. Moulin de Daudet (Daudet's Mill). Open daily, Apr. through Sept., 9–12, 2–7 (to 6 in winter).

GORDES. Château, housing *Musée Vasarély,* (tel. 90-72-02-89). Open daily except Tues., 10–12, 2–6.

Village des Bories (Stone Hut Village). Open daily, Feb. to mid-Nov., 9 to sunset; mid-Nov. through Jan., weekends only, 10 to sunset.

MONTMAJOUR. Abbaye Open daily except Tues. and certain public hols., Apr. through Sept., 9–12, 2–6 (to 5 in winter).

MOUSTIERS-STE.-MARIE. Musée de la Faïence (Pottery Museum). Open daily Apr. through Oct., 9–12, 2–7 (to 5 in winter).

NÎMES. All museums and historic buildings in Nîmes are open Palm Sun. through Sept., 9–12, 2–6 (to 5 in winter); but they are closed Sun. A.M., Oct. through Apr., and most public hols. A convenient single ticket for them all costs around 20 fr.: ask for it at the first place you visit (reduced price for those under 16, students and the disabled).

Chapelle des Jésuites (Jesuit Chapel), Grande-Rue.

Maison Carrée, rue Général-Perrier (tel. 66-67-25-57).

Musée Archéologique (Archeological Museum), 13 blvd. Amiral-Courbet (tel. 66-67-25-57).

Musée des Beaux-Arts (Fine Arts Museum), rue Cité-Foulc (tel. 66-67-38-21).

Musée d'Histoire Naturelle et de Préhistoire (Natural and Prehistory Museum), 13 blvd. Amiral-Courbet (tel. 66-67-39-14).

Musée du Vieux Nîmes (Local History Museum), palais de l'Ancien Evêché (tel. 66-36-00-64).

ORANGE. Arc de Triomphe (Triumphal Arch), av. Arc-de-Triomphe.

Théâtre Antique (Roman theater), pl. Frères-Mounet. Open daily, June through Sept., 9–6.15; Oct. through May, 9–12, 2–5. Closed on public hols.

PONT DU GARD. Guided tours in July and Aug. only, generally at 10 A.M. and 3 and 5 P.M., leaving from tourist office on right bank of river.

ST.-RÉMY DE PROVENCE. Glanum (Greek and Roman ruins). Open Apr. through Sept., daily except Tues., with guided tours at 10 and 11 A.M., 3, 4 and

5 P.M.; extra tours June through Sept. at 9 A.M. and 6 P.M. Open Mar. and Oct. weekends only. Half price on Sun. and public hols.

Hôtel de Sade (museum of finds from Glanum). Open Easter through Sept., 9–12, 4–7. Closed Tues. in summer and weekends in winter.

Tour du Cardinal (Cardinal's Tower), Vieux Chemin d'Arles (tel. 90-92-15-92). Guided visits daily on request (call first).

ST.-MAXIMIN-LA-STE.-BAUME. Couvent Royal (Royal Monastery), (tel. 94-78-01-93). Open Apr. through Sept., daily 9–11.30, 2.30–6. Guided tours at 10.30, 3 and 5. In winter call first.

LES STES.-MARIES-DE-LA-MER. Musée Baroncelli (museum of Camargue traditions), rue Espelly. Open Apr. through Sept., 9–12, 2–7; winter, 9.30–12, 2.30–5 (closed Wed. Oct. through May and Dec.).

SALON-DE-PROVENCE. L'Empéri (château housing Museum of French Military History), (tel. 90-56-22-36). Open 10–12, 2–6 (to 6.30 in summer). Closed Tues., Jan. 1, May 1, Christmas Day.

SÉNANQUE. Abbaye (Abbey), near Gordes (tel. 90-72-02-05). Open daily June through Sept., 10–1, 2–7; Oct. through May, 10–12, 2–6. Guided tours during school vacations.

SILVACANE. Abbaye (Abbey), at La-Roque-d'Anthéron (tel. 42-50-41-69). Open daily except Tues., Apr. through Sept., 10–12, 2–7 (to 5 in winter).

TARASCON. Château du Roy René, (tel. 90-91-01-93). Open daily except Tues. and public hols., Apr. through Sept., 9–12, 2–7 (to 6 in winter). Guided tours only. Half price Sun. and public hols.

LE THORONET. Abbaye (Abbey), Le Luc (tel. 94-73-87-13). Open daily, May through Sept., 10–12, 2–6 (to 4 or 5 in winter). Closed Tues. and certain public hols.

UZÈS. Duché (Castle), (tel. 66-22-18-96). Open daily, Palm Sun. through Sept., 9.30–12, 2–6.30; winter, 10.30–12, 2–4.30.

Musée Municipal, Ancien Evêché (tel. 66-22-68-88). Open June through Sept., daily except Tues., 3–6; rest of year, Sun. only, 3–6.

Muséon di Rodo (Automobile and Rail Museum), at Arpaillargues, 2 km. (1¼ miles) from Uzès. Open daily except Mon., 9–12, 2–7 (to 5 in winter).

Palais Episcopal (Bishop's Residence), housing *Musée d'Art et de Tradition de l'Uzège* (Regional Folklore Museum). Open June through Sept., daily except Mon.; rest of year afternoons only on Sat. and Sun.

VAISON-LA-ROMAINE. Ruines Romaines (Roman Ruins). Open daily, Apr. through June, 9–6 (10–6 on Sun.); July through Sept., 9–6.30 (10–6.30 on Sun.); winter, 9–12, 2–5 (opens at 10 on Sun.). Special *billets globaux* (tickets) for all monuments.

VILLENEUVE-LÈS-AVIGNON. Chartreuse du Val de Bénédiction (Charterhouse), rue de la République (tel. 90-25-05-46). Open daily, Apr. through Sept., 9–12, 2–6.30; winter, 10–12, 2–6.30. Half price on Sun.

Fort-St.-André (tel. 90-25-45-35). Open Apr. through Sept., daily except public hols. 9–12, 2–6.30; winter, 10–12, 2–5. (Combined ticket for Charterhouse and fortress available).

Musée Municipal. Open Apr. through Sept., daily except Tues. and public hols., 10.30–12.30, 3–7.30; winter, 10–12, 2–5.

Tour de Philippe-le-Bel (Philip the Fair's Tower), (tel. 90-25-42-03). Open Apr. through Sept., daily except Tues. and Feb., 10.30–12.30, 3–7.30; winter, 10–12, 2–5.

SHOPPING. Provençal print fabrics are very attractive and can be bought made up into scarves, tea cosies, etc., or in lengths, from shops in Arles (rue Calade and rue Jean-Jaurès) and Aix-en-Provence (Vieil Aix or old town). *Santons* are carved miniature figures in wood or clay for the Christmas crib; you can buy them in the St.-Trophime area of Arles and can also see them being made at *Atelier Ferriol,* 2 chemin de Barriol, Arles (tel. 90-93-31-46), daily, except Sun., 10–8. Good reproductions of Van Gogh's paintings are sold in Arles; the best shop is Hôtel St.-Trophime, 16 rue Calade.

Olive wood articles such as salad bowls can be found in craft shops in all main centers. The lavender of Provence is particularly fragrant, and lavender bags and lavender water make good gifts to take home. Soaps fragrant with natural flower scents are a specialty of Aix: try *La Provence Gourmande,* 66 rue Boulegon in Vieil Aix, where they are prettily packed in little wicker baskets. This store also has some good food specialties: jars of herbs and spices, *caviar d'aubergine* (a tasty spread made with aubergines), and boxes of diamond-shaped marzipan candies, *calissons d'Aix.* Olive oil and local wines are other good, if less transportable, buys in this part of France. So are attractive bunches of dried flowers.

LANGUEDOC AND ROUSSILLON

Modern Resorts and Ancient Fortresses

The region that today bears this name borders the Mediterranean from the Pyrenees to the Rhône delta, and is in two halves. First, the lower Languedoc, around Montpellier, the eastern part of that vast historic province where people spoke "the tongue of *oc*" ("yes" for them was *oc*, not *oïl* or *oui* as in the north). This sun-baked land of vine-clad plains and dry, stony hills has been a crossroads of many civilizations since pre-Roman days. Before the Cathar massacres, it saw the flowering of the gentle, courteous age of troubadours with their courts of love. That glory is now lost, but the local people retain an assertive sense of regional identity, and a mistrust of all that comes from Paris.

For miles on all sides stretch the vineyards. This area produces nearly half of France's cheap wine, but so cheap is it that many growers claim they cannot make a living, and in recent years they have repeatedly been in revolt, blocking the roads with tractors and even attacking the police. They have made common cause with the local separatist movement of young hotheads who dream vaguely of a free Occitania (the historic name for southern France) and daub walls with their "OC" symbol. Politically, their influence is slight.

This is France's deep south, where under the dazzling sun the pace of life is easy; a land of cypress and cicada, where small red-roofed towns lie sleepily beneath the walls of mighty old fortresses, such as Carcassonne. Yet, without losing its charm, Languedoc is now facing modern change. Huge modern seaside resorts line the coast; new factories and new irrigation schemes have arrived. Quiet, aristocratic Montpellier, the regional capital, has mushroomed into a commercial metropolis.

Even further south is the small province of Roussillon, sometimes known as French Catalonia. It is prosperous, thanks to farming and tourism: spas and ski resorts in the Pyrenees vie with the beaches of the Vermilion Coast, while the fertile plain around the capital, Perpignan, has some of the richest farms in France, producing fruit and early vegetables. Like Brittany and the Basque country, Roussillon is a corner of France that feels different: its flavor is Spanish (not surprisingly, for Roussillon belonged to Spain till 1659), and the people here are Catalans, brothers to their neighbors in the much larger Spanish Catalonia around Barcelona. Today, local cultural self-expression is all the rage: the Catalan language has been revived, folk festivals multiply, and the red-and-yellow Catalan flag flies defiantly over Perpignan. A minority—but only a tiny minority—want to politicize this trend, to detach Roussillon from France and federate it with Spanish Catalonia.

From the Cerdagne to Prades

Southeast of Andorra, the Toulouse–Barcelona main road leads to the frontier town of Bourg-Madame. Here the Spanish townlet of Llivia forms an enclave inside France, the result of a concession won by Spain when she ceded Roussillon in 1659. We are now in the Cerdagne, an upland plain of meadows and pine forests, backed by snowy mountains. Its altitude is 1,066 meters (3,500 ft.), yet it seems like a pastoral valley, and its sunshine level is the highest in France. Hence its choice as the main site of French experiments with solar energy. Europe's largest solar furnace, at Odeillo near Font-Romeu, is a massive square building where 62 swiveling mirrors reflect the sun on to one giant concave mirror; some of the scientists live in strange little houses with ugly glass façades, heated by solar energy.

The sun brings skiers as well as scientists to the Cerdagne—Font-Romeu is a superbly equipped resort where Olympic champions often train. From here it is a mile's walk through the forest to the Hermitage, shrine of the strange Vierge de l'Invention. This austere Romanesque madonna is black with age, and through having been buried during the Arab invasions, like many sculptures of that time. The name "Invention" (discovery) comes from the local legend whereby this Virgin was accidentally unearthed, centuries later, by a bull scratching at the ground. Each year, on September 8, the statue is solemnly carried to the church at Odeillo, then back to the shrine on Trinity Sunday.

From the Cerdagne, the road to Perpignan skirts the fortress of Mont-Louis (built by Vauban as a defense against the Spaniards), then descends a steep and winding valley. Just off this road is Vernet-les-Bains, an elegantly laid-out but now fading spa, once much colonized by the British, like Pau. The classic excursion from here is to the remote mountain abbey of St.-Martin-du-Canigou, accessible only by jeep or—preferably—a 30-minute walk up a steep path. Built just after A.D. 1000, the abbey fell into ruins after the Revolution, but has been carefully restored during this century and is now used for retreats by laity and priests alike. Austerely beautiful, it lies lost to view in the folds of Mount Canigou, the highest Pyrenean peak in Roussillon.

Further down the valley is the small town of Prades, the center of a rich district of peach, cherry and apricot orchards. The cellist Pablo Casals lived here for many years before his death, and an annual music festival is held in his honor. Just to the south stands the beautiful abbey of St.-Michel-de-Cuxa, in the 11th century the leading church of Roussillon. During the Revolution it was abandoned and later pillaged, but in 1913 an American sculptor managed to collect many of the missing bits of the cloisters, which today have been reassembled at Fort Tryon Park, Manhattan. The abbey itself has been restored: its cloister, though incomplete, is of rare grace. The place is occupied by Catalan Benedictines, who use it as a center for the propagation of Catalan culture. The Casals Festival concerts are also held in the abbey.

Perpignan, Sardañas, and the Côte Vermeille

Perpignan, capital of the so-called "kingdom of Mallorca" in the 13th century, is today the largest Catalan town (with a population of 120,000) after Barcelona. Legend claims it takes its name from a cowherd, Père Pinya, who was magically guided to found a city on the most fertile spot in the valley. It is a pleasant southerly town, with promenades lined with planes and palm trees. Its most interesting building is the Castillet (citadel), an old brick fortress housing a museum of local arts and traditions. Worth a visit too are the 14th-century cathedral of St.-Jean; the palace of the kings of Mallorca; and the elegant Loge de Mer, built in 1397 and then for centuries used as a trade center where maritime disputes were handled.

In the little square beside the Loge, the locals dance the *sardaña,* the national dance of all Catalonia, on summer evenings. If you want to see more spontaneous *sardañas,* go to almost any local village square on a summer weekend, or to the festivals at Arles-sur-Tech or Amélie-les-Bains (or, better still, to Barcelona). Oddly, this is not a traditional dance but a fairly recent invention.

East of Perpignan the coast is flat, and resorts such as Argelès, a campers' paradise with dozens of huge campsites, have wide sandy beaches backed by pine woods. A few miles south, where the Pyrenees stumble into the sea, is the Côte Vermeille (Vermilion Coast), named after its reddish rocks and hills. Banyuls is a pleasant if cluttered resort, whose vines on their steep slopes produce the famous sweet Banyuls wine (you can visit the old wine cellars, and get a free tasting). The prettiest resort is Collioure, which has kept much of its charm despite the tourist hordes who descend on this picture-postcard fishing village, once lived in (and painted so often), by Matisse, Dufy and others. The village with its narrow cobbled streets lies below a vast 12th-century castle, right on the sea; there are fishing boats drawn up along the pebbly beach, their bows holding the great globes of the special lamps the fishermen use to lure their fish at night.

Places to visit inland from here are Elne, with its superb cathedral cloister, and the delightful old town of Céret, where Picasso worked for some years. Its museum has canvases by him and other painters of his period. North of Perpignan is the fortress of Salses, built by the Spaniards in the 15th century. Important prehistoric remains have been excavated near here.

Narbonne and Carcassonne

North of Salses we cross into Languedoc and are soon in Narbonne, today a quietish little town but in Roman times a major city, the capital of the province of Gallia Narbonensis. Its port, today silted up, was then the busiest in the western Mediterranean. Narbonne's chief glory, and its oddity, is the cathedral of St.-Just, begun in 1272 but never completed: when the choir had been built, the local Consuls refused to let the nave be added—and so it remains today. It is one of the tallest Gothic cathedrals in France, little lower than Beauvais. The cloister leads to the massive fortified Palace of the Archbishops, housing museums of art and ancient history. Visit, too, the lapidary museum (in a deconsecrated church). An elegant 16th-century building, the Maison des Trois Nourrices (House of the Three Wet-Nurses) is so named because the cornice of its fine Renaissance window is supported by Raquel Welch-like caryatids!

Southwest of Narbonne is the superb 11th-century Cistercian abbey of Fontfroide, with a noble cloister and a peaceful garden lined with cypresses. Westward range the strange, wild limestone hills of the Corbières, which give their name to the best wine of Languedoc. Further west is Limoux, a town producing a popular champagne-type wine (the cellars can be visited).

And so to fabulous Carcassonne, Europe's largest medieval fortress and one of the most complete. If you can, see it first at night, from a distance, when the mighty circle of towers and battlements, aloft on their hilltop, are brilliantly floodlit. The newer town, on the plain, is unexciting. Our concern is with La Cité, the walled city, and its epic history. Parts of its walls were first built by the Romans, then the Visigoths enlarged it into a great fortress in the 5th century (the present line of the towers is theirs). Charlemagne laid siege to the place for five years in the 9th century, cutting off all supplies—and thereby hangs a tale. According to an anecdote cooked up later by the troubadours, a certain Dame Carcas broke the siege by ringing an alarm bell, then stuffing a pig with the last grain remaining in the city, in full view of the besiegers. She threw the pig off the battlements: it burst, scattering grain. Charlemagne was thus convinced that the city must have plenty to waste, and called off the siege. So the place, in her honor, was called "Carcas Sonne" (Carcas rings). We need not believe this punning joke: the Romans had long previously known it as Carcaso.

In the 13th century, the fortress fell to the anti-Cathar crusaders, and Simon de Montfort took it as a command post for his routine massacres. St. Louis and his son Philip the Bold then strengthened the fortifications, giving the place the appearance it has today. It was by now self-contained enough to withstand any siege: a wheat-grinding mill was built, smiths forged hinges and armour, a mint coined money, and in the great Narbonne Tower was a cistern able to hold six months' supply of fresh water. The cathedral of St.-Nazaire was built, as well as an open air theater which is still used today.

After the annexation of Roussillon in 1659 the fortress lost much of its military importance and slowly fell into ruin. Finally, in 1844, Viollet-le-Duc was commissioned to rebuild the battlements, towers and cathedral—the world's first restoration on such a scale. This great architect has been much criticized for doing too good a touch-up job; at close quarters much of his detail looks artificial, like a Hollywood cardboard set. But time is finally mellowing his work, which now blends less uneasily with the original elements. And at least he restored the original skyline of towers and turrets, to provide full romantic effect from a distance.

You can take a guide around the city, or wander at leisure, admiring the intricate fortifications of the two castellated walls, one inside the other, about a mile in circumference. The views from the battlements towards the Pyrenees are stunning. Visit the cathedral, over-restored in places, but remarkable for its stained-glass rose windows, fine statues, elegant Romanesque nave and Gothic transepts. The city still has 500 permanent inhabitants, mostly poorer people—and its quaint medieval streets are lined with cheapjack souvenir shops, plus a few more elegant craft boutiques and a couple of pleasant restaurants.

The New Resorts: Pyramids and Nudists

Does this region share something of America's mania for building "the biggest?" Carcassonne, Europe's biggest fortress—and now, in modern times, the 193-km. (120-mile) Languedoc-Roussillon coastline is the scene of the biggest planned tourist development in European history.

This coast has wide sandy beaches, backed by saltwater lagoons, but till recently the mosquito reigned supreme and bathers were few. Then in 1963 the Gaullist government set about creating eight new resorts as an overspill for the near-saturated Riviera. The lagoons were dredged, the mosquitoes wiped out, and new marinas and a new road network built. When the project is finished, by 1990 or so, some 280,000 new tourist beds will have been provided. The futuristic design of resorts such as La Grande Motte may not appeal to lovers of old-world charm. But at least the project is proving a success with hundreds of thousands of foreign tourists, as well as French. And it has given a shot-in-the-arm to the economy of an area still too vulnerably dependent on its badly organized wine industry.

The northerly resorts, near Montpellier, are on the whole more attractive and popular than the southerly ones, near Perpignan, where the architecture is not so inspired and the winds too strong for comfort. From south to north, this is the picture:

St.-Cyprien has a pleasant country club with golf course, a good tennis school and some nice family hotels. At Port-Barcarès a Japanese-owned converted Greek passenger boat, the *Lydia,* has been towed on to the beach to serve as a nightclub, casino and restaurant; at Port-Leucate, the nudist village of Aphrodite is run by the British—of all people! Cap d'Agde, much further north, is in many ways the pleasantest of the resorts, a pastiche of a traditional fishing village, with pretty buildings in pastel shades. Next to it is the showpiece of tourism's fastest growth-sector: nudism. The nudist holiday town here, Europe's largest, has casinos, supermarkets, nightclubs, the lot, and accommodations for 20,000 lovely (or unlovely) bodies.

La Grande Motte, the most sophisticated and highly publicized of the resorts, is Brasilia-on-Sea, a Le Corbusier vision with motor yachts and beach parasols added. Its ranks of ten-story ziggurat pyramids contain holiday apartments, boutiques and discos. Some of the newest blocks are in weird shapes and colors (one resembles a giant fairground wheel). Not everyone may want to spend a holiday in these surrealistic pop-art surroundings, however jolly the colors and lavish the amenities, but La Grande Motte signals unmistakeably the face of the new France, and provides an intriguing contrast with the sleepy, classical hinterland. Nearby Port-Camargue is more exclusive, attracting a well-heeled yachting set.

Along the coast, a few old ports and fishing villages manage to survive the Brave New World. One of the quaintest is Gruissan, built in a circular shape beside a lagoon, and dominated by a ruined tower. But here too a new resort has sprung up on the edge of the sea, harmonizing quite well with the old village. It is a good place to set out for walking or riding excursions in the Clape chain of hills just behind the coast. Sète, further east, a lively, fair-sized town, is France's leading Mediterranean port after Marseille. The outdoor fish restaurants along the main canal are a delight. The poet Paul Valéry was born and lived in Sète, and a museum is devoted to him: beside it, on a hillside facing the sea, is the romantic cemetery where he was inspired to write his greatest poem, *Le cimetière marin*.

Montpellier, and the Surprises of the Hinterland

The regional capital has grown since World War II from dozy provincial town to busy metropolis. Its university is one of France's largest (Rabelais was a student here) and is noted for medicine and chemistry. Off the central square with its pleasant paved piazza is a snazzy commercial and shopping center, the Polygone. Yet Montpellier has not lost its old seigneurial charm. The narrow, largely traffic-free streets of the older quarter, on a low hill, are lined with elegant residences of the 17th and 18th centuries. Here too is one of France's best provincial museums, the Musée Fabre, and a handsome formal garden, the Peyrou.

The hinterland, where the mountains of the Cévennes and the Massif Central meet the plain, offers many fascinating surprises. This is *garrigue* country of stony hills covered with scrub and bush, opening to far horizons. The Pic de St.-Loup is a conical limestone peak rising up from the plain, with a ruined white castle on its ridge. Further north are the Grottes des Demoiselles, among the loveliest caves in France, containing enormous stalactites in many bizarre forms, one of them known as the Virgin and Child because of its shape. Southwest from here, St.-Guilhem-le-Désert is a remote and picturesque village, built in a ravine of the Hérault gorge. Its fine 10th-century abbey church has been shorn of its cloister—sold to the Metropolitan Museum in New York!

On the road from Montpellier to Béziers, take a look at Pézenas, a little town that was once the capital of lower Languedoc and today preserves intact its impressive ensemble of 15th- to 17th-century houses. The great dramatist Molière and his company gave many performances here and a festival is held annually in his honor. Béziers, a big modern city with one of France's best rugby teams, has a Museum of the History of Wine. Just to the west is the remarkable early Celtic settlement of Ensérune, unearthed on a hilltop. It dates back to at least 600 B.C. and had 8,000 inhabitants in the 3rd century B.C. The museum has an interesting collection of Celtic domestic objects.

Finally, on westwards to Minerve, an old village on a limestone cliff, dominating the vineyards below. Its now ruined castle was once a Cathar stronghold, besieged and captured by Simon de Montfort. He and his crusaders then burned 140 Cathars alive, watching the fires "with great joy," according to an eyewitness account. The villagers tell you this story today with seething indignation, as if it happened last year. After 750 years, at Montségur and Minerve, the martyrs' blood is not yet dry.

PRACTICAL INFORMATION FOR
LANGUEDOC-ROUSSILLON

TOURIST OFFICES. The two regional tourist offices for the whole of Languedoc-Roussillon—written enquiries only—are the *Comité Régional de Tourisme,* 12 rue France, 34000 Montpellier (tel. 67-60-55-42) and the *Fédération Régionale des Offices de Tourisme et des Syndicats d'Initiative,* 15 blvd. Camille-Pelletan, 11000 Carcassonne (tel. 68-25-41-32). In addition, the *départements* of Languedoc-Roussillon have their own tourist offices (again, written enquiries only): **Hérault,** *Comité Départemental de l'Hérault,* pl. Marcel-Godechot, 34000 Montpellier (tel. 67-54-20-66); **Aude,** *Comité Départemental de l'Aude,* 39 blvd. Barbès, 11000 Carcassonne (tel. 68-71-30-09); **Pyrénées-Orientales,** *Comité Départementale des Pyrénées Orientales,* Maison du Tourisme, Palais Consulaire, 66005 Perpignan (tel. 68-34-29-95). The Pyrenees area has an office in Paris: Maison des Pyrenees, 15 rue St.-Augustin, 75002 Paris (tel. 42-61-58-18). Five tourist offices on the motorways known as *la Languedocienne* (A9) and *la Catalane* (B9) provide a very useful last-minute hotel reservation service.

There are local tourist offices in the following towns: **Agde,** rue Louis Bages (tel. 67-94-29-68); **Argelès,** pl. Athènes (tel. 68-81-15-85); **Béziers,** 27 rue Quatre-Septembre (tel. 67-49-24-19); **Cap d'Agde,** Centre des Congrès (tel. 67-26-38-58); **Carcassonne,** blvd. Camille-Pelletan (tel. 68-25-07-04), and Porte Narbonnaise (tel. 68-25-68-81), (June through Sept.); and across from the rail station (July to Sept.) (tel. 68-71-44-73); **Castelnaudary,** pl. République (tel. 68-23-05-73), (closed mornings except June through Sept.); **Collioure,** av. C-Pelletan (tel. 68-82-15-47), (closed mornings except June through Sept.); **Font-Romeu,** av. E-Brousse (tel. 68-30-02-74); **La Grande Motte,** pl. ler-Oct.-1974 (tel. 67-56-62-62); **Limoux,** prom. Tivoli (tel. 68-31-11-82), (closed mornings except June through Sept.); **Montpellier,** 6 rue Maguelone (tel. 67-58-26-04); **Narbonne,** pl. Roger-Salengro (tel. 68-65-15-60); **Palavas-les-Flots,** Hôtel de Ville (tel. 67-68-02-34); **Perpignan,** quai De Lattre-de-Tassigny (tel. 68-34-29-94); **Pézénas,** Marché au Bled (tel. 67-88-11-82); **Port Barcarès,** Front de Mer (Barcarès town), (tel. 68-86-16-56); **Port Camargue,** Carrefour 2000 (tel. 66-51-71-68), (Apr. through Sept. only); **St.-Cyprien,** parking nord du Port (tel. 68-21-01-33); **Sète,** 22 quai Alger (tel. 67-74-73-00).

REGIONAL FOOD AND DRINK. The cooking of Languedoc is agreeably varied. All along the coast the fish and shellfish are excellent, and here you find the glorious garlicky fish dishes of the French Mediterranean. Among them are *bouillabaisse* (maybe not quite as good as in its Marseille homeland), *bourride* (another variety of rich fish stew) and *brandade de morue* (salt-cod mousse). The local oysters can be eaten all the year round, unlike in other parts of France. Sète is famous for its mussels, and has special fish dishes of its own, such as *rouille de seiche* (cuttlefish in a garlicky sauce).

In Roussillon, the Catalan cooking is generally better than in Spain. Olive oil here reigns supreme, and a local maxim has it, "The fish must die in oil, as it is born in water." *Civet de langouste* (lobster stew) is a specialty of the Banyuls, while Collioure is noted for its anchovies and fresh sardines. A Catalan national dish is *ouillade,* a soup of beans and cabbage, each cooked separately and mixed just before serving. Try also *perdreau à la Catalane* (partridge with bitter oranges).

Around Carcassonne the great dish is *cassoulet*. The Languedoc hinterland is a country of game dishes (in season) and of unusual peasant soups: *oulade* is a soup of cabbage, potatoes and mushrooms, with a little salt pork; *mourtaîrol* is a chicken bouillon with saffron; and *aîgo bouillido*, in the Cévennes, is a soup of garlic, eggs and herbs. The herding of sheep is age-old, leading to sheep cheeses and piquant lamb, flavored with herbs from the hillside scrub. *Alycuit* is a stew made by simmering the giblets of duck and goose. The remarkable *saucisse à la Languedocienne* consists of skewered sausages, sautéed in goose fat and served with spiced tomato purée. Snails, which inhabit the vineyards, are a great Languedoc favorite.

Languedoc produces vast quantities of cheapish table wine, much of it thin and mediocre, but some of fair quality improving each year with new technology. Best are the full-bodied reds of Corbières and Fitou, from the area southwest of Narbonne, or the gentler Minervois. Around Montpellier, the most drinkable wines tend to be the *Clairettes-du-Languedoc* and the *Coteaux-du-Languedoc*. *Blanquette de Limoux*, from the town of that name, is a sparkling wine made by the champagne method. Roussillon produces some very pleasant reds, and two well-known natural sweet wines, *Rivesaltes* and *Banyuls*, usually drunk on their own, chilled, before meals.

HOTELS AND RESTAURANTS. So many vacationers prefer to rent or camp these days that the new resorts tend to be short on hotel accommodations, though steps are being taken to remedy this. Towns such as Montpellier, Narbonne, Perpignan and Carcassone, however, are plentifully supplied with hotels. Similarly, inland you'll find a fair number of pleasant if modest hotels and inns. Many resort hotels may close in the winter, and a number offer discounts in May and October.

For general notes on hotels and restaurants, see "Hotels" and "Restaurants" in *Facts at Your Fingertips*.

AGDE. At **La Tamarissière**, 4 km. (2½ miles) southwest, *La Tamarissière* (M), (tel. 67-94-20-87). 30 rooms. Closed mid-Dec. to mid-Mar., Sun. for dinner, Mon. (except July and Aug.). Best known for restaurant serving colorful local specialties. AE, DC, MC, V.

AMÉLIE-LES-BAINS. *Castel Emeraude* (M), on road to La Petite Provence (tel. 68-39-02-83). 31 rooms. Closed Jan. and Dec. Well sited just outside town; attractive building set in grounds, with good restaurant. V. *Grand Hôtel Thermes* (M), (tel. 68-39-01-00). 83 rooms. Closed mid-Dec. to mid-Jan. Connected with thermal baths; lovely garden and views; terrace for outdoor meals. MC.

Restaurants. *La Bogavante* (I), quai Bosch (tel. 68-39-08-57). Closed mid-Nov. to mid-Dec., first half of March and Mon. Right by river. AE, DC, MC, V. *Hostellerie Toque Blanche* (I), av. Vallespir (tel. 68-99-00-57). Closed mid-Dec. to mid-Jan. Good-value meals; also has rooms.

ARGELÈS-SUR-MER. *Lido* (M), 50 blvd. Mer (tel. 68-81-10-32). 65 rooms. Closed Oct. to mid-May. Perched above pool and beach, with pleasant restaurant. V. *Plage des Pins* (M), (tel. 68-81-09-05). 49 rooms. Closed Oct. to Whitsun. Good sea views, close to pine woods; pool and (I) restaurant. DC.

Restaurant. *Solarium* (I), av. Vallespir (tel. 68-81-10-74). Closed Oct. through Apr. Dinner only; modest, good value; also has rooms.

BANYULS-SUR-MER. *Catalan* (E), rte. Cerbère (tel. 68-88-02-80). 36 rooms. Closed Nov. through April. All rooms overlook sea; good-value meals. AE, DC. *Cap Doune* (I), pl. Reig (tel. 68-88-03-56). 30 rooms. Closed Oct. through May. Modest, no restaurant.

Restaurants. *Les Elmes* (M), pl. Elmes (tel. 68-88-03-12). Closed Nov. through Mar. Close to sea; fresh fish and good-value *menus*. Also has 21 rooms.

MC, V. *Sardinal* (M), pl. Reig (tel. 68-88-30-07). Closed Jan., second half Oct., Sun. for dinner and Mon. Good traditional dishes. MC, V.

BÉZIERS. *Imperator* (M), 28 allées Riquet (tel. 67-49-02-25). 45 rooms. Pleasant traditional hotel; interior garden; no restaurant. AE, DC, MC. *Midi* (M), 13 rue Coquille (tel. 67-49-13-43). 30 rooms. Closed second half Nov. and restaurant also closed Sat. and Sun. night (except Aug.). Best known for popular seafood restaurant. AE, DC, MC, V. *Concorde* (I), 7 rue Solférino (tel. 67-28-31-05). 25 rooms. Closed mid-Dec. to mid-Jan. Central, modest; no restaurant. V.

Restaurants. *Cigale* (M), 60 allées Riquet (tel. 67-28-21-56). Closed second half June, second half Sept., Mon. for dinner, Tues. Good-value fish and other local produce. AE, DC, MC, V. *L'Olivier* (M), 12 rue Boïeldieu (tel. 67-28-86-64). Good *nouvelle cuisine* served in nice bistro décor; good wines. AE, DC, MC, V.

CAP d'AGDE. *Matago* (M), rue Trésor-Royal (tel. 67-26-00-05). 90 rooms. Closed mid-Sept. to mid-April. Pleasant pool and restaurant (but some rooms have kitchenettes). AE, DC, MC, V. *St.-Clair.* (M), pl. St.-Clair (tel. 67-26-36-44). 82 rooms. Closed Nov. to Mar. New hotel near harbor; rooms with good facilities; pool; restaurant. AE, DC, MC, V.

Restaurants. *Le Braséro* (M), Port Richelieu II (tel. 67-26-24-75). Closed Jan. and Feb., Tues. except July and Aug. Cheerful atmosphere, good fish. AE, DC, V. *Trois Sergents* (M), in *St.-Clair* hotel (tel. 67-26-73-13). Closed Nov. through Feb. Best in resort. MC, V. *Le Boucanier* (I), Tour Vigie (tel. 67-94-73-76). Closed Oct. through Mar., Mon. except for dinner in July and Aug. Family-type restaurant, good value. V.

CARCASSONNE. Inside walls. *Cité* (E), pl. Eglise (tel. 68-25-03-34). 54 rooms. Closed mid-Oct. to mid-Apr.; restaurant closed Mon. Very grand; beautifully furnished rooms with four-posters; garden and restaurant. AE, DC, V. *Donjon* (M), 2 rue Comte-Roger (tel. 68-71-08-80). 36 rooms. Attractive and friendly; beautiful garden inside; restaurant open for dinner only; closed on Wed. AE, DC, MC, V. *Remparts* (I), 3 pl. Grand-puits (tel. 68-71-27-72). 18 rooms. Modest but well located.

Restaurant. *La Crémade* (I), 1 rue Plo (tel. 68-25-16-64). Closed Jan., second half Nov., Sun. for dinner, Mon. (except July and Aug.). Friendly, attractive dining room in old building; local specialties. AE, DC, MC, V.

Outside walls. *Domaine d'Auriac* (E), rte. St.-Hilaire (tel. 68-25-72-22). 23 rooms. Restaurant closed Sun. and for lunch on Mon. 2½ km. (1½ miles) southeast; 19th-century manor-house with garden, pool, tennis; fine cuisine and excellent local wines. AE, DC, MC, V. *Montségur* (M), 27 allée d'Iéna (tel. 68-25-31-41). 21 rooms. Closed mid-Dec. to mid-Jan. 19th-century mansion with well-furnished rooms (some airconditioned); good restaurant. AE, DC, MC, V.

Restaurants. *Auberge Pont-Levis* (M), (tel. 68-25-55-23). Closed part of Jan., and Feb., mid-July to mid-Aug., Sun. for dinner Mon. Just outside walls, by Porte Narbonnaise; attractive regional décor, classical cuisine. AE, DC, MC, V. *Languedoc* (M), 32 allée Iéna (tel. 68-25-22-17). Closed mid-Dec. to mid-Jan., Sun. for dinner, except July and Aug., Mon. In hotel *Montségur;* old-established family-run place with excellent regional dishes; tables outside in summer. AE, DC, MC, V. *Logis de Trencavel* (M), 286 av. Général-Leclerc (tel. 68-71-09-53). Closed mid-Jan. to mid-Feb., and Wed. On edge of town; fine regional specialties, plus some "new" dishes; also has 12 rooms (M). AE, DC, MC, V.

CASTELNAUDARY. *Mapotel Palmes* (M), 10 rue Maréchal-Foch (tel. 68-23-03-10). 20 rooms. Well-run and comfortable; pleasant restaurant is *the* place for *cassoulet,* the local specialty. AE, DC, MC, V.

Restaurant. *Fourcade* (M), 14 rue Carmes (tel. 68-23-02-08). Closed Tues. for dinner, Wed. (except Feb. to Sept.) and Feb. Traditional cooking with famous *cassoulet;* also has 14 (I) rooms. AE, DC, MC, V.

CÉRET. *La Châtaigneraie* (M), rte. Fontfrède (tel. 68-87-03-19). 8 rooms. Closed Oct. to mid-Mar.; restaurant closed Sun. 2 km. (1¼ miles) outside town in delightful country setting with superb views; dinner for residents only (no lunches). Pool. *La Terrasse au Soleil* (M), rte. Fontfrède (tel. 68-87-01-94). 18 rooms. Closed Nov. through Mar.; restaurant closed Mon., Tues. for lunch. On edge of town; peaceful and charming, good food in (M) restaurant; pool. v. *Arcades* (I), 1 pl. Picasso (tel. 68-87-12-30). 21 rooms. Closed second half Nov. Traditional spot with lots of local color; no restaurant. AE, DC, MC.

COLLIOURE. *Casa Pairal* (M), impasse des Palmiers (tel. 68-82-05-81). 26 rooms. Closed Nov. through Mar. Agreeable old house in town with peaceful garden and fountain; swimming pool. v. *Templiers* (M), quai Amirauté (tel. 68-82-05-58). 27 rooms. Restaurant closed Sun. for dinner and Mon., Nov. through Mar. except Christmas. Brimming with atmosphere, paintings and geraniums! Good local fish too; tables on quayside in summer. v. *Terrasses* (I), rue Jean-Bart (tel. 68-82-06-52). 20 rooms. Harbor views; restaurant. MC, v.
   Restaurants. *Balette* (M), rte. Port-Vendres (tel. 68-82-05-07). Closed Nov. through Mar., Sun. for dinner, Mon. (except May through Oct.). Superb position overlooking harbor and castle; the food matches the view! *Bodega* (M), 6 rue République (tel. 68-82-05-60). Closed Nov. to Christmas, Mon. for dinner, Tues. (except July and Aug.). Bustling converted wine cellar with good regional specialties. AE, DC, v. *Le Puits* (I), rue Arago (tel. 68-82-06-24). Closed mid-Nov. to mid-Feb. Just behind harbor; good-value *menu.* v.

FONT-ROMEU. *Carlit* (E), rue Docteur-Capelle (tel. 68-30-07-45). 58 rooms. Closed May and Oct. to mid-Dec. Comfortable and well-run; entertainment some evenings; (M) restaurant. AE, MC. *Clair Soleil* (M), rte Odeillo (tel. 68-30-13-65). 31 rooms. Closed mid-Apr. to mid-May, mid-Oct. to mid-Dec.; restaurant closed Wed.; no lunches. On Odeillo road, with good views; meals outside in good weather. MC, v. *Y Sem Bé* (M), rue Ecureuils (tel. 68-30-00-54). 27 rooms. Closed May, Oct. to mid-Dec.; no lunches. Very pleasant chalet-hotel; lovely mountain views. v.
   At **Odeillo,** 3 km. (2 miles) away, *Romarin* (I), av. Arago (tel. 68-30-09-66). 16 rooms. Closed first half of June. Modest and peaceful; lovely views, on road leading to solar furnace; restaurant. v.

LA GRANDE MOTTE. *Pullman* (E), rue Port (tel. 67-59-90-81). 135 rooms. Closed mid-Nov. to mid-March. Modern, well-planned rooms; overlooking harbor; good (M) restaurant. AE, DC, MC, v. *Méditerranée* (M), 277 allée Vaccarès (tel. 67-56-53-38). 40 rooms. Modern and very pleasant; pool, garden, no restaurant. AE, DC, v. *Azur* (M), terre-plein Capitainerie (tel. 67-56-56-00). 17 rooms. Closed Nov. to mid-Jan. Comfortable, with pool and lovely gardens. No restaurant. DC, v.
   Restaurant. *Alexandre-Amirauté* (E), esplanade Capitainerie (tel. 67-56-63-63). Closed Jan. to mid-Feb., one week in Nov., Sun. for dinner, Mon. (except June through Aug.). Opulent décor, excellent seafood cooked "new"-style; best restaurant in whole area. MC.

GRUISSAN. *Corail* (I), quai Ponant (tel. 68-49-04-43). 32 rooms. Closed Nov. through Feb. Right beside harbor; friendly, with restaurant. AE, v.
   Restaurants. *Chebek* (M), quai d'Honneur (tel. 68-49-02-58). Closed Feb., Sun. for dinner, Mon. (except July and Aug.). On waterfront; good seafood and local wines. AE, DC, MC, v. *Estagnol* (M), (tel. 68-49-01-27). Closed second half Mar., second half Oct., Tues. except dinner in July and Aug. In the old village, attractive, regional specialties. v.

MONTPELLIER. *Métropole* (E), 3 rue Clos-René (tel. 67-58-11-22). 92 rooms. Central, well-modernized; garden and good restaurant. AE, DC, MC, v. *Sofitel* (E), Le Triangle (tel. 67-54-04-04). 98 rooms. In district of modern buildings close to city center; comfortable, functional rooms; no restaurant; air-conditioning. AE, DC, MC, v.
   George-V (M), 42 av. St.-Lazare (tel. 67-72-35-91). 39 rooms. Closed Christmas and New Year period. A bit away from center but very comfortable; no

restaurant. AE, DC, MC, V. *Noailles* (M), 2 rue Ecoles-Centrales (tel. 67-60-49-80). 30 rooms. Closed Christmas and New Year period. 17th-century building in old town; attractive and comfortable; no restaurant. AE, DC, MC, V. *Midi* (M), 22 blvd. Victor-Hugo (tel. 67-92-69-61). 50 rooms. Traditional, well-run hotel in city center; garden and restaurant; air-conditioned. AE, DC, V.

Arceaux (I), 33 blvd. Arceaux (tel. 67-92-61-76). 15 rooms. Near Promenade de Peyrou; modest but pleasant; no restaurant. *Hôtel* (I), 6 rue Jules-Ferry (tel. 67-58-88-75). 55 rooms. Convenient spot opposite station; well-renovated. AE, DC, MC, V.

Out of town. 6 km. (3½ miles) southeast, *Demeure des Brousses* (M), rte. Vauguières (tel. 67-65-77-66). 18 rooms. Closed three weeks in April, and Oct. through Mar. 18th-century building with pleasant rooms; lovely trees in park. Good restaurant in the old orangerie (newly opened). AE, DC.

Restaurants. *Chandelier* (M), 3 rue Leenhart (tel. 67-92-61-62). Closed three weeks in Aug., first half of Feb., Mon. for lunch and Sun. Delicious *nouvelle cuisine* and desserts; near station. AE, DC, V. *Isadora* (M), 6 rue Petit-Scel (tel. 67-66-25-23). Closed Sat. for lunch, Sun. In 12th-century cellar; quite chic. AE, DC, MC, V. *Réserve Rimbaud* (M), 820 av. St.-Maur (tel. 67-72-52-53). Closed first half Jan., Sun. for dinner, Mon. Classical cuisine; lovely terrace overlooking river is popular, so reserve well ahead. AE, DC, V. *Gabelle* (I), 26 rue Ecoles-Laïques (tel. 67-72-35-14). Closed Wed. Good home cooking; nice old décor; very good-value *menus.* AE, DC, MC, V.

Bouchou (I), 7 rue Université (tel. 67-66-26-20). Closed Sun. and Mon. Good-value, home-style cooking; very popular so get there early. *Louvre* (I), 2 rue Vieille (tel. 67-60-59-37). Closed May, Sun., Mon. for lunch in winter. Home-style regional cooking; popular with locals. DC, V.

Out of town. 6 km. (3½ miles) southeast, *Le Mas* (E), rte. de Vauguières (tel. 67-65-52-27). Closed mid-Jan. to mid-Feb., Sun. for dinner, Mon. In the grounds of the *Demeure des Brousses* hotel, but under different management with master-chef Michel Loustau at the helm. A popular spot for country dining for Montpellier folks. Delicious newish cuisine, excellent-value gourmet *menu;* friendly service. AE, DC.

NARBONNE. *Mapotel Languedoc* (M), 22 blvd. Gambetta (tel. 68-65-14-74). 43 rooms. Restaurant closed Jan., Fri. for dinner and Sat. except in July and Aug. Friendly, family-run hotel; good restaurant. AE, DC, MC, V. *Résidence* (M), 6 rue 1er-Mai (tel. 68-32-19-41). 35 rooms. Closed Jan. to mid-Feb. Close to cathedral and archbishop's palace; comfortable and well-furnished; airconditioning; no restaurant. AE, V. *France* (I), 6 rue Rossini (tel. 68-32-09-75). 15 rooms. Traditional city-center hotel; good service, no restaurant. V.

At Narbonne-Plage, 15 km. (10 miles) away, *Caravelle* (I), Narbonne-Plage (tel. 68-49-80-38). 24 rooms. Closed Oct. through Apr. Modest seaside hotel; family-type restaurant. MC, V.

Restaurants. *Réverbère* (E), 4 pl. Jacobins (tel. 68-32-29-18). Closed Feb. and one week in Mar., Sun. for dinner, Mon. One of the best in the area, with superb *nouvelle cuisine.* AE, DC, V. *Alsace* (M), 2 av. Pierre-Sémard (tel. 68-65-10-24). Closed mid-Nov. to mid-Dec., Mon. for dinner (except mid-July through Sept.), Tues. Delicious regional seafood dishes. AE, DC, MC, V.

PERPIGNAN. *Mas des Arcades* (M), av. Espagne, 2 km. (1¼ miles) south (tel. 68-85-11-11). 128 rooms. Closed Christmas and New Year period. Just outside town on Perthus road; pool, tennis courts, nice large rooms and restaurant. DC, MC. *Loge* (M), pl. Loge (tel. 68-34-54-84). 29 rooms. Delightful spot in town center, well renovated; no restaurant. AE, DC, MC, V. *Park* (M), 18 blvd. Jean-Bourrat (tel. 68-35-14-14). 67 rooms. Restaurant closed three weeks in Aug., Christmas period. Sat. for dinner and Sun. Modern and rather chic; with good restaurant *(Chapon Fin);* airconditioned. AE, DC, MC, V. *Athena* (I), 1 rue Queya (tel. 68-34-37-63). 38 rooms. In heart of old town; 14th-cent. building; small pool, patio; no restaurant. AE, DC, MC, V.

Restaurants. *Festin de Pierre* (M), 7 rue Théâtre (tel. 68-51-28-74). Closed Feb., Tues. for dinner, Wed. Classical cuisine served in 15th-century building. AE, DC, V. *Delcros* (M), 63 av. Maréchal-Leclerc (tel. 68-34-96-05). Closed first

half of July, Sun. for dinner, Mon. Chic bistrot setting; *nouvelle cuisine.* V.
François Villon (M), 1 rue Four-St.-Jean (tel. 68-51-18-43). Closed mid-July to
mid-Aug., Sun. and Mon. In old town, close to cathedral; "new" versions of
regional specialties; attractive vaulted dining room. *La Serre* (M), 2 rue Dagobert (tel. 68-34-33-02). Closed Sun. Mixture of classical and *nouvelle* cuisine;
very welcoming; good-value *menus.* AE, DC, MC, V.
 Luigi (I), 11 quai Batillo (tel. 68-35-15-56). Closed New Year period, Mon.
for dinner, Tues., Wed. Officially a pizzeria, but also serves fish, pasta, and other
goodies; popular with local youngsters. AE, DC, MC, V. *Vauban* (I), 29 quai Vauban (tel. 68-51-05-10). Closed Sun. Good, lively *brasserie,* welcoming, excellent
service, good value; terrace. AE, DC, V.

PÉZÉNAS. *Genieys* (I), 9 av. Aristide-Briand (tel. 67-98-13-99). 20 rooms.
Closed first half Mar., most of Nov.; restaurant closed Sun. for dinner, Mon.
(except July and Aug.). Old-established, family-run hotel; traditional cuisine
(M); attractive flower-filled courtyard for outdoor meals. AE, DC, MC, V.
 Restaurant. *Le Pré St.-Jean* (M), 18 av. du Mal. Leclerc (tel. 67-98-15-31).
Closed Jan., Sun. for dinner and Mon. Simple dishes in a simple place. AE, MC,
V.

PORT-BARCARÈS. *Lydia Playa* (M), (tel. 68-86-25-25). 192 rooms. Closed
Oct. through May. Ultra-modern member of PLM chain; beach, pool, tennis
courts; airconditioning; light meals only in restaurant. AE, DC, V.
 Restaurant. *Don Quichotte* (M), (tel. 68-86-06-57). Closed Oct., Nov., first
half Mar., Wed. (except in July and Aug.). Just by yacht harbor; excellent local
fish.

PORT-CAMARGUE. *Chabian* (E), (tel. 66-51-44-33). 47 rooms. Closed mid-
Oct. to mid-Mar. Modern and comfortable, with self-catering apartments as
well as ordinary rooms; pool, tennis court, private beach; restaurant. DC, MC, V.
Spinaker (M), pointe Môle (tel. 66-51-54-93). 20 rooms. Closed Jan. to mid-
Feb., most of Nov.; restaurant closed Sun. for dinner, Mon. Modern, right on
harbor, with pool and good restaurant. MC, V.
 Restaurant. *Rancho* (I), 40 rue Michel Rédarès (tel. 66-51-45-61). In the
main street of this lovely little harbor town; good *menu* and very good value.

PRADES. At **Molitg-les-Bains,** 7 km. (5 miles) away, *Château de Riell* (E),
(tel. 68-05-04-40). Closed Nov. through Mar. Very luxurious and romantic
Relais et Châteaux member; pool, tennis; excellent restaurant. AE, V.
 Restaurants. *Hostalrich* (I), 103 rte. Nationale (tel. 68-96-05-38). Closed
Thurs. Family-type meals; also has some modest rooms. V.
 At **Villefranche-de-Conflent,** 6 km. (4 miles) away, *Grill* (I), rue St.-Jean (tel.
68-96-17-65). Closed mid-Nov. to mid-Jan., Sun. for dinner, and Mon. Good
regional cuisine in this attractive walled town; painting exhibits in dining room.
MC, V.

ST.-CYPRIEN. *Mas d'Huston* (E), Golf de St.-Cyprien (tel. 68-21-01-71). 46
rooms. Closed first half Dec. and Feb. Right on golf course (golfing weekends
a specialty!); with pools, tennis, sailing; good *nouvelle cuisine* in restaurant;
airconditioned. AE, DC, MC, V. *Glycines* (I), rue Delacroix (tel. 68-21-00-11). 37
rooms. Closed Oct. through Mar., Wed. (except July through Sept.). Friendly
family-type hotel, close to beach, with good-value restaurant. V.

ST.-GUILHEM-LE-DÉSERT. **Restaurant.** *Fonzes* (I), 1 av. St.-Benoît-
d'Aniane (tel. 67-57-72-01). Closed Dec. through Feb. Modest spot worth visiting for lovely terrace overlooking gorges.

SÈTE. *Grand* (M), 17 quai de-Lattre-de-Tassigny (tel. 67-74-71-77). 47
rooms. Closed Christmas and New Year period. Old-style "grand hotel," large
rooms; good service; good restaurant (*Rotonde*) with new management. Good

value. AE, DC, MC, V. *Mapotel Impérial* (M), pl. Edouard-Herriot (tel. 67-53-28-32). 43 rooms. 2 km. (1¼ miles) from town on corniche road with views over sea and lagoon; no restaurant. AE, DC, MC, V. *Hippocampe* (I), 3 rue Longuyon (tel. 67-74-51-14). 19 rooms. Close to canal and harbor; no restaurant. V.

Restaurants. *Palangrotte* (M), rampe Paul-Valéry (tel. 67-74-80-35). Closed Feb. to mid-Mar., Sun. eve (except July and Aug.), Mon. On quayside, delicious fish cooked "new"-style; *menu* offers excellent value. AE, DC, V. *Rascasse* (I), 27 quai Général-Durand (tel. 67-74-38-46). Closed Christmas through Jan., Thurs. Good value and lots of atmosphere; also on quayside. AE, DC, V.

VERNET-LES-BAINS. *Mas Fleuri* (M), 25 blvd. Clemenceau (tel. 68-05-51-94). 40 rooms. Closed Nov. to Easter. Modern, with pool and garden; lovely views; no restaurant. AE, DC, V. *Hôtel des Deux Lions et Restaurant Thalassa* (I), blvd. Clemenceau (tel. 68-05-55-42). 12 rooms. Closed Nov. to Christmas. Delightful outdoor meals in summer, by roaring fire in winter; local specialties. AE, DC, MC, V. *Princess* (I), rue Lavandières (tel. 68-05-56-22). 23 rooms. Closed Nov. through Mar. Well-run, with nice little rooms; no restaurant. V.

TOURS AND EXCURSIONS. On Foot. Local tourist offices arrange guided tours of the following towns: Agde, Thurs. afternoons in summer from 4 P.M., for 15 fr. (call tourist office first for appointment); Carcassonne, day and evening tours of the *Cité* (walled town), July to mid-Sept. (schedules at tourist office); Montpellier, personal guides at 320 fr. for a day, 216 fr. for half a day; Narbonne, daily except Sun., July through Sept., daily except Sun., 1½ hour, 3 hour or half-day tours at 10 A.M. and 4 P.M. for 4 to 8 fr.; Perpignan Old Town, mid-June to mid-Sept., daily except Sun., at 4 P.M. in front of the tourist office.

SIGHTSEEING DATA. For general notes on visiting museums and historic buildings in France—and an important warning—see "Sightseeing" in *Facts at Your Fingertips.*

AGDE. Musée Agathois (Agde Museum), 5 rue de la Fraternité, pl. Gambetta (tel. 67-94-82-51). Open daily, except Tues.

BÉZIERS. Musée des Beaux Arts (Fine Arts Museum), pl. de la Révolution (tel. 67-28-38-78). Open daily, except Sun. morning, Mon., most public hols.
Musée Vieux Biterrois et du Vin (Regional and Wine Museum), 7 rue Massol. Open daily, except Mon. and public hols.

CARCASSONE. Château Comtal. Open daily, except public hols., Easter through Sept., 9–12, 2–6.30; Oct. to Easter, daily 10–12, 2–5.
Musée des Beaux Arts (Fine Arts Museum), rue de Verdun. Open daily, except Sun., 9–12, 2–6.

CASTELNAUDARY. Musée d'Archéologie Industrielle (Museum of Industrial Archeology), tel. 68-23-11-16. Opening times from tourist office.

CERET. Musée d'Art Moderne (Museum of Modern Art), 1 av. Clemenceau (tel. 68-87-00-53). Open daily, May through Sept., 10–12, 3–7, closed Tues., Oct. through Apr., Mon. afternoon, Wed., Sat. and Sun. only.

ELNE. Cathédrale. Cloisters open 9–12, 2–6.30 (2–5 in winter and closed Tues. and Sun.).

FONTFROIDE. Abbaye. Open daily 9–12, 2.30–6; closed Tues. and Oct. through Mar.

LA GROTTE DES DEMOISELLES. Open daily, Apr. through Sept., 8.30–12, 2–7; Oct. through Mar., 9–12, 1.30–5.

MONTPELLIER. Musée Fabre, blvd. Sarrail. Open daily, except Mon. and public hols., 9–12, 2–5.

NARBONNE. Donjon Gilles-Aycelin (Gilles-Aycelin Fortress). Open daily, mid-May through Sept., 10–12, 2–6; Oct. through mid-May, 10–12, 2–5, closed Mon.

PERPIGNAN. Le Castillet. Open daily, 9–12, 2–6, except Sun. and public hols., mid-Sept. through mid-June.
  Palace of the Kings of Mallorca. Open daily, except Tues., June through Sept., 9–11, 2.30–5. Oct. through May, 9–12, 2–5.

ST.-MICHEL-DE-CUXA. Abbaye. Open daily, 9.30–11, 2.30–5.

SALSES. Fort de Salses. Open daily, except Tues. (and Wed. in winter), 9–11, 3–6 (2–4 Oct. through Apr.).

SÈTE. Musée Paul Valery. Open daily 10–12, 2–6 (2–5 Oct. through Mar.). Closed Tues. and public hols.

VILLEFRANCHE-DE-CONFLENT. Remparts (City Walls). Open daily, mid-Mar. through Sept., 9–11.30, 2–6.30. Otherwise call 68-96-10-78 to arrange a special visit.

SOUTHWEST FRANCE

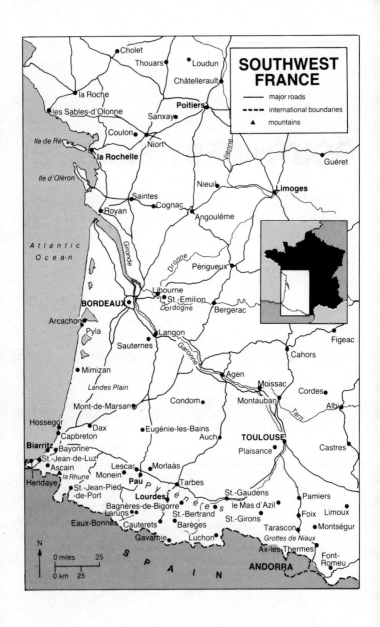

TOULOUSE AND THE
CENTRAL PYRENEES

Tradition as Rugged as the Mountains

The high Pyrenees, separating France from Spain, form one of Europe's great natural frontiers. They are a prime cause of Spain's centuries-old sense of isolation, and to the whole region on the French side of the border they have given the feeling of being in a cul-de-sac. After traveling south from Paris for 800 km. (500 miles) across plains and low hills, you suddenly come to a seemingly impenetrable range of snowy peaks, glowing pink in the early sun or glistening white at noon.

This is still a largely unspoilt region of swift mountain streams, lush valleys, mysterious caves, red-brick Romanesque churches and medieval hilltop castles, and from its long and turbulent history it retains today a sense of being different. In the 13th century it nurtured the famous Albigensian or Cathar heresy, and tribal memories linger of Paris's brutal suppression of those martyrs. Toulouse, the regional capital, known since medieval days as "the counter-Paris," is still the most sullenly hostile to Paris of the larger French towns. And in Pau, to the west, the lords of lower Navarre ruled in independence from France until as late as 1620.

Even within today's centralized State, the spirit of independence persists throughout the region. People are proud, looking on Parisians as a remote and despised breed. They speak with the twangy accent of the Midi (the general term for all southern France) and they like to live at an easy pace, even though the rhythm of the factory-belt is today impinging on that of the slow game of *boules* played in some dusty square. People are excitable and contentious, but though quarrels flare up suddenly they subside as quickly and are buried over a friendly glass or two (or three) of *pastis* in a café. *Boules* (an early version of bowls, played with clinking metal balls) and the drinking of *pastis* (an anisette-based aperitif) are two traditions that strongly survive, and another—notably around Toulouse—is the eating of *cassoulet,* a splendid rich stew of preserved goose, pork, spicy sausage and beans. Try it, but not at lunch unless you plan to take a siesta afterwards. A newer tradition is rugby football, imported from England in the last century and today a cult practised as fervently here as anywhere in the British Isles. Most of the rest of France prefers soccer, but the southwest plays rugby—just to be different!

The Pyrenees, rising to 3,200 meters (10,500 ft.), are Western Europe's highest chain after the Alps. The Romans loved these mountains with their healing springs and fine climate, but during the Middle Ages they were largely forgotten. Only in the 18th century did geologists begin to examine them properly, and the work was continued in Victorian days by such pioneers as Lord Henry Russell, a Franco-Irish peer who staged a romantic ten-year retreat in a grotto.

A state reforestation program has partly made good the damage done by many years of tree-felling and subsequent soil erosion. Other measures too have dispelled some of the old solitude of the mountains. Hydro-electric power has been developed in the upper valleys, and modern roads into Spain have been built over passes or through tunnels. Modern tourism has been making psychological fissures in that historic mountain barrier too; and with Spain's entry into the Common Market in 1986, the breaches are growing wider.

The region is known and loved by countless visitors of many kinds, from climbers to painters, from trout or salmon fishermen to prehistorians. It has spas and ski-slopes, and is served by a modern tourist highway engineered in the best French manner—the Route des Pyrénées. Most of the hotels have been modernized too. No longer, Miranda, will you be asked to remember the fleas that tease, or the spreading of straw for a bedding. A plus for comfort, if not for romance.

Toulouse

The northern gateway to the Pyrenees is the ebullient city of Toulouse, one-time capital of Languedoc, today France's fourth largest town with a population of 500,000. Sprawling astride the river Garonne on a wide plain, it has grown since the war from a quiet market town to a noisy, dusty, industrial metropolis, animated, cosmopolitan, rich in contrasts between old and new. Like some huge Neapolitan ice-cream, it is pink in the middle, white outside: the old inner city, with its elegant Renaissance palaces and Romanesque churches, is mellow rose-pink brick, while around it lies the modern Toulouse of Le Corbusier-inspired housing estates, aircraft factories, student campuses and science centers, gleaming white under the Midi sun. This is France's aviation capital, where the Caravelle and Concorde were built, and today Airbus; it is an electronics center too, and one of the leading

French university towns, with 40,000 students and a special emphasis on modern technology. Toulouse lives late: the downtown sidewalks and outdoor cafés are busy way past midnight with an international throng—Spaniards, Algerians, executives and scientists from Paris, local peasant emigrants, plus a few Germans and British at work on Airbus.

Historic Toulouse has a wealth of interest. The basilica of St.-Sernin is the finest and largest Romanesque church in the Midi, and the richest in relics: its crypt holds the remains of more than 100 saints. The cathedral of St.-Etienne, a strange asymmetrical building, was begun in the 11th century and never completed; other remarkable early churches are the Jacobins and the Dalbade. The leading museum, the Augustins, is noted for its antique sculptures; also worth visits are the Paul Dupuy and St.-Raymond museums, the latter with the best collection of imperial Roman busts outside Italy.

In the narrow streets of the old city are great gateways opening on to courtyards, round which stand imposing Renaissance mansions (finest is the Hôtel Assezat); many are still lived in by their aristocratic owners, and some are topped by the red-bricked towers of the "Capitouls," former consular rulers of the city. On the main square, the town hall, the Capitole, is a stately 18th-century brick palace, home also of one of the best French opera companies. Toulouse prides itself on being a musical center, and all summer concerts are held in enchantingly floodlit old courtyards or on the banks of the Garonne. Try also to see the Ballets Occitans, a polished and lively local folk-dance group.

Armagnac Country: Montauban, Albi, Castres

The open rolling country round Toulouse offers much of interest. To the west is the former county of Armagnac, today producing the brandy of that name which, for many connoisseurs, rivals the best cognacs (to ask for a cognac, rather than an armagnac, can be taken as an insult in this area). North of Toulouse, the market town of Montauban on the river Tarn was a key Protestant citadel in the 16th century: it has pink brick arcades, a graceful 14th-century bridge, and a notable museum devoted chiefly to the works of the town's most famous son, the painter Ingres.

Further upstream, also on the Tarn, is the remarkable city of Albi, dominated by the towering red walls of its famous cathedral. This was formerly fortified, and is an odd mixture of Romanesque and Gothic: don't miss its intricately carved rood screen. The former episcopal palace close by was also once fortified. Today it houses a museum with the world's best collection of works by Toulouse-Lautrec, the painter of Montmartre life who was born in Albi. You can also visit his birthplace, in the street that now bears his name.

Northwest of Albi is a delightful curiosity—the tiny walled medieval town of Cordes, on a high hilltop eyrie above the valley. And to the south is Castres, still a cloth-weaving town as it was in the Middle Ages. Overhanging the river, and reflected in it, are some picturesque old balconied houses. The local museum, surprisingly, has a fine collection of Spanish art, notably Goya. Nearby is the strange plateau of Sidobre, strewn with thousands of smooth rocks in all shapes, providing granite for the local stone-carving workshops.

Pau: French Nobility and English Colonists

This busy and sophisticated city of 125,000 people is a good center for excursions into the Western Pyrenean area: its boulevard des Pyrénées offers beautiful views of the snowy peaks. Pau is the capital of the highly individual region known as Béarn, and it has a royal past, best studied by visiting its great château where the lords of Béarn, Foix and Navarre held sway over a large slice of France in the centuries before 1620. The inscription over the entrance, *Touches-y si tu l'oses* ('Touch this if you dare'), was that of the golden-haired Gaston "Phoebus," flamboyant and volatile count of Foix in the 14th century. He murdered his brother and his only son, but was also a poet and kept open court to writers and troubadours (all this part of France was troubadour country).

Marguerite of Angoulême, a 16th-century *châtelaine,* remodeled the castle in the style of her age, the Renaissance, and its fine furnishings and Gobelin tapestries reflect her taste. This beautiful woman of parts held brilliant balls and banquets, her pastorales were performed in the castle gardens, and she wrote the *Heptaméron,* a collection of 72 tales modeled on Boccaccio. It was said of her, "She has the body of a woman, the heart of a man, the head of an angel," but her virago daughter, Jeanne d'Albret, earned the remark, "She has nothing of woman but the sex." Yet it was Jeanne who gave the world the future Henri IV, amorist, life-lover, benefactor of the common people and one of France's favorite kings—"Our Henry," he is still called in Béarn.

The area round Pau breathes *douceur de vivre:* the countryside is green and gentle, the winters are mild, and it was these qualities that drew thousands of Britons to settle here, after Wellington's officers discovered the place around 1815 on their return from Spain. By the 1860s about a third of Pau's population of 9,000 was British; indeed it was the largest British colony outside the Empire, with its own shops, tea parties, balls and fox hunts. Today Pau is one of the most chic towns in France, mixing civilized elegance with industrial boom. Large deposits of natural gas were discovered in the '50s at Lacq, and a functional new town was built close by at Mourenx to house the workers.

The Pau district offers much of cultural and geological interest. Nearby are the grottoes of Bétharram, with spectacular stalactites; the cathedral of Lescar; and fine old churches at Morlaas and Monein. In the Ossau valley, south of Pau, are the pleasant little spas of Eaux-Bonnes and Eaux-Chaudes, whose sulfurous waters are used to treat rheumatism and chest troubles. At Laruns, on some feast days, the women parade in their elaborate traditional costumes.

Northeast of Pau—take the long straight road from Lannemezan—lies Auch, standing proudly on its hill above the well-farmed plains. The home town of d'Artagnan, of Musketeer fame, Auch is an attractive, busy spot, especially on market days. The cathedral has some magnificent 16th-century stained glass and huge carved-oak choir stalls, thronged with figures.

Lourdes: the Pilgrimage Industry

East of Pau is the industrial town of Tarbes, whose airport receives a non-stop airlift of large jets, to and from such places as Rome, Dublin and Brussels. Why? This is also the airport for Lourdes, and in southwest France there's no growth industry like the pilgrimage industry. Lourdes has more hotel space than any town in France save Paris or possibly Nice. It claims three million pilgrims a year, drawn here by the story of Bernadette, the great churches built near the site of her visions, and the miraculous cures attributed to the spring waters.

In February 1858, Bernadette Soubirous, aged 14, daughter of a local miller, claimed that the Virgin Mary had appeared to her near the Massabielle grotto. A subsequent vision (there were 18 in all) was accompanied by the miraculous gushing of water where no known spring existed. Pilgrims flocked there, drawn by reports of the water's healing powers, and four years later the Church accepted the miracle's authenticity. Bernadette was canonized in 1933.

Of the six annual pilgrimages today, the main one is on August 15, when huge crowds attend daylight and torchlight processions. It is hard not to be impressed by the long winding columns of pilgrims bearing lighted torches, chanting "Ave Maria," and by the fervent faces of poor and rich who have come from the five continents. But some visitors may be distressed by the sight of the armies of cripples hopefully crawling up the wide flight of steps to the Church of the Rosary; or they may be sickened by the town's blatant commercialization, where hundreds of shops sell souvenirs of the saint in every shape and form—a carnival of holy kitsch.

In 1958, the centenary of the first vision, the world's largest underground church, the basilica of Pope Pius X, was completed, able to hold 20,000 people. Through clever use of reinforced concrete, it has one single unsupported vault. You should see also the house where Bernadette was born, and the museum that shows a film of her life. Dominating the town, the fortified château is a fine specimen of medieval military architecture. It has impressive *son et lumière* shows in summer, and also houses the Pyrenean Museum, one of the best of French provincial museums, with a notable collection of peasant costumes, pottery, stuffed animals, and scenes of local life.

The High Pyrenees: Spas and Ski Resorts

From Laruns all the way to Luchon, the Route des Pyrénées takes the motorist up through spectacular mountain scenery, under the brow of the mighty Pic du Midi de Bigorre (2,894 meters/9,500 ft.) and over the Tourmalet pass (1,980 meters/6,500 ft.). Here we are no longer in the Béarn but in neighboring Bigorre, and the valleys are dotted with little spas and ski resorts where the athletic and the rheumatic make common cause. Cauterets, south of Lourdes, is one such ski/spa center: since Roman times its thermal springs have been thought to benefit sterile women. Is it a coincidence that Cauterets is also fertile in literary romance? Victor Hugo womanized here, George Sand discovered the thrills of adultery, Chateaubriand sighed for his "inaccessible Occitan girl."

From Cauterets there are two classic excursions to two of the best-known beauty spots of the central Pyrenees. One is via the Pont d'Espagne to the lake of Gaube. You drive up a steep winding road, then either climb on foot or go by chair-lift to the plateau at the end of which is the famous bright-blue 16-hectare (40-acre) lake. From here, a sturdy walker with a guide can cut over the mountains to the even more famous Cirque de Gavarnie, more easily reached by car from Luz. The road climbs up a narrow valley into rugged country and ends at the village of Gavarnie, at the foot of the Cirque (circus). This is a giant natural amphitheater, set in a ring of mountains: from its cliffs, nearly a mile high in places, plunge numerous waterfalls when the upper snows are melting. The Cirque is one of the world's most remarkable examples of glacial erosion, and has long had an appeal for mountain climbers (in the village is a statue to one of them, Lord Russell).

Barèges, to the north, is in country with streams full of trout and mountains full of partridge. Northeast again, Bagnères-de-Bigorre is both an industrial town and a health resort, and was favored in the past by Montaigne, Rossini and others. It is a good walking center, but the high mountains are not close. Some 64 km. (40 miles) to the east lies the largest and most fashionable of Pyrenean spas, Bagnères-de-Luchon (usually known as Luchon). It has a golf course and luxury shops, and attracts opera singers, barristers, politicians and other windbags (its thermal specialty is treatment of the vocal chords!). The town lies at the head of a lush valley, below the highest of all the Pyrenean peaks, and it is worth driving up the 17 km. (11 miles) of scenic road to Superbagnères, a ski resort perched on a plateau 1,218 meters (4,000 ft.) above Luchon with marvelous views of the Maladeta range.

St. Bertrand-de-Comminges, 32 km. (20 miles) north of Luchon, is also worth a visit. This was an important Roman center (Herod and Herodias were banished here), but in the 6th century the city was wiped out by plague, and its Roman forum, baths, temple and theater were silted over. Now they have been excavated. Nearby is the 9th-century church of St.-Just-de-Valcabrère, half-hidden by cypresses, a marvel of early Romanesque. And a mile away, crowning a tiny walled medieval city, is the 12th-century cathedral built by Bertrand, bishop of Comminges. Its Romanesque cloister, with finely proportioned arches, looks serenely over the valley below; within there are brilliantly carved Renaissance choir stalls.

Prehistoric Caves and Cathar Ruins

The area between Luchon and Foix is rich in prehistory. Some 8 km. (5 miles) from St.-Bertrand is the grotto of Gargas, known as "the cave of cut hands," for its vault is covered with the imprints of mutilated hands, suggesting barbaric rituals during the Aurignacian Age. Perhaps the most remarkable of Pyrenean caves is the Mas-d'Azil, north of St.-Girons. It is a natural tunnel 800 meters (2,640 ft.) long, formed by the river Arize, and in its caves Magdalenian man has left rock engravings of bison, reindeer, horses and cats, as well as the bones and teeth of the prehistoric animals he ate. Early Christians in the 3rd century, Cathars in the 13th, Huguenots in the 17th, all sought refuge in these caverns, which are so vast that they were even used as aircraft factories in World War II.

Near Foix is the underground river of Labouiche, where waters have tunneled for 5 km. (3 miles) through the limestone cliffs: you can take a 90-minute boat-ride, and admire the cleverly floodlit stalactites. Farther south, in the Vicdessos valley beyond Tarascon, the superb Niaux grotto is comparable to Spain's Altamira because of its well-preserved Magdalenian rock paintings, dating to about 20,000 B.C. Scores of horses, deer and bison, simply but elegantly drawn, line a natural gallery just under 1 km. (½ mile) from the entrance. Now that Lascaux can only be seen in reproduction, this is the finest ensemble of prehistoric art in France open to the public; but the constant stream of tourists is damaging these paintings too, and Niaux in its turn may soon have to be closed, unless there is a strict limit on visits.

The capital of this district is the appealing little town of Foix, crowned by its 11th-century castle perched high on a rock above the town center. The castle with its three tall towers has a children's picturebook quality. It was ferociously besieged during the anti-Cathar crusade; today it houses a museum of prehistoric and medieval art. In early September the château is floodlit and colorful folkdancing takes place in the streets below.

Thirty-two km. (20 miles) to the southeast are the ruins of the famous castle of Montségur, scene of the final tragic martyrdom of the Cathars in 1244. All this part of France, from Foix and Toulouse to as far east as Montpellier, was the country of the Cathars (or Albigensians) and the memory of that terrifying episode is still alive in local hearts and minds. Imported from the Middle East and the Balkans, the Albigensian "heresy" flourished in Languedoc in the early 13th century, where it took its name from Albi, one of its main centers. Its believers preached a doctrine of ascetic purity, rejecting earthly life as evil; and its spiritual leaders were known as "the pure ones," *Les Cathares*. They implicitly criticized the worldly ways of the Church. So Pope Innocent III ordered a crusade against them, finding willing executives in the Capetian rulers of France, who identified Catharism with Languedoc nationalism and its rejection of Parisian hegemony. The crusade, under Simon de Montfort, was of appalling severity. Soldiers marched down from the north, burning towns, massacring whole populations whether practising Cathars or not: "Kill them all, God will then recognise his own," was one commander's order-of-the-day.

Toulouse and other centers were subjugated, and the last remaining 200 "pure ones" took refuge in Montségur, where they were besieged, captured and burned alive in March 1244. The castle, today in ruins, stands in lonely splendor on a hilltop amid glorious wooded country, and is worth a visit. In the tiny village nearby is a Cathar museum, and a "spiritualist library" of assorted religions and philosophies, run by ardent local bohemians—for Montségur today is a leading center of the new interest in Catharism. This is linked with political opposition to Paris—the people of this area resent Paris's "colonization" almost as much as their ancestors did, and so they cherish the memory of the Cathar martyrs.

Many years after the Montségur affair, in the early 14th century, Catharism was still so much alive in some upland villages of the area that one local bishop staged an Inquisition to try to wipe it out. The verbatim transcripts of his detailed enquiries in one village, Montaillou, northeast of Ax-les-Thermes, have survived to this day; and the famous French historian Emmanuel Le Roy Ladurie has recently reworked them into a fascinating account of medieval rural life (his book, *Montaillou*, was a bestseller in both French and English).

Many mysteries surrounding the Cathar tragedy continue to haunt the modern imagination. According to one legend, a strange Cathar treasure was smuggled out of Montségur before it fell, and was buried in the area. Some have connected this with the true story of the 19th-century priest in the nearby village of Rennes-le-Château (south of Limoux) who seemingly found the key to some hidden treasure in his church. And some have gone on to link this enigma of the Cathar treasure with the mystery of the Holy Grail.

Andorra, the Last Feudal State

High in the Pyrenees on the southward side of the passes, Andorra is one of Europe's tiniest independent states, with 40,000 inhabitants. It is also Europe's last surviving feudal protectorate: a treaty of 1278 placed it under the joint tutelage of the bishop of nearby Seo d'Urgel in Spain, and of the count of Foix, and this remains in force, save that the count's role has now passed to the president of France. The protectors rarely intervene and Andorra is in practice independent, with her own little army, her own laws and ruling council, but no separate currency: francs and pesetas are both used. Catalan is the official language.

The country's remoteness kept it from being swallowed up by its neighbors. There is still no airport or railroad, and the main road from France follows a series of dizzy hairpin bends over the highest of the Pyrenean passes, the Elvira (2,406 meters/7,900 ft.). This road is closed in winter, but all through the season it is jammed with tourist traffic, and Andorra's once-primitive villages are now a concrete jungle of banks, hotels, snack bars and duty-free supermarkets. For this is a tax-free paradise, where gasoline, liquor, cameras, watches and much else can be bought at little more than half French prices. This draws trippers from France in thousands. Smuggling, too, is an organized industry.

In the side valleys, away from the main road, are a few hamlets where livestock breeding is still practiced and the traditional Andorran way of life has not been totally swamped by the tourist boom. In the capital, Andorra-la-Vella, the House of the Valley where the "parliament" meets is an interesting 16th-century building. But apart from this, the country has little to attract the visitor in search of more than cut-price goods. Even the shrine of the curious Notre-Dame de Meritxell, worshipped by Andorrans as their patroness, was destroyed by fire in 1972. Divine vengeance, maybe.

PRACTICAL INFORMATION FOR TOULOUSE
AND THE CENTRAL PYRENEES

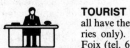

TOURIST OFFICES. The *départements* of the region all have their own regional tourist offices (written enquiries only). These are: **Ariège,** 14 rue Lazema, 09000 Foix (tel. 61-65-29-00); **Gers,** BP 69, 32000 Auch (tel. 62-05-37-02); **Haute-Garonne,** Administrative Centre, 31 rue de Metz, 31066 Toulouse (tel. 61-53-11-22); **Tarn,** Ancienne Préfecture du Tarn, 81013 Albi Cedex (63-54-65-25).

There are local tourist offices in the following towns: **Albi,** 19 pl. St.-Cécile (tel. 63-54-22-30); **Auch,** pl. Cathédrale (tel. 62-05-22-89); **Lourdes,** pl. Champ-Commun (tel. 62-94-15-64); **Montauban,** rue College-Montauban (tel. 63-63-60-60); **Pau,** pl. Royale (tel. 59-27-27-08); **Tarbes,** pl. Verdun (tel. 62-93-36-62); **Toulouse,** Donjon du Capitole—behind pl. Capitole—(tel. 61-23-32-00) and at the rail station (tel. 61-63-11-88).

REGIONAL FOOD AND DRINK. The cuisine of the region is varied, rich, strongly seasoned, with plentiful use of garlic and goose fat. The most famous dish is *cassoulet,* a succulent white bean stew with *confit* (preserved goose), spicy sausage, pork, and sometimes lamb, found in a number of local versions around Toulouse and Carcassone. Like the rest of southwestern France, this is the land of expensive foie gras, delicious when freshly sautéed with grapes. Goose and duck dishes like *magret de canard* (a steak of duck breast), are much enjoyed.

Cheaper specialties include *garbure,* a mixed vegetable soup which comes sometimes as a broth, sometimes as a purée; *farci du lauragais* a kind of pork pancake; and *gigot de sept heures,* where a leg of lamb is braised with garlic for no less than seven hours. Béarn, around Pau, is great eating country, its *poule au pot* of stuffed chicken poached with vegetables made a legend by King Henri IV, the "grand Béarnais;" try the richly marinaded stews, either of wood-pigeon *(civet de palombes),* or of wild goat *(civet d'isnard).* (The famous *sauce béarnaise* is not local, despite its name, but a Parisian invention.) Cakes include *feuilleté béarnaise,* an interesting flaky pastry layered with goose fat or butter, prunes and armagnac.

This is not a region especially noted for its wines. But those of Béarn are pleasant enough, principally the white *Jurançon,* the red *Madiran,* and the *rosés.* East of Toulouse, the best wine is *Gaillac.* To the west of the city lies *Armagnac* country, producing brandy to rival the best cognacs.

HOTELS AND RESTAURANTS. Toulouse has the usual range of big-city hotels and restaurants, with many opportunities for open-air meals; reserve well ahead in spring and fall as hotels get very busy. Most of the region has small, pleasant but not luxurious hotels, often closing in the winter except in the Pyrenees ski resorts.

For general notes on hotels and restaurants, see "Hotels" and "Restaurants" in *Facts at Your Fingertips.*

ALBI. *Hostellerie St.-Antoine* (E), 17 rue St.-Antoine (tel. 63-54-04-04). 56 rooms. Rooms furnished with antiques; pretty courtyard garden; very central and comfortable, belongs to Mapotel group; good restaurant. Pool and tennis at Fonvialane annex. AE, DC, MC, V. *Chiffre* (M), 50 rue Séré-de-Rivières (tel. 63-54-04-60). 39 rooms. Restaurant closed Sun., Nov. through Mar. Old-established, family run place, now carefully modernized; restaurant overlooking beautiful garden. AE, DC, MC, V. *Pujol* (I), 22 av. Teyssier (tel. 63-54-02-92). 21 rooms. Closed mid-June to mid-July, part of Feb.; restaurant closed Fri. evenings and Sat. In town center, with airconditioning and good (M–I) regional cuisine. AE, DC, V.

At **Fonvialane,** 3 km. (2 miles) northwest, *Réserve* (E), rte. de Cordes (tel. 63-60-79-79). 20 rooms. Closed Nov. through March. Under same ownership as St.-Antoine in town; Relais et Châteaux member on the banks of the Tarn, set in big garden with pool and tennis; good newish cuisine (M). AE, DC, MC, V.

Restaurant. At **Marssac,** 10 km. (6½ miles) west, *Francis Cardaillac* (M), (tel. 63-55-41-90). Closed part of Jan., Sun. for dinner and Mon. (except holidays). Marvelous value *nouvelle cuisine* versions of regional dishes; pool and airconditioning; piano bar. Good place to spend the evening, in attractive setting beside Tarn river. AE, DC, MC, V.

AUCH. *France* (E), pl. Libération (tel. 62-05-00-44). 30 rooms. Superb restaurant (E) generally thought to be best in Gascony, with endless duck dishes; closed Jan., Sun. for dinner and Mon. (except public hols.); plus bar (called *Neuvième*) for good value regional food (M). AE, DC, MC, V. *Lion d'Or* (I), 7 rue Pasteur (tel. 62-05-02-07). 16 rooms. Family-type hotel, with restaurant and pleasant bar. V.

Restaurant. At Ste.-Christie, 14 km. (9 miles) north, *Relais du Cardeneau* (M), (tel. 62-65-51-80). Genuine regional cuisine; great *foie gras*. Very good value and worth the trip out of town. AE, DC, V.

BAGNÈRES-DE-BIGORRE. *Résidence* (M), Parc Thermal de Salut (tel. 62-95-03-97). 40 rooms. Closed mid-Oct. through Mar., except for three weeks in Feb. and Easter hols. Open at Easter. Set in lovely grounds, with pool and restaurant. v. *Hostellerie d'Aste* (I), route D935 (tel. 62-95-20-27). 23 rooms. Closed Wed., Nov. to mid-Dec. and most of May. Pleasant, modern amenities; good restaurant. Half-board terms compulsory in season. v.

CASTRES. *Grand* (M), 11 rue Libération (tel. 63-59-00-30). 40 rooms. Closed mid-Dec. to mid-Jan. Restaurant closed Sat. and mid-June to mid-Sept. Old-established hotel beside the river; rooms have now been modernized and in summer the hotel has a "summer restaurant" beside the river (see *Caravelle*, below) instead of the usual classical cuisine served the rest of the year. AE, DC, MC, V. *Occitan* (M), 201 av. Charles-de-Gaulle (tel. 63-35-34-20). 30 rooms. Closed first half of Aug., Christmas and New Year, weekends. A bit away from town center, but pleasant; no restaurant.
Restaurants. *Caravelle* (M), 150 av. Roquecourbe (tel. 63-59-27-72). Closed mid-Sept. to mid-June, Fri. for dinner, Sat. The "summer restaurant" of the Grand Hôtel and delightful for outdoor meals beside the river; good value *nouvelle cuisine*. AE, DC, MC, V.
At **Les Salvages**, 5 km. (3 miles) northeast, *Café du Pont* (I), (tel. 63-35-08-21). Closed Feb., Sun. for dinner and Mon. Riverside restaurant offering rich classical cuisine; also has 6 (I) rooms. AE, DC, MC.

CAUTERETS. *Trois Pics* (M), blvd. Leclerc (tel. 62-92-53-64). 30 rooms. Closed mid-April through May, Nov. to mid-Dec. Well run hotel typical of mountain resort, friendly and cheerful; restaurant. AE, DC, MC, V.
Restaurant. *Fruitière* (I), 6 km. (3½ miles) south (tel. 62-92-52-04). Closed Oct. to mid-May. Secluded setting in Pyrenees National Park; regional cuisine. Also has 8 rooms. AE, V.

CONDOM. *Table des Cordeliers* (M), rue des Cordeliers (tel. 62-28-03-68). 21 rooms. Closed Jan. through Feb., Sun. for dinner, Mon.; well run, with every modern amenity. Restaurant in lovely 14th-century chapel and quite exceptional. Closed Jan. to mid-Mar., Sun. for dinner and Mon. MC, V.

CORDES. *Grand Écuyer* (E), rue Voltaire (tel. 63-56-01-03). 16 rooms. Closed Nov. through March. Restaurant closed Mon. (except summer). Beautiful Gothic-style hotel with wonderfully furnished rooms. Excellent restaurant based on superb local produce. AE, DC, V. *Cité* (M), (tel. 63-56-03-53). 10 rooms. Closed Dec. to mid-Feb.; no lunches, except July and Aug. Quiet spot, with garden and restaurant. v.

FOIX. *Audoye* (I), 6 pl. Duthil (tel. 61-65-52-44). 35 rooms. Closed Sat. in winter. Converted coaching inn; restaurant overlooks river. AE, DC, MC, V. *Barbacane* (I), 1 av. Lérida (tel. 61-65-50-44). 21 rooms. Closed Nov. to mid-March. Rooms vary in quality and comfort. AE, V.
Restaurants. *Phoebus* (M), 3 cours Irénée-Cros (tel. 61-65-10-42). Closed Mon. Enjoy bird's eye view of château while eating tasty regional cuisine. MC, V. *XIXe Siècle* (I), 2 rue Delcassé (tel. 61-65-12-10). Closed Feb. to mid-March, Sat. except July and Aug. Regional cooking, good value *menus*.

LOURDES. *Gallia et Londres* (E), 26 av. Bernadette-Soubirous (tel. 62-94-35-44). 90 rooms. Closed mid-Oct. to mid-April. Comfortable and elegant; garden. AE, DC, V. *Mapotel de la Grotte* (E), 66 rue Grotte (tel. 62-94-58-87). 83 rooms. Closed Nov. through March. All rooms have balconies overlooking basilica; restaurant; beautiful views. AE, DC, MC, V.

Auberge Provençale (M), 4 rue Baron-Duprat (tel. 62-94-31-34). 68 rooms. Comfortable rooms and everything to hand; souvenir shop, bar and cheerful restaurant *(Bella Napoli)* with Italian cuisine (I). AE, DC, V. *Christina* (M), 42 av. Peyramale (tel. 62-94-26-11). 210 rooms. Closed Nov. through March. Modern and pleasant; lovely mountain views; restaurant (I). AE, DC, MC, V. *Galilée-Windsor* (M), 10 av. Peyramale (tel. 62-94-21-55). 170 rooms. Closed Nov. through March. Well run, with large rooms and good service; close to grotto. Restaurant is (I). *Impérial* (M), 3 av. Paradis (tel. 62-94-06-30). 100 rooms. Closed mid-Oct. to mid-April. Stylish décor and nice courtyard-cum-garden; restaurant and good views. AE, DC, MC, V.

Concorde (I), 7 rue Calvaire (tel. 62-94-05-18). 54 rooms. Closed mid-Oct. to Easter. Typical French provincial hotel; good value, with restaurant.

Restaurants. *Ermitage* (M), pl. Mgr.-Laurence (tel. 62-94-08-42). Closed mid-Oct. through April. One of best restaurants in town; mostly *nouvelle cuisine.* AE, DC, MC, V. *Bella Napoli* (I), in Auberge Provençale Hôtel (tel. 62-94-31-34). Cheerful Italian restaurant; good value. AE, DC, V. *Maurice Prat* (I), 22 av. Béguère (tel. 62-94-01-53). Closed mid-Dec. through Feb., Mon. except March to mid-Oct. Modest family restaurant; also has 14 rooms. (M)

LUCHON. *Corneille* (M), av. Alexandre Dumas (tel. 61-79-36-22). 58 rooms. Closed mid-Oct. through March. Traditional and secluded in own lovely grounds; nice big bedrooms and elegant restaurant. AE, DC, V. *Étigny* (M), 3 av. Bonnemaison (tel. 61-79-01-42). 58 rooms. Closed mid-Oct. to mid-March. Opposite spa building, with restaurant, garden and pleasant terrace; best rooms have private balcony. *Bon Accueil* (I), 1 pl. Joffre (tel. 61-79-02-20). 28 rooms. Closed mid-Oct. to mid-Dec. Good value family hotel; pleasant service and restaurant. AE, V.

PAU. *Continental* (M), 2 rue Maréchal Foch (tel. 59-27-69-31). 110 rooms. Large and comfortable rooms; good restaurant. AE, DC, V. *Paris* (M), 80 rue Garet (tel. 59-27-34-39). 41 rooms. Central and well run; rooms are quiet and nicely furnished; no restaurant. AE, DC, MC, V. *Roncevaux* (M), 25 rue Barthou (tel. 59-27-08-44). 42 rooms. Convenient for both château and station; no restaurant. AE, MC, V. *Montpensier* (I), 36 rue Montpensier (tel. 59-27-42-72). 24 rooms. Beautiful house in town center, with well equipped rooms; welcoming; no restaurant. AE, DC, MC, V.

Restaurants. *Pierre* (E), 16 rue Barthou (tel. 59-27-76-86). Closed part of Feb., Sun. Very good classical cuisine, with a few *nouvelle* dishes too; must reserve. AE, DC, MC, V. *Gousse d'Ail* (M), 12 rue Hédas (tel. 59-27-31-55). Closed most of Oct., Sat. for lunch and Sun. Attractive building in old part of town; good-value *menus.* AE, DC. *Lucifer* (M), 1 rue Hédas (tel. 59-27-56-06). Closed Sun., also for lunch Wed. Good regional specialties and lots of fish; good value *menus.* AE, V. *Patrick Jourdan* (M), 14 rue Latapie (tel. 59-27-68-70). Closed Sat. for lunch and Sun. Chic *nouvelle cuisine* restaurant. AE, DC, V.

At **Jurançon**, 2 km. (1¼ miles) southwest, *Chez Ruffet* (M), av. Ch. Touzet (tel. 59-06-25-13). Closed Aug., Sun. for dinner, Mon. Well-known for regional cuisine. AE, DC.

PLAISANCE. Restaurant. *Ripa-Alta* (M), pl. Eglise (tel. 62-69-30-43). Closed Nov. to mid-Dec., Sun. for dinner, except June through Aug., Mon. Deservedly popular for its imaginative cuisine, based on regional specialties, enhanced by most attractive country setting and décor; also has 14 (I) rooms. AE, DC, MC, V.

ST.-BERTRAND-DE-COMMINGES. *Comminges* (M), (tel. 61-88-31-43). 13 rooms. Closed Nov. through Mar. Nice little hotel with lovely views and peaceful rooms. Restaurant.

SAUVETERRE-DE-COMMINGES. *Hostellerie des 7 Molles* (E), (61-88-30-87). 19 rooms. Closed Nov. to mid-Mar. Set in the foothills and hard to find, makes an excellent quiet base for exploration. Relais et Châteaux member. Fine restaurant (M). AE, DC, V.

TARBES. *Henry IV* (M), 7 av. Barère (tel. 62-34-01-68). 24 rooms. Convenient for station; attractive, comfortable rooms; no restaurant. AE, DC, MC, V. *Président* (M), rte. Lourdes (N21) (tel. 62-93-98-40). 57 rooms. Good member of Mapotel chain, modern and comfortable; pool, grillroom for light meals and, up on the 9th floor, with lovely views, full-scale restaurant (see below). AE, DC, MC, V.

Restaurants. *Amphitryon* (M), 38 rue Larrey (tel. 62-34-08-99). Closed 2 weeks in Aug., Sat. for lunch, Sun. Probably best in town and certainly very popular; newish cuisine using local specialties such as wild mushrooms. AE, DC, V. *Toit de Bigorre* (M), in Président Hôtel (tel. 62-93-98-40). Right at the top of the Président Hôtel; good regional cuisine to go with the glorious views. AE, DC, MC, V. *Toup'Ty* (M), 86 av. Barère (tel. 62-93-32-08). Closed July, Sun. for dinner, Mon. Near station; good value regional cuisine with some (I) *menus.*

TOULOUSE. *Atea Wilson* (E), 7 rue Labéda (tel. 61-21-21-75). 95 rooms. Central and comfortable; no restaurant, though light suppers can be served in your room. AE, DC, MC, V. *Grand Hôtel de l'Opéra* (E), 1 pl. Capitole (tel. 61-23-07-76). 49 rooms. Marvelous hotel right in town center and built in Toulouse's famous pink brick; excellent restaurant (see below). AE, DC, MC, V. *Caravelle* (M), 62 rue Raymond IV (tel. 61-62-70-65). 30 rooms. Central, with good facilities including airconditioning in all rooms; no restaurant. AE, DC, MC, V. *Compagnie du Midi* (M), gare de Toulouse-Matabiau (tel. 61-62-84-93). At main rail station, overlooking Canal du Midi, yet close to center; airconditioned rooms, restaurant and brasserie for light meals. AE, DC, MC, V.

Junior (I), 62 rue Taur (tel. 61-21-69-67). 23 rooms. Right by St.-Sernin basilica; small, pretty rooms; no restaurant. *Ours Blanc* (I), 2 rue Victor-Hugo (tel. 61-21-62-40). 37 rooms. Small but fairly quiet rooms in side street in town center; friendly atmosphere; no restaurant. V. *Raymond-IV* (I), 16 rue Raymond-IV (tel. 61-62-89-41). 41 rooms. An old building but rooms well modernized; in town center; no restaurant. AE, DC, MC, V.

At **Vieille Toulouse,** 9 km. (5½ miles) south, *Flânerie* (M), route Lacroix-Falgarde (tel. 61-73-39-12). 15 rooms. Charming and peaceful; set in lovely grounds near golf course and riding stables; no restaurant. AE, DC, V.

Restaurants. *Jardins de l'Opera* (E), in *Grand Hotel de l'Opera,* 1 pl. Capitole (tel. 61-23-07-76). Closed one week in Aug., and Sun. Delicious *nouvelle cuisine* with some regional touches. AE, DC, V. *Vanel* (E), 22 rue Maurice Fonvielle (tel. 61-21-51-82). Closed Mon. for lunch, Sun., and Aug. Perhaps the best restaurant in Toulouse. Very light and imaginative *nouvelle cuisine;* price range includes (M). AE, MC. *Bistrot Van Gogh* (M), 21 pl. St.-Georges (tel. 61-21-03-15). Closed Sun. Popular spot on lively square in town center; bustling brasserie downstairs (tables outside in fine weather); chic restaurant upstairs; some regional specialties. AE, DC, MC, V. *Cahuzac* (M), 21 rue Perchepinte (tel. 61-53-11-15). Closed Sun., Mon. for lunch. Near cathedral and most attractive; reasonably priced *menus* and lots of local dishes. AE, DC, V. *Orsi* (M), 13 rue Industrie (tel. 61-62-97-43). Marvelous fish restaurant right in town center, but also has specialties from the chef-owner's native Lyon. AE, DC, V.

Bibent (I), pl. Capitole (tel. 61-23-89-03). Closed Sun. Delightful up-dated version of old-style brasserie on main square; aproned waiters, mirrors and brass rails galore; open late for stylish suppers. AE, DC, V. *Cassoulet* (I), 40 rue Peyrolières (tel. 61-21-18-99). Closed first half of Jan., Mon. Specializes in, you've guessed it, tasty *cassoulet,* plus other southwestern dishes; good value and cheerful ambience. *Pavillon d'Argent* (I), 42 rue Taur (tel. 61-23-36-48). Closed Mon. for lunch, Aug. and Christmas hols. Welcoming; delicious cooking and excellent value. DC, V.

TOURS AND EXCURSIONS. By Bus. A good bus network in the region includes circular tours to points of interest from such centers as Luchon (including an excursion into Andorra and Spain), Lourdes, Laruns, Foix, Perpignan and the Côte Vermeille (again including trips to Andorra and Spain's Costa Brava). In addition, the S.N.C.F. (French Railways) also operate a series of bus excursions from most principal centers. Details of these and other tours from local tourist offices.

SIGHTSEEING DATA. For general notes on visiting museums and historic buildings in France—and an important warning—see "Sightseeing" in *Facts at Your Fingertips.*

ALBI. Maison Natale de Toulouse-Lautrec (Toulouse-Lautrec Birthplace), 14 rue Toulouse-Lautrec (tel. 63-54-21-81). Open daily, mid-June to mid-Sept. 9–11.45, 3–6.45. Closed mornings on Sun. and public hols.

CASTRES. Palais de l'Evêché, housing **Musée Goya** and **Musée Jaurès** (tel. 63-59-12-43). Closed Mon. and public hols. Open 9–12 (10–12 Sun.), 2–6 (2–5 in winter).

FOIX. Château. Open daily, May through Aug., 8.30–12, 2–6.30; Oct. through Apr., daily, 10–12, 2–6.

GROTTES DE BETHARRAM. Open daily, Easter through Oct., closed at lunchtime.

GROTTES DE NIAUX (tel. 61-05-88-37). Open July through Sept., guided tours every 45 mins. between 8.30–11.30, 1.30–5.15; Oct. through June, tours at 11, 3 and 4.30. Numbers on tours are restricted, so early arrival is recommended.

GROTTES DU MAS D'AZIL. Open daily, July through Oct., 10–12, 2–6; Apr. through June, open afternoons only except Sun. and public hols.

LABOUICHE. Rivière Souterraine (Underground River). Open daily, Easter through Sept., 8.30–12, 2–7; Oct. open Sun. only. Boats leave at frequent intervals. Also evening visits (6–9) for which reservations are essential.

LOURDES. Funiculaire du Pic du Jer (cable railway). Runs every half hour, 9–12, 1.30–7.
Musée Bernadette, 38 rue Grotte. Film show daily in summer; check times locally.
Musee Pyrénéen, in château (tel. 62-94-02-04). Open daily, mid-June to mid-Sept., 9–11, 2–6; mid Sept. to mid-June 9–11, 2–5.

MONTAUBAN. Musée Ingres, Palais Episcopal, 19 rue Mairie (tel. 63-63-18-04). Open Oct. through May, daily except Mon. and Sun. morning, 10–12, 2–6; June and Sept., daily, except Mon., 9.30–12, 1.30–6; July and Aug., daily, except Mon., 9.30–12, 1.30–6.

MONTSÉGUR. Château (tel. 61–01–10–27). Open daily, May through Sept., 9–7. Museum, open daily, May through Sept., 9–12, 2–7.

PAU. Château (tel. 59-27-36-22). Open daily, mid-Apr. to mid-Oct., 9–11.45, 2–5.45; mid-Oct. to mid-April 9.30–11.45, 2–4.45.

TOULOUSE. Musée des Augustins, 21 rue Metz (tel. 61-22-21-82). Open daily, except Tues., Wed. morning and public hols., 10–12, 2–6 (and to 10 P.M. on Wed.).

Musée St.-Raymond, pl. St.-Sernin (tel. 61-22-21-85). Open daily, except Tues. and Sun. morning, 10–12, 2–6; for guided tours, inquire at Musée des Augustins (see above).

Les Jacobins. Open daily except Sun. 10–12, 3–6.30 (5.30 in winter).

WINTER SPORTS. The Pyrenees comprise the second most important ski region in France. Here you have real mountain skiing at lower rates than the more frequented Alps. The weather tends to be warmer and sunnier too. The region is less given to social distinctions than the Alps: fanciest center is Superbagnères, with nearby Luchon. Even there however accommodations are bargain-priced compared with the Alpine centers. The season runs Dec.–Apr., and there are plenty of lifts, ski schools, rinks, etc.

Andorra. Some of the finest virgin skiing fields in the Pyrenees, if not in Europe, are to be found in Andorra. Equipment, however, is rather minimal, and a good skier has soon done everything there is to do. Fine cross-country and powder-snow skiing, on the other hand. There are two ski centers, one at Pas de la Casa and Envalira, the other at Soldeu lift. Season: Dec. into June.

THE ATLANTIC COAST

Two Thousand Years of Wine

With well over 640 km. (400 miles) of coastline, including long sandy beaches stretching right down to the Spanish border beyond elegant Biarritz and picturesque St.-Jean-de-Luz, most of this part of western France is holiday country *par excellence.* The many resorts, catering for every pocketbook, offer an enormous variety of sports opportunities, especially sailing, swimming, fishing, waterskiing and windsurfing, all of which can be practised both in the sea and on the inland lakes. The magnificent sandy beaches running south from Royan are backed by 1,215,000 hectares (3 million acres) of pine forests, through which snakes a chain of lakes, many of them recently developed (but not over-developed) and equipped with every type of holiday amenity.

Yet the Atlantic coast is far more varied than those who come here merely to soak up the sun might realize. That same sun has been bringing prosperity to the region since the time of the Romans, by ripening the grapes that produce the magnificent clarets that are one of the chief glories of France. Bordeaux, the headquarters of the region's wine trade, is a large and prosperous town, with many cultural attractions. The town of Arcachon, by contrast, depends on its splendid oysters beds, while further north La Rochelle is an important fishing port. Right down in the south, the resort of Biarritz still has a smart summer season, a far cry from the fiercely local traditions of the Basque country and the simple life led in the little farmhouses of the Béarn, in what is now known as the Pyrénées Atlantiques. Inland, Poitou, way up in the north of this region, is different again, with much to offer in the way of art and architectural treasures, as well as a haven for seekers of solitude and rural charm.

Beaches and Lakes

Let's start by visiting the coast, which has resorts for all tastes and budgets. Until fairly recently this part of France had escaped the attentions of the developers, except of course for the chic resorts down by the Spanish border. But a government program to increase the area's tourist potential has led to many new yacht marinas, golf courses and the like, none of which, needless to say, is popular with nature lovers and the growing ecology lobby in France. Yet development hasn't so far spoilt this coastline and the sea is still clear and clean. Bathing is a delight (though you should bear in mind that in some places the undertow is such that it's dangerous to swim too far out).

If you start in the north you come first to Les Sables d'Olonne, a fast-growing resort in the Vendée that is only 450 km. (280 miles) from Paris. This little town is a busy fishing port as well as catering for its thriving tourist trade. The fine sandy beach is a delightful place on which to bask in the sun. On special feast days you may see, clattering along the streets in their little wooden shoes, the slim, graceful Sablaise women, with their short pleated skirts and their perky winged hats. Walk along the Remblai esplanade beside the beach, and observe the carefree crowds reveling in the invigorating sea air. In the evening the casino has the usual program of concerts and festivities.

A trip by boat through the waterways of the extraordinary salt marshlands takes you to the forest of Olonne, covering nearly ten km. (six miles), with its serried ranks of stately pines.

Luçon, inland and to the east of Les Sables d'Olonne, has the distinction of having had Cardinal Richelieu as its bishop. Its 13th-century cathedral of Notre-Dame is only the first of the many interesting churches along the Atlantic coast.

La Rochelle

Halfway between Les Sables d'Olonne and Royan is La Rochelle, once one of the most important trading ports of France, through which passed the bulk of the trade with Canada. It was a great Protestant stronghold until its defeat by Cardinal Richelieu, but when France subsequently lost Canada to the English, La Rochelle received a blow from which it has never recovered. In 1891 the port of La Pallice was constructed five km. (three miles) away, with modern amenities designed to restore the former fortunes of the region. The Germans built their enormous submarine bases at La Pallice during the last war (they can still be seen). The town was heavily bombed by the Allies but has been handsomely restored.

La Rochelle still remains the most important fishing port on the Atlantic coast, and it is also the most interesting from the historic and architectural points of view. It is a delightful town with its 16th-century town hall, the rue des Merciers with old wooden houses, the covered market in the place du Marché, and the 14th-century towers at the entrance to the old port. Don't miss the Tour de la Chaîne, which used to help support the chain suspended between it and the Tour St.-Nicolas, which served as an efficient barrier when it was necessary to close the port. For a magnificent view of the town and surrounding countryside, climb to the summit of the Tour de la Lanterne, formerly a lighthouse. A new museum opened here in 1982: the Musée du Nouveau Monde (the Museum of the New World), which is a must for transatlantic visitors.

There is also a beach, and running down to it, the beautiful Parc Charruyer, through which meanders a stream that forms occasional pools inhabited by swans. You can spend many happy days in La Rochelle, exploring its treasures, or lounging in the old port with its picturesque fishing boats and old towers. A visit to the early-morning fish auction, with bidders shouting their prices, is fascinating.

La Rochelle is also a lively little town with chic boutiques and restaurants. It is overcrowded in summer, but very well worth exploring in spring or fall.

Take the ferry to the Ile de Ré, a flat and romantically melancholy island with beautiful wide beaches, ranging from sheltered coves where children can bathe safely to great stretches, like those in southern California, where the surf comes pounding in—and the currents can be tricky. Pine-covered dunes and woods for hiking and cycling, picturesque fishing villages, a couple of old churches, make this island a favorite with fashionable families from Bordeaux and Paris. But beware August: the camp sites are so crowded you can barely plant a tent pole, and the beaches near the towns get dirty. A plan to build a bridge to the island is being fought by lovers of the area.

South of Rochefort, a toll bridge leads to the increasingly popular resort island of Oléron, 32 km. (20 miles) long and six km. (four miles) wide, covered with pine woods, dunes and beaches. Oléron is well provided with hotels for all tastes and purses.

Still farther south, at the mouth of the Gironde, is Royan, which had to be extensively rebuilt after World War II damage. From here, a car-ferry service operates all day long to the Médoc peninsula.

Poitiers and Angoulême

On the way to Poitiers from the north and west, there are many artistic and historical sights to be seen, such as the Roman theater in Sanxay; the old donjons of Loudun and Niort; the Romanesque churches of Aulnay-de-Saintonge, St.-Généroux, Champdeniers and St.-Jouin-de-Marnes; the old stone bridges in Airvault, Parthenay and Châtellerault; a superb 16th-century castle in Oiron; the medieval château of Dampierre-sur-Boutonne; Touffou, a famous Renaissance castle; St.-Médard dominated by a 17th-century château, and Thouars with its venerable old houses and 12th-century church.

For a total change of pace, try the Marais Poitevin, promoted these days under the catchy, and totally inaccurate, name of La Venise Verte—the Green Venice. It is, of course, completely unlike Venice, for it is a spreading area of canal-laced fenland, without a building in sight. The Marais lies westwards from Niort on either side of the Sèvre-Niortaise river, with a few small villages—Coulon, Damvix, Arçais, La Ronde—dotted about. In summer you can travel the canals, called *rigoles* when they are wide, *conches* when narrow, in boats which are poled or paddled silently along; outboard motors are banned from all but one or two main canals. Designated a Nature Park in 1977, the Marais is still a lost world of small fields, curtained by thick green trees, and grazed by cows that have to be transported in by barge. One of the best places to start exploring this dreamlike region is at Coulon; but try and avoid Sundays, when the people of the area throng in for picnics.

Poitiers, the ancient capital of Poitou where English archers displayed their legendary skill and valor in 1356, is one of the most charming little towns in this part of France. Historically and artistically it has few rivals. The 4th-century baptistry of St.-Jean, one of the oldest Christian buildings in France, stands oddly in the middle of a modern thoroughfare; Notre-Dame-la-Grande, a strikingly unusual Romanesque church with an intricately carved 12th-century façade and pinecone-shaped towers, is surrounded by a picturesque flower market; the Gothic cathedral of St.-Pierre with steep steps descending to a huge portal has plump gargoyles and tremendous space and luminosity; Ste.-Radegonde, adorned by frescoes and colored columns, harbors a dark crypt containing the remains of St. Radegonde; St.-Hilaire-le-Grand, built on different levels, has a Romanesque exterior and heavily restored interior; St.-Porchaire, once an old clock tower, has been converted into a square church with interesting carved capitals. The Palais de Justice affords the only entrance to the 12th-century Palais des Ducs. In the vast Salle des Pas Perdus, with its late Gothic windows and the three largest fireplaces in France, Joan of Arc was questioned by the doctors of the university on behalf of Charles VII. Here too Richard the Lion Heart was proclaimed duke of Anjou and count of Poitou in 1170. Poitiers has a particularly interesting street, the Grand'Rue, where you'll find several long-established specialist stores, including what is probably the only place left in France where they make superb, hand-crafted umbrellas, and another, nearly three centuries old, specializing in candles.

Angoulême, a busy little town bedeviled by heavy traffic—the motorway unfortunately sweeps westwards to Saintes before heading south to Bordeaux—is best seen from the southwest, where the Ville Haute, or upper town, perched on a rocky promontory and surrounded by ramparts, is most picturesque. The Ville Basse, or lower town, housing the rail station and the industrial zone, is far less attractive. An enjoyable walk round the ramparts allows you to admire the elaborate carved façade of the cathedral of St.-Pierre in the Poitevin Romanesque style. Take time, and binoculars too, if possible, to study the 70-odd figures peopling the last Judgement centered on a striking Christ in Majesty, and to spot the lively scenes unexpectedly taken from the *Song of Roland*.

Saintes, an ancient Roman city on the river Charente has its magnificent Triumphal Arch of Germanicus, the ruins of a Roman theater, and three beautiful old churches. Close by, Cognac is a small town whose fame is based, of course, on brandy—if your head is strong visit the vaults of Hennessy, Otard, Martell and others. The town has old houses, the lovely park of François I, the Hôtel de Ville, and the ancient château of the Valois family (where François I was born in 1494) with a 13th-century tower and a charming Renaissance fountain.

Bordeaux, the Wine Capital

About 112 km. (70 miles) south of Saintes lies Bordeaux, one of France's largest cities and an important center of trade, industry, and culture. The last is the heritage of a past running back 2,000 years, when Bordeaux was a flourishing Roman city and the Romans drank Bordeaux wine. A reminder of the Roman era is to be seen in the Palais

Gallien, all that remains of the 3rd-century amphitheater. In the 12th century Bordeaux with Aquitaine, of which it was the capital, became English, when Henry Plantagenet, who had married Eleanor, Duchess of Aquitaine, became Henry II of England. The English tongue distorted Aquitaine to Guyenne, and *clairette* (which in French means a sparkling white wine of the south) to claret. Not until 1453 did Bordeaux again become French.

This bustling city on the broad Garonne river has retained a feeling of prosperity and elegance despite its importance as a modern economic center. Many of the buildings date from the 18th century, a period of French architecture when mansions of noble proportions, grouped together to form elegant streets and squares, broad avenues and sweeping vistas, were very much the order of the day. Even the old town, le Vieux Bordeaux, is not medieval, unlike many French towns, but 18th-century. Many of the city's beautiful buildings have recently been restored and add a new charm and interest to a city that was already noted as a place in which to stand and stare. Make sure you stroll in the newly-restored place du Parlement, where all the restaurant and café terraces sport identical creamy-white parasols in summer, with thick wooden poles and spokes resembling ships' masts—a reminder that the quayside and the place de la Bourse, designed by the two Gabriels, is only a few minutes' walk away. Famous landmarks in the Old Town include the Grosse Cloche, or Big Bell, a large bell tower, and the tall Tour St.-Michel, another bell tower once attached to a basilica.

Exploration of the Old Town can be combined with a visit to the cathedral of St.-André, an impressive building of various architectural styles and with some magnificent carvings surrounding the huge portals, the Portail Nord and Porte Royale. Bordeaux's major museums are conveniently grouped just by the cathedral. Right opposite the west front are the Fine Arts Museum, full of major French paintings and sculpture, and the Aquitaine Museum, devoted to the history of the region from the prehistoric period down to recent centuries. The two museums are set on either side of the attractive gardens behind the City Hall, once the bishop's palace. Close by you will also find the Museum of Decorative (or Applied) Art, which in the mid-'80s was expanded to house an important collection of some 20,000 exhibits dating from the Restoration period.

After visiting these museums, you might like to make your way via the elegant, almost oval place Gambetta along the cours de l'Intendance, a chic shopping street, to the place de la Comédie and the city's best-known building, the majestic Grand Théâtre, fronted by a superb colonnade that looks quite magical against a blue sky or illuminated at night. Visit the surprising Eglise Notre-Dame nearby, with its elaborate Baroque facade, before strolling along the leafy Allées de Tourny to reach the huge Esplanade des Quinconces. The effect of this famous esplanade sweeping down to the river is somewhat marred these days by the endless surge of traffic, but it is still impressive with its monumental sculpture groups. From the place Tourny you can follow the cours de Verdun to a large and attractive public garden housing the city's Natural History Museum, from where a short walk will take you to the Palais Gallien, a 3rd-century amphitheater.

Many of these historic buildings are used as the setting for concerts held during the *Mai Musical,* one of France's most important music festivals. Other concerts are sometimes staged in major buildings in the surrounding area such as the Château de la Brède, where Montesquieu was born and spent a large part of every year.

Excursions into the Wine Region

If you are a wine lover, the tourist office in Bordeaux or in the local wine-producing villages will give details of vineyards that can be visited. But the easiest way to combine a trip through the vineyards with some interesting sightseeing is to take an excursion to St.-Emilion, the fortified hilltop town that gives its name to one of the region's richest wine districts.

Scenically situated on the slopes at the very edge of the town is the Château Ausone, whose wines are officially ranked as the greatest of St.-Emilion's 400-odd vintages. The town itself offers many medieval details and several curiosities from times even more remote. Among the latter is the 7th-century hermitage of St.-Emilion. Hollowed out of the rock, this contains crude versions of the basic modern conveniences—a bed, a table, a clothes closet, and a fountain more or less in the form of a bathtub. Giggling girls drop two pins into the "tub," if the pins land in the form of a cross it is a sure sign that the dropper will be married within the year.

Nearby is the entrance to the "monolithic" chapel. This underground shrine, whose nave is separated from the aisles by ten roughly square columns, 38 meters (125 ft.) long, about 20 meters (65 ft.) wide and more than 15 meters (50 ft.) high. The dimensions are impressive when you learn that monks, beginning their work some 900 years ago, hacked the whole church out of solid rock. A subterranean passage, once running from the church, leads to partially excavated catacombs containing clumsily carved columns and many skeletons in superimposed tombs of great antiquity.

North of Bordeaux, on the west bank of the Gironde, is the fabled Médoc area, known to wine connoisseurs the world over. Only a short distance from the city, and also from the little resorts on the coast north of Arcachon, where you might like to base yourself, are such names as Château-Margaux, Château Mouton-Rothschild and Château-Lafite. Wine tastings can often be arranged, but it is wise to plan this in advance because written notice may be required. Fit in some sightseeing too: at Mouton-Rothschild you can pore over a splendid collection of exhibits related to wine and vineyards, ranging from wine glasses to paintings and sculpture in the château's museum. Several châteaux are worth admiring for their architecture alone: Château-Margaux is a large and imposing neo-Classical building, while the 18th-century Château de Beychevelle seems much less massive with its white walls and elegant balustrades.

Another wine pilgrimage can be made to the Sauternais, the area southeast of Bordeaux centered on the little town of Sauternes itself, where you'll certainly want to sample the delectable white wine of the same name (in fact it has a wonderful golden hue), made by allowing the grapes to rot on the vines. A couple of kilometers away, and commanding lovely views, is Château-Yquem, where the most famous —and by far the most expensive—wine in the area has been produced for centuries. You can wander in the courtyard and peep into the cellars with their huge vats and barrels. One of the finest local buildings is the Château de Malle, which is surrounded by large grounds including terraced gardens dotted with sculptures.

Arcachon and Le Pyla, and pleasant little Mimizan-Plage south of Bordeaux, offer delightful beaches (not so self-conscious as Biarritz), the highest sand dunes in Europe, and a variety of sports, ranging from wind-surfing and pine-needle skiing, to yacht racing and Basque *pelote.* Don't be misled by this word *"pelote,"* however; you won't be in the Basque country until you've crossed the strange sandy plain and marsh of the Landes between Bordeaux and Bayonne. Nowadays, it is mostly pine forest, the result of a vast program of land reclamation and afforestation. The Regional Park of the Gascony Landes, covering 10,000 acres, has its own museum, the Ecomusée de la Grande-Lande, well worth a visit. You'll see a collection of furnished houses and farm buildings typical of the region, plus exhibits relating to local crafts, all set in a lovely clearing in the forest.

On the southern fringes of the Landes are the beaches of Hossegor and Capbreton, and Dax, an inland spa, the ancient Roman Aquae Tarbellicae. There are many new holiday centers and campsites round the string of lakes running parallel to the coast. At Bombannes, for example, you'll find a well-equipped recreation center.

The Basque Country

About 120,000 of the nearly two million Basques live in France. They are handsome in their national dress, characterized by the beret, worn frequently by the men, rope-soled shoes called *espadrilles,* and the *makhila,* which is carried on a thong and serves both as a walking stick and as a weapon.

The Basques are famous for their dancing, poetic improvisation, *pelote* and, in recent years, agitation for a measure of autonomy for the Basque provinces in Spain. French Basques rarely have the same craving for autonomy, yet they sympathize with their Spanish brothers and there are strong cultural and linguistic links across the frontier.

While Basque legends and dances have their counterparts in many European countries, the origin of these people remains obscure. The resemblance of their evening call, the *irrinzina,* to that of the Upper Amazon Indians does not solve the mystery; nor does the fact that the Basques reckon in 20s, like the ancient Mayas. Some ethnologists say their language resembles Japanese.

Bayonne, Capital of the Basque Country

Although Bayonne is the official capital of the Pays Basque, it is not typically Basque. During the August festivities and bullfights the city is a colorful blend of Gascon, Spanish and Basque vivacity.

Bayonne's Basque Museum offers a delightful presentation of life and lore in the little country's three states, Labourd, Basse-Navarre and Soule. The Bonnat Museum houses one of France's richest collections of El Greco, Tintoretto, Dürer, Goya and Bonnat. Don't miss the lovely Gothic cathedral of Ste.-Marie.

You'll need several days if you're going to explore the countryside as well as Bayonne's old streets, quays and ramparts. For fine views of the Pyrenees, take a short excursion on foot (one hour for the round trip) to the Hauteurs de St.-Etienne, or drive to La Croix de Mouguerre, about six km. (four miles) south.

Biarritz, Fashionable Seaside Resort

The most frequented of France's Atlantic beach resorts is Biarritz, which stands at the entrance to the Pays Basque. It enjoys an unusually favorable year-round climate and a particularly attractive location, where the sandy pine forests of the Landes merge with the craggy Basque coast. Carlist exiles from Spain put Biarritz on the map in 1838. Unable to visit San Sebastian on the Spanish coast, they sought a recreation spot as close as possible to their old stamping ground. Among the exiles was Eugénie de Montijo, destined to become empress of France, with whom Biarritz found special favor.

It was the Empress Eugénie who gave Biarritz its coming out party, changing the town into an international favorite. Visits by Queen Victoria and Edward VII attracted a fashionable British clientele to Biarritz. Half the crowned heads of Europe slept in Eugénie's villa, now the Hôtel du Palais. After 40 years or so of eclipse Biarritz is now modestly coming back into fashion, and celebrities are again appearing. But its true golden age will never return, and many find it staid and unexciting.

Extending from the Hôtel du Palais to the Côte des Basques is a magnificent promenade that is one of Biarritz's main attractions. Visit the Rocher de la Vierge when the sea is rough, for a dramatic view. Follow the lower promenade, along the boulevard du Prince de Galles, for a glimpse of the foaming breakers that beat constantly upon the sands, giving the name of Côte d'Argent (Silver Coast) to the length of the French Basque coast.

The lighthouse is a few minutes' walk beyond the Hôtel Miramar, on the summit of Cap St.-Martin, and commands a splendid view. When the tide is low you'll be able to continue on to the Plage de la Chambre d'Amour.

St.-Jean-de-Luz, Resort Town and Fishing Port

More intimate and picturesque is the resort and fishing-town of St.-Jean-de-Luz. Some of its fortified houses are several centuries old. The church of St.-Jean is typical Basque architecture, with an aisleless nave, gilded altar screen, and three-tiered wooden galleries reserved for men. Reserved, also, since 1660, is the door through which Louis XIV passed to wed Spanish Maria Theresa. (Their marriage contract is in the Musée du Souvenir, in Ducontenia Park.) The door was then sealed to prevent its being used by common folk.

Sailors of St.-Jean-de-Luz were the first to fish the Grand Banks off Newfoundland—in 1520—and they supplied most of the ships that broke the English blockade of La Rochelle in 1627. The port suffered a mortal blow when the Grand Banks fishing rights were transferred to Great Britain in 1713, but the new harbor has since become an important sardine-fishing port and center of the French tuna industry. Much of the town's interest is centered on the harbor. In the place Louis XIV is the 17th-century Château Lohobiague (or de Louis XIV), and overlooking the harbor is the turreted Maison de l'Infante, where the Infanta Maria Theresa stayed before her marriage.

The celebration of *Toro del Fuego,* which begins on June 24, is in itself sufficient reason for a visit to the Basque country. For three days and nights the entire populace dances the *fandango,* that stunning exhibition of restrained passion, in the streets. And best of all, the Bull of St.-Jean, a crazy, fire-spitting creature made of papier-mâché, is carried about the town, lashing about in a frenzy of pseudo rage and real sparks.

A favorite excursion is to the mountain of La Rhune (898 meters/2,950 ft.)—you can climb it in three hours—and to the little Basque village of Ascain, where Pierre Loti wrote his novel, *Ramuntcho*. The Col de St.-Ignace is the starting point of a cog-wheel railway to La Rhune, a 30-minute trip. Beyond (13 km./eight miles) is another characteristic village, Sare, whose caves are well worth visiting.

Hendaye and the Spanish Frontier

At Hendaye, on the Ile-des-Faisans in the middle of the river Bidassoa, which separates France from Spain, François I shamefully purchased his release from Spanish captivity by delivering his two small sons as hostages, with no intention of keeping his side of the bargain. Some hundred years later the island witnessed a scene of great splendor when Louis XIV met his bride, Maria Theresa, and her father, Philip IV of Spain.

From Hendaye you can look across the Bidassoa to Spanish Fuentarrabia. A scant 24 km. (15 miles) away along the magnificent coast is Biarritz's rival, San Sebastian. If you're driving, you can stop to enjoy the panorama that spreads below the Haya, or Mount of Three Crowns, and the curious fortified church of Renteria. And you can wander in the old towns of San Pedro and San Juan, which guard the narrow entrance to the Bay of Pasajes.

Once beyond the coastal villas you find, in the mountain towns, charming Basque houses. Neat, white-washed dwellings, often decorated in peasant fashion, with hearts, flowers and birds, they crowd around the village church, beside which there is always a well for *pelote*. The Basques blithely mingle religion with their beloved national sport; they also have a fine, philosophical attitude toward death. You often see the inscription, *"Orhait hilceaz"*—"Remember death." Indeed, you can almost feel this peaceful acceptance of fate in the country graveyards, so silent and so timeless, with their strange tombstones. The finest examples of these faceless antiquities are found in the cemeteries of Bidarray and Urrugne. At the pass of Roncevaux—remember your *Song of Roland?*—is the enchanting town of St.-Jean-Pied-de-Port, an ideal place for rambling, fishing, or just sitting in the sun.

Before you leave the Pays Basque you may want to linger in Soule, to see its three-spired churches—especially those of Gotein and Aussurucq—and, if you're lucky the most lavish, as well as the oldest, Basque dance, the *mascarade*. For five centuries this strange tradition has persisted, with the same masques, the most curious of which is that of the *zamalzain*, who wears a wooden horse strapped about his waist. If you happen to be in Itxassou, Bidarray or Louhossoa on the Sunday after Corpus Christi, you will see all this, amidst dancing, singing and popping of shotguns.

PRACTICAL INFORMATION FOR THE ATLANTIC COAST

TOURIST OFFICES. All the *départements* of the Atlantic Coast have their own regional tourist offices (written enquiries only). These are: *Vendée, Poitou and Charente*—**Deux-Sèvres,** 18 rue du Rempart, 79000 Niort (tel. 49-24-76-79); **Charente-Maritime,** 11 bis rue des Augustins, BP 1152, 17008, La Rochelle Cedex (tel. 46-41-43-33); **Vendée,** Préfecture, 85000 La Roche-sur-Yon gare (tel. 51-05-45-28). *Bordelais-Landes*—**Gironde,** 21 cours de l'Intendance, 33080 Bordeaux Cedex (tel. 56-52-61-40); **Landes,** 22 rue Victor-Hugo, 40011 Mont-de-Marsan (tel. 58-75-38-67). *Pays Basque*—**Pyrénées-Atlantiques,** Parlement de Navarre, rue Henri-IV, 64000 Pau (tel. 59-27-32-19).

There are local tourist offices in the following towns: **Angoulême,** City Hall (tel. 45-95-16-84) and at rail station (tel. 45-92-27-57); **Arcachon,** pl. Franklin-Roosevelt (tel. 56-83-01-69); **Bayonne,** pl. Liberté (tel. 59-59-31-31); **Biarritz,** sq. Ixelles (tel. 59-21-20-24); **Bordeaux,** 12 cours 30-Juillet (tel. 56-44-28-41); **Poitiers,** 11 rue V.-Hugo (tel. 49-41-58-22); **La Rochelle,** 10 rue Fleuriau (tel. 46-41-14-68); **St.-Jean-de-Luz,** pl. Maréchal-Foch (tel. 59-26-03-16); **St.-Jean-Pied-de-Port,** pl. Charles-de-Gaulle (tel. 59-37-03-57).

REGIONAL FOOD AND DRINK. Needless to say, the coastal regions specialize in fish dishes, but that is almost the only culinary link between the northern and southern ends of France's Atlantic coast. In the Vendée and Poitou, mussels are cooked with saffron and cream in a *mouclade,* while *chaudrée* fish chowder recalls the fish stews of Brittany just to the north, and poached fish is served with a *beurre blanc* sauce based on the famous Charentes butter.

From near Bordeaux come the famous oysters of Marennes, green from the algae on which they feed, scallops and crayfish are cooked *à la bordelaise* with shallots, brandy and white wine. Indeed, shallots and onions are a Bordeaux trademark, appearing together with wine and cognac, in a wide variety of meat and poultry dishes and with wild *cèpes* (boletus) mushrooms. In the Landes you find all sorts of little birds such as the famous roast *ortolan* (bunting), as well as *foie gras* liver *pâtés.* (The distinctive flavor of much of this southwest region of France comes from the use of goose fat.)

Characteristic flavors of the Basque country are *piment basquais,* a dried red pepper, and the renowned ham of Bayonne. Red and green peppers are used in *pipérade,* a thick purée of scrambled eggs flavored with tomato, onions and garlic. Beef, lamb, poultry, and fish (cod and hake are favorites) are cooked with peppers, while *tioro* fish stew is spiced with hot pepper and topped with mussels. Squid *(chipirones)* are appreciated, stuffed or cooked in their ink, and you'll often find fresh trout from the mountains. For dessert, try *gâteau basque,* (pastry with a custard and often fruit filling), or one of the excellent chocolates of Bayonne.

The Atlantic coast is not cheese country. However Poitou and Charentes make goat cheeses, and a few sheep cheeses come from the Pyrenees.

The Basque region produces several wines, one of the best-known being *Irouléguy,* but they cannot of course compare with the superb clarets of the Bordeaux region, which include the most famous names in the world. The wines of Bordeaux are classified in five *crus* or growths. Preeminent are the *premier grand cru* wines of the Médoc peninsula, *Château Lafite* and *Château Latour,* at Pauillac, and *Château Margaux,* at Margaux. Equally good is *Château Haut-Brion,* in the Graves district at Pessac. Queen of the white wines is the matchless *Château Yquem,* sweet but never cloying, from the Sauternes district. Also good are the rich wines of St.-Emilion and the red and white wines of the Graves district, so-called after the gravelly soil from which they spring. The district of Entre-deux-Mers, between the Dordogne and the Gironde, also produces good quality red and white wines. The Cognac region naturally produces wonderful brandy, and you'll also find cognac-flavored chocolates here.

HOTELS AND RESTAURANTS. The Atlantic Coast can offer accommodations to suit every pocket, ranging from the luxury hotels of a resort like Biarritz to modest but comfortable little hotels in the family resorts, and small inns in the inland districts, where prices can be substantially lower than on the coast. Most resort hotels are closed in winter, though not in Bordeaux. This is also a good area for camping; addresses are available from tourist offices.

For general notes on hotels and restaurants, see "Hotels" and "Restaurants" in *Facts at Your Fingertips.*

ANGOULÊME. *France* (M), 1 pl. Halles (tel. 45-95-47-95). 60 rooms. Restaurant closed Christmas, New Year, Sun. for lunch and Sat. Centrally located in Ville Haute; good views from garden; service a bit distant but efficient; classical cuisine. AE, DC, MC, V. *Novotel* (M), 6 km. (3½ miles) north (tel. 45-68-53-22). 100 rooms. Usual functional rooms and light meals, plus pool and garden. AE, DC, MC, V. *Epi d'Or* (I), 66 blvd. Chabasse (tel. 45-95-67-64). 30 rooms. Just outside Ville Haute; no restaurant. AE, DC, MC, V. *Trois Piliers* (I), 3 blvd. Bury (tel. 45-92-42-11). 50 rooms. Central; no restaurant.

At **Asnières-sur-Nouère,** 10 km. (6 miles) west, *Moulin du Maine Brun* (E), (tel. 45-96-92-62). 20 rooms. Closed Nov. to Dec. 15 and Sun. night, Mon. (Dec. 15 through March). Exceptionally pleasant converted mill on road to Cognac, is now a Relais et Châteaux member; excellent restaurant too (M). AE, DC, V.

Restaurant. *Ruelle* (I), 6 rue Trois Notre-Dame (tel. 45-92-94-64). Closed Sat. for lunch, Sun. and Mon. New and very good restaurant in town, with *nouvelle cuisine* and good-value *menus.* V.

ARCACHON. *Arc* (E), 89 blvd. Plage (tel. 56-83-06-85). 30 rooms. Right by yacht harbor, with pool; and terraces to all rooms; no restaurant, but some rooms have kitchenettes. AE, DC, MC, V. *Richelieu* (M), 185 blvd. Plage (tel. 56-83-16-50). 43 rooms. Closed Nov. to mid-March. Stylish turn-of-the-century place, now well modernized; no restaurant, though light meals available in the evenings. AE, DC, V. *Roc et Moderne* (M), 200 blvd. Plage (tel. 56-83-07-43). 54 rooms. Closed mid-Oct. through March. Close to beach, with one modern wing, one older but well renovated; restaurant is (I).

At **Pyla-sur-Mer,** 4 km. (2½ miles) southwest, *La Guitoune* (M), (tel. 56-22-70-10). 22 rooms. Closed mid-Nov. to mid-Dec. Surrounded by pine trees and close to sea; cuisine is good but can be over-elaborate. AE, DC, MC, V.

Restaurants. *Mareyeur* (E), 89 blvd. Plage (tel. 56-83-35-45). Closed Oct. through March, Sun. for dinner (except July and Aug.), Mon. Stylish and inventive regional cuisine; must reserve. AE, DC, MC, V. *Chez Boron* (M), 15 rue Professeur-Jolyet (tel. 56-83-29-96). Closed mid-semester vacations in Feb., first half of Dec., Wed. (except July and Aug.). Lovely fresh fish; very popular. AE, DC, MC, V. *Gérard Tissier* (M), 222 blvd. Plage (tel. 56-83-41-82). Closed mid-Nov. to mid-Dec., Mon. (except for dinner in July and Aug.). A new find and quite delightful; right by beach; specializes in fish, but meat dishes are good too. AE, DC, MC, V. *Chez Yvette* (I), 59 blvd. Gal Leclerc (tel. 56-83-05-11). Closed Jan. Welcoming, best for oysters and sorbets.

At **Pyla-sur-Mer,** 4 km. (2½ miles) southwest, *Corniche* (M), (tel. 56-22-72-11). Closed mid-Oct. through April, Wed. (except July and Aug.). Sea views and pleasant meals; also has 15 peaceful rooms. (M)

BAYONNE. *Agora* (M), av. Jean Rostand (tel. 59-63-30-90). 110 rooms. Modern, with garden overlooking river; light meals only. AE, DC, MC, V. *Deux Rivières* (M), 21 rue Thiers (tel. 59-59-14-61). 62 rooms. Friendly service; central but reasonably quiet; no restaurant. AE, DC, MC, V.

Restaurants. *Beluga* (M), 15 rue Tonneliers (tel. 59-25-52-13). Closed Sun. Chic, tasty *nouvelle cuisine.Tanière* (M), 53 av. Resplandy (tel. 59-25-53-42). Closed mid-Feb. to mid-March, second half June, Mon. for dinner, Tues., except in July and Aug. Friendly ambiance and good specialties from the southwest. AE, DC, V. *Euzkalduna* (I), 61 rue Pannecau (tel. 59-59-28-02). Closed second half of May, Oct., Mon. for lunch, and every evening except Sat. for dinner (but check). Good Basque name and good Basque food; good value too.

BERGERAC. *Flambée* (M), route de Périguex (tel. 53-57-52-33). 21 rooms. Closed Jan. through Mar.; restaurant closed Sun. Beautiful country house with park and pool. AE, DC, MC, V.

At **St. Julien de Crempse** (12 km., 7½ miles from Bergerac by D107), *Manoir Grand Vignoble* (M), (tel. 53-24-23-16, or in Paris 42-27-66-26). 26 rooms. 17th-century house; huge park; horse-riding, cycling, tennis, pool. Restaurant.

Restaurant. *Cyrano* (M), 2 blvd. Montaigne (tel. 53-57-02-76). Closed first half July, Dec., Mon., Sun. evening (except July and Aug.). Unusual food with inventive variations on regional specialties. Also has 10 (I) rooms. AE, V.

BIARRITZ. *Miramar* (L), ave. Impératrice (tel. 59-24-85-20). 105 rooms. Opened early '80s and ostentatiously modern; pool, saltwater cure center, good restaurant (see below). AE, DC, MC, V. *Palais,* (L), av. Impératrice (tel. 59-24-09-40). 120 rooms. Closed mid-Nov. to mid-Apr. Napoleon III and the Empress Eugenie once lived here, and it's still pretty much like a royal palace. Excellent restaurant (see below). AE, DC, MC, V.

Eurotel (E), 19 ave. Perspective (tel. 59-24-32-33). Closed Nov. to mid-Mar. Restaurant closed Sun. and Mon. for lunch. Modern, very convenient for beach; with restaurant, though some rooms have kitchenettes. AE, DC, V. *Régina et Golf* (M), 52 ave. Impératrice (tel. 59-24-09-60). 45 rooms. Closed Nov. through April. Old-established and charming, now thoroughly modernized; close to beach, with restaurant; direct access to golf course. AE, DC, V. *Windsor* (M), Grande Plage (tel. 59-24-08-52). 37 rooms. Closed Nov. through March. Modern, close to casino and beach; with restaurant. AE, DC, MC, V.

At **Anglet,** 4 km. (2½ miles) away, *Château de Brindos* (L), (tel. 59-50-17-68). 16 rooms. Pseudo-medieval castle, beautifully located on lake with pool and classical cuisine; Relais et Châteaux member. AE, DC, MC, V.

Restaurants. *Café de Paris* (E), 5 pl. Bellevue (tel. 59-24-19-53). Closed Feb., Mon. (except July and Aug.). best-known restaurant in town, serving *nouvelle cuisine;* stylish service, chic clientele. AE, DC, V. *Palais* (E), in Palais Hôtel (tel. 59-24-09-40). Closed Nov. through March. Very elegant; mostly *nouvelle cuisine.* AE, DC, MC, V.

Alambic (M), 5 pl. Bellevue (tel. 59-24-53-41). Closed mid-Nov. through Mar., Mon. except July and Aug. Brasserie-type sister-restaurant of Café de Paris, open all day and very good value. *Coq Hardi* (M) in El Mirador Hôtel (tel. 59-24-13-81). Closed Dec. to mid-March. Excellent for fish. AE, DC, V. *Chez Maurice* (M), 87 av. Marne (tel. 59-24-01-61). Closed Sun. for dinner, Mon. (except in July and Aug.). Lots of local color and atmosphere; delicious fish; stays open late. AE, V. *Relais Miramar* (M), in Miramar Hôtel (tel. 59-24-85-20). Chic, overlooking pool. AE, DC, MC, V. *Auberge du Relais* (I), 44 av. Marne (tel. 59-24-85-90). Closed Feb. Very good value; also has 14 rooms. AE, DC, V.

At **airport,** 8 km. (5 miles) southwest, *Relais de Parme* (E), (tel. 59-23-93-84). Closed Sat. A very superior airport restaurant, under same ownership as Café de Paris in town. AE, DC, V.

At **Bidart,** 6 km. (3½ miles) away, *Chistera* (M), (tel. 59-26-51-07). Closed Nov. to mid-May, Tues., except July and Aug. No lunches. Most attractive, with lovely old furniture and lots of atmosphere; excellent fish. AE, V.

BORDEAUX. *Aquitania* (E), quartier du Lac (tel. 56-50-83-80). 204 rooms. Restaurant closed Aug. and Sun. At Exhibit Center, modern and comfortable, with good-value restaurant and various bars; airconditioned. AE, DC, MC, V. *Grand Hôtel de Bordeaux* (E), pl. Comédie (tel. 56-90-93-44). 98 rooms. Right opposite Grand Théâtre; extensively modernized but rooms are small; no proper restaurant, but brasserie for quick meals. AE, DC, MC, V.

Mapotel Terminus (M), at Gare St.-Jean (tel. 56-92-71-58). 81 rooms. Right by rail station; old-established but well modernized; restaurant *(Relais St.-Jean)* has good regional dishes. AE, DC, V. *Mercure* (M), quartier du Lac (tel. 56-50-90-30). 98 rooms. At Exhibit Center, north of town, modern with pool, tennis courts and restaurant; airconditioned. AE, DC, MC, V. *Royal Médoc* (M), 3 rue Sèze (tel. 56-81-72-42). 45 rooms. Close to esplanade des Quinconces in town center, but reasonably quiet; efficient service; no restaurant. AE, DC, MC, V.

Bayonne (I), 4 rue Martignac (tel. 56-48-00-88). 37 rooms. Closed second half Dec. Modern, good location in town center; no restaurant. V. *Ibis* (I), quartier du Lac (tel. 56-50-96-50). 119 rooms. At Exhibit Center; usual functional rooms in this impersonal but well run chain; restaurant for light meals. V.

Restaurants. *Clavel* (E), 44 rue Domercq (tel. 56-92-91-52). Closed school Feb. and Easter vacations, second half July, Sun. and Mon. Opposite rail station and one of best in town; mostly *nouvelle cuisine*. AE, DC, V. *Dubern* (E), 42 allées Tourny (tel. 56-48-03-44). Closed Sun. Superb classical cuisine with regional flavor; very elegant; chef is Christian Clément. AE, DC, MC, V.

Estaminet (M), 42 allées Tourny (tel. 56-48-03-44). Closed Sat. for lunch, Sun. Cheaper version of the chic Dubern, in same building; open late, home-style cooking. AE, DC, MC, V. *Tupina* (M), 6 rue Porte-de-la-Monnaie (tel. 56-91-56-37). Closed Sun. Old favorite for regional dishes; small but airconditioned. V. *Vieux Bordeaux* (M), 27 rue Buhan (tel. 56-52-94-36). Closed Aug., one week in Feb., Sat. for lunch, Sun. Very popular place for *nouvelle cuisine,* on edge of Old Town. AE, DC, V.

Ombrière (I), 14 pl. Parlement (tel. 56-44-82-69). Closed Aug., Sun. and Mon. Chic clientele, ideal for openair meals on pretty square in heart of Old Town; newish cuisine. AE, DC, V.

At **Pessac,** 8 km. (5 miles) away, *Réserve* (M), (tel. 56-07-13-28). Closed Nov. through Mar. Good for outdoor meals in lovely garden setting; also has 19 comfortable (E) rooms. MC, V.

CHOLET. At **Saint-Laurent-sur-Sèvre,** 11 km. (7 miles) south, *Baumotel* (M), (tel. 51-67-88-12). 20 rooms. Attractive country hotel with terrace overlooking Sèvre Nantaise; good classical restaurant called *Chaumière* (M), quick grills also available (I). AE, DC, MC, V.

COGNAC. *Logis de Beaulieu* (M), on N141 road (tel. 45-82-30-50). 21 rooms. Closed second half Dec. Rich classical cuisine in restaurant and comfortable rooms, some with antique furniture; huge garden; wine tastings arranged. AE, DC, MC, V. *Auberge* (I), 13 rue Plumejeau (tel. 45-32-08-70). 27 rooms. Closed Christmas and New Year period. Restaurant closed Sat. Peaceful, with good value restaurant. MC, V.

At **Fleurac,** 24 km. (15 miles) east, *Domaine de Fleurac* (M), (tel. 45-81-78-22). 16 rooms. Closed Oct., Sun. night and Mon. (Sept. 15 to May 15). Elegant 16th-century manorhouse in lovely grounds; pleasant restaurant. DC, MC, V.

Restaurants. *Pigeons Blancs* (M), 110 Jules-Brisson (tel. 45-82-16-36). Closed first half Jan. and Sun. (restaurant only). Converted coaching inn owned by same family since 17th century; regional dishes cooked "new"-style; good value. AE, DC, V.

At **Cierzac,** 13 km. (8 miles) away, *Moulin de Cierzac* (M), (tel. 46-83-01-32). Closed Feb., Mon. (except in July and Aug.). One of most pleasant restaurants in area, in converted watermill; also has 10 rooms. DC, V.

At **Jarnac,** 15 km. (10 miles) away, *Château* (M), (tel. 45-81-07-17). Closed second half Aug., second half Feb., Sat. for lunch, Sun. for dinner and Mon. Friendly family-style place, ideal for lunch out. MC, V.

DAX. *Parc* (M), 1 pl. Thiers (tel. 58-74-86-17). 41 rooms. Typical spa hotel with direct access to thermal baths; pleasant river setting and good restaurant (closed Sun. and Dec. 15 to Jan. 15). AE, DC, MC, V. *Regina* (M), blvd. Sports (tel. 58-74-84-58). 132 rooms. Closed mid-Dec. through Feb. Direct access to spa building; garden, restaurant. AE, DC. *Splendid* (M), cours Verdun (tel. 58-74-59-30). 180 rooms. Closed Dec. through Feb. Old-style "grand hotel," sensitively modernized; lovely big rooms, garden, pool and restaurant. AE, DC, MC.

At **Magesq,** 17 km. (10 miles) away, *Relais de la Poste* (M), (tel. 58-47-70-25). 15 rooms. Closed mid-Nov. to Christmas. Restaurant closed Mon. for dinner, Tues. (except July and Aug.). Lovely hotel with pool, tennis, and outstanding restaurant serving good classical and regional food. AE, DC.

Restaurants. *Richelieu* (M), 13 av. Victor-Hugo (tel. 58-74-81-81). Regional dishes and décor; very pleasant; also has 20 (M) rooms. AE, DC, V. *Bois de Boulogne* (I), allée Bois-de-Boulogne (tel. 58-74-23-32). Closed Oct., Sun. for dinner, Mon. Good value *menus,* with some regional specialties.

EUGÉNIE-LES-BAINS. *Prés d'Eugénie-Michel Guérard* (E), (tel. 58-51-19-01). Closed mid-Nov. to early Mar. One of best in country, run by super-chef Michel Guérard of *cuisine minceur* fame; reserve well ahead; now has 7 luxury apartments and 28 almost as luxurious rooms to tempt you into a long stay (you won't get the *minceur* menu unless you're staying). AE, DC.

HENDAYE. *Liliac* (M), Rond-Point at Hendaye-Plage (tel. 59-20-02-45). 23 rooms. Comfortable and quite elegant; no restaurant; right on beach. AE, DC, MC, V. *Chez Antoinette* (I), pl. Pellot (tel. 59-20-08-47). 24 rooms. Closed Oct. through May. In town; restaurant offers filling regional dishes; good value.

Restaurant. At **Biriatou,** 4 km. (2½ miles) south, *Bakea* (M), (tel. 59-20-76-36). Closed Oct. to mid-May. Right by Spanish border, with lovely views and tasty regional cuisine; also has 15 (M) rooms. AE, DC, MC, V.

HOSSEGOR. *Beauséjour* (M), av. Genets (tel. 58-43-51-07). 46 rooms. Closed mid-Sept. through May. No lunches. Modern, in peaceful pine forest setting; pool and restaurant (I), open for dinner only. *Mercédès* (I), av. Tour-du-Lac (tel. 58-43-52-23). 40 rooms. Closed mid-Sept. to mid-June. Modern rooms with views; pool, garden; good restaurant. V.

Restaurant. *Huitrières du Lac* (M), 1187 av. Touring-Club (tel. 58-43-51-48). Closed Dec. through Feb., and Wed. (except in July and Aug.). Marvelous oysters and other seafood; also has 9 (I) rooms with views over lake.

LANGON. Restaurant. *Darroze* (M), 95 cours Leclerc (tel. 56-63-00-48). Closed mid-Oct. to mid-Nov., Sun. for dinner (except July and Aug.). Still one of the nicest restaurants in the area, with marvelous regional cuisine; also has 16 (I) rooms. AE, DC, MC, V.

MIMIZAN. *Côte d'Argent* (M), 4 av. Maurice-Martin (tel. 58-09-15-22). 40 rooms. Closed Oct. through May. Right by sea with views from "panoramic restaurant"; modern, comfortable rooms. AE, DC, MC, V. *Au Bon Coin du Lac* (I), 34 av. Lac (tel. 58-09-01-55). 8 rooms. Closed Feb. Restaurant closed Sun. for dinner and Mon. Attractive rooms; terrace for summer meals; superb regional cooking (M); try the *menus.* AE, V.

NIEUIL. *Château de Nieuil* (E), rte. de Fontagie, on the left (tel. 45-71-36-38). 13 rooms. Closed mid-Nov. to end of year, Jan. to mid-Apr., Wed. for lunch. Elegant Relais et Châteaux member with beautifully furnished rooms and excellent regional cuisine adapted to light, *nouvelle cuisine* style. AE, V.

OLÉRON, ILE DE. *Grand Large* (E), La Rémigeasse (tel. 46-75-37-89). 26 rooms. Closed mid-Oct. through March. Stylish Relais et Châteaux member with excellent restaurant, *Amiral,* serving marvelous fish; sea views; pool, tennis. *Pins du Vert-Bois* (M), Plage du Vert-Bois (tel. 46-75-34-98). 22 rooms. Closed mid-Sept. through May. No lunches. Most attractive setting in huge, flower-filled garden with pool, tennis courts and restaurant. AE, DC, V.

Restaurant. *Trois Chapons* (M), St.-Georges (tel. 46-76-51-51). Closed Mon. for dinner, Tues. (except July and Aug.) and Dec. to mid-Jan. Mixture of classical and more inventive cuisine; particularly good fish. AE, DC, V.

POITIERS. *France* (E), 28 rue Carnot (tel. 49-41-32-01). 87 rooms. Traditional provincial hotel in town center, with large, modernized rooms and good restaurant; very welcoming; interior garden and terrace. AE, DC, MC, V. *Europe* (I), 39 rue Carnot (tel. 49-88-12-00). 50 rooms. Central yet peaceful; no restaurant. V.

Restaurants. *Poitevin* (M), 76 rue Carnot (tel. 49-88-35-04). Closed July, Sun., Sat. for lunch. Good regional cuisine at reasonable prices. MC, V. *Maxime* (I), 4 rue St.-Nicolas (tel. 49-41-09-55). Good classical cuisine with some *nouvelle* touches; very popular so must reserve. AE, DC, MC, V.

At **La Croutelle**, 6 km. (4 miles) south, *Pierre Benoist* (M), (tel. 49-57-11-52). Closed second half Feb., first half Aug., Sun. for dinner and Mon. Converted farmhouse, very popular for carefully cooked classical cuisine with regional flavor; good-value *menu*. V.

RÉ, ILE DE. *Richelieu* (E), La Flotte (tel. 46-09-60-70). 30 rooms. Closed Nov. through Mar. Marvelous spot with pool; rooms in bungalows dotted round grounds overlooking sea; excellent restaurant specializing in seafood. V. *Atalante* (M), Ste.-Marie-de-Ré (tel. 46-30-22-44). 65 rooms. Hotel complex right on beach; some rooms in bungalows; good restaurant, golfcourse, tennis, sauna, heated saltwater pool and saltwater cure center next door under same management. AE, DC, MC, V. *Auberge de la Marée* (M), Rivedoux-Plage (tel. 46-09-80-02). 30 rooms. Closed Oct. through April. Delightful, with pool and flower-filled grounds; good restaurant with some (I) *menus*. V.

LA ROCHELLE. *Champlain* (M), 20 rue Rambaud (tel. 46-41-23-99). 36 rooms. Closed Nov. through Jan. Charming mansion converted into chic hotel; central, nice garden; no restaurant. AE, DC, MC, V. *France-Angleterre* (M), 22 rue Gargoulleau (tel. 46-41-34-66). 76 rooms. In Old Town, but modern building; very good restaurant (called *Richelieu*). Closed Sun. and Mon. for lunch. AE, DC, MC, V. *Le Port* (M), 22 quai Duperré (tel. 46-41-25-95). 9 rooms. Tiny place with some rooms overlooking the harbor. No restaurant. *St.-Nicolas* (M), 13 rue Sardinerie (tel. 46-41-71-55). New hotel, quiet, near the old harbor; no restaurant. AE, DC, V.

Restaurants. *Richard Coutanceau* (E), pl. Concurrence (tel. 46-41-48-19). Closed Sun., Mon. for dinner. Opened mid-80s and soon became smartest place in town; *nouvelle cuisine.* AE, DC, V. *Le Pré Vert* (I), 43 rue St.-Nicolas (tel.46-41-24-43). Closed first half Nov., and last week of Feb., Sun. for dinner in Nov. and Dec. Excellent value *menus.* AE, DC, MC. *Marmite* (M), 14 rue St.-Jean-du Pérot (tel. 46-41-17-03). Closed second half Jan., Wed. Small and quite elegant; *nouvelle cuisine.* AE, DC, MC, V. *Serge* (M), 46 cours Dames (tel. 46-41-18-80). Closed mid-Jan. to mid-Feb., Tues. (except in July and Aug.). Tasty fish; popular, must reserve. AE, DC, MC, V. *Quatre Sergents* (I), 49 rue St.-Jean-du-Pérot (tel. 46-41-35-80). Closed Sun. for dinner, Mon. Some good regional dishes; splendid turn-of-the-century glass-domed roof. AE, DC, MC, V.

At **St.-Ouen-d'Aunis**, 14 km. (9 miles) west by RN11 and D102, *Auberge Breuil* (tel. 46-37-04-31). Good-value *menu* and good food generally.

ROYAN. *Family Golf* (M), 28 blvd. Garnier, Grande-Conche (tel. 46-05-14-66). 27 rooms. Closed Oct. through March. Right by beach, with restaurant and modern rooms, most with balcony. For a pleasant stay. V.

LES SABLES D'OLONNE. *Atlantic* (E), 5 promenade Godet (tel. 51-95-37-71). 30 rooms. Well run and friendly, popular with readers for good value restaurant, *Sloop.* AE, DC, MC, V.

Restaurants. *Beau Rivage* (M), 40 promenade Clemenceau (tel. 51-32-03-01). Closed first half Oct., mid-Dec. to mid-Jan., Sun. for dinner, Mon., except June through Sept. By sea, and good value if you stick to *menus,* newish cuisine; also has 21 rooms. AE, DC, MC, V. *Capitaine* (M), 5 quai Guiné (tel. 51-95-18-10). Closed Oct., second half Dec., Sun. for dinner (except in July and Aug.). Marvelous fish, very popular; beside fishing harbor. AE, DC, MC, V.

ST.-EMILION. *Plaisance* (E), pl. Clocher (tel. 57-24-72-32). 12 rooms. Elegant, right in center of village; good restaurant (M); air-conditioned. AE, DC, MC, V. *Auberge de la Commanderie* (I), rue Cordeliers (tel. 57-24-70-19). 15 rooms. Closed mid-Dec. to mid-Feb. Pretty rooms, some overlooking garden and meadows; pleasant little restaurant, closed Tues. (except July and Aug.), not always open in Feb.

    Restaurants. *Chez Germaine* (M), pl. Clocher (tel. 57-24-70-88). Closed mid-Dec. to mid-Jan., Sun. for dinner, Mon. Good for regional specialties; elegant upstairs dining room with terrace. AE, DC. *Logis de la Cadène* (I), pl. Marché-aux-Bois (tel. 57-24-71-40). Closed second half June, first half Sept., three weeks in Jan., Mon. Dinners served only in July and Aug. Good regional cuisine, right by church; very popular; good value *menus*.

ST.-JEAN-DE-LUZ. *Chantaco* (E), Golf de Chantaco (tel. 59-26-14-76). 24 rooms. Closed Nov. through March. Most attractive, overlooking France's finest golfcourse; good restaurant (called *El Patio*). AE, DC. *Madison* (M), 25 blvd. Thiers (tel. 59-26-35-02). 25 rooms. Old-established and very pleasant, near beach; no restaurant. AE, DC, MC, V.

    Restaurants. *Léonie* (M), 6 rue Garat (tel. 59-26-37-10). Closed Mon. Very popular with summer visitors; good for plainly cooked fish. Excellent value. AE, DC, V. *Chez Pablo* (I), 5 rue Etcheto (tel. 59-26-37-81). Closed Wed. Tasty regional cuisine, lots of atmosphere.

    At **Ciboure,** just outside town, *Arrantzaleak* (I), (tel. 59-47-10-75). Closed mid-Dec. to mid-Jan., Mon. for dinner and Tues. Delicious fresh fish served in huge quantities; Basque songs, cheerful ambience. AE, DC.

ST.-JEAN-PIED-DE-PORT. *Central* (I), pl. de Gaulle (tel. 59-37-00-22). 14 rooms. Closed mid-Dec. to mid-Feb. Modest, with good value restaurant. AE, DC.

    Restaurants. *Etche-Ona* (M), 15 pl. Floquet (tel. 59-37-01-14). Closed Nov. to mid-Dec., Fri. (except in July and Aug.). Now serves mostly "new" cuisine; also has 13 (I) rooms. *Pyrénées* (M), 19 pl. de Gaulle (tel. 59-37-01-01). Closed Jan. and first three weeks of Dec., Mon. for dinner Nov. through Mar. and Tues. (except July and Aug.). Marvelous regional cuisine; deservedly popular with locals, so must reserve; also a hotel with 31 (M) rooms. AE, V.

SAUTERNES. Restaurant. *Vignes* (I), pl. Eglise (tel. 56-63-60-06). Closed mid-Jan. to mid-Feb., Mon. for dinner. Perfect little village restaurant with red-checked tablecloths, open fire and cottagey feel; very good value *menus* and wine by the glass if you prefer to sample different ones with each course.

TOURS AND EXCURSIONS. By Bus. The S.N.C.F. (French Railways) run excursions from Arcachon ("Tour des Bassins," "Oyster Beds"); Bordeaux (the Landes nature reserve and a cruise on the Garonne river); Dax (the Basque Country); Ile d'Oléron (Palmyre zoo); La Rochelle (Ile de Ré, Ile d'Oléron, and around the Marais Poitevin); Royan (La Coubre, Talmont); and Tarbes (the Basque coast).

    By Boat. Sea trips from St.-Jean-de-Luz and La Tranche-sur-Mer are operated by a number of companies, the S.N.C.F. among them. There are also "wine cruises" on the Garonne river from Bordeaux through the wine growing districts. Trips on the Charente river from St.-Savinien are also available. Full details are available from tourist offices.

SIGHTSEEING DATA. For general notes on visiting museums and historic buildings in France—and an important warning—see "Sightseeing" in *Facts at Your Fingertips.*

BAYONNE. Musée Basque, rue Marengo. Open daily, except Sun. and public hols., 9.30–12.30, 2.30–6.30 (to 5.30 Oct. through May).

Musée Bonnat, rue Jacques-Lafitte. Open daily, except Tues., 10–12, 4–8 (summer); Mon. to Thurs., 1–7, Fri. 4–10, Sat. and Sun. 3–7 (winter).

BORDEAUX. Centre Jean-Moulin, pl. Jean-Moulin. Open Mon. to Fri. only, 2–6.

Musée d'Aquitaine, 20 cours Albert. Open daily except Tues. and Sun., 2–6.

Musée des Arts Decoratifs, 39 rue Bouffard. Open daily, except Tues., 2–6.

Musée des Beaux Arts, Jardin de la Mairie (City Hall). Open daily, except Tues. and public hols. 10–12, 2–6.

Musée d'Histoire Naturelle, Jardin Public. Open daily, except Tues. and public hols., 2–5.30 (2–6 mid-June to mid-Sept.).

DAMPIERRE-SUR-BOUTONNE. Château (tel. 46-33-82-24). Open June through Sept., daily, 9–12, 2.30–7; Oct. through May, Sun. and public hols. only, 10–12, 2.30–5. Closed on Thurs. except summer.

GRANDE LANDE. Ecomusée, Marqueze. Open daily, mid-June to mid-Sept.; Apr. to mid-June and mid-Sept. through Oct., Sat. afternoon, Sun. and public hols. only.

OIRON. Château (tel. 49-66-71-25). Open daily, except Tues. 9–12.15, 2–7 (closes at 5.30 Oct. through Mar.).

PAUILLAC. Château Mouton-Rothschild, housing **Musée du Vin.** Open Mon. to Fri. only, 9–12, 2–5; closed Aug. For **Musée du Vin** write or call Bordeaux tourist office for appointment first.

POITIERS. Baptistère St.-Jean. Open daily, except Wed. and mid-Jan. through Feb. 10.30–12.30, 2.30–6.

Palais de Justice. Open 9–12, 2–7 most days, but check first as may be closed if major session is in progress.

LA ROCHELLE. Musée du Nouveau Monde, 10 rue Fleuriau (tel. 46-41-46-50). Open daily, except Tues., 10.30–6.

Tour de la Chaine. Open Easter through Sept. only.

ST.-EMILION. Ermitage and **Monolithic Church.** Guided tours set out from tourist office at various times depending on demand.

 WINE TASTING. The opportunities for sampling the world-famous Bordeaux wines are legion. The key address is that of the well-run *Maison du Vin de Bordeaux,* 1 cours 30-Juillet (tel. 56-52-82-82). It's right in the center of the town and is open Mon. to Sat. The helpful and efficient hostesses will supply details of excursions and of estates that can be visited by individuals, as well as maps, lists of dealers and vineyard owners, and descriptions of the wines and vintages. Tastings may be made here too if you want to buy but have no time to visit the estates.

CORSICA

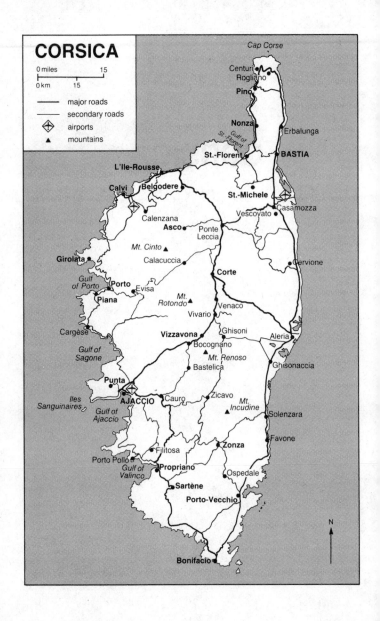

CORSICA

The Scented Isle

Corsica, the third-largest and, many think, the loveliest of the Mediterranean islands, well deserves such titles as "the Isle of Beauty" and "the Scented Isle." Now officially a *département* of France, with a population of about 220,000, Corsica is a very popular vacation spot, particularly for families looking for action-packed holidays where the accent is more on sport than sightseeing.

The major attractions of the island are natural rather than manmade. Its rugged grandeur is a refreshing change after the more "civilized" delights of many mainland regions. Almost the entire island is covered with jagged, forested mountains. Perched on the sides of peaks and nestled in the valleys are numerous little villages that look like a picture out of the Middle Ages. Many of the smaller bays are still quite inaccessible except by boat, because of the high rocky coastline.

The first thing that will strike you about the island, whether you come by air or sea, will be the mountains, which seem to spring straight up from the ocean. The highest peak is Monte Cinto (2,700 meters/ 8,890 ft.), but it is only 24 km. (15 miles) from the sea. The approach by air is superb—Ajaccio resembles an amphitheater, with the port occupying the stage and the houses perched where the seats should be.

Sprawling coastal beaches are fringed with palm trees, ancient buildings, and cafés; Genoese watchtowers dot the coast, and houses and boats sparkle with the wild, bright Corsican reds, greens, yellows, blues. The air is full of the scent of rosemary and thyme, and songs that are half-French, half-Genoese. All combine to give Corsica great individuality.

Another unusual feature that will soon strike you is the number of cemeteries. For generations, Corsicans have had to travel abroad to find work—to Marseille, Paris or even New York. But most of them have dreamt throughout their exile of returning to their beloved island in retirement. When they do so, one of the first claims on their large or small fortunes amassed overseas is the building of a tomb in which their family can take pride. Many a visitor to Corsica has walked or driven to what appears to be a picturesque hill village perched high above a rocky valley, only to find that it is a well-tended cemetery full of huge tombs in the shape of houses and other more elaborate buildings. It may seem macabre, but these strange, ghost villages are well worth a visit.

The true hill villages and towns vary in size from a mere cluster of houses to fairly large towns, but the tall stone houses with their heavy slate roofs, narrow slit windows and heavy doors give the impression of an old fortress. Indeed, the houses were often built to form a solid defensive fortress wall, for the Corsicans fought their Genoese masters for generations before the island was sold to France. Once upon a time the word *vendetta* was almost synonymous with Corsica. The streets are narrow alleys, built more for donkeys and goats than for modern vehicles.

But the island's chief glory is undoubtedly its wild countryside: the chalky cliffs at Bonifacio, where in the 15th century the inhabitants resisted a long Spanish siege, the crimson mountains that rise straight up from the sea at Piana, the fertile vineyards in the valleys. From the dense undergrowth (called *maquis*), the rich scent of myrtle, honeysuckle, lavender, eucalyptus, cyclamen and wild mint carries far out to sea during the spring. "I would recognize Corsica, eyes closed, only because of its perfume," said Napoleon.

Corsica produces mixed reactions in some people. Some find the island oppressive because of the absence of many men of working age and the presence of so many elderly people. Others have difficulties with the local people, whom they find not only cautious and insular—characteristics they share with many islanders—but only too ready to milk tourists for all they are worth. And you should be aware that excursions with locals—boat trips and the like—may sound tempting, but should only be undertaken after careful consideration. Reports in French newspapers suggest that many such jaunts have ended unpleasantly for the tourists who were involved in them.

But the picture is far from being all black. Other visitors adore Corsica and would not dream of going elsewhere for their vacations. The wisest approach is probably to go with an open mind, to concentrate on the fabulous scenery, the unspoilt beaches and all the delights that are hard to find in other places these days. That way you are sure to find much to enjoy, and the occasional irritations concerning such "civilized" preoccupations as service and cleanliness will fade into insignificance.

A final word on prices: the growth of tourist facilities and holiday villages has inevitably led to prices that would startle those who knew Corsica not so long ago as a budgeteer's paradise. In particular, restaurants often seem surprisingly expensive. But, on the other hand, the island is marvelous for campers, and, with a bit of care, you should be able to enjoy a vacation costing considerably less than on the mainland Mediterranean coast.

Ajaccio, Birthplace of Napoleon

The chief town of the island is Ajaccio, a cross between an overgrown village and a busy modern city. It is a fine winter resort, but you will find it interesting no matter when you are there. Located on a protected gulf, it is surrounded by green mountains and rocky crags covered with snow during the winter.

The place Fesch, opposite the steamer landing, is a good place to start your tour of the town. In the Hôtel de Ville, the Town Hall, there is a Napoleonic museum containing a collection of family portraits, as well as the Emperor's baptismal certificate and the bronze deathmask made at St. Helena by his Corsican doctor. Follow the rue Charles to the little street in which stands Napoleon's birthplace, facing a small garden. Here you will see the couch upon which he was born in 1769, his study and bedroom, complete with trap door. At the end of the street is the 16th-century cathedral where he was baptized. In the rue Fesch is the home of Cardinal Fesch, Napoleon's uncle, now a museum. The right wing contains the imperial chapel, the left wing is a museum with an exceptional collection of early-Italian paintings (13th to 15th century), as well as 17th-century Roman and Neapolitan paintings. But you should be warned that in Corsica museums seem to spend a lot of time closed for restoration or for other unexplained reasons. One that is usually open throughout the tourist season is the Musée du Capitellu, opposite the citadel, a fascinating collection of paintings, sculpture, engravings, ivory and lace, providing a well-rounded picture of 18th- and 19th-century Ajaccio through the eyes and mementoes of a distinguished local family.

The market on boulevard du Roi Jérôme, behind the Hôtel de Ville, is a good place to buy some of the local *brocciu* cheese, sausages, delicious peaches, fresh almonds by the kilo, and regional pastries. The fish market, just below the building, offers the usual Mediterranean display of tempting seafood.

From Ajaccio to Bonifacio

Southward from Ajaccio the road turns and twists, offering wonderful views of the gulf of Ajaccio and the Iles Sanguinaires (to which an attractive boat trip may be arranged). On the gulf of Valinco is the busy fishing port and tourist resort of Propriano, now well endowed with modern hotels. Sartène, 82 km. (51 miles) from Ajaccio, is a typical old Corsican town, with several streets that retain something of the atmosphere of the Middle Ages. Perched magnificently in the mountains, it has a splendid view of the bay below and the distant mountain ring. It is well known for its Good Friday "Catenaccin Procession," a religious parade dating back to the Middle Ages, in which a red-robed and hooded penitent, weighed down with chains and dragging a huge wooden cross, takes on the role of Christ at Calvary as he zigzags through the narrow streets of the dark and often eerie Old Town. Those interested in prehistoric times, should make sure of visiting the town's *Corsican Prehistory Museum,* as well as exploring the area west and southwest of Sartène, towards the sea, where the countryside is strewn with megalithic dolmens, menhirs and stone circles. Another "must" is Filitosa, inland from Porto-Pollo, a major religious center in prehistoric times and now extensively excavated. You can visit a small museum on the site housing many of the finds from Filitosa, as well as a local craft center. With its restaurant and well-designed documentation center, it makes a most interesting day out. You can even stay there if you feel like thoroughly absorbing yourself in the prehistoric ambiance. The southerly route branches east to Cauro, thence via Zonza and Porto-Vecchio to Bonifacio.

Bonifacio, 37 km. (23 miles) further south, is an ancient fortress town set spectacularly on high chalk cliffs. It still maintains an active garrison, including some Foreign Legionnaires in their white *képis.* Still largely medieval in atmosphere, the citadel withstood many sieges, the most famous vestiges of which are the steps cut in the high rock face during the 15th century by the troops of Alphonse d'Aragon (take a boat trip outside the harbor to see these, and the famous grottoes). Bonifacio citadel also has a number of old churches, and in the rue Longue you can see the façades of the houses where Emperor Charles V stayed in 1541 and where Napoleon was billeted at one point in his army career. There is a yacht harbor and a sailing school.

Northward from Ajaccio to Bastia

Another side trip from Ajaccio, perhaps even more picturesque than the excursion to Bonifacio, takes you north up the western coast to Porto, Calvi and L'Ile-Rousse. The road is frequently steep and twisting, but magnificent panoramas meet the eye at every turn. Along the coast from Piana to Porto, the *calanques* (*calanches*) or coves of red-tinted rocks form a startling contrast to the vivid blue sea into which they plunge and the verdant greens of the surrounding vegetation. Inland from Porto, a magnificent scenic road leads to Calvi via Evisa, the Spelunca gorge, the spectacular gorge known as the Scala di Santa Regina and Ponte-Leccia. Porto, a little fishing town 80 km. (50 miles) from Ajaccio on the gulf of Porto, is thought by many visitors to be the most beautiful spot in Corsica. The mild climate of Calvi, its setting on the sea, and the high mountains that surround its landward perimeter have long made it a tourist resort. The old citadel, with its 16th-century walls and narrow streets, is a fine place to wander. In the rue Colombo is the alleged birthplace of Columbus. L'Ile-Rousse, only 24 km. (15 miles) from Calvi, has an interesting convent that dates from the end of the 15th century; its climate and its beauty have helped to make it one of the most fashionable resorts in Corsica. Nearby St.-Florent has become one of the busiest pleasure-craft harbors on the island. It also has a beautiful Romanesque cathedral.

On the northeast coast is Bastia, the island's largest town and its commercial capital. The most interesting part is the old harbor area. Most of the buildings date from the 17th and 18th centuries, and the citadel was built during the 16th and 17th centuries. Be sure to see the old governor's place (1453); the churches of Ste.-Marie, Ste.-Croix, St.-Roch and la Concepcion, the citadel, and place St.-Nicolas.

One of the most beautiful excursions from Bastia is the circuit of Cap Corse, the finger-like peninsula that points north toward France. The road parallels the sea almost to the tip of the cape, and all along there are lovely little bays and coves, and many valleys leading up into the forest-covered mountains that form the backbone of the peninsula. The scenery is spectacular at every bend in the road. Old Genoese watchtowers, villas, lime trees and olive groves contrast with rocky fiords and the *maquis,* stunted and warped by the force of the northeast wind called the *libeccio*. The tiny port of Centuri is one of the marvels of the Cap.

From Bastia to Bonifacio

There are several ways south from Bastia. The most scenic route goes via Casamozza, Corte, Ghisoni, Ghisonaccia, Solenzara, Zonza and Porto-Vecchio. This road crosses a corner of the coastal plain for 19 km. (12 miles), but at Casamozza you climb up into the wonderful Corsican mountains. An excursion to Corte, the island's largest inland town, involves mountain roads and breathtaking scenery. Overhanging the town are the fantastic 15th-century citadel and the brooding crags of Monte Rotondo.

From Corte to Ghisonaccia it is mountain driving most of the way, but at the latter town you return to the coastal plain. At Solenzara the road swings inland once again and takes you over the Col de Bavella to Zonza, considered by many to be the most spectacularly beautiful drive in the island. From Zonza you head through beautiful forested country to the rather chic resort of Porto-Vecchio on the coast with its granite walls, cork-oak plantations and elegant marina.

One more trip, made by almost every visitor to Corsica, is the drive or train ride from Bastia to Ajaccio via Corte. Of course, you can travel in either direction, but if you start out from Bastia, the drive to Corte is the same as the one mentioned for the Bastia–Bonifacio excursion. After leaving Corte the road flanks several high peaks. It passes through the town of Vivario, the jumping-off point for tours of the Inzecca Gorge, then climbs up into the heavily forested mountain country around the town of Vizzavona, a lovely area. From Vizzavona it is only a little over 48 km. (30 miles) to Ajaccio. The road leads past Bocognano, a favorite summer resort of the people of Ajaccio, then runs through a forest of chestnut trees as it drops into the valleys that lead to the gulf of Ajaccio.

PRACTICAL INFORMATION FOR CORSICA

TOURIST OFFICES. It is notoriously difficult to get up-to-date information about Corsica, and the tourist authorities are slow in issuing leaflets and in answering letters, though most staff will do their best to help. There is a new service which covers the whole of the island, dealing with accommodations and packages, as well as general information: *Loisir Accueil Région Corse,* 24 blvd. Paoli, Ajaccio (tel. 95-22-70-79).

There are local tourist offices in the following towns: **Ajaccio,** av. Antoine-Sérafini (tel. 95-21-40-87); **Bastia,** 35 blvd. Paoli (tel. 95-31-02-04); **Calvi,** esplanade Gare (tel. 95-65-05-87); **L'Ile-Rousse,** pl. Paoli (tel. 95-60-03-72); **Porto,** 9 rte. Marine (tel. 95-26-10-55); **Porto-Vecchio,** 2 rue Maréchal-Juin (tel. 95-70-09-58); **Propriano,** 17 av. Général-de-Gaulle (tel. 95-76-01-49); **Sartène,** cours Saranelli (tel. 95-77-05-37).

TELEPHONE CODES. The Corsican telephone system is fully slotted into the mainland system and operates in exactly the same way. The old area code for the whole island was 95, so if you're given a 6-digit number, merely add that to the beginning to get the full new number.

REGIONAL FOOD AND DRINK. Corsica does not boast any luxury restaurants and the local cuisine, although tasty and copious, can hardly be called gastronomic. Seafood is abundant and delicious, but many foods have to be imported and restaurant prices are therefore comparatively high. Much of the cooking is done with olive oil, and has a distinctly Italian flavor.

The sea provides the staple diet of Corsica, and you'll be served with all varieties of Mediterranean fish—grilled, baked, broiled or fried. Sardines fried in batter are good, provided you don't mind head, tail, bones, and the lot. Shellfish include cockles, limpets, winkles, sea urchins *(oursins),* apart from the delicious oysters and crayfish (sold by weight in restaurants, and an expensive addition to your bill). *Ziminù* is the Corsican *bouillabaisse,* its simpler form being *soupe de poisson. Suppa* is a thick vegetable and herb soup.

The local cheeses are delicious; apart from the *Brocciù,* which is used in both sweet and savory dishes, look for the mild *Bastelicaccis* and the *Bleu de Corse.* Try also an omelet filled with cream cheese and mint.

Among the notable Corsican charcuterie products are *figatelli* (small dry sausages made of pork), salami sausage, and pork *lonzu* (filet) or *coppa* (shoulder). You will find pork, lamb and even blackbird stews, often with a *pebronata* sauce of bell peppers, garlic and tomato. Kid comes drenched in herbs, there's wild boar, and mushrooms in great variety. Ham, leg of lamb with garlic and a brandy sauce, and artichoke hearts stuffed with chopped meat and topped with *brocciù* are other island specialties.

Corsican confectionery features a whole galaxy of *pisticcine, torta, canestrone, rappi* and *pane biscottù*—fritters, tarts, biscuits, and so on—made with chestnut or wheat flour, raisins, nuts, butter and eggs. The pastries known as *fiadonu, imbrocciatta* and *cocciula* are flavored with *brocciù* and brandy.

Good wines are the white and *rosé* wines of Patrimonio, in the Bastia region, the *Malvoisie* and *Muscat* of Cap Corse, also *Cédratine* and *Myrtle* liqueur, and *eau de vie* (brandy).

HOTELS AND RESTAURANTS. The tourist boom in Corsica has resulted in much building of new hotels in hitherto undeveloped areas. These are generally modern and impersonal, clean but occasionally haphazard in service; meals are good and are served in generous portions. There are few hotels that can be called deluxe, yet prices are fairly high, not much lower than on the Côte d'Azur, the Riviera, on the mainland. Most hotels close for nearly half the year (from Oct. or Nov. to Easter). In the high season (July and Aug.), most hotels in all price ranges insist on half-board or even full-board terms. Most hotels will provide a packed lunch, though, and eating in your hotel is certainly advisable in smaller places anyway, as there are few restaurants, and those that do exist are fairly expensive. Best check your hotel or restaurant bill for every item.

Corsica also has a number of holiday villages of varying degrees of comfort and ranging from small (20 beds) to huge (2,000 beds, at Lozari). There are even two nudist villages. Full details available from the regional tourist office in Ajaccio.

AJACCIO. *Albion* (M), 15 av. Général-Leclerc (tel. 95-21-66-70). 63 rooms. Well-run; near beach and city center; no restaurant. AE, DC, MC, V. *Etrangers* (M), 2 rue Rossi (tel. 95-21-01-26). 40 rooms. Peaceful, with lovely garden; nicest rooms are in villa annex; no restaurant. *Fesch* (M), 7 rue Fesch (tel. 95-21-50-52). 77 rooms. Closed mid-Dec. through Jan. At the center of the old part of town and full of local color; close to beach; no restaurant. AE, DC, MC, V. *Impérial* (M), 6 blvd. Albert-Ier (tel. 95-21-50-62). 44 rooms. Closed Nov. through Mar. On the boulevard at the beginning of rte. des Sanguinaires; garden and restaurant. AE, DC.

Five km. (3 miles) east, *Campo dell'Oro* (E), rte. Aéroport (tel. 95-22-32-41). 138 rooms. Restaurant closed Jan. and Feb. Deluxe spot overlooking the beach; pool, sauna, two (M) restaurants (one right on the beach). AE, DC, MC, V.

Eight km. (5 miles) southwest, *Eden Roc* (E), rte. des Sanguinaires (tel. 95-52-01-47). 30 rooms. Closed Oct. through Apr. Full-board terms only; Relais et Châteaux member with garden, pool, and fine sea views; restaurant. AE, DC, V.

Restaurants. *Amour Piattu* (M), 8 pl. Gal. de Gaulle (tel. 95-51-00-53). Good restaurant serving dinner only. Closed Sun. and Oct. Mostly regional cooking; excellent Corsican wines; terrace. V. *Grange* (M), 4 rue Notre-Dame (tel. 95-21-25-32). Closed Dec. through Feb., Mon. (except July and Aug.). Right behind cathedral and very busy. AE, DC, V. *Pardi* (I), rue Fesch (tel. 95-21-43-08). Closed mid-Dec. through Jan., Sun. Very popular, and deservedly so for its good-value *menus* with plenty of local specialties. *St.-Hubert* (I), 3 rue Colonel-Colonna-d'Ornano (tel. 95-23-23-78). Closed Christmas and the New Year, Sun. dinner (except during July and Aug.). Good fixed-price meals with some local specialties; good range of *menus*. AE, MC, V. *U Scalone* (I), 2 rue Roi-de-Rome (tel. 95-21-50-05). Closed Dec. and Sun. Lively place specializing in dishes from the Lyon region.

BASTELICA. *Castagnetu* (I), tel. 95-28-70-71. 15 rooms. Closed Nov. and Tues. (except June through Sept.). Mountain setting in southern Corsica; peaceful center for riding, skiing and hiking; good restaurant offering superb views; half-board terms compulsory in season. AE, V.

Restaurant. *Chez Paul* (I), (tel. 95-28-71-59). Great little spot for regional food; *menus* only; extremely good value; Corsican wines; terrace.

BASTIA. *Bonaparte* (M), 45 blvd. Général-Graziani (tel. 95-34-07-10). 22 rooms. Near ferry and Air France terminals; no restaurant. AE, DC, MC, V. *Ostella* (M), 4 km. (2½ miles) south on the Ajaccio road (tel. 95-33-51-05). 30 rooms. Modern, just outside town; all rooms have balconies. AE, V.

At **Pietranera**, 3 km. (2 miles) north, *Pietracap* (M), tel. 95-31-64-63. 22 rooms. Closed Dec. through Feb. Pool, but no restaurant; all rooms have balconies. AE, DC, V.

Restaurants. *Chez Assunta* (I), pl. Neuve Fontaine (tel. 95-31-67-06). Closed Jan., Sun. and public holidays. In a 17th-century chapel; chic, with good, straightforward cuisine at reasonable prices. AE, DC, V. *Taverne* (I), 9 rue Général-Carbuccia (tel. 95-31-17-87). Closed Mon. Mouth-watering Corsican specialties; overlooking the harbor. AE, DC, V.

BONIFACIO. *Club des Pêcheurs* (E), Ile Cavallo (tel. 90-70-36-39). 14 rooms. Closed mid-Sept. through May. On island and reached by boat from quai Plantarella; restaurant is (M). AE, DC, V. *Résidence du Centre Nautique* (M), tel. 95-73-02-12. 10 rooms. Closed Nov. to mid-Mar. Beside harbor, with most attractive rooms on two floors; no restaurant. *Etrangers* (I), av. Bohn (tel. 95-73-01-09). 30 rooms. Closed mid-Nov. through Mar. (except Christmas and New Year). Modest, no restaurant. V.

Restaurant. *Rascasse* (I), 6 quai Comparetti (tel. 95-73-01-26). Closed mid-Oct. through Apr. Right by harbor and specializing in fish and shellfish. AE, DC, V.

CALVI. *Grand* (E), blvd. Président-Wilson (tel. 95-65-09-74). 58 rooms. Closed Oct. to mid-Mar. Close to town center and beach, with lovely views; rather elegant rooms, but no restaurant. AE, DC, MC, V. *Kallisté* (M), av. Commandant-Marche (tel. 95-65-09-81). 24 rooms. Closed Oct. through May. Peaceful rooms overlooking garden; restaurant. AE, V. *Résidence des Aloës* (I), 1 km. (½ mile) southwest in Donateo district (tel. 95-65-01-46). 25 rooms. Closed Oct. through Apr. Modern, a bit away from the center but worth it for the peace and quiet of its garden and rooms; some rooms have kitchenettes. AE, DC, V.

Restaurants. *Ile de Beauté* (E), quai Landry (tel. 95-65-00-46). Closed Oct. through Apr., Wed. (except mid-July to mid-Sept.). Views of harbor and worth the rather high prices for the marvelous fish. AE, DC. *U Spuntinu* (M), rte.

Bonifato (D251), tel. 95-65-07-06. Closed mid-Oct. through May. Converted farmhouse specializing in Corsican cuisine; good value and lots of atmosphere.

CENTURI. *Vieux Moulin* (I), tel. 95-35-60-15. 14 rooms. Closed Nov. through Feb. Attractive little hotel by peaceful harbor on the northern tip of the island; half-board terms compulsory in season; good fish in (M) restaurant. AE, DC, V.

CORTE. *Paix* (M), av. de Gaulle (tel. 95-46-06-72). 64 rooms. Closed Oct. to Apr. Typical Corsican architecture, attractive rooms; restaurant. *Sampiero Corso* (I), av. Président-Pierucci (tel. 95-46-09-76). 31 rooms. Closed Oct. through Mar. Modest but friendly; no restaurant.

FAVONE. *U Dragulinu* (M), tel. 95-57-20-30. Closed mid-Oct. through mid-April; restaurant also closed Apr. to mid-May. Attractive modern version of regional architecture on a lovely bay; well-planned rooms and rustic-style restaurant, closed Oct. to mid-May. V.

FERAYOLA. *Auberge Ferayola* (M), (tel. 95-62-01-52). 10 rooms. Closed Oct. to mid-May. Quiet, in the Maquis, a mile from the sea; good home cooking. V.

L'ILE-ROUSSE. *Napoléon-Bonaparte* (E), 3 pl. Paoli (tel. 95-60-06-09). 100 rooms. Closed Nov. to mid-Feb. Plenty of old-style comfort; close to beach, with garden, pool, and tennis courts. Restaurant beside the pool. AE, DC, MC, V. *Pietra* (M), rte. Port (tel. 95-60-01-45). 40 rooms. Closed Nov. through Mar. Right by the sea; comfortable rooms, each with kitchenette; no restaurant. AE, DC, V. *Grillon* (I), av. Paul-Doumer (tel. 95-60-00-49). 16 rooms. Closed Dec. and Jan.; restaurant closed Tues. Small and well-run, with restaurant.

Restaurant. *California* (I), rte. Port (tel. 95-60-01-13). Closed Nov. through Feb., Wed. Good views and good-value meals, too.

PORTICCIO. *Sofitel* (L), tel. 95-25-00-34. 100 rooms. Worth the high prices for comfortable rooms and many amenities: private beach, saltwater coves, etc.; half-board terms only; good restaurant, *Caroubier*. AE, DC, MC, V. *Maquis* (E), tel. 95-25-05-55. 22 rooms. Closed Jan. and Feb. Half-board terms only; modern building forms annexe to delightful older place housing good restaurant; pool and tennis. AE, DC, V.

Restaurant. *Dorbera* (M), in **Vesco**, just south of town (tel. 95-25-02-39). Closed mid-Oct. through April. Friendly bistrot specializing in tasty pasta and Corsican wines. AE, DC, V.

PORTO. *Flots Bleus* (M), at Porto-Marine (95-26-11-26). 20 rooms. Closed mid-Oct. through Mar. Half-board terms only in July and Aug.; facing sea with good-value restaurant specializing in fish. *Bella Vista* (I), tel. 95-26-11-08. 20 rooms. Closed mid-Oct. through Apr. Really does have lovely views; no restaurant. MC, V. *Capo d'Orto* (I), tel. 95-26-11-14. Closed Oct. through Mar. Pool, sea views, and good-value restaurant.

At **Piana,** 12 km. (7½ miles) southwest, *Capo Rosso* (M), tel. 95-26-82-40. 57 rooms. Closed mid-Oct. through Mar. Glorious setting with sweeping sea vistas; pool, big terrace, and restaurant specializing in fish. AE, DC, V.

PORTO VECCHIO. *Cala Verde* (E), in Poretta district (tel. 95-70-11-55). 40 rooms. Closed Oct. through Apr. Big garden and balconies to all rooms; no restaurant. AE, DC, MC, V. *Ziglione* (E), rte. Picovaggia (tel. 95-70-09-83). 52 rooms. Closed Oct. through Apr. Pleasant, with lovely garden right by the sea; delightful restaurant with stunning views.

At **Cala Rossa,** 10 km. (6 miles) northeast, *Grand Hôtel Cala Rossa* (E), tel. 95-71-61-51. 50 rooms. Closed Oct. through mid-May. Modern, airconditioned, stylish; big gardens and fine restaurant (tables in garden during the summer); one of the island's best bets. AE, DC, V.

At **La Trinité,** 7 km. (4½ miles) northeast, *Stagnolo* (M), on the road to Cala Rossa (tel. 95-70-02-07). 23 rooms. Closed Oct. through Mar. Half-board terms compulsory in July and Aug.; right on the sea, with lovely sea and mountain views; some rooms (in modern annex) have kitchenettes, but there's also a restaurant. Closed Oct. to mid-June. AE, DC, V.

On road to **Bastia,** 2 km. (1¼ miles) out, *Roi Théodore* (M), tel. 95-70-14-94. 39 rooms. Closed Nov. through Mar. Bungalow-style; rooms all have balconies overlooking pool; 2 restaurants; tennis. AE, DC, V. *San Giovanni* (M), rte. Arca, 3 km. (2 miles) out (tel. 95-70-22-25). 26 rooms. Closed Nov. through Mar. Bungalow-type in attractive setting, with pool and tennis; restaurant has some Corsican recipes and good fish.

Restaurants. *Lucullus* (M), 17 rue Général-de-Gaulle (tel. 95-70-10-17). Closed mid-Jan. through Feb., Sun., Mon. lunch. Genuine Corsican specialties and friendly atmosphere. AE, DC, MC, V. *Troquemuche* (M), on road to Bastia (tel. 95-70-12-19). Closed Nov. and Dec., Sun. Attractive little bistrot with tables outside; some regional dishes. AE, V.

PROPRIANO. *Miramar* (E), rte. Corniche (tel. 95-76-06-13). 29 rooms. Closed Oct. to Easter. Modern, with large, comfortable rooms, garden, pool, and restaurant. DC. *Roc E Mare* (E), tel. 95-76-04-85. 60 rooms. Closed Oct. through April. Modern, facing sea, with private beach and restaurant. AE, DC, MC, V.

Restaurants. *Lido* (M), tel. 95-76-06-37. Closed Oct. through Apr. Excellent shellfish in restaurant right on the sea, plus 17 good-value (M) rooms with direct access to beach (half-board terms compulsory in July and Aug.). AE, DC, V. *Thalassa* (M), 14 av. Général-de-Gaulle (tel. 95-76-08-39). Closed Nov. to Mar. Good seafood and regional specialties; always crowded.

ST.-FLORENT. *Dolce Notte* (M), on Bastia road (D81), tel. 95-37-06-26. 25 rooms. Closed mid-Nov. to mid-Mar. You will indeed spend "gentle nights" in your pretty room right by the beach; no restaurant.

Restaurant. *Rascasse* (I), Résidence Arcades (tel. 95-37-06-99). Closed Mon. (Apr. to mid-June) and Nov. through Mar. One of the best places in the area for fish; terrace. AE, V.

SARTÈNE. Restaurant. *Chaumière* (M), 39 rue Capitaine-Benedetti (tel. 95-77-07-13). Closed Jan., Sun. (except June through Sept.). Good place for lunch during an excursion to this picturesque town; lots of Corsican specialties and a good (I) *menu.* AE, DC, V.

VENACO. *Paesotel E Caselle* (M), 5 km. (3½ miles) east (tel. 95-47-02-01). 47 rooms. Closed Oct. through April. Lovely, secluded hotel in wild scenery; pool, tennis, riding; some rooms have kitchenettes; good simple restaurant. AE, DC, V.

 HOW TO GET AROUND. By Train. Corsica's rail system is simple, consisting of one main route and two branches. It runs from Ajaccio via Corte to Ponte Leccia in the northern central part of the island and then divides, one line going to Ile-Rousse and Calvi, the other to Bastia. Ajaccio to Bastia takes around four hrs., to Calvi around five hrs. Trains are clean and moderately comfortable, and the scenery is spectacular along most of the route. A service called *Trains et Tramways de la Bologne* runs between Calvi and Ile-Rousse in summer, stopping at many little resorts and beaches.

By Car. The first point to bear in mind is that driving is a slow business in Corsica: you can rarely get above a speed of 50/60 k.p.h. (35 m.p.h.) as the roads are winding and mountainous, and surfaces often poor. When planning an excursion, take a tip and double the time you first thought of! That way you should be about right, and won't find yourself having to make an unexpected overnight stop.

For more specific information on driving itineraries, see "Tours and Excursions" below.

By Bus. Despite the rapid expansion of tourism on the island, public transport facilities are inconvenient from the tourist angle as they are mostly geared to locals coming into main centers in the morning and returning in the evening, rather than the other way about. However, traveling on public buses can be fun—you will meet the people and all the highlights will be pointed out to you. Services run between main towns and from popular resorts such as Propriano to Ajaccio.

 TOURS AND EXCURSIONS. By Car. Despite the warnings given above concerning poor road surfaces and steep, winding ascents, the views are everywhere on the island frequently stupendous and practically every corner of the island is rewarding for the motorist. Here are a few suggestions for excursions: from Ajaccio to Sagone (fast road for this first stretch), then on to Vico, Evisa, and the Spelunca gorges, then the road to Ota with its Genoese bridge, Porto, and Piana. An interesting excursion taking in Propriano and Filitosa follows the coast road via Porticcio and Coti-Chiavari, with the return journey via Petreto-Bicchisano. An excursion north along the coast road to Cargèse and back can be fitted comfortably into a day. If you plan a trip right to the southern tip of the island, best take the fairly good direct road (N196) to Sartène, then on from there via Roccapina.

From Porto-Vecchio, a definite must is the journey inland to Zonza (RF11, lovely but very slow), then on via the glorious Col de Bavella to the coast at Solenzara and back by the coast road.

From Bastia, the classic excursion is the Cap Corse Tour. Start by driving to lovely Erbalunga, an old Genoese town, then right on round the peninsula to Nonza, almost opposite Erbalunga, and to St.-Florent. You might like to return via Patrimonio, where the island's best-known wine comes from. Another interesting tour is to the "Désert des Agniates" (where it gets very hot in summer); you can't visit the coast here without a boat. Then on to Ile-Rousse and the return journey inland via Ponte Leccia, then the N197 towards La Porta, then on to Cervione and back via the coast road. Some enchanting little chapels can be visited on the way.

From Propriano, apart from the obvious excursions to Ajaccio, Sartène, and Bonifacio, don't miss the lovely drive to the Aiguilles de Bavella, with many possibilities for spectacular sidetrips.

By Bus. Several operators organize bus excursions in Corsica. The classic half-day excursions are to the prehistoric site at Filitosa from Ajaccio, via the Col de Bellavelle, Pila-Canale, Calzola, Taravo Valley, Sena-di-Ferro, Zivignola, the Col de Giradello, Pietrosella, Isolella, and Porticcio. Another popular half-day trip is the pleasant "forest tour" covering Cauro, Zipitoli forest, the Col de Menta, Bastelica, the Lac de Tolla, Prunelli gorges, and Bastelicaccia.

The most attractive but also the most tiring of the whole-day excursions, offering superb scenery but a lot of dizzying mountain roads, takes in the Col de Vizzavona, Vivario, Venaco, Corte, the fantastic Scala di Sante Régina, Calacuccia, the forest of Valdoniello, the Col de Vergio (where lunch is usually available), the Aitone Forest, Evisa, La Spelunca, Porto, Piana, Cargèse, Sagone, and Tiuccia. A shorter and less tiring version of this tour is available some days, but this misses out Scala di Santa Régina. Day trips from Ajaccio to Bonifacio, taking in Porto Vecchio, and to Calvi, taking in some glorious scenery, are also regular features of most operators' programs.

"Corsica Tours," lasting a week, with full-board terms, are tiring but give you an excellent view of the island. Two different circuits are generally available, from Apr. to around mid-Oct., and you will be picked up at the harbor or airport upon arrival.

By Boat. There are regular boating excursions from Ajaccio, Bonifacio, Calvi, Porto, and Propriano. From Ajaccio, there are trips to Iles Sanquinaires; from Bonifacio, Dragon Grottoes and Venus' Bath (1-hour trips set out every 15 min. during July and Aug.), also Lanezzi Islands excursion (half-day or whole-day); from Calvi, whole-day tours to Girolata, the Gulf, and Scandola, as well as a two-hour excursion round Calanques de Piana; and finally from Propriano, half-day excursions to Porto-Pollo and Compomoro, and whole-day trips to Tizzano.

On Foot. There are many beautiful possibilities, but you should bear in mind that Corsica's forests are not well-maintained, so some portions of even well-marked paths will involve tiring plods through undergrowth. Leaflets covering paths and trails in the Parc Naturel Régional de Corse are available from tourist offices. Ask for *Da Paese a Paese* ("From Village to Village") maps and brochures.

SIGHTSEEING DATA. Corsica's museums have a nasty habit of closing at unexpected times and/or for several weeks at a time, with no advance warning. Always check at tourist offices to insure that the place you want to visit really is open as advertised.

AJACCIO. Maison Bonaparte (Napoleon Bonaparte's House), rue St.-Charles (tel. 95-21-43-89). Open daily except Sun. afternoon and Mon. morning, Oct. to mid-June, 9–12, 2–5; mid-June through Sept., 2–6. Half price on Sun.

Musée du Capitellu (Museum of Old Ajaccio), 18 blvd. Danielle-Casanova. Open daily, except Sun. afternoon and Mon. morning, 9–12, 3–7.

Musée Fesch, 50 rue Cardinal-Fesch. Closed at presstime for renovations; inquire locally whether it has yet re-opened.

Musée Napoléonien, in the Hôtel de Ville (tel. 95-21-90-15). Open daily, Oct. through Apr. 9–12, 2–5; May through Sept. 2.30–6. Closed Sun. and public hols.

BONIFACIO. Phare du Pertusato. Open daily 8–12, 2–6 (winter 10–12, 2–4).

FILITOSA. Fouilles Préhistoriques (Prehistoric Excavations and Museum), tel. 95-74-00-91. Open daily from 8 A.M. to sunset.

MARIANA. Canonica Church. Ask for key at the cafe next to the church.

SARTÈNE. Musée de la Pré- et Proto-histoire (Prehistory Museum), tel. 95-77-01-09. Open daily, mid-June to mid-Sept., 10–12, 2–6; mid-Sept. to mid-June, 10–12, 2–5. Closed weekends and public hols.

SPECIAL INTEREST ACTIVITIES. Horseback Riding. Corsica is famous riding country and equestrians will delight in its scenic trails. An association called *Casa di a Muntagna,* 9 rue Colonel-Ferracci, 20250 Corte, publishes details of riding tours accompanied by expert guides.

Wine-tasting. Corsica has its own "Wine Road" (Route des Vins de Corse); leaflets give details of estates where local wines may be tasted and purchased.

VOCABULARY

ENGLISH-FRENCH TOURIST VOCABULARY

Basics

yes	oui
no	non
please	s'il vous plaît
thank you	merci
thank you very much	merci bien
excuse me, sorry	pardon
I'm sorry	je suis désolé(e), je regrette
good morning, good afternoon, hello	bonjour
good evening	bonsoir
good night	bonne nuit
goodbye	au revoir

Numbers

1	un	16	seize
2	deux	17	dix-sept
3	trois	18	dix-huit
4	quatre	19	dix-neuf
5	cinq	20	vingt
6	six	21	vingt-et-un
7	sept	30	trente
8	huit	40	quarante
9	neuf	50	cinquante
10	dix	60	soixante
11	onze	70	soixante-dix
12	douze	80	quatre-vingts
13	treize	90	quatre-vingt-dix
14	quatorze	100	cent
15	quinze	1000	mille

Days of the Week

Sunday	dimanche
Monday	lundi
Tuesday	mardi
Wednesday	mercredi
Thursday	jeudi
Friday	vendredi
Saturday	samedi

Months

January	janvier
February	février
March	mars
April	avril
May	mai
June	juin
July	juillet
August	août
September	septembre
October	octobre
November	novembre

Useful Questions and Answers

Do you speak English?	Parlez-vous anglais?
What time is it?	Quelle heure est-il?
Is this seat free?	Est-ce que cette place est libre?
How much does it cost?	Quel est le prix, s'il vous plaît?
Would you please direct me to . . . ?	Quel est le chemin pour . . . ?
Where is the station, museum . . . ?	Pour aller à la gare, au musée, s'il vous plaît?
I am American, British	Je suis américain(e), anglais(e)
It's very kind of you	Vous êtes bien aimable
I don't understand	Je ne comprends pas
I don't know	Je ne sais pas
Please speak more slowly	Parlez plus lentement, s'il vous plaît
Please sit down	Asseyez-vous, je vous en prie

Everyday Needs

cigar, cigarettes	cigare, cigarette
matches	allumettes
dictionary	dictionnaire
key	clef
razor blades	lames de rasoir
shaving cream	mousse à barbe
soap	savon
city plan	plan de la ville
road map	carte routière
country map	carte géographique
newspaper	journal
magazine	magazine, revue
telephone	téléphone
telegram	télégramme
envelopes	enveloppes
writing paper	papier à lettres
airmail writing paper	papier avion
post card	carte postale
stamp	timbre

Services and Stores

bakery	boulangerie
bookshop	librairie
butcher's	boucherie
delicatessen	charcuterie
dry cleaner's	pressing
grocery	épicerie
hairdresser, barber	coiffeur
laundry	blanchisserie
laundromat	laverie automatique
shoemaker	cordonnerie
stationery store	papeterie
supermarket	supermarché

Emergencies

ill, sick	malade
I am ill	Je suis malade
My wife/husband/child is ill	Mon épouse/mon mari/mon enfant est malade

doctor	médecin
nurse	infirmier/infirmière
prescription	ordonnance
pharmacist/chemist	pharmacien
Please fetch/call a doctor	Veuillez chercher/appeler un médecin
accident	accident
road accident	accident de la route
Where is the nearest hospital?	Veuillez m'indiquer l'hôpital/la clinique le/la plus proche
dentist	dentiste
X-ray	radio

Pharmacist's

pain-killer	analgèsique
gauze pads	carré de gaze
bandage	pansement
bandaid	sparadrap
scissors	ciseaux
hot-water bottle	bouillotte
sanitary pads	serviettes hygiéniques
ointment for bites/stings	pommade pour les pîqures
coughdrops	pastilles pour la gorge
cough mixture	sirop anti-tussif
laxative	laxatif

Traveling

plane	avion
hovercraft	aéroglisseur
train	train
boat	bateau/ferry
taxi	taxi
car	voiture
seat	place
reservation	réservation
smoking/non-smoking compartment	salle fumeurs/non-fumeurs
rail station	gare
subway station	station
airport	aéroport
harbor	port
town terminal	terminus en ville
shuttle bus/train	navette
sleeper	wagon-lit
couchette	couchette
porter	porteur
baggage/luggage	bagages
baggage trolley	chariot
single ticket	aller
return ticket	aller-retour
first class	première classe
second class	deuxième/seconde classe
When does the train leave?	Le train part à quelle heure?
What time does the train arrive at . . . ?	Le train arrive à . . . à quelle heure?
When does the first/last train leave?	À quelle heure part le premier/le dernier train?

Hotels

room	chambre
bed	lit
bathroom	salle de bains
bathtub	baignoire
shower	douche
toilet, lavatory	toilettes, WC (*pron.* vay-say)
toilet paper	papier hygiénique
pillow	oreiller
blanket	couverture
chambermaid	femme de chambre
breakfast	petit déjeuner
lunch	déjeuner
dinner	dîner

Do you have a single/double /twin-bedded room?	Auriez-vous une chambre single/à grand lit/à deux lits?
I'd like a quiet room	Je voudrais une chambre calme
I'd like some pillows	Je voudrais des oreillers
What time is breakfast?	On sert le petit déjeuner de quelle heure à quelle heure?
Come in!	Entrez!
Are there any messages for me?	Auriez-vous un message pour moi?
Would you please call me a taxi?	J'aurais aimé un taxi, s'il vous plaît
Please take our bags to our room	Veuillez emmener nos bagages à la chambre

Restaurants

menu	carte
fixed-price menu	menu
wine list	carte des vins
waiter	serveur
Waiter!	Monsieur, s'il vous plaît
bill/check	addition/note

ON THE MENU
Starters

crudités	raw vegetables
escargot	snail
hors d'oeuvres variés	mixed hors d'oeuvre
melon	melon
pâté	finely chopped and pressed meat, baked
potage	soup
terrine	a rougher version of pâté

Meats (Viande)

agneau	lamb	jambon	ham
biftec	steak	lapin	rabbit
boeuf	beef	lard	bacon
brochette	kebab	mouton	mutton
charcuterie	pork cold cuts	porc	pork
châteaubriand	fillet steak	rosbif	roastbeef
côte, côtelette	chop	saucisse	sausage
entrecôte	rib steak	saucisson	salami

| gigot d'agneau | leg of lamb | veau | veal |

Poultry (Volaille) and Game (Gibier)

caille	quail	oie	goose
canard	duck	perdreau	partridge
caneton	duckling	pintade/pintadeau	guinea hen/fowl
coq	young cockerel	poule	boiling fowl
faisan	pheasant	poulet	chicken
marcassin	wild boar	poussin	spring chicken

Variety Meats, Offal (Abats)

cervelle	brains	ris	sweetbreads
foie	liver	rognon	kidney
langue	tongue	tripes	tripe

Fish (Poisson)

anguille	eel	merlan	whiting
cabillaud	cod	perche	perch
daurade	sea bream	saumon	salmon
lotte	monkfish	truite	trout
loup de mer	sea bass	truite saumonée	salmon trout
maquereau	mackerel		

Shellfish (Coquillages, Crustacés)

bouquet	prawn	huîtres	oysters
crevettes	shrimp	langouste	spiny rock
ecrevisses	crawfish	langoustines	lobster, crayfish
escargots	snails	moules	scampi
fruits de mer	mixed shellfish	oursin	sea urchin
cuisses de gren-		palourdes	cockles
ouilles	frogs' legs	praires	clams
homard	lobster		

Vegetables (Légumes)

artichaut	globe artichoke	haricot blanc	white haricot bean
asperge	asparagus	haricot vert	French bean
aubergine	eggplant	lentille	lentils
carotte	carrot	navet	turnip
champignon	mushroom	oignon	onion
chou	cabbage	oseille	sorrel
choucroute	sauerkraut	pomme de terre	potato
choufleur	cauliflower	petit pois	pea
courgette	zucchini	poireau	leek
cresson	watercress	poivron	green/red pepper
endive	chicory	riz	rice
épinards	spinach	salade	lettuce
fève	broad bean	tomate	tomato
flageolet	kidney bean (green)	topinambour	Jerusalem artichoke

Fruit

| ananas | pineapple | mûr | blackberry (bramble) |
| cassis | blackcurrant | myrtille | bilberry |

cerise	cherry	orange	orange
citron	lemon	pamplemousse	grapefruit
fraise	strawberry	pastèque	watermelon
fraise des bois	wild strawberry	pêche	peach
framboise	raspberry	poire	pear
groseille	redcurrant	pomme	apple
groseille à maquereau	gooseberry	prune	plum
		pruneau	prune

Desserts

beignet	fritter	mousse au chocolat	chocolate mousse
crème caramel	caramel custard	salade des fruits	fruit salad
gâteau	cake	sorbet	water ice
glace	ice cream	tarte	pie/tart/flan

Sauces and Styles

aïoli	garlic mayonnaise	au gratin	browned under grill (perhaps with grated cheese)
béarnaise	sauce made from egg, butter and herbs		
bien cuit	well done	indienne	curried
bordelaise	prepared with red claret, garlic, onions and mushrooms	niçoise	prepared with oil, garlic, tomatoes and onions
à la broche	spit-roasted	poêlé	fried, sautéed
bleu	very rare (steak)	a point	medium (steak)
Chantilly	with whipped cream	rose	lightly roasted
croustade	baked pastry shell	rôti	roast
flambé	flamed with warmed brandy	saignant	rare (steak)
fricassé	braised, fried	vinaigrette	with oil and vinegar dressing
fumé	smoked		

INDEX

**The letter H indicates Hotels and other accommodations.
The letter R indicates Restaurants.**

General Information

FODOR'S TRAVEL GUIDES

Here is a complete list of Fodor's Travel Guides, available in current editions; most are also available in a British edition published by Hodder & Stoughton.

U.S. GUIDES

Alaska
American Cities (Great Travel Values)
Arizona including the Grand Canyon
Atlantic City & the New Jersey Shore
Boston
California
Cape Cod & the Islands of Martha's Vineyard & Nantucket
Carolinas & the Georgia Coast
Chesapeake
Chicago
Colorado
Dallas/Fort Worth
Disney World & the Orlando Area (Fun in)
Far West
Florida
Forth Worth (see Dallas)
Galveston (see Houston)
Georgia (see Carolinas)
Grand Canyon (see Arizona)
Greater Miami & the Gold Coast
Hawaii
Hawaii (Great Travel Values)
Houston & Galveston
I-10: California to Florida
I-55: Chicago to New Orleans
I-75: Michigan to Florida
I-80: San Francisco to New York
I-95: Maine to Miami
Jamestown (see Williamsburg)
Las Vegas including Reno & Lake Tahoe (Fun in)
Los Angeles & Nearby Attractions
Martha's Vineyard (see Cape Cod)
Maui (Fun in)
Nantucket (see Cape Cod)
New England
New Jersey (see Atlantic City)
New Mexico
New Orleans
New Orleans (Fun in)
New York City
New York City (Fun in)
New York State
Orlando (see Disney World)
Pacific North Coast
Philadelphia
Reno (see Las Vegas)
Rockies
San Diego & Nearby Attractions
San Francisco (Fun in)
San Francisco plus Marin County & the Wine Country
The South
Texas
U.S.A.
Virgin Islands (U.S. & British)

Virginia
Waikiki (Fun in)
Washington, D.C.
Williamsburg, Jamestown & Yorktown

FOREIGN GUIDES

Acapulco (see Mexico City)
Acapulco (Fun in)
Amsterdam
Australia, New Zealand & the South Pacific
Austria
The Bahamas
The Bahamas (Fun in)
Barbados (Fun in)
Beijing, Guangzhou & Shanghai
Belgium & Luxembourg
Bermuda
Brazil
Britain (Great Travel Values)
Canada
Canada (Great Travel Values)
Canada's Maritime Provinces plus Newfoundland & Labrador
Cancún, Cozumel, Mérida & the Yucatán
Caribbean
Caribbean (Great Travel Values)
Central America
Copenhagen (see Stockholm)
Cozumel (see Cancún)
Eastern Europe
Egypt
Europe
Europe (Budget)
France
France (Great Travel Values)
Germany: East & West
Germany (Great Travel Values)
Great Britain
Greece
Guangzhou (see Beijing)
Helsinki (see Stockholm)
Holland
Hong Kong & Macau
Hungary
India, Nepal & Sri Lanka
Ireland
Israel
Italy
Italy (Great Travel Values)
Jamaica (Fun in)
Japan
Japan (Great Travel Values)
Jordan & the Holy Land
Kenya
Korea
Labrador (see Canada's Maritime Provinces)
Lisbon
Loire Valley
London

London (Fun in)
London (Great Travel Values)
Luxembourg (see Belgium)
Macau (see Hong Kong)
Madrid
Mazatlan (see Mexico's Baja)
Mexico
Mexico (Great Travel Values)
Mexico City & Acapulco
Mexico's Baja & Puerto Vallarta, Mazatlan, Manzanillo, Copper Canyon
Montreal (Fun in)
Munich
Nepal (see India)
New Zealand
Newfoundland (see Canada's Maritime Provinces)
1936 . . . on the Continent
North Africa
Oslo (see Stockholm)
Paris
Paris (Fun in)
People's Republic of China
Portugal
Province of Quebec
Puerto Vallarta (see Mexico's Baja)
Reykjavik (see Stockholm)
Rio (Fun in)
The Riviera (Fun on)
Rome
St. Martin/St. Maarten (Fun in)
Scandinavia
Scotland
Shanghai (see Beijing)
Singapore
South America
South Pacific
Southeast Asia
Soviet Union
Spain
Spain (Great Travel Values)
Sri Lanka (see India)
Stockholm, Copenhagen, Oslo, Helsinki & Reykjavik
Sweden
Switzerland
Sydney
Tokyo
Toronto
Turkey
Vienna
Yucatán (see Cancún)
Yugoslavia

SPECIAL-INTEREST GUIDES

Bed & Breakfast Guide: North America
Royalty Watching
Selected Hotels of Europe
Selected Resorts and Hotels of the U.S.
Ski Resorts of North America
Views to Dine by around the World

AVAILABLE AT YOUR LOCAL BOOKSTORE OR WRITE TO FODOR'S TRAVEL PUBLICATIONS, INC., 201 EAST 50th STREET, NEW YORK, NY 10022.